Cases on Performance Measurement and Productivity Improvement:

Technology Integration and Maturity

Mehdi Khosrow-Pour
Information Resources Management Association, USA

BUSINESS SCIENCE Reference

Managing Director:	Lindsay Johnston
Senior Editorial Director:	Heather A. Probst
Book Production Manager:	Sean Woznicki
Development Manager:	Joel Gamon
Assistant Acquisitions Editor:	Kayla Wolfe
Typesetter:	Lisandro Gonzalez
Cover Design:	Nick Newcomer

Published in the United States of America by
Business Science Reference (an imprint of IGI Global)
701 E. Chocolate Avenue
Hershey PA 17033
Tel: 717-533-8845
Fax: 717-533-8661
E-mail: cust@igi-global.com
Web site: http://www.igi-global.com

Library of Congress Cataloging-in-Publication Data

Cases on performance measurement and productivity improvement : technology integration and maturity / Mehdi Khosrow-Pour, editor.
    p. cm.
  Includes bibliographical references and index.
  Summary: "This book present a variety of teaching cases that provide essential research on applied innovations in the business and IT management fields"--Provided by publisher.
   ISBN 978-1-4666-2618-8 (hardcover : alk. paper) -- ISBN 978-1-4666-2619-5 (ebook : alk. paper) -- ISBN 978-1-4666-2620-1 (print & perpetual access . alk. paper) 1. Business enterprises--Technological innovations--Case studies. 2. Information technology--Technological innovations--Case studies. 3. Information technology--Management--Case studies. 4. Performance--Measurement--Case studies. 5. Industrial productivity--Case studies. I. Khosrowpour, Mehdi, 1951-

  HD45.C375 2013
  658.5'03--dc23
                          2012024331

British Cataloguing in Publication Data
A Cataloguing in Publication record for this book is available from the British Library.

The views expressed in this book are those of the authors, but not necessarily of the publisher.

Table of Contents

Section 2
Managerial Approaches and Practices

Section 3
Implementation and Interactions

Detailed Table of Contents

Section 1
Innovation and Design

Chapter 1

Michael Workman, Florida Institute of Technology, USA

The literature on technology innovation adoption and diffusion is vast. In this chapter, we organize and summarize some of the major perspectives from this body of literature, contrasting various theoretical perspectives on how innovations are adopted and shaped by organizational processes and structure. We first introduce the technology acceptance model, and innovation diffusion theory; and then we categorize viewpoints about organizational innovativeness. Drawing from this framework, for our case study background we introduce adaptive structuration theory, redefining some of its conceptual relationships in "structuration agency theory," putting primacy on the actions of agents and the means by which they operate through and around institutional structures. We then present a case study example of an expert decision support system, and we conclude with a discussion of implications for managers and entrepreneurs.

Chapter 2

Mustafa Alshawi, University of Salford, UK
Hafez Salleh, University of Malaya, Malaysia

This chapter explains the concept of an IT/IS readiness maturity model including particular requirements in terms of four domains, embracing nine attributes: IT infrastructure (top management perception, systems and communication), people (skills, roles and responsibility of IT staff, user involvement), process, and work environment (organization behaviour, IT department, leadership). Each of the attributes consists of 14 factors: top management perception (drivers, systems requirements definition), systems and communication (focus, network communication), skills (type of skills, capability building), roles and responsibility of IT staff (position of IT/IS heads, roles of IT staff), user involvement, process (practices), organizational behaviour (characteristics), IT policy (control of IT/IS activities), and leadership (communication, participation). The following section describes the concept of readiness and maturity, the resources used for element extraction/adoption and the description of the model.

Faced with increasing competitive pressures, a logistics company in the United States sought to reduce its cost structure by implementing two information systems. The Labor Management System (LMS) was specifically designed to improve warehouse worker efficiency and the Radio Frequency Identification (RFID) system tracked the movement of products, pallets, and shipment. This case presents an overview of the logistics industry, background on the business need to consider new systems, and the requirements of the company in its system selection. Details of the technologies considered are included. The reader is then faced with the challenge of analyzing the options, and making a recommendation for systems selection.

This case describes the implementation of an online travel management system at FED-AK, the Alaska office of a U.S. government agency. The previous system was intended to accomplish the same functionality, but due to employee resistance, it was used only as a forms generator in conjunction with a paper- and mail-based process. The new system is integrated, which compels employees to use all the functionality provided. It also incorporates many lessons learned from the old system—in particular, extensive training and online help functions. The system is expected to significantly reduce the cost of travel by minimizing errors, enforcing policies, and reducing transaction costs. The system will also lead to faster reimbursement of employee travel expenses.

This chapter aims at presenting the results of an empirical study, linking the fields of technology-enhanced learning (TEL), Web 2.0 technologies and organizational learning, and their impact on the financial and non-financial business performance. The chapter focuses on the presentation of the conceptualization of a structural model that was developed to test the impact of technology-enhanced learning and Web 2.0 technologies on the organizational learning and business performance of companies with more than 50 employees. The paper provides detailed definitions of technology-enhanced learning, Web 2.0 technologies and technical terms related to it, its scope and the process of organisational learning, as well as a method for business performance assessment. Special attention is given to the findings related to the observed correlations between the aforementioned constructs. The results of the study indicate a strong impact of ICT and technology-enhanced learning on organizational learning and the non-financial business performance.

Chapter 6

Amit Agrahari, Indian Institute of Management, India
Saket Jhunjhunwala, Accenture, India

This case captures inventory management process in an Indian convenience store. Unlike retail stores in developed countries, Indian convenience stores are a special format of organized retailing, where retailers open multiple smaller stores in a town instead of one big centralised store. An excellent inventory management process is the key to make such stores perform well. This case describes inventory management problems faced by an Indian convenience store chain and asks students to propose solutions to these problems. This case illustrates how processes realities and their IT solutions differ in an emerging economy. Using inventory management process as an example, this teaching case can introduce students to the process and technological realities in an Indian context and differences between India and the West.

Section 2
Managerial Approaches and Practices

Chapter 7

Ahu Genis-Gruber, TOBB University of Economics and Technology, Turkey
Ramazan Aktas, TOBB University of Economics and Technology, Turkey

Organizations operating worldwide adopt different strategies and marketing techniques in various geographic areas, depending on the cultural perception of the country in which they are active. There are diverse reasons for implementing different management strategies, even under the same organizational umbrella. Responsiveness to customers, market adaptability, and competitiveness with other organizations operating in the same sector are some of the most important.

The current case examines the management strategies of a leading furniture company that started off as a small business and rapidly expanded globally. The success the company has achieved through its innovative marketing strategies and use of international management techniques is presented. The case highlights the company's flexibility in adapting its organizational structures to the nature of the market in different countries, and its reliance on a cross-cultural management approach to marketing in order to increase product acceptance by consumers across the world.

Knowledge management represents a strategic vision for developing an organization's performance and its likelihood of success in dealing with future challenges in its industry. The case starts by discussing the importance of knowledge management in improving the competitive edge of firms in general and of consulting firms in particular. Then, the case discusses the process of building a knowledge management system in the structural engineering department at a leading engineering design consulting firm, based in the Republic of Lebanon. The knowledge, both tacit and explicit, needed during the design phase is identified and mapped according to the adopted design process, and an expert system was built to capture some of the tacit knowledge needed in the conceptual design stage of the process. In addition, an intranet Web-based knowledge management system was developed with the aim of helping diffuse both explicit and tacit knowledge.

With the invention of Internet, supply chains have become more comprehensive, global, and faster than ever before. Traditionally, companies used to cut costs through manpower reduction, waste reduction, process automation, and inventory control. However, today those companies that reduce costs in their supply chain are the ones who can remain competitive in the market and provide their customers with a superior quality product. Cost reduction in supply chain is not a new concept. Dell worked with just-in-time systems to make its supply chain both time and cost efficient. Companies have sought to make their supply chains both lean and agile and thus become cost efficient as well as responsive to customer demands. Although there are so many examples of modern global supply chains, most of the supply chains in Indian sub-continent still suffer from a number of inefficiencies. The multi-layered market structure, as well as the lack of resilience among supply chain partners, aggravates the issue. Lack of experience and confidence in modern supply chains precludes the supply chain partners to introduce any innovation in the supply chains.

This chapter presents several case studies of the multilayered system in India and shows how the prevalent distribution system preclude any means of cost reduction and making these supply chains efficient. Supply chains of perishable goods, electronic products, FMCG products and Pharmaceutical products are discussed in this chapter. Each of these supply chains present unique challenges and issues that need attention. The three main objectives in these studies are to understand the distribution systems as well as cost economics of the supply chains, identify potential conflicts and issues in their distribution system, and to study the effect of macro-environment on the distribution system. Apart from these objectives, these cases are also meant to prepare those venturing into such supply chains to come up with efficient solutions for improving these supply chains.

Chapter 10

    Sami Akabawi, American University in Cairo (AUC), Egypt
    Heba Hodeeb, American University in Cairo (AUC), Egypt

To compete successfully in today's retail business arena, senior management are often demanding fast and responsive Information Systems that enable the company not only to manage its operations but to provide on-the-fly performance measurement through a variety of tools. Use of (ERP) systems have been slow in responding to these needs, despite the wealth of the internally generated business databases and reports as a consequence of functional integration. The specific nature and demands by those senior management staff require the congregation of many external data elements and use data mining techniques to provide fast discovery of performance slippages or changes in the business environment. Data Warehousing and Business Intelligence (BI) applications, evolved during the past few decades, have been implemented to respond to these needs. In this case write-up, we present how the ERP system was utilized as the backbone for use by BI tools and systems to provide Sales and Marketing units in a transnational company subsidiary in Egypt to actively respond to the demands for agile information services. The Egypt subsidiary is the HQ of the African region's operations of several franchises and distributers of the company products, in addition to operating a beverage concentrate manufacturing plant in Egypt, which services the entire region's beverage products needs.

Chapter 11

Harald Fardal, Vestfold University College, Norway
Jan Oddvar Sørnes, Bodø Graduate School of Business, Norway

In large, geographically dispersed organizations, achieving a successful Information Systems (IS) strategy can prove very challenging. This case describes how a CIO in such an organization met that challenge by focusing on actions rather than plans, and on bottom-up processes rather than top-down decisions. The CIO keyed on benefitting from employees' competencies. The organization, here called "NorConstruct," has few long-term IS strategic plans. Instead, it has developed five different IS strategic themes on a general level. It's actual IS strategy takes place through different IS projects. The case is told through the CIO and provides rich descriptions of IS strategic processes in NorConstruct, as well as the CIO's thoughts on the pros and cons. Throughout the case, several relevant reflections are described.

Section 3
Implementation and Interactions

Chapter 12

Tanja Arh, Jožef Stefan Institute, Slovenia
Vlado Dimovski, University of Ljubljana, Faculty of Economics, Slovenia
Borka Jerman Blažič, Jožef Stefan Institute, Slovenia

This chapter aims at presenting the results of an empirical study, linking the fields of technology-enhanced learning (TEL), Web 2.0 technologies and organizational learning, and their impact on the financial and non-financial business performance. The chapter focuses on the presentation of the conceptualization of a structural model that was developed to test the impact of technology-enhanced learning and Web 2.0 technologies on the organizational learning and business performance of companies with more than 50 employees. The paper provides detailed definitions of technology-enhanced learning, Web 2.0 technologies and technical terms related to it, its scope and the process of organisational learning, as well as a method for business performance assessment. Special attention is given to the findings related to the observed correlations between the aforementioned constructs. The results of the study indicate a strong impact of ICT and technology-enhanced learning on organizational learning and the non-financial business performance.

Chapter 13

Neven Vrček, University of Zagreb, Croatia
Ivan Magdalenić, University of Zagreb, Croatia

Many benefits from implementation of e-business solutions are related to network effects which means that there are many interconnected parties utilizing the same or compatible technologies. The large-scale adoption of e-business practices in public sectors and in small and medium enterprises (SMEs)-prevailing economic environments will be successful if appropriate support in the form of education, adequate legislative, directions, and open source applications is provided. This case study describes the adoption of e-business in public sectors and SMEs by using an integrated open source approach called e-modules. E-module is a model which has process properties, data properties, and requirements on technology. Therefore e-module presents a holistic framework for deployment of e-business solutions and such e-module structure mandates an approach which requires reengineering of business processes and adoption of strong standardization that solves interoperability issues. E-module is based on principles of service-oriented architectures with guidelines for introduction into business processes and integration with ERP systems. Such an open source approach enables the spreading of compatible software solutions across any given country, thus, increasing e-business adoption. This paper presents a methodology for defining and building e-modules.

Eskandar Tooma, American University in Cairo (AUC), Egypt
Aliaa Bassiouny, American University in Cairo (AUC), Egypt
Nourhan El Mogui, American University in Cairo (AUC), Egypt

Despite its success in creating a strong market for its product and growing its customer base, PICS is going through a restructuring phase to overcome a variety of operational and financial challenges. This case study examines the concept of value-based management (VBM) and how applying it to the company's restructuring process would help PICS'S management track its performance and make sound strategic decisions for the company. The protagonist is PICS CEO Mr. Paul Antaki, who is being presented with a proposal from 'Val-U' consultants on how VBM would create value for all PICS stakeholders.

The case follows through the history of PICS, presenting the business model and the market for its products. It then moves on to outline the financial position of PICS over the period 2002-2005,which shows that, despite double-digit growth in revenue, the company has suffered from poor bottom lines that have put the company in severe financial distress.

Suryadeo Vinay Kissoon, RMIT University, Australia

This chapter introduces the CTIO (Concern-Task-Interaction-Outcome) Cycle as a means of studying team member interaction using face-to-face and virtual interaction media in retail banking. The type of interaction is discussed in terms of different conceptual cycles having a linkage in the framing of the CTIO Cycle. In the past, routine teamwork using face-to-face communication was important. Today, with emerging technologies for retail banking organizations, teamwork through virtual communication has been gaining importance for increased productivity. This chapter addresses different problem-solving cycles, each of which relates to the mode of interaction medium (whether face-to-face or virtual) used by team members, facilitators, or managers to resolve problems in the workplace. The chapter focuses on understanding the relationship between face-to-face and virtual interaction variables. This is important to researchers in identifying retail banking trends using hybrid teams and virtual group networks with routine teamwork. Using virtual over face-to-face interactions in the different data life cycles linkages are gaining importance from the perspectives of data and information quality. This can be attributed to the increased use of technologies and virtual network features. Current trends are leading to the triangulation of continuous improvement, routine teamwork, and virtual teamwork in support of retail banking organizations achieving productive performance.

Chapter 16

Inge Hermanrud, Hedmark University College, Norway

Organizations today are looking for new ways to support knowledge-sharing and learning activities among their employees by the use of IT. The case describes how inspectors share their work experiences, reflect upon them, and learn from each other at a distance by using stories, pictures, and documents, which is made possible by the GoToMeeting tool™. In this case the GoToMeeting™ tool supports learning activities across geographical and organizational boundaries and contributes to efficient conditions for sharing inspection practices. The issues covered are learning activities facilitated by IT as well as the limitations of the tool in use.

Chapter 17

Anna Filipi, Australian Council for Educational Research, Australia
Sophie Lissonnet, Australian Council for Educational Research, Australia

This chapter reports an investigation of online interactions occurring in the context of the development of a suite of foreign language tests known as the Assessment of Language Competence (ALC) (http://www.acer.edu.au/alc/). The interactions took place in a wiki environment from 2007 to 2009. The aim of the investigation was twofold. The first was to identify the features of the organization of online postings in an asynchronous online environment and to compare them with the organization of face-to-face interaction. The second was to examine how expertise is invoked in interactions centered on the vetting of test items. The chapter uses selected findings from Conversation Analysis and applies them to the postings on the wiki. Findings from the analysis include the rarity of self-repair, similarities in the organization of sequence structure and the same orientations to affiliative behavior found in conversation.

Chapter 18

A Use Case for Ontology Evolution and Interoperability: The IEC Utility
Standards Reference Framework 62357 387

Mathias Uslar, OFFIS – Institute for Information Technology, Germany
Fabian Grüning, OFFIS – Institute for Information Technology, Germany
Sebastian Rohjans, OFFIS – Institute for Information Technology, Germany

Within this chapter, the authors provide two use cases on semantic interoperability
in the electric utility industry based on the IEC TR 62357 seamless integration
architecture. The first use case on semantic integration based on ontologies deals
with the integration of the two heterogeneous standards families IEC 61970 and
IEC 61850. Based on a quantitative analysis, we outline the need for integration and
provide a solution based on our framework, COLIN. The second use cases points
out the need to use better metadata semantics in the utility branch, also being solely
based on the IEC 61970 standard. The authors provide a solution to use the CIM as
a domain ontology and taxonomy for improving data quality. Finally, this chapter
outlines open questions and argues that proper semantics and domain models based
on international standards can improve the systems within a utility.

Chapter 19

Streamlining Semantic Integration Systems 416

Yannis Kalfoglou, Ricoh Europe Plc, UK
Bo Hu, SAP Research CEC Belfast, UK

Yannis Kalfoglou and Bo Hu argue for the use of a streamlined approach to integrate semantic integration systems. The authors elaborate on the abundance and
diversity of semantic integration solutions and how this impairs strict engineering
practice and ease of application. The versatile and dynamic nature of these solutions
comes at a price: they are not working in sync with each other neither is it easy to
align them. Rather, they work as standalone systems often leading to diverse and
sometimes incompatible results. Hence the irony that we might need to address the
interoperability issue of tools tackling information interoperability. Kalfoglou and Hu
also report on an exemplar case from the field of ontology mapping where systems
that used seemingly similar integration algorithms and data, yield different results
which are arbitrary formatted and annotated making interpretation and reuse of the
results difficult. This makes it difficult to apply semantic integration solutions in a
principled manner. The authors argue for a holistic approach to streamline and glue
together different integration systems and algorithms. This will bring uniformity
of results and effective application of the semantic integration solutions. If the
proposed streamlining respects design principles of the underlying systems, then
the engineers will have maximum configuration power and tune the streamlined
systems in order to get uniform and well understood results. The authors propose
a framework for building such streamlined system based on engineering principles
and an exemplar, purpose built system, CROSI Mapping System (CMS), which
targets the problem of ontology mapping.

Chapter 20

The Interplay between Practitioners and Technological Experts in the Design
Process of an Archaeology Information System

Tommaso Federici, Università degli Studi della Tuscia, Italy
Alessio Maria Braccini, Università LUISS Guido Carli, Italy

This case describes the design and development process of a computer-based information system for the management of archaeological finds and related documents. Adaptive Structuration Theory is used as the conceptual framework to analyse the role and actions of different people involved in the design and development process, during the different stages of the case. The case addresses key issues, such as an initiative taking place in an organizational context where users show different needs, profiles and levels of information technology literacy. It focuses primarily on the interactions between practitioners and technological experts during the design and development process. Another matter of interest comes from the fact that, in this sector, no other information system for finds management was already available. Moreover, this case targets the domain of archaeology that has not received so much attention by Information Systems literature to date.

Preface

Creating an interactive business environment that intelligently assists workers and mangers as they respond to threats, needs, and opportunities is a possibility that can be realized as never before. However, as business systems advance, they leave in their wake a myriad of pitfalls, inefficiencies, and potential confusion, especially if the design and implementation, managerial concerns, and daily interactions are not properly understood. Often, to gain the best understanding of these exchanges, the only proper teacher is experience and first-hand interaction. While it would be impossible to put this invaluable asset into a book, this collection of cases attempts to do just that by presenting a useful distillation of the context, actions, and results of innovations applied by business professionals.

This casebook, made up of 20 cases, provides an active look into the successes and failures which shape the modern business. It couples the theory and planning required before designing and implementing a system or technological solution. It presents managerial pitfalls that were addressed as well at the opportunities that these systems opened up. And lastly, it outlines the daily interaction, frustration, and success of endeavors as they are fully adopted and become integral to the operations or outcome of the organization as a whole.

The first section is "Innovation and Design" and covers the beginning stages of understanding problems that technology can address, finding the opportunities for innovation, and ensuring that the technological solutions can and are implemented at a procedural level. The first chapter, *Technology Innovation Adoption and Diffusion: A Contrast of Perspectives,* organizes and summarizes the literature on technology innovation adoption and diffusion, which is vast. Some of the major perspectives from this body of literature, contrasting various theoretical perspectives on how innovations are adopted and shaped by organizational processes and structure are presented. The authors first introduce the technology acceptance model, and innovation diffusion theory; and then they categorize viewpoints about organizational innovativeness. Drawing from this framework, for their case study background they introduce adaptive structuration theory, redefining some of its conceptual relationships in "structuration agency theory," putting primacy on the actions of agents and the means by which they operate through and around institutional structures. The authors then present a case study example of an expert decision support system, and conclude with a discussion of implications for managers and entrepreneurs.

The second chapter, *IT/IS Readiness Maturity Model,* explains the concept of an IT/IS readiness maturity model including particular requirements in terms of four domains, embracing nine attributes: IT infrastructure (top management perception, systems and communication), people (skills, roles and responsibility of IT staff, user involvement), process, and work environment (organization behaviour, IT department, leadership). Each of the attributes consists of 14 factors: top management perception (drivers, systems requirements definition), systems and communication (focus, network communication), skills (type of skills, capability building), roles and responsibility of IT staff (position of IT/IS heads, roles of IT staff), user involvement, process (practices), organizational behaviour (characteristics), IT policy (control of IT/IS activities), and leadership (communication, participation). The following section describes the concept of readiness and maturity, the resources used for element extraction/adoption and the description of the model.

Faced with increasing competitive pressures, a logistics company in the United States sought to reduce its cost structure by implementing two information systems. The Labor Management System (LMS) was specifically designed to improve warehouse worker efficiency and the Radio Frequency Identification (RFID) system tracked the movement of products, pallets, and shipment. Chapter 3, *RFID and Labor Management Systems Selection in the Logistics Industry,* presents an overview of the logistics industry, background on the business need to consider new systems, and the requirements of the company in its system selection. Details of the technologies considered are included. After analyzing this case study, the reader should be able to, define logistics functions, supply chain management, and third party logistics (3PL) services; describe LMS and RFID systems; identify the expected costs and benefits of the proposed technologies; develop a multi-factor evaluation for vendor selection; and make a recommendation based on the evaluation, financial data, and other considerations.

Chapter 4, *Adoption of a New Online Travel Management System for FED-AK,* describes the implementation of an online travel management system at FED-AK, the Alaska office of a U.S. government agency. The previous system was intended to accomplish the same functionality, but due to employee resistance, it was used only as a forms generator in conjunction with a paper- and mail-based process. The new system is integrated, which compels employees to use all the functionality provided. It also incorporates many lessons learned from the old system—in particular, extensive training and online help functions. The system is expected to significantly reduce the cost of travel by minimizing errors, enforcing policies, and reducing transaction costs. The system will also lead to faster reimbursement of employee travel expenses.

Chapter 5, *ICT and Web 2.0 Technologies as a Determinant of Business Performance,* provides detailed definitions of technology-enhanced learning, Web 2.0 technologies and technical terms related to it, its scope and the process of organizational learning, as well as a method for business performance assessment. Special attention is given to the findings related to the observed correlations between the aforementioned constructs.

The next chapter, *Inventory Management Process: Problems in an Indian Convenience Store* captures inventory management process in an Indian convenience store. Unlike retail stores in developed countries, Indian convenience stores are a special format of organized retailing, where retailers open multiple smaller stores in a town instead of one big centralized store. An excellent inventory management process is the key to make such stores perform well. This case describes inventory management problems faced by an Indian convenience store chain and asks students to propose solutions to these problems. This case illustrates how processes realities and their IT solutions differ in an emerging economy. Using inventory management process as an example, this teaching case can introduce students to the process and technological realities in an Indian context and differences between India and the West.

The next section, "Managerial Approaches and Practices," explores the role that management plays in the success or failure of many innovations. The first case in this section, *Path to Success: Innovative Managerial Approach,* discusses the various reasons for implementing different organizational strategies, such as responsiveness to customers, adaptability to market, and competitiveness with other competitors. It explores the factors that encourage a company to diversify its organizational structure in different countries. Further, it highlights the important differences between organizational structure at headquarter as compared to that in foreign subsidiaries.

Building a Knowledge Management System in a Design Firm: The Case of XYZ Structural Department shows how knowledge management represents a strategic vision for developing an organization's performance and its likelihood of success in dealing with future challenges in its industry. This case starts by discussing the importance of knowledge management in improving the competitive edge of firms in general and of consulting firms in particular. Then, the case discusses the process of building a knowledge management system in the structural engineering department at a leading engineering design consulting firm, based in the Republic of Lebanon. The knowledge, both tacit and explicit, needed during the design phase is identified and mapped according to the adopted design process, and an expert system was built to capture some of the tacit knowledge needed in the conceptual design stage of the process. In addition, an intranet Web-based knowledge management system was developed with the aim of helping diffuse both explicit and tacit knowledge.

Chapter 9, *Multilayered Distribution System in India: Practice and Issues,* presents several case studies of the multilayered system in India and shows how the prevalent distribution system preclude any means of cost reduction and making these supply chains efficient. Supply chains of perishable goods, electronic products, FMCG products, and pharmaceutical products are discussed in this chapter. Each of these supply chains present unique challenges and issues that need attention.

Current severe competition in the market forced senior management to give much care to acquiring quick and efficient Information Systems that enable the company not only to manage its operations but to provide on-the-fly performance measurement through a variety of tools. Chapter 10, *Implementing Business Intelligence in the Dynamic Beverages Sales and Distribution Environment,* explains how the ERP system was used as the backbone by BI systems to help Sales and Marketing units in Transnational Company subsidiary in Egypt successfully meet the demands for nimble information services.

Lastly in this section, Chapter 11 *IS Strategic Processes: Benefitting from People's Competencies in a Geographically Dispersed Organization - A CIO's Challenge,* provides rich descriptions of IS strategic processes, as well as the CIO's thoughts on the pros and cons, as told through the CIO. In large, geographically dispersed organizations, achieving a successful Information Systems (IS) strategy can prove very challenging. This case describes how a CIO in such an organization met that challenge by focusing on actions rather than plans, and on bottom-up processes rather than top-down decisions. The CIO keyed on benefitting from employees' competencies. The organization, here called "NorConstruct," has few long-term IS strategic plans. Instead, it has developed five different IS strategic themes on a general level. It's actual IS strategy takes place through different IS projects. Throughout the case, several relevant reflections are described.

Section three, Implementation and Interactions, describes some of the necessary "growing pains" of successful implementation of IS strategies. This sections provides a broad sampling from many different types of enterprises and organizations working to achieve long-term benefits from the technological possibilities . For example, Chapter 12, *ICT and Web 2.0 Technologies as a Determinant of Business Performance,* examines key issues surrounding the management and implementation of health information systems (HIS) outsourcing in Taiwanese hospitals and identify issues that are crucial in managing and implementing HIS outsourcing in hospitals. Four key issues and problems were identified in the HIS outsourcing process: lack of implementation in IS investment evaluation process, problems in managing HIS outsourcing contracts, lack of user involvement and participation in HIS outsourcing process, and failure to retain critical HIS contract management skills and project management capabilities in-house.

Many benefits from implementation of e-business solutions are related to network effects which means that there are many interconnected parties utilizing the same or compatible technologies. The large-scale adoption of e-business practices in public sectors and in small and medium enterprises (SMEs)-prevailing economic environments will be successful if appropriate support in the form of education, adequate legislative, directions, and open source applications is provided. This case, Chapter 13, *Methodology and Software Components for E-Business Development and Implementation: Case of Introducing E-Invoice in Public Sector and SMEs*, describes the adoption of e-business in public sectors and SMEs by using an integrated open source approach called e-modules. E-module is a model which has process properties, data properties, and requirements on technology. Therefore e-module presents a holistic framework for deployment of e-business solutions and such e-module structure mandates an approach which requires reengineering of business processes and adoption of strong standardization that solves interoperability issues. E-module is based on principles of service-oriented architectures with guidelines for introduction into business processes and integration with ERP systems. Such an open source approach enables the spreading of compatible software solutions across any given country, thus, increasing e-business adoption. This paper presents a methodology for defining and building e-modules.

Chapter 14, *Premium International for Credit Services: Application of Value-Based Management,* proposes the implementation of the Value-Based-Management approach as a tool to monitor performance and improve decision making. It thoroughly explains the business model of Premium International Credit Card Services Company (PICS), a well-established Egyptian consumer credit card service provider. PICS has been undertaking a restructuring process to overcome its financial and operational problems. The company's management has been presented with a proposal to apply value based management to improve the company's performance and create value to stakeholders.

The next chapter, *Use of the Concern-Task-Interaction-Outcome (CTIO) Cycle for Virtual Teamwork,* introduces the CTIO (Concern-Task-Interaction-Outcome) Cycle as a means of studying team member interaction using face-to-face and virtual interaction media in retail banking. The type of interaction is discussed in terms of different conceptual cycles having a linkage in the framing of the CTIO Cycle. In the past, routine teamwork using face-to-face communication was important. Today, with emerging technologies for retail banking organizations, teamwork through virtual communication has been gaining importance for increased productivity.

Organizations today are looking for new ways to support knowledge-sharing and learning activities among their employees by the use of IT. The case *Sharing Work Practice in the Distributed Organization* describes how inspectors share their work experiences, reflect upon them, and learn from each other at a distance by using stories, pictures, and documents, which is made possible by the GoToMeeting™ tool. In this case the GoToMeeting™ tool supports learning activities across geographical and organizational boundaries and contributes to efficient conditions for sharing inspection practices. The issues covered are learning activities facilitated by IT as well as the limitations of the tool in use.

In Chapter 17, *Investigating the Online Interactions of a Team of Test Developers Working in a Wiki Environment, w*e get to take a close look at the online collaboration of experts developing a test in order to (1) compare the online, asynchronous communication to face-to-face, and (2) uncover how expertise is displayed online. Filipi and Lissonet use the method of conversation analysis to get at matters of structure and identity in the online interactions of experts working together.

The authors of Chapter 18, *A Use Case for Ontology Evolution and Interoperability: The IEC Utility Standards Reference Framework 62357,* provide two use cases on semantic interoperability in the electric utility industry based on the IEC TR 62357 seamless integration architecture. The first use case on semantic integration based on ontologies deals with the integration of the two heterogeneous standards families IEC 61970 and IEC 61850. Based on a quantitative analysis, the authors outline the need for integration and provide a solution based on our framework, COLIN. The second use cases points out the need to use better metadata semantics in the utility branch, also being solely based on the IEC 61970 standard. The authors provide a solution to use the CIM as a domain ontology and taxonomy for improving data quality. Finally, this chapter outlines open questions and argues that proper semantics and domain models based on international standards can improve the systems within a utility.

Yannis Kalfoglou and Bo Hu in Chapter 19, *Streamlining Semantic Integration Systems,* argue for the use of a streamlined approach to integrate semantic integration systems. The authors elaborate on the abundance and diversity of semantic integration solutions and how this impairs strict engineering practice and ease of application. The versatile and dynamic nature of these solutions comes at a price: they are not working in sync with each other neither is it easy to align them. Rather, they work as standalone systems often leading to diverse and sometimes incompatible results. Hence the irony that we might need to address the interoperability issue of tools tackling information interoperability. Kalfoglou and Hu also report on an exemplar case from the field of ontology mapping where systems that used seemingly similar integration algorithms and data, yield different results which are arbitrary formatted and annotated making interpretation and reuse of the results difficult. This makes it difficult to apply semantic integration solutions in a principled manner. The authors argue for a holistic approach to streamline and glue together different integration systems and algorithms. This will bring uniformity of results and effective application of the semantic integration solutions. If the proposed streamlining respects design principles of the underlying systems, then the engineers will have maximum configuration power and tune the streamlined systems in order to get uniform and well understood results. The authors propose a framework for building such streamlined system based on engineering principles and an exemplar, purpose built system, CROSI Mapping System (CMS), which targets the problem of ontology mapping.

Lastly, Chapter 20, *The Interplay between Practitioners and Technological Experts in the Design Process of an Archaeology Information System,* describes the design and development process of a computer-based information system for the management of archaeological finds and related documents. Adaptive Structuration Theory is used as the conceptual framework to analyze the role and actions of different people involved in the design and development process, during the different stages of the case. The case addresses key issues, such as an initiative taking place in an organizational context where users show different needs, profiles and levels of information technology literacy. It focuses primarily on the interactions between practitioners and technological experts during the design and development process. Another matter of interest comes from the fact that, in this sector, no other information system for finds management was already available. Moreover, this case targets the domain of archaeology that has not received so much attention by Information Systems literature to date.

When considered as a whole, these cases provide a collection of insights and real-world examples for guiding any professional or future professional on the design, implementation and management of technology related innovation. With the understanding that is available in these cases one can capitalize on the many improvements to productivity and the opportunities uniquely possible with today's technology.

Mehdi Khosrow-Pour
Information Resources Management Association, USA

Section 1
Innovation and Design

Chapter 1

Technology Innovation Adoption and Diffusion:
A Contrast of Perspectives

Michael Workman
Florida Institute of Technology, USA

EXECUTIVE SUMMARY

The literature on technology innovation adoption and diffusion is vast. In this chapter, we organize and summarize some of the major perspectives from this body of literature, contrasting various theoretical perspectives on how innovations are adopted and shaped by organizational processes and structure. We first introduce the technology acceptance model, and innovation diffusion theory; and then we categorize viewpoints about organizational innovativeness. Drawing from this framework, for our case study background we introduce adaptive structuration theory, redefining some of its conceptual relationships in "structuration agency theory," putting primacy on the actions of agents and the means by which they operate through and around institutional structures. We then present a case study example of an expert decision support system, and we conclude with a discussion of implications for managers and entrepreneurs.

INTRODUCTION

An innovation is defined as the act of changing the established order, or introducing something new (Webster's Dictionary, 1978). Thus there are two sides to the innovation coin, the diffusion of them, and the production of them. One aspect these two sides of the coin share in common is some measure of risk-taking behavior, but the

DOI: 10.4018/978-1-4666-2618-8.ch001

creation of innovations tends to be an individualized thought put into action, whereas the diffusion of them tends to be the result of a set of institutionalized and collective socialized actions, although sometimes initiated by a "champion" (Lake, 2009).

In this chapter, we will concentrate on the adoption and diffusion of technological innovations within organizations. We will first briefly introduce innovation research situated in the field of management science and briefly discuss how it has evolved relative to our topic. In the sections that follow, we will review two seminal streams of innovation adoption theory by introducing the technology acceptance model (Davis, 1989) and diffusion of innovations theory (Rogers, 1983). We will then categorize and summarize the major theoretical perspectives on how innovations develop from, or are shaped by, organizational processes and structures –referred to as organizational innovativeness (Chakravarthy, 1997). We will then present a brief case study to illustrate adoption and diffusion theory and structuration with an expert decision support system in an organization, and conclude with a discussion of implications.

The study of innovations has its basis in management science. Some of the most frequently cited examples are novel approaches or inventions such as Henry Ford's mass production of the automobile, or Eli Whitney's approach to the mass assembly of rifles, or his cotton gin, or about Thomas Edison and the invention the light bulb, or Alexander Graham Bell and the telephone; but the development of innovations occur with much less fanfare and more frequently than we might expect, with many failing to gain enough traction to be adopted or diffuse in organizations.

Management science has evolved from its early roots in the 19th-Century scientific management era to embrace the notion that an organization adapts and structures itself according to its business environment and needs, and that human actions emerge from, and business conditions grow out of, dynamic organizational systems (Sine, Mitsuhashi & Kirsch, 2006). This evolution in managerial thinking began in the 1970s and gave rise to "systems theory." As part of that renaissance, in the 1980s and early 90s, socio-technical systems theory (Trist, 1971) began to make its way into management practice in which both the technical and socio-cultural aspects of organizational systems were considered to be interdependent (Manz & Stewart, 1997). Socio-technical systems:

"...reflects the goal of integrating the social requirements of people doing the work with the technical requirements needed to keep the work systems viable with regard to their environments. These are considered interdependent because arrangements that are optimal for one may not be optimal for the other. Also tradeoffs are typical, and thus there is a need for both dual focus and joint optimization" (Fox, 1995, p. 92).

Although dual focus and joint optimization were imagined to be an ideal, socio-technical systems-driven practices initially ran counter to the entrenched mechanistic ones (Burns & Stalker, 1961) and was met with much resistance (Quinn, 1992). While process engineers, total quality management proponents, and members of process standards bodies fought to maintain their control over processes and developments throughout the 1980s and 1990s by means of certifications that tested conformance to a given standard with a presumed single correct solution, many organizations began concentrating instead on innovation through diversity of inputs in reaction. According to Hamel and Prahalad, (1993), there was a growing rejection of the notion that through benchmarking and standardization, everyone should have a race down identical paths where no one wins.

Consequently, creativity was touted as the means to achieve innovativeness. Creativity is by definition variation or deviation from the norm (Daft & Lengel, 1986); and since it often evolves out of crises (Kuhn, 1996), the phrase *necessity is the mother of invention* was an appropriate cliché. Thus newer organizational models came to operate less from a systematic perspective and more from a systemic one. In other words, while it was well recognized that standardization and striving toward some well-defined end using some well-defined means were crucial in certain areas and aspects within an organization, by and large, this forced convergence was too constraining to enable, let alone encourage, innovation (Stacy, 1992).

In that light, the drives toward innovation and differentiation became the over-arching goals of many organizations (Porter, 1996), and organizational strategies were formulated and aligned to generate a level of variety that matched the level of flexibility required by the organization's purpose and environment (Denton & Wisdom, 1992). It was perceived that any innovation was strategic in nature and would need to combine flexible technologies, processes, and people to accommodate the spectrum of issues across multiple system boundaries (Mintzberg, 1994). This was an important concept because even "modest increases in variety usually produce dramatic increases in flexibility and in the capacity for adaptive response" (Pava, 1983, p. 55).

Nevertheless, the alignment and optimization of organizational systems meant that technological systems had to diffuse rapidly throughout organizations. Innovation theory (Rogers, 1983) postulates that the adoption of a technological innovation encompasses many facets spanning personal, social, and strategic aspects of organizations, and can derive from either an administrative core or from the "grass roots" level. Along with globalization and multiculturalism found in many organizations as the result of multinational conglomerations and outsourcing, it led to increased complexity, necessitating that managers and entrepreneurs attend not only to the technological aspects of variety but the socio-cultural aspects of variety as well (Semler, 1997).

By the time socio-technical systems theory had taken hold in organizational practice, it was firmly believed that inadequate attention to a particular technological environment or their impacts on social structures in organizations would result in problems such as a lack of *ownership* of, or lack of commitment to, organizational goals and innovations (Manz & Stewart, 1997). Consequently a marriage was made of the rational-technological elements of innovation and the socio-cultural and qualitative viewpoints about innovativeness such as those espoused by adaptive structuration theory (DeSanctis & Poole, 1994).

By emphasizing the role that social systems played in technology adoption, innovation, and organizational structuring, this ultimately led to an ideational integration about the technical, behavioral, and social systems in management science (Ngwenyama & Lee, 1997). This was considered to be important because dynamic interrelationships among people (their beliefs, values, intentions, and behavior) and their social and technological systems all collide in organizations and have direct bearing on an organization's innovativeness (Boxall, 1996; Porter, 1979).

THEORY FRAMEWORKS

Technology Acceptance Model

The study of how innovations are adopted and spread through organizations has been widely studied, primarily guided by two seminal sets of work, the technology adoption model (Davis, 1989) and the diffusion of innovations theory (Rogers, 1983), although other theories have also been utilized such as Ajzen's (1991) theory of planned behavior. The technology acceptance model (Davis, 1989), or TAM, describes how innovative technology impacts people at work. In his foundational study, Davis (1989) presented two variables as predictive constructs of technology adoption and implementation behavior, which were called "perceived usefulness" of technology and "perceived ease of use" of technology.

In his model, perceived usefulness and perceived ease of use predict attitudes about innovations that in turn predict people's intentions to adopt and use them. The perceived usefulness construct is defined as "the degree to which a person believes that using a particular system would enhance his or her job performance, whereas perceived ease of use refers to the degree to which a person believes that using a particular system would be free of effort" (p. 320). Davis (1989) also emphasized the subjectivity in innovation adoption since "a decision maker's choice of strategy is theorized to be based on subjective as opposed to objective accuracy and effort" (p. 321). Thus, TAM focused almost exclusively on individual acceptance of innovations in organizations.

Innovation Diffusion Theory

Besides the TAM, one of the most influential among the seminal works on innovation adoption and diffusion was the lineage of research conducted by Rogers (1983), known as the innovation diffusion theory. Unlike the TAM, rather than concentrating exclusively on individuals and their roles in adoption of innovations, innovation diffusion theory is generally studied as an organization-level construct, although individuals and their characteristics are still considered to be important components of this theory framework (Wolfe, 1994). To highlight this, an innovation in this sense is "an idea, practice, or object that is perceived as new by an individual or other unit of adoption" (Rogers, 1983, p. 11).

From innovation diffusion theory, the factors purported to influence diffusion of new technologies include adopter characteristics, the social network to which the adopters belong, innovation attributes, environmental characteristics, the process by which an innovation is communicated, and the characteristics of those who are promoting the innovation (Rogers & Kincaid, 1981). According to Wolfe (1994), innovation adoption falls under administrative or technological domains. Administrative innovations involve changes in the organization's structure or administrative processes, and tend to derive from management. Technological innovations derive from technical needs, and often from the "grass roots" level in the organization.

Innovation diffusion occurs in stages: initiation, adoption, implementation and institutionalization (Rogers, 1983). Adoption entails a decision making influence or force. Implementation involves the details of the innovation reflecting organizational contingencies. When an innovation becomes routine, it becomes an institutionalized structure (Chakravarthy, 1997). According to Taylor and Todd (1995), three characteristics of an innovation relate to technology adoption and diffusion (implementation) behavior. These characteristics are complexity, compatibility, and perceived relative advantage. Complexity in this framework is akin to the TAM perceived ease of use; and compatibility is akin to the TAM perceived usefulness.

The perceived relative advantage is a product of a cost-benefit assessment. "As the perceived relative advantages and compatibility of information technology usage increase, and as complexity decreases, attitude towards information systems usage should become more positive, and such an outcome would be consistent with the general diffusion of innovations literature and with specific results observed for information technology" (Taylor & Todd, 1995, p. 152). Elaborating on the concept of perceived relative advantage, other research on decision making about innovations (Gustafson & Reger, 1995) has included the maximization of benefits and the minimization of costs adjusted by or filtered through cognitive schematic frames.

According to this view, people do not simply adopt an innovation from rational aspects such as economics alone, but from perceived relative advantage influenced by their cognitive schema and previous experiences. These schematic frames represent preferences and affect, and are therefore not part of a formalized or systematic choice; consequently, the decisions about adopting new technological innovations may be subject to overconfidence errors such as optimism in response to perceived risks (c.f. Tversky & Kahneman, 1983). Thus, while (according to this theory) innovation adoption and diffusion decision making may be deliberate processes, they may not always be rational processes (Gustafson & Reger, 1995).

Finally, Rogers (1983) defined what has become commonly referred to as the "adoption curve" in which he articulates five categories of adopters. This is sometimes referred to as the S-curve adoption of an innovation because of its non-linear plotting over time. The categories Roger's defined were: innovators, early adopters, early majority, late majority, and laggards. Each has associated with it a category of risk tolerance, or risk homeostasis. That is to say, people differ in their assessments of risk (Wilde, 2001) and some people have a greater risk tolerance than others (Lauriola, Levin, & Hart; 2007), which can be plotted on the technology adoption curve –from innovators to laggards.

Innovation as a Socio-Cultural Phenomenon

Another important body of literature has considered the socio-cultural influences in technology innovation adoption and diffusion. For instance, Sheppard, et al. (1988) conducted a meta-analysis in which they revealed that when people perceive that they have little control over an outcome such as the adoption of a new technology, there is negative impact on intentions regarding the necessary risk-taking to adopt an innovation, and that they may make attempts to dissuade others from adoption of an innovation as well, either directly or through normative actions. The perception of control has socio-cultural components called "contextual adequacy" and "symbolic meaning."

Contextual adequacy relates to the sufficiency of an innovation to satisfy perceived needs (Fussell & Benimoff, 1995). The symbolic meaning aspect of an innovation may influence perception of constituent's control in a related but separate way from contextual adequacy (Ngwenyama & Lee, 1997). That is, the mental models people formulate about what the innovation may mean for a given adopter goes beyond the innovation's technological characteristics, such as how they "feel" about it, the implications for their jobs, or relates to their intrinsic resistance to change. To summarize the technology innovation adoption and diffusion theory, according to Webster (1998):

"Innovation characteristics theory assumes that individuals adopt innovative technologies to perform individual tasks and therefore technologies need to be designed

with the correct characteristics of these individuals, while implementation processes theory assumes that groups perform interdependent tasks and therefore managerial effort needs to be focused on the process of implementation" (p. 258).

BACKGROUND

From the preceding section on innovation adoption and diffusion theory, we suggested that the research bases on innovation diffusion have been influenced largely by concentrating on individuals acting in their organizational structural and social environments. In this section, we will examine and contrast several perspectives on how technological innovations "come about" and become institutionalized in organizations, referring to this as organizational innovativeness. The purpose of this section is to provide the background for our case study.

We will begin with the view that is consistent with the individual-focused approach, where an individual or a small group of actors are presumed to drive or shape innovation adoption, and then progress into a more systemic view of how collective social action may do this. We conclude this section by considering the possibilities for how actors may affect innovation adoption and diffusion either directly or indirectly, but ultimately, we propose that technology innovation adoption and diffusion are the result of collective social activity governed in part by how actors utilize organizational processes and structures to influence adoption and diffusion of innovations.

Innovation as a Deliberative Strategic Plan

As might be inferred from the innovation adoption theory in the previous section, an innovation is widely assumed to be a strategic organizational concept (c.f. Jarzabkowski, 2008). Still, the concept of strategic innovative behavior has little consensus in the literature about what it means (Raisch & Birkinshaw, 2008). To some, it a process that *can be engineered* (Mintzberg, 1994) while to others it is the characteristic of *future visioning* (Denton & Wisdom, 1992) and for others it is exploiting *core competencies* (Hamel & Prahalad, 1993). Regardless, the body of research literature on strategic innovation divides along the lines in a continuum where at one polar end consists of processes that are scientific, planned or structured (e.g. Semler, 1997) and on the other polar end are forms of artistry, imagination, and intuition (e.g. Stacy, 1992). Thus there are different perspectives about strategic organizational innovativeness.

In a deliberative paradigm, a strategic innovation is a product development or service activity that (1) is used to gain competitive advantage (Porter, 1979, 1997), and (2) requires "long-term" commitment in time and resources to produce, provide, or implement (Simon & Houghton, 2003). Strategic innovations therefore differ from tactics and operations in that the former is a blend of various analyses, behavioral techniques, and the use of power and organizational politics to bring about broadly conceived outcomes (Quinn, 1992). Tactics are managerial actions that enact a strategic innovation (Greer, 1995), and operations are the daily routines that result from management actions such as planning and production and quality control (Synnott, 1987).

From this point of view, realizing a strategic innovation in organizations comes by way of a deliberative process through a "value chain" (Porter, 1979), either as a formalized and structured procedure or as an imaginative and creative visioning process. In either case, from this perspective, innovation adoption and diffusion is a focused and systematic method (Simon & Houghton, 2003).

Innovation as a Convergent Set of Processes

In the 1970s as part of the Tavistock studies that took place in the United Kingdom, a new view of organizations as parts of interconnected systems emerged (Trist, 1971). From this socio-technical systems theory perspective, strategic innovation results from organizational alignment of strategic and operational activities (Semler, 1997). In this sense, it shares the perspective of the strategic innovation planning lens in which innovativeness is a formalized and deliberative action. It differs however in the sense that this is not seen as a single deliberative process but rather as a convergence of many (and possibly disparate) processes (Greer, 1995).

In realizing an innovation from the convergence perspective, managers and entrepreneurs apply principles defined in socio-technical systems theory, first by performing a system scan (Fox, 1995) in which the mission of the organization is identified and stakeholders' interests are reconciled by what is viable with regard to the outside environment. Various techniques ranging from "Delphi" to stochastic modeling technology have been used for this (along with their cousin "action planning") and continue to be popular approaches employed by many managers and entrepreneurs.

The *systems scan* is followed by a technical analysis in which the technology inputs and outputs (rather than tools, processes or techniques) are defined. In an end-to-end process the systems are analyzed separately from jobs and people –from the input side of the system to the output side, and from this activity a unit-operations flow chart is produced. Variances are noted (other than those representing human error or breakdowns) and recorded and a key-variance matrix table is generated with the primary goal of eliminating deviations. This way, it can be determined what actions are necessary to control the variances. Finally, the social analysis is performed. This function (called focal-role analysis) determines the role-expectations and work-related interactions of those in positions most involved with the control of key variances (Fox, 1995).

Simultaneously with this effort to drive out variance and gain conformity to a given set of standards, the process seeks to establish sets of core competencies, and align the collective values and beliefs of the organizational members with organizational objectives, and the social relationships are noted for work-related interactions of "focal persons and four survival criteria: sound key-variance control, adaptation to the external environment, integration of in-system people activities, and long-term development" (Fox, 1995, p. 99). The product of this activity is called a "grid of social relations."

Once the system is defined in this manner, social-technical systems innovations could be implemented, which according to Pava (1983, p. 64) involve: (1) Guiding the explicit acknowledgement and designation of major deliberations and their corresponding discretionary coalitions. (2) Establishing responsibilities of each coalition for every deliberation. (3) Delineating human resource policies that support effective deliberations among discretionary coalitions. (4) Suggesting structural changes in the organization pertaining to responsibilities and coordination that enhances major deliberations and their associated coalitions, and, (5) proposing technical enhancements to assist discretionary coalitions engaged in major deliberations about innovations.

Innovation as an Emergent Phenomenon

The notion that innovativeness is an emergent phenomenon discards the concept that organizational activities are static enough to record and asserts that capturing or bracketing its fluid structures is impractical, if possible. The view of innovation through emergence is more akin to the strategic innovation perspective in-so-far as innovations are seen as the product of imagination and creativity, but it differs in the sense that these processes are not considered part of a formal deliberative or systematic method. Also in contrast to the socio-technical systems approach which suggests that innovations are driven through the alignment of organizational systems, from the emergent perspective, innovation evolves out of chaos and crises (Stacy, 1992).

According to Kuhn (1996), when a normative approach to solving problems (which Kuhn called a paradigm) becomes insoluble, a radical transformation occurs (which Kuhn coined a paradigm shift). During the latter 1990s, it became apparent in the literature on strategic innovations that it was not feasible in the manner of socio-technical systems theory to maintain a peaceful coexistence between those who believed that innovation could be designed and those who believed innovation was pure serendipity. To put it another way, the efforts to drive out variance and drive towards conformance to a standard regarding innovative development, versus generating the variety needed for continuous innovation do not peacefully coexist (Mintzberg, 1994).

As an example, it became apparent that trying to maintain a "grid of social relations," let alone make note of all the interrelated organizational objectives involving those social relationships was impractical if even possible (Stacy, 1992). In addition, new organizational structures had evolved including the notion of teamwork and extreme forms of organizational autonomy such as self-managed teams (Workman & Bommer, 2004). The emphasis on teamwork relies on the essential thought that deliberations are democratic and that ideational generation and decisions about them require consensus rather than compromises. In this way, all organizational behaviors were perceived as strategic, and that values and beliefs of participants would help to foster innovativeness through the collective efforts and activities, including conflicts (Mintzberg, 1994).

Thus from this vantage point, since organizations are comprised of people, ultimately, it is the collective capabilities of those people that orchestrate the achievements in organizations. Here, the development of capabilities results from dynamic and active processes that happen *ad hoc*. This contrasts with the convergent prescriptive, which was criticized by Antonacopoulou and FitzGerald (1996) because, they asserted, it is misleading to consider innovation as a narrowly defined and rigid process that can be formulated *a priori*. To them –innovativeness is an open-ended activity. In this way it is not be the capabilities of people that are developed and applied in building an innovation, but rather it constitutes the capabilities of people in action through continuous learning and experimentation that produces radical mutations we call innovation (Stacy, 1992).

In a more contemporary form, the view of innovativeness embodies a holistic "open systems" perspective that neither concentrates exclusively on converging mechanistic efficiencies nor on fostering creative effectiveness (Sine, et al., 2006). Instead it embraces self-organization and the informal and fluid processes that germinate spontaneous ideas, but it also recognizes that these seemingly "chaotic" organizations and reorganizations have structure to them. More particularly, the continuous establishment and disestablishment of social networks and the natural shifts in organizational power energizes action through both cooperation and conflicts that erupt and dissipate. And fundamental to this more organic view of innovation as an emerging phenomenon is the realization of the differences between problems that have a single correct solution and are programmable, and those that are equivocal and involve multiple subjective points of view about innovative solutions (Daft & Lengel, 1986).

Innovation through Structuration

Structuration theory helps to explain the role of human agency in the reciprocal relationship between human social systems and their social structures, which Giddens called the "duality of structure." It is important to note that structuration theory (Giddens, 1984, 1991) has taken some criticism in the "post-modern" management theory literature for being poorly operationalized (Gephart, Boje, & Thatchenkery, 1996; Ritzer, 2005; Stones, 2005), and as well in the information technology literature for having difficulty bracketing actions and transitions in structures, especially in light of technological advances that can affect structuration (De Sanctis & Poole, 1994; Orlikowski, 1996).

Consequently, adaptive structuration theory (De Sanctis & Poole, 1994) was developed from structuration theory to capture how people adapt to technology as well as adapt the technology to their own usage behaviors. For instance, studies (c.f. Maznevski & Chudoba, 2000) have shown that the social structures and power distributions affected how people utilize new technology. Other studies (De Sanctis & Poole, 1994; Orlikowski, 1996) have demonstrated how groups used the same decision support system differently for determining project priorities.

In these studies, depending on the social structures, the use of power, and the results of conflicts that arose within the groups, very different structuration took place. More specifically, some group members tended to rely more on influence and persuasion while others tended to use force. Therefore, from a socio-cultural perspective, adaptive structuration theory, or AST, (Desanctis & Poole, 1994) has provided "a model that describes the interplay among advanced information technologies, social structures, and human interaction in the adoption of innovations" (p. 125). The social context provides the rules and resources that serve as templates for a group's actions relative to how they might respond to changes, such as in the introduction of an innovation.

Note that according to AST, the social context of technology adoption and their use relies heavily on leader support and on task structures (Kahai, Sosik & Avolio, 1997). In this way, AST explains the use of information technology and its resulting outcomes (Desanctis & Poole, 1994). These structures are also important to technology innovations; for example, innovation theory generally suggests that innovations are typically derived from the administrative core where leader support is an essential (Wolfe, 1994). In terms of task structure, technology adoption would be impacted by the suitability of the technology to the worker's tasks, and the worker's group interactions. Leader support and task structure "pertain to the systems normative framework for appropriate behaviors" (Kahai, et. al., 1997, p. 123). But this theory alone has not fully explained how innovation becomes "embraced" by organizational members, as illustrated by Workman (2007) in the façade exposed concerning the use of an innovative expert system foisted upon network engineers by their management, as described in our case study that follows. It is important therefore to consider structuration from an agency (social-actor) perspective.

Structuration Agency Theory

Agency in a structuration theory sense is anyone who acts within the formalized social structure of the organization (Jarzabkowski, 2008). The structuration agency use of the term "agency" represents individual behaviors that operate within a broad network of socio-structural influences (Bjorklund, 1995; Chomsky, 1996), which can be within or outside the formally defined organizational structures. Bandura (2001) described this triadic phenomenon as "agentic transactions, where people are producers as well as products of social systems" (p. 1). As defined in this theory, agency exists on three levels: (1) direct personal agency (an individual's actions), (2) proxy agency, which relies on others to act on one's behalf to secure individually desired outcomes, and (3) collective agency, which is exercised through socially coordinative and interdependent effort (Chomsky, 1996; Bandura, 2001). The notion of agency from this perspective contrasts with non-deterministic (chaotic) and non-rational "natural" processes that generate the environments in which people operate either formally or informally (Beck, Giddens & Lash, 1994).

The reciprocal relationships between agentic action and social structures are referred to as the "duality of structure" by Giddens (1984). In these terms, structure is defined by the regularity of actions or patterns of behavior in collective social action, which become institutionalized, and agency then is the human ability to make rational choices and to affect others with consequential actions based on those choices that may coincide with or run counter to institutionalized structures.

Structuration on the other hand is a dynamic activity that emerges from social interaction (Giddens, 1984). Particularly, social action relies on social structures, and social structures are created by means of social action. Thus structures derive the rules and resources that enable form and substance in social life, but the structures themselves are neither form nor substance. Instead, they exist only in and through the activities of human agents. For example, people use language for communications with one-another, and language is defined by the rules and protocols that objectify the concepts that people convey to each other (Chomsky, 1996). The syntax structure of language is the arrangement of words in a sentence, and by their relationships one to another (e.g. subject-predicate noun-verb phrase) the sentence structure establishes a well-defined grammar that people use to communicate (Verspoor & Lowie, 2003).

However, language is also generative and productive and an inherently novel activity, allowing people to create sentences using the syntax rather than to simply memorize and repeat them (Chomsky, 1996). In similar fashion, institutionalized

Figure 1. Structuration Agency Framework

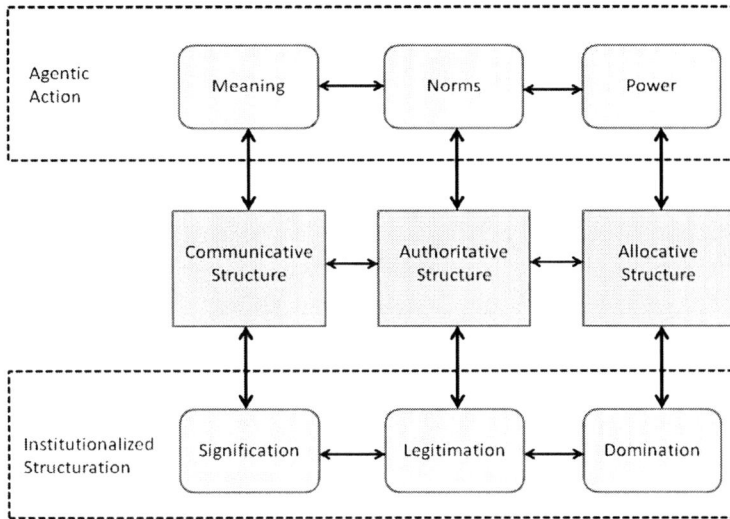

structures regulate agentic behavior, but agents may also disrupt institutionalized structures (Jarzabkowski, 2008). The defining features of structuration theory that explain how these processes work are: signification, legitimation and domination. Signification concerns how meaning is co-created and interpreted by agents, legitimation encompasses the norms and rules for acceptable behavior, and domination refers to power, influence, and control over resources (Giddens, 1991). Collectively, the signification, legitimation and domination constitute the institutionalized structuration processes. Agentic interaction with these processes creates the communicative structure, authoritative structure, and allocative structure, respectively. In the next section we present a case study to illustrate an example of agency and structuration related to technology innovation adoption and diffusion.

CASE STUDY

Globetel (a pseudonym) operates the world's second-largest computer network. Network engineers residing in various parts of the world often need to make changes to the network, but given the vast complexity of the network, a change made to a network segment in one geographical location might have a significant negative impact on another network segment in a different geographical location. In one particularly critical incident, network engineers made a change in the Dallas Texas network operations center (NOC) that led to a collapse of the entire Illinois network segment, causing that segment of the network to be out of operation for several days.

Because network outages such as these were extremely costly and disruptive to many organizations, executive management created a "skunk works" team, which was a term given by Kelly Johnson at Lockheed Martin to an advanced development team that bypassed traditional organizational processes and structures to shorten the development time for innovations. The skunk works team set out to build an expert decision support system (EDSS) that could make predictions about how a proposed network change might impact the overall network infrastructure and traffic.

An EDSS is similar in many ways to conventional decision support systems (DSS). Like DSS, EDSS usage consists of a series of analytical modeling steps that define the problem context and gather relevant information (Taylor & Karlin, 1993). Going beyond DSS, however, EDSS does not terminate with the gathering and rendering of information for human consumers. Instead, the EDSS operates upon the information with reasoning and inference to generate solutions to given problems in the form of stochastic models and prescribed steps and courses of action for the users to follow (Gregor & Benbasat, 1999).

The literature on innovation adoption and diffusion (e.g., Taylor & Todd, 1995) has frequently commented on the importance of innovative technology use in organizational outcomes. For example, technologies can be instrumental in facilitating decision making (DeSanctis & Poole, 1994), may improve communication (Kraut et al., 1998), and may enhance effectiveness, productivity and job performance (Goodhue & Thompson, 1995); yet because the social and communicative structures are often ignored in the introduction of innovations, even with a "champion" for an innovation, systems that are shown to be effective may not diffuse throughout an organization (Brown & Duguid, 2000).

When the EDSS technology was introduced by management into the engineering organization, many were skeptical that the technology could be more accurate than the experience and knowledge of the engineers, and there were outward expressions of distrust. Since the EDSS originated from the administrative core in Globetel, and because the EDSS dictated to the engineers what actions to take, there was initially a strong resistance to adopt the innovation. Some of the engineers expressed that they felt "left out" of the skunk works, and some worried about the meaning of the technology relative to their jobs, and some stating that management was "trying to shove the technology down their throats." There were also expressions that the technology was too rigid. Since the technology required well-defined progressive stages confined to a usage paradigm, the perception of rigidity negatively affected some attitudes towards the technology. In such cases, social communicative and normative influences may impinge on the adoption of the technology (Taylor & Karlin, 1993; Taylor & Todd, 1995).

Unlike pressure levied through an allocative structure that tends to produce resistance, using the communicative and authoritative structures, people sometimes strive more progressively to conform to normative pressures as social influences increase (Salanick & Pfeffer, 1978). Combined with the use of power and force to gain compliance, negative peer normative influence can create an amplification of the resistance. A sample of a dissuasive statement given by a case study participant was, "Can't you figure it out? Why do you have to use the tool for that?" Thus strong sentiment against adopting a technology by peers may increase dissuasive influences and inhibit diffusion. Yet in spite of this, management's response to try to overcome the resistance was to further increase the pressure through the allocative structures by threatening to levy punishments on those who neglected to use the technology.

As indicated in adoption and diffusion theory, human-technology and human-information usage represent different contexts (Gregor & Benbasat, 1999; Morris & Venkatesh, 2000; Tan & Hunter, 2002). For instance, people may utilize a technology because it is expected as part of standard organization practices (legitimation) having coming from an administrative (and authoritative structure), or acceded to by domination (through the use of power to reward or punish), but this forced compliance may lead to counterproductive behaviors in protest (Brown & Duguid, 2000).

When human-induced errors continued at high rates and network outages persisted, a study was initiated by management to find out if the technology was effective. As investigators studied the technology logs and compared them to courses of action engineers took, along with "trouble tickets" called into the technology support center, they determined that the technology was effective in reducing human-induced errors. However, they also learned that the more pressure managers placed on engineers through the use of force to utilize the technology there was a concomitant non-linear relationship between executing the EDSS and ignoring the technology recommendations. In addition, investigators found that negative attitudes toward the EDSS acted as a "social contagion" and spread throughout the engineering organization even among those who had not yet tried the technology, further inhibiting diffusion (Workman, 2005).

In summary therefore, in this case, managers had operated primarily through the use of power and force, relying on authoritative and allocative structures to require the use of the technology. As greater pressure was placed on engineers to use the EDSS, many engineers would simply use the technology to generate the models and procedures, but instead of following the directions given by the technology, they would often ignore the directions and perform their tasks according to their own judgments.

In retrospect, signification from the communicative structure was seen as an important missing focus in this case because technology use does not necessarily lead to the use of the information manipulated or produced by the technology

(Plumlee, 2003). It has been found, as in this case, that social influences and individual attitudes may interact in such a way that when people have poor attitudes or perceptions about a technology and yet social forces strongly encourage its use, people may feign the use of technology but without commitment or without following its prescription (Terry, Hogg & White, 1999). Thus management realized the need for joint optimization by communicating, negotiating, and cooperating with the constituents in the organization for introduction of the innovation.

A task force was established to gather input from the engineers and to address their concerns. The engineers were incorporated into further developments of the EDSS technology, providing for example, input into the knowledgebase and user interface changes. Eventually expressions about the EDSS then began to change. A sample of a persuasive supporting statement given by a participant in the case study was, "Why do you do it the hard way? Just use the tool for that." Ultimately, the EDSS became widely utilized and recognized by engineers as an important facilitation in reducing errors.

DISCUSSION AND LESSONS LEARNED

Technology innovation adoption and diffusion have been actively researched; however, given the vast of body literature it can be difficult to determine under what circumstances innovations are adopted and diffused, and what factors may lead to resistance. In this chapter, we summarized and organized major streams of theory and perspectives on innovation and adoption and diffusion. We utilized structuration agency as a framework in our case study to show how actors and structures play out in the adoption and diffusion of an innovative technology.

In the case presented, we observed that if an innovative technology is not utilized, the potential benefits from the technology may be lost, or may contribute to the failure of the technologies to live up to their promised payback (Brown & Duguid, 2000). Innovations such as EDSS not only have ability to perform the more mundane tasks such as data gathering, they also enhance the ability to more effectively solve problems with the technology (Taylor & Todd, 1995). Nevertheless, because EDSS provides a structured approach to problem solving and decision-making within a particular usage paradigm, some users may develop negative attitudes towards the technology (e.g., DeSanctis & Poole, 1994).

When peers or groups of individuals have positive or negative perceptions of an innovation, they tend to use the communicative and authoritative structures to encourage or discourage diffusion by conveying meaning and normative expressions. This process may occur either directly or by proxy agency. Direct and indirect agency levies social influences in different ways, but in either case, they may encourage or discourage performance of a behavior to varying degrees that correspond to the amount of social force applied (Ajzen, 1991; Salanick & Pfeffer, 1978). Moderate approval or disapproval of performing an act may be viewed as encouragement or discouragement, whereas when expressed or normative social forces reach extremes, social influences become perceived as pressure to act or refrain from acting (Terry et al., 1999).

Finally, in addition to the normative influences on technology adoption, social influences are also exerted through observational models. For instance, watching the successful effort by others is likely to increase one's own effort towards that behavior, as well as the converse (Bandura, 1977).

Hence, in addition to individual assessments of what "important others" think about one performing a behavior, observation of these peoples' behavior likewise influences the performance of the behavior such as adopting and using an innovative technology (Ajzen, 1991). As a result, people who observe others using a system with positive results are encouraged to use the new system (Compeau & Higgins, 1995; Kraut et al., 1998).

REFERENCES

Ajzen, I. (1991). The theory of planned behavior. *Organizational Behavior and Human Decision Processes, 50*, 179–211. doi:10.1016/0749-5978(91)90020-T

Antonacopoulou, E. P., & FitzGerald, L. (1996). Reframing competency in management development. *Human Resource Management Journal, 6*, 27–46. doi:10.1111/j.1748-8583.1996.tb00395.x

Bandura, A. (2001). Social cognitive theory: An agentic perspective. *Annual Review of Psychology, 52*, 1–26. doi:10.1146/annurev.psych.52.1.1

Beck, U., Giddens, A., & Lash, S. (1994). *Reflexive modernization. Politics, tradition and aesthetics in the modern social order*. Cambridge: Polity Press.

Bjorklund, D. F. (1995). *Information processing approaches: An introduction to cognitive development*. Washington, D.C.: Brooks-Cole.

Boxall, P. (1996). The strategic HRM debate and the resource-based view of the firm. *Human Resource Management Journal, 6*, 59–70. doi:10.1111/j.1748-8583.1996.tb00412.x

Brown, J. S., & Duguid, P. (2000). *The social life of information*. Boston: Harvard Business School Press.

Burns, T., & Stalker, G. M. (1961). *The management of innovation*. London: Tavistock.

Chakravarthy, B. (1997). A new strategy framework for coping with turbulence. *Sloan Management Review*, (Winter): 69–82.

Chomsky, N. (1996). *Language and problems of knowledge*. Mendocino, CA: MIT Press.

Compeau, D. R., & Higgins, C. A. (1995). Computer self-efficacy: Development of a measure and initial test. *Management Information Systems Quarterly*, *19*, 189–211. doi:10.2307/249688

Daft, R. L., & Lengel, R. H. (1986). Organizational information requirements, media richness and structural design. *Management Science*, *32*, 554–571. doi:10.1287/mnsc.32.5.554

Davis, F. D. (1989). Perceived usefulness, perceived ease of use, and user acceptance of information technology. *Management Information Systems Quarterly*, (September): 319–338. doi:10.2307/249008

De Sanctis, G., & Poole, M. S. (1994). Capturing the complexity in advanced technology use: Adaptive structuration theory. *Organization Science*, *5*, 121–147. doi:10.1287/orsc.5.2.121

Denton, D. K., & Wisdom, B. L. (1992). Shared vision . In Thompson, A. A. Jr, Fulmer, W. E., & Strickland, A. J. III, (Eds.), *Readings in strategic management* (pp. 52–56). Boston: Irwin.

Fox, W. M. (1995). Sociotechnical system principles and guidelines: past and present. *The Journal of Applied Behavioral Science*, *31*, 91–105. doi:10.1177/0021886395311009

Fussell, S. R., & Benimoff, I. (1995). Social and cognitive processes in interpersonal communication: Implications for advanced telecommunications technologies. *Human Factors*, *37*, 228–250. doi:10.1518/001872095779064546

Gephart, R. P., Boje, D. M., & Thatchenkery, T. J. (1996). Postmodern management and the coming crises of organizational analysis . In Gephart, R. P. (Eds.), *Postmodern Management and Organization Theory* (pp. 1–20). Thousand Oaks, CA: Sage.

Giddens, A. (1984). *The constitution of society: Outline of the theory of structuration*. Cambridge, UK: Polity Press.

Giddens, A. (1991). *Modernity and self-identity. Self and society in the late modern age*. Stanford, CA: Stanford University Press.

Goodhue, D. L., & Thompson, R. L. (1995). Task-technology fit and individual performance. *Management Information Systems Quarterly*, (June): 213–232. doi:10.2307/249689

Greer, C. R. (1995). *Strategy and human resources. A general managerial perspective*. Englewood Cliffs, NJ: Prentice-Hall.

Gregor, S., & Benbasat, I. (1999). Explanations from intelligent systems: Theoretical foundations and implications for practice. *Management Information Systems Quarterly*, *23*, 497–527. doi:10.2307/249487

Gustafson, L. T., & Reger, R. K. (1995). Using organizational identity to achieve stability and change in high velocity environments. *Academy of Management Journal, Best Papers Proceedings,* 464-468.

Hamel, G., & Prahalad. (1993). Strategy as stretch and leverage. *Harvard Business Review*, (March-April): 75–85.

Jarzabkowski, P. (2008). Shaping strategy as a structuration process. *Academy of Management Journal*, *51*, 621–650.

Kahai, S. S., Sosik, J. J., & Avolio, B. J. (1997). Effects of leadership style and problem structure on work group process and outcomes in an electronic meeting system environment. *Personnel Psychology*, *50*, 121–146. doi:10.1111/j.1744-6570.1997.tb00903.x

Kraut, R. E., Rice, R. E., Cool, C., & Fish, R. S. (1998). Varieties of social influence: The role of utility and norms in the success of a new communication medium. *Organization Science*, *9*, 437–453. doi:10.1287/orsc.9.4.437

Kuhn, T. S. (1996). *The structure of scientific revolutions*. Chicago: University of Chicago Press.

Lake, M. (2009). The art of creation in science: A consonant paradox. *Market Times*, *19*, 278–197.

Lauriola, M., Levin, I. P., & Hart, S. S. (2007). Common and distinct factors in decision making under ambiguity and risk: A psychometric study of individual differences. *Organizational Behavior and Human Decision Processes*, *104*, 130–149. doi:10.1016/j.obhdp.2007.04.001

Lee, P. M., & O'Neill, H. M. (2003). Ownership structures and R&D investments of US and Japanese firms: Agency and stewardship perspectives. *Academy of Management Journal*, *46*, 195–211.

Manz, C. C., & Stewart, G. L. (1997). Attaining flexible stability by integrating total quality management and socio-technical systems theory. *Organization Science*, *8*, 59–70. doi:10.1287/orsc.8.1.59

Maznevski, M. L., & Chudoba, K. M. (2000). Bridging Space Over Time: Global Virtual Team Dynamics and Effectiveness. *Organization Science*, *11*, 473–492. doi:10.1287/orsc.11.5.473.15200

Mintzberg, H. (1994). The fall and rise of strategic planning. *Harvard Business Review*, (January-February): 107–114.

Morris, M. G., & Venkatesh, V. (2000). Age differences in technology adoption decisions: Implications for a changing work force. *Personnel Psychology*, *53*, 365–401. doi:10.1111/j.1744-6570.2000.tb00206.x

Ngwenyama, O. K., & Lee, A. S. (1997). Communication richness in electronic mail: Critical social theory and the contextuality of meaning. *Management Information Systems Quarterly*, (June): 145–166. doi:10.2307/249417

Orlikowski, W. J. (1996). Improvising organizational transformation over time: A situated change perspective. *Information Systems Research*, *7*, 63–92. doi:10.1287/isre.7.1.63

Pava, C. (1986). Redesigning sociotechnical systems design: Concepts and methods for the 1990s. *The Journal of Applied Behavioral Science*, *22*, 201–221. doi:10.1177/002188638602200303

Pfeffer, J., & Salancik, G. R. (1978). *The external control of organizations: A resource dependence perspective*. New York: Harper & Row.

Plumlee, M. A. (2003). The effect of information complexity on analysts' use of that information. *Accounting Review*, *78*, 275–296. doi:10.2308/accr.2003.78.1.275

Porter, M. E. (1979). *How competitive forces shape strategy*. New York: Free Press.

Porter, M. E. (1996). What is strategy? *Harvard Business Review*, (November-December): 61–78.

Quinn, J. B. (1992). Managing strategic change. In A. A. Thompson, Jr., W. E. Fulmer & A. J. Strickland III (Eds.), *Readings in Strategic Management* (4th ed., pp. 19-42). Boston: Irwin. (Reprinted from *Sloan Management Review, 21,* 3-20).

Raisch, S., & Birkinshaw, J. (2008). Organizational ambidexterity: Antecedents, outcomes, and moderators. *Journal of Management*, *34*, 375–409. doi:10.1177/0149206308316058

Ritzer, G. (2005). Structuration theory. *Contemporary Sociology: A Journal of Reviews, 36*, 84-85.

Rogers, E. M. (1983). *Diffusion of innovations*. New York: Free Press.

Rogers, E. M., & Kincaid, D. L. (1981). *Communication networks: Toward a new paradigm for research*. New York: Free Press.

Semler, S. W. (1997). Systematic agreement: a theory of organizational alignment. *Human Resource Development Quarterly, 8*, 23–40. doi:10.1002/hrdq.3920080105

Sheppard, B. H., Harwick, J., & Warshaw, P. R. (1988). The theory or reasoned action: A meta-analysis of past research with recommendations for modifications and future research. *The Journal of Consumer Research, 15*, 325–343. doi:10.1086/209170

Simon, M., & Houghton, S. M. (2003). The relationship between overconfidence and the introduction of risky products: Evidence from a field study. *Academy of Management Journal, 46*, 139–149.

Sine, W. D., Mitsuhashi, H., & Kirsch, D. A. (2006). Revisiting Burns and Stalker: Formal structure and new venture performance in emerging economic sectors. *Academy of Management Journal, 49*, 121–132.

Stacy, R. D. (1992). *Managing the unknowable. Strategic boundaries between order and chaos in organizations*. San Francisco: Jossey-Bass.

Stones, R. (2005). *Structuration theory*. New York: Palgrave-Macmillan.

Synnott, W. R. (1987). *The information weapon: Winning customers and markets with technology*. New York: John Wiley & Sons.

Tan, F. B., & Hunter, M. G. (2002). The repertory grid technique: A method for the study of cognition in information systems . *Management Information Systems Quarterly, 26*, 39–57. doi:10.2307/4132340

Taylor, H., & Karlin, S. (1993). *Introduction to stochastic modeling*. London: Academic Press.

Taylor, S., & Todd, P. A. (1995). Understanding information technology usage: A test of competing models. *Information Systems Research, 6*, 144–176. doi:10.1287/isre.6.2.144

Terry, D. J., Hogg, M. A., & White, K. M. (1999). The theory of planned behavior: Self-identity, social identity and group norms. *British Journal of Psychological Society, 38*, 225–244. doi:10.1348/014466699164149

Tihanyi, L., Johnson, R. A., Hoskisson, R. E., & Hitt, M. A. (2003). Institutional ownership differences and international diversification: The effects of boards of directors and technological opportunity. *Academy of Management Journal, 46*, 195–211.

Trist, E. (1971). New directions of hope. *Regional Studies, 13*, 439–451. doi:10.1080/09595237900185381

Tversky, A., & Kahneman, D. (1983). Extensional versus intuitive reasoning: The conjunction fallacy in probability judgment. *Psychological Review, 90*, 293–315. doi:10.1037/0033-295X.90.4.293

Verspoor, M., & Lowie, W. (2003). Making sense of polysemous words. *Journal of Language Learning, 53*, 547–586. doi:10.1111/1467-9922.00234

Webster, J. (1998). Desktop video teleconferencing: Experiences of complete users, wary users, and nonusers. *Management Information Systems Quarterly,* (September): 257–286. doi:10.2307/249666

Webster's Dictionary. (1978). *Webster's new 20th century dictionary*. New York: Harper-Collins.

Wilde, G. J. S. (2001). *Target risk*. Toronto: PDE Publications.

Wolfe, R. A. (1994). Organizational innovation: Review, critique and suggested research directions. *Journal of Management Studies, 31*, 405–427. doi:10.1111/j.1467-6486.1994.tb00624.x

Workman, M. (2005). Expert decision support system use, disuse, and misuse: A study using the theory of planned behavior. *Journal of Computers in Human Behavior, 21*, 211–231. doi:10.1016/j.chb.2004.03.011

Workman, M. (2007). Advancements in technology: New opportunities to investigate factors contributing to differential technology and information use. *Journal of Management and Decision Making, 8*, 221–240.

Workman, M., & Bommer, W. (2004). Redesigning computer call center work: A longitudinal field experiment. *Journal of Organizational Behavior, 25*, 317–337. doi:10.1002/job.247

Chapter 2
IT/IS Readiness Maturity Model

Mustafa Alshawi
University of Salford, UK

Hafez Salleh
University of Malaya, Malaysia

EXECUTIVE SUMMARY

This chapter explains the concept of an IT/IS readiness maturity model including particular requirements in terms of four domains, embracing nine attributes: IT infrastructure (top management perception, systems and communication), people (skills, roles and responsibility of IT staff, user involvement), process, and work environment (organization behaviour, IT department, leadership). Each of the attributes consists of 14 factors: top management perception (drivers, systems requirements definition), systems and communication (focus, network communication), skills (type of skills, capability building), roles and responsibility of IT staff (position of IT/IS heads, roles of IT staff), user involvement, process (practices), organizational behaviour (characteristics), IT policy (control of IT/IS activities), and leadership (communication, participation). The following section describes the concept of readiness and maturity, the resources used for element extraction/ adoption and the description of the model.

DOI: 10.4018/978-1-4666-2618-8.ch002

DESCRIPTION OF MODEL

The Purpose of IT/IS Readiness Model

A. The model is intended to be used prior to IS/IT project implementation
B. The model is a holistic in nature and focuses on soft issues which embrace all the key organizational elements such as IS/IT, people, business processes and work environment.
C. The model adopts the maturity-level techniques to facilitate the measurement of the "Readiness Gap", i.e. the gap between the current and the required state of readiness, prior to the implementation of a selected IS/IT project.
D. Each maturity level provides guidelines for managers to improve the readiness status and progress through the maturity levels.

The proposed model is a maturity model composed of six progressive stages of maturity that an organization can achieve in their investment and implementation of IT/IS. These maturity stages are cumulative; which means, in order to get a higher position in the maturity stages, the organization must comply with the pre-ordained requirements for that stage (in addition to those for all the lower stages).

What is being Evaluated?

The model is based on assessing four organizational elements and is shown in Table 1.

A. IT infrastructure
B. Business process
C. People
D. Work environment

The proposed model is a maturity model composed of six progressive stages of maturity that an organization can achieve in their investment and implementation of IT/IS. These maturity stages are cumulative; which means, in order to get a higher position in the maturity stages, the organization must comply with the pre-ordained requirements for that stage (in addition to those for all the lower stages).

IT Infrastructure

Top Management Perceptions

Level 1. Small IT/IS are developed or purchased where the decision regarding their acquisition tends to be ad-hoc in nature. They are made at low levels within the

Table 1. The characteristics of the key elements of the IT/IS readiness model

Key Elements	Attributes	Characteristics
IT Infrastructure	Top management perception	Describes top management's (business executives) strategic thinking and direction towards the development and utilization of IS/IT in their organizations
	Systems and communication	The development and utilization of applications and the organizations' direction and strategic plan
People	User Involvement	The level of involvement of staff in the IS/IT developments in organizations
	Roles and responsibility of IT staff	The roles and responsibility of IT staff in organizations
	Skills	Acquiring and development of human capacity
Process	Processes	Represented by the process "Practices" within the organization
Work Environment	Organizational behaviour	Actual implementation pattern of IT/IS in organization
	Leadership	The leadership style at both operational and strategic levels
	IT Department	The unit group to provide IT/IS services including infrastructure and applications

organization, mainly at group level, and are based on what the management sees taking place within other external organizations.

Level 2. An increased number of IT/IS are being developed or purchased through a small number of IT/IS development plans.

Level 3. Short term development of IT/IS starts to appear with management welcoming user involvement to define needs and requirements.

Level 4. The management begins to consider the long term development of IT/IS with an attempt to align business strategy and IT strategy.

Level 5. The development of IT/IS is used to add value to products or services and to support supply chain activities.

Level 6. The development of IT/IS used to support strategic and innovative business objectives.

System and Communication

Level 1. Most of the systems are small, off-the-shelf financial packages which tend to be independent of each other (i.e. stand-alone) and built/purchased in isolation from other IT/ISs located in the organization or even in the same group.

Level 2. The IT/IS application is more focused on the operational system within the financial area, while a small number of other business-oriented systems are being developed.

Level 3. In-house IT/IS applications cover most business operation areas but the IT/IS support varies between the business units. Some new systems are developed, installed, and operated by the central IT/IS department.

Level 4. All required communication protocols such as standard e-mail format is mostly in place, and some EIS, DSS start to appear throughout the organization which indicates the beginning of dependency on the organization-wide network in conducting formal communication.

Level 5. Strategic IT/IS applications are developed with external-oriented data through the use of standard communication such as EDI with external entities such as customers, government and suppliers.

Level 6. The organization uses intra-organizational systems with outside entities (government, suppliers, etc.) with 'sharing' IT/IS services such as the internet, e-commerce technology, etc.

People

Skill

Level 1. The work requires few IT/IS skills. No IT/IS training is provided. User skill is improved by individual effort.

Level 2. IT/IS skills are needed to develop and maintain the system such as programming, analysis and programming skills and being able to install off-the-shelf, ready made packages.

Level 3. Users develop project management skills.

Level 4. Business users start to gain IT understanding. The user gains a proper insight into IT/IS related issues.

Level 5. The business/IT/IS staff gain cross-disciplinary experience. Core technical skills developed. Very knowledgeable IT/IS users.

Level 6. The workgroups are optimizing their IT/IS capability and competency for performing their work processes.

Roles and Responsibility of IT Staff

Level 1. No individual responsible for the IT/IS department. No IT/IS manager. No dedicated IT staff. Small number of low-level technicians and programmers. External contactors may be used to develop/install small systems.

Level 2. The IT/IS manager is responsible for the IT department. Small numbers of IT/IS staff comprising of systems analysts recruited. The IT/IS staff are responsible for adequately understanding the user requirements for systems development.

Level 3. A technically oriented IT/IS manager is appointed. Dedicated IT/IS planners and database administrators are appointed. Adequate technical and specialist staff are to coordinate between current and future IT/IS needs.

Level 4. Apart from programmers, systems analysts and data base administrators, the organization has business analysts. A high level manager for the IT/IS services area is appointed with middle management status.

Level 5. IT/IS managers with senior management status. The organization seeks to develop and retain core hybrid staff.

Level 6. The IT/IS manager becomes a full member of the board of directors and plays an active part in determining strategic direction. The IT/IS staff keep up with the strategic needs of the group.

Users Involvement

Level 1. The IT Department has little control over the users' IT/IS related activities and little user participation in IT/IS decisions.

Level 2. The relationship may exist between users and the IT Department and begin to look at users' knowledge and skills.

Level 3. The IT Department recognizes and welcomes user involvement over the users' needs and requirements concerning IT/IS matters.

Level 4. The users have a significant degree of involvement in IT/IS-related decisions. IT/IS investments are derived from users' stated needs. The IT Department supports the user's activities.

Level 5. Partnerships exist between the IT Department and user groups. The IT Department and users cooperate on an equal basis as partners and continuous striving exists for the integration of organizational workgroups.

Level 6. Central coordination of the strategic coalition between the IT Department and user groups.

Process

Level 1. No standard business process and no alternative plan during crises, and this often leads to compromises on quality. Heavily depends on individual skills to perform the business tasks.

Level 2. Policies and standard procedures established for major business activities.

Level 3. Most business activities are documented and standardized within workgroups.

Level 4. Well-defined business process activities, including standard business descriptions, and models for performing the work tasks within the organization.

Level 5. Established and maintained quantitative objectives for the process about quality and measuring the product/services, the degree of customer satisfaction, and the level of harmony across the supply chain.

Level 6. Ensuring continuous improvement of the process of fulfilling the relevant strategic business goals.

Work Environment

Organizational Behaviour

Level 1. IT/IS is to be used as a tool for performing a single work task

Level 2. IT/IS applications are technology driven

Level 3. IT/IS is one of the many ways to reduce costs in the firm and expenditure on IT/IS is seen as a way to reduce costs

Level 4. IT/IS is vital for streamlining business processes

Level 5. IT/IS is one of the vital elements that lead to competitive advantage

Level 6. IT/IS is the single most critical factor to success in business through knowledge sharing and dissemination

IT Policy

Level 1. Little or no control in IT/IS function and / or no formal IT/IS organizational structure

Level 2. An IT/IS Department is introduced within the organization.

Level 3. The IT/IS Department becomes centralized and IT/IS staff seek control of IT/IS matters.

Level 4. The IT/IS function is well established, and IT/IS services begin to be decentralized with central standards and a policy for co-ordination, implementation, and utility.

Level 5. The central IT/IS department provides an organization-wide communication system, major data processing, and large scale hardware within a large organization. A decentralized management structure exists with the flexibility to support IT/IS initiatives.

Level 6. Coalition between co-ordinated inter-organizational systems

Leadership

Level 1. There is a lack of consistency in the management of IT/IS activities.

Level 2. Management of IT/IS activities with necessary measures and in an ad-hoc manner

Level 3. Management of IT/IS activities with organization wide-policies and standards

Level 4. Management of IT/IS activities with well-defined organizational standards

Level 5. Established management of IT/IS activities with performance measurement

Level 6. Continuous improvement of IT/IS activities management

The Factors/Variables Investigated

A variety of factors need to be achieved in order to get to a higher position in the maturity stages, i.e. the organization must comply with the requirements for that stage (in addition to those for all the lower stages). All factors are contained at each stage to represent their maturity, and the importance of these factors has been discussed in the previous section. Table 2 shows the criteria for each element.

Drivers

These are the factors that drive or trigger the management to make new IT/IS investments. For example, the management decides to invest in the new IT/IS to save operational costs, space reduction, reduce data duplication & redundancy, enhance the company image, etc.

A.   **Systems Requirements Definition (SRD):** To identify the requirements of the stakeholders (customers and users) for a new system or proposed system

Table 2. The criteria/variables for the IT/IS readiness model

Element	IT Infrastructure		People		
Attributes	Top Management Perception	Systems and Communication	Skill	Roles & Responsibility of IT staff	User Involvement
Factors	• Drivers • Systems requirements definition	• Focus • Network communication	• Type of skills • Capability building	• Positions of IT/IS heads • Roles of IT staff	• User involvement
Element	Process	Work Environment			
Attributes	Process	Organization Behaviour	IT Policy	Leadership	
Factors	• Practices	• Characteristics	• Control of • IT/IS activities	• Communication • Participation	

alteration such as *functional requirements* (specific behaviour; what the system can do such as data processing, data manipulation, graphical user interface, ease of use, security etc.) and *non-functional requirements* (to judge the operation of a system such as reliability, performance and cost). SRD is an important part of the system design process, whereby business analysts along with the stakeholders and system developers identify the needs of a client. Among popular techniques used to identify SRD are the stakeholder's interview, workshops, prototypes etc.

B. **Focus:** The utilization of IT for the organization's improvement such as to improve internal efficiency; enhance overall organizational effectiveness; extend geography and market reach; change the industry or market place (Tallon et al, 2000).

C. **Network Communication:** A computer *network coverage* within the organization that is capable of exchanging information electronically between individuals, groups, and business units.

D. **Process:** A workflow, or group of activities (sometimes called methods and procedures), that produce an outcome valued by an internal or external customer'. (Hammer and Champy, 1993; Harrington, 1991). They (a work flow or group of activities) are generally cross-functional and horizontal in nature with no single person having responsibility for the entire process (Innovative Manufacturing Initiative, 1994).

E. **Types of Skills:** A specific range of IT/IS skills needed by the user to maximize the potential of IT systems and meet the requirements of a specific job.

F. **Capability Building:** The mechanism for an organization improving their learning capabilities of IT/IS skills (Murray and Donegan, 2003).

G. **Position of IT/IS Head:** The position of the IT/IS Head in the organization structure.

H. **Roles of IT Staff:** The roles and responsibility of IT staff including technicians, programmers, analysts, managers, etc.

I. **User Involvement:** The approach of user involvement in the IT/IS development process by an individual or members of the target user group.

J. **Organization Behaviour Characteristics:** The actual implementation pattern of IT/IS within working environments in the organization.

K. **Control of IT/IS Activities:** The pattern of enterprise decision making authority on IT resources (infrastructure and application) among IT departments and business units.

L. **Communication:** The communication planning throughout the organization at all levels of the management regarding the IT/IS implementation/activities.

M. **Participation:** The participation of top and middle management in the IT/IS initiatives.

The summary of IT/IS readiness model can be found in Tables 4, 5, 6, and 7.

Table 3. Summary of research model – Information Technology infrastructure element

	Top Management Perceptions *Top management (business executive's) strategic thinking and direction towards the development and utilization of IT/IS in their organizations*	**Systems and Communication** *The development and utilization of applications and systems to facilitate the organization's direction and strategic plan*
Level 6	**STRATEGIC OBJECTIVES** *The development of IT/IS used to support strategic and innovative business objectives.* • **Drivers:** Global competition. • **System Requirements Definition:** Full in-house with minimum intervention from company's partners.	**INTRA-ORGANIZATIONAL SYSTEMS** *Organization uses intra-organizational systems with outside entities (government, suppliers, etc) sharing IT/IS services such as the internet, e-commerce technology etc.* • **Focus:** Managing information for strategic business core-capabilities. • **Network Communication:** Intra-Organizational networking.
Level 5	**ADDED VALUE** *The development of IT/IS is used to add value to products or services and to support supply chain activities.* • **Drivers:** Partner's supply chain. • **System Requirements Definition:** Mainly in-house with intervention from supply chain partners and vendors.	**STRATEGIC SYSTEM** *Strategic IT/IS applications are developed with external-oriented data through the use of standard communication such as ERP, SCM, EDI with external entities such as customers, government and suppliers.* • **Focus:** Managing supply-chain. • **Network Communication:** Supply-chain with partners.
Level 4	**LONG TERM BUSINESS INVESTMENT** *The management start to consider long term development of IT/IS with an attempt to align business strategy and IT strategy.* • **Drivers:** Business process improvement. • **System Requirements Definition:** Mainly in-house with intervention from vendor.	**COMMUNICATION PROTOCOLS** *All required communication protocols such as standard e-mail format is mostly in place and some EIS, DSS start to appear throughout the organization which indicates the beginning of dependency on the organization-wide network in conducting formal communication.* • **Focus:** Manipulating information to assist managers in decision making. • **Network Communication:** Organizational-network systems.
Level 3	**SHORT TERM BUSINESS INVEST-MENT** *Short term development of IT/IS start to appear with management welcoming user involvement to define needs and requirements.* • **Drivers:** Organization communication. • **System Requirements Definition:** Mainly in-house with intervention from vendors.	**WORK GROUP SYSTEM** *In-house IT/IS applications cover most business operational areas but the IT/IS support varies between the business units. Some new systems are developed, installed, and operated by the central IT/IS department.* • **Focus:** Full integration of application organizational-wide. • **Network Communication:** Organizational-network systems.

continued on following page

Table 3. Continued

	Top Management Perceptions *Top management (business executive's)* *strategic thinking and direction towards the* *development and utilization of IT/IS in their* *organizations*	Systems and Communication *The development and utilization of applications* *and systems to facilitate the organization's* *direction and strategic plan*
Level 2	**PROJECT-ORIENTED INVESTMENT** *An increasing number of IT/IS being developed or purchased through small number of IT/IS development plans.* • **Drivers:** Work task requirements. • **System Requirements Definition:** Partially from in-house and mostly form vendor.	**ADMINISTRATION SYSTEM** *The IT/IS application focus is more on the operational system within the financial area while a small number of other business-oriented systems are being developed.* • **Focus:** Co-ordination information activities. • **Network Communication:** Networking within business unit.
Level 1	**AD-HOC INVESTMENT** *Small IT/ISs are developed or purchased where the decision regarding their acquisition tend to be ad-hoc in nature, made at low levels within organization, mainly at group level and are based on what the management sees taking place within other external organizations.* • **Drivers:** Copying/duplication. • **System Technical Requirements Definition:** Heavily depends on vendor.	**STAND-ALONE SYSTEM** *Almost all systems are small and off-the-shelf financial packages, which tend to be independent of each other (stand-alone) and built/purchased in isolation from other IT/ISs located in the organization or even in the same group.* • **Focus:** Financial activities. • **Network Communication:** Stand-alone.

Table 4. Summary of research model – Process element

	Process *Represented by the process "practices" within the organization*
Level 6	**INSTITUTIONALISE AN OPTIMISING PROCESS** *Ensuring continuous improvement of the process in fulfilling the relevant strategic business goals.* • The entire supply chain is focused on continuous business process improvement (strength, weakness and evaluation).
Level 5	**INSTITUTIONALISE QUANTITATIVELY MANAGED PROCESS** *Establish and maintain quantitative objectives for the process of quality and measuring the product services, the degree of customer satisfaction, and the level of harmony across the supply chain.* • The capability to set quality goals and measures on business process activities.
Level 4	**INSTITUTIONALISE DEFINED PROCESS** *Well-defined business process activities including standard business descriptions and models for performing the work tasks within the organization.* • A well-defined business process includes standard descriptions and models for performing work.
Level 3	**INSTITUTIONALISE MANAGED PROCESS** *Most business activities are documented and standardized within workgroups.* • Business process is documented, standardized and integrated organization-wide.
Level 2	**ACHIEVE SPECIFIC GOALS** *Policies and standard procedures established for major business activities.* • Business process scope is identified and improved as the work progresses.
Level 1	**AD-HOC LEVEL** *No standard business process and no alternative plan during crises which often leads to compromises on quality. Heavily dependant on individual skills to perform the business tasks.* • Business process is unpredictable and constantly changed or modified as the work progresses.

Table 5. Summary of research model – People element

	Skill *The acquisition and development of human capacity*	**Roles and Responsibility of IT Staff** *The roles and responsibility of IT staff in organizations.*	**Users' Involvement** *The level of involvement of staff in the IS/IT developments in organizations*
Level 6	**SKILLS ENHANCEMENT** *The workgroups are optimizing their IT/IS capability and competency for performing their work processes.* • **Type of skills:** Acquiring skills to develop IT core capabilities. • **Capability Building:** Intra-organizational sharing experience.	**EXECUTIVE BOARD STAFF** *The IT/IS manager becomes a full member of the board of directors and plays an active part in determining strategic direction. The IT/IS staff keep up with the strategic needs of the group.* • **Position of IT/IS Head:** IT Manager with full membership of the board of directors. • **Roles:** To align IT/IS strategy and business strategy.	**STRATEGIC** *Central coordination of the strategic coalition between the IT Department and user groups.* • **User Involvement:** User group establishes their role and become central reference in IT/IS project team looking at aligning IT/IS strategy and business strategy.
Level 5	**SKILLS INTEGRATION** *The business/IT/IS staff gains cross-disciplinary experience. Core technical skills developed. Very knowledgeable IT/IS users.* • **Type of skills:** Gains cross-disciplinary experience to support supply-chain activities. • **Capability Building:** Knowledge sharing and knowledge management (multi-disciplinary).	**HYBRID STAFF** *IT/IS manager with senior management status. The organization seeks to develop and retain core hybrid staff.* • **Position of IT/IS Head:** IT Manager with senior management status. • **Roles:** To set-up IT/IS strategy.	**PARTNERSHIP** *Partnership exists between IT Department and user groups. IT Department and users cooperate on an equal basis as partners and continuously strive to integrate the organizational workgroups.* • **User Involvement:** User group become permanent in the IT/IS project team looking at IT/IS strategy.
Level 4	**SKILLS DEPLOYMENT** *Business users start to gain IT understanding. A user gains a proper insight into IT/IS related issues.* • **Type of skills:** Using IT/IS to make decisions. • **Capability Building:** Centrally integrated training program within the organization.	**BUSINESS-ORIENTED STAFF** *Apart from programmers, systems analysts and data base administrators, the organization has business analysts. A high level manager for the IT/IS services area is appointed with middle management status.* • **Position of IT/IS Head:** IT Manager with middle management status. • **Roles:** To manage information across organization.	**CONSULTATIVE** *The users have a significant degree of involvement in IT/IS-related decisions. IT/IS investments are derived from users' stated needs. The IT Department supports user's activities.* • **User Involvement:** Focus group consultation on managing information across organization.

continued on following page

Table 5. Continued

	Skill *The acquisition and development of human capacity*	Roles and Responsibility of IT Staff *The roles and responsibility of IT staff in organizations.*	Users' Involvement *The level of involvement of staff in the IS/IT developments in organizations*
Level 3	**IT/IS PROJECT MANAGEMENT SKILLS** *Users developed project management skills.* • **Type of Skills:** Considerable technical and project management skills. • **Capability Building:** Centrally integrated training programs within organizations.	**TECHNICAL-ORIENTED STAFF** *A technically oriented IT/IS manager is appointed. Dedicated IT/IS planners and database administrators are appointed. Adequate technical and specialist staff to coordinate between current and future IT/IS needs.* • **Position of IT/IS Head:** Technical IT Manager. • **Roles:** To set-up purchasing policy and centralized IT/IS activities.	**REPRESENTATIVE** *The IT Department recognizes and welcomes user involvement on the users needs and requirements concerning IT/IS matters.* • **User involvement:** Focus group consultation on purchasing and centralized IT/IS activities.
Level 2	**IT/IS SKILLS DEVELOPMENT** *IT/IS skills are needed to develop and maintain systems such as programming, analysis and programming skills and being able to install off-the-shelf, ready made packages.* • **Type of skills:** Purely technical skills. • **Capability building:** Team based/effort within workgroups.	**LIMITED ROLE** *The IT/IS manager is responsible for the IT department. Small numbers of IT/IS staff comprised of systems analysts recruited. The IT/IS staff are responsible for adequately understanding the user requirements for systems development.* • **Position of IT/IS Head:** IT Manager at IT department. • **Roles:** Providing technical support.	**AD-HOC INVOLVEMENT** *A relationship may exist between users and the IT Department and begin to look at users' knowledge and skills.* • **User Involvement:** Individual consultations on technical support.
Level 1	**BASIC IT/IS SKILLS** *The work requires few IT/IS skills. No IT/IS training provided. User skill is improved by individual effort.* • **Type of skills:** Basic IT/IS skills. • **Capability Building:** Individual based/effort.	**NO ROLE** *No individuals responsible for the IT/IS department. No IT/IS manager. No dedicated IT staff. Small numbers of low-level technicians and programmers. External contactors may be used to develop/install small systems.* • **Position of IT/IS Head:** No IT Manager. • **Roles:** No role.	**BASIC INVOLVEMENT** *IT Department has little control over users IT/IS related activities and little user participation in IT/IS decision.* • **User Involvement:** No user participation in IT/IS improvement/enhancement.

Table 6. Summary of research model – Work environment element

	Organization Behaviour *Actual implementation pattern of IT/IS in an organization*	IT Governance *The unit group to provide and control IT/IS services including infrastructure and application*	Leadership *The leadership communication and participation level*
Level 6	**KNOWLEDGE - CULTURE** *IT/IS is the most single critical factor to success in business through knowledge sharing and dissemination.* **Characteristics:** • IT benefit is measured quantitatively (financial cost/profit ratio) and qualitatively (usefulness for all members of the company). • Information is shared and exchanged for product and process innovation and improvements, decision making and organizational adaptation and renewal. • 'Informational culture' - design the system according the explicit and implicit knowledge that individuals possess.	**ESTABLISHED HYBRID MODEL/FEDERAL STRUCTURE** *Coalition between co-ordinated inter-organizational system.* • **IT/IS Activities Control:** Centralized IT/IS infrastructure and decentralized application to support intra-organizational IT/IS activities.	*Continuous improvement of IT/IS activities management.* • **Communication:** Continuous improvement of the communication process. • **Participation:** Participates actively in the continuous improvement of IS/IT projects such as using the data obtained from efficiency and effectiveness matrices for strategic decision making.
Level 5	**CAPABILITY APPROACH** *IT/IS is one of the vital elements that lead to competitive advantage.* **Characteristics:** • IT/IS used to provide better products/services to customers. • Staff encouraged to input IT/IS driven ideas to improve products/services. • IT/IS investment influenced by competition.	**HYBRID MODEL/FEDERAL STRUCTURE** *Central IT/IS departments provide an organization-wide communication system, major data processing, and large scale hardware within large organizations. A decentralized management structure exists with the flexibility to support IT/IS initiatives.* • **IT/IS Activities Control:** Centralized IT/IS infrastructure and decentralized application to support supply chain activities.	*Established management of IT/IS activities with performance measurement.* • **Communication:** Well documented and integrated communication planning for overall organizational structure. • **Participation:** Participates in performance measurement of IS/IT projects such as efficiency and effectiveness.
Level 4	**ORGANIZATION - APPROACH** *IT/IS is vital for streamlining business processes.* **Characteristics:** • The focus is on ensuring all organization functions and operations are running smoothly. • Process oriented. • Sharing processes for particular tasks within the organization.	**ESTABLISHED IT DEPARTMENT** *IT/IS function is well established and IT/IS services begin to decentralize with central standards and a policy for co-ordination, implementation and utility.* • **IT/IS Activities Control:** Centralized IT/IS infrastructure and decentralized application (policy).	*Management of IT/IS activities with well-defined organizational standards.* • **Communication:** A communication plan is expected for all activities. • **Participation:** Participation of all IS/IT activities within the organization such as project prioritization, change control, risk identification etc.

continued on following page

Table 6. Continued

	Organization Behaviour *Actual implementation pattern of IT/IS in an organization*	**IT Governance** *The unit group to provide and control IT/IS services including infrastructure and application*	**Leadership** *The leadership communication and participation level*
Level 3	**COST - APPROACH** *IT/IS is one of the many ways to reduce costs in the firm and expenditure on IT/IS is seen as a way to reduce costs.* **Characteristics:** • IT benefits are measured quantitatively (financial cost/profit ratio). • Profit driven - every project is based on its feasibility to gain profit. • Tight budget control - centralized (top management) monitoring on expenditure.	**IT DEPARTMENT CENTRALISED** *IT/IS Department become centralized and IT/IS staff seek control of IT/IS matters.* • **IT/IS Activities Control:** Centralized purchasing policy and support (policy).	*Management of IT/IS activities with organization wide-policies and standards.* • **Communication:** There are an organization-wide policy and standards for communications. • **Participation:** Participation on large scale and high cost IS/IT activities such as cost and schedule etc.
Level 2	**TECHNOLOGY - APPROACH** *IT/IS applications are technology driven.* **Characteristics:** • Technology-led. • 'Informatics culture' - designs the system from technical point of view, then persuades staff to adapt to it. • IT success is measured in IT terms rather than the impact made on the business.	**IT DEPARTMENT RECOGNISED** *IT/IS Department is introduced within the organization.* • **IT/IS Activities Control:** Technical support.	*Management of IT/IS activities with necessary measures and in an ad-hoc manner.* • **Communication:** No established standards in place for communications planning. • **Participation:** Ad-hoc participation basis by individual managers such as IS/IT project status (milestone - plan and actual) etc.
Level 1	**AD-HOC APPROACH** *IT/IS is thought of as a tool for performing single work tasks.* **Characteristics:** • Users determine their needs and requirements. • No data sharing culture exists. • Each individual has their own separate processes.	**NO FORMAL IT DEPARTMENT** *Little or no control in IT/IS functions and or no formal IT/IS organizational structure.* • **IT/IS Activities Control:** No control on policy.	*Lack of consistency in the management of IT/IS activities.* • **Communication:** No communication. • **Participation:** No participation.

REFERENCES

Hammer, M., & Champy, J. (1993). *Reengineering the corporation: A manifesto for the business revolution*. New York, NY: Harper Business.

Harrington, H. J. (1991). *Business process improvement*. US: McGraw-Hill.

Murray, P., & Donegan, K. (2003). Empirical linkages between firm competencies and organisational learning. *The Learning Organization*, *10*(1), 51. doi:10.1108/09696470310457496

Tallon, P. P., Kraemer, K. L., & Gurbaxani, V. (2000). Executives' perceptions of the business value of information technology - A process-oriented approach. *Journal of Management Information Systems*, *16*(4), 145–173.

Chapter 3

RFID and Labor Management Systems Selection in the Logistics Industry

Cheryl A. Tibus
Mercer University, USA

Linda L. Brennan
Mercer University, USA

EXECUTIVE SUMMARY

Faced with increasing competitive pressures, a logistics company in the United States sought to reduce its cost structure by implementing two information systems. The Labor Management System (LMS) was specifically designed to improve warehouse worker efficiency and the Radio Frequency Identification (RFID) system tracked the movement of products, pallets, and shipment. This case presents an overview of the logistics industry, background on the business need to consider new systems, and the requirements of the company in its system selection. Details of the technologies considered are included. The reader is then faced with the challenge of analyzing the options, and making a recommendation for systems selection.

DOI: 10.4018/978-1-4666-2618-8.ch003

After analyzing this case study, the reader should be able to:

- *Define logistics functions, supply chain management, and third party logistics (3PL) services*
- *Describe LMS and RFID systems*
- *Identify the expected costs and benefits of the proposed technologies*
- *Develop a multi-factor evaluation for vendor selection*
- *Make a recommendation based on the evaluation, financial data, and other considerations.*

ORGANIZATIONAL BACKGROUND

A2B Logistics (A2B) is headquartered in the Southwestern United States, with locations, primarily warehouses with transportation management functions, across the United States. The company is considered a third party logistics (3PL) services provider, with a stated mission of "helping customers through the management of change and information in the supply chain" (A2B Logistics, 2008).

Logistics and Supply Chain Management

According to the Council of Supply Chain Management Professionals (www.cscmp. org), the logistics function includes sourcing and procurement, production planning and scheduling, packaging and assembly, and customer service. It is involved in all levels of planning and execution—strategic, operational and tactical. Logistics management is an integrating function, which coordinates and optimizes all logistics activities, as well as integrates logistics activities with other functions including marketing, sales manufacturing, finance, and information technology.

Logistics definitions vary by perspective. Russell (2000) contrasts the way the term is used in common culture as, "handling the details of an activity," with a customer perspective of "getting the right product to the right customer, in the right quantity, in the right condition at the right place, at the right time, and at the right cost" (p. 15). Meeting customer service requirements is the primary value driver for a logistics provider. This must be accomplished while minimizing the supply chain costs while maximizing the profits to the provider (Rutner & Langley, 2000).

Coyle, Bardi, and Langley (2003) suggest that a logical extension of the logistics concept is supply chain management. Supply chain management encapsulates the flow of activities, data, raw materials, finished products and various services in an effective and efficient manner as they travel through a variety of organizations in route to the final customer.

Third Party Logistics

Third party logistics (3PL) companies are used as an integral step in an organization's supply chain:

- Supply chain management encompasses the planning and management of all activities involved in sourcing and procurement, conversion, and all logistics management activities. Importantly, it also includes coordination and collaboration with channel partners, i.e. suppliers, intermediaries, third party service providers, and customers.
- Logistics management activities typically include inbound and outbound transportation management, fleet management, warehousing, materials handling, order fulfillment, logistics network design, inventory management, supply/demand planning, and management of third-party logistics services providers (Council of Supply Chain Management Professionals, 2008).

3PLs are considered the third party between the supplier and the customer, handling varying degrees of the logistics involved in the storage, transportation and delivery of raw materials and/or finished goods. In order for a manufacturer to outsource this function, a 3PL must be able to "add more value to their customer's business than the customer would be able to achieve themselves" (Berglund, Laarhoven, Sharman & Wandel, 1999, p. 64). This value added is manifest as improved customer service and reduced costs, resulting from a combination of outsourced functions including (Vaidyanathan, 2005):

- Transportation
- Warehousing
- Freight consolidation and distribution
- Product marketing, labeling, and packaging
- Inventory management
- Traffic management and fleet operations
- Freight payments and auditing
- Cross docking
- Product returns
- Order management
- Packaging
- Carrier selection
- Rate negotiation
- Logistics information systems.

The industry is growing. A survey of 3PL leaders reported that over 80 percent have experienced a 10 percent sales growth during the past year, and 36.6 percent report growth in excess of 20 percent. Profitability still lags behind sales, a reality attributed to rising operational costs, ongoing consolidation in the segment, and, as one 3PL reports, customers are experiencing pressure to reduce costs that pressure is then passed down to the supply chair provider to reduce costs as well (O'Reilly, 2007). A2B's need to reduce costs was a typical challenge across the industry (Sauvage, 2003).

A2B Service Offerings

As an asset based company, A2B can be classified as an Integrated Vendor. Even though they own trucks and warehouses they will also contract with other providers to meet the long and short term requirements of their customers (Razzaque & Sheng, 1998). Like many 3PLs, A2B Logistics provides a range of services customized for each customer. Primarily, services provided include (A2B Logistics, 2008):

- Logistics Center Management: This is the core function of most 3PLs and is the end-to-end operation of the warehousing facility, spanning from the time the inbound shipment of product to the facility is planned, to the outbound shipment of product to various distribution centers or stores is completed and reported. This is typically the most labor-intense dimension of a 3PL as this service maintains responsibility for the physical inventory movement and management, customer service, and the security and safety of the facility.
- Transportation Management: The 3PL performs this role by managing the inbound and outbound shipments to optimize the throughput of product shipments and utilization of the fleet. This movement of products through the supply chain requires the coordination, execution, tracking and reporting of shipments throughout the process, whether domestic or international.
- Value-Added Services: This broad category of service really customizes product configurations according to specific customer needs. This may include display building for specific in-store promotions, labeling cases with new information, or assembling various products into a new combined selling unit.
- Information Technology Services: The effective use of technology automates and integrates supply chain business processes, electronically captures and delivers all related data to A2B's customers, partners, employees and management in the format, frequency and detail level needed to optimize the supply chain.

Management Structure

The company is led by James Janns, Chief Executive Officer (CEO). Other members of the executive team include: Ed Larson, Chief Financial Officer; Michael Benson, Sr. VP Operations; Joe Wolenski, VP Sales; Dennis McAdam, VP Information Technology; Carley Johnson, VP Human Resources; and Kathy Hawkins, General Counsel. The organizational chart is presented in Figure 1.

Since 3PLs frequently facilitate relationships between several partners, the culture of the 3PL plays an important role in the success of each interaction. The shared values that the employees follow, the beliefs and assumptions inherent in the organization, and certain patterns of behavior are all elements of the culture (Schein, 1992). With over 2000 workers, including full-time, part-time and contract support, the culture of the daily work environment impacts the relationships workers have with customers, supplies and other employees.

The A2B company culture can be characterized as "conflicted." While the portrayed pattern of behavior to the marketplace is customer-centric and proactive, in recent years the company has functioned in a reactive or market-follower mode playing "catch-up" to competing 3PLs in growth, technology and profitability. The lack of strong focused leadership and the rate of executive turnover contribute

Figure 1. A2B Organization Chart

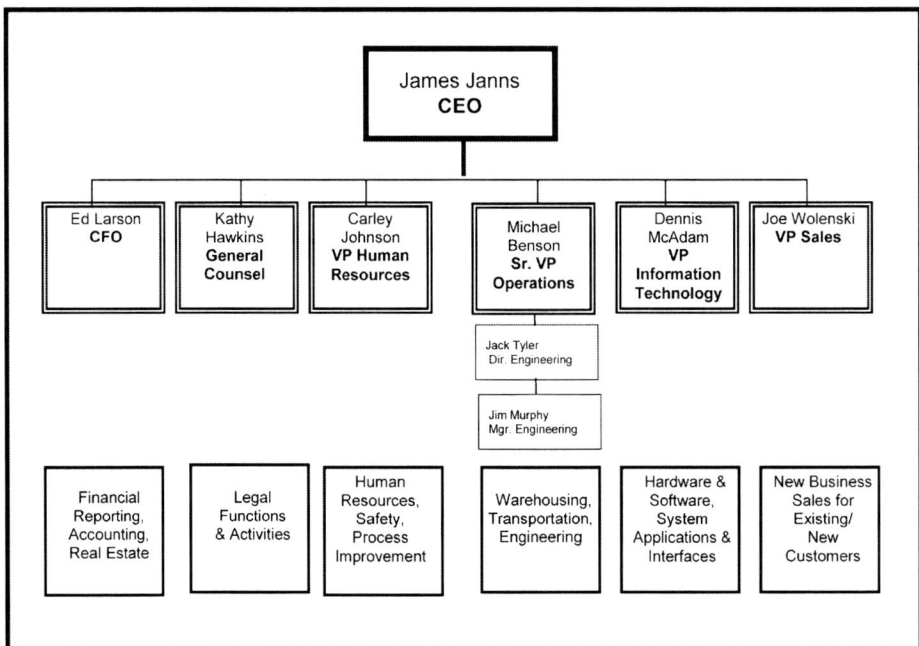

to the conflicted culture: "Human resource management policies, which directly influence and are influenced by corporate culture, also significantly impact supply chain members" (McAfee, Glassman, & Honeycutt, 2002, p. 1).

The company is privately held, so available financial data are limited. Founded as a warehouse storage provider in 1975, it expanded into transportation services five years later and has grown ever since. In the mid 1990s, the current CEO consolidated the 15 subsidiaries into one company and one identity. Profit margins, however, have declined in recent years. Of immediate concern is an increasing trend of losing new business because competitors are more cost-effective.

SETTING THE STAGE

Vice President of Sales Joe Wolenski slammed down the telephone receiver in frustration. "I can't believe it!" he grimaced, as he walked down the hall to the office two doors down. "This has got to stop!"

Carley Johnson, A2B's Vice President of Human Resources, looked up from her computer. "What's wrong, Joe?"

Wolenski slumped into a chair in her office. "We have lost another contract. We were on the short list of 3PLs bidding on Bohannan's Big Box wholesale chain—a huge contract for us—and we lost out to EXEL, again. I called McKenzie Bohannan to see if she would share what the deciding factors were. Basically, she said she liked us better, but couldn't justify the incremental cost of our contract over EXEL's. I am getting so frustrated—we have to do something to reduce our operating costs!"

Johnson leaned back in her chair and sighed. "Joe, we know what we have to do – but perhaps we can use this loss to create a greater sense of urgency. We have known for months that we need to invest in additional information technologies to change our cost structure. You and I both have staff researching the options, trying to define the requirements and projecting costs and benefits. Let's pull the Steering Committee (comprised of the VP of IT, VP of HR, VP of Sales, Director of Engineering and Sr. VP of Operations) together to see if we can gain some traction on this effort."

A2B's Executive Team had previously developed what they called a "strategic viewpoint of supply chain execution." This included A2B's vision of supply chain offerings that ensured that any information technology solution would not only address the immediate need, but be robust enough to support the longer term strategy. "The key criterion to justifying an investment in technology successfully is to determine whether the project objective is consistent with the strategic direction of the corporate objectives" (Triggs, 1993, p. 25). Any investment in a LMS and/or RFID would therefore have to meet both the short and longer term needs of A2B

Logistics. The attractiveness of supply chain management software is that the flow of the product and the related information can be monitored and tracked in real time throughout the supply chain (Kahl, 1999).

The hope was that new technology could position A2B's customized services to better meet the customers' needs at a more attractive price. According to Sauvage (2003) "technological effort becomes a key variable and a significant means of differentiation for logistics service providers" (p. 239).

A key part of the supply chain execution included a project to research labor management systems. This effort was lead by Jim Murphy, Engineering Manager. His team was charged with developing the vendor selection criteria, managing the vendor relationships (i.e., organize demonstrations, validate references, visit site installations), documenting the budget and return on investment (ROI) for the project and making a recommendation for vendor selection and implementation plans. Since there is a high cost to technology "complete calculation of ROI including hardware depreciation, staff savings, and any assumptions and constraints statements regarding personnel and operations" (Allen, 2007, p. 38) is necessary to ensure that the project would achieve its goal.

Similarly, Art Ricca, IT Manager, led the team with a charge for using RFID tags on products and pallets in the A2B Logistics operation. The motivation for this supply chain execution project was slightly different. In addition to labor reduction through increased automation and product identification, it was also a compliance issue. Both government and consumer regulations were requiring more accuracy in the tracking of products and shipments. "Operationally, RFID allows data from a tag attached to a pallet, case, or individual product to be captured by a reader device" (Niederman, Mathieu, Morley, & Kwon, 2007, p. 94). Unlike traditional bar codes, RFID tags can store product information on a chip that can be read without opening the package or passing it over a scanner (Jessup & Valacich, 2006). Knowing where product was in the supply chain regardless of the number of handlers was becoming more of a focus due to both security and product recalls. More and more consumer goods manufacturers and retailers were moving towards the use of RFID and wanted the 3PLs to comply. Some even reported that they would not accept product if it did not have an RFID readable tag.

Wal-Mart, Target and Albertsons Inc., as well as the Department of Defense, launched the initial initiatives in 2004. Manufacturers including Proctor & Gamble and Kimberly-Clark had strategic initiates focused on RFID. It seemed inevitable that this would become a requirement of large retailers. Albertsons expected their top 100 suppliers to join the program within a year (Gonsalves, 2004).

Together, a LMS and the implementation of RFID were needed to reduce the operating cost of A2B if they were to continue to compete and ultimately be awarded contracts for new business. A2B executives were aware that information technology solutions would help address the high cost of their services, as research showed, they "automate and lower the costs of supervision and information processing" (Sauvage, 2003, p. 239) which are ultimately passed on to the customer.

Johnson and Wolenski met with the two other members of the Steering Committee that afternoon. Jack Tyler, Director of Engineering, was responsible for engineering the warehouse layout and determining the labor needs and Dennis McAdam the VP of the Information Technology. The four of them agreed that based on the team's work of reviewing various consulting firms it looked like there were really only two contenders that could offer both a LMS and RFID solution. They also had potential to expand into other supply chain information systems, a consideration consistent with the strategic viewpoint of supply chain execution.

Current Information Systems and Technology

A2B's current hardware platform is a network of nine leased IBM Application System/400s (AS/400). A2B's warehousing and corporate locations were assigned to a specific AS/400 and linked to a second for backup.

The primary software run on the system was an aging "legacy" or "home grown" warehouse management system (WMS) used for inventory management. The WMS had little documentation and systems programmers to support the application were difficult to find. An i2 Technologies solution software supported the transportation management function while a variety of email, accounting, human resources and customer relationship management software supported activities at the corporate headquarters.

The selection of a new system would have to "fit" in the existing environment. It also seemed to make sense to go with a single vendor solution, to minimize interfaces with the existing system. The two most impressive vendors had very different strengths, but it was time to make a decision.

CASE DESCRIPTION

As outsourcing continues to grow in popularity, the companies who are the recipients of this outsourced work need to be keenly aware of their cost/benefit equations. 3PL is no exception. As 3PLs handle the movement of product from manufacturer to distribution center or store, the biggest expense is labor. The industry exists because manufactures don't want to be in the "logistics" business. They seem to prefer to focus on marketing, research & development, manufacturing and sales. Therefore, 3PLs must keep their pricing low enough to be competitive and gain new business but high enough to earn what are often only single digit margins.

Technology, in particular the latest software systems, have been an enticing approach to both monitoring and minimizing labor expense. In recent years, two programs have been reviewed by many 3PLs for implementation feasibility: RFID and LMS. This cases will explore the journey that one 3PL took in their decision to select a vendor and systems implementation to reduce their labor expense.

Labor Management Requirements

Reducing labor costs and improving labor productivity were key concerns at A2B Logistics. Johnson had convinced the executive team that using a labor management program would help them to address this concern with the philosophy, "you can't manage what you can't measure." The intent was to create a culture of continuous improvement, whereby methods were developed based on best practices, standards were created, goals were set, measurements were taken, and opportunities for improvement were identified.

This was typical for a 3PL. It has long been acknowledged that the labor intensity of warehouses is one of the largest contributors to the cost of logistics operations (Wunnenberg, Jr., 1977; Murphy & Poist, 1993; Autry, Griffis, & Goldsby, 2005). One estimate suggests that warehouse and distribution center employees account for more than 60% of total operating costs (Drickhamer, 2005). One of the primary reasons a manufacturer chooses to outsource to a 3PL firm is to reduce costs (Vaidyanathan, 2005). To remain competitive, a 3PL must address labor costs and make increasing labor productivity an ongoing initiative.

Labor management systems typically provide the capability for planning and reporting labor requirements, as part of managing the overall workflow in the warehouse. A key ingredient to the implementation is the establishment of performance standards, e.g., number of orders filled/day; time to receive a new shipment; time to pick and palletize a shipment. These standards can be based on historical performance, suggestions from the vendor, or benchmarks from other companies. These may be refined over time, tied to incentive systems, and shared with customers.

The expected benefits of such capability are labor cost-savings, workload balancing, and paperwork reduction (Min, 2006). Drickhamer (2005) reports, "productivity improvements from implementing labor management systems range from 10% to more than 20%, and a return on investment between 3 and 12 months" (p. 1). In one case study he mentions, the company found that the improvement in labor visibility, i.e., who was doing what and how long it was taking, gave an instant increase in productivity as a result of employees by seeing how they compared to others.

Another way in which an LMS can reduce costs is by enabling warehouse managers to identify optimal staffing levels. For example, assume that a product is brought into the warehouse, stored into a specific location and/or picked and prepared for shipment from the warehouse. The LMS would then calculate the number of minutes to perform the task based on an engineered standard. Warehouse supervisors could use this data to determine the number of workers needed for each shift. No longer would workers stand around waiting at the start, middle or end of the shift. With this data labor expense could be predicted, monitored and managed. Supervisors could also ensure that there is sufficient staffing for the completion of all the tasks on a particular shift. No orders will be delayed and customers dissatisfied due to insufficient staffing.

The short term and ongoing benefit is the ability to understand and control the costs of labor. The longer term benefit is to have a body of data that will allow for accurate pricing to customers and a clear understanding of when additional services are being provided. The system was automated to capture the start and end times of each task eliminating the need for workers to complete manual timecards, again eliminating unproductive time. Each of these would help A2B manage the costs associated with every logistics activity. Total annual labor savings for A2B were projected to be $3,000,000. This estimate was based on a time study done by the engineering department. The saving was projected to be 10% of the overall hourly labor costs for those warehousing accounts that have variable pricing. (If an account was "cost-plus," savings generated as a result of the project would be passed directly to the customer.) The time study identified three areas that were an unproductive use of people:

1. Manual completion of time cards
2. Wasted time in each shift
3. Idle time at the end of each shift.

It was also noted that the implementation of such a system might encounter some resistance by the employees. Min (2006) summarizes reported pitfalls in terms of "a lack of standards/compatibility, limited functionalities, frequent updates/modifications, and employees' resistance to change" (p. 112). Employees might resent the oversight, feel dehumanized and be concerned about the impact on their pay. However, Drickhamer (2005) notes that employee's morale could also improve with the implementation of a LMS, because of perceived fairness and objectivity in the data. Regardless, A2B management knew this was an implementation that had to be handled with some sensitivity.

The Labor Management team had identified several categories of requirements for the system, with importance weights, as presented in Table 1. Because of the concern about the warehouse workers' support for the system, the user functionality, training, and support were key considerations.

Table 1. Labor Management System Requirements and Weights.

Requirement	Definition	Weight
User Functionality	All User Aspects of Software	35%
Training/Ease of Use	All User, Technical, and Documentation Related to Training	18%
Engineering	Methods, Standards, and Facility Mapping	18%
Reporting	Standard, Scheduled, Ad-Hoc, and Alert Reporting	12%
Support – Initial	Initial Implementation Support – Tools, Training, and Documentation	8%
Support – Ongoing	Addressing User Issues and Driving Improvements to System	4%
Integration	Constructing and Testing Interfaces	5%
	Total	**100%**

The team identified six potential vendors, and researched them extensively. As a result, four of them were eliminated from further consideration. The team then applied a multi-factor evaluation approach to compare the offerings of the remaining contenders, Canton Partners and Orion, LLC.

Radio Frequency Identification (RFID) Requirements

The business requirements for the RFID team were less clearly defined but the discussion by the team centered around:

- Sales Capability: Would our system demonstrate our ability to meet potential customer needs both from the manufacturer (i.e. Kellogg, Kimberly-Clark) and from the retailer (i.e. Wal-Mart, Target)?
- Tracking Granularity: If you tag each case of product, can you link all the cases to a specific pallet?
- Scalability: Can this be expanded for all of our current RFID needs and be able to meet the increasing demands of retailers?
- Data Transmission: Can we transmit data to customers and other trading partners?
- Reporting: Can we generate reports that will allow us to analyze our activities and improve our supply chain partnerships?
- Cost: Is there a payback?

While the universal product code (UPC) system has been the dominate product tracking standard since the early 1990's, RFID provided manufacturers and 3PLs the opportunity to automate the industry-wide standard product "tags" that were both readable and writeable using radio frequency (RF) waves. In 2003 EPC Global assumed leadership for the development of industry wide standards for electronic product codes (EPC) specifically for RFID. This is the system that Wal-Mart mandated certain suppliers use (Neidermann et al., 2007).

For RFID success, the tags must function properly in various environments including weather, products and outside radio frequency interference. Since tag performance was crucial to RFID performance, A2B needed to investigate "read-rates." Read rates tend to be affected by location factors as well as factors inherent in the environment (Powanga & Powanga, 2008).

There is a significant concern to not over-invest in a proprietary technology, while still maintaining the ability to respond to customers' requirements and to demonstrate to potential customers this important capability. "The biggest challenge for widespread use of RFID technology is the ability to control the costs while still realizing the perceived benefits." (Jones, Clarke-Hill, Shears, Comfort, & Hillier, 2004; Vijayaraman & Osyk, 2006, p. 8) Over the past two years, the team had been researching different vendors' approaches and collaborating with customers on their RFID initiatives. What they learned is that:

- RFID "standards" may vary.
- Most of the manufacturers providing RFID tags to retailers are doing so for only a small subset of stock keeping units (SKUs).
- There is no opportunity for a return on investment (ROI) for the 3PL in the short term.

Scalability continued to be an important consideration in the RFID implementation. If A2B made the investment in a system, would that system have the ability to be expanded across multiple products, retailers and/or logistics centers (O'Brien & Marakas, 2005)? The two approaches considered were the "Manual Slap and Ship" and the "Automated RFID Labeling Line".

"Slap and Ship" was appealing due to its simplicity, ease of implementation and cost. A warehouse worked would "slap" a readable RFID tag on a case of product and then the product is "shipped" to the retailer. This approach requires a minimum configuration appropriate for low volumes; therefore, low equipment costs and high labor costs. This is illustrated in Figure 2.

"From a management perspective, it will be important to build systems that are robust enough that such data will be collected and integrated even when pressured human operators are more concerned with "getting the job done" than ensuring accurate acquisition of information needed only at later stages in the business process." (Niederman et al., 2007, p. 97).

Figure 2. RFID: Manual Slap and Ship

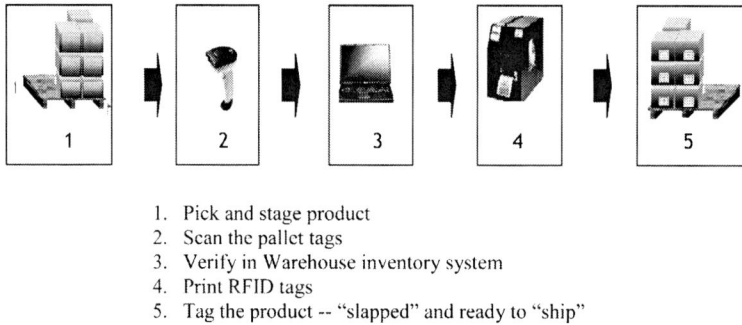

1. Pick and stage product
2. Scan the pallet tags
3. Verify in Warehouse inventory system
4. Print RFID tags
5. Tag the product -- "slapped" and ready to "ship"

But could a "slap & ship" RFID implementation grow, as the volume of tags in the system increased? The team was concerned about this issue of scalability, particularly given the A2B strategic viewpoint that investments should meet immediate needs <u>and</u> support longer-term strategies. "While "slap & ship" may appear to be the easiest short-term choice to make in order to satisfy mandates, organizations are also looking at how to convert the potential of RFID into a business case to that does not attempt to simply recover the costs but also can resulting a positive ROI" (Vijayaraman, 2006, p. 6).

The "Automated RFID Labeling Line", with a somewhat higher equipment investment and lower labor costs, is more appropriate for moderate volumes, as shown in Figure 3. The automation moves the cases across a conveyor where writable tags are applied, encoded and verified to ensure that they are readable. The product is then put on a pallet and a "RFID pallet tag" is generated to identify all the cases that are on the pallet. While the initial cost is higher than "slap & ship," the elimination of some of the manual labor would make it attractive of medium volume applications.

The RFID team had also identified an initial list of six (6) vendors, eliminating four (4) for various reasons such as scalability, flexibility, and experience. The remaining two were again Canton Partners and Orion, LLC. Both vendors seemed to have an understanding of the 3PL industry, and had been selected as partners by several of A2B's customers or competitors. Their technologies were compatible with A2B's network. To evaluate their differences, the team considered several factors (Table 2).

The weights were determined by the relative importance of each factor to the project objective. Most important to A2B and assigned a weight of 50% was the need for the RFID system to meet business requirements. The weight was significantly high to ensure that a new system would, in fact, solve the business issues related to not having RFID. Next important was the maturity of the solution. Having a system that had demonstrated performance over time as well as in various

Figure 3. Automated RFID Labeling Line

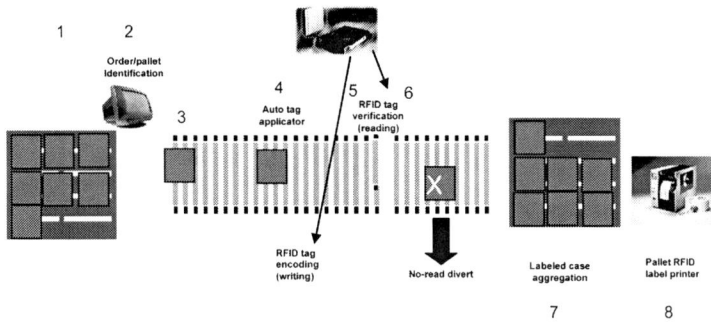

1. Pick and stage product
2. Scan the pallet tag/verify in warehouse inventory system
3. Place cases on conveyor
4. RFID Tag is applied
5. RFID Tag is encoded with data
6. RFID Tag is scanned to ensure readability. All unreadable tags are diverted.
7. Cases are placed on Pallet
8. RFID pallet tag is generated and applied

Table 2. RFID System Requirements and Weights

Requirement	Definition	Weight
Business Requirements	Compliance with customer needs	50%
Training	Complete participant and leader manuals	5%
Integration	Construction and testing of interfaces	10%
Technology Platform	Compatible with A2B's network	5%
Support	Initial and ongoing vendor supplied knowledge and tools	10%
Documentation	Compete system standards	5%
Solution Maturity/Vendor Intangibles	Meet current and future needs	15%
	Total	**100%**

applications would help A2B minimize risk. Less important, due to the fact the A2B could address these factors internally were training, documentation and technology platform, all at 5%.

Both vendors proposed two solutions. They were the "slap & ship" and "automated labeling line" approaches. While the proposals were similar in principle, the underlying system, integration with A2B's current technology, and ability to expand as the marketplace demanded were the differentiators.

MULTI-FACTOR EVALUATION

It was important to everyone involved that the system evaluations be thorough, fair, and explainable. To accomplish this, the project teams scored both alternatives using the weightings of the multiple requirements (i.e., multi-factors) that had been identified. In this way, the "winner" would have the highest score.

Labor Management System Evaluation

Based on the evaluations, the vendors were given scores (presented in Table 3). Technically, in terms of functionality and engineering, the Orion solution is stronger. The Canton Partners is considered slightly better in the support factors.

While training may be the difference between success and failure of the implementation and Canton Partners training material and support were slightly better than Orion, LLC, Orion, LLC had a superior product in the areas of functionality, engineering and reporting. Orion's score was 11% higher than Canton Partners.

RFID System Evaluation

The team's multi-factor RFID system evaluation is presented in Table 4. In establishing the weight assigned to each category, the project team considered the overall objectives of the project, the level and competency of the workers, the staff support available, the potential vendor's ability to provide short and long-term support as well as the ability and ease with which their solution can be integrated into the existing A2B systems.

Both vendors demonstrated similar features that were important to the project. They both had solutions in place for several current A2B customers, they understood the 3PL industry, they were key members of the EPC Global organization, their solutions are scalable for different business profiles and functions and the technology is compatible with A2B's network.

While the vendor assigned weight appeared similar, the ability of the Canton Partners' system to meet business requirements impressed the evaluation team significantly giving Canton Partners a score 3% higher than Orion, LLC. The score for Solution Maturity/Vendor Intangibles highlighted a strength of Canton Partners. While both vendors provided RFID systems to A2B customers, Canton Partners had a longer track record of success. Canton Partners' implementation team appeared to be a better 'cultural fit' for A2B giving Canton Partners an overall score 3% higher than Orion, LLC in the category.

Table 3. Labor Management System: Assessment of Vendors

Category	Description	Weight	Orion, LLC	Orion, LLC	Canton Partners	Canton Partners
User Functionality	All user aspects of software	35%	Strong planning tools. Robust real time feedback. Incentives. Basic clock-in/out feature.	29%	Basic planning tools. Limited real-time feedback. Incentives. Strong clock-in/out feature.	23%
Training/ Ease of Use	All user, technical, and documentation related to training	18%	Strong soft skills. Little to no PC skills required to operate system. No formal training to address change management.	11%	Strong technical skills. Little to no PC skills required to operate system.	12%
Engineering	Methods, standards, and facility mapping	18%	Integrated approach. MSD based. Orion, LLC provides all engineering support.	16%	Non-integrated Approach. Time study based. Canton hires outside firm for all engineering support.	12%
Reporting	Identify standard, scheduled, ad-hoc, and alert reporting	12%	Strong reporting. Drill down & graphical capabilities. Intuitive reporting tools.	11%	Basic reporting. Stronger historical reporting vs. real time reporting.	7%
Support – Initial	Initial implementation support: tools, training, and documentation	8%	Documentation required prior to and contractual agreement to ensure.	6%	Strong commitment during sales cycle. Documentation required prior to agreement.	7%
Support – On Going	Addressing user issues and driving improvements to system	4%	A2B will need to push for on-going management support. 24/7 technical support included.	2%	Strong commitment. A2B would become an integral member of vertical industry group. 24/7 support included.	3%
Integration	Constructing and testing interfaces	5%	FTP or sockets	4%	FTP or sockets	4%
Total		**100%**		**79%**		**68%**

Table 4. RFID Weights by Vendor

Category	Weight	Orion, LLC	Canton Partners
Business Requirements	50%	46%	43%
Training	5%	2%	3%
Integration	10%	7%	7%
Technology Platform	5%	4%	4%
Support	10%	6%	7%
Documentation	5%	4%	4%
Solution Maturity / Vendor Intangibles	15%	8%	12%
Total	**100%**	**77%**	**80%**

Financial Considerations

To compare the costs of the two options, the teams prepared a series of budgets. Budget estimates were based on the assumption of existing departmental staffing being sufficient to support the implementation as well as ongoing operations. These are presented in the Appendices.

Other Considerations

When using a multi-factor evaluation, it makes sense to only consider factors that distinguish the alternatives. With any systems implementation certain issues will present themselves, and are really independent of the vendor selection. For example, ensuring the reliability of the RFID system in the relatively harsh environment of warehouses would be necessary for either choice. Similarly, A2B was ready to address the employee compensation and incentives systems that the LMS would present, regardless of the vendor.

Beyond the multi-factor evaluations and the cost analyses, the steering committee raised additional considerations before making the decision. It was not a decision to be made strictly on the basis of numbers. This "buying behavior" of rational factors coupled with subjective variables is not unusual (Gustin, Daugherty & Ellinger, 1997).

In this case, vendors hired by A2B must pass an implicit and subjective image test. The CEO of A2B had spent the past decade creating an image that was consistent with the business vision. The CEO placed significant importance on professional appearance, behavior and communication. To have vendors working for the company who did not demonstrate the appearance, professionalism and work ethic of A2B, would undermine the success of the effort and could drain the energy from other efforts pursued by the company.

Arguably, this consideration could have been made explicit in the multi-factor evaluation, but it would be hard to measure. So, while these dimensions were not explicitly evident in the requirements, they were implicit and significant conversation regarding them took place in decision meetings as the weights were determined. In the eyes of the CEO, the image of Canton Partners was clearly a better fit for A2B.

Another informal factor was reputation. The CEO's significant network in the logistics arena also played an important role in vendor selection. The network provided candid, off the record information regarding the vendors, their employees, their customers and their challenges. These were readily shared with the evaluation team. Once again, Canton Partners emerged as having the best evaluations.

Should A2B go with a single-vendor solution? If so, which vendor should it be? Why?

REFERENCES

Allen, D. (2007). Cost/Benefit analysis for implementing ECM, BPM systems. *The Information Management Journal*, *41*(3), 34.

Autry, C. W., Griffis, S. E., & Goldsby, T. J. (2005). Warehouse management systems: Resource commitment, capabilities, and organizational performance. *Journal of Business Logistics*, *26*(2), 165–182. doi:10.1002/j.2158-1592.2005.tb00210.x

Berglund, M., Laarhoven, G., & Wandel, S. (1999). Third-party logistics: Is there a future? *International Journal of Logistics Management*, *10*(1), 59–71. doi:10.1108/09574099910805932

Council of Supply Chain Management Professionals. (2008). *CSCMP*. Retrieved from http://www.cscmp.org

Coyle, J. J., Bardi, E. J., & Langley, C. J. Jr. (2003). *The Management of Business Logistics: A Supply Chain Perspective*. Cincinnati, OH: South-Western.

Drickhamer, D. (2005, September). Labor management software: The final profit frontier. *Material Handling Management*. Retrieved January 28, 2009, from http://mhmonline.com

Gonsalves, A. (2004, March 5). *Albertsons Launches RFID Initiative*. Retrieved January 29, 2009, from http://www.networkcomputing.com

Gustin, C., Daugherty, P., & Ellinger, A. (1997). Supplier selection decisions in system/software purchases. *International Journal of Purchasing and Materials Management*, *33*(4), 41–47.

Jessup, L., & Valacich, J. (2006). *Information Systems Today: Why IS Matters* (2nd ed.). Old Tappan, NJ: Prentice Hall.

Jones, P., Clarke-Hill, C., Shears, P., Comfort, D., & Hillier, D. (2004). Radio frequency identification in the UK: Opportunities and challenges. *International Journal of Retail & Distribution Management*, *32*(3), 164–171. doi:10.1108/09590550410524957

Kahl, S. (1999). What's the 'value' of supply chain software? *Supply Chain Management Review*, *4*(4), 59–67.

McAfee, R., Glassman, M., & Honeycutt, E. (2002). The effects of culture and human resource management policies on supply chain management strategy. *Journal of Business Logistics*, *23*(1), 1–18. doi:10.1002/j.2158-1592.2002.tb00013.x

Min, H. (2006). The applications of warehouse management systems: An exploratory study. *International Journal of Logistics: Research and Applications*, *9*(2), 111–126.

Murphy, P. R., & Poist, R. E. (1993). In search of warehousing excellence: A multi-variate analysis of HRM practices. *Journal of Business Logistics, 14*(2), 145–164.

Niederman, F., Mathieu, R., Morley, R., & Kwon, I. (2007). Examining RFID applications in supply chain management. *Communications of the ACM, 50*(7), 93–101. doi:10.1145/1272516.1272520

O'Brien, J., & Marakas, G. (2005). *Introduction to Information Systems* (13th ed.). New York: McGraw-Hill.

O'Reilly, J. (2007). Market insight survey: 3PL perspectives. *Inbound Logistics, July,* 107.

Powanga, M., & Powanga, L. (2008). Deploying RFID in logistics: Criteria and best practices and issues. *Business Review (Federal Reserve Bank of Philadelphia), 9*(2), 1–10.

Razzaque, M., & Sheng, C. (1998). Outsourcing of logistics functions: A literature survey. *International Journal of Physical Distribution & Logistics Management, 28*(2), 89–107. doi:10.1108/09600039810221667

Russell, S. H. (2000). Growing world of logistics. *Air Force Journal of Logistics, 24*(4), 15.

Rutner, C., & Langley, J. Jr. (2000). Logistics value: Definition, process and measurement. *International Journal of Logistics Management, 11*(2), 73–83.

Sauvage, T. (2003). The relationship between technology and logistics third-party providers. *International Journal of Physical Distribution & Logistics Management, 33*(3), 236–253. doi:10.1108/09600030310471989

Schein, E. (1992). *Organizational Culture and Leadership*. San Francisco: Jossey-Bass.

Triggs, D. (1993). Justifying investment in technology. *Logistics Information Management, 6*(5), 20–27. doi:10.1108/09576059310045934

Vaidyanathan, G. (2005). A framework for evaluating third-party logistics. *Communications of the ACM, 48*(1), 89–94. doi:10.1145/1039539.1039544

Vijayaraman, B., & Osyk, B. (2006). An empirical study of RFID implementation in the warehousing industry. *International Journal of Logistics Management, 17*(1), 6–15. doi:10.1108/09574090610663400

Wunnenberg, C. A. Jr. (1977). Productivity in the warehouse: Who needs to automate? *Management Review,* (October): 55–59.

APPENDIX

Table 1. Labor Management Budget - Pilot Site Only

	Canton Partners	**Orion, LLC**	**Orion, LLC**
	(Outsourced Engineering Support)		(Outsourced Engineering Support)
Vendor Costs	247.5	155.0	156.0
A2B External Costs	24.5	24.5	24.5
Annual Ongoing Expense (12 Months)	39.0	40.5	40.5
Labor Management External Project Costs	311.0	220.0	221.0
A2B Internal Costs	130.0	130.0	130.0
Total	**441.0**	**350.0**	**351.0**

Table 2. Labor Management Budget - 14 Sites with 4 Site Vendor Support

	Canton Partners	**Orion, LLC**	**Orion, LLC**
	(Outsourced Engineering Support)		(Outsourced Engineering Support)
Vendor Costs	759.0	583.5	603.5
A2B External Costs	237.5	237.5	237.5
Annual Ongoing Expense (12 Months)	127.5	131.5	131.0
Labor Management External Project Costs	1,124.0	952.5	972.0
A2B Internal Costs	352.0	352.0	352.0
Total	**1,476.0**	**1,304.5**	**1,324.0**

Table 3. Labor Management Budget - 14 Sites with 14 Site Vendor Support

	Canton Partners	**Orion, LLC**	**Orion, LLC**
	(Outsourced Engineering Support)		(Outsourced Engineering Support)
Vendor Costs	1,122.5	1,145.0	1,023.5
A2B External Costs	187.5	187.0	187.5
Annual Ongoing Expense (12 Months)	128.0	131.0	131.0
Labor Management External Project Costs	1,438.0	1,463.0	1,342.0
A2B Internal Costs	352.0	352.0	352.0
Total	**1,790.0**	**1,815.0**	**1,694.0**

Table 4. RFID Project Costs - Pilot Site Only

	Canton Partners	Orion, LLC
RFID Software License	20.0	20.0
RFID Integration/Implementation	25.0	34.5
RFID External Expenses Equipment		
Server	6.5	6.5
Conveyor	5.0	5.0
Automatic Tag Applicator	5.0	10.5
Readers	3.5	3.5
Misc Equipment	4.5	4.5
Installation Equipment	2.0	2.0
Operational Startup	3.0	3.0
Vendor Services		
Vendor Installation Services	-	4.0
Vendor Travel & Meals	7.0	6.0
Sub-Total	**81.5**	**99.5**
RFID Internal Expenses		
IT Hours	38.0	38.0
Process Improvement Hours	5.0	5.0
Engineering Hours	10.0	10.0
Operations Hours	3.0	3.0
Customer Service Hours	2.0	2.0
Travel Expenses	19.0	13.0
Sub-Total	**77.0**	**71.0**
Total RFID Project Costs	**158.5**	**170.5**
Annual Maintenance Agreement	8.0	8.0
Annual Hardware Maintenance	3.0	4.0
Total Annual Recurring Expenses	**11.0**	**12.0**

This work was previously published in the Journal of Cases on Information Technology, Volume 12, Issue 1, edited by Mehdi Khosrow-Pour, pp. 31-49, copyright 2010 by IGI Publishing (an imprint of IGI Global).

Chapter 4

Adoption of a New Online Travel Management System for FED–AK

Aundrea Kell
University of Alaska Anchorage, USA

Shari Pierre
University of Alaska Anchorage, USA

Bogdan Hoanca
University of Alaska Anchorage, USA

EXECUTIVE SUMMARY

This case describes the implementation of an online travel management system at FED-AK, the Alaska office of a U.S. government agency. The previous system was intended to accomplish the same functionality, but due to employee resistance, it was used only as a forms generator in conjunction with a paper- and mail-based process. The new system is integrated, which compels employees to use all the functionality provided. It also incorporates many lessons learned from the old system—in particular, extensive training and online help functions. The system is expected to significantly reduce the cost of travel by minimizing errors, enforcing policies, and reducing transaction costs. The system will also lead to faster reimbursement of employee travel expenses.

DOI: 10.4018/978-1-4666-2618-8.ch004

ORGANIZATION BACKGROUND

The organization discussed in this case is Federal Environment Department - Alaska (FED-AK), the Alaska office of a United States federal government agency, Federal Environment Department - USA (FED-USA), which is part of the Department of the Interior (DOI). In addition to the references indicated, much of the information in the case is from personal interviews and from internal agency documents.

With the widespread use of the Internet for business and personal interactions, many national and local governments are offering citizens access to government resources via electronic channels (Evans & Yen, 2005). A well-established model (Laine & Lee, 2001) organizes Electronic Government (e-Government) offerings along four stages: cataloging, simple transactions, vertical integration within one functional area and full vertical and horizontal integration in a truly one-stop shopping experience. According to the most recent report on e-Government around the world (West, 2008), the level of e-Government service varies tremendously, from simply a web presence with limited or no catalog access, to full transactional capability (available in at least one service area in 50% of the government websites worldwide). A comprehensive survey of services offered by city governments in Europe tracks 67 different types of e-Government services available to citizens (Torres, Pina & Acerete, 2005).

A number of studies have evaluated the readiness, the usability, the usage levels and the effectiveness of e-Government, using empirical surveys theoretical models, or a combination of the two (Wang, Bretschneider & Gant, 2005). Srivastava and Teo (2007) go even one step further, showing a link between e-Government adoption and two metrics for national performance: reduction of social divide and increase of business competitiveness. Titah and Barki (2005) provide a good review of both theoretical and experimental e-Government research results published up to 2005.

At the same time, e-Government initiatives are facing several roadblocks, including privacy and confidentiality, usability, ease of navigation and ingrained habits of citizens. These roadblocks are significant even in the most technologically advanced countries, such as the United Kingdom (Kolsaker & Lee-Kelley, 2007). As one might expect, more e-Government functionality is available in developed countries, but variability in the level of service is also higher in developed countries (Siau & Long, 2006). For example, a United Nations survey (UN, 2008) ranks the United States as fourth in the world in e-readiness, and first in e-participation.

In February 2002, President George W. Bush presented a series of measures intended to streamline the government and to increase transparency and accountability through widespread use of Electronic Government (e-Gov). Internet-based technologies have the ability to improve citizens' access to government resources, to increase efficiency and effectiveness of the government, and to improve the results of taxpayer interactions with agencies (U.S. Government, n.d.). The e-Gov initiative in the US encompasses four areas of service: government to citizens, government to business, government to government, and intra-government efficiency and effectiveness (U.S. Government, 2002). In the area of increasing efficiency and effectiveness, the main drivers for e-Government initiatives are cost savings, service innovation, better control and decision making, improved service delivery, and modernization (UN, 2008). The UN survey gives examples of several successful e-Government initiatives worldwide. One example particularly relevant for the case study below is that of the Treasury Board of Canada Secretariat website that makes public information about travel and hospitality expenses for Canadian government officials (Proactive Disclosure, n.d.).

Among the initiatives intended to improve intra-governmental effectiveness, the e-Travel initiative is designed to provide government-wide travel management services. Travel, along with timekeeping, is one of the key expenses that can be misrepresented by government employees, and not only in the United States: Shallert (2003) presents the initial stages of business process reengineering to solve a similar problem in the Australian government. In September 2007, the U.S. General Accounting Office (GAO) reported to Congress that internal control weaknesses led to at least $146 million in improper premium travel government-wide during the fiscal year ending June 30, 2006. Most of this premium travel involved business class airline fares (General Accounting Office, 2007). Although an exact number is not available, a common rule of thumb is that coach travel would have cost as little as 25% of this amount.

Federal employee travel is governed by the Federal Travel Regulations (FTR), which are administered by the General Services Administration (GSA) (General Accounting Office, n.d.). Through an Interagency Travel Management Committee (ITMC), GSA coordinates an exchange of information among federal agencies to ensure compliance with federal rules as well as with internal agency policies. For example, GSA sets per diem levels and reimbursement policies. However, since the GSA doesn't specify any standard processes, U.S. Federal Executive Departments such as the Department of the Interior (DOI) are allowed to define their own policies and rules within the confines of the FTR framework.

To comply with the requirements of e-Travel, all agencies must implement travel management with an e-Gov travel provider by October 1, 2008 (this is an extension from the original date of September 30, 2006 – E-travel, 2003). This case study discusses the process currently being implemented for Federal Environment Department Alaska (FED-AK), the Alaska component of FED-USA. FED-USA is a government agency that has a state office and several district offices in Alaska. Despite being part of the same organization, travel management practices differ from office to office across the states with FED-USA offices. The goal in implementing the new information system is to be able to handle the end-to-end travel process for all offices, from authorization through reimbursement. The system was scheduled to go live in summer of 2008.

SETTING THE STAGE

To accomplish the FED-USA agency goals, many employees of FED-AK must travel extensively. Summer is a particularly heavy travel season in Alaska because many surveys, assessments, and data collection studies can only be performed at this time due to weather restrictions. Additionally, employees travel year-round to attend training, conferences, workshops, and meetings. The highest travel expenses for the FED-AK are lodging, per diem, and airplane tickets.

The most frequent users of the travel system are managers, who must travel throughout the state to represent the government at public forums. As shown in Table 1, FED-AK travel expenditures exceeded $4 million during fiscal year 2007. In the period 2000-2007, travel costs have been close or slightly over this $ 4 million figure. Considering that air travel represents one-third of travel expenses each year, improved measures to track usage and enforce policies on travel will benefit the agency. This attention to airline costs is expected to become even more important as fuel prices and airline charges surged in early 2008, with little hope for a reduction in the near future.

Table 1. Travel Cost For FED-AK FY 2007

ATM/Bank Fees	$1,280.04
Agent Fees	$102,861.26
Plane Tickets	$1,416,171.55
Hotel, Per Diem, Excess Baggage	$2,145,025.91
Rental Car Gasoline, Parking	$103,487.64
POV[1] Mileage	$11,918.71
Rental Car	$201,170.85
Shuttles, Taxi Cabs	$9,369.03
Local Travel, not Airplane	$3,183.88
Other	$283,830.77
Total Spent on Travel FY07	$4,278,299.64

CASE DESCRIPTION

Overview

The case is set in late 2007 when about half of the FED-USA offices are using an e-Gov travel vendor, which standardizes travel reimbursement documents and tracks travel expenditures electronically. However, the end-to-end travel process involves a combination of methods, such as printed paper forms, electronic forms using Microsoft Excel or Microsoft Word, standalone travel agencies, online booking engines and various off-the-shelf products.

According to the FED-AK Travel Coordinator, FED-AK used one of these off-the-shelf products, Gelco's Travel Manager, since the late 1990s to create travel documents. Travel Manager began as a solution to standardize the travel management process. Although it could have been used to electronically route, sign, and upload completed documents to a financial system for payment, it was been used primarily as a forms generator. According to the Travel Coordinator, employee resistance to change and the absence of a senior-level travel liaison were the two main causes for the failed implementation of Travel Manager as a fully online system.

Employee Resistance to Change

Employee resistance was a problem mainly in the auditing team in Denver, the major hub for the federal travel management process. Documents from all DOI agencies are sent to contract workers in Denver for reimbursement. Denver employees were reluctant to accept the new forms included in Gelco's Travel Manager program because they would have had to re-learn how to read vouchers and authorizations. The Denver team was familiar with the location of every item they audited, which made it easy for them to spot errors. These contract employees rejected full implementation of a digital travel management process because they claimed that Gelco Travel Manager's forms were not easy to audit. Not all government agencies reported the same problem: other DOI agencies, including U. S. Geological Survey (USGS) and U. S. Fish and Wildlife Service had no problems using the forms produced by Gelco Travel Manager.

Lack of Executive Leadership for the Travel Program

The second reason for the failure of Travel Manager is related to the senior level leadership structure in key FED-AK positions. According to the FED-AK Travel Coordinator, travel is the only program in the DOI that does not have a representative in Washington. Therefore, many program decisions and policy-making duties have been passed down to the contract and full-time employees in Denver because of their position in the chain of command in the travel management process.

The travel team in Denver receives all travel vouchers within the DOI and must approve each document before issuing a reimbursement. This team consists of both full time and contract employees, but it does not include any senior level employees. Contract workers make up the majority of the team. They audit vouchers and make sure no federal travel regulations (FTR) have been broken. All of the financial transactions are handled by full-time employees. Although the full-time employees are required to review vouchers after the contract auditors, before issuing a reimbursement, this does not happen in many routine situations. However, whenever red flags appear on a voucher, a more thorough audit is done by both groups of employees. Although the team is working well together, the lack of senior level employees has led to a lax enforcement of policies. This includes a willingness to tolerate the current hybrid process combining electronic Travel Manager functionality with paper-based steps.

Because of employee resistance, only a limited set of the Travel Manager's functionality is currently in use. The mix of electronic and paper-based procedures greatly slows down the process. Using a combination of Gelco's Travel Manager, printing, and FedEx shipping, the current travel reimbursement process for the FED-AK can take 7-15 days.

Problems with the Current Process

Appendix A1 illustrates the current travel management process (as of the end of 2007). As with many other internally-developed systems, it involves several redundant steps that add time, expense and potential for human error. The agency manages travel inefficiently, by relying on a complex and slow process that involves hard copies, handwritten signatures, FedEx delivery of original documents and work outsourced to contract employees. As an example, travelers must fill out a separate travel voucher for reimbursement with much of the same information that had already been submitted in a travel authorization. This is just the opposite of what research shows is needed for achieving positive results with e-Government: adopt "processes that enable collecting data once for multiple uses" and eliminate redundant processes (Van Wert, 2002). While redundancy may exist where it is not needed, it is sometimes absent where it would enhance reliability. The organizational structure includes a single Travel Coordinator responsible for all travel within the FED-AK. A bottleneck occurs when this person is out of the office or unable to expedite the paperwork on to the next step.

The Road to GovTrip

In August 2003, GSA awarded a first set of travel contracts for US government agencies to Carlson Wagonlit and Northrop Grumman (U.S. General Services Administration, 2003). Six months later, GSA added a third vendor, EDS, to the list of contract awardees (Michael, 2004). At the Department of the Interior (DOI), the process of selecting a travel vendor took several months. First, the DOI issued a proposal request from any Travel Management Center that wished to submit a bid for the government contract. All three GSA-approved vendor companies submitted proposals in response to an agency-developed questionnaire. Each company had to demonstrate compliance with the requirements for DOI online booking engines. Second, the questionnaire assessed the company's compatibility with governmental policies and procedures. After receiving the company responses to the questionnaire, the DOI set up vendor presentations for a committee that included the FED-AK Travel Coordinator. The committee listened to three days of presentations, and then had an opportunity to ask questions to the companies submitting proposals. The particular concerns from the Alaska agencies included:

- How to accommodate employees without Internet access
- How to deal with a large number of accounting codes and charge accounts on one transaction (many companies were prepared to work with up to 5 different codes, but some FED-AK travelers with special needs can generate up to 27 codes per transaction)
- Whether the online booking engine (OBE) was set up to book Alaska Marine Ferry tickets (frequently used by FED-AK travelers, but not available on many online search engines)

The vendors were evaluated based on their paper submission to the questionnaire and their presentations. An evaluation sheet for the presentations ensured consistency and fairness in the application of the evaluation criteria. A team of four to five committee members evaluated each vendor on the criteria presented on the questionnaire and presentation evaluation sheet.

Although Carson Wagonlit was the current travel vendor for DOI, the Department selected Northrop Grumman's product, GovTrip, in July 2007. Northrop Grumman's Gov Trip application was chosen because it offered the best overall value as far as technical requirements, past performance with other government agencies, and price (GovTrip, 2007). For example, Carson Wagonlit charged more per transaction, as it involved interactions with a human operator. Ironically, FED-AK still requires using Carson Wagonlit for special reservations, such as small local airlines in Alaska that are not available on the major booking engines.

Northrop Grumman's Information Technology (IT) division manages many of the contracts that deliver technology to federal agencies. This company is the largest non-manufacturing provider of IT products and services to the United States government. It supports U.S. civilian agencies and departments such as the IRS tax systems, air traffic control, and the U.S. Postal Service (Northrop Grumman, n.d.). Northrop had an additional qualification for DOI because it had recently purchased the rights to the source code for the Gelco Travel Manager system, the system then in use at DOI.

Among the less successful implementations of Northrop Grumman systems, the Department of Defense (DoD) implemented a travel system that was intended to save $56 million per year from 2009 to 2016, but instead ended up several years late, costing over $500 million and failing to meet the intended goals (Williamson, 2006). The government report and Northrop Grumman seem to disagree on the actual situation, but the savings initially projected by DoD to occur through automating existing processes will not materialize: the Navy and Air Force anticipate no staff reductions despite the automation (Rogin, 2006). A common complaint about e-government systems is that they are "shallow e-commerce applications and portals overlaid as a thin veneer on top of massive, outdated organizations and aging IT systems. They all too often fail to transform a way of doing business or fail to deliver outstanding return on investment" (Hoeing, 2001)."

For FED-USA, Northrop will be responsible for booking travel reservations, automating the processing of travel authorizations and travel vouchers, and forwarding travel transactions from GovTrip to the DOI's core financial systems (GovTrip, 2007). All agencies within the DOI will be mandated to convert to GovTrip, starting with the U.S. Geological Survey. GovTrip is supposed to reduce reimbursement time from up to fourteen business days to as few as three days, and also to make the entire travel process paperless. For GovTrip to be successful, FED-USA had to implement digital signatures, which will allow the travel management system to accept electronic documents as valid originals.

Description of the Information System

GovTrip is a web-based, self-service travel system accessed via User ID and Password. It uses American Express for traditional reservations support and TRX, a leading global technology company, for automated booking processes. Real-time availability for air, lodging, and rental cars is built into GovTrip. The travel system interfaces with government accounting systems, which is one of the main reasons why reimbursement time can be reduced.

A federal traveler logs into GovTrip and completes a trip itinerary by selecting flights and placing the reservations on hold. The request is routed to a Travel Management Center (TMC), where a travel agent checks the reservation cost against federal travel regulations (FTR) rules and completes the reservation. The reservation is automatically forwarded to an approving official who digitally stamps his/her approval. The status of the document is automatically updated so the federal traveler is informed, and the reservation is routed to a queue for ticketing. After travel, these automated "route and review" features use digital signatures to approve and distribute travel reimbursements.

Benefits of GovTrip

According to Northrop Grumman's Document Processing Manual (Northrop Grumman, 2007), GovTrip allows federal travelers and travel preparers to:

- Input and update travel documents at their workstations
- Update travel preferences in a personal profile
- Use GovTrip information to prepare a voucher
- Input and digitally sign actual trip information
- Determine the status of an authorization or voucher at any time

Using GovTrip, approving officials are able to:

- Preview, review, and approve authorizations and vouchers
- Cancel a travel authorization
- Return a travel document to a traveler for changes/corrections
- Edit travel documents for a traveler
- Delegate and revoke signature authority
- Certify funds available

Because each itinerary is reviewed to ensure all costs are within the regulations, travelers and their supervisors have limited ability to select improper premium travel arrangements. GovTrip audits a trip before it is confirmed so travelers are in compliance with the FTR. This helps to identify fraud and reduce unauthorized travel expenditures by government employees.

According to the FED-AK Travel Coordinator estimates, GovTrip is expected to reduce the cost from \$28 to \$14 per self-service transaction. Because of the clear cost advantage, the GSA has mandated use of the new online travel system except in the following special cases:

- Employees without Internet connectivity
- Travel requiring complex, multi-leg domestic or international flights

- Emergency travel
- Complicated group travel
- Travelers requiring disability accommodations
- Special lodging requirements
- Permanent change of station

In these special cases, travelers and travel arrangers are able to call Carlson Wagonlit to arrange travel over the phone. Appendix A2 illustrates FED-AK's future travel management process using GovTrip. In addition to reducing the transaction costs, GovTrip is also estimated to cut in half the time it takes for government employees to receive reimbursements. This is possible because GovTrip will make the entire process paperless.

As a side benefit of the new system, employees will be compelled to use the entire functionality of the system. They will be unable to pick and choose parts of the system (such as forms), as they do with Travel Manager. GovTrip does not allow data entry from existing manual systems and requires all of its components to be used in the workflow to successfully complete travel arrangements.

Implementation

Northrop Grumman Mission Systems (NGMS) is responsible for the implementation of the travel management systems at the FED-AK. An efficient and effective implementation is critical to the success of large-scale projects. NGMS developed its implementation process based on the experience of more than 70,000 users at 21 pilot sites (GovTrip, n.d.).

The entire implementation process can be completed in as little as four weeks. Following the task order from the client company, NGMS conducts a series of workshops and training classes, starting with travel managers, then with travel administrators and finally with end users. NGMS reviews business processes, sets up the system and secures acceptance from the client. Issue resolution occurs within a period of continuing support during the six months following the client acceptance.

Training

In deploying the new system, training received particular attention. Especially important to the success of the project was to overcome existing resistance and negative perceptions from employees, in particular from those who did not use travel programs before. Employees at FED-AK had already been offered training in using online booking engines when the system was upgraded from Gelco Travel Manager 8.2 to version 9.0. At the time, the training program had developed a negative reputation, because there was only one trainer for a widely dispersed user population. Also, since the upgrade was completed on an accelerated schedule, not all users were trained before the system went live. Additionally, the team responsible for the e-Gov Travel initiative purposely modified the layout of Gelco 9.0 to get the users accustomed to dealing with change. All these issues caused frustration among some employees and led to slower adoption of the new system.

Since GovTrip is a web-based solution, it uses an Enterprise Web Training system as a training portal for travelers, routing officials, and administrators. The effort to expand eTraining is among the 24 presidential e-Gov initiatives that include e-Travel. An article in the American Society for Training and Development's journal *T+D*, states that federal agencies are among the learning innovators (Galloway, 2006). The author found that learning successes in government agencies were the direct result of cross-organizational, collaborative initiatives. Also, agencies are seeking ways to stretch training budgets by identifying common learning needs and capitalizing on shared services. This implementation of GovTrip attempts to use progressive and cost-saving online training methods as discussed below.

Training for GovTrip for the Federal Environment Department Alaska began the week of November 5, 2007. The Travel Coordinator was solely responsible for preparing the local organization for this new all-digital travel management system. Training and support is available through several channels, including hands-on (in person), video, online, and e-mail consultations.

Hands-on Training

This type of training session is designed for individuals who are less comfortable with technology and change. Users are taken step-by-step through the username and password setup process and shown first-hand the functionality of the program. Training materials for this class consist of screen snapshots so that the trainee knows exactly what to expect throughout each stage of the process. The employees are encouraged to ask questions as they learn how to log in to the system. These training sessions last between 40 and 90 minutes.

Video Training

This type of training session is designed for employees who are proficient using online engines and is especially effective for visual learners. These individuals don't require as much one-on-one instruction as the trainees for hands-on training. They learn the program at their own pace and can call the Travel Coordinator if they have any problems. The brochures that accompany the training videos show each step of setting up a username and password, along with additional information about the online booking engine. The video is one hour long.

Online Training

GovTrip provides online training on its website http://www.govtrip.com. The site includes training manuals and demonstration slides.

Email "Quick Start" Guides

Some employees will not be arranging their own travel and hence are not interested in learning the system. A staff assistant or travel arranger can be designated to set up a person's profile or username/password. Therefore, the travel coordinator emailed everyone a quick one-page document laying out the steps to create usernames and passwords.

CURRENT CHALLENGES/PROBLEMS FACING THE ORGANIZATION

Since training has begun, things have been running smoothly, but there are still a few problems that FED-AK is dealing with.

New Problems Faced

Limitations in the ability to audit system usage

Use of GovTrip is scheduled to become mandatory only in the summer of 2008. In the meantime, employees can continue arranging travel using the current system. While both systems are available, it is not clear how many employees are already using the new system, or have at least set up their username and password on it. Unlike with Travel Manager, the Travel Coordinator does not have the authority to see who has or has not set up a password. While this is beneficial for security reasons, this inability to audit usage is expected to make it more difficult to manage users in the long run. According to the Travel Coordinator many people may wait until the last minute to try to set up usernames/passwords, but the Coordinator has no way of identifying the laggards to anticipate problems. Given the problems that are happening now on the small scale with the early adopters, the Coordinator expressed concern that many more mistakes and lockouts will occur during the final stages of implementation, when all users are finally forced to migrate to the new system.

Setting up Usernames and Passwords

User authentication is a critical and often problematic step in the operation of information systems (Ardagna, Damiani, Frati & Reale, 2007). Although a single sign-on approach is preferred, where users can use the same password to access all the linked information systems they need, organizational and sometimes technological problems prevent this from happening. GovTrip interfaces with the government accounting system, but it does not link to non-accounting systems to allow a single sign on for all users. Thus, access to GovTrip requires a separate user name and password for FED-AK employees.

One of the main problems reported by FED-AK employees is in the first step of setting up usernames and passwords. GovTrip requires a "token" to log in to the system the first time, as well as a username and password (Northrop Grumman Systems, 2007). However, many people are confusing the token with the password and they end up locked out of the system. Unlike with the previous system, when an employee is locked out of GovTrip that person must wait one hour for GovTrip to reset his/her account. This delay has caused much frustration and resistance from the workforce. Experiencing such delays and problems with just the basics of setting up a username and password, has led to the perception that the rest of the system will be even more difficult to use. The Travel Coordinator has received several email messages expressing frustration with this first step in using the new system. However, the Coordinator stated that only a small percentage of the workforce is experiencing this problem. The percentage of reported problems might increase as the deadline for using the current system is getting closer, as explained above.

Constantly Locked Documents

Another anticipated problem is the constant locking of documents. When an employee sends a document to his supervisor (Mary) for approval, the supervisor receives a message requesting her authorization. Normally, Mary opens the document, approves it and sends it out to the next step in the process. Problems can arise when Mary opens the document, but she leaves the office before completing the authorization process. The document remains locked and unavailable for access by another supervisor. While Mary is out of the office, a designated backup or alternate supervisor (Paul) is charged with performing the same duties in her absence. If the document is locked by Mary, the information system will prevent Paul from completing the process, even though he has the delegated authority to do so. Clear communication between authorizing officials is required to avoid problems and delays with documents locked in the system.

Perceptions of Professional Employees

FED-AK has several classes of employees. Professional employees such as scientists, analysts, and lawyers have advanced academic degrees and specialized training. Many of these employees are not used to arranging their own travel, and many do not want to learn a new travel arrangement system. They would rather focus on their specialty and leave the travel arrangement process to staff assistants. They feel that time spent arranging travel is wasted, and they would rather use work time for their specialty. Such employees might delegate authority to administrative assistants to use the system on their behalf.

Employees without Internet Access

Most employees throughout the FED-AK offices have Internet access; however, employees who are in the field, especially in remote areas, do not generally have access to the Internet. Problems are expected to arise when these employees require changes in their flight itinerary, for example if they finish work early or if they need to extend their stay. These employees can still call the Carlson Wagonlit Travel Management Center to purchase airplane tickets, request hotel stays, and make car rental reservations. However, a higher transaction fee is charged to the agency for this service.

Overcoming Current Issues

FED-AK has already experienced resistance to change from some of its employees. It is expected that all organizations experience pushback from users who persist in using a legacy system, even as the system has become less useful and less efficient over time. The FED-AK expects to have to address these resistance issues from users, especially considering the problems with the previous Gelco upgrade experience, and the resentment it generated among the users.

Art Murray, writing in *KMWorld* (2007), offers some useful techniques to turn the weight of resistance into positive momentum:

- Keep people, processes, and technologies closely aligned and in balance. Focus efforts on areas having the greatest impact on the implementation's success.
- Make change habitual to the point where nobody has to think about doing things the new way; they just do it. Don't allow users to fall back to doing things the old way.

- Keep the leading change agents visible and dedicated to convincing others of the benefits of the new system.

As explained above, one issue that the Travel Coordinator may face in the next few months is non-participation in setting up usernames and passwords until the GovTrip system becomes mandatory. It may be that only a few comments and complaints have been received because employees are choosing to wait until it is mandatory for them to use the system. Two recommendations for dealing with this problem are: i) set up a schedule to phase everyone into active use and ii) get management involved in the implementation process before the go-live date.

ASSESSMENT AND NEXT STEPS

The project was expected to be completed in April 2008, but that date was extended to June of 2008. Training schedules have been set up to help everyone become familiar with the functionality of the new system. The goal was to get everyone trained on the new system early on, before it becomes mandatory for making travel arrangements. So far, only one week of training has been conducted for the workforce; however, several additional training sessions are planned for the near future.

Employees who have used GovTrip to produce vouchers and authorizations, have few complaints. However, persons who have used the system end-to-end have the following complaints:

- The system is complicated - Changes are difficult to make because of the many nested windows. To make a change users have to click through many windows to get to a line item's entry screen.
- It is hard to remember how to use GovTrip because of the reduced usage. The average traveler may go on a trip once or twice every year. This is not nearly enough time in GovTrip to become familiar and comfortable with the program.
- Program is not intuitive- People who are not computer savvy have a difficult time navigating through GovTrip. Most of the workforce at FED-AK is familiar mainly with the Microsoft Office® suite. Since GovTrip is not designed with an interface similar to Microsoft Office®, it presents itself as a steep learning curve for those not familiar with different software programs. The system does attempt to navigate a user through the entire process of completing a transaction, but problems arise when a changes need to be made.
- Lack of Control - If users get locked out of the system due to consecutive failed login attempts, they are locked out of the system for an hour for secu-

rity purposes. Before GovTrip, with Gelco, the Travel Coordinator was able to reset user passwords, but now users and the Travel Coordinator have no control during the lockout period. This is even more of an issue as people tend to forget their passwords due to long periods of inactivity between trips.

- Time may not be saved- Currently, travel vouchers and authorizations do not go through an audit procedure before they are sent to Denver. This makes the process quick, but only until an error is found. When employees in Denver find errors, they send the vouchers back to the traveler to fix. When resubmitted, the voucher goes back in the long line of new vouchers. This could double or triple the amount of time an employee might have to wait to receive their reimbursement, eliminating any time savings in the process.

- Lack of Education in Travel Regulations- Frustration is caused mostly due to a lack of knowledge of the Federal Travel Regulations. It's nice that GovTrip prevents people from making mistakes, but it does not always make it clear to the traveler what rule they are violating. Prior to GovTrip, travel arrangers were required to take a class on the Federal Travel Regulation that lasted a week. With all users now being expected to be their own travel arrangers, regulation training has mistakenly been left out of the implementation process.

With the new system, the federal government expects that accountability will increase, premium travel expenses will decrease, paper usage will decrease, and the administrative process will be more streamlined and consistent agency-wide. GovTrip's auditing features are intended to provide data on the level of employee adherence to policy. The system has the ability to track travel class (coach, business and first) and will flag reservations for premium travel requiring special approval from supervisors. The benefits of the system will be clearer for federal employees once they are familiar with the system: a much shorter turnaround time for reimbursements and a more efficient travel planning interface.

It is too early to evaluate the success of the GovTrip implementation. At this early stage, it is difficult to identify real, systemic problems in the face of transition-induced stress and the steep learning curve associated with a new system. The success of GovTrip at FED-AK will be more precisely evaluated over the course of the next fiscal year.

Questions:

- Will the potential time savings be lost to added delays caused by errors in vouchers?
- How could management ensure that problems are solved during the transition period and do not linger into the long-term use of the system?

- What kinds of administrative functions could be granted so that the Travel Coordinator has better ability to monitor the system?
- Will the system be able to deliver on the intended benefits?
- How might FED-AK make sure it maintains control over its costs with Carlson Wagonlit so that exceptions are managed appropriately?
- What would have been a better alternative to using the Denver contract workers?
- Considering the expected user resistance, how should FED-AK manage the training phase with NGMS? Should it be more customized? Should the agency allow more time than usual for training?

REFERENCES

Ardagna, C. A., Damiani, E., Frati, F., & Reale, S. (2007). Secure Authentication Process for High Sensitive Data E-Services: A Roadmap. *Journal of Cases on Information Technology*, *9*(1), 20–35. doi:10.4018/jcit.2007010102

Evans, D., & Yen, D. C. (2005). E-government: An analysis for implementation: Framework for understanding cultural and social impact. *Government Information Quarterly*, *22*(3), 354–373. doi:10.1016/j.giq.2005.05.007

Galloway, L. (2006). E-Learning Winter Showcase and Learning Symposium Highlights Best Practices and Innovative Approaches. *T+D, 60*(2), 14.

General Accounting Office. (2007). *Internal Control Weaknesses Governmentwide Led to Improper and Abusive Use of Premium Class Travel*. Washington, DC: Author.

General Accounting Office. (n.d.). *Federal Travel Regulations.* Washington, DC: U.S. Government Printing Office. Retrieved June 25, 2008, from http://www.gpoaccess.gov/cfr/

GovTrip. (2007). *The Department of the Interior Selects Northrop Grumman's GovTrip!* Retrieved June 25, 2008, from http://www.govtrip.com/govtrip/site/document.jsp?docID=807

GovTrip. (n.d.). *Implementation*. Retrieved June 25, 2008, from http://www.govtrip.com/govtrip/site/section_more.jsp?sid=4

Hoeing, C. (2001). Beyond e-government: building the next generation of public services. *Government Executive*, *33*(14), 49–60.

Kolsaker, A., & Lee-Kelley, L. (2007). G2C e-Government: Modernisation or transformation? *Electronic Government*, *4*(1), 68–75. doi:10.1504/EG.2007.012180

Layne, K., & Lee, J. (2001). Developing fully functional e-Government: A four stage model. *Government Information Quarterly, 18*(2), 122–136. doi:10.1016/S0740-624X(01)00066-1

Michael, S. (2004). GSA E-Travel mandatory. *Federal Computer Week, 18*(1), 14.

Murray, A. (2007). Overcoming Resistance to Change. *KM World, 16*(9), 24.

Northrop Grumman. (2007). *Complete Document Processing Manual*. Retrieved November 5, 2007, from http://www.govtrip.com/govtrip/site/redir.jsp?docID=717

Northrop Grumman. (n.d.). *Federal Civilian Agencies*. Retrieved June 25, 2008, from http://www.it.northropgrumman.com/serve/agencies.html

Northrop Grumman Systems. (2007). *Online Booking Engine Sign In*. Retrieved November 5, 2007, from http://www.govtrip.com

Rogin, J. (2006). GAO: DOD overstated travel system savings. *Federal Computer Week, 20*(34), 12.

Schallert, M. (2003). Business process redesign in travel management in an SAP R/3 upgrade project--a case study. *Annals of Cases on Information Technology, 5*, 319–327. doi:10.4018/978-1-59140-061-5.ch021

Siau, K., & Long, Y. (2006). Using Social Development Lenses to Understand E-Government Development. *Journal of Global Information Management, 14*(1), 47–62. doi:10.4018/jgim.2006010103

Srivastava, S. C., & Teo, T. S. H. (2007). E-Government Payoffs: Evidence from Cross-Country Data. *Journal of Global Information Management, 15*(4), 20–40. doi:10.4018/jgim.2007100102

Titah, R., & Barki, H. (2005). E-Government Adoption and Acceptance: A Literature Review. *International Journal of Electronic Government Research, 2*(3), 23–57. doi:10.4018/jegr.2006070102

Torres, L., Pina, V., & Acerete, B. (2005). E-government developments on delivering public services among EU cities. *Government Information Quarterly, 22*(2), 217–238. doi:10.1016/j.giq.2005.02.004

Treasury Board of Canada Secretariat. (n.d.). *Proactive Disclosure*. Retrieved December 30, 2008, from http://www.tbs-sct.gc.ca/pd-dp/index-eng.asp

UN. (2008). *United Nations e-Government Survey 2008*. Retrieved December 30, 2008, from http://unpan1.un.org/intradoc/groups/public/documents/un/unpan028607.pdf

U.S. General Services Administration. (2003, August 15). Bush Administration's E-Travel Initiative Under Way: GSA Awards E- Travel Contract Expected to Save Millions. *PR Newswire, 1.* Retrieved December 4, 2008, from http://www.gsa.gov/Portal/gsa/ep/contentView.do?contentType=GSA_BASIC&contentId=12920&noc=T

U.S. Government. (2002). *E-government strategy: Implementing the President's* management *agenda for e-Government: Simplified delivery of services to citizens.* Retrieved September 30, 2008, from http://www.whitehouse.gov/omb/inforeg/egovstrategy.pdf

U.S. Government. (n.d.). *About E-Gov.* Retrieved November 12, 2007, from http://www.whitehouse.gov/omb/egov/g-1-background.html

Van Wert, J. M. (2002), E-government and performance: a citizen-centered imperative. *The Public Manager,* 16-20.

Wang, L., Bretschneider, S., & Gant, J. (2005) Evaluating Web-Based E-Government Services with a Citizen-Centric Approach. In *Proceedings of the 38th Annual Hawaii International Conference on Systems Sciences,* Big Island, Hawaii.

West, D. M. (2008). *Improving Technology Utilization in Electronic Government around the World, 2008.* Retrieved December 29, 2008, from http://www.brookings.edu/~/media/Files/rc/reports/2008/0817_egovernment_west/0817_egovernment_west.pdf

Williamson, E. (2006, September 27). Report Criticizes Pentagon's New Travel Booking System. *The Washington Post*, A.25.

KEY TERMS AND DEFINITIONS

DOI: Department of the Interior

FTR: Federal Travel Regulations

GAO: U.S. General Accounting Office

GSA: General Services Administration

NGMS: Northrop Grumman Mission Systems, the company responsible for the implementation the travel management systems at the FED-AK

Per Diem Allowance: The amount of money that the government estimates a traveler will spend for hotel and meals. The government will reimburse an authorized traveler up to the listed per diem amount while in travel status. For special cases where listed per diem is too low, actual costs up to 300% over per diem can be requested. Per diem allowance amounts change per state, county, region, and country, and sometimes by time of the year.

Privately Owned Vehicle (POV): This is when an employee uses his/her personal vehicle for transportation while on official business. POV mileage rates are included in the FTR.

Travel Management Center (TMC): Travel Management Centers are companies that provide full service travel arrangements for the Government (airfare ticketing services, hotel registration, car rental registration, and cancellations.)

ENDNOTES

[1]   Privately Owned Vehicle. See the glossary for a definition of the term.

APPENDIX A

Figure 1. Current Process Flow: Travel Reimbursement for FED-AK

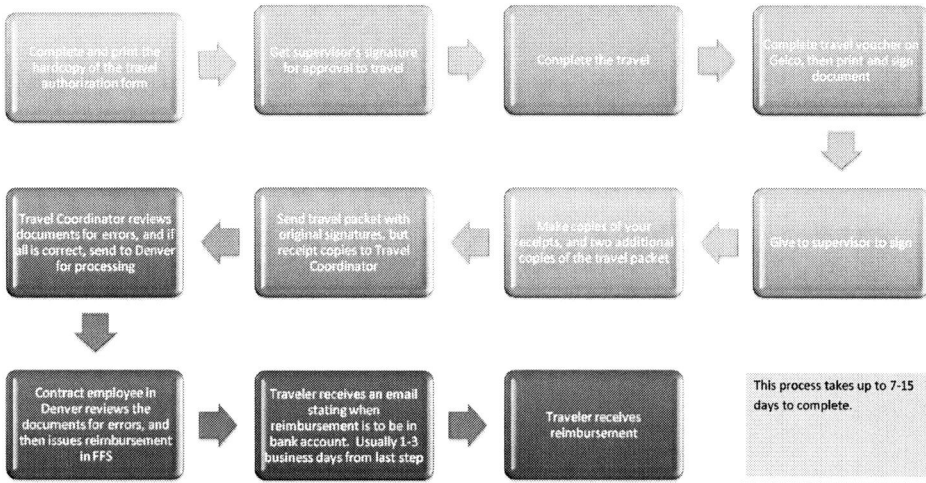

APPENDIX B

Figure 2. Future Process Flow: Travel Reimbursement for FED-AK

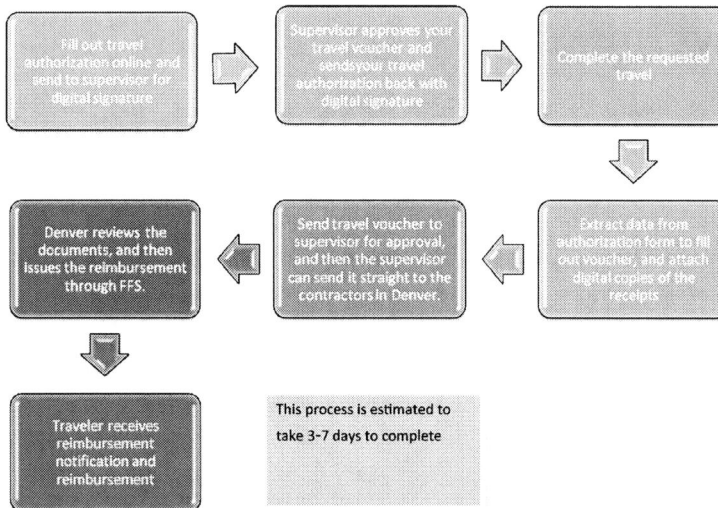

This work was previously published in the Journal of Cases on Information Technology, Volume 12, Issue 1, edited by Mehdi Khosrow-Pour, pp. 1-16, copyright 2010 by IGI Publishing (an imprint of IGI Global).

Chapter 5
ICT and Web 2.0 Technologies as a Determinant of Business Performance

Tanja Arh
Jožef Stefan Institute, Slovenia

Vlado Dimovski
University of Ljubljana, Faculty of Economics, Slovenia

Borka Jerman Blažič
Jožef Stefan Institute, Slovenia

EXCUTIVE SUMMARY

This chapter aims at presenting the results of an empirical study, linking the fields of technology-enhanced learning (TEL), Web 2.0 technologies and organizational learning, and their impact on the financial and non-financial business performance. The chapter focuses on the presentation of the conceptualization of a structural model that was developed to test the impact of technology-enhanced learning and Web 2.0 technologies on the organizational learning and business performance of companies with more than 50 employees. The paper provides detailed definitions of technology-enhanced learning, Web 2.0 technologies and technical terms related to it, its scope and the process of organisational learning, as well as a method for business performance assessment. Special attention is given to the findings related to the observed correlations between the aforementioned constructs. The results of the study indicate a strong impact of ICT and technology-enhanced learning on organizational learning and the non-financial business performance.

DOI: 10.4018/978-1-4666-2618-8.ch005

INTRODUCTION AND BACKGROUND

Success in a highly dynamic environment requires a more efficient response to customers from the side of the companies, more flexible approaches in facing their business circle and more focus on their core competencies (Smith, 2008). What are companies expected to do in order to introduce the necessary changes in the whole business circle? The answer definitely lies in people. The employees' knowledge and competencies significantly contribute to the company's ability to react to the requirements of the fast changes markets, customer needs and successful business processes. With this in view, companies are obliged to manage and maintain the knowledge of their employees. Maintaining the knowledge means to evaluate the employees' tacit and explicit knowledge, and provide knowledge within the company with the suitable tools (Reychav & Weisberg, 2009).

To perform this approach effectively, employees and all members of the company are expected to continuously refresh and enhance their skills and knowledge (Collins & Smith, 2006). As the human capital replacing the physical capital as the source of competitive advantage, organizational learning emerges as a key element for success (Varney, 2008). Only by making learning a truly strategic investment we can ensure an organization in which every person within the company is fully enabled to perform effectively and meet the ever changing demands.

When companies devise their strategies for the employee knowledge acquisition, they can find the most suitable solutions among the methods based on information and communication technologies (ICT), Web 2.0 technologies and technology-enhanced learning (TEL). Technology-enhanced learning as a way of acquiring knowledge and competences has been adopted by many companies as a promising time and cost saving solution providing learn-on-demand opportunities to individual employees, TEL enables workers to access various on-line databases, tools and e-services that help them find solutions for work-related problems (Zhang, 2002; 2003). The term Web 2.0 was coined by O'Reilly (2005) as a common denominator for recent trends heading towards the 'Read-Write Web', allowing everyone to publish resources on the web using simple and open, personal and collaborative publishing tools, known as the social software: blogs, wikis, social bookmarking systems, podcasts, etc. The main features of these tools are dynamism, openness and free availability. According to MacManus and Porter (2005), the power of social software lies in the content personalization and remixing with the other data to create much more useful information and knowledge. The continuously growing dissemination of social and open software in technology-enhanced learning is expected to reshape the technology-enhanced learning landscapes that are currently based on closed, proprietary, institutionalized systems. Thanks to the web evolution, the use of social and open software for learning is becoming an increasingly feasible alternative to these closed, proprietary, institutionalized systems.

However, earlier authors (Roach, 1987) argued that ICT still had not paid off in terms of the required productivity growth. The phenomenon was called the 'productivity paradox' and it asserted that the ICT investments did not result in productivity gains (Navarette & Pick, 2002). Carr (2003) believes that 'ICT may not help a company gain a strategic advantage, but it could easily put a company at a cost disadvantage.' Indeed, the latest empirical studies (Dewan & Kraemer 1998; Navarette & Pick 2002; Dimovski & Škerlavaj 2003) tend to reject the productivity paradox thesis – the phenomenon of organisational learning can be seen as a way out of the dilemma called the productivity paradox. In the last few decades the field of organisational learning has attracted a lot of interest from academics as well as practitioners. A key question in this context is the connection between ICT and organisational learning, and the impact they both have on the business performance (Škerlavaj & Dimovski, 2006).

In the past decade, quite a lot of research studies dealt with the influence of ICT (investments, usage, etc.) on (mainly financial) business performance. We can divide them into four streams of research based on the observed units: business, industry, national and international levels. The results were mixed. Some recent studies in our context (Dimovski & Škerlavaj, 2003) that analysed the influence of hardware, software, telecommunications and knowledge investments on value added per industry in Slovenia for the period 1996-2000, demonstrated a statistically significant, positive influence of hardware and telecommunication investments on value added (Škerlavaj & Dimovski, 2006). Dimovski (1994) confirmed the positive impact on both – the financial and non-financial performance aspects, using a one-industry research design and a stratified sample of 200 credit unions in Ohio, based on the asset size criterion (Škerlavaj & Dimovski, 2006). This study investigated the determinants, processes and outcomes of organisational learning, as well as the relationship between organisational learning and performance. Sloan et al. (2002), Lam (1998) and Figueireido (2003) also arrived at similar conclusions. Simonin (1997) found strong effects of learning on the financial and non-financial performance in the context of strategic alliances.

This chapter has four parts. The first section provides definitions of technology-enhanced learning and Web 2.0 technologies, technical terms related to it, its scope and the process of organisational learning, as well as a method for the business performance assessment in order to develop a set of constructs and an empirical basis for the relationships among them. In the second part, the model's operationalisation through the development of a measurement sub-model is presented. In the third section, the model is tested using a structural linear modelling technique. We conclude with a discussion on the implications of the results and offer some guidelines for future research.

CONCEPTUALISATION OF STRUCTURAL SUB-MODEL

A complete research model normally consists of two sub-models: measurement and structural (Jöreskog, Sörbrom, 1993). The measurement sub-model shows how each latent variable is operationalised through observations of corresponding indicators, and also provides data on validity and reliability of the variables observed. The structural sub-model describes relationships between the latent variables, indicating the amount of unexplained variance. Development of a quality model requires first to establish a structural framework, which is usually implemented in two steps: presentation of fundamental constructs and review of potential correlations between them. Results of the final analysis greatly depend on good conceptualisation of a research model (Jöreskog, Sörbrom, 1993).

Technology-Enhanced Leaning and Web 2.0 Technologies

Technology-enhanced learning is a term introduced along with the introduction of information and communication technology for educational purposes. Up to date companies have widely used this term as a synonym for e-learning (Arh, Pipan & Jerman-Blažič, 2006). Definitions of technology-enhanced learning are various, diverse and lack unity, consequently, it is of outmost importance to provide precise definitions of technology-enhanced learning and related notions. Hereby we refer to the process of studying and teaching as technology-enhanced learning when it includes information and communication technology, regardless of the mode or the scope of its use (Henry, 2001).

Kirschner and Paas (2001) defined technology-enhanced learning as a learning process in which the Internet plays the key role in the presentation, support, management and assessment of learning. Rosenberg (2001) defines technology-enhanced learning as a learning process in which information technology partially or fully undertakes the role of a mediator between different stakeholders involved in the learning process. We refer to the process of studying and teaching as technology-enhanced learning when it includes information and communication technology, regardless of the mode or the scope of its use (Henry, 2001; Dinevski & Plenković, 2002). Technology-enhanced learning extends the company out to ever-widening circles of impact. The companies are participating in a radical redefinition of industries, markets and the global economy itself. Today, organizations are investing great efforts into the making of proper adjustments to the changing business environment in order to enhance their competitiveness. In an attempt to keep up with the development of information technology and the Internet, many businesses are replacing traditional vocational training with e-learning to better manage their workforce. However, it is questionable whether training programs actually change employee behaviour after the implementation. In the case of the US companies, only 10-15% of training is applied to work (Sevilla & Wells, 1988).

When we talk about technology-enhanced learning we cannot overlook the impact of the Web 2.0 technologies on the process of technology-enhanced learning. The Web 2.0 technologies are changing the way messages spread across the web. A number of online tools and platforms are now defining how people share their perspectives, opinions, thoughts and experiences. The Web 2.0 tools, such as instant messaging systems, blogs, RSS, video casting, social bookmarking, social networking, podcasts and picture sharing sites are becoming more and more popular. One major advantage of the Web 2.0 tools is that the majority of them are free. There is a large number of the Web 2.0 tools, some of the more popular ones are: instant messaging systems, blogs, video-wiki and xo-wiki, Doodle, podcasting, RSS, etc.

Instant Messaging Systems (IMS)

The need for communication tools in the learning process is often underestimated by educators, especially those who feel comfortable with the traditional, instructive way of teaching. However, even with their 'traditional' approach learners need to communicate with each other when working together. At the beginning of the 90s, digital communication tools were rather limited: apart from the direct face-to-face meetings, the main way to communicate was through the plain old telephone. Sharing course materials was only enabled by a copy or a fax machine. However, these devices were rarely available in ordinary households. The only barriers to communication that exist today are the lack of skills needed to operate the new technologies. This barrier goes mostly unnoticed with the younger generations that have grown up as digital 'natives', rarely pulling themselves away from their computers (even out on the street they keep the mobile phones in their pockets), but it is definitely still a serious obstacle for many educators. However, the new technologies are inevitably permeating our everyday lives, and it is probably not necessary to explain the purpose of instant messaging to anyone in 2009. The number of users of the world top 10 instant messaging systems is counted in hundreds of millions according to the Wikipedia (2008) statistics, e.g. QQ 783 million total, 317.9 million active, 40.3 million peak online (mostly in China), MSN 294 million active, Yahoo 248 million active, Skype 309 million total, 12 million speak online, etc. The decisive factor for choosing an instant messaging system by an ordinary user is a friend recommendation (most people start using the same system the majority of their friends are already using). The IMS are used for any kind of information exchange including communication between employees or students regarding their study or learning environment. This is the reason this practice is included in the technology that contributes to the personalized learning environment.

Blogs

A blog is a type of a web site in which entries are made as in a journal or a diary and are displayed in reverse chronological order. Basically, an individual maintains his or her own weblog and it functions as a sort of a personal online diary. Regular entries such as comments, descriptions of events, or other types of materials combined with text, images, and links to other weblogs and web sites are the typical weblog ingredients. Blogs have attracted a lot of attention within the educational circles, where they are experienced as the tools that support several pedagogical aims and scenarios, ranging from an individual knowledge management and competence development to group-based learning activities. Therefore, blogs have become an important educational tool in recent years, providing an opportunity for both facilitators and employees to publish their ideas, essays, or simply providing a space to reflect upon their particular learning processes and reading materials. In the context of teaching and learning, blogs can do much more than just deliver instructions or course news items to employees. They can be an interesting collaboration tool for employees who can join relevant community and find people to collaborate with, give feedback to the management and others. In a learning environment blogs are most frequently used for content publishing and sharing. The blog technology can be improved by plug-ins such as the FeedBack tool used to track and integrate the content of other authors within one blog. FeedBack is a standard plug-in piece of code developed within the framework of the iCamp project (www.icamp-project. eu). In a simple way it is used to enable blog users to subscribe to each others' blogs. The blogging technology, in combination with innovations such as the FeedBack specification, has definitely a high potential to be considered a powerful tool for learning with others.

Video-Wiki and Xo-Wiki

Publishing or presenting someone's thoughts online usually means writing some text and illustrating it with pictures. Still, the most natural form of communication for humans is face to face, and for most people the majority of information is presented orally, directly facing the presenter, whose non-verbally communicated information is often even more important than the words they utter. Video could serve as a replacement for the face-to-face presentation, since it can convey the visible behaviour and important non-verbal information. In the past, recording a video and making sure it reached the target audience was quite a big challenge. Depending on the number of intended users, TV broadcasts or video tapes could be used. Employees taking part in an e-learning course work in groups, and are suggested to form groups by getting to know each other and discover some common topics. The mentor/tutor usually uses VideoWiki to record for ex. short self-introduction videos in which employees present their background, or explain their expectations regarding some specific topic for the group assignment. VideoWiki is based on the Red5 open-source Flash server written in Java and Flash. It allows video recording, searching and playback through the main system web page or via the standard URL links. VideoWiki also provides RSS feeds for each name, space or author, and videos can be embedded on any web page using special code snippets. Collaborative creation and maintenance of knowledge artefacts is one of the emerging phenomena of the online Internet communities, such as Wikipedia.org, MediaWiki.org, LyricWiki.org, Microformats.org and Wikitravel.org. A collection of web pages (a so-called wiki) can also be very useful for the teaching and learning purposes; for instance if learners need to collaborate to work on certain topics, or if facilitators wish to develop and share their learning content with others. Consequently, a contemporary approach to technology-enhanced learning requires tools which can enable learners to work on artefacts collaboratively, either by allowing them to publish small posts which can be reused and combined with others (see the blog-based solution presented in the previous section) or by providing real wiki functionality. XoWiki is one such wiki implementation, realized as a component of OpenACS (Open Architecture Community System), a framework for building scalable, community-oriented web applications. XoWiki includes a rich text editor for easy creation and editing of wiki pages, and provides features for structuring, commenting, tagging and visualisation of the wiki-based content.

Doodle

When employees work on a group project they need to divide tasks among the members of the group and monitor the progress of work. This requires the employees to engage in collaboration, discussion and decision making processes. In the context of bringing different cultures, educational systems, levels of teaching, languages and technology skills into a common virtual learning space, planning a series of meetings several weeks in advance may simply not work. Taking this into account, employees must adopt simple solutions to meet their needs. There are plenty of solutions which can help make a project run smoothly. One of them is Doodle. Doodle can be described simply as a web-based tool for finding suitable appointment dates. Doodle allows employees to plan their meetings with partners, suppliers and other employees. In addition to time management, it can be used as a voting tool for any other issue that arises as a part of the distance learning process; for example, the literature that needs to be selected and analysed in order to complete a particular task.

Searching the Net: ObjectSpot

ObjectSpot is a meta-search engine designed to facilitate different types of research. It can be used to find publications and other learning resources on the web. Object-Spot realizes federated searches over an ever-increasing number of digital libraries and learning object repositories. It provides access to more than 10 million learning objects spread across famous libraries such as the Directory of Open Access Journals (DOAJ), OAIster, EBSCO, ACM, CiteBase and IEEE. Some of these repositories are open access, whilst others require registration or subscription.

Organisational Learning

In recent years, the concept of organizational learning has enjoyed a renaissance among both academics and practitioners seeking to improve organizations. Early proponents (e.g. Argyris & Schön, 1978) found their ideas largely confined to the periphery of management thought during the 1980s, but the 1990s witnessed a rebirth of interest. The current renaissance is evident in the creation of a journal about organizational learning (*The Learning Organization*) as well as in the devotion of special issues of several journals to the topic (e.g., *Organization Science*, 1991; *Organizational Dynamics*, 1993; *Accounting, Management and Information Technologies,* 1995; *Journal of Organizational Change Management*, 1996). The appearance of several major review articles is testimony to organizational learning's growing stature in the research community (see Crossan, Lane & White, 1999; Dodgson, 1993; Fiol & Lyles, 1985; Huber, 1991; Jones, 2000; Levitt & March, 1998; Miner & Mezias, 1996). Moreover, a large number of articles in professional periodicals describing the design and management of learning organizations attest to the popularity of organizational learning and knowledge management among practitioners. New theories of knowledge creation have become prominent (Nonaka, 1994; Raelin, 1997), and formal knowledge management programs have been undertaken in many companies (Davenport, De Long & Beers, 1998). As we head into the twenty-first century, therefore, organizational learning promises to be a dominant perspective with influence on both organizational research and management practice (Argyris & Schön, 1996).

Defining Organizational Learning

Organisational learning is defined in numerous ways and approached from different perspectives. The pioneers (Argyris, & Schön, 1996; Senge, 1990) defined organisational learning as an individual's acquisition of information and knowledge, and development of analytical and communicational skills. Understanding organisational learning as a process, which can take up different levels of development, makes the learning organisational structure an ideal form of organisation, which can only be achieved once the process of organisational learning is fully optimised and the organisation is viewed as a system (Senge, 1990). Jones (2000) emphasizes the importance of organizational learning for the organizational performance, defining it as "a process through which managers try to increase organizational members' capabilities in order to better understand and manage the organization and its environment and accept the decisions that would increase organizational performance on a continuous basis." The aforementioned statements regarding the lack of unity of organisational learning definitions are also supported by the findings of Shrivastava, 1983 and Dimovski, 1994. The former states that extensive research carried out in the field of organisational learning has mostly been fragmented, while the latter adds the fragmentation lead to the multitude of definitions (for ex. Nonaka & Takeuchi, 1996 and Wall, 1998), differing according to the criteria of inclusion, scope and focus (Škerlavaj, 2003). Dimovski (1994) and Dimovski & Colnar (1999) provided an overview of previous research and identified four varying perspectives on organizational learning. Dimovski's model managed to merge informational, interpretational, strategic and behavioural approaches to organizational learning, and defined it as a process of information acquisition, information interpretation and the resulting behavioural and cognitive changes which should, in turn, have an impact on the company performance.

Development of our research model is based on DiBella and Nevis' model (DiBella & Nevis, 1998) of integrated approach, according to which the organisational learning factors are divided into study guidelines and study promoters, and on the Dimovski approach (Dimovski, 1994), which combines the aforementioned four aspects of organisational learning.

In this sense the organisational learning can be defined as a dynamic process of the acquisition, transfer and use of knowledge (Crossan, Lane & White, 1999; Dibella & Nevis, 1998), which starts at the core of the organisation – related to individual and team performance – and enable companies to strengthen the efficiency of the financial and non-profit (non-financial?) business achievements (Tippins & Sohi, 2003).

Business Performance

Business performance assessments have advanced over the past years, and developed from traditional, exclusively financial criteria, to modern criteria, which include also the non-financial indicators. Due to numerous disadvantages of the classical accounts and the growing need for quality information on company performance, the theory of economics started developing improved models for performance assessment, taking into account all shareholders: employees, customers, supplier employees and the wider community, also advocated by the Freeman's shareholders theory (Freeman, 1994; 1984). There are several approaches to the non-financial indicator selection, the most established of which is the Balanced Scorecard – BSC (Kaplan & Norton, 1992). The existing models, based on the accounting categories, combine with the non-financial data and the assessment of the so called 'soft' business areas, which mostly improve the assessment of companies' perspective possibilities. For a good performance of a modern company we need to introduce the non-financial indicators along with the financial ones.

Relationship among Constructs

Findings based on a rather wide overview and systematisation of literature has shown that we can expect positive impact of ICT and technology-enhanced learning on organisational learning and business performance. Robey et al. (2000) do warn that technology-enhanced learning and relative ICT may take either the role of a promoter or the role of an inhibitor of organisational learning, so the following hypothesis can be posed:

H_1: Technology-enhanced learning has positive impact on organisational learning.

H_2: Technology-enhanced learning has positive impact on financial performance.

H_3: Technology-enhanced learning has positive impact on non-financial performance.

Correlation between organisational learning and business success is often a controversial issue when we begin to deal with the company management (Inkpen & Crossan, 1995). Some authors believe better performance is related to organisational learning, though their definitions of business results differ greatly. In relation to this we can mention the capacity of organisational learning to have a positive impact on the financial results (Lei et al., 1999; Slater & Narver, 1995), on the results related to shareholders (Goh & Richards, 1997; Ulrich et al., 1993) and on the business results, such as innovativeness and greater productivity (Leonard-Barton, 1992). Mintzberg (1990) says the company performance is an important piece of feedback information on effectiveness and efficiency of the learning process. The study of Perez et al. (2004) has shown organisational learning has a significant impact on the company performance. On this basis, the following hypotheses can be put forward:

H_4: Organisational learning leads to improved financial results.

H_5: Organisational learning leads to improved non-financial results.

CONCEPTUALISATION OF MEASUREMENT SUB-MODEL

Having understood the hypothesized correlations between the latent variables, the following question is logically raised: 'How should these four constructs be operationalised and measured?' There are certainly various approaches available, since the number and the type of indicators to be used for the assessment of a certain construct, the number and the type of items to be included under an indicator and the methods for their integration are decided on the basis of validity and variability of specific measuring instruments. Table 1 presents constructs, indicators used for construct assessment, number of items summed up to give the value of an indicator and the theory or empirical research on the basis of which the measurement items were developed.

In short, the hypothesized model shall be composed of four constructs and 13 indicators, and will be of recursive nature, meaning that there shall be no cases of two variables appearing simultaneously, i.e. as a cause and a consequence to one another.

Development of Research Instrument

The questionnaire used has been under constant development and validation for more than 10 years. Dimovski (1994) used it on a sample of Ohio credit unions in order to measure the organizational learning process as a source of competitive advantage. Škerlavaj (2003) upgraded it to include the measures of non-financial performance, while he replaced the industry-specific measures of financial performance with two

Table 1. Specification of constructs

Latent Variables	Indicators and Number of Items from Questionnaire
Technology-Enhanced Learning	Information and communication infrastructure (ICI) – 9 items Education technology (ET) – 10 items Learning contents (LC) – 3 items
Organisational Learning	Knowledge acquisition (KAc) – 9 items Knowledge transmission (KTt) – 10 items Use of knowledge (UoK) – 10 items
Financial Performance	Return on assets (FP1) – 1 item Return on capital (FP2) – 1 item Value added per employee (FP3) – 1 item
Non-Financial Performance	Employee fluctuation (NFP1) – 1 item Share of loyal customers (NFP2) – 1 item Number of customer complaints (NFP3) – 1 item Supplier relations (NFP4) – 1 item

measures valid for all companies. For this study the operationalisation of all four constructs involved was improved and applied on a sample of Slovenian companies with more than 50 employees in 2007. The reason to include smaller companies is to improve the generalizability of the research findings. The measurement instrument used in this study has 22 items for the technology-enhanced learning construct, 29 items for the organizational learning construct, 3 items for the financial and 4 items for the non-financial performance. The pre-testing procedures were conducted in the form of interviews and studies with managers and focus groups of research and academic colleagues.

RESEARCH HYPOTHESES AND MODEL

Once the theoretical frame of the model is devised, illustration of conceptualisation by the means of a flow chart is to be tackled (Arh, Dimovski & Jerman-Blažič, 2008). Flow chart is a graphical representation of interrelations between various elements of a model. Measurement variables belonging to exogenous latent variables are marked with an x, while their measurement deviations are marked with a δ. Endogenous latent variable indicators are marked with a y, and measurement deviations with an ε. Structural equation deviations are ζ, exogenous latent variables are ξ, endogenous constructs are η, and one-way influence of exogenous latent variables on exogenous are γ. To describe relations between latent variables and their indicators (measurement variables) we use λ. The Figure 1 below is showing a conceptualised research model, presenting all basic constructs and hypothesized correlations between them.

Figure 1. Conceptualised research model

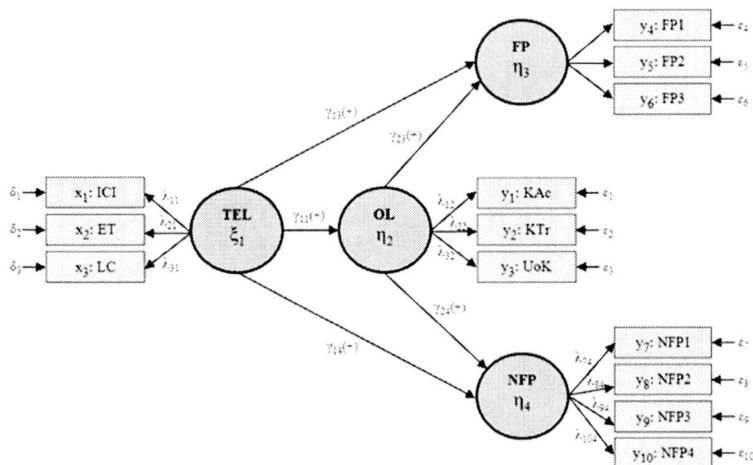

We aim at proving: (1) that the latent variable of technology-enhanced learning (TEL) has positive impact on organisational learning (OL), (2) financial (FP) and (3) non-financial performance (NFP); (4) that the latent variable of organisational learning (OL) as a process of knowledge creation leads to improved financial results (FP), as well as to (5) improved non-financial results (NFP); (6) that it is impossible to expect significant statistical correlations between financial performance (FP) and non-financial (NFP) performance.

RESEARCH PROCEDURE

The methodology applied to test our research model was structural equation modelling (SEM). This involves a combination of confirmatory factor analysis (CFA) and econometric modelling, which aims to analyse hypothesised relationships among the latent constructs, measured with observed indicators (measurement variables). Table 2 provides the procedure for data analysis.

First, the item analysis was performed to describe the sample characteristics, to investigate the item means, and to assess item-to-total correlations. Second, exploratory factor analysis was performed to explore whether the items load highly on their intended latent construct, and have low cross-loadings. After the exploratory factor analysis, reliability of the underlying factors was discussed in terms of Cronbach's alphas. Third, confirmatory analysis (CFA) was performed to ensure that the constructs are valid and reliable; this refers to the measurement part of the model.

Table 2. Research pocedure

Stage	Analysis	Purpose
1.	**Item Analysis**	Investigation of sample characteristics Investigation of item means Investigation of item-to-total correlations
2.	**Exploratory Factor Analysis**	Exploration of loadings; removal of items with low loadings and high cross-loadings; Assessment of number of latent factors Assessment of reliability (Cronbach's alpha)
3.	**Confirmatory Factor Analysis**	Assessment of convergent validity Assessment of discriminant validity Assessment of construct reliability Assessment of correlations and multicollinearity
4.	**Testing Hypothesis**	Assessment of structural relationship (H1-H5) Parameter Estimates for Overall Measurement Model Convergent and Discriminant Validity
5.	**Presentation of Results**	Discussion of findings

Consequently, CFAs (without any structural relationships) were performed with LISREL 8.80 to check whether the items meet the criteria for convergent and discriminant validity, as well as construct reliability. Properties of the four research constructs in the proposed model (Figure 1) and the five hypotheses were tested using LISREL 8.80 and PRELIS 2.30 packages for structural equation analysis and procedures. As estimation method for model evaluation and procedures, the maximum likelihood (ML) method was utilized. Structural equation modelling (SEM) is designed to evaluate how well a proposed conceptual model that contains observed indicators and hypothetical constructs explains or fits the collected data. It also provides the ability to measure or specify the structural relationships among the sets of unobserved (latent) variables, while describing the amount of unexplained variance. Clearly, the hypothetical model in this study was designed to measure structural relationships among the unobserved constructs that are set up on the basis of relevant theories, and prior empirical research and results. Therefore, the SEM procedure is an appropriate solution for testing the proposed structural model and hypotheses for this study.

Data Gathering and Sample

Based on the model's conceptualisation, a measurement instrument (questionnaire) was developed and sent in June 2007 to the CEOs or board members of all Slovenian companies with more than 50 employees, which accounted for 1215 companies. In the first three weeks 356 completed questionnaires were returned, five out of which were excluded from further analysis due to missing values. The response rate was 29.7%, which can be considered successful in the Slovenian context (using our primary data collection technique and no call backs). It is an indication that, beside academia, managers are also interested to know whether and in which circumstances investments in ICT and technology-enhanced learning pay off. We aimed at an audience of top and middle managers bearing in mind the idea of a strategic and to some degree even an interdisciplinary perspective of the companies in question, although there is some discrepancy between the desired and the actual structure of respondents. Based on the criterion of the average number of employees, in 2006 73.88% of the selected companies had between 50 and 249 employees, followed by 14.61% with 250 to 499 employees, while 11.51% of the companies had 500 to 999 employees. According to the company revenues in 2006, 33.15% of the Slovenian companies had the annual revenue of 2 to 7.3 million EUR. A somewhat smaller proportion (32.87%) of companies had the net income of 7.3 to 29.2 million EUR in this same period, 19.94% had the annual turnover of more than 29.2 million euro, and only 14.04% have not reached the annual revenue threshold of 2 million

Table 3. Structure of respondents (by industry)

Industry (EU NACE Rev.1)	Frequency	Percent (%)
A Agriculture, hunting and forestry	7	2
B Fishing	0	0
C Mining and quarrying	7	2
D Manufacturing	158	44.4
E Electricity, gas and water supply	15	4.2
F Construction	49	13.8
G Wholesale & retail, repair of motor vehicles, personal & household goods	41	11.5
H Hotels and restaurants	12	3.4
I Transport, storage and communication	14	3.9
J Financial intermediation	7	2
K Real estate, renting and business activities	16	4.5
M Education	2	0.6
N Health and social work	1	0.3
O Other community, social and personal services	27	7.6

euro. The questionnaire was mostly completed by middle management respondents (directors of functional departments). The top and middle management were almost equally represented within the sample.

Table 3 demonstrates the industry structure of the companies in question. Our respondents reported in almost half of all cases that their main industry was manufacturing, followed by 13.8% of companies in the construction business and 11.5% in the wholesale & retail, repair of motor vehicles, personal & household goods. One out of fifteen industries have only one company representative, there was no company from the fishery sector and only two companies working the field of education. This is logical since we excluded the non-profit and small businesses from our analysis.

Parameter Value Estimates

The results of structural equation analysis by LISREL were utilized to test the hypotheses proposed in this study. As discussed in the previous section, the relationships between the constructs were examined based on t-values associated with path coefficients between the constructs. If an estimated t-value was greater than a certain critical value ($p < .05$, t-value = 1.96) (Mueller, 1996), the null hypothesis that the associated estimated parameter is equal to 0 was rejected. Subsequently, the hypothesized relationship was supported.

The maximum likelihood (ML) method was used to estimate the parameter values. In this phase, the hypotheses posed in the conceptualisation phase are tested. Even though several methods can be used for this purpose, ML is the one most often used and has the advantage of being statistically efficient and at the same time specification-error sensitive because it demands only complete data and does not allow for missing values. All methods will, however, lead to similar parameter estimates on the condition that the sample is large enough and that the model is correct (Jöreskog & Sörbrom, 1993). Figure 2 shows a path diagram of our model (with completely standardised parameter estimates).

The Tpu construct demonstrated a statistically significant, positive and strong impact on the Ou. Namely, the value of the completely standardised parameter almost equals the margin of 0.70. However, Tpu did not exhibit any statistically significant impact on the Fp, meaning that the hypothesis 2 must be rejected. The OI construct demonstrated a statistically significant positive and strong impact on the Fp and an even stronger one on the Nfp. This means that the hypotheses 4 and 5 can be considered empirically supported by the data at hand.

Global Fit Assessment

Bollen (1989) explained that the model fit relates to the degree to which a hypothesised model is consistent with the available data – the degree to which the implicit

*Figure 2. Research model (completely standardised parameter values, *significant at p > 0.05)*

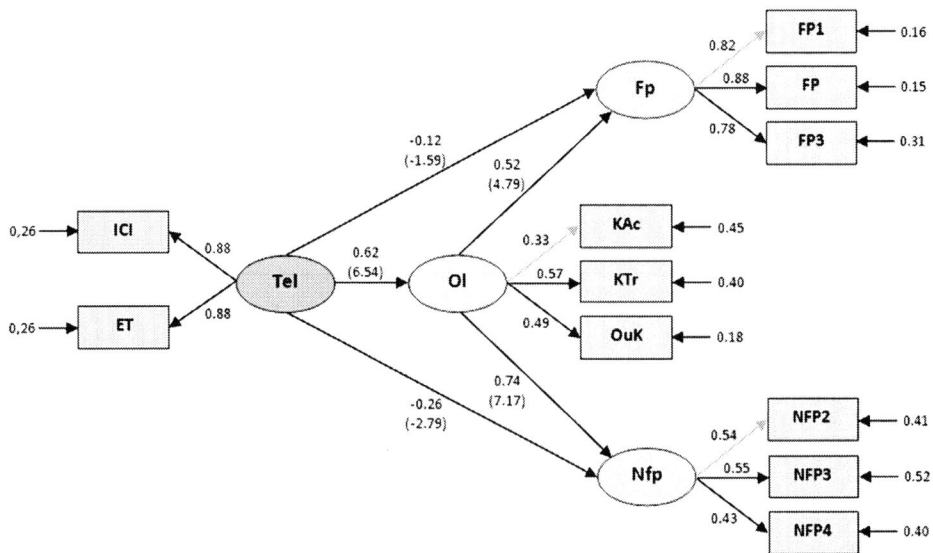

matrix of covariances (based on the hypothesised model) and the sample covariance matrix (based on the data) fit. The aim of the global fit assessment is to determine to what degree is the model as a whole consistent with the data gathered. Over the years numerous global fit indices have been developed. To every researcher's regret, none of them is superior to the others. Different authors favour different measures. Diamantopoulos and Siguaw (2000) recommend using several measures and at the same time provide reference values for every one of them (Table 4).

The most traditional value is χ^2 statistics. Using this fit indicator we test the hypothesis that the implicit covariance matrix equals the sample covariance matrix. Our goal was not to reject this hypothesis, however, in our case this hypothesis must be rejected (at a 5% level of significance). Nonetheless, quantifying the degree of misfit is often more useful than testing the hypothesis of exact fit, which χ^2 statistics are designed for. All other indices lead to the conclusion that the model is an appropriate representation of reality. The root means square error of approximation (RMSEA) is the most widespread measure of the global fit and in our case points to the acceptable fitness of the model. The consistent Akaike information criteria (CAIC) of the model needs to be compared against the CAIC of the saturated and independent model, where smaller values represent a better fit. Standardised root mean square residual (standardised RMR) is a fit index calculated on the basis of

Table 4. Fit indices

Fit Indices	Reference Value	Model Value	Global Fit
Chi-square ($\chi2$) of estimate model	($\chi^2/df < 2$)	89.29 (df = 38) = 2.34	No
Goodness-of-fit index (GFI)	$\geq .90$	.96	Yes
Root mean square residual (RMR)	$< .05$	.023	Yes
Root mean square error of approximation (RMSEA)	$\leq .05$	.062	Yes
CAIC	CAIC saturated model CAIC independent model	281.79	Yes
Adjusted goodness-of-fit index (AGFI)	$\geq .90$	.92	Yes
Non-normed fit index (NNFI)	$\geq .95$	.97	Yes
Normed fit index (NFI)	$\geq .90$	.96	Yes
Parsimony goodness-of-fit index(PGFI)	$\geq .50$	.55	Yes
Comparative fit index (CFI)	$\geq .90$	.98	Yes
Critical (CN)	N = 248.77	356	Yes

standardised residuals (differences between elements of the sample and implicit covariance matrixes). The goodness-of-fit (GFI) index and the adjusted goodness-of-fit (AGFI) index are absolute fit indices which directly assess how well the co-variances based on the parameter estimates reproduce the sample covariances (Gebring &Anderson, 1993). All of the indices described above lead to the conclusion that the model can be regarded as an appropriate approximation of reality (at a global level).

SOLUTIONS AND RECOMMENDATIONS

The aim of this paper was to present the conceptualisation of a model for the assessment of the impact of technology-enhanced learning, and the respective information and communication technology on the business performance of Slovene companies with more than 50 employees. The theoretical and empirical grounds were studied in order to demonstrate the correlations between the aforementioned constructs with the basic aim to present a hypothesized research model as a concrete result.

The study focuses on the findings achieved through the estimation of the relations between information and communication technology and technology-enhanced learning, organizational learning and business performance, and their operationalisation. In accordance with stakeholder theory and balanced scorecard, both the financial and non-financial aspects of business performance are considered. Within this approach, a structural equation model was conceptualised based on the prior theoretical and empirical foundations.

In the study, five hypothesis were tested: (1) technology-enhanced learning has a positive impact on organizational learning, (2) technology-enhanced learning has a positive impact on the financial business results, (3) technology-enhanced learning has a positive impact on the non-financial business results, (4) organizational learning as a process of knowledge creation has a positive impact on the financial performance, and (5) organizational learning has a positive effect on the non-financial performance. A sample of data collected was used through the survey questionnaire, which was circulated among the CEOs and presidents of the management boards of Slovenian companies with more than 50 employees in June 2007. Out of a total of 1215 questionnaires sent, 356 correctly completed questionnaires were returned, which means that the response rate was 29.7%. The questionnaire was structured in four parts. The first construct (technology-enhanced learning) was based on 22 measurement variables, the second construct (organizational learning) on 29 measurement variables related to the acquisition of knowledge, knowledge transfer and the use of knowledge. The third and the fourth constructs were designed with the intention of measuring the financial and non-financial company results (three measurement variables for the financial and four measurement variables for the non-financial results). Equation modelling methodology was used for the analysis in the empirical part of the study. The methodology of structural equation modelling enabled us to concretely determine whether the hypothetical links between the constructs or latent variables are valid or not.

The results of the survey prove a statistically significant, strong and positive impact of ICT and technology-enhanced learning on organizational learning, and a decisive influence of organizational learning on the financial and non-financial business results. The companies which systematically incorporated various advanced educational tools and systems into their daily work, and ensured high quality information and communication technology equipment recognized the importance of organizational learning as the most effective process for the production, dissemination and application of knowledge. Furthermore, the positive effects of organizational learning on the financial and non-financial business results confirm that this concept really guarantees the achievement of higher performance both in financial and non-financial terms. Knowledge is definitely one of the most important criteria of the competitive advantage, which is confirmed by the results of the study.

The study contributes to the technology-enhanced learning and organizational learning base of knowledge in the following three dimensions: (1) theoretical, (2) methodological, and (3) practical. Technology-enhanced learning contributes to sustainable competitive advantage through its interaction with other resources. Recent literature suggests that organizational learning is a process that plays an important role in enhancing company's competitive advantage (Lei, Slocum & Pitts, 1999), which may benefit from the judicious application of technology-enhanced learning. It has also been argued that a prerequisite for the firms to be successful is the completion of Tel with Ol. Within the broader conceptual framework, this study focuses on the relationship between technology-enhanced learning, organizational learning and business performance. As such, the conceptual model offers several research opportunities and provides a solid base for further empirical testing of hypotheses related to technology-enhanced learning and organizational learning.

REFERENCES

Argyris, C., & Schön, D. A. (1978). *Organizational Learning: A Theory of Action Perspective*. Reading, MA: Addison-Wesley.

Argyris, C., & Schön, D. A. (1996). *Organizational Learning II: Theory, Method and Practice*. Reading, MA: Addison-Wesley.

Arh, T., Dimovski, V., & Jerman-Blažič, B. (2008). *Model of impact of technology-enhanced organizational learning on business performance. V P. Cunningham, M. Cunningham (ur.), Collaboration and the knowledge economy: issues, applications, case studies, (str. 1521–1528)*. Netherlands: IOS Press.

Arh, T., Pipan, M., Jerman-Blažič, B. (2006). Virtual learning environment for the support of life-long learning initiative. *WSEAS transactions on advances in engineering education*, 4(4), str. 737–743.

Bollen, K. A. (1989). *Structural equations with latent variables*. New York: Wiley.

Carr, N. G. (2003). IT doesn't matter. *Harvard Business Review*, *81*(5), 41.

Collins, C. J., & Smith, K. G. (2006). Knowledge exchange and combination: the role of human resource practices in the performance of high-technology firms. *Academy of Management Journal*, *49*(3), 544–560.

Crossan, M., Lane, H. W., & White, R. E. (1999). An organizational learning framework: from intuition to institution. *Academy of Management Review*, *24*(3), 522–537. doi:10.2307/259140

Davenport, T. H., De Long, D. W., & Beers, M. C. (1998). Successful knowledge management projects. *Sloan Management Review*, *39*(2), 43–57.

Dewan, S., & Kraemer, K. L. (1998). International dimensions of the productivity paradox. *Communications of the ACM*, *41*(8), 56–62. doi:10.1145/280324.280333

Diamantopoulos, A., & Siguaw, J. A. (2000). *Introducing LISREL*. London: SAGE Publications.

DiBella, J. A., & Nevis, E. C. (1998). *How Organizations Learn – An Integrated Strategy for Building Learning Capability*. San Francisco, CA: Jossey-Bass.

Dimovski, V. (1994). *Organisational learning and competitive advantage*. Unpublished doctoral dissertation, Cleveland State University.

Dimovski, V., & Colnar, T. (1999). Organizacijsko učenje. *Teorija in Praksa*, *5*(36), 701–722.

Dinevski, D., & Plenković, M. (2002). Modern University and e-learning. *Media, culture and public relations, 2*, 137−146.

Dodgson, M. (1993). Organizational learning: a review of some literatures. *Organization Studies*, *14*(3), 375–394. doi:10.1177/017084069301400303

Figueiredo, P. N. (2003). Learning processes features: How do they influence inter-firm differences in technological capability - Accumulation paths and operational performance improvement? *International Journal of Technology Management, 26*(7), 655–689. doi:10.1504/IJTM.2003.003451

Fiol, C. M., & Lyles, M. A. (1985). Organizational learning. *Academy of Management Review, 10*(4), 803–813. doi:10.2307/258048

Freeman, E. R. (1984). *Strategic Management – A Stakeholder Approach*. London: Pitman.

Freeman, E. R. (1994). Politics of Stakeholder Theory: Some Future Directions . *Business Ethics Quarterly, 4*, 409–422. doi:10.2307/3857340

Gerbing, D. W., & Anderson, J. C. (1988). An updated paradigm for scale development incorporating unidimensionality and measurement error. *JMR, Journal of Marketing Research, 25*, 186–192. doi:10.2307/3172650

Goh, S., & Richards, G. (1997). Benchmarking the learning capability of organizations. *European Management Journal, 15*(5), 575–583. doi:10.1016/S0263-2373(97)00036-4

Henry, P (2001). E-learning technology, content and services. *Education + Training, 43*(4), 251–259.

Huber, G. P. (1991). Organizational Learning: The Contributing Processes and the Literatures. *Organization Science, 2*(1), 88–115. doi:10.1287/orsc.2.1.88

Inkpen, A., & Crossan, M. M. (1995). Believing is seeing: Organizational learning in joint ventures. *Journal of Management Studies, 32*(5), 595–618. doi:10.1111/j.1467-6486.1995.tb00790.x

Jones, G. R. (2000). *Organizational Theory* (3rd ed.). New York: Prentice Hall.

Jöreskog, K. G., & Sörbrom, D. (1993). *LISREL 8: Structural Equation Modelling with the SIMPLIS Command Language*. London: Lawrence Erlbaum Associates Publishers.

Kaplan, R. S., & Norton, D. P. (1992). Balanced Scorecard – Measures That Drive Performance. *Harvard Business Review, 1–2*, 71–79.

Kirchner, P. A., & Pass, F. (2001). Web enhanced higher education: a Tower of Babel. *Computers in Human Behavior, 17*(4), 347–353. doi:10.1016/S0747-5632(01)00009-7

Lam, S. S. K. (1998). Organizational performance and learning styles in Hong Kong. *The Journal of Social Psychology, 138*(3), 401–403. doi:10.1080/00224549809600392

Lei, D., Hitt, M. A., & Bettis, R. (1996). Dynamic core competencies through meta-learning and strategic context. *Journal of Management, 22*(4), 549–569. doi:10.1177/014920639602200402

Lei, D., Slocum, J. W., & Pitts, R. A. (1999). Designing organizations for competitive advantage: The power of unlearning and learning. *Organizational Dynamics, 27*(3), 24–38. doi:10.1016/S0090-2616(99)90019-0

Leonard-Barton, D. (1992). The factory as a learning laboratory. *Sloan Management Review, 34*(1), 23–38.

Levitt, B., & March, J. G. (1998). Organizational learning. *Annual Review of Sociology, 14*, 319–340. doi:10.1146/annurev.so.14.080188.001535

MacManus, R., & Porter, J. (2005): *Web 2.0 for design: bootstrapping the social web*. Retrieved April 15th 2008, from: http://www.digital-web.com/articles/web_2_for_designers

Miner, A. S., & Mezias, S. J. (1996). Ugly duckling no more: pasts and futures of organizational learning research. *Organization Science, 7*(1), 88–99. doi:10.1287/orsc.7.1.88

Mintzberg, H. (1990). Strategy formation: Schools of thought . In Frederickson, J. W. (Ed.), *Perspectives of strategic management* (pp. 105–235). New York: Harper Business.

Mueller, R. O. (1996). *Basic Principles of Structural Equation Modelling: An Introduction to Lisrel and EQS*. New York: Springer.

Navarette, C. J., & Pick, J. B. (2002). Information technology expenditure and industry performance: The case of the Mexican banking industry. *Journal of Global Information Technology Management, 5*(2), 7–28.

Nonaka, I. (1994). A dynamic theory of organizational knowledge creation. *Organization Science, 5*(1), 14–37. doi:10.1287/orsc.5.1.14

Nonaka, I., & Takeuchi, H. (1996). A Theory of Organizational Knowledge Creation . *International Journal of Technology Management, 11*(7/8), 833–846.

O'Reilly, T. (2005). *What Is Web 2.0. Design Patterns and Business Models for the Next Generation of Software*. Retrieved November 10, 2009, from http://oreilly.com/web2 /archive/what-is-web-20.html

Péréz López, S., Montes Peón, J. M., & Vázquez Ordás, C.Managing knowledge: The link between culture and organizational learning. *Journal of Knowledge Management*, *8*(6), 93–104. doi:10.1108/13673270410567657

Raelin, J. A. (1997). A model of work-based learning. *Organization Science*, *8*(6), 563–578. doi:10.1287/orsc.8.6.563

Reychav, I., & Weisberg, J. (2009). Good for workers, good for companies: How knowledge sharing benefits individual employees. *Knowledge and Process Management*, *16*(4), 186–197. doi:10.1002/kpm.335

Roach, S. (1987). *America's technology dilemma: A profile of the information economy. Economics Newsletter Series*. New York: Morgan Stanley.

Robey, D., Boudreau, M., & Rose, G. M. (2000). Information Technology and Organizational Learning: a Review and Assessment of Research. *Accounting . Management and Information Technologies*, *10*, 125–155. doi:10.1016/S0959-8022(99)00017-X

Rosenberg, M. (2001). *E-Learning, Strategies for Developing Knowledge in the Digital Age. New York*. McGraw-Hill.

Senge, P. M. (1990). *The fifth discipline: art and practice of the learning organization*. New York: Doubleday.

Sevilla, C., & Wells, T. D. (1988). Contracting to ensure training transfer. *Training & Development*, *6*(1), 10–11.

Shrivastava, P. A. (1983). Typology of Organizational Learning Systems. *Journal of Management Studies*, *20*, 1–28. doi:10.1111/j.1467-6486.1983.tb00195.x

Simonin, B. L. (1997). The importance of collaborative know-how: An empirical test of the learning organization. *Academy of Management Journal*, *40*(5), 1150–1173. doi:10.2307/256930

Škerlavaj, M. (2003). *Vpliv informacijsko-komunikacijskih tehnologij in organizacijskega učenja na uspešnost poslovanja: teoretična in empirična analiza*. Unpublished Master's theses. Ljubljana: Ekonomska fakulteta.

Škerlavaj, M., & Dimovski, V. (2006). Study of the Mutual Connections among Information-communication Technologies, Organisational Learning and Business Performance. *Journal for East European Management Studies*, *11*(1), 9–29.

Slater, S. F., & Narver, J. C. (1995). Market orientation and the learning organization. *Journal of Marketing*, *59*(3), 63–74. doi:10.2307/1252120

Sloan, T. R., Hyland, P. W. B., & Beckett, R. C. (2002). Learning as a competitive advantage: Innovative training in the Australian aerospace industry. *International Journal of Technology Management, 23*(4), 341–352. doi:10.1504/IJTM.2002.003014

Smith, R. (2008). Aligning Competencies, Capabilities and Resources. *Research Technology Management: The Journal of the Industrial Research Institute*, September-October.

Tippins, M. J., & Sohi, R. S. (2003). IT competency and firm performance: Is organizational learning a missing link? *Strategic Management Journal, 24*(8), 745–761. doi:10.1002/smj.337

Ulrich, D., Jick, T., & von Glinow, M. A. (1993). High-impact learning: Building and diffusing learning capability. *Organizational Dynamics, 22*(2), 52–66. doi:10.1016/0090-2616(93)90053-4

Varney, S. (2008). Leadership learning: key to organizational transformation. *Strategic HR Review, 7*(1), 5–10. doi:10.1108/14754390810880471

Wall, B. (1998). Measuring the Right Stuff: Identifying and Applying the Right Knowledge. *Knowledge Management Review, 1*(4), 20–24.

Zhang, D. *Media structuration – Towards an integrated approach to interactive multimedia-based E-Learning.* (Ph.D. dissertation, The University of Arizona, 2002. Zhang, D., & Nunamaker, J. F. (2003). Powering e-learning in the new millennium: an overview of e-learning and enabling technology. *Information Systems Frontiers, 5*(2), 207–218.

KEY TERMS AND DEFINITIONS

Balanced Scorecard (BSC): The balanced scorecard (BSC) is a strategic performance management tool – a semi-standard structured report supported by proven design methods and automation tools that can be used by managers to keep track of the execution of activities of staff within their control, and monitor the consequences arising from these actions. It is perhaps the best known of several such frameworks, and was widely adopted in the English speaking western countries and Scandinavia in the early 1990s. The BCS based on the use of three non-financial topic areas as prompts to aid the identification of the non-financial measures in addition to the one looking at the financial measures. The four perspectives are: financial, customer, internal business, and innovation and learning.

Confirmatory Factor Analysis: Confirmatory factor analysis (CFA) is a powerful statistical technique. CFA allows researchers to test the hypothesis of the existence of a relationship between the observed variables and their underlying latent construct(s). Researchers apply their theoretical knowledge, empirical research, or both, postulate the relationship pattern a priori and then tests the hypothesis statistically.

LISREL: LISREL is the pioneering software for structural equation modelling which includes statistical methods for complex data survey. LISREL was developed in 1970s by Karl Jöreskog and Dag Sörbom, both professors at the Uppsala University, Sweden.

Organizational Learning: Organizational learning is an area of knowledge within the organizational theory that studies models and theories about the ways an organization learns and adapts. Argyris and Schön (1978) were the first to propose models that facilitate organizational learning; others have followed in the tradition of their work. They distinguished between the single- and double-loop learning. In the single-loop learning, individuals, groups, or organizations modify their actions according to the difference between the expected and obtained outcomes. In the double-loop learning, entities (individuals, groups or organizations) question the values, assumptions and policies that led to the actions in the first place; if they are able to view and modify those, then the second-order or the double-loop learning has taken place. The double-loop learning is the process of learning about the single-loop learning.

Structural Equation Modelling: Structural equation modelling, or in short SEM, is a statistical technique for testing and estimating causal relationships using a combination of statistical data and qualitative causal assumptions. SEM allows both confirmatory and exploratory modelling, meaning it suits both theory testing and theory development. Factor analysis, path analysis and regression all represent special cases of SEM.

Technology Enhanced Learning: Technology-enhanced learning (TEL) refers to any learning activity supported by technology. TEL is often used as a synonym for e-learning, however, there are significant differences between the two; namely, TEL focuses on the technological support of any pedagogical approach that utilizes technology. However, it rarely includes the print technology or developments related to libraries, books and journals occurring in the centuries before computers.

Web 2.0: Web 2.0 is a category of new Internet tools and technologies created around the idea that those who consume the media, access the Internet, and use the web should not just passively absorb what is available; they should be rather active contributors, helping customize the media and technology for their own purposes, as well as those of their communities. Web 2.0 marks the beginning of a new era in technology – one that promises to help the nonprofits operate more efficiently, generate more funding, and affect more lives. These new tools include blogs, social networking applications, RSS, social networking tools, and wikis.

This work was previously published in Cases on ICT Utilization, Practice and Solutions: Tools for Managing Day-to-Day Issues, edited by Mubarak S. Al-Mutairi & Lawan A. Mohammed, pp. 59-77, copyright 2011 by Information Science Reference (an imprint of IGI Global).

Chapter 6
Inventory Management Process:
Problems in an Indian Convenience Store

Amit Agrahari
Indian Institute of Management, India

Saket Jhunjhunwala
Accenture, India

EXECUTIVE SUMMARY

This case captures inventory management process in an Indian convenience store. Unlike retail stores in developed countries, Indian convenience stores are a special format of organized retailing, where retailers open multiple smaller stores in a town instead of one big centralised store. An excellent inventory management process is the key to make such stores perform well. This case describes inventory management problems faced by an Indian convenience store chain and asks students to propose solutions to these problems. This case illustrates how processes realities and their IT solutions differ in an emerging economy. Using inventory management process as an example, this teaching case can introduce students to the process and technological realities in an Indian context and differences between India and the West.

DOI: 10.4018/978-1-4666-2618-8.ch006

ORGANISATION BACKGROUND

In India, retail sector has witnessed an unprecedented change and growth in the last 10 years. From small family-owned and unorganized stores to organized and corporate-owned store chains; rise of retail sector in India has been partially fuelled by the rise in middle class population and increase in their purchasing power. With over 15 million retail outlets, India has the highest retail outlets density in the world (Mukherjee & Patel, 2005). Though retail sector is still dominated by traditional mom and pop stores, corporate owned retail chains are fast catching up (Table 1). Multinational corporations such as Wal-Mart, Shoprite, and Tesco are also foraying into Indian retail sector.

This is a story of an Indian convenience store chain, which is a small sized organised retail format in India. Convenience stores are relatively small stores that are easily accessible to the middle class neighbourhood. Traditional Indian retail stores are family owned small shops, with an average size ranging from 100 to 500 square ft, located in the neighbourhood which provides convenient shopping experience to the customers. Given the high traffic congestion and underdeveloped public transport infrastructure in the country, neighbourhood convenience store is the most preferred format for the Indian consumers. Hence for organized sector opening multiple convenience stores instead of one large store in a city seems to be a better strategy. As a result, Indian retailers such as Spence's, Aditya Birla and Reliance Retail are opening several such convenience stores so that people don't have to travel long distances for their grocery needs. However, some Indian retailers such as Future Group (with brand stores big bazaar and food bazaar) and Hypercity are focusing on opening up large stores (typically one or two in each town, similar to a Wal-Mart in USA), possibly in an uptown area.

Table 1. Grocery retailers company shares: Percentage value (Euromonitor International, 2009)

Retailers	2004	2005	2006	2007	2008
Pantaloon Retail India Ltd	0.1	0.2	0.3	0.5	0.9
Spencer's Retail Ltd	-	-	0.1	0.2	0.7
Subhiksha Trading Services Pvt Ltd	0.1	0.1	0.1	0.3	0.6
Aditya Birla Retail Ltd	-	-	-	0.1	0.5
Reliance Retail Ltd	-	-	0.0	0.3	0.5
REI Agro Ltd	-	-	-	0.0	0.2
Mother Dairy Fruit & Vegetable Ltd	0.1	0.1	0.1	0.1	0.1
Others	99.7	99.7	99.3	98.4	96.4
Total	100.0	100.0	100.0	100.0	100.0

Higher operational efficiency and excellent supply chain management are the success mantra in retail business. Though convenience stores are easily accessible, they cannot charge any premium for that, as Indian middle class consumers are very price sensitive. Due to their smaller size, convenience stores do not have the same procurement aggregations and economy of scope benefits that large format retail stores enjoy. In addition to that convenience stores do not have adequate space to hold stock and hence excellent inventory management and on-demand deliveries are imperative to their survival and success.

Setting the Stage

There are couple of interesting inventory management problems that retail stores face across the world. Raman, DeHoratius, and Ton (2001) classified them as inventory record inaccuracy and misplaced SKU (stock keeping units) in stores. SKU is a term used to describe uniquely identifiable article (e.g., 75gm soap bar of brand X). However because of its unique characteristics as described below, Indian convenience stores need redefined processes and IT solutions to cope with the following problems

Format: Organized retail sector in western world is only familiar with large format retail chains. Indian organized retail sector is experimenting with large format retail chain and small format convenience store chain. Convenience stores are much smaller in size, with each store developed in an area of around 3000 square feet and having about 4500 stock keeping units (SKU) and average SKU density of 1.5 sku/sq ft. This case discusses the problems faced at convenience store chains.

Pack size: Pack size refers to the quantity that one unit of an SKU contains. Owing to factors such as lower prices and convenience, it makes sense in western world to sell a SKU in larger quantity and some time in cases. However the business logic at the bottom of the pyramid requires just the opposite perspective. For example, 60% of all shampoos sold in India, in terms of value, are in single-serve packet. They are sold for about a penny a piece and are a very profitable business (Prahalad, 2004). In general, because of smaller pack sizes, average price of a unit sold in retail store is equal to Rs 40 (almost equal to 1 USD). In a store, average shelf size of a SKU is 500 cubic centimetre. Therefore a sophisticated RFID tool is ruled out in this scenario.

Information Technology (IT): Despite of India's dramatic rise in IT and enabled services industry, Indian organizations spend very little on IT infrastructure and application. Inexpensive manual labour is preferred over capital intensive IT solutions. While point of sale and ERP systems are a norm in Indian retail sector, technology integration with business partners remains a big challenge. Most vendors do not have very sophisticated IT tools. Twenty percent of the SKUs which the stores carry do not even have a manufacturer's EAN or Bar code.

People: India is the second most populated country and could claim to have a large number of engineers and graduates fuelling its outsourcing industry. However getting skilled human resource is a big concern for Indian retail sector. Unlike other countries, there is very little emphasis on vocational training in India. Students do not choose to work part time as parents financially support their children. To keep cost at the lowest possible level, stores recruit unskilled people on minimum wage rate. These unskilled workers are recruited from relatively lower strata of the society and have to be trained and groomed to work in an urban retail store. Further product labelling is predominantly in English language and majority of the store staff have very limited reading and writing command on the language. As a result they get confused in product identification and fail to help the customers in product search. In lot of cases the staffs does not understand the utility or usage of the products as they have never used such products themselves.

Case Description

This case focuses on a convenience store chain that has Pan- India presence. It has convenience stores in 30 Indian cities and meets the grocery needs of its customers. The key product categories offered by the store chain include food (fruits and vegetables, staples and processed food), non food fast moving consumer goods (home care and personal care) and basic house wares (plastic and metal ware needs for kitchen).

Stores need not carry similar products and SKUs present in a given store is a subset of the master assortment for the entire retail chain which comprises of 54,000 SKU (refer to Appendix A for detailed store layout). Each store carry inventory worth Rs. 2,500,000 in value terms and 50,000 to 60,000 units in terms of quantity. Each SKU has a unique European Article Number (EAN) printed by the vendor. SKUs also carry a unique article code assigned by the retailer as per the inventory management process. Unit of measurement is a count (of pieces) for 95% of the SKUs and Kilograms (KG) for the balance 5% SKUs. Target inventory for 90% SKUs in a store is less than or equal to twelve units (count). For the balance 10% the inventory varies from 13 to 240 units. Re-order quantity and target inventory is defined in the IT application at SKU-in-store level for replenishment purpose. 2-5% SKUs are of high value, smaller size and prone to shirk loss. These SKUs are easily tradable in the market at a petty handsome resale realization, e.g., Shaving blades, processed dairy products such as small cheese pack worth RS. 80-100, chocolates, etc.

Inventory flows from the collection centre to the stores based on the indents generated by the stores. The stock is received at the store and sold to the custom-

Figure 1. High level view of inventory management process at store

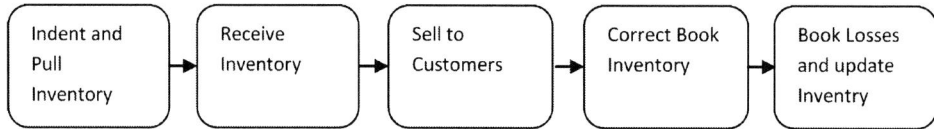

```
┌─────────────┐   ┌─────────────┐   ┌─────────────┐   ┌─────────────┐   ┌─────────────┐
│ Indent and  │   │ Receive     │   │ Sell to     │   │ Correct Book│   │ Book Losses │
│ Pull        │──▶│ Inventory   │──▶│ Customers   │──▶│ Inventory   │──▶│ and update  │
│ Inventory   │   │             │   │             │   │             │   │ Inventry    │
└─────────────┘   └─────────────┘   └─────────────┘   └─────────────┘   └─────────────┘
```

ers. Entire stock received in the store need not get sold in the store; some of it get damaged and is recorded as damage loss at the time of inventory correction in the store. While some quantity may simply vanish from the shelves, stolen by customers or store staff, this loss is booked as shrink loss in the inventory book. This high level inventory movement is summarised (Figure 1).

Inventory flows to store either as "delivered directly" from the vendors or through the collection centres. Direct delivery mode is followed for SKUs where vendors have a very comprehensive supply chain network covering every nook and corner of the city. Direct delivery is also followed for local products (which are produced by micro industries with annual turnover of less than Rs. 500,000). Typical example of direct delivery SKUs are milk, soft drinks, etc. To achieve aggregation benefits in inventory management, store chain routes a lot of inventory through collections centres (CC). Each collection centre services a specific geography and typically one CC serves 60-70 stores. In case the number of stores in any given geography is more than 60-70, there would be two collection centres to feed inventory to the stores. The broad design principle is that each CC should serve stores in a radius of 100 km. This further reduces the economies of scale as the CC covers much smaller radius and limited number of stores unlike other developed countries with evolved organised retail. Collection centres are typically situated outside the city boundaries to reduce the land and labour cost. This retail store chain has 400 odd stores serviced by 10 collection centres.

Direct Delivery from Vendor (DDV)

SKUs that are delivered directly from the vendors can be further classified based on the product shelf life into two broad buckets, products that require daily replenishment (e.g., milk, bakery products, etc.) and products that require periodic replenishment (e.g., soft drinks, ice cream, etc.). For all such deliveries, stores need to place an order to the vendor, as all inward inventories in the store can be delivered only against purchase order (PO) raised on the vendor. Some of these vendors may have advanced IT applications that are capable of talking to the store's IT applications. However majority of the vendors are local and do not have any advanced IT applications which can talk to the store's IT applications. Purchase order for daily replenishment SKUs (10-15 SKUs) has to be created every day, factoring in the lead time for delivery. This is a cumbersome activity since creating and communicating purchase orders on daily basis involves time and cost. As a good inventory management practice, these SKUs have maximum stocking parameters that should not be altered. The store ERP system does not allow receiving inventory without a corresponding PO.

Another 50-75 SKUs require periodic replenishments. Given the work load in the store, sales focus of the store staff and high number of SKUs, it is difficult for the store staff to keep track of the SKUs that require periodic replenishment and also decide on the required quantity and raise the PO on the vendor. DDV process is described in Figure 2.

Collection Centre

Collection Centres do not push inventories to the stores; rather stores pull inventories from the collection centres. At CC, replenishment indents are automatically generated by an IT application, which has a real time access to every store's inventory informa-

Figure 2. DDV indenting process at store

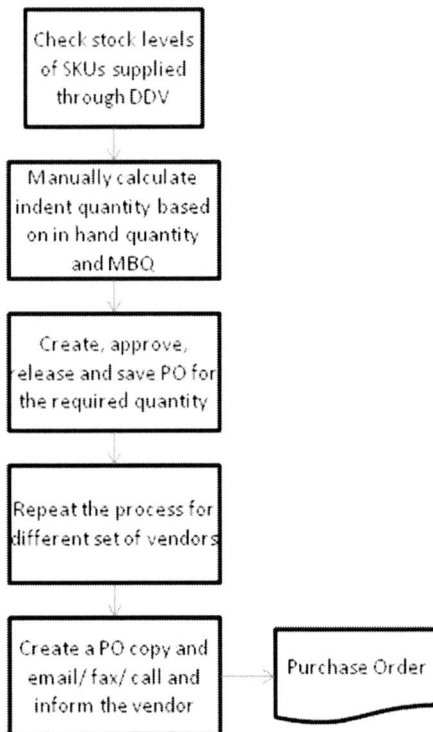

tion. Once store's inventory goes below the re-order quantity, replenishment indent is automatically created by this application for the difference in quantity between the target inventory and in-hand book inventory. For example, target inventory for SKU "Brand G Biscuit 490 grams pack" is 60 pieces and re-order level is 24 for store code 08456. Assuming that on August 24, 2009 the closing book inventory is 26. Since the book inventory is greater than the re-order level, no replenishment indent would be created. Suppose on August 25, 2009 the store sells another 8 pieces and the closing book inventory is 18. On August 26, 2009 an auto indent will be created for 42 pieces (target inventory minus inventory in hand). From this example it is evident that the accuracy of book stock is a prerequisite for auto indenting and availability of stock in store. When collection centre dispatches inventories to stores, it books them as sales in the IT application and generates an invoice on the receiving stores. Figure 3 describes replenishment process at collection centre.

Pulling inventory from the collection centres

Supplies are made by the collection centre based on their internal process which includes, indent consolidation, pick list generation, actual SKU picking and pack-

Figure 3. Replenishment process at the collection centre

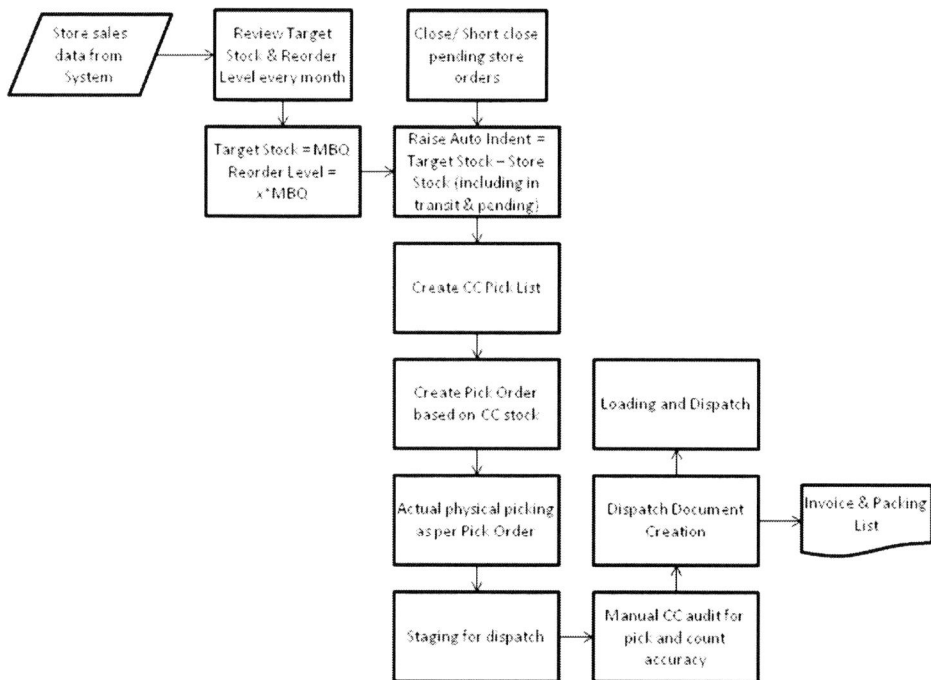

ing, picking audit, delivery creation, invoicing, loading and dispatch. The picking of required inventory, from the storage locations (bins/ racks) in CC (as per the quantity mentioned in replenishment indent) is a manual activity carried out by pickers in the CC (unlike western markets where picking is an automated process due to large volumes involved). This activity is prone to human error and could result in wrong quantity and wrong SKU picking. Though collection centres have their internal checks and balances to minimize such errors, however due to sub-standard manpower in the collection centres the error rate is high.

Due to high attrition rate and lack of skilled resources in the market, improving the quality and skills of pickers in the collection centres is not a cost efficient solution and has been explored in length by the store chain. Stores continuously complain that the supplied quantity is less than the invoice quantity. In addition the stores also complain of receiving damaged or near expiry or expired inventories from the collection centres. This is in spite of implementing state-of-art batch management process in the collection centres. In the batch management process the minimum shelf-life requirement for each product category is pre-defined in the IT application. A SKU (which belong to a specific product category) with less than the required shelf-life is blocked by the IT application for picking, e.g., for a product category with shelf life of 90 days, application would not allow picking in the CC if the balance shelf-life is less than 50% that is 45 days. It is imperative to say that the target inventory and re-order levels for each SKU is defined based on the shelf-life of the SKU, average daily sales of the SKU and lead time for delivery.

Inventories are supplied to the stores in covered and sealed trucks through 3rd party logistics. There is a separate security team to ensure that there is no transit loss by the 3rd party. On an average, each store is supplied 4 to 5 times in a week based on the sales in the store. The average load of one delivery is 120-150 cartons containing 350-400 SKUs and worth Rs. 80-100 thousand. The delivery cycle and delivery window is pre-planned, agreed and signed by the store operations and collection centre operations. However there is a perennial dispute between the collection centre and the stores on the actual quantity with claims and counter claims. Stores continuously claim that the supplied quantity is short by 2-6% and there is another 1-2% damage and expiry/ near expiry supply. While collection centres claim to have 99.8% accuracy in picking (correct SKU and correct quantity). Collection centres further claim that the probability of dispatching damaged or expiry/ near expiry SKUs is less than 0.10%. Figure 4 illustrates receiving process in store for CC deliveries.

Store needs a cost and time efficient receiving process so that there is no dispute between stores and collection centre, and to do that stakeholder's roles can be redefined for the process. This can also be achieved by redefining product category wise balance shelf life criteria and rules for the same. The shelf-life of products

Figure 4. Receiving process in store for CC deliveries

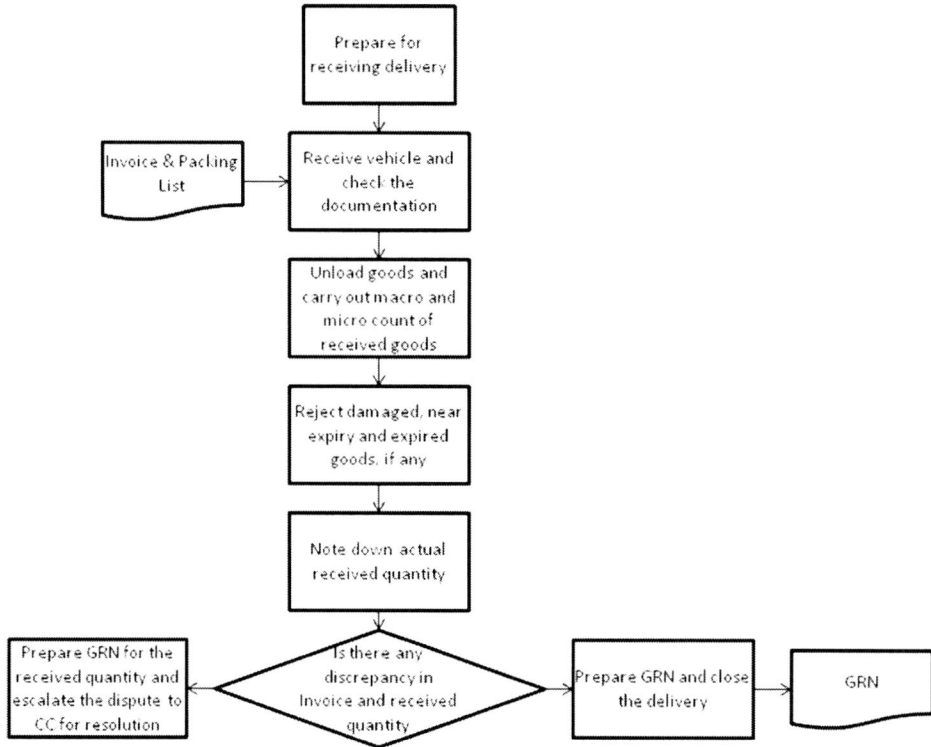

```
                    ┌─────────────────┐
                    │   Prepare for   │
                    │ receiving       │
                    │ delivery        │
                    └────────┬────────┘
                             │
                             ▼
┌─────────────────┐ ┌─────────────────┐
│ Invoice & Packing│─▶│Receive vehicle and│
│ List            │ │ check the        │
└─────────────────┘ │ documentation    │
                    └────────┬────────┘
                             │
                             ▼
                    ┌─────────────────┐
                    │ Unload goods and │
                    │ carry out macro and│
                    │ micro count of   │
                    │ received goods   │
                    └────────┬────────┘
                             │
                             ▼
                    ┌─────────────────┐
                    │Reject damaged, near│
                    │ expiry and expired│
                    │ goods, if any    │
                    └────────┬────────┘
                             │
                             ▼
                    ┌─────────────────┐
                    │ Note down actual │
                    │ received quantity │
                    └────────┬────────┘
                             │
                             ▼
```

Prepare GRN for the received quantity and escalate the dispute to CC for resolution ◀── Is there any discrepancy in Invoice and received quantity ──▶ Prepare GRN and close the delivery ──▶ GRN

varies from 2 days to 2 years. Minimum shelf-life is a function of number of inventory turn for a SKU and the total shelf life of the SKU. For example if the total shelf life of the product is 6 months and the inventory turn is 3 months it implies that the inventory in store takes 3 months to sell out. Therefore if SKUs with balance shelf-life of less than 3 months are shipped, there is a very high probability that the products would expire on the shelf before being sold out.

Selling it to the customers

Since indenting process is automated, once store's inventory goes below the re-order quantity, indent is created for the difference in quantity between the target inventory and in-hand book inventory. With each passing day there is a gradual drift between the in-hand inventory as per IT application and the actual physical inventory available in the store. Store's target inventory is not very high. Fast moving SKUs have high number of inventory cycles and low target inventory is maintained to save on store space, Demand for slow moving SKUs is as such low and there is no point in having high inventory levels and associated carrying cost for such SKUs.

The drift between actual inventory and book inventory is primarily due to picking inefficiencies in the collection centres, shoplifting by customers and staff theft, which is a perennial problem of the retail industry, and wrong product identification for SKUs without barcode. A recent global retail theft barometer has reported that the Indian retail industry has highest shrink loss in the world (Centre for Retail Research, 2009). Replenishment is badly impacted as the auto indents are not generated for SKUs where inventory reflected in IT application is more than the reorder level, whereas the actual physical inventory is lower than reorder level. This problem is resolved periodically through the stock take of physical inventory (STPI) process, where the physical inventory and book inventory (as reflected in IT application) is synced and matched. Though this process is carried out once every quarter, the physical and book inventory starts drifting the very next day. The immediate outcome of the drift is poor replenishment, stock-out in the store and Loss of Sale. The drift on account of theft typically affects fast moving or high value SKUs.

Manual indenting is one of the possible ways to manage the stock outs on account of book and physical stock mismatch. However manual identification of such SKUs and indenting is a very time consuming and intellectual process. In addition manual indenting is not a sustainable solution. The process of correcting the book inventory through the STPI process can't be carried out on a monthly basis as the entire process is very time consuming and has a huge cost associated with it. At the same time we can't do stock take of limited number of SKUs as it results into financial booking of loss and daily booking of loss on account of shrink is not a right approach to maintain the financial books. A possible solution is to develop a process to easily identify top selling SKUs with the drift and correct it for continuous replenishment and availability.

Store inventory is stocked in the sales floor and a small part is stored in storage area in the back office. On the sales floor, SKUs are placed on the fixtures called bays which have shelves on them. Each SKU has a designated place in the store as per planogram. A planogram is a diagram of fixtures and products that illustrates how and where retail products should be displayed, usually on a store shelf in order to increase customer purchase. A planogram defines which product is placed in which area of a shelving unit along with facing, depth and height measures. However customers generally misplace items while shopping. Some SKUs are more or less identical with similar packaging size, colour and design hence they can be differentiated only on the basis of SKU description. Store has business KPI defined with respect to how much loss can be booked by the store due to shrink loss. To meet the targets, the store staffs tend to under report losses by over reporting the actual inventory.

The stock take is carried out during the non trading hours, i.e., between 22:00 hrs to 08:00 hrs. Therefore the manpower planning is another focus area with respect to stock take preparation and scheduling. For staffing, store follows thumb rule of one employee per 180sq.ft. Store is open from 8:00 a.m. to 9:00 p.m. for customers and there are 2 shifts in the store of 9 hours each. First Shift starts at 6:00 a.m. and ends at 3:00 p.m., second shift starts at 2:00 p.m. and ends at 11:00 p.m. Each shift is manned by 8 to 10 store staff and a weekly roaster is made by the store manager based on the monthly buying cycle, leaves and activities on hand. Given the trading hours and the total manpower power strength of the store, store manager cannot allocate more than 10 staff for the extra night shift to carry out the stock take process.

Since stock take process should be carried out only for the store assortment of 4500 SKUs and not the entire assortment of SKU (54000 SKUs), there is a need to generate a list of store assortment SKUs for which stock take should be carried out. Store also needs to ensure that the book inventory is correct and reflects goods received note (GRN) for all deliverable inventories, goods return vouchers (GRV), and sales of the day. In the physical stock take process, entire physical inventory in the store is manually counted and compared against the book inventory and difference, if any, is analyzed. In case book inventory is greater than physical inventory, it means some units are missing, so book stock needs to be reduced and booked as shrink loss in the financial books. However in case book inventory is less than physical inventory then the problem gets compounded as it is possible only due to some manual errors in other store processes.

Information technology infrastructure

Convenience store chain operates on SAP retail Enterprise Resource Planning (ERP) platform. All the stores and collection centres have individual server and are connected to the main server through VSAT or broadband as the case may be. Stores update central server data at periodic interval of every two hours for sales revenue, store receiving, etc. However, the store inventory is adjusted for the sales of the day, at the end of the day through a batch process. Subsequently the auto indents are raised, through another batch process, in the system for stock delivery from CC to the stores. The limited bandwidth is allocated via V-SAT to keep the IT cost low. Because of lower bandwidth, network performance is severely affected and results in data update delays. To save cost, same bandwidth is also used for mail exchange between stores and the state/ corporate office. Stores have handheld devices with barcode reading capabilities. Because of significant hardware and training costs, each store is allocated limited number of handheld devices (2 for 10 employees). Unlike western context data entry and stock counting activities are performed by two different individuals, which might lead to another source of error in SKU inventory records.

Daily sales are recorded in separate sales software at the point of sales (POS). This sales record is migrated to ERP overnight using a batch processing system at midnight and simultaneously the auto indents are generated by the IT application based on the closing book inventory, re-order levels and target stock. However due to limited bandwidth, at times there are technical issues and sales data migration gets delayed till the next day morning. In the ERP system, inventory is posted in various tables, called virtual storage locations (SLoc). All good and saleable inventories are stored in SLoc 100. All receiving in the store is done on SLoc 100 and all sales in the store use inventory maintained in SLoc 100. Since there is no physical segregation of goods in the store, stock take of physical inventory process should only work on inventories mentioned in SLoc 100. All damaged inventory in a store is transferred to a separate SLoc (SLoc 090) and is dumped after approval from the VP – Store Inventory. If there is any dispute in quantity received (excess or shortage), then disputed quantities are parked in SLoc 080 (Appendix C). To illustrate further, damaged units are transferred to SLoc 90 in IT application to correct the in-hand inventory and ensure replenishment in a proper manner. However the damaged pieces are physically available in the store and could be counted by the store staff during the stock take process. Therefore the damaged inventory in SLoc 90 should be written-off from the books as dump loss and the physical pieces should be salvaged in the store as per the company policy or the inventory should be transferred back to SLoc 100 and included in stock take.

The store chain uses the best and most advanced technology available in the market; however, it does not intend to use RFID as it is not an economically and operationally feasible option given the average cost of each unit of inventory in the store and number of units sold in a day.

Current Challenges/Problems Facing the Organization

Convenience store chain needs to re-define business processes for the entire inventory management process along with applicable business rules. New business process should resolve the process problems captured in Appendix B, specifically reduction in workload of store staff. Store also needs a high level design of new IT capabilities to implement the redesigned business process. Daily PO creation for DDV SKUs is not a desirable process. Conflicts between collection centres and stores not only result in loss of inventory but also valuable working hours. A better process should save time that is lost in resolving the inventory disputes. Further, to tackle mismatch between actual and book inventory, store needs a stock take of physical inventory process which easily identifies top selling SKUs and corrects it periodically.

The problems illustrated in this case are similar to challenges faced by the western retailers, but the solutions are specific to Indian scenario. The proposed solution

Table 2. List of KPIs for the store

KPI	Calculation	Target Value
Dump %	Dump loss as a percentage of sales (monthly)	0.50%
Shrink %	Shrink loss as a percentage of Sales (monthly)	1.0%
Manpower cost per sq.ft.	Total salary cost of all store staff/ size of the store in sq.ft.	Rs. 20/-

should design human centric processes with active aid from technology, rather automating work to minimize errors. Unlike western context, Indian organizations work on relationship and trust rather than mere market dynamics. Successful business processes utilize these relationships and augment them using information systems. So while a "right first time" might not be achievable in Indian context, "right over a period of time" might make more sense for this emerging economy (Table 2).

REFERENCES

Centre for Retail Research. (2009). *The global retail theft barometer 2009*. Nottingham, UK: Author. Retrieved November 10, 2009, from http://www.globalretailtheftbarometer.com/pdf/GRTB_2009_ENGLISH.pdf

Euromonitor International. (2009). *Convenience Stores - India*. London, UK: Author.

Mukherjee, A., & Patel, N. (2005). *FDI in retail sector*. New Delhi, India: Academic Foundation.

Prahalad, C. (2004). Why selling to the poor makes for good business. *Fortune*, *150*(10), 70–72.

Raman, A., DeHoratius, N., & Ton, Z. (2001). Execution: The missing link in retail operations. *California Management Review*, *43*(3), 136–152.

APPENDIX A

Figure 5. Typical Store Layout

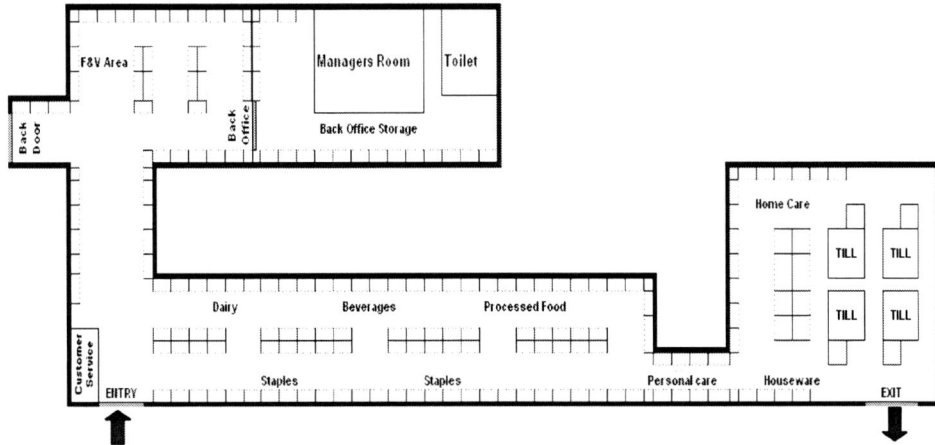

APPENDIX B

Table A1. List of Issues

Indent and Pull Inventory	Receive Inventory	Stock Correction for replenishment	Book Losses and Update Inventory
Define a new process for DDV to raise PO on vendors along with rational to decide PO quantity. Should PO be raised on daily basis or periodic and need basis? Difficult to keep track of periodic replenishment .	Collection centres dispatch wrong SKU and in wrong quantity. SKUS shipped by CC are damaged or near expiration. Redefine product category based on the shelf-life and minimum balance shelf-life limits for picking in the CC. Indent picking at collection centre is a high error prone process.	Unequal distribution of work between store staff . A process to resolve drift between actual and book inventory so that replenishment is not impacted and there is no loss of sales in the store on account of inventory mismatch.	Almost no sync between inventories in IT application and physical inventories. Identification of 4500 SKUs out of 54000 odd SKUs for stock take. Error proof process for physical stock count recording such that entire physical stock in the store is counted and recorded. Error proof process for physically counted stock and the book stock comparison. Incorrect reporting of shrink loss by store employees.

APPENDIX C

Figure 6. Virtual Store Locators

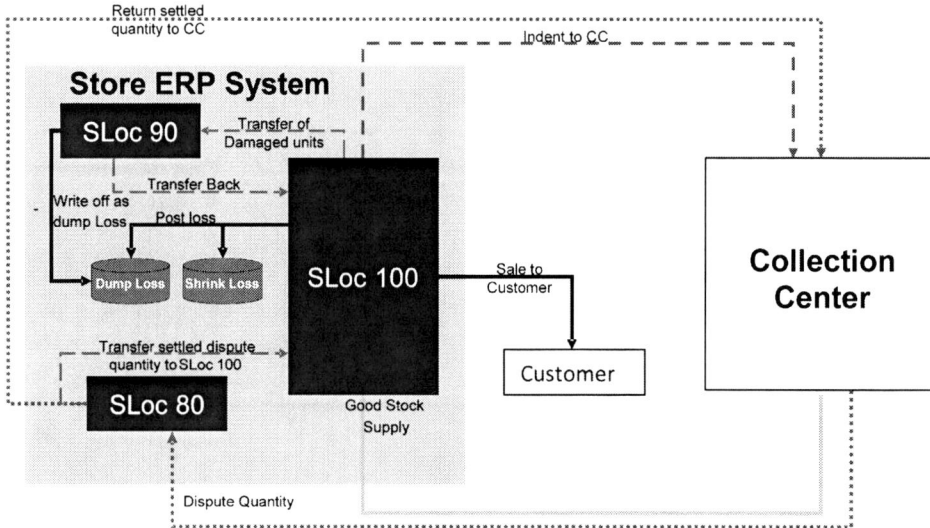

Table A2. In hand inventory of Brand K 500gm Mixed Fruit Jam, as per application is 14 pieces. Actual physical quantity present in the store is 11 pieces. Out of the 11 pieces, two are damaged and could not be sold.

IT Application Inventory		Physical Inventory	Actual Shrink Loss	Booked Shrink Loss
SLoc 100	SLoc 80			
12	2	11	3	None
If write-off the damaged inventory from SLoc 80 and then do the Stock Take				
12	0	9	3	3
If we don't write-off the damaged inventory and neither transfer it back to SLoc 100				
12	2	11	3	1 (12 – 11units)
If we don't write-off the damaged inventory but transfer it back to SLoc 100				
14	0	11	3	3

This work was previously published in the Journal of Cases on Information Technology, Volume 14, Issue 1, edited by Mehdi Khosrow-Pour, pp. 1-14, copyright 2010 by IGI Publishing (an imprint of IGI Global).

Section 2
Managerial Approaches and Practices

Chapter 7
Path to Success:
Innovative Managerial Approach

Ahu Genis-Gruber
TOBB University of Economics and Technology, Turkey

Ramazan Aktas
TOBB University of Economics and Technology, Turkey

EXECUTIVE SUMMARY

Organizations operating worldwide adopt different strategies and marketing techniques in various geographic areas, depending on the cultural perception of the country in which they are active. There are diverse reasons for implementing different management strategies, even under the same organizational umbrella. Responsiveness to customers, market adaptability, and competitiveness with other organizations operating in the same sector are some of the most important.

The current case examines the management strategies of a leading furniture company that started off as a small business and rapidly expanded globally. The success the company has achieved through its innovative marketing strategies and use of international management techniques is presented. The case highlights the company's flexibility in adapting its organizational structures to the nature of the market in different countries, and its reliance on a cross-cultural management approach to marketing in order to increase product acceptance by consumers across the world.

DOI: 10.4018/978-1-4666-2618-8.ch007

ORGANIZATIONAL BACKGROUND

History of the Company

Founded in 1995 in the Inegöl district in the Marmara region of Turkey, Çilek is generally acknowledged as Turkey's leading company in the children's furniture industry and the design of children's rooms. Çilek was established with the aim of developing furniture products and accessories for children. It is the first brand to create products in the furniture sector specially designed for a particular age group. The company caters to the newly born all the way up to youth aged 24.

Çilek's mission is to offer the most functional, most secure and most economical furniture and to set the standard at all times and in all places for the sector in which it operates. The company's vision is to be a unique and unrivalled Turkish brand in its field.

Çilek, which has its own production lines, is the first brand in the children's furniture design and production sector to operate at a global level. The company launched its first exports in Switzerland in 1996. Having become a well-known brand, Çilek went on to open its very first retail store in Malta in 2001. That same year, the company's logo, brand and products were registered in 70 countries in the world.

Çilek's expansion policy is based on a franchise system. The company has a total of 150 concept stores in Turkey. It also operates in 68 countries - including countries in the Middle East and North Africa (MENA) - with a total of 135 concept stores. In addition, Çilek has institutional clients like Alghanim Ind in Kuwait, Kika Leiner in Austria, Möbel Pfister in Switzerland, Moniflor in Portugal, Elburg in Russia and Sweet Dreams in the United Kingdom (UK).

Çilek has clear requirements for specific age groups. The furniture should be practical, of high quality, original, different and durable. Since Çilek produces furniture for children, the most essential quality criteria are the use of anti-carcinogenic, anti-allergenic and anti-bacterial materials in production, a five-year guarantee period and a Geprüfte Sicherheit (GS) Quality Certificate. Hundreds of Çilek products are constantly subjected to tests in laboratories to ensure reliability. Çilek has received the GS Quality Certificate by certifying its products to GS standards one piece at a time.

In 2005, the high quality of Çilek's products earned the company the Superbrands International award in the furniture industry. Superbrands are determined by Turkey's Superbrands Selection Board, which is made up of professionally respected and qualified individuals. The board members assess all brands operating in Turkey, both domestic and international, against Superbrands International criteria.

Çilek has also been accepted into the Turquality Support Program. The program selects leading companies in their field to support Turkish brands in their work processes, offer vocational training to companies working in the same sector to help

Figure 1.

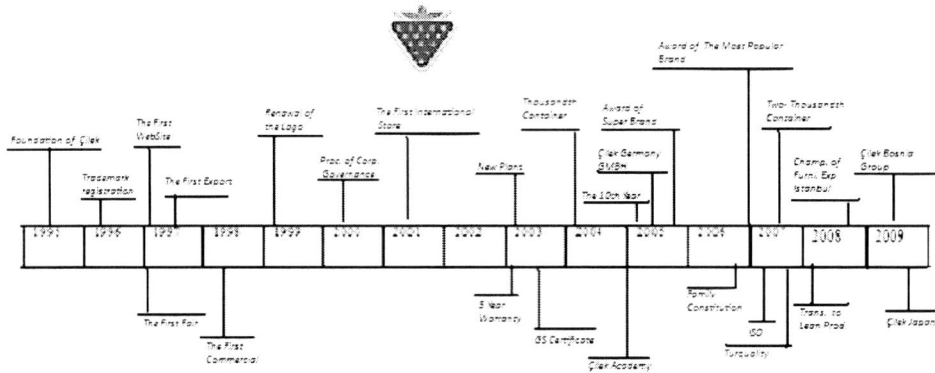

them gain competitive advantage in the global market, offer companies coaching services, and support companies financially on their path to becoming a global brand. Çilek was the first to get accepted into this program as a leader in the furniture sector.

Today, with 444 sales points, 2,200 employees, a sales area of 60,000 m² and a retail turnover of 110 million Euros, Çilek, which started off as a small, family-owned business, is on its way to becoming the leading international company in the furniture sector.

The history of the company is presented in Figure 1.

Çilek Companies

Çilek has different companies in various countries. These include:

- Çilek Mobilya A.Ş.:→ Founded in 1995. The general management and head-quarters, sales & marketing departments are located in Istanbul and the factory and product support departments are located in Inegöl-Bursa.
- Çilek Germany GmbH:→ Founded in 2005
- Çilek USA Inc:→ Founded in 2007
- Çilek Bosnia Doo:→ Founded in 2009
- Çilek Japan Corp:→ Founded in 2009

Factory

Çilek's factory, which extends over 33,000 m², is located in the Inegöl region. The factory employs 900 workers to produce 150,000 bedroom furniture sets annually. Despite the global economic crisis, Çilek has decided to expand its facilities to cover an area of 45,000 m² in response to the growing demand.

Child Safety

Through the use of advanced technologies, the company produces child-safe furniture that meets, and even exceeds, the standards set forth by the European Union. Çilek products are produced using the highest quality raw materials that consist of anti-carcinogenic, anti-allergenic and anti-bacterial melamine-coated chipboards. Specially tempered glass is also used. This way, the risk of accidental breakage that would normally result in sharp and jagged pieces that may cause harm to children is reduced. The fabrics used in Çilek products are not only fire retardant but also easy to clean. A costly process in production has allowed for the successful reduction of E1 formaldehyde levels to the point that its use in materials has become harmless.

Market and Competition

Çilek's aim is to become a worldwide brand in the niche market for unique furniture designs for infants, children and youth up to the age of 24. The company defines its customers as educated families from big cities who belong to the middle-to-high income bracket.

Çilek has created a new concept-store[1] perspective for entrepreneurs in the world and has opted to be an alternative brand. The company aims to increase brand awareness and expand its market share in all target markets using the same concept-store strategy.

Brand Values

i.   *Conscious:* Çilek is determined to focus on the niche of furniture for the 0-24 age group and has succeeded in becoming the world leader in this sector.
ii. *Determined:* Çilek is a corporation that knows what it wants, provides the most functional, safest, and most economic furniture and tries to set the standard in all places and at all times.
iii. *Innovative:* Çilek is the first furniture brand in the world to focus on a specific age group and implement unique designs and products for this group.
iv. *Expert:* Çilek has introduced the term "young rooms" to Turkey. Çilek has identified its target age groups as infants, kids and youth, and is an expert in this niche.
v.   *Leader:* Çilek is the first and only leader of the young-rooms concept-store chain in the world.
vi. *Passionate:* Backed by a hardworking and innovative team, Çilek is passionate about doing its best.

vii. *Visionary:* Çilek is an international brand that exports to 68 countries. It has 135 foreign subsidiaries and 110 franchised stores in Turkey. Çilek products are in more that 2 million children's rooms in various parts of the world.

Despite the major market challenges facing SMEs in Europe in general and Turkey in particular, and the host of management challenges facing small and large business as they expand their operations internationally, Çilek has been able to successfully expand its market to 68 countries in 9 main geographic areas in a relatively short time. Countries in which its products are sold include Algeria, Australia, Denmark, Egypt, Indonesia, Japan, Kuwait, Mexico, Panama, Russia, South Africa, and the USA, to name a few. In order to expand and increase its market penetration, the company is adopting a more aggressive marketing strategy in existing markets by opening new subsidiaries, not only in Turkey but also in different geographic areas around the world.

With its focus on the niche of furniture for a specific age group, its product diversification and emphasis on quality, Çilek has a competitive advantage over local and global competitors. The main challenge Çilek faces is low-quality imitation of its products. Other companies globally produce furniture for children using cheaper materials, imitating Çilek's concepts and designs.

SETTING THE STAGE

Overview of SMEs in Europe and Turkey

A strong and vibrant private sector is acknowledged as vital to educe economic dynamism, improve productivity and reduce poverty in developing and emerging economies. Accordingly, various strategies are being implemented to develop the private sector and promote SMEs that trigger the economy. SMEs create employment, maintain social stability and favor both entrepreneurial spirit and innovation. (Alkin & Okay, 2008)

In the European Union, SMEs are defined as companies that employ less than 250 people, whose annual turnover does not exceed 50 million Euros and/or whose annual balance sheet total does not exceed 43 million Euros. Under this definition, 23 million SMEs represent 99% of all companies in the EU and provide around 75 million jobs. (Alkin & Okay, 2008)

Turkey boasts a strong entrepreneurial culture. Indeed, SMEs constitute the backbone of the Turkish private sector, making up 99.5% of the total number of enterprises and 61.1% of total employment, and contributing about 36% of GNP (TUIK, 2003).

Table 1. Definition of an SME

	Number of Employees	Annual Turnover	or	Balance-Sheet Size	Independence
Micro Enterprise	Less than 10	Up to 2 million Euros		Up to 2 million Euros	Shareholding by another firm not to exceed 25%
Small Enterprise	Less than 50	Up to 10 million Euros		Up to 10 million Euros	
Medium-Sized Enterprise	Less than 250	Up to 50 million Euros		Up to 43 million Euros	

Source: REX/264 EU-Turkey Joint Consultative Committee Access to financing for SMEs in the EU and Turkey, 25th meeting of the EU-Turkey Joint Consultative Committee Paris, France 18-19 November, 2008, pp.4

SMEs have been a key element in the social and economic structures of their countries in terms of industrialization, urbanization, efficient and equitable distribution of resources, elimination of interregional gaps in development, creation of employment and development of trade. Thus, they play an effective role in the processes of policy-making and strategy formulation in their respective countries. Unlike large enterprises, since they do not depend on high-cost investments, SMEs can adapt more easily and rapidly to technological developments, administrative and process changes, and market preferences. This characteristic of SMEs enables them to be more flexible during economic fluctuations, to rapidly adapt to demand and to control costs (Keskin, 2008).

Various market failures work against European SMEs, notably lack of infrastructure, limited access to financial resources and to innovation, shortage of skilled labor, the costs of market research, lack of bargaining power, and legislative impediments, including national and EU regulations concerning intellectual property rights, labor, and taxation. These market failures often generate costs that are difficult for individual SMEs to bear. (Alkin & Okay, 2008)

In terms of financial resources, alternative sources of financing, including capital market instruments, have not been created for SMEs. Macroeconomic factors are another important cause of the financing problems of SMEs. In an environment of increased financial vulnerability and instability, increases in exchange rate and interest rate have an adverse effect on the financial condition and profitability of these firms. (Alkin & Okay, 2008)

In the developing economies, the overall education level in SMEs is low and entrepreneurs with an engineering background are limited. A partnership culture is also not common; thus, the whole capital is provided by the entrepreneur himself. (Alkin & Okay, 2008)

A survey covering 40,000 SMEs in Turkey conducted by the Small and Medium Industry Development Organization (SMIDO) in 2005 revealed that 56% of the SMEs do not or cannot export their products. In addition, although 46% suffer from lack of funds and 63% need additional financing, 70% do not take any loans. It also revealed that 56% of SMEs have no registered trademark, utility model or patent, while 60% do not benefit from statistical quality control, 72% from performance management, and 76% from computer-supported production and sales planning (Alkin & Okay, 2008).

The SME sector in Turkey is characterized by great geographical imbalances. SMEs are very unevenly spread across the country. The Marmara region (which includes Istanbul) and Izmir together account for about 65% of the SMEs in the country. The Eastern regions, on the other hand, harbor less than 20% of all SMEs. But whereas those concentrated in the less developed regions represent the majority of smaller enterprises, the Marmara region attracts most of the medium-sized enterprises (Alkin & Okay, 2008).

Due to their capital structures, SMEs in Turkey have certain disadvantages in terms of self-financing. Since they have low capital intensity and operate mainly in labor-intensive sectors, the amount of depreciation set aside on fixed assets is low. As a result, they are able to set aside fewer funds in this way and cannot benefit from the capacity extension effect of depreciation (Alkin & Okay, 2008).

An exploration of the biggest challenge facing Turkish SMEs points to institutionalization. The general form of SMEs in Turkey is family-owned businesses, while the chances that the next generation will take over the business are limited to 5%. According to the literature, the main reason that micro enterprises go bankrupt is their conservative attitude towards production and new product lines; their resistance to innovation causes them to decline. An analysis of small enterprises, on the other hand, shows that their tendency to cover their expenses with their own resources results in limited investment. As for medium-sized enterprises, institutionalization appears to be the biggest challenge. Institutionalization requires knowledge at the management level. The lack of management know-how results in dependency on one person, mainly the enterprise owner. (Alkin & Okay, 2008) Production and production lines are learnt throughout the production process, though without an in-depth analysis of managerial requirements. Most of the time, the board of directors consists of family members, and financial and accounting functions are carried out by these members.

Going International

Globalization, the process of increased integration among countries, continues at an accelerated pace. Daily, more companies are going global and trying to increase their share in the global economy through international trade. As evidenced by the statistics, international trade and investments have been increasing over the past decades. An increasing percentage of total revenue comes from overseas markets.

Internet technologies have played a key role in globalization. They have changed the way organizations operate, making it easier for them to keep up-to-date and to communicate with each other. They have also changed the structure of the competitive environment, facilitating access of all organizations to information and raw materials and allowing them to provide goods and services worldwide.

Surviving in international markets is a challenge for small companies and multinational corporations alike. The challenges of going international include the need to adapt management strategies to the economic systems of different countries and regions; the strategy at headquarters may not achieve the same results in another country. Thus, international management - the process of applying management techniques and concepts in a multinational environment - has become crucial (Luthans & Doh, 2009).

Foremost among the issues to be considered in international management is the structure of the business. In the global world, there is no magic organizational formula that can be implemented anywhere and everywhere and guarantee success. As a result, new organizational theories are constantly being analyzed and implemented. Strict matrix organizational structures have given way to more flexible hybrid structures, and more flexible marketing strategies that are adapted to the cultural perceptions of the society in which the organization is active have come into being.

The literature on international management also presents various approaches to marketing. Levitt (1983) stated that the worldwide success of a growing list of products that have become household names is evidence that customers, despite cultural differences, are becoming homogenized. As a result, a multinational corporation's strategy of tailoring its products to the needs of multiple markets may put it at a severe disadvantage vis-à-vis competitors who apply marketing imagination to the task of developing advanced, functional, reliable standardized products, at the right price, on a global scale.

Levitt's argument was based on the assumption that consumer behavior is rational (De Mooij, 2003). Assumptions of consumer rationality are, however, a matter of debate and ignore cultural aspects (McCracken, 1989; Suerdem, 1993; Antonides; 1998). De Mooij stated that despite the converging economic and demographic systems, consumer behavior is diverging in Europe; both convergence and divergence take place at macro level depending on the various regions. Thus, if products converge across countries, convergence is weakest in economically heterogeneous regions and strongest in economically homogeneous regions. De Mooij noted that consumption differences between countries can be explained by culture.

Donnelly (1970) analyzed the impact of cultural differences on international advertising, showing the significance of such differences and indicating that these differences should weigh heavily in a firm's international advertising decisions. Donnelly's study results revealed that the importance advertising managers give to cultural variables is significantly related to their approach to international advertising in two specific areas: 1. The degree of autonomy given to local branch officials in making major advertising planning decisions for the local area. 2. The approach used in the preparation and placement of non-domestic advertisements. The study indicates that the approach taken by an international advertising manager to plan and place a foreign ad is affected by the manager's assumptions about the importance of cultural variables. If this is the case, then it is vital that the assumptions a manager makes about the role of culture be valid ones.

CASE DESCRIPTION

In this section, we analyze the management strategies of Çilek, which started off as a small family-owned business in Turkey and quickly expanded to become one of the leading companies in the sector at the global level. In particular, we examine how the company has positioned itself in international markets as a high-quality furniture manufacturer for infants, kids and youth using international management techniques and a cross-cultural marketing approach.

Organization and Management

Management Team

Çilek was founded by three brothers: Mr. Mustafa Çilek, an engineer who is responsible for the production process, Mr. Muzaffer Çilek, who has in-depth experience in the retail sector and is responsible for the company's work processes, and Mr. Muharrem Çilek, a specialist in international marketing who is responsible for developing the company's expansion strategies. All three brothers have equal shares in the company.

In terms of management, Çilek has not shown the typical features of SMEs in Turkey. Despite being a family-founded and family-owned business, the management of the business is carried out professionally. The brothers have shared responsibility for running the company, each in accordance with his experience and educational background. The rest of the management team is chosen from among a qualified pool of candidate managers.

Organization and Management at Headquarters

Çilek's organizational structure at headquarters is presented in Figure 2. The structure is typical of a functional structure, that is, one in which similar activities are grouped together from the bottom to the top of the organization. With a functional structure, all knowledge and skills related to specific activities are consolidated, providing valuable depth of knowledge for the organization.

A functional structure is most effective when in-depth expertise is crucial to meeting organizational goals, when the organization needs to be controlled and coordinated through a vertical hierarchy, and when efficiency is important. Such a structure can be quite effective when there is little need for horizontal coordination (Daft, 2007). With a functional structure, economies of scale can be achieved. Employees working in similar activities are gathered in one specific area, and can thus share facilities, resulting in cost savings. Working closely together also allows employees to learn from one another, and working on one specific function enables employees to gain more knowledge about the function and related subjects and to develop their respective skills. In this intense working environment, the in-depth

Figure 2.

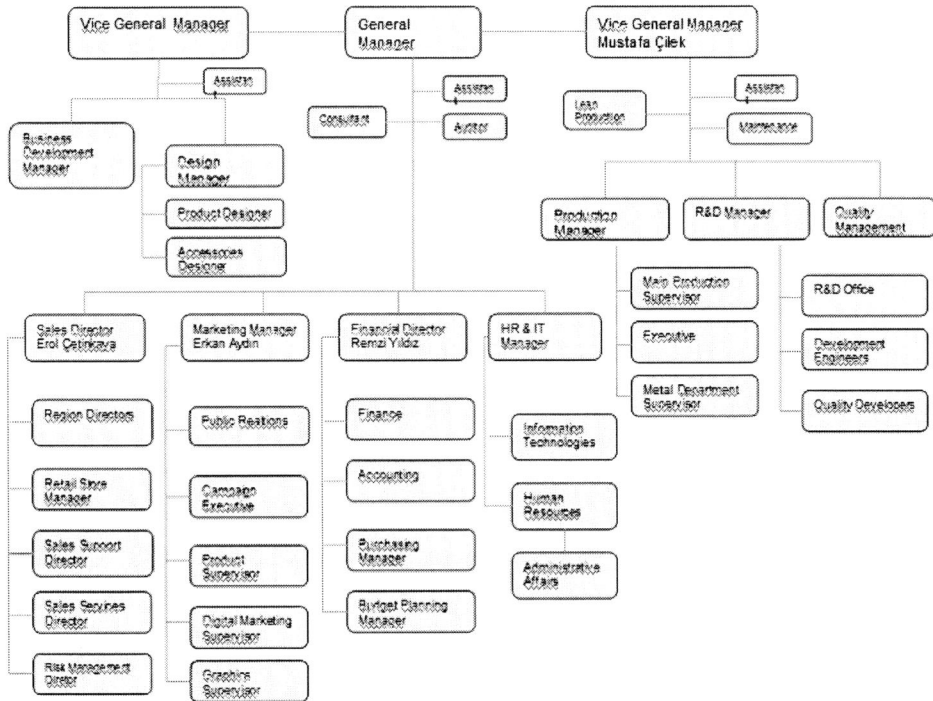

knowledge of employees increases. Thus, the functional structure works well with one or a few production lines.

In this regard, the functional structure is the right choice for Çilek. Since the company's business focuses on the production of children's furniture, in-depth expertise is required. The existing structure allows the employees to respond to market needs with a limited number of production lines.

It can be observed that Çilek consists of functional units that allow for teamwork in a vertical manner. Each department is associated with the function, and lines of reporting work horizontally upward to the responsible functional manager. Strategic decisions and organizational goals, however, are determined by top management.

An in-depth analysis of Çilek's organizational structure shows that:

- Management levels are set horizontally in the organizational structure.
- Management areas are set vertically at the top management level.
- Communication channels flow from top to bottom along the pre-determined functional line.
- Span of control is set at most effective.

Çilek's management is made up of five levels:

- *General Manager*: The most influential person in the organization. He is the only authority who plans, organizes, coordinates and controls activities in the big picture.
- *Department Managers*: The most influential persons in their own departments. They are responsible for planning, organizing, leading, coordinating and controlling activities in their own departments. They report to the General Manager.
- *Vice Managers*: They perform their duties within a predefined framework. They report directly to the Department Managers and hold responsibility in second degree.
- *Executives:* They perform their set activities in accordance with their authority level. They hold responsibility in third degree for the activities undertaken by their department.
- *Employees:* They perform their activities within the framework of the authority given them.

Organization and Management of Foreign Subsidiaries

Çilek's foreign subsidiaries show different organizational features depending on system needs specific to the area. These needs may include location, turnover and number of stores in the area. The structure can be made up of:

Stores executive, warehouse executive, store executive, sales adviser, maintenance employees

Or;

Store manager, sales adviser, maintenance employees

In this regard, the organizational structure in international markets shows diversification depending on the needs of the market. A geographical structure is also applied in various markets. In sum, a hybrid structure can be identified.

During the process of setting up a new foreign subsidiary, an advisor manager from headquarters is assigned to establish and implement the system. Teams are formed to adjust the organizational structure at the subsidiary. The store manager and warehouse manager employed by the foreign subsidiary are trained in Turkey and work for a period of time in one of Çilek's stores in the country. The advisor manager also gives on-the-job training to the subsidiary's team. The coverage and duration of the on-the-job training and orientation programs are planned by Çilek's human resources manager and department manager. On-the-job training is provided throughout the production process and, with each new product or implementation, allied training is given at the subsidiary where the store is performing.

Regional managers forward decisions made at headquarters, project information and all issues requiring communication to the related subsidiaries. Likewise, each month, Çilek's foreign subsidiaries send their warehouse and store inventory lists, product sales and order reports, employee-based turnover reports and financial reports to headquarters. The department manager visits the subsidiaries periodically and evaluates the reports with the store managers on the spot. The reports are consolidated at headquarters and form the basis for performance evaluation.

Corporate Business Strategy

Çilek's strategy is to be a unique Turkish brand, get the biggest share in the market through successful implementation of its unique designs in its field of expertise and become the most profitable corporation in the furniture sector. To this end, Çilek works to:

- Analyze its competitors' strategies;
- Evaluate sales channels;
- Identify target markets in the global area;

- Increase brand awareness;
- Set a good example by generating its own retail channels;
- Expand by contracting the best retailers in their own countries;
- Become a profitable brand for investors; and
- Understand the needs and expectations of individuals and provide products beyond those needs and expectations.

Çilek's five-year strategic plan is prepared with the participation of the management board and top managers. The plan, which is updated annually, covers the following issues:

- Promotion of the company
- Target markets
- Customer, product, distribution channels and competitor analysis
- Market-entry strategies
- Brand strategy
- Sales, marketing and operational plans
- Financial projections

Marketing Strategy

Çilek's marketing strategy is "to open more foreign subsidiaries and sell more Çilek products to more people". For Çilek, this poses the following question: "In today's democratic market where entrepreneurs and consumers have the choice, what can we do to be the chosen brand?" In response to the question, the company has determined the main features of its marketing strategy to be the following:

- Çilek should be present in markets where the potential is high (in malls, in zones where there is a concentration of children furniture shops, in the children's section of corporate clients, in e-commerce, and in catalogue sales)
- Çilek stores should be in the best locations
- Çilek stores should be of the highest quality, decorated with enthusiasm and always tidy
- Çilek store windows should be decorated attractively in accordance with the season
- Çilek sales team should provide entrepreneurs and customers with the best quality service
- Çilek stores should be highly profitable for investors
- Çilek products and accessories should be on the agenda of the target group

- Çilek should always ask existing and potential customers about their needs and expectations regarding the company's products, and design its products accordingly.

Brand Strategy

Çilek's brand strategy is to focus on a niche market and be an expert brand in this sector. Çilek differentiates itself from its competitors by producing a variety of furniture and furniture accessories for the 0–24 age group.

Requirements of the Brand Strategy:

What can be done?

- Communication among girl-boy or age classification
- Development of Social Responsibility projects and sponsorships
- Joint promotion with well-known children and youth brands
- Participation in design-focused fairs; sponsorship of such fairs
- Use of the smell and taste of strawberry ("strawberry" in Turkish is "Çilek")
- Opening of new stores in big cities in the world

What cannot be done?

- Cannot produce or sell any rooms other than for infants, kids and youth
- Cannot focus on luxurious and upper-class products and consumer segments
- Cannot focus on cheap products and lower-income consumer segments
- Cannot renounce its furniture or accessories product-line
- Cannot produce below European Union standards
- Cannot engage in custom manufacturing

Market-Entry Strategy

Çilek's market-entry strategy is implemented by comparing the entry policies of local and global competitors. In this regard, under the framework of the customer segment analysis data set, Çilek has analyzed its positioning strategies in relation to those of two other local competitors. The analysis is presented in Figure 3.

As can be seen in the graph, Çilek has created an important difference by implementing its concept-store and furniture & accessories combination model. Çilek plans to execute this strategy in its upcoming market entries.

Table 2.

Business Strategy
Çilek's strategy is to be a unique Turkish brand. Through the successful implementation of innovative designs in its field of expertise, Çilek aims to get the biggest market share and become the most profitable company in its sector. Achieving this entails analyzing the strategies of competitors, evaluating sales channels, determining the right markets in a particular global area, increasing brand awareness, setting a good example by generating the company's own retail channels, expanding by contracting the best retailers in their own countries, being a profitable brand for investors, understanding the needs and expectations of individuals and providing products beyond these needs and expectations. After all, Çilek aims to expand globally.

↓

Brand Strategy
Focusing on the niche of furniture for the 0-24 age group and being an expert brand in the sector.
↓
Çilek rooms are the furnished environment of infants, kids and youth, responding to all expectations of the age group through a combination of furniture and accessories.

↓

Brand Awareness
"Furniture and accessories for infants, kids and youth"

↓

Brand Promise
"We provide them with the room of their dreams; thus, they prepare themselves for life with joy."

Figure 3.

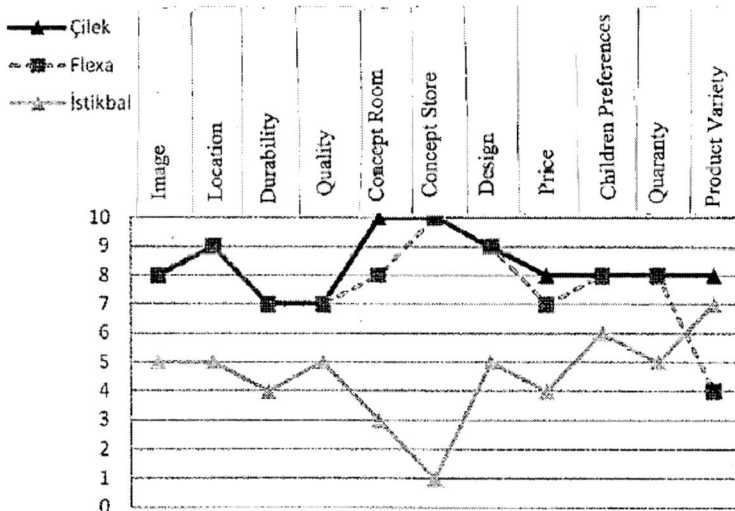

Product Development

Çilek has gained a close understanding of the market for children's furniture in different parts of the world. Designers work jointly with psychologists to produce unique designs that are adjusted to the needs of children in different geographic areas. Ultimately, Çilek aims to create a dream world for infants, children and youth through common design features that make up "*Çilek Fashion*".

Basic Product Specifications that Result in Sales

Five-Year Guarantee

All Çilek products have a five-year guarantee against deterioration, breakages and discoloration.

Quality

Çilek produces furniture in conformity with European Union standards, and the specially produced melamine-coated chipboards Çilek uses in its raw materials are anti-carcinogenic, anti-bacterial and anti-allergenic. Because of this, Çilek is the first brand in its sector in Turkey to have received Geprüfte Sicherheit (GS) certification. The GS Quality Certificate is granted by Landesgewerbeanstalt Bayern (LGA) in Germany for high-quality and high-security products.

Security

Çilek uses specially tempered glass to reduce the risk of accidental breakage that would normally result in sharp and jagged pieces that may cause harm to children. The fabrics used on Çilek products are not only fire retardant but also easy to clean.

Concept Unity and Design Focus

Each Çilek room has a different character and mood. The designs are ergonomic and functional and rely on a combination of color and theme models. All products are designed jointly with psychologists and designers to produce unique designs that appeal to those aged 0-24.

Segmentation

The 0-24 age category is segmented into infants, children and youth. Çilek products are designed differently for girls and boys, with a different concept for each.

After Sales Services

The Çilek Service Support Center has been set up to facilitate communication with customers who have bought Çilek products.

Promotional Strategy

All Çilek advertising and communication activities are carried out in Turkey. Through original ads that distinguish the company from its competitors in the sector, Çilek seeks to increase brand awareness, strengthen the positioning of the company and reach its target markets. The ads, which target all customers in a particular global area, are designed to associate the brand in the minds of the target group with dream rooms for infants, kids and youth up to the age of 24.

Like other leading world brands, Çilek uses a universal language for kids. In all its advertising campaigns, the company uses a positive tone that respects the intelligence of children. Children from different geographic areas are casted in the ads, as a part of the company's cross-cultural management approach. However, the children all sing the same song and send the same message, creating a strong feeling of belonging to the Çilek brand.

In the promotions it carries out globally, Çilek is attentive to regional differences. The company takes into account local traditions, culture and values during the preparation of campaigns in a specific region. Consumer behavior tendencies and preferences in the region are also analyzed and the ads adjusted accordingly.

In Europe, for example, where consumers rank high on reading habits, Çilek's efforts to increase brand awareness focus on ads in newspapers as well as ads and special interviews in sector-specific magazines. Çilek also engages in sponsorships and celebrates special days of the region.

In Saudi Arabia, Çilek's promotional activities focus on ads in newspapers, since Saudi Arabian consumers tend to read newspapers more than they watch TV. Çilek ads targeting Saudi Arabian customers are designed to create an image of colorful, funny, high-quality furniture, in keeping with cultural preferences. Since Saudi consumers tend to change the furniture in their homes during the month of Ramadan, Çilek's marketing efforts in the country accelerate before and during Ramadan.

In Japan, standards are high and the Japanese consumer gives great importance to the quality and packaging of the product, rather than to price. A market analysis shows that Japanese female consumers tend to choose products that are promoted on the Internet and in magazines. Once they use a product, they will often share their experience about it on their personal websites and blogs. Consequently, in addition to placing ads in newspapers, Çilek's promotional efforts in Japan focus on the Internet and magazines. The emphasis is on presenting the company's high-quality products in as attractive a package as possible.

Pricing Strategy

Çilek products are priced individually and sold by the piece. The products are in the middle-to-high price range. As the leader in the furniture industry for the 0-24 age category, Çilek sets the prices in the sector. The company, however, has not adopted an international pricing strategy, so its high-quality products are sold at a price that is considered reasonable outside Turkey.

Financial Strategy

An analysis of Çilek's financial status, including annual company sales, expenses and profit, shows that the company enjoys very high liquidity. Çilek operates with its own equity capital. As a result, the company was not affected by fluctuations in the market during the economic crisis. Since Çilek has a high percentage of equity capital, its debt payback capacity, especially short-term liability is high. Inventory and credit turnover rate, as well as active turnover rate, are high. The conservative approach the company has adopted, however, is a survival strategy that leads to a liquidity reserve rather than a high profit margin over a short period. While Çilek has become a well-known brand, its active profit margin and equity capital profit margin are below what would be expected. In order to reach the desired profit level, Çilek's preferred strategy is to increase its asset turnover rate by focusing on exports.

Çilek operates with a JIT (Just-in-Time) system that does not allow for great amounts of inventory. Under normal circumstances, when the inventory turnover rate is low, the company faces late delivery problems that might lead customers to choose another brand. Çilek, however, has not experienced such a scenario. Customers have trust in Çilek products and tend to show brand loyalty.

CURRENT CHALLENGES FACING THE ORGANIZATION

Economies play an incremental role in shaping an organization's future. Fluctuations in an economy affect strategic and investment plans, while global economic crises change the path of organizations, affecting them in a number of ways, including their investment, human resource and expansion plans and their marketing and promotion strategies. Sector-specific challenges also play an important role in the growth and development of an organization. As a Turkish company that started off as a small enterprise, Çilek had to cope with many of the market failures and challenges facing SMEs in Turkey. As a company that is quickly expanding globally, the main challenges it faces today are organizational, management, marketing and financial ones.

1. *Organizational Challenges*

According to Peter Drucker (2006), to create and keep a customer, a company must be wedded to the ideal of innovation. A global company should shape the vectors of technology and globalization into its strategic richness. Organizational theory points to the fact that innovation in SMEs depends on the decision of the manager himself. Due to lack of institutionalization, an innovative approach is generally lacking. Teamwork is not seen often; rather, small working groups and individuals that report directly to the manager are appreciated, giving the manager direct control. Motivation techniques are not used much. The work process is labor-intensive. (Alkin & Okay, 2008)

This is not the case with Çilek, which consists of functional units that allow for and encourage teamwork. But while the company has adopted a functional structure at headquarters - the most efficient structure to respond to fewer production lines – adjustments to the organizational structure of subsidiaries sometimes need to be made, depending on the requirements of the geographic area in which Çilek is operating. In some cases, the need for a more flexible and horizontal structure has led the company to develop a hybrid structure for foreign subsidiaries. For multinationals or transnational companies, the search for an appropriate organizational structure might last a while, which makes for a costly period. In the case of an expanding organization, the organizational structure at headquarters can sometimes not respond in a timely way to the expansion of production lines and to local adjustments. For Çilek, choosing the right organizational structure may be considered the main organizational challenge facing the company and has an impact on its marketing and human resource activities abroad.

2. *Management Challenges*

During the assignment of regional managers, a polycentric approach is implemented and local managers are employed based on their knowledge of the area and the environment. Prior to startup, on-the-job training is offered to local managers in Turkey in order to introduce them to Çilek's production lines, and these managers work in a Turkish store for a certain period of time.

In the global era, the necessity of employing the right manager locally might present a challenge and a polycentric approach could shift to a geocentric approach. However, acceptance of the new manager by local staff might pose new challenges.

3.   *Marketing Challenges*

In terms of marketing, Çilek implements a cross-cultural marketing strategy. Local requirements are taken into account and local people are hired for the ads. In this regard, searching for new strategies, finding adequate means of promotion, and developing culturally appropriate advertising and promotional campaigns are costly processes. Moreover, the need to develop new sales channels, such as e-commerce, is accelerating. Means of transportation, delivery and payment also need to be developed and adjusted to new sales lines, posing additional challenges.

In terms of market competition, the greatest challenge Çilek faces is niche imitation using low-quality products. Other companies globally produce furniture for children using cheaper materials, imitating Çilek concept designs. In some cases, customer segmentation differs and price awareness also takes over.

4.   *Financial Challenges*

Çilek enjoys very high liquidity and operates with its own equity capital. As a result, the company remained unaffected by fluctuations in the market during the economic crisis. The challenge is that the company's gross profit margin is low while its operational costs are high. The company's high marketing budget, promotional efforts, and the use of high-quality raw materials for production, coupled with administrative costs, push operational costs up. The highly competitive environment leads to a decrease in profit margins, as the market is shared with many companies operating in the same sector. The company's financial leverage is low compared to other companies operating in the same sector, which causes a growth deficit. Loans would help improve the ratio of net profit to equity.

CONCLUSION

Çilek started off as an SME in Turkey in 1995. The company differentiated itself in the furniture sector by focusing on the niche of furniture for the 0-24 age bracket. Çilek's high-quality products, costly production processes, right customer segmentation and international awards and certificates have reinforced the company's positioning in the market. Today, with its unique designs and themes, Çilek is the leading brand in Turkey in the sector.

Çilek's expansion strategy through foreign subsidiaries has opened up new markets for the company in 68 countries. By taking advantage of being the first in a niche market, adopting innovative and flexible management styles and organizational structures, and developing appropriate marketing strategies that rely on cross-cultural management techniques, the company has succeeded in positioning itself in international markets as a high-quality furniture manufacturer for children between the ages of 0 to 24. Çilek's successful positioning has relied on a rational analysis of the sector, a market-entry analysis that focuses not only on the competition but also on cultural features that would increase the rate of acceptance of Çilek products by the target group in the foreign market, and adequate financial strategies. Despite the challenges facing SMEs in general, Çilek has become a big brand company that enjoys tremendous popularity, both locally and internationally.

REFERENCES

Alkin, K., & Okay, E. (2008). *The process of alignment with Basel II by SMEs in Turkey and recommendations* (pp.68, 74). (Istanbul Chamber of Trade, Publication No: 2008-4).

Antonides, G. (1998). *An attempt at integration of economic and psychological theories of consumption. European Perspectives on Consumer Behavior*. Prentice Hall, Europe.

Daft, R. (2007). *Understanding the theory and design of organizations*. Thomson South-Western.

De Mooij, M. (2003). Convergence and divergence in consumer behavior: Implications for global advertising. *International Journal of Advertising*, *22*(2), 183–202.

Donnelly, J. H. (1970). Marketing notes and communications: Attitudes toward culture and approach to international advertising. *Journal of Marketing*, 60–63.

Drucker, P. (2006). *Classic Drucker*. Harvard Business School Publishing Corporation.

Keskin, E. (2008). *Access to financing for SME's in the EU and Turkey*. REX/264 EU-Turkey Joint Consultative Committee, 25th meeting of the EU-Turkey Joint Consultative Committee Paris, France, 18-19 November, 2008.

Levitt, T. (1983). The globalization of markets. *Harvard Business Review*, 92–102.

Luthans, F., & Doh, J. P. (2009). *International management, culture, strategy, and behavior*. McGraw Hill.

McCracken, G. (1989). Culture and consumer behavior: An anthropological perspective. *Journal of the Market Research Society. Market Research Society, 32*(1), 56–73.

Suerdem, A. (1993). Social de(re)construction of mass culture: Making (non) sense of consumer behavior. *International Journal of Research in Marketing, 11*, 423–443.

TUIK- Turkish Statistical Institute. (2003). *General census of industry and establishments*. Retrieved from https://www.tuik.gov.tr

ENDNOTES

[1]   In the late 1990s, some European retail traders developed the idea of tailoring a shop towards a lifestyle theme, in the form of "concept stores" that specialized in cross-selling without using separate departments.

This work was previously published in Cases on Business and Management in the MENA Region: New Trends and Opportunities, edited by El-Khazindar Business Research and Case Center, pp. 99-114, copyright 2011 by Business Science Reference (an imprint of IGI Global).

Chapter 8

Building a Knowledge Management System in a Design Firm:
The Case of XYZ Structural Department

Toufic Mezher
American University of Beirut, Lebanon

M.A. Abdul-Malak
American University of Beirut, Lebanon

Mohamad Khaled
XYZ Engineering Company, Lebanon

Ibrahim El-Khatib
XYZ Engineering Company, Lebanon

EXECUTIVE SUMMARY

Knowledge management represents a strategic vision for developing an organization's performance and its likelihood of success in dealing with future challenges in its industry. The case starts by discussing the importance of knowledge management in improving the competitive edge of firms in general and of consulting firms in particular. Then, the case discusses the process of building a knowledge management system in the structural engineering department at a leading engineering design consulting firm, based in the Republic of Lebanon.

DOI: 10.4018/978-1-4666-2618-8.ch008

The knowledge, both tacit and explicit, needed during the design phase is identified and mapped according to the adopted design process, and an expert system was built to capture some of the tacit knowledge needed in the conceptual design stage of the process. In addition, an intranet Web-based knowledge management system was developed with the aim of helping diffuse both explicit and tacit knowledge.

ORGANIZATION BACKGROUND

As engineering becomes more complicated and advanced in application, a vision must be drawn to meet tomorrow's consulting needs. Engineering companies must look forward to adopt new technologies as well as improve available technical skills in order to accelerate the work process and compete with other consulting companies. The goal of any engineering firm is to attract as many projects as possible and deliver the services required on such projects to the clients' established standards and within the limited timeframes allowed. One key approach to achieve such an objective is for a company to leverage its knowledge, by adopting proven knowledge management practices.

Knowledge management is known as an evolving field that has currently attracted much attention. Knowing that skilled employees are considered as real assets for their organizations, wise management can be characterized as one that shall always uphold such values and resources. However, these assets usually live in the collective human memory and are poorly reserved and managed (Augier & Knudsen, 2004; Raub & Von Wittich, 2004).

The objective of this case is to share the experience of building a knowledge management system (KMS) in a consulting firm, mainly, the Structure Engineering Department at XYZ consulting firm, one of the top 100 engineering firms operating worldwide.

XYZ is a multidisciplinary architectural and engineering consulting company that offers clients an integrated approach towards the ever-increasing need for concrete and reliable project delivery systems. The firm provides consulting services in architecture & planning; structural, electrical, mechanical, transportation, environmental, telecommunication, industrial, and process engineering; geographic information systems (GIS); and information technology (IT).

Figure 1 presents the knowledge level and decision-making process for each position inside the structural department. It has a hierarchical form starting from the lowest position (Junior Engineer) and increasing to reach the highest position (Head of Department) inside the department. As the task increases in value, the responsibility will automatically gain more importance. The figure also shows the knowledge of engineers at each position level of XYZ's structural department. It

Figure 1. Level of knowledge and experience in Structure Engineering Department at XYZ

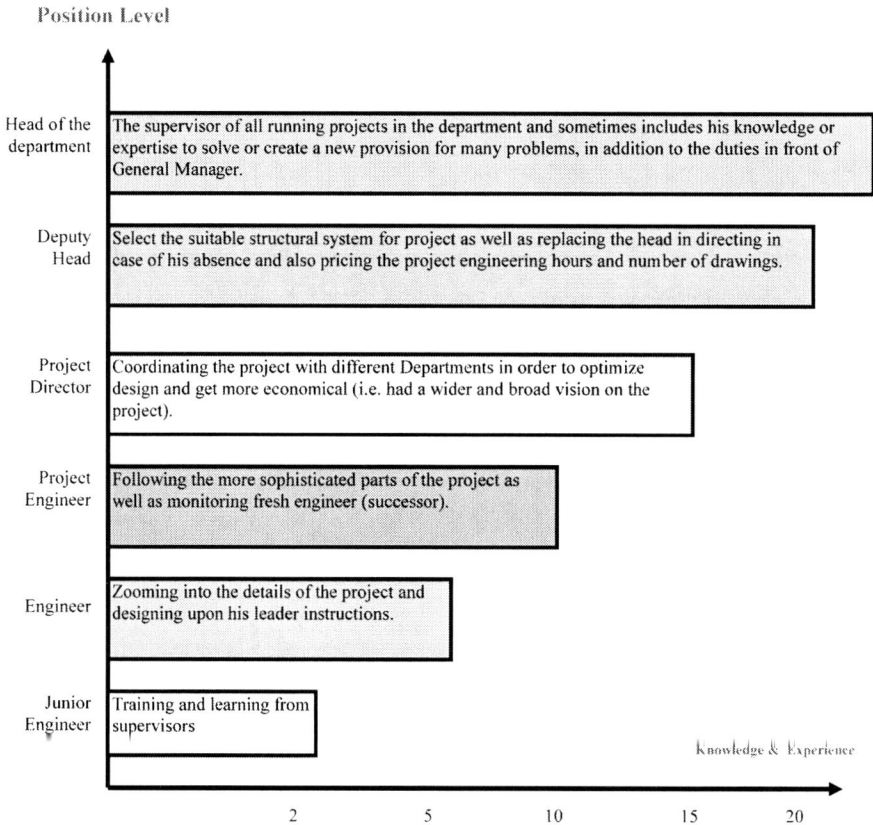

Position Level

Position	Description
Head of the department	The supervisor of all running projects in the department and sometimes includes his knowledge or expertise to solve or create a new provision for many problems, in addition to the duties in front of General Manager.
Deputy Head	Select the suitable structural system for project as well as replacing the head in directing in case of his absence and also pricing the project engineering hours and number of drawings.
Project Director	Coordinating the project with different Departments in order to optimize design and get more economical (i.e. had a wider and broad vision on the project).
Project Engineer	Following the more sophisticated parts of the project as well as monitoring fresh engineer (successor).
Engineer	Zooming into the details of the project and designing upon his leader instructions.
Junior Engineer	Training and learning from supervisors

Knowledge & Experience

2   5   10   15   20

is noticeable that as the number of years in service increases, a wide knowledge of design is developed. In other words, each stage has its own determinants and characteristics. For engineers to reach a higher position, they must upgrade their knowledge level as well as their contribution to the decision-making process of the department.

The company has many servers for administrative and engineering purposes. The existing servers include proxy, FTP, e-mail, Web, anti-spam and anti-virus, database, and Veritas back up. In addition, there are many servers used to manage current and existing engineering projects. Other servers are used to manage all related business.

SETTING THE STAGE

In its most basic form, knowledge can be thought of as information that is contextual, relevant, and actionable (Anwar, Kanok-Nukulchai, & Batanov, 2005). It is a process of converting the extracted data into information, and the information, in turn, to relevant and actionable knowledge (Turban, Aronson, Liang, & Sharda, 2007; Dalkir, 2005).

In changing markets and rapid technological advances, many organizations have changed their strategies to become more flexible in coping with such trends in order to be competitive; a certain way of doing so is to strengthen their potential to learn as organizations. In this context, knowledge plays an essential role for value creation and as an organizational driver. Increased emphasis must be placed on expanding the organizational knowledge-base level, either by learning from others (colleagues, partners, etc.) or by creating new knowledge through innovation (Turban at al., 2007; Awad & Ghaziri, 2004).

Basically, there are two types of knowledge: explicit and tacit. The first is defined by a knowledge embodied in a code or a language, and as consequence it can be communicated, processed, transmitted, and stored relatively in a useful manner. The latter is deeply rooted knowledge of people's experience and know-how. This knowledge is acquired by sharing experiences and observations (Awad & Ghaziri, 2004).

Knowledge management (KM) is the systematic and formal management of knowledge related to activities, practices, programs, and policies within the enterprise. The main goal of KM is to effectively apply an organization's knowledge to create new knowledge for achieving and maintaining competitive advantage. KM is the aimed coordination of knowledge as a component of production, and the management of the environment to support individual knowledge transfer and the following creation of collective knowledge. So knowledge management is not only the management of knowledge itself, but the management of the organization with a particular focus on the knowledge issue (Bose, 2004).

There are many challenges facing business acceptance of KM. Software and hardware technologies are advancing at a rapid speed, and many organizations are under pressure to stay up to date. In addition, knowledge is dynamic and developing rapidly, and it is very difficult to capture new knowledge as it occurs (Awad & Ghaziri, 2004; Tuban et al., 2007). Edwards, Handzic, Carlsson, and Nissen (2003) mention that the most important challenges facing practice over the next three years are evaluation and measurement, creating a trust-based organizational culture, demonstrating the value of and motivating people to share, demystification, gaining acceptance, regaining credibility, and making KM a part of practice and daily processes of an organization. All these challenges can hinder KM acceptance in business, and more coordination and planning are needed before initiating KM projects.

Knowledge Management Cycle

KM tends to follow a logical progression, or cycle. Dalkir (2005) proposes the major phases involved in the knowledge management cycle: encompassing the capture, creation, codification, sharing, accessing, application, and reuse of knowledge within and between organizations. This KM cycle is an integration from four major approaches to KM cycles that are presented by Meyer and Zack (1996), Bukowitz and Williams (2000), McElroy (2003), and Wiig (1993).

This case follows the KM cycle proposed by Turban et al. (2007). The six phases are:

1. *Create knowledge.* Knowledge is created as people determine new ways of doing things or develop know-how. Sometimes external knowledge is brought in.
2. *Capture knowledge.* New knowledge must be identified as valuable and be represented in a reasonable way.
3. *Refine knowledge.* New knowledge must be placed in context so that it is actionable. This is where human insights (tacit qualities) must be captured along with explicit facts.
4. *Store knowledge.* Useful knowledge must then he stored in a reasonable format in a knowledge repository so that others in the organization can access it.
5. *Manage knowledge.* Like a library, knowledge must be kept current. It must be reviewed to verify that it is relevant and accurate.
6. *Disseminate knowledge.* Knowledge must be made available in a useful format to anyone in the organization who needs it anywhere and anytime. As knowledge is disseminated, individuals develop, create, and identify new knowledge or update old knowledge, which they return to the system. Knowledge must be updated. Thus, the knowledge repository grows over time.

Knowledge Management Systems in Engineering Consulting Firms

In general, consulting firms, usually considered to be highly knowledge-intensive companies, have been increasing their information technology expenditure, developing intranets and data warehousing, and using the Internet in an effort to create knowledge management systems (Alavi & Leidner, 1997; Edenius & Borgerson,

2003; Mezher, Abdul-Malak, Ghosn, & Ajam, 2005). The personal (informal) networks that had sustained knowledge sharing across consultants and engagements were increasingly seen as insufficient, especially as consulting firms are recognizing that much of the key knowledge is held by individuals, unless there is some structure to retain it within the organizational memory (Davenport & Hansen, 1998). In other words, when a person leaves the organization, that knowledge leaves with that person (Pasternack & Viscio, 1998).

The first generic challenge facing a consulting firm seeking to establish an effective knowledge management system is to ensure that the quality of information in the system is high. However, for KM to work, it may require a shift in mindset and culture, away from hoarding knowledge and towards sharing ideas. Consultants are likely to be influenced in their behavior by the reward structure of the firm. When consultants are faced with a choice between serving clients and collecting the internal "connecting knowledge," the incentives typically line up in favor of serving clients. The second generic challenge facing a consulting firm that is seeking to establish an effective knowledge management system is to ensure that the system, once established, is used. Despite the substantial commitment of resources to the establishment of such systems, not all consultants are willing to use the implemented systems. A large variation in the level of use of, and contribution to, KMS has been observed. Often the sheer volume of information available online is a problem (Weiss, 1999). The elimination of obsolete knowledge can also be problematic.

The Need for KMS in a Structural Engineering Design Environment

The demand for more complex engineering of buildings and structures is resulting in an increase in their required structural performance. Analysis techniques are becoming more complicated and structural engineers are becoming more specialized in their structural engineering analysis. However, specialists must make interrelated decisions regarding geometric configuration, material properties, loading and boundary conditions, in addition to appropriate type of analyses needed to predict structural behavior. In a typical project, the design process flows by relying on complex interactions between predicted analytical and behavior, available experimental test data, and the previous design experience of a number of diverse experts. The complexity tends to cause difficulties in coordinating the efforts of a multidisciplinary design analysis process and increases the demand for a limited number of skilled designers, which results in a longer design lifecycle.

KMS can be used as an important tool to disseminate expert knowledge to the needed designers. The key to performance is the knowledge utilized in problem solving. When this knowledge is "routine," KMS functions as an assistant. If the knowledge is elicited from the expert, the KMS will be more able to solve difficult problems such as simulating the performance of an expert in the specific problem-solving situation.

Two types of knowledge are represented in KMS: (1) explicit knowledge, and (2) tacit knowledge that is converted to explicit knowledge. Explicit knowledge can represent the description of an engineering system, including the physical structure and its components; this will be explained by a structural frame in building that includes knowledge about both geometry and material properties of many structural elements. Tacit knowledge varies from highly structured knowledge with established scientific theoretical rules to weakly structured knowledge such as that gained by long years of experience. Many different methods for representing the different scientific laws associated with engineering disciplines have existed to organize and ease analysis type problems.

CASE DESCRIPTION

Stages of Design Phase in the Structure Department at XYZ

Figure 2 shows the main stages of the structural engineering work throughout the project lifecycle. These phases are Conceptual Phase, Embodiment Phase, Detail Phase, and Construction Phase (Tender Documents). They highlight the relevant activities needed to run the project and deliver proper design documents. They are sorted depending on each type. For XYZ's structural department, the design process is part of the overall planning and designing that drives the construction and maintenance of constructed projects.

In the normal procedure, these items can be linked together sequentially. Each element is dependent on the previous package and induces information to the next package in line. Figure 3 shows the path of information flow in the structure department for a specified project lifecycle. It shows that information can be monitored at each stage and engineering can make use of knowledge gained during the design of a specific project. The structural work begins by having an architectural concept and its design functions. Based on this concept, structural work can be formulated—in other words, the structural model and analysis can take place—then followed by designing the different structural elements and detailing it properly in order to reach the best executable design. Moreover, the drafting process has a contributing role in this process to present the materials captured to the external environment. Upon submittal of the drawings, an estimated calculation by the engineer is required to value the project cost in all of its forms.

Figure 2. The structural engineering work process

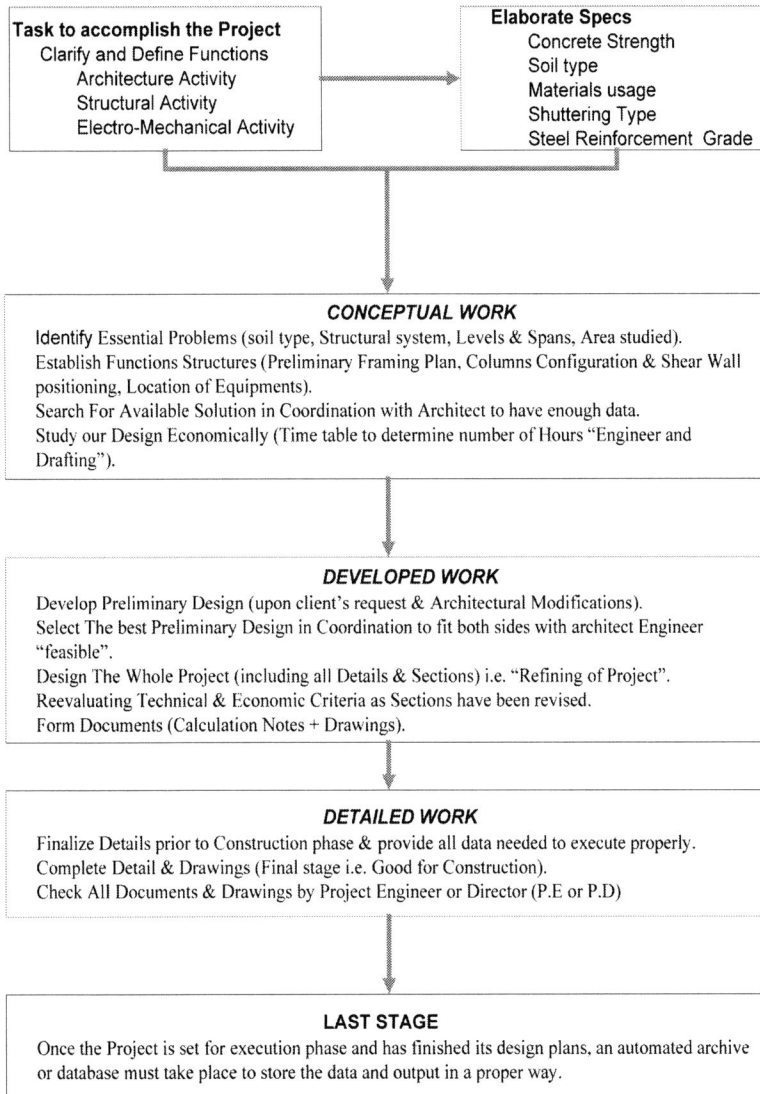

Task to accomplish the Project	Elaborate Specs
Clarify and Define Functions Architecture Activity Structural Activity Electro-Mechanical Activity	Concrete Strength Soil type Materials usage Shuttering Type Steel Reinforcement Grade

CONCEPTUAL WORK

Identify Essential Problems (soil type, Structural system, Levels & Spans, Area studied).
Establish Functions Structures (Preliminary Framing Plan, Columns Configuration & Shear Wall positioning, Location of Equipments).
Search For Available Solution in Coordination with Architect to have enough data.
Study our Design Economically (Time table to determine number of Hours "Engineer and Drafting").

DEVELOPED WORK

Develop Preliminary Design (upon client's request & Architectural Modifications).
Select The best Preliminary Design in Coordination to fit both sides with architect Engineer "feasible".
Design The Whole Project (including all Details & Sections) i.e. "Refining of Project".
Reevaluating Technical & Economic Criteria as Sections have been revised.
Form Documents (Calculation Notes + Drawings).

DETAILED WORK

Finalize Details prior to Construction phase & provide all data needed to execute properly.
Complete Detail & Drawings (Final stage i.e. Good for Construction).
Check All Documents & Drawings by Project Engineer or Director (P.E or P.D)

LAST STAGE

Once the Project is set for execution phase and has finished its design plans, an automated archive or database must take place to store the data and output in a proper way.

In general, Figure 4 shows the various types of work carried out by the structure department at XYZ. These works vary from buildings and towers to bridges and water structures. Each circle describes a sort of analysis and design undertaken to represent the manner of delivering materials for many projects.

The structural work inside this department involves multiple functions treating different types of structures, for instance, buildings, towers, bridges, and water structures, as mentioned above. In each type of structure, several tasks must be ac-

Figure 3. Information flow model for structural design process

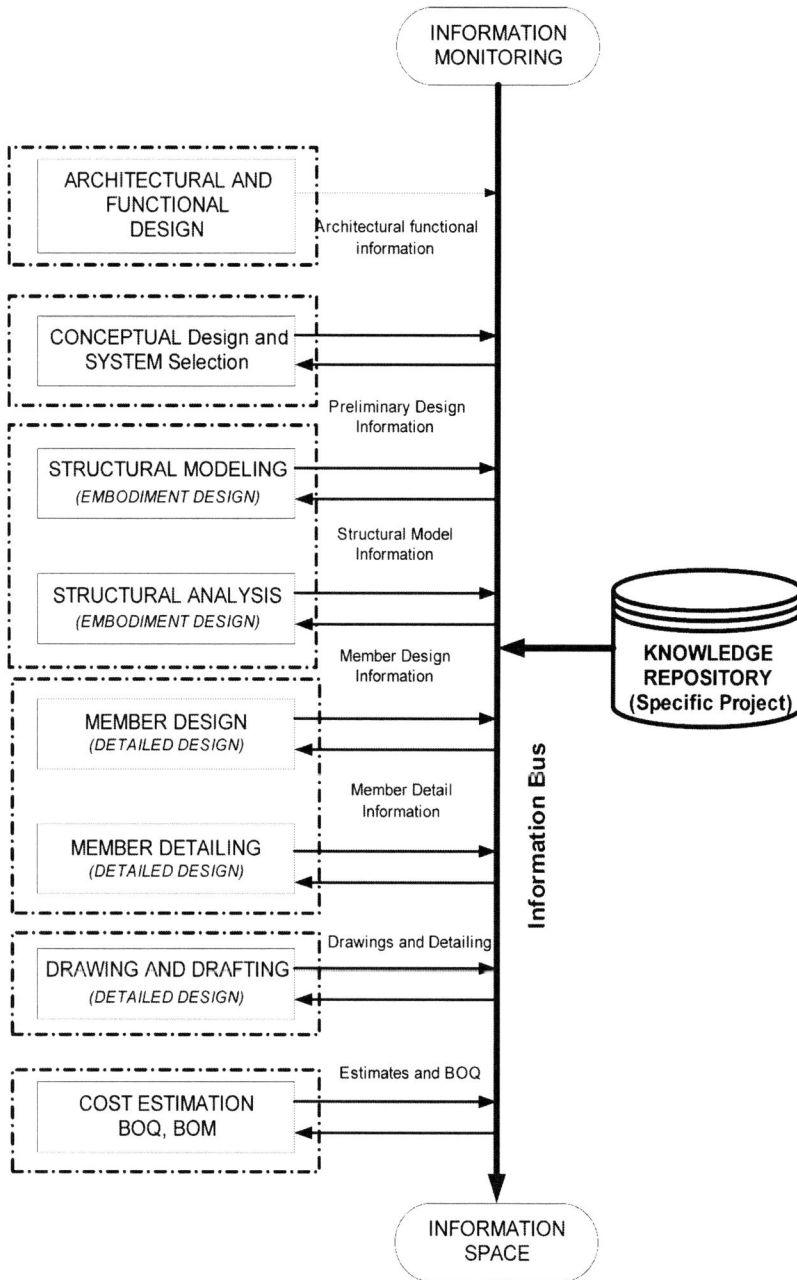

complished in coordination with other disciplines. For example, Figure 5 reveals the different tasks running to reach the final stage of tower design. The work starts

Figure 4. Types of work carried out by Structure Engineering Department at XYZ

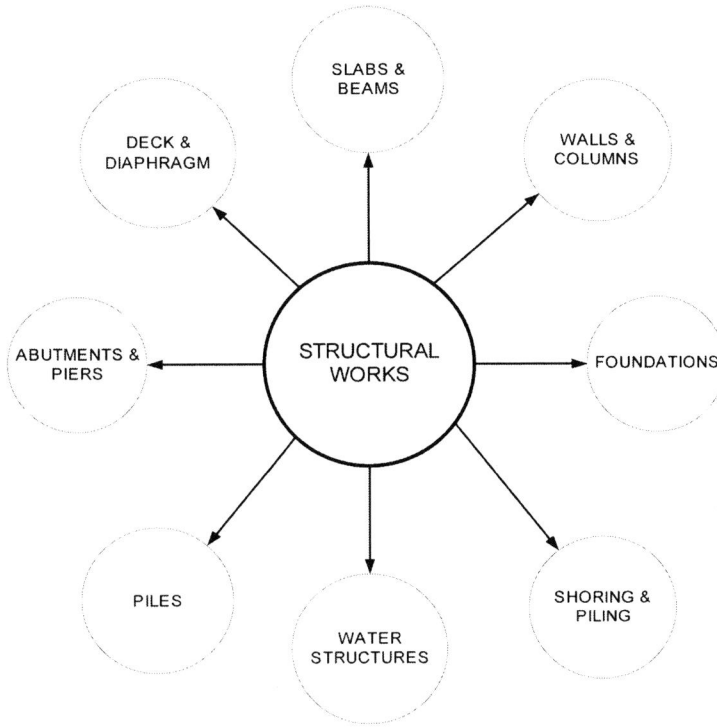

by defining the substructure system (piling package, foundation) and continues in designing the columns, walls needed to carry the building mass, as well as for slabs and beams to frame the floor. The work ends up by detailing the different structural elements progressed through the design phase prior to the construction stage. The different parameters required to analyze a tower design include: frame the slab system and determine its type, analyze the vertical supporting elements (walls and columns), check the lateral drift induced from seismic and wind effects, design the

Figure 5. Different tasks in designing towers

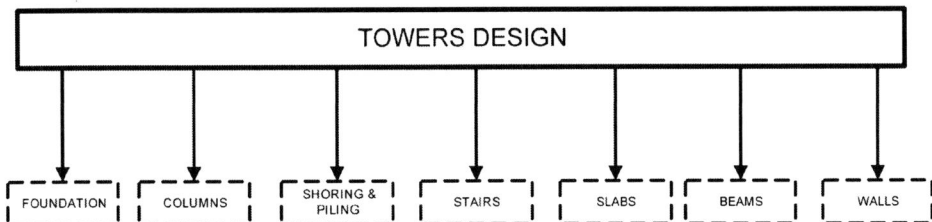

foundation and shoring system adopted, analyze the framing system and the beams (if any), design the stairs and reinforce the wall sections, and design steel members and outriggers when needed.

Knowledge Mapping at XYZ

A simple intranet Web page hierarchical structure was used for the KMS. The system will direct engineers to the knowledge needed to perform a specific task at any stage of the design process Figures 2 and 4 show the structural design process, and information and knowledge flow at XYZ respectively. Therefore, identifying and mapping knowledge, both tacit and explicit, at each phase of the design process is an important step in building a KMS. For example, in a tower design, in the conceptual design phase, the knowledge is needed to: identify basic criteria (soil type, structural system, and materials applied); establish functions (structural) and preliminary framing plan, columns layout, and wall distribution; frame an optimized solution (system) in collaboration with other disciplines; and evaluate proposed design feasibility (workability and financially) by computing the timeframe and anticipated man-hours in addition to estimated number of drawings.

In the embodiment design, the knowledge is needed to: develop the conceptual design based on the client's review and municipality requirements; optimize the selection, meeting other disciplines' functions (plans, sections, etc.); refine the project scope by producing more plans and design sections; and create/form documents and drawings to purify the cost value.

The knowledge is needed in the detail design phase to: finalize details prior to the construction phase in order to provide all the required data for proper execution, and revise the work done and approve it as "Good for Construction" (this is done under the supervision of the project director).

Finally, the knowledge needed in the last phase to prepare the whole document (technically) needed for pricing, prepare the general conditions of the contract, and determine its relevant specifications are in compliance with code regulations. Tables 1, 2, and 3 identify the tacit and explicit knowledge that is needed in the different phases of the design process in general.

Building KMS at XYZ

In principle, a knowledge management system provides strong potential for any organization to leverage its knowledge assets. Based on this potential, XYZ chose to adopt such technology in the field of engineering, and viewed it as necessary in order to remain competitive in the market. This KMS will enable knowledge accumulated from past projects to be used on present and future ones.

Table 1. Availability of explicit and tacit knowledge in conceptual phase

Knowledge Type	Engineer Assistance	Standards (Criteria)	Design Aids (Experience)	Design Codes (References)	Design Method (Work Schedule)	Detailed Activity
Tacit	Provide Interaction with Others/Informal Discussion	-Meet project budget (\$). -Safer and executable design. -Respect timeframe. -Adopt the required specs.	-Previous experience and expertise with similar past projects. -System or process in design phase.	---	---	-Provide proper coordination among different departments to reach an executable structure.
Explicit	---	---	-Basic rules and equations to estimate the different structural components (foundation sizes, slab thickness, etc.). -Guidelines for system design.	-Templates (loads definition meeting code requirements and architectural functions). -Design forms for seismic/wind zoning to determine the demands for each system. -Requirements for strength and serviceability for structural design. -Computer software (Safe, Etabs, etc.) to enhance manual design.	-Templates (CAD drawings, PDF, Excel, MathCAD, and Word files) captured from previous and similar projects.

Knowledge Management Cycle at XYZ

The KM cycle starts with knowledge creation. This phase begins with knowledge mapping (Tables 1, 2, and 3), as shown previously, which should identify all possible needed explicit and tacit knowledge (noticed or previously unnoticed) to complete each step in the structure engineering work process shown in Figure 2. Once the needed knowledge is identified as valuable to the organization, it should be captured and refined, which are the next two phases. All needed explicit knowledge is placed in context that is actionable. For example, basic formulas and equations, design templates and forms, and drawings are placed in a format that engineers can use when needed. Tacit knowledge is also captured in this phase.

For example, an expert system was built to help determine the best system for tower lateral analysis. Many times expert engineers in structure tower design are not available to help novice designers, therefore, the expert knowledge is captured and used in an expert system so the designers can have instant access to it whenever it is needed.

The next phase in the KM cycle is storing knowledge. After converting all the needed fact and tacit knowledge into explicit knowledge, the knowledge is stored in

Table 2. Availability of explicit and tacit knowledge in the development phase

Knowledge Type	Engineer Assistance	Standards (Criteria)	Design Aids (Experience)	Design Codes (References)	Design Procedure (Work Process)	Detailed Activity
Tacit	Provide Interaction with Others /Informal Discussion	-Meet safety and economy. -Study thermal and acoustics insulation. -Consider time factor (speed of construction). -Determine local availability of materials. -Have the technical skills (labor). -Coordinate the flexibility in changing functions. -Emphasize on the end use of the structure (residential, office, hospital, hotel, etc.).	-Experience in defining the framing system and determining the structural components such as floor depth, minimum column dimensions.	---	---	-Ability to build up a system that meets conflicting requirements for different disciplines.
Explicit	---		-Reverse design to predetermine the input parameters such as bar spacing, ratio of sizes for columns and walls.	-Basic formulas and primary equations to estimate the structural components (minimum dimensions and ratio of dimensions, span-depth ratio, wall thickness, column sizes, etc.).	-Templates (loads definition meeting code requirements and architectural functions). -Design forms for seismic/wind zoning to determine the demands for each system. -Meet strength and serviceability for structural design.	-Templates (CAD drawings, Excel, MathCAD, PDF, and Word files) captured from previous and similar projects.

repositories so that engineers can have access to them in an efficient and effective manner to facilitate their use. Storing the knowledge is subjected to the approval of the auditors and other experts in the field. This will ensure that validity of the stored knowledge.

Managing knowledge management is the next phase in the KM cycle. The system will not survive without continuous updating. Feedback from knowledge workers is very important for updating to succeed. It is also important to archive obsolete knowledge.

Table 3. Availability of explicit and tacit knowledge in the detailed and tender phases

Design Phase	Knowledge Type	Engineer Assistance	Standards (Criteria)	Design Aids (Experience)	Design Codes (References)	Design Method (Work Schedule)	Detailed Activity
Detailed Design Phase	Tacit	Provide Interaction with Others / Informal Discussion	-Meet Project Budget ($). -Safe and executable design. -Submit project deliverables on time. -Adopt the required specs.	-Increase in coordination process to reach an improved and workable design. -Previous experience to solve some particular problems faced in previous projects.	---	---	-Ability to build up a system that meets conflicted parts for different disciplines.
	Explicit		---	---	Equations, formulas, and code regulation to determine different parameters for detailed design such as (slab and beam dimensions, reinforcement, details, wall dimensions, foundation sizes, etc.).	-Spreadsheets distributed among engineers to define the required sections. -3D model analysis to verify results and study lateral effect.	Preparation for plans layout, schematic drawings, and different detail sections.
Tender Phase	Tacit	Determine Needed Specs to Meet the Quality Objective.	-Confirm contractual documents and subparticulars. -Engineer estimate about project cost ($).	-Define the critical clauses in the project contract. -Identify the impacted materials in the specs document. -Suggest solutions and approaches for value reduction.	---	---	Link to detailed work from different disciplines to calculate BOQ value.
	Explicit		Preserve and respect the specs mentioned in the design drawings.	---	-Excel Sheets, PDF files, and CAD drawings. -FIDIC regulations. -BOQ calculation.	Spreadsheets to compute the project cost as well as specify its allocated materials.	Determine all parameters relevant to cost and quality as well.

Dissemination of knowledge is the last phase of the KM cycle. Knowledge gained from previous projects is available to all designers to help in solving current and future problems. Therefore, it is imperative that all knowledge workers have access to the KMS.

The KMS at XYZ

Making the KMS accessible through the intranet in the Structural Engineering Department at XYZ was deemed to be the best collaborative approach to assist designers in finishing their work more effectively and efficiently. Their work entails two main activities: design and detailed. Figure 6 shows the main menu of the KMS. Designers may choose to use the system by clicking on the left-hand menu.

The Design Activity

The design activity includes four categories mainly: criteria (standards), design aids (experience), design codes (references), and work process and engineer assistance.

Figure 6. The main window of the intranet in Structural Engineering Department at XYZ

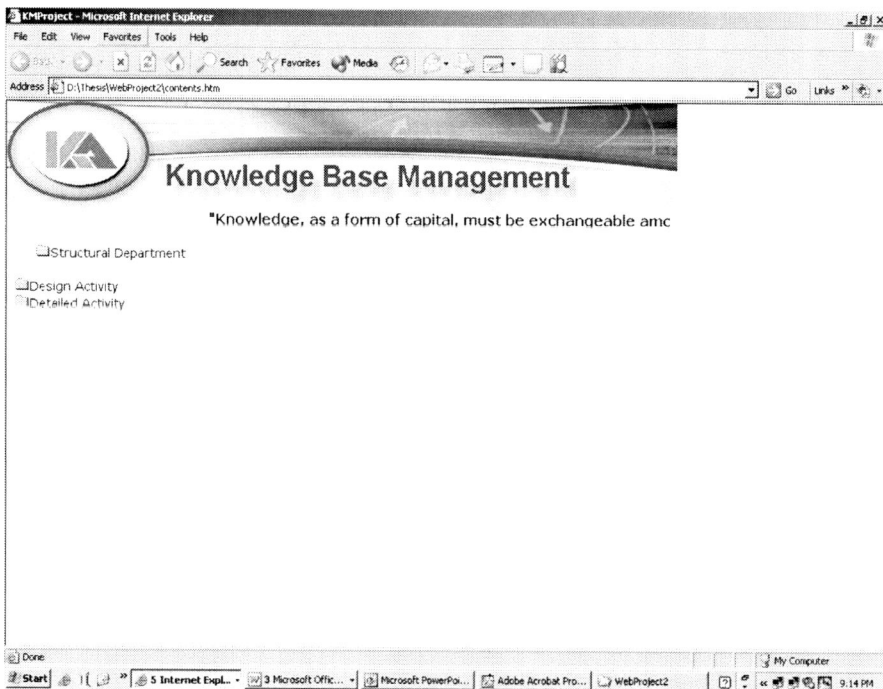

The criteria are defined by some constraints and rules of thumb that the designer should have at the onset of the project to properly perform in the design—for example, to compute the approximate period value for a certain tower subjected to seismic excitation in a considered direction. Figure 7 shows an example of the main key elements that affect the integrity of the design. From a structural point view, these criteria are encapsulated by a definite conceptual report (functions, materials, structural system, etc.), added to the code of practice for each project.

Design aids are considered as key tools used to reach a pure design, free of defects or problems. This can be achieved by the performance of the engineers and the wide knowledge captured by the experts, as they are considered the most knowledgeable and informed people about the various past projects and their complications. For example, to avoid using a pre-stressing approach in the design of basement floors, as its efficiency will be minimal, surrounding basement walls are suggested. Figure 8 shows Excel® sheets and MathCAD® models generated to facilitate the engineers' work. These forms are later modified and checked for applicability for future projects.

Design codes are defined by all available resources and references contributed to fulfill the design based on code requirements and municipality regulations. In other words, all the engineering equations or formulas that are used at this stage will be extracted from the design codes. An example here is to determine the

Figure 7. An interface layer for criteria folder under the title of engineering work

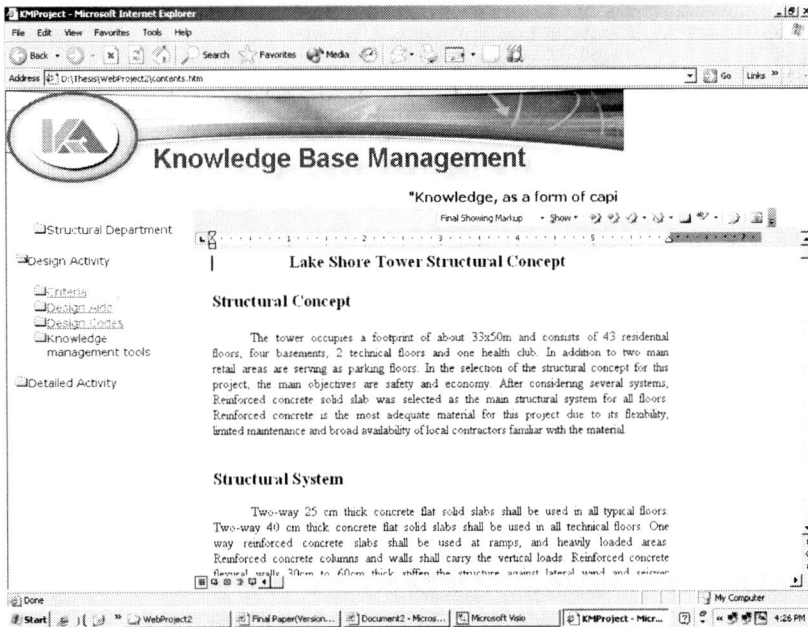

Figure 8. An example of design aids (Excel sheets and MathCAD models)

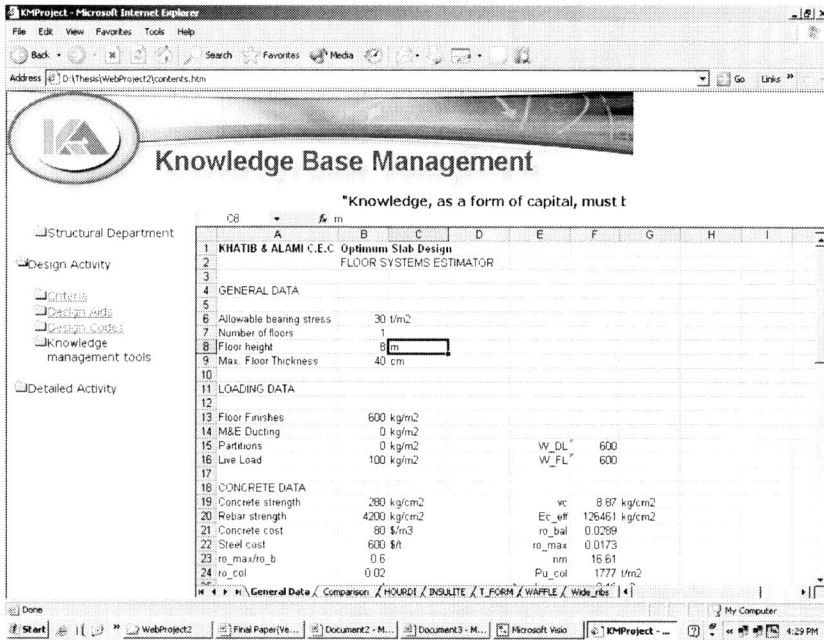

minimum floor thickness required to satisfy deflection control based on the slab system (solid, ribbed, waffle, flat plate, etc.).

Work process and engineer assistance are performed as one unit aiming to define the framework of the work process. In this process, several spreadsheets and calculation methods are installed by the expert engineers to be more useful for other engineers in running their design plans and accelerating the productivity level. After data has been entered by junior engineers, this work must be validated by senior engineers.

Detailed Activity

The detailed activity uses two main folders—Computer Aided Design (CAD) drawings and Calculation Notes—which are the main deliverables of any project. Thus, the aim of this phase is to store the resulting information in an organized form that guides the engineer to reach the solution in an efficient time. This phase also includes the allocated materials to specifications and contractual documents such as Bill of Quantity (BOQ) forms, General Conditions of Contract, and its sub-particulars. The end result will be an interface layer to present the materials in a digital format (CAD drawings, PDF and Word® files, etc.).

The KMS at XYZ did create added value to the organization, because the system:

- Facilitates better and more informed decisions,
- Contributes to the intellectual capital and organizational learning,
- Encourages free flow of ideas which leads to better insights,
- Improves client service and efficiency,
- Accelerates the productivity of the work,
- Organizes the knowledge in a structured way which eliminates redundancy,
- Allows access for the knowledge seeker to the needed knowledge at any time and from anywhere, and
- Keeps knowledge from going outside the door when experienced engineers retire.

The success of the KMS implementation was due to the real commitment from all the engineers in the structural department to share, organize, and capture the knowledge needed to improve their design work. In addition, top management support was also essential to building the KMS; this will eventually lead to building other KMSs in different departments in the future.

CURRENT CHALLENGES FACING THE ORGANIZATION

As discussed earlier, tacit knowledge related to the structure design of towers (see Figure 5) is needed. This knowledge is based on years of experience in designing high-rise buildings. Table 1 shows that in the conceptual design phase, design aids that are based on previous experience and know-how on similar projects can be very useful for new and inexperienced tower designers. Therefore, capturing this tacit knowledge and converting it to explicit knowledge in order to make it available when needed is crucial to the design process, especially when expert engineers are not available.

The challenge here is two-fold. First, you must have experts that are willing to share their knowledge. Second, an organization should have the infrastructure needed to capture and make the knowledge explicit, and integrate the knowledge into the KMS. The knowledge in this case was captured and converted into production rules in a rule-based expert system and then integrated into the KMS. The purpose of the expert system is to determine the best system for tower lateral analysis. When needed, designers can access the expert system from the knowledge management tools menu as shown in Figures 7 and 8. More detailed information of the expert system is found in Khaled (2005).

Even though there was excitement for building the KMS, more work is still needed when it comes to improving the communications between engineers in order to improve knowledge-sharing capabilities. Therefore, there is a need to establish formal communities of practice (Wenger, 1998) or knowledge networks (not just informal) at XYZ to advance knowledge sharing through the intranet. Today, low-cost and open-source tools already exist such as blogs, wikis, and other knowledge base facilitators (Scarff, 2006).

REFERENCES

Alavi, M., & Leidner, D. (1997). Knowledge management systems: Emerging views and practices from the field. *Proceedings of the 32nd IEEE Hawaii International Conference on System Sciences.*

Anwar, N., Kanok-Nukulchai, W., & Batanov, D. (2005). Component based, information oriented structural engineering applications. *Journal of Computing in Civil Engineering, 19*(1), 45–57. doi:10.1061/(ASCE)0887-3801(2005)19:1(45)

Augier, M., & Knudsen, T. (2004). The architecture and design of the knowledge organization. *Journal of Knowledge Management, 8*(4), 6–20. doi:10.1108/13673270410548450

Awad, E., & Ghaziri, H. (2004) *Knowledge management.* Upper Saddle River, NJ: Prentice Hall.

Bose, R. (2004). Knowledge management metrics. *Industrial Management & Data Systems, 104*(6), 457–468. doi:10.1108/02635570410543771

Bukowitz, W., & Williams, R. (2000). *The knowledge management fieldbook.* London: Prentice Hall.

Dalkir, K. (2005). *Knowledge management in theory and practice.* Amsterdam: Elsevier.

Davenport, T., & Hansen, M. (1998). *Knowledge management at Andersen consulting.* Case 9-499-032, Harvard Business School Press, Boston.

Edenius, M., & Borgerson, J. (2003). To manage knowledge by intranet. *Knowledge Management, 7*(5), 124–136. doi:10.1108/13673270310505430

Edwards, J. S., Handzic, M., Carlsson, S., & Nissen, M. (2003). Knowledge management research and practice: Visions and directions. *Knowledge Management Research & Practice, 1*(1), 49–60. doi:10.1057/palgrave.kmrp.8500005

Khaled, M. (2006). *Toward building a knowledge management system in a design firm: The case of Khatib and Alami structural department.* Master's thesis, American University of Beirut, Lebanon.

McElroy, M. (2003). *The new knowledge management: Complexity, learning and sustainable innovation*. Boston: Butterworth-Heinemann.

Meyer, M., & Zack, M. (1996). The design and implementation of information products. *Sloan Management Review, 37*(3), 43–59.

Mezher, T., Abdul-Malak, M. A., Ghosn, I., & Ajam, M. (2005). Knowledge management in mechanical and industrial engineering consulting: A case study. *Journal of Management Engineering, 21*(3), 138–147. doi:10.1061/(ASCE)0742-597X(2005)21:3(138)

Pasternack, B., & Viscio, A. (1998). *The center less corporation: A new model for transforming your organization for growth and prosperity.* New York.

Raub, S., & Von Wittich, D. (2004). Implementing knowledge management: Three strategies for effective CKOs. *European Management Journal, 22*(6), 714–724. doi:10.1016/j.emj.2004.09.024

Scarff, A. (2006). Advancing knowledge sharing with Intranet 2.0. *Knowledge Management Review, 9*(4), 24–27.

Turban, E., Aronson, J. E., Liang, T. P., & Sharda, R. (2007). *Decision support and business intelligence systems*. New York: Prentice Hall.

Weiss, L. (1999). *Collection and connection: The anatomy of knowledge sharing in professional service firms.* Chicago.

Wenger, E. (1998). *Learning, meaning, and identity*. Cambridge, UK: Cambridge University Press.

Wiig, K. (1993). *Knowledge management foundations.* Arlington, TX: Schema Press.

This work was previously published in the Journal of Cases on Information Technology, Volume 11, Issue 3, edited by Mehdi Khosrow-Pour, pp. 1-17, copyright 2010 by IGI Publishing (an imprint of IGI Global).

Chapter 9

Multilayered Distribution System in India:
Practice and Issues

Sumeet Gupta
*Shri Shankaracharya Institute of
Technology and Management, India*

Priyanka Jain
*Shri Shankaracharya Group of
Institutions, India*

Tushar Agrawal
*Shri Shankaracharya Group of
Institutions, India*

Dolly Jaisinghani
*Shri Shankaracharya Group of
Institutions, India*

Ritika Rathi
*Shri Shankaracharya Group of
Institutions, India*

EXECUTIVE SUMMARY

With the invention of Internet, supply chains have become more comprehensive, global, and faster than ever before. Traditionally, companies used to cut costs through manpower reduction, waste reduction, process automation, and inventory control. However, today those companies that reduce costs in their supply chain are the ones who can remain competitive in the market and provide their customers with a superior quality product. Cost reduction in supply chain is not a new concept. Dell worked with just-in-time systems to make its supply chain both time and cost efficient. Companies have sought to make their supply chains both lean and agile and thus become cost efficient as well as responsive to customer demands. Although there are so many examples of modern global supply chains, most of the supply chains in Indian sub-continent still suffer from a number of inefficiencies.

DOI: 10.4018/978-1-4666-2618-8.ch009

The multi-layered market structure, as well as the lack of resilience among supply chain partners, aggravates the issue. Lack of experience and confidence in modern supply chains precludes the supply chain partners to introduce any innovation in the supply chains.

This chapter presents several case studies of the multilayered system in India and shows how the prevalent distribution system preclude any means of cost reduction and making these supply chains efficient. Supply chains of perishable goods, electronic products, FMCG products and Pharmaceutical products are discussed in this chapter. Each of these supply chains present unique challenges and issues that need attention. The three main objectives in these studies are to understand the distribution systems as well as cost economics of the supply chains, identify potential conflicts and issues in their distribution system, and to study the effect of macro-environment on the distribution system. Apart from these objectives, these cases are also meant to prepare those venturing into such supply chains to come up with efficient solutions for improving these supply chains.

CASE I: DISTRIBUTION SYSTEM OF PERISHABLE GOODS: VEGETABLES

Perishable goods present the biggest challenge for supply chains partners because if such goods are not properly handled they perish before reaching the end customer. Therefore, the supply chain partners have to keep some margin for the amount that perishes on the way. The supply chain of vegetable is very simple but the supplier base and the customer base is very complex. In a broad sense the partners in the supply chain of vegetables are the local producers, big farm owners and cold storages which supply vegetables to a central marketplace in a city. In every city there are a few wholesale marketplaces (commonly termed as mandi) which act as a hub for supplying vegetables to small markets and stores in the city. Here, the vegetables are auctioned throughout the day till the supply of vegetables for that day is finished. The vegetables are then supplied to malls, vegetable shops, and small marketplaces in the city. Sometimes small vendors purchase vegetables and deliver them from door-to-door. Figure 1 shows a simple supply chain of a vegetable market, although in reality the supply chain would be much more complex.

Here we discuss the vegetables supply chain in a farm rice state of India – Chhattisgarh. The case study has been conducted for Peesegaon farm which is a sprawling farm of around 20 acres and supplies various kinds of vegetables and fruits to the vegetable marketplaces. Fresh vegetables from local farms are harvested a day before or early in the morning. And those vegetables that are transported from far off places are harvested 2-3 days prior to reaching mandi. Big farm owners also

Figure 1. The vegetable supply chain

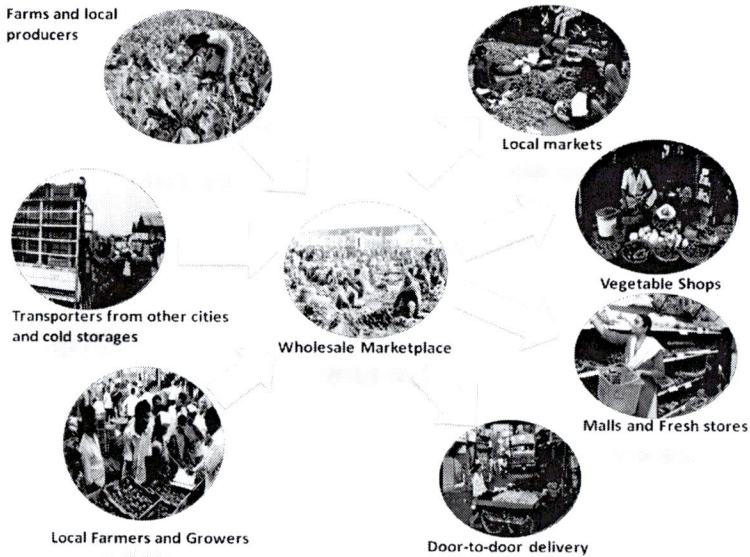

utilize cold storage facilities where they can store and export their vegetables for international markets. Many farm owners grow and sell their vegetables for Metropolitan markets of India and they do not intend to sell them in the local markets. The fork of farmers requires hard labor as they have to work in an open area. Different vegetables require different treatment. Some require more water and some less. Likewise some require shed whereas others do not.

Figure 2. The vegetables are harvested by people paid specifically for harvesting

Figure 3. Transportation of vegetables and fruits using small trucks to Mandi

Generally vegetables are supplied to *mandi* from nearby farms. Some vegetables which have low production in Chhattisgarh are supplied from places like Jabalpur, Bangalore etc. outside the state. The intra-state transportation is mostly done by small trucks in case of big farm owners and commissioning agents and by cycle or pushcart by farmers. The vegetables from outside the state are delivered using truck transportation.

Mandi opens at 6:00 am and ends at 3:00 pm. From morning onwards farmers bring their vegetables to Mandi. The vegetables are supplied to the commissioning agents who act as intermediary between the farm suppliers and the bulk purchase customers. These commissioning agents work on a fixed commission of 8% of the total sales. There are a number of commissioning agents who operate in the mandi and therefore there is no monopoly. Moreover, since they compete among each other, no cartels are formed but there are chances of price signaling by big commissioning agents. The big farm owners post their own commissioning agents. Most commissioning agents have developed relationship with farms and farmers and they work closely with them.

Early in the morning when vegetables are fresh and there are a number of sellers (commissioning agents) and buyers, sellers auction their vegetables. The buyers bid for the vegetables and the highest bidder sets the price of the vegetables. At mandi the sales are always done in bulk quantities. Although vegetables are auctioned every day, the weekly variation in price is usually low. During the season the prices are usually low and during off-season the prices of vegetables and fruits pick up very heavily.

Figure 4. Vegetables arrive at the Mandi from various parts of the state as well as other states

Figure 5. Tomatoes being auctioned by commissioning agents to the local bulk purchasers

The various types of bidders bid for vegetable including the pushcart owners, marketplace hawkers, vegetable shop owners, and mall retailers. The transportation is usually privately arranged by the bidders and they sell their purchases at various local marketplaces. As the day ends, the left over vegetables are generally purchased

Table 1. Prices of vegetables across the supply chain

Vegetable	Mandi Rate	Rate at Local Marketplace	Rate at Local Vegetable Shop	Push Cart Owners
Spinach	Rs 100 for 25 Kg.	10 Rs/Kg	14 Rs/Kg	12 Rs/Kg
Tomato	Rs 65 for 22 Kg	12 Rs/Kg	14 Rs/Kg	12 Rs/Kg
Lemon	Rs 50 for 100 pieces	2.5 Rs/piece	Rs 3-4/piece	Rs 2.4 /piece
Potato	Rs 100 for 25 Kg	10 Rs/Kg	12 Rs/Kg	10 Rs/Kg
Onion	Rs 320 for 40Kg	9 Rs/Kg	10 Rs/Kg	10 Rs/Kg
Beans	Rs 500 for 20 Kg	30 Rs/Kg	40 Rs/Kg	----
Carrot	Rs 240 for 20 Kg	15 Rs/Kg	20 Rs/Kg	20 Rs/Kg
Brinjal	Rs 500 for 20 Kg	35 Rs/Kg	40 Rs/Kg	40 Rs/Kg
Cauliflower	Rs 500 for 25 Kg	25 Rs/Kg	30 Rs/Kg	30 Rs/Kg
Lady's finger	Rs 400 for 20 Kg	20 Rs/Kg	30 Rs/Kg	25 Rs/Kg
Chilli	Rs 160 for 10 Kg	18 Rs/Kg	25 Rs/Kg	20 Rs/Kg
Ginger	Rs 200 for 5 Kg	45 Rs/Kg	60 Rs/Kg	50 Rs/Kg
Capsicum	Rs 120 for 10 Kg	16 Rs/Kg	20 Rs/Kg	20 Rs/Kg
Cabbage	Rs 720 for 40 Kg	25 Rs/Kg	30 Rs/Kg	25 Rs/Kg
Pointed Gourd	Rs 480 for 40 Kg	20 Rs/Kg	30 Rs/Kg	30 Rs/Kg

by restaurant owners, hostel or mess workers etc. who get lower price for the left over vegetables and those vegetables which are about to perish.

Economics of Vegetable Supply Chains

In the case study conducted by us, some of the cost figures are available below which gives an indication of the price economics of vegetable supply chains. However, these prices vary and therefore can only be taken as an indication (Table 1).

Generally the vegetable shop owners in posh areas of the city charge 20% more than the local marketplace. Marketplaces run during specific hours (4 PM to 10 PM) in different locations in the city (twice in a week in the same place). The prices charged at different locations are different depending upon the community in that specific area. If the people living in an area are wealthy then prices charged are higher as compared to other areas. In other words, in a vegetable marketplace all forms of pricing mechanisms can be seen. As the marketplace begins, prices are high so as to skim as much as of the market as possible. Towards the end, the prices come down so as to sell as much as possible i.e., a type of penetration pricing. During the marketplace activities, sellers use competitive pricing and set prices according to competitors. Some sellers use target-profit pricing mechanism and do not allow any bargains while others do now lower the prices beyond a certain cost-plus margin.

There are various direct costs involved on the side of a hawker and that adds to the cost of vegetables procured from the mandi. A small marketplace hawker earns around Rs. 500 per day by selling vegetables for half a day.

- Transportation cost (Around Rs. 40-Rs. 100)
- Marketplace Tax (Rent in case of a vegetable shopkeeper could be Rs. 3000-Rs. 5000 per month). For the place they have to pay to the Government's coordinators who are authorized by the Government to collect taxes on its behalf. These coordinators pay money to the Government on a yearly basis and take money from hawkers on a daily basis.
- Polythene bags (Nominal cost of around Rs. 0.50 per transaction)
- Electricity cost (Around Rs. 5 - Rs. 10 per seating in a marketplace). In case of a vegetable shop keeper such cost may run to about Rs. 500 per month.
- Hidden cost
  ◦ Arising out of perished vegetables during transportation as well as the portion of vegetables trimmed after purchase.
  ◦ Left over vegetables are sold at very low prices

Indirect costs are usually low and involve the cost of weighing scale and related accessories.

New Formats in Vegetable Supply Chains

Owing to tremendous appreciation of prices a few new retail formats have sprung up in the vegetable supply chains. These formats are discussed below:

Direct to Door format was developed by Sabzeewala.com. The format includes direct procurement from farm, consolidation at a central warehouse and delivery to the home. The various costs involved between farm and home delivery are thus reduced drastically. Sabzeewala.com charged its service subscribers Rs. 120.00 per month for the home delivery service and thus earned heavily in the transaction. The subscribers could get vegetables delivered to their home twice a day through a delivery van and Rs. 120 is very small price for getting vegetables delivered to home. The prices of vegetables are usually marked slightly lower as compared to a local marketplace. However, after successfully running this format for one year sabzeewala.com closed down its services for various unknown reasons one of which was the various hidden costs involved in providing this service (including office rent, telephone charges, website renting charges and salary for persons employed for providing this service).

Reliance Fresh is a retail mall which attempted to provide direct from farm to retail malls and thus removing intermediaries from the picture. They purchase directly from the farm and supply to its own outlets at various parts of the cities. However, they faced tremendous opposition from various small retailers and shop keepers and hence this format is running only in big cities.

Issues in Vegetable Supply Chains

Political Issues

Big farm owners face the problem of bribery to keep the Government officials happy. These are the major problem facing the farmers as they have to rely on Government policies and procedures to sell their vegetables in the market. Problem arises during harvesting the vegetables where politicians create troubles. Sometimes Government take farms under its possession for the development of the city/state/country. The farms are taken over by the Government at prices much lower than the market price. If they want to raise their voice against the politician then they have to go to court for the justice. They have to bear losses in most of the condition as politicians are in power. A farmes has to bear all these losses.

Hybrid vs Organic

It has become a major problem in today's era. A farmer has to decide whether to grow vegetable for the welfare of the country or to fill his own pocket. The good thing about organic vegetables is that they are good for health. But they rot very soon once taken from the farm. In other words they have to be sold as early as possible. Moreover, their production is less as compared to hybrid vegetables. The production in case of hybrid vegetables is large and taken less time. Moreover, they do not rot as early as organic vegetables. However, they do not taste as good as organic and are also not good for health. They do not add as much to health as organic vegetables. Most of the public in small cities prefer organic vegetables as compared to hybrid. Hybrid vegetables are preferred for party and where show is important.

Labor Problem

There is an acute labor problem in the state of Chhattisgarh because the lower sections of the society get heavily susbidised ration from the Government. Therefore, laborers do not work as much and even when they work their efficiency is low. The amount they earn is usually spent in liquor etc. The absenteeism has become an acute problem in vegetable supply chains.

Subsidy Problem

Generally farmers get subsidy from the Government in various agricultural products including hybrid seeds and manure. However, in reality getting a subsidy is a hard struggle for them. Government employees are notorious for asking bribes for passing on these subsidies to farmers. At the end a farmer is left with half or even less than half of the subsidy marked for him.

Germs and Insects Problem

Production of vegetables requires specific care from germs and other insects. Insecticide and pesticides have to be used in right amount and at the right time. If they amount used is more than the vegetables being grown could be contaminated with chemicals or in some cases the plants also die. Under use of insecticide may leave the vegetables infected.

Other Problems

Sometimes the people around create problem for no reasons or out of enmity and envy. The cattle also enter the farm and destroy the production and these have to be specifically taken care of by the farmer.

Demand and Supply Economics

There are daily variations in the prices of the vegetables. It depends upon the quantity of vegetables supply in the mandi. If the quantity is large prices will be low and if quantity is small, prices will be high. Higher prices are charged when a customer wants quick delivery of vegetables as the commissioning agent has to call the farmer for urgent supply to the mandi. Prices also vary due to changes in the price of petrol and other commodities. On seasons and festivals also the prices are high.

Theft

Generally there are less chances of theft in mandi as the mandi is very crowded from 6:00am to 3:00pm and after no one leaves any of his belongings there.

Rotten Stuff

Mostly the rotten stuff is purchased by hostels and small restaurants because they wish to save money in these things. The rotten vegetables which cannot be taken by anyone as left over for cows and other animals.

Summary

This case discusses about vegetable supply chains and the related cost economics. The prices become 3-5 times from the farm to the customer and therefore there are possibilities of grabbing this inefficiency by reducing intermediaries. The study presents the economics of vegetables supply chains to give an indication of margins that can be gained by using other business models. There are tremendous hidden costs involved in these supply chains. Direct sourcing is one of the business models being mulled over by various businessmen to reduce these hidden costs. However, so far these models have not been very successful.

CASE II: DISTRIBUTION SYSTEM OF ELECTRONIC GOODS: MOBILE PHONES

India is among the world's fastest-growing markets for mobile phones (Knowledge @ Wharton, n.d.). Among major players in the mobile handsets market are Nokia, Samsung, Motorola, Sony-Ericsson, Siemens and LG. Among the recent addition to this list are Videocon, Spice and Micromax. Several other China made mobile handsets are also available in the market. The country has some 170 million subscribers and adds 6 million to 7 million more each month (Businses Maps of India, 2010). Recognizing this potential, several global telecom giants jumped into the fray when the Indian government first opened up the country's telecom market to private enterprise in 1994. Finland based Nokia forged ahead of rivals and today commands a 58% market share for mobile phones (also called "handsets"). In specific segments, such as GSM (GSM, which stands for Global System for Mobile, is the world's most popular standard for mobile communications.) telephony.

Market Dynamics of Mobile Phone Industry

Figure 6 shows the market dynamics of mobile phone industry in terms of Porter's five forces model. The threat of new entrants in high because the state of Chhattisgarh is progressing rapidly in the telecom industry and the Government give special privileges to those involved in this industry. The potential of mobile phone

Figure 6. Porter's 5 forces model

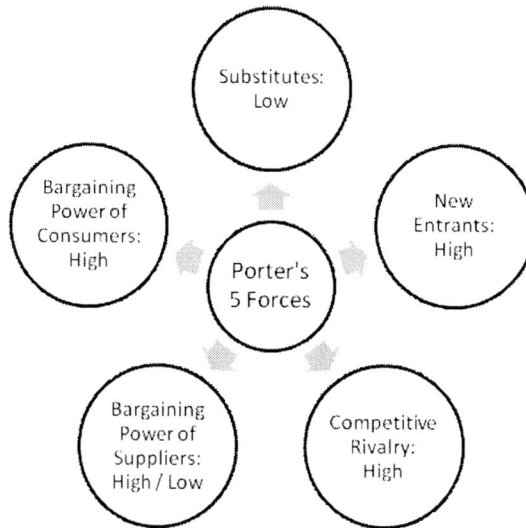

is also very high owing to low penetration in rural areas. The bargaining of customer is also very high because there are a number of competitors with varieties of handsets. There are cheaper versions of Blackberry mobiles which sell at as low as Rs. 5000 and provide a number of facilities available in high-end mobile phones. The competitive rivalry is also very high as the competitors can easily differentiate themselves in terms of technology. For example, Micromax's mobile phones sell at very cheap rate, but provide functionality similar to high end mobiles. The VAT rate is high and therefore customers prefer to purchase mobiles from other states.

The bargaining power of suppliers depends on the size of the supplier. For example, market leader like Nokia, Samsung etc. command high bargaining power as compared to China or India made hand-sets. Big manufactures command the supply chain by fixing targets for their distributors and can provide discount on bulk purchases by micro-distributors. They can also promote SIM card of a particular telecom service provider along with the mobile phone. The threat of substitutes is low because customers still prefer branded mobile phones owing to their superior product quality as well as customer service. Value-added differentiation exists in various brands of mobile phones. For example, local brands offer dual SIM phones which are not usually available in branded mobile phones.

Demand Side of Supply Chain of Mobile Phone

The demand-side supply chain of a mobile phone consists of five main partners, namely the manufacturing company itself, the distributor center (also known as rural superior distributor), the micro distributor, the retailer and the end customer. Figure 7 presents a schematic representation of the demand side of the mobile phone supply chain.

The mobile phone manufacturing company is the major and a powerful entity in the supply chain. Most of the mobile phone manufacturing companies in India are global firms and therefore they control the entire supply chain. The local companies (e.g., Micromax, Spice) and companies from China, however, have lesser control over the supply chain owing to their lower bargaining power.

The mobile phone manufacturing company supplies the manufactured or assembled mobiles to a rural superior distributor which performs the task of a distribution warehouse including sorting, break bulk and packaging, if necessary. A company opens its priority center as well as service center in big cities which provide various models of the company as well as the related services. The transportation charges to a rural superior distributor are borne by the company. There are only a few rural superior distributors in the state (usually located district wise; In Chhattisgarh there

Figure 7. Demand-side supply chain of mobile phones

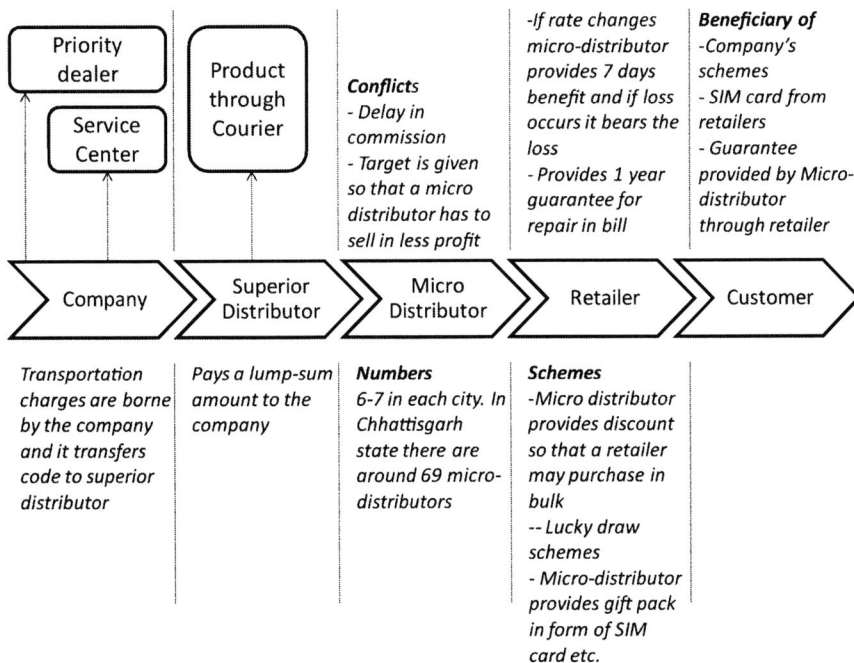

175

are 7 rural superior distributors) which supply to micro-distributors located in big cities. The rural superior distributors receive product through courier services according to the specifications provided by them to the company. They have to make advance payment for receiving the products.

In each city there are around 6-7 micro-distributors who obtain license from a rural superior distributor. The information about each micro-distributor is kept by the company which provides a code to the micro distributor for functioning on behalf of the company. Minimum two persons are required for a micro-distributor to work. The micro-distributor earns mainly on value added services and remits 14% VAT to the rural superior distributors. The VAT rate may differ from state to state. Various incentives are provided by the manufacturer and passed on throughout the supply chain for increased sales of mobile phones. A manufacturer sets a target for their rural superior distributors beyond with specific incentives and bonuses are provided. A manufacturer also provides various lucky draw schemes on various sets. It also provides various schemes (such as quantity discounts on bulk purchases) on a specific targeted purchases conducted by the distributor. It also promotes SIM card of mobile service providers with the handset. However, sometimes conflict arises between manufacturer and distributors because of changes in prices of similar products of competitors which mandates manufacturers to reduce their prices.

The micro-distributors are responsible for distribution of mobile phones throughout the city to the retailers. The retailers generally set a margin of 5-6% before selling to the end customer (Table 2). The distributor also provides various gift packs in the form of trips, tours, SIM cards etc. They also provide bulk discount to the retailers as well as incentives such as lucky draw schemes in which they provide handset, clock, watch etc. Retailer sells the products as per the terms and conditions given by the micro distributor and provides various services to the customers as given by the company as the service centre for the servicing of mobile phones if required. Micro distributor provides various benefits and schemes to the retailer as they have to attain the target given by the company to avail various extra benefits given by the company.

Table 2. Dealer prices and retailer prices

Set no.	D.P	14% VAT	Dealer Price	Retailer
2700	3882	543	4425	4689
5130-c	5084	712	5796	6139
1202 c	1201	168	1369	1451
1203	1201	168	1369	1451
1209	1341	188	1529	1620
7210 c	4578	641	5219	5532

Conflicts in Mobile Supply Chain

Conflicts arise in the supply chain when promises are not kept or there is breach of contract. The attempt to sell directly to the end-customer (such as through online store) cannibalizes the sales of the distributors. The competitive environment also induces conflicts between manufacturers and distributors. For example, when the prices of similar products of competitors fall, the sales of distributors suffer and they are bound to make loss unless specifically compensated by the manufacturers. Similarly, frequent updating of prices also creates conflicts in the supply chain with the manufacturer.

Another reason for conflict is the non-availability of parts for repairing, particularly when the handset is in guarantee period. This puts-off the customer and jeopardizes the sales of the retailer.

Conflicts also arise when manufacturers of distributors do not meet their promises. For examples, sometimes handsets are not produced as per the requirement. Sometimes mobiles are not delivered on due dates and this creates conflicts in the supply chain. When there are delays in payment or in getting commission, there are conflicts between micro distributor and the manufacturer. Inability to complete target also induces conflicts among supply chain members. For example, to complete the target micro distributor and retailers are compelled to sell at lower than normal profit earning rate.

Conflicts also arise is micro-distributors do not have 2 people to manage as it's a rule to have at least 2 people under micro distributor.

New Formats in Mobile Phone Distribution System

With the emergence of mall culture and internet shopping it seems that the inefficiencies of a multi-layered distribution system could be overcome to a great extent. A number of malls carry multiple brands of mobile phone and offer heavy discounts which are difficult for small retailers to provide. These malls procure directly from manufacturing firms or rural superior distributor and thus save on the commission for other partners down the supply chain. The savings are then passed on to the customers.

Another unsuccessful format that has been attempted is that of direct sales through Internet (www.indiatimes.com) or mobile (www.ngpay.com). However, the model is relatively unsuccessful because the delivery time is more and people generally wish to examine the model closely before making purchase decision. Also, the prices offered by these websites are almost that same as that of an online store. Moreover, the penetration of mobile phone is quite high and they are available very easily within close vicinity of customers.

Summary

Demand side Mobile Supply Chains in India consists of multi-tiered distribution system. Multi-tiered system is generally considered to be inefficient because of cost addition at every stage of supply chain. Direct sales model through Internet has not been so successful, although malls offer greater discounts as compared to small shops or company's priority dealers.

CASE III: DISTRIBUTION SYSTEM OF FMCG PRODUCTS: THE CASE OF SOAP INDUSTRY

The soap industry includes companies primarily engaged in making soap, synthetic organic detergents, inorganic alkaline detergents, and crude and refined glycerine from vegetable and animal fats. This study focuses on the distribution system of personal wash soaps (Wikipedia, n.d.).

Overview of the Indian Soap Industry

India is a vast country with a population of 1,030 million people. Household penetration of soaps is 98%.

History of Soap in India

Soap manufacturing was started by North American Companies around 200 years ago. In India the first soap industry was established by North West Soap Company in 1897 at Meerut following the Swadeshi movement.

Cold process soaps are manufactured by mixing all ingredients (soap base, perfume, fillers, actives, etc.) in a large pot and heating them up to 70 degrees while they are stirred manually. Once the mixture is ready, the soap is plodded based on its size with the logo by a machine. In a machine made soap, the mixing process is called milling and this is done by a rotary operated machine.

Soap manufacturers originally targeted their products to the lowest income strata in urban as well as rural areas, positioning their brands as a way to remove dirt and clean the body. For some brands, that positioning persists even today with a focus on removal of body odour and keeping the user healthy. However, soap positioning is moving towards skin care as a value-added benefit

Marketing

Soap is primarily targeted towards women, as they are the chief decision-makers in terms of soap purchase. Medicated positioning like germ killing and anti-bacterial are marketed to families (How Products are Made, 2011). About 75% of soap can be bought through these different types of outlets:

Kirana Store

This is the most common source for buying soap, which usually forms a part of the month's grocery list (which is purchased from these Kirana Stores). Consumers exhibit loyalty to these stores, which is largely dependent on proximity to consumers' homes. Here consumers buy across the counter and do not have an option of browsing through display shelves.

Pan-Beedi Shops

These are really small shops, almost like handcarts, and they are primarily set up to dispense cigarettes and chewing tobacco. However, one would find such a shop at every corner and they are the main sources of soap purchase for the lower socio-economic classes. These kinds of shops exist by the dozen in rural areas.

Department Store

In India, there are very few department stores and the "Indianised" version of department stores is called "Sahakari Bhandars." It is still a fairly new concept. However, department stores have good display counters and this is the only place where consumers get a firsthand experience of shopping and choosing from available options. Here soap prices are also discounted below the retail prices.

Market Dynamics of Soap Industry

Threat of new Entrants

The major raw material required for toilet soap is palm oil which is required to be imported from countries like Malaysia. Palm oil is an expensive ingredient and this gives a low cost advantage to the soap industry of countries like Malaysia, China etc. The new entrants generally cater to small markets for e.g. there are a large number of soap manufacturers catering the local markets of southern states. Most of these players are a part of the large unorganized sector, which directly purchases fatty acids of palm oil from the Indian manufacturers. The capital required for manufacturing process is very high in this sector especially if one needs to manufacture standardized quality soap. Most manufacturers in the organized sector like import the machinery from Italy. Distribution is the key factor in this sector. Companies having a good distribution network are able to cater to a wider market across the country. Sales are volume driven and not value driven. The specialty about this sector is that it has a high level of learning curve that improves with experience and therefore soap manufacturing is quite often called an art rather than a science. The duties applicable to this sector are very high and thus prove to be major barrier for the new entrants.

Competitive Rivalry

In soap industry the competition is high and the competitors differentiate themselves in terms of technology and raw material procurement. Those who have advanced technology they can operate in three shifts. In terms of raw material procurement, companies stock raw material when it is available at a cheaper price. These firms have competitive edge over others when there is a shortage of raw material.

Bargaining Power of Suppliers

The major input for the soap manufacture is vegetable oil (around 80% of the raw materials). Earlier animal Fat was used which was even cheaper, but after the Indian government banned animal fat, one had to shift to vegetable oils. They are not available in India and thus have to be imported from countries like Malaysia, Indonesia and China. There are only few players who export palm oil from these countries and as such these exporters have a commanding position. There are various grades of palm oil available and the manufacturer can switch between these grades to save on the cost of inputs. Companies like Godrej and who previously used to supply soaps to other bigger companies have gone for forward integration and started selling their own brands. Small players cannot afford to import oils as the price of oil keeps on fluctuating. These fluctuations, if on the higher side, cannot be incorporated in the price of the product in this age of cut-throat competition. So they directly purchase fatty acids of oils from large-scale Indian manufacturers who import oil and convert them to fatty acids (Robinson, 1904).

Bargaining Power of Buyers

To a large extent, premium Soap is a price sensitive market. Off late there has been an increasing trend towards down trading. And this has forced the manufacturers to lower the prices or offer temporary discounts to woo the consumers who are either down trading from the popular segment or graduating upwards from carbolic soaps. This sector faces low level of brand loyalty. Switching costs is very low and these results in price war and people are concentrating on value-for-money. This forces players to frequently implement promotional schemes, such as 3-on-1 or 2-on-1. Earlier the decision for purchasing the soaps was equally balanced between man and woman (50:50). Now the decision ratio is 60:40 in the favour of woman purchaser. This proves the fact that today most companies target their soaps towards Indian woman. The buyers, even in the rural area, are subjected to the media invasion and are well informed about the basket of products available in the market and thus take a rational decision.

PEST ANALYSIS

Political Factors

Earlier the soap industry was under the Licence-raj restrictions. But, after liberalization of economy by the Narshima Rao government there has been a spurt in the number of players in the organized as well as the unorganized sector. The political system in India is undergoing major change. There has been competition between various states like Maharashtra, Gujarat, Andhra Pradesh and Madhya Pradesh. The new entrants are given several incentives, like sales tax concessions that encourage them to produce in these states.

Economic Factors

Soaps in India are costly as compared to other countries like Indonesia. For example, a 100 gms of soap in Indonesia cost Rs 4.25, whereas in India it cost Rs 10 approximately. This is primarily attributed to high cost of import duty. India players are lobbying with the government agencies to reduce this duty which can bring down the cost of final product.

Social Factors

The social factor is very important when it comes to premium soaps segment of the soap market. With the rising education and disposable income levels, the need for hygiene and personal / skin care has become important. Premium soaps are thus targeted at the audience to change their habits by raising their aspiration levels.

Technological Factors

The industry though capital intensive is not very technology intensive. Premium soap manufacturing though compared with other soaps manufacturing relies to an extent on technology (especially in the finishing stage). The more important is logistics management where marketing and distribution play a pivotal role. Here technology like (SCM) Supply Chain Management and (E-CRM) Electronic Customer Relationship Management plays a pivotal role. Companies like HLL are working very hard towards such a system to rope up the entire small stores and retailers (Kirana Stores).

Distribution Supply Chain of Soap

The case study is conducted at Chattisgarh Soap Industries, located at Suddu (Raipur) in Chhattisgarh State of India. It has another manufacturing unit at Dehradun (U.P.). The goods from the factories goes directly to the distributors and then to retailer, and from retailer to consumers. The main raw materials (Soap Nodules) are purchased from India (Mumbai) and Malaysia in bulk quantity. This raw material is then processed at the soap factory and mixed with other ingredients for making soap. Once the processing is completed, it is transported to the distributor or wholesaler who then passes it down to the retailers and end customers. In soap industry the distribution system is multilayered and depends on the manufacturer selling policies. Mostly, soap factory owners provide their soaps to distributors on 1 month or 15 days credit.

The Manufacturer

Usually local manufacturers of soap give fancy names to their soap as well as international packaging so that the soap looks like a premium one. These soaps can be easily sold in villages as compared to cities where global brands do not permit local brands to permeate. In village these can be easily sold because of attractive looks and cheaper price. A soap of 100gms costs around Rs. 10. Toilet soaps are not well differentiated by consumers. The market can be divided into four segments, namely, premium, popular, discount and economic. During the soap making soap process following expenses are incurred beginning from the purchase of raw material to the transportation cost all are added and then sales price is decided. The cost structure of soaps is given below. There are three grades of soap, namely, first grade (bathing soap), second grade (hand wash soap) and third grade (clothes washing soap).

182

- First Grade: TFM (Total Fatty Material), 75% pure oil is added along with starch.
- Second Grade: TFM, 40 to 64.99%.
- Third Grade: TFM, 30 to 39.99%.

The quality of soap is linked to total fatty material, which increases the cost of soap. This is because this fatty material is imported which attract high import duty. These costs can be controlled by good procurement system that will minimize the inbound logistics cost soaps (Voice of Words, 2010).

Supply Chain Issues Faced by the Manufacturer

The major supply chain issue faced by the manufacturer is related to the raw material. Raw material is prone to deterioration and theft during supply to the factor. In case of damage the owner can negotiate on prices with the supplier. If the raw material gets deteriorated in quality then it is not useful. The suppliers are prone to sending low quality raw material. However, in case the manufacturer receives low grade raw material, he can adjust that in supplier's bill. Increases in raw material prices also introduce pricing issues. Generally, the contracts are drawn for longer terms. If there is an increase in price after the order has been finalised the supplier and manufacturer enter into a conflict situation. The manufacturer also bears the transportation cost of supplying finished soaps to the distributor. The transportation charges greatly increase the cost of soap. Moreover, if the transportation is within the state, the buyer has to bear VAT and if interstate, buyer has to bear other taxes. In other words the transportation costs are major constituent of cost of soaps. The transportation cost comes to around 1% within Chhattisgarh and to around 3-4% to other states of India.

The Distributor

The distributor receives supplies from the factory and then sells them to retailers in small villages within and outside the state. The distributor gets commission of around 6% from the manufacturer. From time to time the distributor receives incentives (such as watches, calendar, and free samples of soap) from the manufacturer for selling beyond target.

There are 25 distributors in Chhattisgarh. They are allowed a credit of 15 days to 1 month by the seller. They purchase products from the company and in turn deliver them to the further channel members at their own cost. They have to maintain their own sales force as well as all other necessary infrastructure or the manpower necessary for selling the goods smoothly and in time to the customers.

The efficiency of the distributors can be judged by ROI that they achieve. ROI or Return on Investment is the net profit that a distributor saves for itself. In FMCG industry the healthy ROI is said to be anything between 18%-24%. But in most cases the distributors can only maintain a ROI of <15%. It is mainly because of the inefficiency of the distributor in his distribution of Goods from the company to the other members of the distribution channel. A distributor reduces his ROI if he maintains a high credit period and his rotation of the working capital is very less. If the rotation is twice a month then the ROI is said to be 24%. This can be achieved by maintaining a credit period of 10-15 days.

Retailer

The retailer purchases either directly from the manufacturer or from the distributor and sells to the end customer. The retail market of soaps is very large because from a large mall to even a small *kirana* (general goods) store all stock soaps. They cater to residents largely and visitors and passerby's. Their reach and ability to cater to the occasional customers mandate their existence. They generally stock those products which are in demand from the customers and have a good consumer pull. The company replenishes the stocks on a fortnightly/ weekly basis and has little influence over the portfolio maintained by the retailers. These outlets are the largest in number and are key points for the company in terms of reaching the masses. In FMCG products, retailers have a margin of 15-25% and are allowed to sell to the extent of maximum retail price marked on the good.

Economics of Distribution System in FMCG Products

The manufacturer carries a margin of 4% in the manufacturing process that include transportation cost. An approximate cost of soap manufacturing is provided below for production of one batch of soap (Around 120 soaps of 95gms). The total cost of production is shown in Table 3.

Production of a 95 gms soap costs around Rs. 7-8.00 to the manufacturer which he sells to the distributor for Rs. 9.00 and the distributor in turn sells it to the customer for Rs. 10.00. Thus, there are huge margins in soap industry. But because the industry is very competitive, the marketing and sales of soap is very difficult.

CONCLUSION

Soaps manufacturers who have good technology and good quality of raw material are able to perform well in this industry. The focus at soap manufacturer is equal on

Table 3. Production costs

Cost of Ingredients	Amount (Kg)	Cost (Rs/Kg)	Total Amount (Rs)
Noodles	100 Kg	45	4500
Talcum Powder	3 Kg	8	24
Starch	3 Kg	20	60
CBEX Chemicals	100 gms	12500	1250
Fragrance	4 Kg	400	1600
Water	2 Kg	-	-
Salt	2.5 Kg	12	30
Glycerin	2.5 Kg	45	115
Color	1 Kg	30	30
EDTA	2.5 Kg	45	115
Total cost			*7724*
Other costs like processing costs are not included in management cost			
Taxes: 12.5% Packaging costs: 8-12% Management cost: 4% Transportation Cost: 3-4%			
Overall Cost: Rs. 9800 to Rs. 10230			
Selling Price (Rs. 1025 per Carton of 120 soaps of 95 gms each)			

all pest factors as there are interlinked. The soap industry of Chhattisgarh consists of few producers. Price of the soap is affordable by villagers and urbanites alike. Chhattisgarh Soap Industries manage their distribution network in an efficient manner. The factory has some future plans to improve its distribution management. The margins are good but marketing is tough.

CASE IV: DISTRIBUTION SYSTEM OF PHARMACEUTICALS PRODUCTS

Distribution system of pharmaceuticals is one of the very complex distribution systems. Case study of pharmaceutical supply chain is conducted here to understand the chain, identify the conflicts within the chain, cost structure of pharmaceutical supply chain, and the impact of external environment on its supply chain.

Pharmaceutical Industry

India's emerging pharmaceutical industry has appeared as the world leader in the fabrication of standard generic drugs, ever since the Patent Act 1970 permitted India to seriously approach and contributes in the pharmaceutical market worldwide. India is the preferred nation for pharmaceutical generation, with low charges for research and development as well as production of drugs. And the pharmaceutical companies in India have made full use of the favorable environment offered by the country to make it big[1]. In the year 2008, Indian pharmaceutical market was assessed at \$7,743m which witnessed an augmentation of 4.0% over 20071. Pharmaceutical industry displayed increasing growth rates in the years 2005-2009. The Indian pharmaceuticals market generated total revenues of \$10,838.7 million in 2009, representing a compound annual growth rate (CAGR) of 11.3% for the period spanning 2005-2009. However, according to Datamonitor report, Indian pharmaceutical industry will perform decelerating growth over the years up to 2014. Alimentary/metabolism sales proved the most lucrative for the Indian pharmaceuticals market in 2009, generating total revenues of \$1,498.8 million, equivalent to 13.8% of the market's overall value. In comparison, cardiovascular sales generated revenues of \$1,285.5 million in 2009, equating to 11.9% of the market's aggregate revenues. The performance of the market is forecast to decelerate, with an anticipated CAGR of 6.5% for the five-year period 2009-2014, which is expected to drive the market to a value of \$14,867.2 million by the end of 2014. India has also appeared as the preferred location for the pharmaceutical companies of the world because of its towering growth scenario furnished by elderly population, alteration in disease profile, developing patent system and socio-economic circumstances.

Industry analysis reveals that the bargaining power of customer is low because a customer has to depend on drugs available in the market, particularly prescription drugs. For non-prescription drugs there are a number of players in the market and

Table 4. India pharmaceuticals market value (\$ billions, 2005-2009)

Year	\$ billion	INR billion	% Growth
2005	7.1	309.4	
2006	7.7	335.5	8.40%
2007	8.6	374.7	11.70%
2008	9.6	422.3	12.70%
2009	10.8	474.9	12.50%
CAGR, 2005-2009			**11.3%**

Source: Datamonitor

Figure 8. Pharmaceutical firms and their earnings (2007)

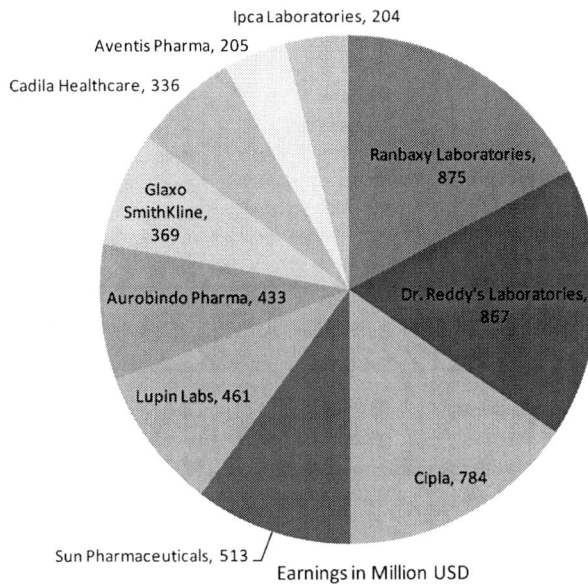

customer can easily switch to other brands. However, in most cases, customers depend upon the prescription of a medical practitioner and the pharmaceutical retailer for purchasing drugs. The organized retail in this sector accounts for a very small percentage and is operating only in big cities. The competition in the Indian pharmaceutical market is cutthroat and the market is divided among the top 10 pharma companies accounting for 36.1% of the overall R&H sales in the fiscal year 2008[1]. The top 10 pharma companies in India and their profits (in million USD) are shown in Figure 8.

Owing to such big players in the market, the bargaining power of suppliers is high because they supply drugs to doctors through medical representatives who influence doctors for prescribing their drugs. They promote various gift items with their medicines as well as provide various schemes if the purchases are made in bulk. The threat of substitutes is low because of heavy investment in research on new drugs with improved potency. The manufacturers tend to promote latest drugs (particularly in prescription drugs) for remaining competitive in the market. Particularly, for cardiac diseases, cancer and other terminal diseases the drugs are extremely costly. However, allopathic drugs face threats from yogic and herbal cures which generally cure very-very difficult to cure diseases also.

Figure 9. Distribution supply chain in a pharmaceutical industry

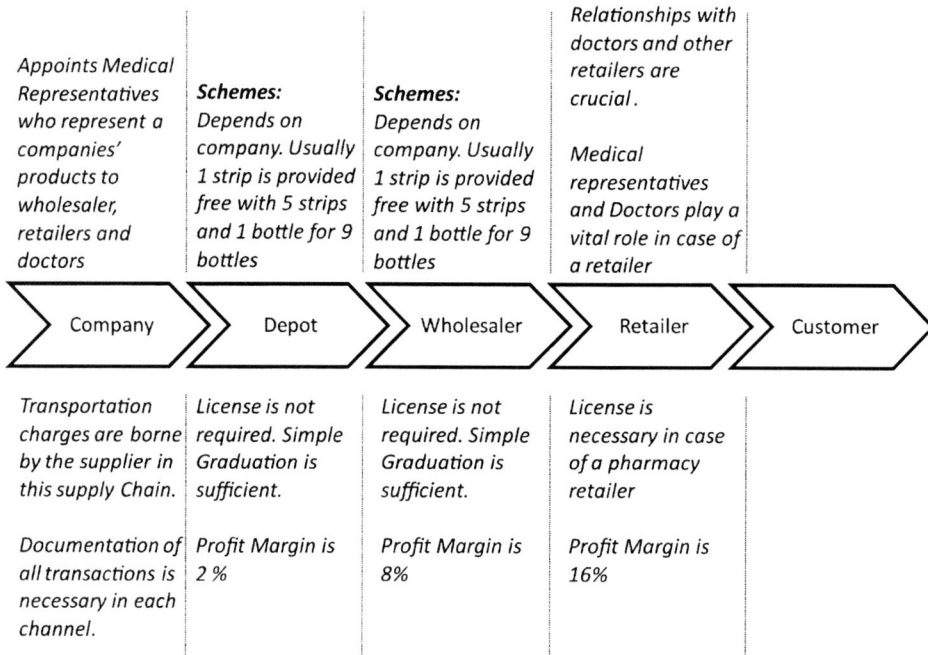

Appuints Medical Representatives who represent a companies' products to wholesaler, retailers and doctors

Schemes: Depends on company. Usually 1 strip is provided free with 5 strips and 1 bottle for 9 bottles

Schemes: Depends on company. Usually 1 strip is provided free with 5 strips and 1 bottle for 9 bottles

Relationships with doctors and other retailers are crucial.

Medical representatives and Doctors play a vital role in case of a retailer

Company → Depot → Wholesaler → Retailer → Customer

Transportation charges are borne by the supplier in this supply Chain.

Documentation of all transactions is necessary in each channel.

License is not required. Simple Graduation is sufficient.

Profit Margin is 2 %

License is not required. Simple Graduation is sufficient.

Profit Margin is 8%

License is necessary in case of a pharmacy retailer

Profit Margin is 16%

Distribution Supply Chain in the Pharmaceutical Industry

Company / Manufacturer

The distribution side of the supply chain in the pharmaceutical industry begins with a manufacturer (Figure 9). It supplies medicine to the depot and bears the cost of transportation. The manufacturer has the responsibility of safe storage and transportation of goods to the Depot, in accordance with legal procedures such that the identity of the product is not lost, the product does not contaminate and does not get contaminated by other products, adequate precautions are taken against spillage, breakage, misappropriation and theft, and appropriate temperature and relative humidity conditions are maintained in the case of pharmaceutical products. In other words, the transportation process should not have a negative effect on the integrity and quality of pharmaceutical products.

The manufacturer has to keep documentation of all the works performed by them as well as all the transactions of medicines performed by them. Each medicine should be distinctively identifiable by its name, active ingredients, type and amount, batch number, expiry date, special storage conditions or handling precautions, directions for use, warnings, and precautions, names and addresses of the manufacturer and/or the supplier. This helps in product recall when there are defects in the product or complaints of serious adverse reactions to the product. The storage and transportation requires utmost precautions. All pharmaceutical products should be stored in containers which do not have an adverse effect on the quality of the products, and which offer adequate protection from external influences, including microbial contamination. Moreover, pharmaceutical products should only be sold and/or distributed to persons or entities that are entitled to acquire such products in terms of applicable national, regional and international legislation. Written proof of such authority must be obtained prior to the dispatch of products to such person or entities. Rejected products and those returned to a distributor should be appropriately identified and quarantined till an appropriate decision has been.

Manufacturing companies also appoint their medical representatives who promote their new products in the market as well as selling of the product to the wholesaler and retailer. A medical representative takes the order from the supply chain partner and sends it to the previous supply chain partner.

Depot

Generally manufacturing firms set up their own Depots which functions like a distribution warehouse. These depots provide medicines to the wholesaler in bulk. No specific degree is required for a Depot holder and graduation is enough. Earlier the taxes were not included in the MRP of the medicine and they were charged according the prevailing tax laws of the state. In Chhattisgarh 4% VAT is paid on most of the items. However, these days taxes are included in MRP and are being paid by the company itself thus reducing the burden over Depot holder. Depot does not suffer the loss of any expired medicine. The expired medicines can be returned to the company and the relevant records of the returned, rejected or destroyed pharmaceutical products need to be maintained. In case there are counterfeit products, they must be segregated immediately from other pharmaceutical products and recorded. The storage area should of sufficient capacity to allow the orderly storage of the various categories products, namely bulk and finished products, products in quarantine, and released, rejected, returned or recalled products

Wholesaler

The wholesaler purchases goods from depot in bulk and then sells it to various retailers in its zone of distribution. They can simultaneously deal with more than one company. The transportation costs to the wholesaler are borne by the Depot and the wholesaler just needs to ensure that the medicine is being delivered to the required place by the depot holder. The operational details for a wholesaler are almost the same as that of a Depot holder. The wholesaler could be any graduate without holding any specific degree. He has to maintain all the records as per legislation of the received and delivered goods, goods returned, expired or rejected. The wholesaler benefits usually by bulk transactions with low commission and other benefits. For example, a wholesaler usually gets 1 bottle free for every 5 bottles purchased from the company and 1 strip for every nice strips of medicine purchased from the company. However, it is beneficiary only when the retailer does not purchase the same quantity. Otherwise, he is liable to pass on this benefit to the retailer. The wholesaler must review all complaints and other information concerning potentially defective and counterfeit pharmaceutical products according to written procedures that describe the action to be taken, including the need to consider a recall when appropriate. Any counterfeit or suspected counterfeit medicines found in the pharmaceutical supply chain should be segregated immediately from other pharmaceutical products and recorded. The medicine storage areas should be of sufficient capacity to allow the orderly storage of the various categories products, namely bulk and finished products, products in quarantine, and released, rejected, returned or recalled products.

Retailer

The retailer receives medicine from the wholesaler and sells it to the customer. The transportation costs are borne by the wholesaler. A retailer simply needs to ensure that the medicine is being delivered according to the order. Other requirements of storage, dealing with returns and counterfeit products, taxes, expired medicines etc. are the same as in the case of a wholesaler or Depot holder. However, a retailer must hold graduate or diploma in pharmacy and must hold a license to operate the pharmacy because it comes in direct touch with the customer. The retailers also get benefitted by various schemes floated by the company. Usually a retailer receives a free bottle on every purchase of 5 bottles and 1 strip of medicine for every 9 strips of medicine. The retailer is responsible for maintaining all instructions and records which document all activities relating to the distribution of pharmaceutical products, including all applicable receipts and issues. The name of the applicable entity should appear on all relevant documents. Documents, in particular instructions and procedures relating to any activity that could have an impact on the quality of pharmaceutical products, should be designed, completed, reviewed and distributed with care. Also, all complaints and other information concerning potentially defective and potentially counterfeit pharmaceutical products should be reviewed carefully according to written procedures describing the action to be taken, including the need to consider a recall where appropriate. If there are any counterfeit medicines they must be quarantined for further action.

Table 5. Profit margins of the supply chain

Channel	Price	Profit margin
Manufacturer	102	2% margin
Depot	106.08	4% margin
Whole seller	114.487	8% margin
Retailer	132.807	16% margin
Maximum retail price	132.807	

Economics of Pharmaceutical Supply Chains

The profit margins in this supply chain are healthy although tight. Retailer receives a margin of 16% on the MRP. A wholesaler gets a margin of 24% out of which it keeps 8% and passes on the rest to the retailer. A Depot holder receives a margin of 28% out of which it keeps 4% for itself and passes on the rest to the wholesaler. An example is shown in Table 5.

For example suppose the manufacturing cost of medicine is ` 100 then:

Issues in a Pharmaceutical Supply Chain

Various issues arise in a pharmaceutical supply chain as it essentially deals with public health. If a retailer sells expired or wrong medicine to a customer, the customer can sue the retailer. Similarly, there are some medicines (such as purgatives and laxatives) that are allowed only to be sold under the prescription of a doctor. Sometimes some medicines like Alprex require that the retailer keeps a photocopy of doctor's prescription.

The doctors play an important role in the acceptance and prescription of the medicines. Mostly, the retailers enter into an agreement with a nearby doctor whereby doctors are asked to prescribe only those medicines that are available with the retailer and those which carry higher margins for the retailer. Doctors grab a portion of the profits earned by the retailers as well as receive non-monetary benefits from them. However, from a social perspective this is not an ethical practice.

There are losses due to theft which results in difficulty in matching the stock on a daily basis.

The maintenance of relationships in this industry is crucial so that these relationships come handy during periods of emergency.

Summary

Since the profit margin is high in each element of the distribution channel, it is possible to pass on the profits to the customers through suitably designed distribution system. However, difficulty may arise because of maintenance of legal documents which may preclude removal of layers in the distribution system. Medicine is a necessity which cannot be avoid or substituted. Government policies control the effective distribution of medicines and it is in the interest of the public. However, the problem arises when Doctors consider their personal interest in prescribing medicines to patients according to the prescriptions of a retailer. The report reveals that the profit margin which is being offered by various companies is quite good because of number of competitors in the market (Knowledge @ Wharton, n.d.).

OVERALL CONCLUSION

The various cases discussed above present the multi-layered distribution system as is practiced by firms in India. The general multi-layered distribution system consists of the manufacturer, distributor, wholesaler and retailer. Generally the margins for wholesalers are fixed and they earn on quantity sales although with lower margin. The margins for retailers are high and they earn on total sales. In case of perishable products there is a huge increase in cost from the producer to the end customer because of the perishable nature of products. However, in case of mobile phones the margins are more or less fixed for wholesaler and retailer as the industry is heavily competitive and customer switching is very easy (Businses Maps of India, 2010).

Attempts have been made to improve margins through removing intermediaries by direct sourcing from the manufacturer and selling to customer (in case of large malls), direct selling through one's online channel (sabzeewala.com). However, the Indian conditions demand the presence of multi-layered system because direct sales require that customers have access to the manufacturer through online channel or phone. In India people are still averse to purchasing online, particularly when the purchase is related to high involvement products (such as mobiles, cars etc.). Moreover, most of the population is not used to online purchase and neither has access to online store. Another reason is that the stores are located a few yards away and a customer can get most of his daily needs fulfilled easily. The purchasing is a means of spending time and refreshing the mind from the boredom of daily work. Also, direct sales require that the manufacture locate itself near its customers, a difficult proposition. A kirana shop is however, located in near vicinity with deep penetration throughout India. These stores also extend credit to their customers, which a big mall would not do. In other words, to improve margins a different approach to multi-layered system is required rather than attempting to remove intermediaries.

The market structure of India also makes the implementation of direct sales method difficult. There are millions of customers with various background and therefore to satisfy everyone is almost impossible. Therefore, wholesalers are required to break bulk and sell to multiple retailers who cater to a large number of consumers.

ACKNOWLEDGMENT

This research is funded and supported by AICTE research grant RID/PRES-(G-7)/2007-08/RPS-263.

REFERENCES

Business Maps of India. (2010). Pharmaceutical companies in India. Retrieved November 11, 2011, from http://business.mapsofindia.com/india-company/pharmaceutical.html

Fordham University. (n.d.). *Royal licenses to export and import, 1205-1206*. Retrieved from http://www.fordham.edu/halsall/source/carol-devillis.html

How Products are Made. (2011). *The manufacturing process of soap*. Retrieved October 13, 2011, from http://www.madehow.com/Volume-2/Soap.html#ixzz3qH1Q5YLh

Knowledge @ Wharton. (n.d.). *Home page*. Retrieved November 12, 2011, from http://knowledge.wharton.upenn.edu

Robinson, J. H. (1904). *Readings in European history* (*Vol. I*). Ginn and Co.

Voices of Words. (2010). Blog. Retrieved November 15, 2011, from http://ahssan.wordpress.com

Wikipedia. (n.d.). *Soap*. Retrieved November 12, 2010, from http://en.wikipedia.org/wiki/Soap

ENDNOTES

[1]   http://business.mapsofindia.com/india-company/pharmaceutical.html

This work was previously published in Cases on Supply Chain and Distribution Management: Issues and Principles, edited by Miti Garg & Sumeet Gupta, pp. 116-146, copyright 2012 by Business Science Reference (an imprint of IGI Global).

Chapter 10
Implementing Business Intelligence in the Dynamic Beverages Sales and Distribution Environment

Sami Akabawi
American University in Cairo (AUC), Egypt

Heba Hodeeb
American University in Cairo (AUC), Egypt

EXECUTIVE SUMMARY

To compete successfully in today's retail business arena, senior management are often demanding fast and responsive Information Systems that enable the company not only to manage its operations but to provide on-the-fly performance measurement through a variety of tools. Use of (ERP) systems have been slow in responding to these needs, despite the wealth of the internally generated business databases and reports as a consequence of functional integration. The specific nature and demands by those senior management staff require the congregation of many external data elements and use data mining techniques to provide fast discovery of performance slippages or changes in the business environment.

DOI: 10.4018/978-1-4666-2618-8.ch010

Data Warehousing and Business Intelligence (BI) applications, evolved during the past few decades, have been implemented to respond to these needs. In this case write-up, we present how the ERP system was utilized as the backbone for use by BI tools and systems to provide Sales and Marketing units in a transnational company subsidiary in Egypt to actively respond to the demands for agile information services. The Egypt subsidiary is the HQ of the African region's operations of several franchises and distributers of the company products, in addition to operating a beverage concentrate manufacturing plant in Egypt, which services the entire region's beverage products needs.

BACKGROUND

Company Overview

The case firm considered in this chapter is a transnational company subsidiary in Egypt, which is located in the Free Zone in Nasr City district, in the country's capital, Cairo. The company owns and operates a beverage concentrate plant within the domain of its facility for producing the concentrate syrup used in all its beverage products. These concentrates are then delivered to many bottling operators in African countries for the production of the final product mixing, bottling, packaging and trade fleet distribution in their respective territories. The concentrate plant is among the few plants of the transnational company world-wide, where the technical know-how formula of the company is produced, and the plant caters for the supply of concentrate syrup for the entire African, Middle East and Asian bottling territories.

The company is divided into a number of business units (BU). Egypt's subsidiary assumes the function of the head office to the African business unit which constitutes more than 25 franchises and distributers in many African countries. In this case-paper, we consider the analysis and evaluation of the information systems categories used in the head office of the company's subsidiary in Egypt for the Sales and Distribution management in the region. In particular, we detail how the backbone Enterprise Resources Planning (ERP) and business intelligence systems (BI) are integrated and used to leverage the need for agile management of the operations in the Sales and Distribution functions within the highly dynamic competitive beverage market.

Brief Economic Outlook of the Country
Where the Case Company Operates

Forecasts put Egypt's food and drink exports growing by 59.4 percent between 2007 and 2012, which is not only a reflection of the free trade agreements ratified by the government of Egypt since late 90's, but also the country's improving food and drink processing industry. Regional trade agreements such as the Greater Arab Free Trade Area (GAFTA) have also given producers access to a far larger market. Having gone into effect in 2005, GAFTA has gradually lowered customs on locally produced food across a broad range of Middle Eastern countries. These agreements opened larger markets for Egyptian producers, given the similarity of diets and lack of language barrier. Meanwhile, Africa is also becoming another key export market, mainly for its proximity and lack of domestic production capacities in the African countries.

Sharply rising food prices have been the cause of growing unrest in Egypt over the past two years.

Though the Egyptian government has taken a number of measures to deal with the mounting public discontent, inflation hit the 20 percent mark and food prices skyrocketed, and a dire situation has evolved in the country.

Egypt is a rather unique market for the region as it benefits from a very large population (over 80mn) and an unsaturated food and drink market. However, the food and drink trade balance is highly dependent on imports. In addition, inflation, in a country with national poverty rate of 22.9 percent according to the World Bank Development Data Group, (2002) and Earth Trend Country profile estimating 20 percent of the population below the poverty line, led to increased levels of political risk and unrest. Against a backdrop of worsening global financial market turmoil and rapidly accelerating inflation, particularly in emerging markets, Egypt has significantly more economic hardship clouds on the horizon. Nonetheless, Egypt receives a pretty high score in the region for its food and drink market due to its per capita food consumption growth. Egypt does not fare well for the country structure indicator, with low GDP per capita, although the size of its population and lack of market maturity help pull up its score.

SETTING THE STAGE

Companies in the beverage industry often operate as producers and distributors of canned and bottled soft drinks, concentrate and other juices and liquid beverage products. They experience rapid changes in the way they have to do business. For one thing, increased commoditization and diversification of beverage products has made it more difficult than ever for beverage manufacturers to differentiate their products and their brands against rivals and competing brands.

In addition, beverage consumers are demanding greater product variety, higher levels of service and more value for their money (Bingham, 1999). The increased global competition, escalating retailer demands and increasingly stringent government regulations have added to the pressure on those companies, making it harder for them to compete globally. With growing concerns with food safety issues, these companies are also finding it necessary to monitor and track every phase of operation – from raw ingredients through finished product, to packaging, storage and distribution – to ensure compliance with the higher safety standards.

Driven by these challenges, beverage producing and distribution companies are looking more and more to their manufacturing processes and supply chain in an effort to increase production efficiency, reduce operational costs and effect better overall management of the enterprise and its assets to sustain desired levels of profitability and growth.

Business Imperatives

Historically, there has been resistance to the introduction of technology in the beverage industry except perhaps to automate certain production processes (e.g. mixing, canning, bottling and packaging). In many large companies, use of information technology (IT) has been limited to off-the-shelf or custom-tailored systems implemented to assist employees with such discrete business processes as accounting, corporate finance, human resources and purchasing. However, in the past few decades, many firms have implemented Electronic Data Interchange (EDI) and host of functional separate systems, often in response to customer and vendors demands or management directives for adopting business-to-customer (B2C) and business-to-business (B2B) e-business functionalities. Despite all of the information flowing through these disparate systems across the enterprise, the information services to operational and top management more often than not lacked integration, timeliness and comprehensiveness.

The lack of timely financial information, integrated with order and production flow would hamper the ability of firms to know where they stand from day to day, both from financial and operations point of views. In most companies, by the time financial information becomes available in a report, it's historical and too late to change course to correct problems. In today's fast-paced global economy and rapidly changing marketplace, the lack of integrated, real-time information to provide business and market analysis, business intelligence and decision support tools negatively impact profitability, growth and ability to act quickly to external marketing forces. Moreover, efficient order entry, materials and inventory control and fast turnover dictate the need for agile and responsive information systems to minimize waste and delivering efficient customer service. In market-driven industries, once the product is made, time is not nearly so critical – but storage, transportation and distribution are.

On the beverage industry side, we see an astonishing level of diversification fragmenting this industry. Where once there were a finite number of carbonated and non-carbonated soft drinks occupying the competitive landscape, today there is an almost infinite explosion of choices – from pure juice and juice blends, to sodas of every kind, waters, and host of beverages. Sales in this area are market-driven, so producers tend to rely on special packaging, competitive pricing, event-driven promotions and other attention-getting techniques to differentiate themselves. For these firms, forecasting and timing of product-to-market are crucial. Market-driven companies thus need to be able to put a product out on the shelves, see how it sells, then turn to adjust production to match demand.

The preceding characteristics illustrate that each segment of the beverage industry has its own challenges to overcome whether it competes in local, national, regional or global markets. However, to retain customer loyalty and grow market share, all beverage manufacturers and distributors need greater flexibility to respond quickly – whether to changing customer expectations, government regulations, or fluctuations in the marketplace resulting from seasonal changes in drinking patterns. In short, beverage producer and distributer companies are finding they have to increase the speed or decrease the lag time between when their products are made and when they are out on the market. To coordinate their production capabilities, manufacturers also need to increase their ability to handle different materials and product lines simultaneously. If they are to improve procurement and inventory control, they must find a way to accurately track both raw materials and finished goods. And, to build their company and product brands among customers and consumers, they must be able to ensure consistency of quality across product lines.

On the business end, optimizing plant operations can be a tremendous source of savings. Companies attaining high visibility and close control of key production elements opt to simplify complexity and better manage cash flows. They need to be able to forecast more closely to customer demands – avoiding either overextending or under-producing – to improve their return on corporate assets. The use of enterprise resources planning (ERP) systems becomes the natural choice for fulfilling such needs (Davenport, 1998). ERP systems operate on enterprise-wide domain to ensure integration among all business functions and result in one large single view of the company's data resources. If those systems are well matched to the business and well implemented, many benefits can be accrued such as: decreased reaction times, better logistics flow, increased responsiveness to market and customer changes and improved supply chain management (SCM).

Information Systems Backbone Implementation in the Case Firm

By early 2000, the case company presented in this chapter planned to acquire an ERP system to replace its aging legacy systems. The company looked for a proven technology platform for its business applications with strong functionalities in areas such as financial applications, procurement, order entry and fulfillment, planning and scheduling, inventory management and optimization, product configuration, flexible product costing, manufacturing, EDI capabilities, and support of multiple plants and/or warehouses and complex distribution system. To that end, a blanket, multilayer deal with highly reputed ERP vendor was selected and configured to run several business application modules to cut costs and share data through multiple distributed systems located in multiple regional datacenters, with secured global access. These applications are built around ERP, customer relationship management (CRM) and SCM modules as well as set of integration middleware tools. The system aimed at helping improve the logistics of store deliveries, sales orders and the back office operations of the networked company's manufacturers, bottlers and distributors around the globe. This distributed approach targeted the improvement of market execution, better service to consumers, in addition to giving a more integrated system platform to serve the information needs at the store level and account level, and more effective management of the business on the street. The implemented distributed ERP systems provided the following application and service tiers:

1. The back office tier which included several modules. The African region implementation provided the following modules:
    a. Marketing Expenses Management
    b. Business Travel Management (BTM)
    c. Human Resources (HR)
    d. Financials and Sales
    e. Logistics
    f. Supply chain and Manufacturing
2. Data warehouse and decision support tier which included the following modules to serve the African business unit:
    a. Value chain modeling, the module manages everything that adds value to a product. Starting from raw material used to produce the product such as sugar, water, vitamins and caramel, to the time employees spend on various functions and the salaries of employees, to the trucks used to distribute the product and the gasoline needed for the trucks. It uses all those individual costs to know how much the product should sell.
    b. Forecasting module, the sales business intelligence module is responsible for everything related to sales. It manipulates three types of data: historical data, which include the actual weekly sales; the business plan data, which constitutes the forecasting for the sales of the year; finally, the rolling estimate data, which is a more accurate prediction of the sales based on the discrepancy between the actual sales and the business plan.

c. Decision support System, this module helps sales function managers in making decisions based on sales by providing the following services:

- Sales flash report issued on specific day of the week. Sales reports of the week are sent to employees on company-provided blackberries. The weekly sales updates are given versus business plan predictions or versus prior years. In addition, sales is always directly related and translated into market share. The company used push strategy to alert the employee that he/she has received an email.

- Telecom reporting is used to control the escalating costs of telecommunications within the African business unit. Managers get periodic data from mobile service operators to determine how much their units pay for mobile services. This particular application used the EDI facility provided by the system through the middleware layer.

- Margin minder report is used to track sales in every outlet, and provides small outlets with data on how to make more profit. For example if a small café is buying more of a certain Stock Keeping Unit (SKU) but the reports show that the café is not selling much of it, the system then recommends that the outlet buys less of this SKU and buys another one that seems to be selling good at the particular café. In addition, it does the 'Right Execution Daily' (RED) that manages the product display and the picture of success (pos), i.e., to make sure that company logo is put at the entrance of sites, that the temperature of the product is set at the prescribed temperature, that the company refrigerators given to sites have their products only.

d. Business Intelligence (BI) tools which perform activities such as collecting and transforming data from a variety of systems, consolidates and aggregate these data in readiness for reporting to assist in decision making. A visual reporting component was missing from this battery of tools for presentation of knowledge to assist with decision. At this stage of implementation, as such, this tier did not incorporate dashboard to provide visual summary of the operations key performance indicators (KPIs). This particular shortage is the subject of the additional development addressed in this chapter.

Additionally, there are some applications used in the African region Egypt HQ that the IT manager referred to as 'ko' which literally means 'knock-out', but what it actually meant is that it is site-specific, internally developed by the company, for the network of sites in the African business unit

A middleware tier was deployed by the company to achieve integration among these disparate enterprise applications through using several reporting and communications layer comprising:

- Mail: the mail system used by the company is 'lotus notes' platform. This platform provides a collaborative work environment as well as email service.
- Microsoft office: the end-user productivity tool for the client side hardware (PCs, laptops, PDAs, etc.)
- Share point portal service: used as the gateway/ portal through which authorized employees can gain access to the various service provided by the host of applications in site or globally.

The architecture of the technology service layers after the implementation of the ERP system in the datacenter accessed by Egypt subsidiary HQ is shown in Figure 1. Some of the modules were implemented in a "vanilla" standard mode while others were customized to adapt to the beverage industry-specific operations. The company gets, through a blanket contract, upgraded versions of the modules on a periodic basis (for the standard application modules only).

The network and communications infrastructure provided connectivity to the corporate datacenter for all sites in the African BU. Business transactions are entered on real-time basis into the respective ERP module. Each site must thus secure the health status of its internet/private connectivity and monitor its operational effectiveness and availability of its links.

Figure 1. Architecture of the IS layers used in the company before the new BI dashboard implementation

The Sales Reporting System Prior Implementing the New Dashboard Facility

For each regional site, the specific reporting and operational needs (which included manufacturing supply chain, sales force management, marketing, inbound and outbound logistics), are accessible remotely from the regional datacenter of the company in Africa. Several functionalities were considered for the management of the African BU in Egypt's HQ site, which is concerned, among other business functions, with the consolidated sales within its domain. The process with which this objective was initially achieved is described in Figure 2. In this process, sales data exchanged between the franchises/bottlers and the HQ constituted:

- Actual sales figures: These are the actual sales volume reported by the bottlers. Actual sales were communicated on a daily basis through e-mails, via Excel templates, sent to every franchise analyst.
- Rolling estimates (RE) figures which reflect the adjusted sales on a monthly basis to adjust targets during the course of a year, thus reflecting changes in the market and used to predict sales volume for the balance of year. These figures are confirmed after communication between the franchise managers, the business planning manager and the HQ office. Once confirmed, the business

Figure 2. Sales reporting process before implementation of the IDB system

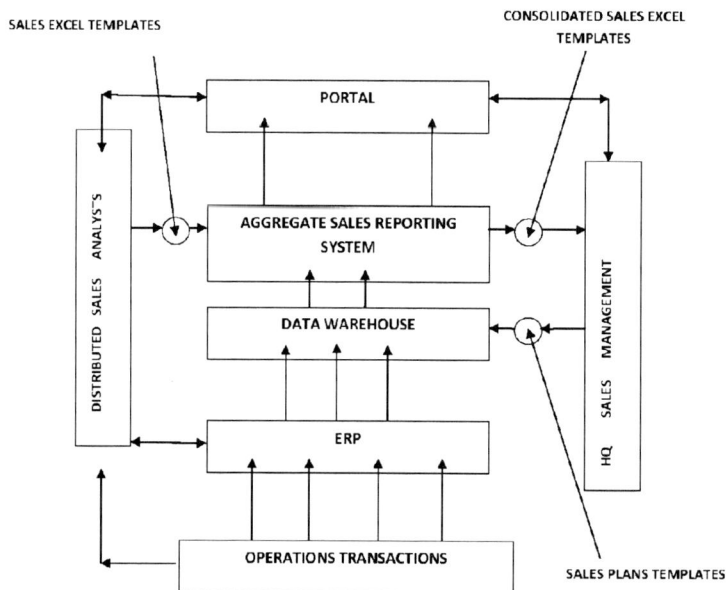

planning manager sends the final confirmed version of the file which contains the actual sales so far and the balance of year figures on a monthly basis for all sites in the domain countries

- Business Plan (BP) figures are set by the BU management at the beginning of the year. They do not change during the course of the year. The BP dictates target sales per brand per pack per month.

Sales Excel sheets Templates which are formatted by the sales analyst of each franchise/bottler liberally, are used by the company for sales reporting. These templates constitute the following reports:

1. Daily Reports

Bottlers of each country send daily sales reports that include the daily actual sales volume in both physical and unit case volumes to the franchise sales analyst. If they send it in physical cases, the franchise analyst converts it into unit cases using the unit case conversion factors. The reports include sales by brand and pack for every day of the week. The drawback of this reporting scheme is that there is no fixed template format for the daily reports sent by bottlers, who communicate the daily sales volume to the HQ.

2. Weekly Reports

The franchise Sales Analyst prepares and sends weekly reports after consolidating the daily sales sent by the bottlers to get total weekly figures. The reports also display the rolling estimates split weekly in addition to the weekly budget split and prior year weekly split. The Business Planning managers use the data communicated through those reports and consolidates data of all franchises to send consolidated weekly reports to HQ.

3. Monthly Reports

Every franchise analyst is requested to submit monthly reports as per deadlines dictated by a quarterly reporting calendar communicated by sales analyst. Those monthly reports include the following:

- Best estimate for current month, draft of upcoming month RE and upcoming month weekly split. This data is usually communicated before the current month is closed.

- RE volume by brand and pack. This report is submitted after the month is closed, it communicates the 'Actuals' of the closed month in addition to the RE figures of the balance of the year data. All 'Actuals' and RE figures are provided with a brand/pack split.

The HQ Sales Analyst then consolidates monthly brand/pack data sent from all franchisees to prepare brand/pack monthly RE updates.

As noted from this process, there are many countries involved in the reporting cycle of the sales results and many reports are communicated back and forth, using email and non-standardized Excel sheet templates between the country sales analysts and their corresponding managers in the HQ site. Many errors and inefficiencies continuously existed due to the use of those sales templates. The oft problems encountered included the following:

- Data inconsistencies due to inconsistency in product coding and Excel template variations led to lateness in reporting;
- Miscommunication due to network problems, variable semantics and other inconsistencies resulted in many duplicate data items (same data repeated in several reports);
- Consolidating non-uniform templates data and variable-semantics led to waste of time and efforts;
- Lack of analysis due to meager analytical competence of sales analysts;
- Lack of standardization led to too many data but no information;
- Redundant processes resulted in data chaos (too many templates causing confusion).

To that end, the focus of this case write up is to determine how the company utilized a new business intelligence dashboard tool, to provide the Sales and Marketing units with the necessary agile and fast decision making platform and to respond to the dynamic market and consumer changes over a wide geographic area; at the same time overcome the critical impediments illustrated in the process described earlier and schematically diagramed in Figure 2.

Literature Review

During the past two decades, many organizations adopted the ERP as their preferred backbone information system for data and information management, since then world ERP market poised to command a little under $65 billion by the end of 2009, according to AMR Research Market Analytix Report (2005). The use of ERP systems by those organizations targeting cost reduction, increase productivity, improve customer satisfaction and suppliers relations in the drive to improve competitiveness in the global networked market space (Davenport, 1998). The cost expended for the acquisition and implementation of ERPs exceed millions of dollars and affect the overall firms' earnings and revenues (Davenport, 1998) and their market values, (Chatterjee et al. 2002). With such huge capital investments, many firms are forced to assess carefully their return of investment (ROI) of such an infrastructure.

The impact of adopting ERP normally goes beyond the immediate control of the business resources, it sets the grounds for organizational changes and the way business processes are performed, (Kallinikos, 2004). As noted by Brazel and Dang (2008), the implementation and use of ERP systems represent a radical change from the operation of legacy systems. Many researchers have therefore studied ERP use and adoption from various perspectives. As a category of information system, several authors approached research on ERP from the perspective of information systems success model (DeLone and McLean, 1992, 2003; Gable, et al. 2001 and 2003; Seddon, 1997; Sedera, et al. 2004; Ifinedo, et al. 2006a and 2007; Robey, et al, 1999).

ERP implementation is a challenging endeavor for many organizations, spanning many functional areas (Yen, et al. 2002), demanding high level of coordination among all stakeholders and adjusting to changes and synergy in the procedural workflow by every business function. Use of such systems implies changes in the workflow of business processes (Kallinikos, 2004). To that end, success of the implementation projects and the critical factors influencing this success was studied by many researchers to investigate ERP implementation success factors, (Bancroft et al, 1996; O'Leary, 2002; Ptak, et al, 2000). Other studies aimed at identifying the critical factors impacting implementing ERP projects (Fryling, 2005). Factors such as those influencing successful implementation, from the operational (rather than technical) point of view were addressed by many researchers, for example, the business operations coverage of the package and the number of licensed users (Francalanci, 2001; Kumar, et al. 2001; Markus, et al. 1988; Parr and Schanks, 2000).

The impact of system configuration and/or setup revisions and enhancements was also studied by Fryling (2005), Nicolaou, et al. (2004 and 2007), Light (2001), Mensching, et al. (2004) and Nah, et al. (2001); impacts of organizational and national cultures (Krumbholtz et al. 2000; Soh, et al. 2000); the configuration and setup of the package's parameters tables and their overall impact on the architecture and flexibility of the ERP packages for rapid adaptation (Fan et al. 2000; Spott, 2000). Some articles also addressed the impact of ERP process standardization and the restructuring of organization tasks or business processes reengineering (Kumar and Van Hillgersberg, 2000). The ability of the system to provide quality and trusted information for operational and executive management decision making has been identified by many researchers (Xu, 2003; Madapusi, et al. 2007).

ERP integrates all functional areas of the organization, acting as the backbone of the information management platform of the organization (Chou, 2005). With its integrated database, ERP systems integrate other functional business components such as Customer Relationship Management (CRM) and SCM systems data resources to support informational needs for decision making. Since ERP system is internally looking, the need to accommodate access to data across the organization boundary is required for decision making at the strategic and organization-wide levels. It is not that ERP systems don't have wealth of information, they do; the challenges lie in the ways of mining them. ERP cannot facilitate real-time decision support function for several operational reasons. Since information is the foundation of every critical business decisions, Decision Support Systems (DSS) are vital for any organization (Drucker, 1998). Report writers can access data from multiple ERP modules and consolidate them with other data elements for decision support. Business Intelligence (BI) is about getting the right information, to the right decision makers, at the right time (Alter, 1980). It is an enterprise-wide platform that supports multi-dimensionality reporting, analytics and decision modeling leading to fact-based decision making and enabling to get a "single version of the truth" (Rasmussen et al., 2001). The common pain points that BI is used to solve are typical examples of what most organizations experience:

- Data everywhere, information no where
- Different users have different needs
- Excel versus PDF
- Pull versus push
- On demand – on schedule
- Your format – my format
- Takes too long – wasted resources/efforts
- Security
- Technical "mumbo jumbo" … Why I just can't get it to you when you want it.

By integrating business intelligence (BI) tools and ERP modules, data flows directly from the ERP database on real-time basis. However, some reliability, availability and scale efficiency may arise as a consequence – particularly due to the excessive access load that may hinder transactional operations. Separating the active ERP database from that of the BI resulted in embracing a second data storage tier, a data warehouse (McDonald et al., 2002). The ERP-BI, On-line Analytics Processing (OLAP) and DSS tools integration framework is based on congregating all needed data from the ERP system and other external data resources, load them into a Data Warehouse or a data Mart, then link to several BI tools, such as OLAP, data mining, analytics tool and reporting systems to create more consistent and knowledge-centric data reporting. BI tools provide such functionalities. More and more organizations extend their ERP beyond the level of back-office to improve sales, customer satisfaction, and decision making (Stedman, 2002).

Integration of the BI and ERP system contributes additional values to businesses (Chou, 2005). According to Holsapple and Whinston (1996), characterization of common DSS features, BI generates different views for available data systems, a scaled data mart or data warehouse providing rich, timely and well structured and cleansed information to the BI. Bolt-on BI systems are also used to view financial, marketing and sales queries by using different tools (CRM2day.com, 2004). Customer Experience Management (CEM) in retailing has also been researched within the framework of BI by score of researchers such as Ding, et al. (2006) and Kamaladevi, B. (2010). Issues of integration of SCM with customer experience management were dealt with by Chou (2005). Approaches to building and implementing BI systems were investigated by Celena Olszak, et al. (2007) being an important decision to many implementing organizations.

CASE DESCRIPTION

Technology Concerns and Needs

Within the context of the studied case, a new Sales Reporting process was developed to address the inefficiencies and pitfalls of the template based sales reporting system described earlier. Egypt's HQ IT department together with the Sales unit, embarked on the development of a new BI tool which was code-named the IDB (information dashboard). The new IDB tool was designed to provide enhanced method for uploading sales data, address the inconsistencies of the country sales figures and the cumbersome method of obtaining the consolidated reports at the HQ. Analysts were trained to upload data on the new IDB platform using a newly developed product coding system. They get the codes from commonly accessible codes database. The coding system is based on a code consisting of 10 digits. The first four digits represent the brand type and flavor. The last four digits represent the package size and type. The two digits in the middle represent the type of syrup whether liquid for normal packages or powder supplied to machines. This level of breakdown for any product provided an easy and efficient facility for tracking Stock Keeping Unit level since it embedded all the necessary information regarding the product whether in terms of brand type, flavor, package size, type, format……etc.

The implementation of the IDB tool availed single unified interface for users to upload the sales data from the respective country to provide aggregate reporting of sales for the HQ in Egypt. The tool allowed drill-down granularity for users. We will first analyze the structure of this implemented information dashboard tool (IDB) and then describe the new sales reporting process. The IDB acted as the single "database" view for all trade related information used by all franchisees and is used through applying several data mining techniques. It is a customized web based application built to access the warehouse database and allowed access from anywhere through the company's network. Furthermore, the IDB is used as the reporting vehicle to management - globally, retiring the use of once prevalent sales templates and the use of the email for posting these templates. Access to the IDB is achieved via web browser using specific URL or via the Company Portal (based on MS Share Point platform). Users log in through their IDs and passwords. After updating the system with the daily, weekly or quarterly sales, figures, respective users can log in and retrieve any report needed at any granularity level for any specific period.

The sales reporting process constituted several activities. Every franchisee analyst is to prepare the weekly sales data using the relevant codes and upload the data on the IDB. The upload is performed automatically through an Autoloader and scheduled on Mondays every week. The system decodes the uploaded codes and maintains the actual data on the system. Business plan figures and rolling estimates figures are also uploaded in the same format and manner. Whenever any discrepancy in the uploaded data on the IDB of a single country affect the accuracy of the data of the total business unit, control measures are promptly carried out to assure the integrity and accuracy of data on the system. After all franchisees upload their weekly figures on the IDB, the HQ Sales Analyst verifies the data on the system and adjusts/deletes any discrepancies found by detecting the countries responsible for the discrepancies and suggests methods for resolving these conflicts with the concerned analyst. The Sales Analyst can also report any variance detected on the IDB due to any error in the application engine through Business Applications Call Logging system, used by the IT department as the support tool for any encountered technical problems while using the IDB.

The HQ sales analyst is also responsible for planning and coordinating all IDB activities with all franchisee analysts in terms of training analysts, installing new IDB applications and communicating with IT to resolve encountered problems. The HQ sales analyst is also responsible for issuing new codes for newly launched packs that are not on the system by filling a request form. The HQ Analyst also monitors the status of expired codes and de-activates them.

Developing the IDB Dashboard Layer

The described new sales business process is depicted in Figure 3. Upon upload of the sales data on IDB, users can simply log into the system from anywhere and access the reports menu via the portal or the specially provided URL and pick the type of

Figure 3. Sales reporting process after implementation of the IDB system

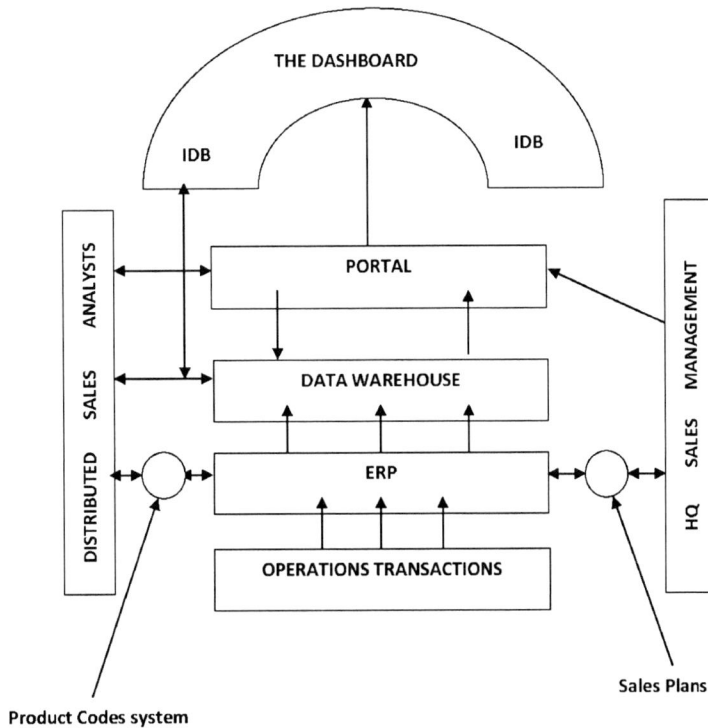

report required using drop down lists. These lists include all product parameters. The IDB system enabled users to get any type of information by selecting the specific criteria needed in the downloaded report with any degree of granularity. In other words, users can customize the reports retrieved from the system by choosing the appropriate parameters from the displayed scroll down lists. Drill down lists may include, but not limited to, parameters such as:

- Country
- Bottler
- Period (Year/Month/Week)
- Brand
- Flavor
- Package type
- Pack size
- Historical data
- Business plan data
- Rolling Estimate (RE) data
- Analysis of sales performance versus prior years, BP, RE…..etc.

Access to the facilities offered in the IDB system is granted though a robust and premeditated authorization scheme. IT unit provides authorized users with their respective personal user name and password for authentication, however accessing and retrieving information at various data-granularity levels are subject to authorization policies. This authorization scheme is set by the respective country management, and communicated to the IT department, to provide various access privileges for the various organizational hierarchical levels.

The Impact of the IDB System on the Effectiveness of the Sales Reporting Process

The use of the IDB facility as a component of the battery of BI tools of the Company's IS platform enhanced the Sales reporting cycle in many ways and had increased the overall efficiency of the Sales Reporting Process. The major areas of improvement IDB offered are:

- First of all, it has eliminated the redundant process of sending the former sales reports templates that were subject to various interpretations, wasting time and effort and causing inconsistencies and mistrust of data.
- Using IDB as an outer shell of the data warehouse provided a very useful tool as it integrates all types of information required whether historical data, brand information, package information, business plan figures…etc. Before using IDB, managers and analysts had to go through many Excel files and sheets to obtain information which is time consuming and some of the required data were lost or hidden. Besides, the same information was sometimes obtained with different values from different sources causing confusion.
- Provided multi-dimensionality reporting using "slice and dice" operations by the analysts.
- IDB acted as a timely and trustworthy reporting tool with a single source of sales data which is not subject to various interpretations. All analysts are bound by specific deadlines to upload their data, so the managers are confident to find the data on time and to retrieve it in a standard format to facilitate the data integration and the decision making process.
- IDB provided analysis facility. Reports retrieved facilitated comparisons and analytical measures that can be used to help managers in the decision making process.
- IDB helped in determining profitable trading partners through the use of multi-dimensionality data mining
- Augmented and replaced cumbersome previous spreadsheet-based system.

- Enabled driver-based planning to streamline and focus efforts around HR plans, manufacturing requirements, or sales resources.
- Enabled use of rolling forecasts to increase forward visibility.
- Reduced the need for consolidation, close and reporting cycles by days or weeks..
- Facilitated conducting what-if scenarios for different revenue projections or changes in business lines.
- Facilitated tracking key corporate performance indicators from desktop.

Beside these impacts on the performance of the Sales function, it enabled giving brand, marketing, and sales managers the knowledge they need to strongly impact the top line through the use of brand, sales, promotion/marketing and delivering a full range of sales management analyses. With the IDB tool, near-real time measures by account, channel/channel segment, promotion, and campaign - can be used to improve the effectiveness of other business cycles such as the full range of brand, portfolio, and product analyses along with the ability to ask random, ad hoc questions and alert when actual performance varies substantially from plan.

In a nutshell, the IDB tool enabled getting the right information, to the right decision makers, at the right time. It is an enterprise-wide platform that supported multi-dimensionality reporting, analytics and decision modeling leading to fact-based decision making and getting a "single version of the truth."

The integration of the marketing data warehouse with the IDB tool also resulted in many benefits such as:

1. Financial process management of annual marketing budgets. Through the marketing Business Warehouse the brand managers gained autonomy in managing this process themselves through accessing this option on the IDB, where they would directly input their budgets online and the embedded workflow would proceed to request granting the necessary approvals. Budget managers were also able to perform internal budget shifts if need be as well as raising new purchase orders where previously it was done manually.
2. Ensuring internal system adherence to corporate financial and procurement procedures, there was no need for manual issuance any more as the ERP system provided the necessary constraints through budget coding, online approval requirements through a hierarchy workflow.
3. Monitoring marketing spend per brand and ensuring correct allocation across the marketing mix. The IDB reports were very malleable in their structure - can be driven by specific periods, campaign types, seasonality, segmentation by below the line marketing activities, or above the line, even by media type

which allowed brand managers and marketing managers a better ability to assess the direct impact of a campaign spend over sales in a particular moment in time.

4. Providing budget reporting across franchise functions. Again, this has been a dissolved manual role as the new system allowed for automatic retrieval as explained in the point above.

5. Reporting on brand contribution and profitability per brand, pack, flavor and concentrate. The integration with the company-wide planning system allowed further report segmentation by account, for example, how each cost contributed to the overall profitability of a brand by integrating other operating expenses (OPEX), capital expenses (CAPEX) reports- this type of reports are high level top-line data that were accessed by top managerial staff and also depended on the level of data-breakdown details that were fed in by accountants.

The final Information Systems infrastructure architecture of the company after the IDB implementation is depicted in Figure 4.

CURRENT CHALLENGES FACING THE CASE FIRM

The ERP system has been put in place in the company for many years. Employees did not have an option, they had to use it. Though the company managed to stream-

Figure 4. Architecture of the IS layers used in the company after IDB implementation

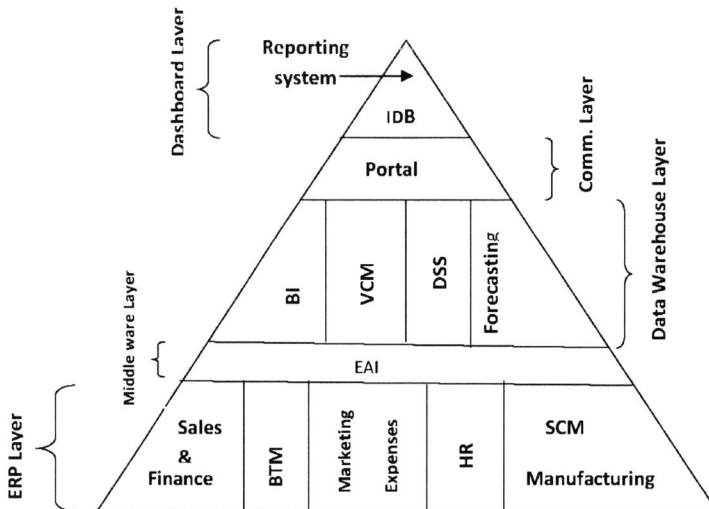

line and align some of its business processes and operations to the "best practice" processes embedded in the ERP, with minimum changes, to adapt to the specific nature of the beverage industry, customized bolt-in additional tools were inevitably used to cater for those specific characteristics. This was quite evident in the sales and marketing functions. As a result of the deployment of the new IDB system, several problems showed up.

The following obstacles and challenges were observed after installing the IDB

- User reluctance to abandon the use of old Excel templates increased resistance of the use of the new developed data entry facility.
- Training analysts to use IDB was a challenging feat. The dispersed remote locations of analysts made it difficult and costly to provide them with the necessary skills for optimum use of the new tool. Though conference calls and video-conferencing were used to tackle this obstacle, the level of operational excellence in using the tool was less than satisfactory as postulated by the management. Incompetency of use of the facilities of the system was also observed due to the lack of analytical proficiency.
- Unrealistic expectations were anticipated in a relatively short period.
- Lack of in-house technical expertise (The IDB support team is remotely located).
- Real-Time data reporting was accessible once accounting inputs are uploaded into the system in due course. Errors in data entry may thus lead to wrong information and decisions. As one employee contends:

"The initial step when we switched from the legacy system to the new setup involved data migration. This was a very tedious task and involved many months of intricate detailed work where existing data had to be assigned codes similar to the coding on the ERP to allow smooth transition. The challenge was to transition with almost zero error and entailed at certain moment of time to halt transactions entry to ensure all real-time data is captured. There was a mechanism to double check on validity of data after transition."

- Employees were not receptive to adapt to change and resisted system implementation by initially rejecting the idea for months. Advanced training technology-based methods were adopted to allow for virtual help where global ERP Power Users were able to access local employees' screens to guide them through a step by step process. Adaptability took about one whole year as the users gained more confidence in system maneuver.

- Although the idea of the ERP is to eliminate a lot of paper work, the case was not so in Egypt in some areas as the embedded ERP workflow involved external as well as internal stakeholder's input in the system. For example, marketing assistants raising new purchase orders through the transaction modules were required to attach three different quotations from three different suppliers. The idea is that suppliers were to send those quotations through an interface mechanism that allowed automatic attach to the purchase order. Given that the business climate in Egypt is still underdeveloped in terms of technology maturity, many continued to send their quotations manually by courier messenger, or fax, rarely few at the time were used to the idea of sending through email. This created a bottle neck since the marketing assistant had to then scan those documents and upload them manually to process the purchase order – where a purchase order raising should have taken about an hour for completion ended up consuming a whole day while it has still not been sent to the brand manager for approval. In some situations this produced further time bottlenecks as some suppliers required down payments prior to activation of the required job on the system.

- Brand managers viewed their newly added task of managing the input-output process of budgets themselves and purchase order requisitions as a waste of time as they previously did not do so. They viewed it as a purely transactional administrative task that should be performed by the accounting department or rather assigned to a department secretary for coordination. In the beginning, they did try to perform the processing themselves, but later, decided that this administrative tasks have impeded their focus on managing the brand with consumers from a marketing perspective.

- An operational issue of ERP is currency variations. Although the system allowed for multiple currency input, the final marketing budget to be approved by division heads and headquarters had to be submitted and received in dollars. This created some issues where brand managers initially prepared their budget in Egyptian pounds per the various local quotations and pricing they received. This total amount however did not sometimes equate for the same amount assigned by global HQ on the ERP which was in dollars. The challenge for the finance was to constantly adjust rates according to fluctuations in exchange rates and other market factors such as inflation and so forth which also resulted in some chunks of the budget in Egyptian pounds being eaten away due to these adjustments. It continues to be an ordeal as concentrate pricing is also in US dollars while other transactions are in multiple currencies.

- The deployment of technology into everyday business is still not very mature within people's mindset in Egypt. For example, the lack of trust still persisted in the Egyptian ideology, where the deployment of online signatures through ERP protocol was still viewed with a suspicious eye. Middle managers especially in the accounting unit still requested a pen-written on paper signature-it made them feel secure. However this required that paper formats of ERP documents were printed and managers were requested put their pen signatures. This did not help in achieving a more lean and streamlined operation which the system was supposed to create.

- End-User Support and Maintenance

A few years ago, for an employee to report an IT problem they had to call the local help desk and technical staff will attend to the call to solve the problem for him or her. However, the company HQ has developed a new process that employees experiencing problems will have to make a call to call center, give their employee ID and describe the technical problem about the software or the hardware. The call center, remotely accessed, will give the employee a ticket number with the problem code and send them an email summarizing the problem. The problem could be simple enough to be solved over the phone (i.e., the center tells the employee on the phone what he or she could do to solve the problem). If it's not then the center directs the problem to the local help desk to solve it. Then the center sends the employee an email asking if the problem has been solved or not to close the ticket. Some employees found this process difficult and time consuming

Future Measures to Enhance the Reporting Cycle and Recommendations

The preceding analysis revealed that key success measures that may help the company to overcome the obstacles cited and leads to turning the IDB system into a success story include the following:

- Executive management involvement and support
- Clear project ownership by including sales analysts in the project management team
- Proper planning
- Hard working and focus by all member countries' analysts
- Clear communication between business and IT by setting meetings, discussing problems and analyzing issues and providing continuous feedback
- Clear role definition for both analysts and IT professionals
- Instituting efficient and effective change management process
- Proper and continuous staff and analysts training

To that end, the company is planning to install new version of the IDB system in the upcoming years. The new system will allow users to create their own queries with specific design and more advanced sales breakdown. Also, the company is planning to use more advanced analytical tools such as the "Instant Visual Analysis" tool which is a simple versatile tool that will make volume analysis and graphic representation faster, easier and more flexible. The Instant Visual Analysis tool uses pivot table reports to help analyze and graph numerical data, answering questions, exhibiting trends, etc. With a few mouse clicks users can see who sold the most where, which brands were the most successful, and which pack sold best.

REFERENCES

Alter, S. (1980). *Decision support systems: Current practice and continuing challenge*. Reading: MA Addison Wiley.

Bancroft, N. (1996). *Implementing SAP R/3*. Greenwich, CT: Manning Publication Co.

Bingham, D. (1999). *Food and beverage companies need to integrate information enterprise-wide*. Beverage Online.

Brazel, J. F., & Dang, L. (2008). The effect of ERP system implementations on the management of earnings and earnings release dates. *Journal of Information Systems, 22*(2), 1–21. doi:10.2308/jis.2008.22.2.1

Chatterjee, D., Grewal, R., & Sambamurthy, V. (2002). Shaping up for e-commerce: Institution enablers of the organizational assimilation of Web technologies. *Management Information Systems Quarterly, 26*(2), 65. doi:10.2307/4132321

Chou, D., Tripuramully, H., & Chou, A. (2005). BI and ERP integration. *Information Management & Computer Security, 13*(5), 340–349. doi:10.1108/09685220510627241

CRM2day. (2004). *Business intelligence*. Retrieved from www.crm2day.com/bi

Data monitor. (2001). *Business intelligence from data to profit*. Retrieved from www.researchandmarkets.com

Davenport, T. (1998). Putting the enterprise into the enterprise system. *Harvard Business Review, 76*(4), 121–131.

DeLone, W., & McLean, E. (1992). Information systems success: The quest for the dependable variable. *Information Systems Research, 3*(1), 60–95. doi:10.1287/isre.3.1.60

DeLone, W., & McLean, E. (2003). The DeLone and McLean Model of Information Systems success: A ten-year update. *Journal of Management Information Systems*, *19*(4), 9–30.

Ding, D., & Chen, J. (2007). Supply chain coordination with contracts game between complementary suppliers. *International Journal of Information Technology & Decision Making*, *6*(1), 163–175. doi:10.1142/S0219622007002332

Drucker, P. (1998). The next information revolution. *Forbes.* Retrieved from www.forbes.com

Fan, M., Stallaert, J., & Whinston, A. (2000). The adoption and design methodologies of component-based enterprise systems. *European Journal of Information Systems*, *9*, 25–35. doi:10.1057/palgrave.ejis.3000343

Francalanci, C. (2001). Predicting the implementation effort of ERP projects: Empirical evidences on SAP R/3. *Journal of Information Technology*, *16*(1), 33–48. doi:10.1080/02683960010035943

Fryling, M. (2005). ERP implementation dynamics. *Information Science and Policy.* University at Albany. State University of New York, Oct. 2005.

Gable, G., Sedera, D., & Chan, T. (2003). Enterprise systems success: A measurement model. *Proceedings of the 24th ICIS,* (pp. 576-591). Seattle, Washington.

Gable, G., van Den Heever, R., Erlank, S., & Scott, J. (2001). Large packaged application software maintenance: A research framework. *Journal of Software Maintenance and Evolution: Research and Practice*, *13*(6), 351–371. doi:10.1002/smr.237

Holsapple, C., & Whinston, A. B. (1996). *Decision support systems: A knowledge based approach.* Minneapolis, MN: West Publishing.

Ifinedo, P. (2006a). Extending the Gable et al. enterprise systems success measurement model: A preliminary study. *Journal of Information Technology Management,* *17*(1), 14-33.

Ifinedo, P., & Nahar, N. (2007). ERP system success: An empirical analysis of how two organizational stakeholder groups prioritize and evaluate relevant measures. *Enterprise Information Systems*, *1*, 25–48. doi:10.1080/17517570601088539

Kallinikos, J. (2004). Deconstructing information packages: Organizational and behavioral implications of ERP systems. *Information Technology & People*, *17*, 8–30. doi:10.1108/09593840410522152

Kamaladevi, B. (2010). Customer experience management in retailing. *Business Intelligence Journal*, *3*(1), 37–54.

Krumbholz, M. (2000). Implementing enterprise resource planning packages in different corporate and national cultures. *Journal of Information Technology*, *15*(4), 267–280. doi:10.1080/02683960010008962

Kumar, K., & Van Hillegersberg, J. (2000). ERP: Experience and evolution. *Communications of the ACM*, *43*, 23–26.

Kumar, V., Maheshwari, B., & Kumar, U. (2001). An investigation of critical management issues in ERP implementation: Empirical evidences from Canadian organizations. *Technovation*, *23*(10).

Light, B. (2001). The maintenance implications of the customization of ERP software. *Journal of Software Maintenance and Evolution: Research and Practice*, *13*(6), 415–429. doi:10.1002/smr.240

Madapusi, A., & Kuo, C. (2007). Assessing data and information quality in ERP systems. *Proceedings of the Decision Sciences Institute Annual Meeting*, Arizona.

Madapusi, A., Kuo, C., & White, R. (2007). A critical factors approach to ERP information quality and decision quality. *Proceedings of the Decision Sciences Institute Annual Meeting,* Arizona.

Markus, M., & Robey, D. (1988). Information Technology and organizational change: Causal structure in theory and research. *Management Science*, *34*, 583–598. doi:10.1287/mnsc.34.5.583

McDonald, k., et al. (2002). *Mastering SAP business information warehouse.* Canada: Wiley Publishing.

Mensching, J., & Corbitt, G. (2004). EPR data archiving- a critical analysis. *Journal of Enterprise Information Management*, *17*(2), 131–141. doi:10.1108/17410390410518772

Nah, F. H., Faja, S., & Cata, T. (2001). Characteristics of ERP software maintenance: A multi-cause study. *Journal of Software Maintenance and Evolution: Research and Practice*, *13*(6), 339–414. doi:10.1002/smr.239

Nicolaou, A. (2004). *ERP system implementation drivers of post-implementation success.* Decision Support in an Uncertain and Complex World: The IFIP TC8/WG8.3 International Conference, 2004, (pp. 589-597).

Nicolaou, A., & Bhattacharya, S. (2007). Organizational performance effects of ERP systems usage: The impact of post-implementation changes. *International Journal of Accounting Information Systems*, *7*(1), 18–35. doi:10.1016/j.accinf.2005.12.002

O'Leary, D. (2002). *Enterprise resource planning systems: System lifecycle, electronic commerce, and risk*. Cambridge, UK: Cambridge University Press.

Olszak, C., & Ziemba, E. (2007). Approach to building and implementing business intelligence system. *Interdisciplinary Journal of Information, Knowledge, and Management*, *2*, 135–148.

Olszak, C., & Ziemba, E., (2006). Business intelligence systems in the holistic infrastructure development - supporting decision-making in organizations. *Interdisciplinary Journal of Information, Knowledge, and Management, 1*.

Parr, A., & Schanks, G. (2000). A model of ERP project implementation. *Journal of Information Technology*, *15*(4), 289–304. doi:10.1080/02683960010009051

Ptak, C., & Schragenheim, E. (2000). *ERP: Tools, techniques and applications for integrating the supply chain*. London, UK: Series on Resources Management, St Lucie Press/APICS.

Rasmussen, N., Goldy, P., & Solli, P. (2002). *Financial business intelligence: Trends, technology, software selection and implementation*. New York, NY: Wiley.

AMR Research (currently part of Gartner inc.). (2005). *Market Analytix Report: ERP 2004-2009*.

Robey, D., & Boudreau, M. (1999). Accounting for the contradictory organizational consequences of information technology. *Information Systems Research*, *10*, 167–185. doi:10.1287/isre.10.2.167

Seddon, P. B. (1997). A re-specification and extension of the DeLone and McLean model of IS success. *Information Systems Research*, *18*(3), 240–253. doi:10.1287/isre.8.3.240

Sedera, D., Gable, G., & Chan, T. (2004). Measuring enterprise systems success: The importance of a multiple stakeholder perspective. *Proceedings of the 12th European Conference on Information Systems*, (pp. 1-13). Turku, Finland.

Soh, C., & Tay-Yap, J. (2000). Cultural fits and misfits: Is ERP a universal solution? *Communications of the ACM*, *43*(4), 47–51. doi:10.1145/332051.332070

Spott, D. (2000). Componentizing the enterprise applications packages. *Communications of the ACM*, *43*(4), 63–90. doi:10.1145/332051.332074

Stedman, C. (1999, November 1). Failed ERP gamble haunts Hershey. *Computerworld*. Retrieved April 16, 2006, from www.computerworld.com

Stedman, C. (2002). Maximizing the ERP investment. *Competitive Financial Operations: The CFO Project, 1*, 1–6.

Xu, H., Nord, J., Brown, N., & Nord, D. (2002). Data quality issues in implementing an ERP. *Industrial Management & Data Systems, 102*(1), 47–58. doi:10.1108/02635570210414668

Yen, D. C., Chou, D. C., & Chang, J. (2002). A synergic analysis for Web-based enterprise resource planning system. *Computer Standards & Interfaces, 24*(4), 337–346. doi:10.1016/S0920-5489(01)00105-2

KEY TERMS AND DEFINITIONS

Business Intelligence (BI): Refers to computer-based techniques used in analyzing business data, such as sales by products and/or departments or associated costs and incomes. In addition, BI technologies avail historical, current, and predictive views of business operations. Common functions of Business Intelligence technologies are reporting, online analytical processing, analytics, data mining, business performance management, benchmarking, text mining, and predictive analytics.

Dashboard: Is the application of visual iconic tools that indicate the status of a particular measurable quantity, event or value. Within the context of business performance measurement, the use of the dashboard may aide decision makers in quickly spotting the status of some KPIs of interest to them.

Data Mining: Is the process of extracting patterns from data. Data mining is becoming an increasingly important tool to transform the data into information. It is commonly used in a wide range of profiling practices, such as marketing, surveillance, fraud detection and scientific discovery. Data mining is often used to uncover patterns in data pertaining to functional or departmental data sets.

Data Warehouse: Is a repository (collection of resources that can be accessed to retrieve information) of an organization's electronically stored data, designed to facilitate reporting and analysis. Data warehousing arises when an organization need reliable, consolidated, unique and integrated analysis and reporting of its data resources, at different levels of aggregation.

Decision Support Systems (DSS): Constitute a class of computer-based information systems including knowledge-based systems that support decision-making activities. DSSs serve the management, operations, and planning levels of an organization and help to make decisions, which may be rapidly changing and not easily specified in advance.

Enterprise Resources Planning (ERP): Is an integrated computer-based software system used to manage organizational internal and external resources. It is an architecture which facilitates the flow of information between all business functions within the boundaries of the organization and manages the interfaces with outside stakeholders.

Key Performance Indicators (KPI): Measures commonly used to help organizations define and evaluate how successful their businesses are, typically in terms of making progress towards long-term organizational goals. KPIs can be specified by answering the question, "What is really important to different organizational stakeholders?"

Chapter 11

IS Strategic Processes:
Benefitting from People's Competencies in a Geographically Dispersed Organization – A CIO's Challenge

Harald Fardal
Vestfold University College, Norway

Jan Oddvar Sørnes
Bodø Graduate School of Business, Norway

EXECUTIVE SUMMARY

In large, geographically dispersed organizations, achieving a successful Information Systems (IS) strategy can prove very challenging. This case describes how a CIO in such an organization met that challenge by focusing on actions rather than plans, and on bottom-up processes rather than top-down decisions. The CIO keyed on benefitting from employees' competencies. The organization, here called "NorConstruct," has few long-term IS strategic plans. Instead, it has developed five different IS strategic themes on a general level. It's actual IS strategy takes place through different IS projects. The case is told through the CIO and provides rich descriptions of IS strategic processes in NorConstruct, as well as the CIO's thoughts on the pros and cons. Throughout the case, several relevant reflections are described.

DOI: 10.4018/978-1-4666-2618-8.ch011

ORGANIZATION BACKGROUND

This study examines the Information Systems (IS) practices of a major Scandinavian corporation ("NorConstruct"). At the time of writing, NorConstruct employed 6,000 people, approximately half of whom were daily using a variety of ISs. NorConstruct's is one of Scandinavia's leading construction and property development companies. It is the leading company in its field in Norway and the fourth largest in Denmark, and it has extensive operations in growth regions in Sweden. NorConstruct's business concept is to create value by designing, building and managing projects in partnership with customers who inspire growth and development. NorConstruct aims to continue to develop its position as one of the leading construction and property development companies in Scandinavia. In 2009 its profit reached NOK 523 million before taxes (approx. $89 million) of a total turnover of approximately NOK 15.5 billion ($2.6 billion). Its stock value on the Oslo stock market had remained above $1 billion for the last few years. Moreover, NorConstruct had its own internal stock program designed to encourage its employees to buy into the company, and they then owned around 20% of it. NorConstruct consisted of several highly self-driven units, or divisions, unevenly spread between Norway, Sweden, and Denmark. Most of NorConstruct's operations were in Norway, site of its corporate headquarters. Figure 1 gives an overview of NorConstruct's organization. Each division had its own CEO who reported to NorConstruct's top CEO. The CIO, meanwhile, whom we'll meet in this case, was a member of the top CEO's staff but not a member of the top management group, which was limited to just the top CEO and the division CEOs. However, the CIO served the whole corporation as there was no local IT or IS departments in the different divisions.

NorConstruct, competing in the open market, would land contracts from private investors as well as publicly funded projects. In the Norwegian market of its core construction business, it faced about five regular competitors on a national level with Skanska and NCC being the biggest of them. However, they faced local competition from strong regional constructions companies. Its real-estate division faced local competition wherever its projects happened to be, but also had to face the competition of Skanska's and NCC's real estate departments. Both Skanska and NCC are multinational corporations, but smaller than NorConstruct in the Norwegian operation. Table 1 gives an overview of some key figures for NorConstruct over the past few years, showing growth up to 2008. Although Norway only have had slight set backs due to the global financial crisis, the areas that felt the effects of the crisis the most was within construction and real estate and probably explains the reduction of NorConstruct's lower figures in 2009. Because NorConstruct's construction projects were scattered all over Norway (with some also in Sweden and Denmark), it relied heavily on local sub-contractors and suppliers.

Figure 1. Organizational map of The Firm

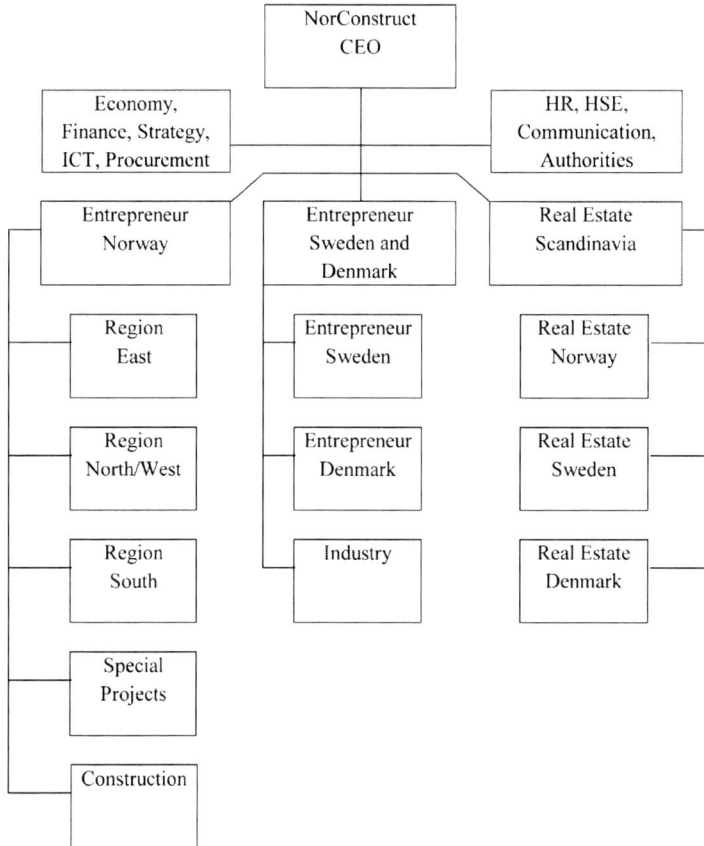

Table 1. Turnover and profit are in million $. Numbers are originially in NOK and calculated using $1 = 5.85 NOK.

Key figures	2009	2008	2007	2006	2005
Turnover (in mil. $)	2652	3306	3296	2803	2485
Profit before taxes	89	139	201	157	121
No. of employees	5821	6244	6475	6351	5598

The action-oriented and bottom-up practice at NorConstruct reflects both national and organizational characteristics of the Norwegian culture (Hall, 1977, 1983; Hofstede, 1980, 1991; Schein, 1985). Hofstede's dimension of Power Distance and Uncertainty Avoidance helps us understand how the Norwegian culture emphasized the importance of cooperation and encouraging individuals to take greater responsibility for their actions – thus more freedom. The action-oriented approach seen in this case can also be understood based on Schein's work on organizational culture, where Norway (and other Scandinavian countries) tends to approach possible conflicts/challenges through negotiations and compromise – where considerable discretionary powers prevail.

NorConstruct's IS management strategy was built around five IS strategic themes, or goals, which will be elaborated upon later: (1) achieve a solid solution for all projects, (2) focus on joint corporate solutions, (3) maintain strong IS department support, (4) allow profession-specific applications when applicable, and (5) be an industry leader in IS competence. As for the general management strategy, the core was local decision-making and the solid anchoring of those decisions. In NorConstruct, solid anchoring of decisions involved the employees as much as managers, meaning that they strived for consensus before making final decisions. For example, our visits to NorConstruct were made possible only due to several employees and managers agreeing that it was a good idea. In NorConstruct it would be unthinkable for one single manager to grant access for two researchers like us. Then we wouldn't have been able to reach the people we wanted to. Achieving wide acceptance and anchoring of decisions was not only a strategy, but had developed into being an important cultural trait of NorConstruct. However, this way of approaching IS strategizing gave NorConstruct some challenges in regards to decision-making time, project time and overview of IS need. Throughout the case description these challenges arise through the CIO's story, and in light of that we discuss them at the end of the paper.

So, too, was the importance NorConstruct attached to teams and collaboration. To enrich the interplay of ideas, it had started hiring people with other types of competencies than its core need (engineering). Several economists and sociologists, for example, had been recruited to participate in projects that traditionally would consist only of engineers, simply (or not so simply) to introduce fresh ways of thinking into a working environment prone to conformity and homogeneity in innovation and project development.

SETTING THE STAGE

Technological Status

NorConstruct's CIO, here named "Birger," whom we interviewed at length for this study, said that his company wasn't interested in being an information technology (IT) leader, since its focus remained steadily on its core business: construction. For this reason, it outsourced both its IT support services and its IT infrastructure services. The outsourced operations were, on a day-to-day basis, mainly managed and regulated through contracts and good relations between the two parties. On a strategic level, NorConstruct had the decision power, but the supplier of the outsourced services were in charge of implementing any changes within the outsourced areas. At the time of our study, NorConstruct had four major IS projects going. Two were corporate-wide: converting its e-mail platform to Microsoft Exchange and introducing a new intranet. The other two—readjusting the HR salary system and the calculation system—concerned just parts of the organization. The CIO and his staff, a total of 11 persons at the time of our visit, owned only the corporate-wide ISs, whereas the divisions owned their task-specific ISs themselves. Corporate-wide ISs included the e-mail system (Lotus Notes), a document handling system (Lotus Notes), the inter- and intranet and MS Office 2003 including MS Project. Birger didn't have a complete overview of all the ISs owned by the different departments and divisions, and claimed he didn't need to either. He said: "We have numerous different ISs out there, especially if you include all the advanced Excel spreadsheets and Access database applications that people have developed on their own initiative".

While NorConstruct had organized its IS activities through a central IS department, an IS board, composed of members from all divisions and from top management in addition to the CIO, had the final say in the prioritizing of IS issues. But the board rarely took upon itself to supply IS ideas; it mostly just discussed the ideas and proposed projects initiated by others. Only in situations of real conflict between the divisions did the IS board interfere with the priorities set by the IS department. Moreover, the CIO was not a member the top management group, and he actually expressed no desire to be one, either. He considered the IS board sufficient in terms of having top management commitment in relation to IS. As long as he knew he enjoyed the required support from the top management group, he had no desire to spend time on those meetings and problems. He wanted to focus on his core activities of developing IS in a good direction for NorConstruct.

So basically Birger faced the challenge of transforming a highly decentralized organization, whose primary activity was fairly independent of its ISs, into one where ISs were fully integrated in the various production processes. Adding to that challenge, Birger told us, was the fact that his company spent only about 0.6% of its total annual turnover on IS; thus funding, or the lack of it, was an important issue as well. Because of these budgetary constraints, the IT-infrastructure operation had been outsourced to a large company of IT specialists, and the in-house competencies had been built around identifying and managing IS projects. Thus Birger and his staff could focus on IS strategic issues rather than on user support and server maintenance.

The CIO of NorConstruct was our primary focus here—specifically, how he handled the numerous IS strategic challenges in his organization. The case is told through Birger's eyes together with our additions. Birger had overall responsibility for the IT infrastructure, the IS portfolio, and of course for delivering proper services to the organization. It was a challenging set of tasks, in part because NorConstruct was dispersed throughout Scandinavia and because large parts of it were sited in temporary locations, depending on wherever its contracts landed. Our case shows how such diversity can be managed, and discusses the various IS strategic challenges that the CIO faced. As our focus was on the CIO's everyday challenges, there's no specific timeline for the case.

Birger saw both his staff and himself as serving primarily as a service unit to the rest of the organization, providing competencies—e.g., IS project management, training, and technical skills—not readily found in the different divisions. Birger felt that moving IS strategic thinking close to the IS needs not only provided better solutions than a centralized system would have, but it also allowed him and his staff to focus more on corporate-wide IS challenges, such as developing a new intranet and introducing a new e-mail platform.

While Birger's approach seems fairly straightforward, it posed several challenges as well, which we will elaborate on later:

- Sometimes two or more divisions needed ISs to solve similar problems.
- Local solutions at times prevented the introduction of new ISs.
- The divisions sometimes had problems getting their ideas relayed to Birger and his staff.
- If employees were to follow up on the good ideas they contributed, they needed the time to do so, which meant sacrificing some of their regular job activities.
- Because Birger and his staff had limited human and monetary recourses, they faced prioritizing issues.
- They also faced budgeting and cost issues. For example, who should pay when two or more divisions were involved?
- And who should be the owner of the IS when two or more divisions were involved?

Birger's practice as a CIO was focused on action—i.e., accomplishing specific tasks or resolving specific problems. He was not very focused on long-term planning or other heavy planning processes. As a support to the reader we will add some theoretical insights in light of what Mintzberg (1987) called "emerging strategies," and also in light of Stacey's (2007) theory of complex responsive processes and its consequences for strategic work in organizations.

CASE DESCRIPTION

As CIO, Birger was responsible for NorConstruct's IS strategy. "We have a very simple strategy," he said. "A few years back we did a job to create some basic IS strategic guidelines, as they were non-existent when I started working here. It resulted in a four-year plan containing five main points of IS strategic-focus areas." Birger emphasized that they had to keep this overall IS strategic plan simple due to NorConstruct's widely dispersed organization and the differing needs throughout it. For example, he said, "The guys building houses don't have the same needs as those selling them." Particularly compelling was Birger's description of how the IS strategy was developed. He said they followed the same procedure there as they had used in their business strategy development. All together, they spent a year on this process, drawing on people from various parts of the organization. Spending an entire year just to develop a few main points may seem disproportionate, but Birger argued that it's just the focus they have on the process that conduces to an IS-strategy that might appear trivial, but that captures needs of the organization and IT opportunities for improving business. Such a length of time also bespeaks the cooperative process they use for agreement, which always takes time.

The Five IS-Strategic Themes

Birger appeared very enthusiastic when explaining the main points of NorConstruct's IS strategy. Following Earl's (1996) terminology, we prefer to call them "themes" instead of "main points." However, Earl considers themes to be emergent by nature, appearing through everyday practices—for example, when someone finds a new way of solving a problem through IT. In the case presented here, the themes have evolved through a defined process and are supposed to serve as IS-strategic guidelines. The strategic themes were defined for a three-year period with annual revisions. At the time of our visit to NorConsult, it was soon time for the first revision. So to keep clear the distinction between Earl's use of the term themes and the usage here, we will use the term *strategic themes*. Here, then, are NorConstruct's five IS strategic themes as explained to us by Birger:

1. We shall deliver good solutions for our building projects.
    - Birger noted that delivering IT-services to building projects is a heady challenge in itself: "The building projects are usually large operations popping up somewhere in the bush, existing for maybe just a year or two yet still needing a full IT-infrastructure." Given that situation, this theme was a no-brainer for Birger.

2. We want joint corporate solutions, meaning that Internet, intranet, and e-mail systems should be the same corporate-wide.
3. The IS department aims to provide support for, and ensure proper realization of, application projects, including profession-specific applications. It's important, Birger said, that our profession-specific applications support business in the best possible way.
4. Profession-specific applications don't have to be corporate-wide, but wherever we believe there will be economical or managerial synergies, we will strive for common solutions.
5. We want to be best on industry-specific IS competence.

Let us now turn to how NorConstruct conducts its IS projects.

Moving from IS-Strategic Themes to Action

Given these strategic themes, one might assume that deciding on projects was a fairly straightforward task for Birger and his colleagues. But experience taught him that this process was all too often both complex and time-consuming. Briefly summarized, Birger said, the projects could be divided into three separate types:

1. Projects regarding the whole corporation.
2. Projects involving at least two divisions.
3. Projects running in only one division.

Furthermore, Birger insisted that they followed the same philosophy of how to conduct an IT project regardless of the type of project. The philosophy was geared toward two main elements. First, they acknowledged that the organization is geographically spread among many scattered locations in Scandinavia, with several being just temporary construction sites. Yet even with all this decentralization, NorConstruct wished somehow to maintain its strong focus on democratic processes within the organization. Second, time wasn't an issue. The important thing was the processes themselves, meaning that they didn't set any absolute deadlines for their projects; they just spent whatever time was necessary to complete them. These two elements, Birger said, proved essential in ensuring that the IT projects were ultimately successful.

Corporate-Wide Projects

For Birger, these projects were the easiest to identify and to decide upon, as the responsibility for them fell solely to him as CIO and to his staff. Moreover, he said, when he started working for NorConstruct in 2004, the challenges were so numerous that identifying projects was actually quite easy. As Birger said: "We have been in, and still are in, the situation where we have a portfolio of some major projects. These are things we believe we must do." Hence, actually going through with the project was the main challenge, he said. As an example, he cited the process of introducing a common platform for basic IT services such as e-mail and intranet throughout the organization. "We want e-mail, intranet, and Internet to be based on one common platform," he said. "We are working on that. Today it's very fragmented, so we are working on converting everything to a Microsoft platform. That will enable us to collaborate better between divisional and regional borders." But given the organizational challenges described earlier, Birger assured us that they ran into several big bumps along the way. Technically, he said, it's not so difficult, but achieving the goals of the project is. He gave us three main reasons aside from those mentioned in the previous paragraph:

1.   We're a project-based corporation, and changing business processes in the middle of a project usually creates more trouble than solutions. So we've converted to Microsoft only on new and long-term projects that will still run for more than a year.
2.   Since we're such a decentralized organization, people are used to do things their own way. Through this conversion to Microsoft project, we have to create common business processes throughout the organization—and educate people to accept them.
3.   A lot of information and documentation is still being sent back and forth though the e-mail system. So we face a huge job in collecting all that stuff and transferring it to the intranet system for better archiving and accessibility.

Birger said that they had already started several processes, but he was sure that the project would last at least a year or two.

Multidivisional Projects

The second type of projects Birger identified in NorConstruct was those involving at least two divisions. One thing separating these projects from the corporate-wide projects was the ownership issue. While the corporate-wide projects were owned by the central IS department, Birger explained, usually multidivisional projects involved profession-specific ISs, and NorConstruct's policy was that such applications should be owned by the divisions themselves, meaning that the project ownership was divisional, too. Having ownership includes bearing the costs of the IS and owning the project. Even so, the project manager was usually someone from the central IS department. Birger saw several challenges with this type of project:

1. How to decide ownership between divisions?
2. Resources. The divisions themselves can't alone decide on which projects to go for, as they depend on other divisions and the central IS department.
3. The divisions involved have different requirements from those of the IS.

The ownership issue was usually solved by assigning ownership to whichever division would be the IS's heaviest user, with possible financial contributions from the other participating divisions being subject to negotiation. Every participating division did, however, have to make human recourses available during the project period. The most challenging part of multidivisional projects, Birger said, was when requirements differed between the participating divisions. In those situations, it was hard to prioritize between the different requirements, so that phase of a project received a lot of attention. Birger said: "The requirement specification we bring to the vendor stems from a very thorough process, and the specifications have been tuned according to organizational needs. Our philosophy usually has been that specifying the requirements takes as long as is takes. It's more important that the process is good, that it results in something we agree upon, rather than we speed things up." Moreover, Birger emphasized that the requirement-specification process often depended on industry-specific IS competence, so that proved its importance as a strategic theme. This competence, however, would mainly be found in the different divisions, not in the central IS department.

Single Division Projects

These projects were the easiest to launch, as fewer stakeholders meant less complex ownership and funding issues. But the focus on requirement specification remained the same as for the multidivisional projects. Furthermore, a division couldn't initiate an IS project without clearing it with the central IS department, as the IS department usually supplied the project manager and handled the technical aspects of the projects. Practically speaking, then, even though the divisions owned their own projects, they had to rely on central resources to conduct them. In other words, the decision to initiate a project often was made outside of the organizational unit that the project was run in.

Of course, this situation was the same for multidivisional projects. To deal with it, NorConstruct had established an IT council that was composed of members from all division and central management in addition to Birger. The IT council's job was to select which projects to run in the near future, thereby avoiding allocating to one or more divisions a disproportionate slice of the central IT department's resources pie.

Project Process

Regardless of the type of IS project in question, Birger explained that they used practically the same project methodology: "Well, it isn't rocket science what we do here. We have a general methodology that focuses on the process that leads to choosing the vendor. What we have experienced is that if we have a good process up to that point, the rest of the project is fairly easy. If we ignore that phase, then we most certainly will experience some kind of failure later. As soon as the vendor is introduced, we often follow the vendor's methodology." Birger used the introduction of a new calculation application as an example of the project process. The first step was to gather some people and organize them into a project group—or more precisely, at this stage, a pilot project group—whose task was to describe the present business processes. They would collaborate with a reference group composed of various future users of the system. When the groups had finished describing the present situation, they'd move on to the important phase of describing the desired future situation. Birger told us that this stage provided the foundation for the requirement specification process that was to follow.

Although they weighed this process fairly heavily, it doesn't mean that they slighted the implementation phase of their projects. Birger said that the best way to ensure a successful implementation of an IS is through a thorough preface and through nurturing vendor relationships: "It's not a good project if we squeeze the vendor and they don't make money on it. That presupposes that we have vendors who do a good job. We actually have kicked vendors out of projects and started all over because we weren't satisfied." So, according to Birger, a successful IS project is not related to squeezing the costs, but rather to building relationships with the involved parties, like employees and vendors.

IS-Strategy as Action

Besides describing the five strategic themes, our focus thus far has been on IS projects, for the strategic themes, while lofty, give no account of NorConstruct's IS strategic actions. Instead, they are just some very general descriptions of intended areas of focus. In Birger's view, what NorConstruct actually *did* represents the IS strategy, and not the strategic themes. But his action-oriented view of IS strategy is hardly common in IS strategy literature. In fact, the opposite seems to dominate the field, as a lot of the mainstream IS literature—in both research papers and textbooks—holds that IS strategy, properly considered, is a thorough, rational planning and strategy-development process. Furthermore, this view contends that if the process is properly done, following those strategic plans will be fairly simple. Consequently, much effort has been put into researching IS strategic planning in order to develop the best planning procedures—ones that will ensure optimal ISs for the organization (e.g. B. Galliers, 1999; R. D. Galliers, Swatman, & Swatman, 1995; Gottschalk, 1999; Teubner, 2007). However, holding that view on strategy implies one's accepting that strategies can in fact fail, and more importantly implies a belief that the future can be predicted. March (2006), a skeptic, argues that the traditional rationality concept ignores alternative logic and human emotions. In this argument lies the assumption that rationality can't fully explain action. If that's true, it means credibility problems for the strategy literature, which presupposes rationality. Stacey (Stacey, 2001, 2007) and his associates, with their theory of Complex Responsive Processes (CRP), have taken the criticism of the rationality perspective even further. Stacey argues that strategy normally unfolds, or evolves, through everyday actions and hence a strategic *plan* is hardly the same as the *actual* strategy. Humans interact in the living present and thereby shape the future by a continuous reinterpretation of the past. Moreover, Stacey argues that strategic plans often get abandoned, and that the strategic decisions and actions humans make can't be understood as resulting from plans but from local interactions between human beings. In the case of NorConstruct, it means that we'd be smarter to study what they have *done* rather than what they have only planned.

The Idea of a Rational Process vs. what Actually Happened

In the previous paragraph we briefly discussed some different perspectives on strategy, indicating that there are several ways to approach this field. To build further on Birger's story we want to dwell on an inconsistency evident in NorConstruct— the inconsistency between what was planned vs. what was actually done. As NorConstruct's IS strategy only described some IS strategic themes and set forth no detailed description of what they actually should do, they annually developed an action plan for the forthcoming year containing descriptions of the projects they had decided upon. It was the IT council's responsibility to make that plan; however, it was based on demands from the different divisions. The process thus far fits perfectly with the rationality scheme. But what's really interesting here is how those projects were identified and finally chosen.

When we asked Birger if the IT council members were the ones actually identifying the projects, he said that, no, most of the projects were first conceived at lower levels in the organization by the people who needed a new IS to do their job better. As one example, he cited the decision to procure a Customer Relationship Management (CRM) system for the real-estate department. When the construction department had finished a project of building apartments or houses, the people there usually handed it over to the real-estate department. Their responsibility was to sell apartments and houses, and to closely follow up on each customer individually. They found that a daunting challenge, as every customer had different needs. Some wanted wooden floors, others wanted tiles. Some had complaints, other not, and so forth. Until recently all this customer information was stored in different Excel files with no standardized structure or common storage space. In practice, it was next to impossible for one executive officer to stand in for a colleague when he or she was out of office. And for the customer it meant that they were tied to one specific executive officer. Clearly, it was not a very flexible or customer-oriented system. Some of the executive officers soon realized that this way of working could cost many a lost customer, so they started researching different CRMs on the market and eventually found just the one they wanted. This process was done without the help or interference of managers and IS staff. The next step was to get the project accepted by managers and the IT council. For this, they had to use an informal channel: they relied on their personal relationships with the right managers to convince them that this was a project well worth its costs.

The whole process from the time when the executive officers first identified their need until the time the project got started actually took more than two years. *But it was never planned for*; it just appeared in the action plan at a time when there really was no way around the project. The pressure from the executive officers of the real-estate department had reached the boiling point, and if nothing had been done they would probably have reached a level of frustration so high as to make them quite incapable of doing their jobs properly. It should also be noted that when the project started, the executive officers were in the driving seat of the project.

Each IS-Project is a Strategic Choice

The example from the real-estate department shows that IS projects can be initiated through bottom-up processes. It also shows that one can't always rationally plan what to do. Through our talk with Birger, we found that NorConstruct, while it had something it called an IS strategy, was actually much more oriented toward its projects. That's what it spent its time on. And its projects were not always planned. To use Mintzberg's (Mintzberg, 1987, 1996; Mintzberg & Ghoshal, 2003) terminology, they emerged from bottom-up in the organization. Mintzberg's point is that you can plan all you want, but the plan is bound to change due to the emergence of new ideas. He argues that those new ideas often lead to some strategic choice being made. Hence, the real strategy turns out to be almost after the fact: it lies in what has been done, not in the original plan, which basically exists only to be modified or even thoughtfully scrapped. Mintzberg explains:

Strategies grow like weeds in the garden. They take place in all kinds of places, wherever people have the capacity to learn (because they are in touch with the situation) and the resources to support that capacity (1987, p. 70).

However, Mintzberg doesn't explain what the "situation" is and what actually happens when people are "in touch with the situation." The process of self-organization from CRP theory might just be what he has missed out on. "Self-organization" refers to the process of communicative interaction and power-relating that humans constantly engage in, which in turn sustains and changes our individual and collective identities (Stacey, 2005). Mintzberg seems to miss this part when he argues that strategies become organizational when they become collective. Just how they get collective doesn't seem to concern him.

In the case of NorConstruct, the IS strategy containing the strategic themes didn't provide much insight into what they were intended to *do*. It merely represented some general guidelines and goals. It was only through the IS projects that the real IS strategy showed itself, and as such each project represented an IS strategic choice. Furthermore, several of the decisions made throughout the project period influenced the outcome to such a degree that it's fair to label them strategic, too.

The CIO Role

Following Stacey (2007) and Mintzberg (1987) and Mintzberg and Ghoshal (2003), one can argue that IS strategy is action. What one *does* is what finally matters. That doesn't mean that planning is a total waste of time, but referring to an IS plan as an IS strategy seems naive, since actions are so often different from plans, and the IS field is no different from others in that regard. Still, in many published papers on IS strategic planning researchers underline the importance of their study to help organizations implement their IS plans. Viewing IS strategy as action calls for a shift of focus from prescriptive models and the controlling manager to the reflexive, participating manager who's focused on action. To us, Birger epitomized this action-oriented manager, and throughout the interview he was much more enthusiastic when we discussed the projects (action) than when we talked about the document he referred to as the "IS strategic plan." Neither Stacey nor Mintzberg rejects the need for managers to make plans or intentions for future actions, but Stacey's micro-analytic approach to organizational communication provides insight into why plans and intentions often gets abandoned and why what's actually done differs from what was planned. Insight, too, into how power relations and local interactions throughout an organization shape it into what it is at a given point in time.

Birger represented the kind of CIO who pays more attention to what he might accomplish than to technicalities and formalities. When we asked him if he was a part of the top management group in NorConstruct, he said: "I think that the discussion whether a CIO should be a part of the top management group is a bit silly. In some organizations it's natural; in others, it's not. Here [in NorConstruct] it's not natural because our core activities have nothing to do with IT." Moreover Birger emphasized that he was satisfied with not being a part of the top management group as long as his relationships with the top executives were good. He argued that it gave him more freedom to focus on his job, because he could distance himself from the responsibilities that naturally followed from being a part of the group. However, he didn't mean that CIOs should distance themselves from business processes and questions. On the contrary, he said: "What's clear is that a CIO must be curious about the business and the business processes. That's important. One has to be interested, understand, and engage in dialogues with people throughout the organization. If one joins in and understands what the business is all about, is interested in knowing just that, is interested in thinking about how to do things better and seek opportunities, then you're on the right track." Birger really focused on dialogues, having repeatedly learned that a CIO and his staff can't think of everything. Through dialogue, good ideas can emerge, and he considered that his most important task in that regard was to bring some value into the discussions. As a CIO he was very clear that his competence needed to be more than just IT. He needed competence that enabled him to be an important team player for the whole organization.

Basically Birger argued that a CIO must spend more time on things that aren't directly connected to IT than on the technology itself. He explained that an average day for him ranged from planned staff meetings, projects meetings and meetings with other managers to report reading and writing. Additionally he had a lot of ad hoc activities and meeting with suppliers and other external connections.

An important area for Birger was increasing the users' IS competence, and he strongly believed that this could be achieved through good project processes. In the next section we will dive deeper into those processes and get to know Birger's beliefs about how users can best increase their IS competence through doing things "right," as he put it.

Good Processes Give Good Users (and Vice Versa)

To date, little or no research has focused on how and if users improve their IS competence through IS strategic processes. Birger, however, was a strong believer in good processes as a key to developing competence. Birger told us: "At the time of speaking, the IS competence amongst the users varies a lot. Especially senior staff members sometimes struggle in regard to using the different ISs properly. However, by having good processes we can strengthen it." As an example, he used the introduction of a new salary and HR system. The process of registering an employee's salary was really old- fashioned and largely done manually. But the people doing it were comfortable with its familiarity and hence were skeptical of modernizing the process. By spending time with them and introducing them to the opportunities this new system could provide, the IS staff gradually helped them become more positive and enthusiastic toward it. In the end, these previous foot-draggers actually were the ones suggesting new functionality, and infused the whole project with creativity and ideas. Birger argued that if his team had neglected this stage in the project, they would have ended up with a great IS that the potential users wouldn't know how to use. Moreover, Birger told us, when the users started to feel enthusiastic, the project itself benefitted from their increased competence, so the result was a win-win. Birger told us that they considered as absolutely crucial this up-front, hands-on way of doing things. He didn't believe in post-project training programs, having found that when people spend a day or two off-site in training, they soon forget much of what was taught, so why bother? Furthermore, Birger considered post-project training as a potential amplifier of bad attitudes toward an IS. How? Well, if the process of involving staff during the project period failed, training could serve as an arena where people could merely get their skepticism toward the IS confirmed Birger wasn't against training, mind you, but he believed that doing the project processes right gave far better outcome in the form of IS competence than just focusing on post-project training. For him, the ideal was doing the project processes right combined with well thought-out training programs. The matrix in Table 2 provides an overview of his thoughts in this issue.

The considerations in Table 2 reflect Birger's experiences from several years of managing IS projects and IS strategic processes. As a consequence, NorConstruct spent little on post-project training programs in the traditional sense, where employees are sent off for a day or two of intensive training. Birger firmly stated that they found spending a lot of money on this was unnecessary as long as they focused on doing the project processes right. Using in-house resources and establishing "super users" throughout the organization was, to Birger, a far more effective, and cheaper, way of increasing the users' competence. He told us that the super users were selected among the staff that was actively involved in the given project. The super users were afforded special training in using the IS correctly, and throughout the project period they had the responsibility of helping their colleagues getting

Table 2. How different approaches give IS competence.

\ Good processes Training	Yes	No
Yes	Ideal	Bad
No	Good	Worst

started with the new IS and providing user support whenever needed. The training given to the super users was often provided by the vendor, so it was a part of the overall project implementation cost. Birger explained that because certain ISs were used differently in different divisions, the super users were trained accordingly. To illustrate the point, he cited NorConstruct's new calculation software. Its main purpose was to support the building-project processes. However, the different divisions, and the departments within those divisions, were involved in different stages of the projects. Moreover, the application was used by economists as well as engineers, and naturally the two groups were involved in different sides of a building project. What the IS department did was to ensure that all super users were given training that enabled them to use most modules of the system, but they were also given special training in the areas directly connected to their professional life. Throughout the project period they had the responsibility of training their colleagues as more and more functionality was introduced. According to Birger, people throughout the organization said they really appreciated being introduced to a new IS from a colleague as opposed to being sent away for an intensive training program run by some outsider.

A Matter of Costs?

Offering training in a new IS on site via super users sounds far cheaper than sending employees away for pricey training courses, and it is. But Birger firmly stated that doing it this way wasn't primarily a question of economy. NorConstruct's focus was on getting the best results from its projects. He said, "As long as the costs are reasonable, we focus on doing good projects." In Birger's view, sending people away for training represented an unreasonable cost compared to the outcome of such arrangements (see Table 2). He considered the overall cost benefit picture to be better using the model with super users without post-project training programs. The super users, however, still had the responsibility of keeping their colleagues up to date and providing user support after a project had finished. Birger also emphasized that even if they had chosen a strategy of external training programs, they would have met with lots of resistance from the employees, who rarely felt they had the time to undergo such courses. By following Birger's super-user, on-site program, the employees felt that they didn't have to sacrifice as much and were more able to combine training with their everyday work activities.

So Birger's basic experience as a CIO was that IS competence and IS strategic processes have a circular relationship that can be either positive or negative depending on what is done. Doing the processes right will improve staff's IS competence, and their increased competence will in turn help improve the processes.

CHALLENGES/PROBLEMS FACING THE ORGANIZATION

Throughout this case we have described a way of doing IS strategic processes that for the most part was accepted and appraised by members of the organization. However, NorConstruct was not without challenges and improvement potential. We consider the following three issues to be the most critical:

Decision Time

Even in this action-oriented firm, it can be a very long time between when an IS need is first identified and when the decision to procure it occurs. For example, the need for a new salary and HR system was first identified some 15 years ago. During that period, almost everybody agreed that such a project merited prompt initiation. However, due to demands on other projects needing it even more, the project remained on the back burner, a task for tomorrow. In NorConstruct, those people in need of an IS are responsible for pushing the launching process forward, and that policy has occasionally led to slow IS strategic decision-making processes. At the time of the case study, this remained an unsolved issue. But it also says a lot about NorConstruct's intense focus on productive projects. Since the HR problem didn't qualify as one, it got easily postponed, year after year.

Project Time

As Birger said, it was more important for NorConstruct to get its IS projects finished satisfactorily than to get them finished posthaste. But this policy carried the possibility of staff getting worn out if the projects dragged on. Most staff had their everyday work tasks to fulfill besides any given IS projects they were engaged in. Moreover, staff not directly involved in the project could get tired of waiting for the new IS to be implemented, especially if the decision time had been long as well. Birger explained that the calculation system project arose from a need identified many years earlier, and it had weathered a long implementation period, too. Not surprisingly, then, some staff members expressed irritation when the system, once finally implemented, still had inevitable kinks that needed reporting and fixing. The balance between quality and time could grow still more important in NorConstruct, since even more advanced ISs were on the verge of being introduced there, and such projects usually take an inordinate amount of time to put in place.

Overview of Needs

In NorConstruct it was Birger, as CIO, and the IS council that were supposed to prioritize and keep the overview of the IS needs in the organization. But Birger came to learn that a lot of the needs never got to the IS council or to him. Why? Because of time and distance, he explained. People in the organization tended to be unusually dedicated to their job, plus they had very busy work schedules, so they didn't have the time to follow up on IS needs. So they developed work-arounds for their problems—everything from making their own small and private ISs in a spreadsheet or a simple database program like MS Access—or they just ignored those annoyances until someone finally had the energy to address them. As CIO, Birger found this situation a challenge, because he would never know if his overview of organizational IS needs was in complete alignment with the actual needs.

REFERENCES

Earl, M. J. (1996). Information Systems Strategy…Why Planning Techniques are not the Answer. *Business Strategy Review*, *7*(1), 54–58. doi:10.1111/j.1467-8616.1996. tb00115.x

Galliers, B. (1999). Towards the integration of e-business, knowledge management and policy considerations within an information systems strategy framework. *The Journal of Strategic Information Systems*, *8*(3), 229–234. doi:10.1016/S0963-8687(00)00023-8

Galliers, R. D., Swatman, P. M. C., & Swatman, P. A. (1995). Strategic Information-Systems Planning - Deriving Comparative Advantage from Edi. *Journal of Information Technology*, *10*(3), 149–157. doi:10.1057/jit.1995.19

Gottschalk, P. (1999). Strategic information systems planning: the IT strategy implementation matrix. *European Journal of Information Systems*, *8*(2), 107–118. doi:10.1057/palgrave.ejis.3000324

Hall, E. T. (1977). *Beyond Culture*. Garden City, NY: Anchor Press/Doubleday.

Hall, E. T. (1983). *The Dance of Life*. Garden City, NY: Anchor Press/Doubleday.

Hofstede, G. (1980). *Culture's Consequences: International Differences in Work-Related Values*. London: Sage Publications.

Hofstede, G. (1991). *Cultures and Organizations: Software of the Mind*. New York: McGraw-Hill.

March, J. G. (2006). Rationality, foolishness, and adaptive intelligence. *Strategic Management Journal*, *27*(3), 201–214. doi:10.1002/smj.515

Mintzberg, H. (1987). Crafting Strategy. *Harvard Business Review*, 66–75.

Mintzberg, H. (1996). Learning 1, planning 0. *California Management Review*, *38*(4), 92–93.

Mintzberg, H., & Ghoshal, S. (2003). *The Strategy Process: Concepts, Contexts, Cases*. Upper Saddle River, NJ: Pearson Education.

Schein, E. H. (1985). *Organizational Culture and Leadership*. San Francisco: Jossey Bass.

Stacey, R. D. (2007). *Strategic Management and Organisational Dynamics: The Challenge of Complexity* (5 ed.). Upper Saddle River, NJ: Prentice Hall.

Stacey, R. D. (2001). *Complex Responsive Processes in Organizations: Learning and Knowledge Creation (Complexity & Emergence in Organizations)*. London: Routledge.

Stacey, R. D. (2005). Values, spirituality and organizations: a complex responsive processes perspective. In D. Griffin & R. Stacey, D. (Eds.), *Complexity and the Experience of Leading Organizations* (pp. 93-123). London: Routledge.

Teubner, A. (2007). Strategic information systems planning: A case study from the financial services industry. *The Journal of Strategic Information Systems*, *16*(1), 105–125. doi:10.1016/j.jsis.2007.01.002

This work was previously published in the Journal of Cases on Information Technology, Volume 12, Issue 4, edited by Mehdi Khosrow-Pour, pp. 50-64, copyright 2010 by IGI Publishing (an imprint of IGI Global).

Section 3
Implementation and Interactions

Chapter 12

ICT and Web 2.0 Technologies as a Determinant of Business Performance

Tanja Arh
Jožef Stefan Institute, Slovenia

Vlado Dimovski
University of Ljubljana, Faculty of Economics, Slovenia

Borka Jerman Blažič
Jožef Stefan Institute, Slovenia

EXCUTIVE SUMMARY

This chapter aims at presenting the results of an empirical study, linking the fields of technology-enhanced learning (TEL), Web 2.0 technologies and organizational learning, and their impact on the financial and non-financial business performance. The chapter focuses on the presentation of the conceptualization of a structural model that was developed to test the impact of technology-enhanced learning and Web 2.0 technologies on the organizational learning and business performance of companies with more than 50 employees. The paper provides detailed definitions of technology-enhanced learning, Web 2.0 technologies and technical terms related to it, its scope and the process of organisational learning, as well as a method for business performance assessment. Special attention is given to the findings related to the observed correlations between the aforementioned constructs. The results of the study indicate a strong impact of ICT and technology-enhanced learning on organizational learning and the non-financial business performance.

DOI: 10.4018/978-1-4666-2618-8.ch012

INTRODUCTION AND BACKGROUND

Success in a highly dynamic environment requires a more efficient response to customers from the side of the companies, more flexible approaches in facing their business circle and more focus on their core competencies (Smith, 2008). What are companies expected to do in order to introduce the necessary changes in the whole business circle? The answer definitely lies in people. The employees' knowledge and competencies significantly contribute to the company's ability to react to the requirements of the fast changes markets, customer needs and successful business processes. With this in view, companies are obliged to manage and maintain the knowledge of their employees. Maintaining the knowledge means to evaluate the employees' tacit and explicit knowledge, and provide knowledge within the company with the suitable tools (Reychav & Weisberg, 2009).

To perform this approach effectively, employees and all members of the company are expected to continuously refresh and enhance their skills and knowledge (Collins & Smith, 2006). As the human capital replacing the physical capital as the source of competitive advantage, organizational learning emerges as a key element for success (Varney, 2008). Only by making learning a truly strategic investment we can ensure an organization in which every person within the company is fully enabled to perform effectively and meet the ever changing demands.

When companies devise their strategies for the employee knowledge acquisition, they can find the most suitable solutions among the methods based on information and communication technologies (ICT), Web 2.0 technologies and technology-enhanced learning (TEL). Technology-enhanced learning as a way of acquiring knowledge and competences has been adopted by many companies as a promising time and cost saving solution providing learn-on-demand opportunities to individual employees, TEL enables workers to access various on-line databases, tools and e-services that help them find solutions for work-related problems (Zhang, 2002; 2003). The term Web 2.0 was coined by O'Reilly (2005) as a common denominator for recent trends heading towards the 'Read-Write Web', allowing everyone to publish resources on the web using simple and open, personal and collaborative publishing tools, known as the social software: blogs, wikis, social bookmarking systems, podcasts, etc. The main features of these tools are dynamism, openness and free availability. According to MacManus and Porter (2005), the power of social software lies in the content personalization and remixing with the other data to create much more useful information and knowledge. The continuously growing dissemination of social and open software in technology-enhanced learning is expected to reshape the technology-enhanced learning landscapes that are currently based on closed, proprietary, institutionalized systems. Thanks to the web evolution, the use of social and open software for learning is becoming an increasingly feasible alternative to these closed, proprietary, institutionalized systems.

However, earlier authors (Roach, 1987) argued that ICT still had not paid off in terms of the required productivity growth. The phenomenon was called the 'productivity paradox' and it asserted that the ICT investments did not result in productivity gains (Navarette & Pick, 2002). Carr (2003) believes that 'ICT may not help a company gain a strategic advantage, but it could easily put a company at a cost disadvantage.' Indeed, the latest empirical studies (Dewan & Kraemer 1998; Navarette & Pick 2002; Dimovski & Škerlavaj 2003) tend to reject the productivity paradox thesis – the phenomenon of organisational learning can be seen as a way out of the dilemma called the productivity paradox. In the last few decades the field of organisational learning has attracted a lot of interest from academics as well as practitioners. A key question in this context is the connection between ICT and organisational learning, and the impact they both have on the business performance (Škerlavaj & Dimovski, 2006).

In the past decade, quite a lot of research studies dealt with the influence of ICT (investments, usage, etc.) on (mainly financial) business performance. We can divide them into four streams of research based on the observed units: business, industry, national and international levels. The results were mixed. Some recent studies in our context (Dimovski & Škerlavaj, 2003) that analysed the influence of hardware, software, telecommunications and knowledge investments on value added per industry in Slovenia for the period 1996-2000, demonstrated a statistically significant, positive influence of hardware and telecommunication investments on value added (Škerlavaj & Dimovski, 2006). Dimovski (1994) confirmed the positive impact on both – the financial and non-financial performance aspects, using a one-industry research design and a stratified sample of 200 credit unions in Ohio, based on the asset size criterion (Škerlavaj & Dimovski, 2006). This study investigated the determinants, processes and outcomes of organisational learning, as well as the relationship between organisational learning and performance. Sloan et al. (2002), Lam (1998) and Figueireido (2003) also arrived at similar conclusions. Simonin (1997) found strong effects of learning on the financial and non-financial performance in the context of strategic alliances.

This chapter has four parts. The first section provides definitions of technology-enhanced learning and Web 2.0 technologies, technical terms related to it, its scope and the process of organisational learning, as well as a method for the business performance assessment in order to develop a set of constructs and an empirical basis for the relationships among them. In the second part, the model's operationalisation through the development of a measurement sub-model is presented. In the third section, the model is tested using a structural linear modelling technique. We conclude with a discussion on the implications of the results and offer some guidelines for future research.

CONCEPTUALISATION OF STRUCTURAL SUB-MODEL

A complete research model normally consists of two sub-models: measurement and structural (Jöreskog, Sörbrom, 1993). The measurement sub-model shows how each latent variable is operationalised through observations of corresponding indicators, and also provides data on validity and reliability of the variables observed. The structural sub-model describes relationships between the latent variables, indicating the amount of unexplained variance. Development of a quality model requires first to establish a structural framework, which is usually implemented in two steps: presentation of fundamental constructs and review of potential correlations between them. Results of the final analysis greatly depend on good conceptualisation of a research model (Jöreskog, Sörbrom, 1993).

Technology-Enhanced Leaning and Web 2.0 Technologies

Technology-enhanced learning is a term introduced along with the introduction of information and communication technology for educational purposes. Up to date companies have widely used this term as a synonym for e-learning (Arh, Pipan & Jerman-Blažič, 2006). Definitions of technology-enhanced learning are various, diverse and lack unity, consequently, it is of outmost importance to provide precise definitions of technology-enhanced learning and related notions. Hereby we refer to the process of studying and teaching as technology-enhanced learning when it includes information and communication technology, regardless of the mode or the scope of its use (Henry, 2001).

Kirschner and Paas (2001) defined technology-enhanced learning as a learning process in which the Internet plays the key role in the presentation, support, management and assessment of learning. Rosenberg (2001) defines technology-enhanced learning as a learning process in which information technology partially or fully undertakes the role of a mediator between different stakeholders involved in the learning process. We refer to the process of studying and teaching as technology-enhanced learning when it includes information and communication technology, regardless of the mode or the scope of its use (Henry, 2001; Dinevski & Plenković, 2002). Technology-enhanced learning extends the company out to ever-widening circles of impact. The companies are participating in a radical redefinition of industries, markets and the global economy itself. Today, organizations are investing great efforts into the making of proper adjustments to the changing business environment in order to enhance their competitiveness. In an attempt to keep up with the development of information technology and the Internet, many businesses are replacing traditional vocational training with e-learning to better manage their workforce. However, it is questionable whether training programs actually change employee behaviour after the implementation. In the case of the US companies, only 10-15% of training is applied to work (Sevilla & Wells, 1988).

When we talk about technology-enhanced learning we cannot overlook the impact of the Web 2.0 technologies on the process of technology-enhanced learning. The Web 2.0 technologies are changing the way messages spread across the web. A number of online tools and platforms are now defining how people share their perspectives, opinions, thoughts and experiences. The Web 2.0 tools, such as instant messaging systems, blogs, RSS, video casting, social bookmarking, social networking, podcasts and picture sharing sites are becoming more and more popular. One major advantage of the Web 2.0 tools is that the majority of them are free. There is a large number of the Web 2.0 tools, some of the more popular ones are: instant messaging systems, blogs, video-wiki and xo-wiki, Doodle, podcasting, RSS, etc.

Instant Messaging Systems (IMS)

The need for communication tools in the learning process is often underestimated by educators, especially those who feel comfortable with the traditional, instructive way of teaching. However, even with their 'traditional' approach learners need to communicate with each other when working together. At the beginning of the 90s, digital communication tools were rather limited: apart from the direct face-to-face meetings, the main way to communicate was through the plain old telephone. Sharing course materials was only enabled by a copy or a fax machine. However, these devices were rarely available in ordinary households. The only barriers to communication that exist today are the lack of skills needed to operate the new technologies. This barrier goes mostly unnoticed with the younger generations that have grown up as digital 'natives', rarely pulling themselves away from their computers (even out on the street they keep the mobile phones in their pockets), but it is definitely still a serious obstacle for many educators. However, the new technologies are inevitably permeating our everyday lives, and it is probably not necessary to explain the purpose of instant messaging to anyone in 2009. The number of users of the world top 10 instant messaging systems is counted in hundreds of millions according to the Wikipedia (2008) statistics, e.g. QQ 783 million total, 317.9 million active, 40.3 million peak online (mostly in China), MSN 294 million active, Yahoo 248 million active, Skype 309 million total, 12 million speak online, etc. The decisive factor for choosing an instant messaging system by an ordinary user is a friend recommendation (most people start using the same system the majority of their friends are already using). The IMS are used for any kind of information exchange including communication between employees or students regarding their study or learning environment. This is the reason this practice is included in the technology that contributes to the personalized learning environment.

Blogs

A blog is a type of a web site in which entries are made as in a journal or a diary and are displayed in reverse chronological order. Basically, an individual maintains his or her own weblog and it functions as a sort of a personal online diary. Regular entries such as comments, descriptions of events, or other types of materials combined with text, images, and links to other weblogs and web sites are the typical weblog ingredients. Blogs have attracted a lot of attention within the educational circles, where they are experienced as the tools that support several pedagogical aims and scenarios, ranging from an individual knowledge management and competence development to group-based learning activities. Therefore, blogs have become an important educational tool in recent years, providing an opportunity for both facilitators and employees to publish their ideas, essays, or simply providing a space to reflect upon their particular learning processes and reading materials. In the context of teaching and learning, blogs can do much more than just deliver instructions or course news items to employees. They can be an interesting collaboration tool for employees who can join relevant community and find people to collaborate with, give feedback to the management and others. In a learning environment blogs are most frequently used for content publishing and sharing. The blog technology can be improved by plug-ins such as the FeedBack tool used to track and integrate the content of other authors within one blog. FeedBack is a standard plug-in piece of code developed within the framework of the iCamp project (www.icamp-project. eu). In a simple way it is used to enable blog users to subscribe to each others' blogs. The blogging technology, in combination with innovations such as the FeedBack specification, has definitely a high potential to be considered a powerful tool for learning with others.

Video-Wiki and Xo-Wiki

Publishing or presenting someone's thoughts online usually means writing some text and illustrating it with pictures. Still, the most natural form of communication for humans is face to face, and for most people the majority of information is presented orally, directly facing the presenter, whose non-verbally communicated information is often even more important than the words they utter. Video could serve as a replacement for the face-to-face presentation, since it can convey the visible behaviour and important non-verbal information. In the past, recording a video and making sure it reached the target audience was quite a big challenge. Depending on the number of intended users, TV broadcasts or video tapes could be used. Employees taking part in an e-learning course work in groups, and are suggested to form groups by getting to know each other and discover some common topics. The mentor/tutor usually uses VideoWiki to record for ex. short self-introduction videos in which employees present their background, or explain their expectations regarding some specific topic for the group assignment. VideoWiki is based on the Red5 open-source Flash server written in Java and Flash. It allows video recording, searching and playback through the main system web page or via the standard URL links. VideoWiki also provides RSS feeds for each name, space or author, and videos can be embedded on any web page using special code snippets. Collaborative creation and maintenance of knowledge artefacts is one of the emerging phenomena of the online Internet communities, such as Wikipedia.org, MediaWiki.org, LyricWiki.org, Microformats.org and Wikitravel.org. A collection of web pages (a so-called wiki) can also be very useful for the teaching and learning purposes; for instance if learners need to collaborate to work on certain topics, or if facilitators wish to develop and share their learning content with others. Consequently, a contemporary approach to technology-enhanced learning requires tools which can enable learners to work on artefacts collaboratively, either by allowing them to publish small posts which can be reused and combined with others (see the blog-based solution presented in the previous section) or by providing real wiki functionality. XoWiki is one such wiki implementation, realized as a component of OpenACS (Open Architecture Community System), a framework for building scalable, community-oriented web applications. XoWiki includes a rich text editor for easy creation and editing of wiki pages, and provides features for structuring, commenting, tagging and visualisation of the wiki-based content.

Doodle

When employees work on a group project they need to divide tasks among the members of the group and monitor the progress of work. This requires the employees to engage in collaboration, discussion and decision making processes. In the context of bringing different cultures, educational systems, levels of teaching, languages and technology skills into a common virtual learning space, planning a series of meetings several weeks in advance may simply not work. Taking this into account, employees must adopt simple solutions to meet their needs. There are plenty of solutions which can help make a project run smoothly. One of them is Doodle. Doodle can be described simply as a web-based tool for finding suitable appointment dates. Doodle allows employees to plan their meetings with partners, suppliers and other employees. In addition to time management, it can be used as a voting tool for any other issue that arises as a part of the distance learning process; for example, the literature that needs to be selected and analysed in order to complete a particular task.

Searching the Net: ObjectSpot

ObjectSpot is a meta-search engine designed to facilitate different types of research. It can be used to find publications and other learning resources on the web. Object-Spot realizes federated searches over an ever-increasing number of digital libraries and learning object repositories. It provides access to more than 10 million learning objects spread across famous libraries such as the Directory of Open Access Journals (DOAJ), OAIster, EBSCO, ACM, CiteBase and IEEE. Some of these repositories are open access, whilst others require registration or subscription.

Organisational Learning

In recent years, the concept of organizational learning has enjoyed a renaissance among both academics and practitioners seeking to improve organizations. Early proponents (e.g. Argyris & Schön, 1978) found their ideas largely confined to the periphery of management thought during the 1980s, but the 1990s witnessed a rebirth of interest. The current renaissance is evident in the creation of a journal about organizational learning (*The Learning Organization*) as well as in the devotion of special issues of several journals to the topic (e.g., *Organization Science*, 1991; *Organizational Dynamics*, 1993; *Accounting, Management and Information Technologies,* 1995; *Journal of Organizational Change Management*, 1996). The appearance of several major review articles is testimony to organizational learning's growing stature in the research community (see Crossan, Lane & White, 1999; Dodgson, 1993; Fiol & Lyles, 1985; Huber, 1991; Jones, 2000; Levitt & March, 1998; Miner & Mezias, 1996). Moreover, a large number of articles in professional periodicals describing the design and management of learning organizations attest to the popularity of organizational learning and knowledge management among practitioners. New theories of knowledge creation have become prominent (Nonaka, 1994; Raelin, 1997), and formal knowledge management programs have been undertaken in many companies (Davenport, De Long & Beers, 1998). As we head into the twenty-first century, therefore, organizational learning promises to be a dominant perspective with influence on both organizational research and management practice (Argyris & Schön, 1996).

Defining Organizational Learning

Organisational learning is defined in numerous ways and approached from different perspectives. The pioneers (Argyris, & Schön, 1996; Senge, 1990) defined organisational learning as an individual's acquisition of information and knowledge, and development of analytical and communicational skills. Understanding organisational learning as a process, which can take up different levels of development, makes the learning organisational structure an ideal form of organisation, which can only be achieved once the process of organisational learning is fully optimised and the organisation is viewed as a system (Senge, 1990). Jones (2000) emphasizes the importance of organizational learning for the organizational performance, defining it as "a process through which managers try to increase organizational members' capabilities in order to better understand and manage the organization and its environment and accept the decisions that would increase organizational performance on a continuous basis." The aforementioned statements regarding the lack of unity of organisational learning definitions are also supported by the findings of Shrivastava, 1983 and Dimovski, 1994. The former states that extensive research carried out in the field of organisational learning has mostly been fragmented, while the latter adds the fragmentation lead to the multitude of definitions (for ex. Nonaka & Takeuchi, 1996 and Wall, 1998), differing according to the criteria of inclusion, scope and focus (Škerlavaj, 2003). Dimovski (1994) and Dimovski & Colnar (1999) provided an overview of previous research and identified four varying perspectives on organizational learning. Dimovski's model managed to merge informational, interpretational, strategic and behavioural approaches to organizational learning, and defined it as a process of information acquisition, information interpretation and the resulting behavioural and cognitive changes which should, in turn, have an impact on the company performance.

Development of our research model is based on DiBella and Nevis' model (DiBella & Nevis, 1998) of integrated approach, according to which the organisational learning factors are divided into study guidelines and study promoters, and on the Dimovski approach (Dimovski, 1994), which combines the aforementioned four aspects of organisational learning.

In this sense the organisational learning can be defined as a dynamic process of the acquisition, transfer and use of knowledge (Crossan, Lane & White, 1999; Dibella & Nevis, 1998), which starts at the core of the organisation – related to individual and team performance – and enable companies to strengthen the efficiency of the financial and non-profit (non-financial?) business achievements (Tippins & Sohi, 2003).

Business Performance

Business performance assessments have advanced over the past years, and developed from traditional, exclusively financial criteria, to modern criteria, which include also the non-financial indicators. Due to numerous disadvantages of the classical accounts and the growing need for quality information on company performance, the theory of economics started developing improved models for performance assessment, taking into account all shareholders: employees, customers, supplier employees and the wider community, also advocated by the Freeman's shareholders theory (Freeman, 1994; 1984). There are several approaches to the non-financial indicator selection, the most established of which is the Balanced Scorecard – BSC (Kaplan & Norton, 1992). The existing models, based on the accounting categories, combine with the non-financial data and the assessment of the so called 'soft' business areas, which mostly improve the assessment of companies' perspective possibilities. For a good performance of a modern company we need to introduce the non-financial indicators along with the financial ones.

Relationship among Constructs

Findings based on a rather wide overview and systematisation of literature has shown that we can expect positive impact of ICT and technology-enhanced learning on organisational learning and business performance. Robey et al. (2000) do warn that technology-enhanced learning and relative ICT may take either the role of a promoter or the role of an inhibitor of organisational learning, so the following hypothesis can be posed:

H₁: Technology-enhanced learning has positive impact on organisational learning.
H₂: Technology-enhanced learning has positive impact on financial performance.
H₃: Technology-enhanced learning has positive impact on non-financial performance.

Correlation between organisational learning and business success is often a controversial issue when we begin to deal with the company management (Inkpen & Crossan, 1995). Some authors believe better performance is related to organisational learning, though their definitions of business results differ greatly. In relation to this we can mention the capacity of organisational learning to have a positive impact on the financial results (Lei et al., 1999; Slater & Narver, 1995), on the results related to shareholders (Goh & Richards, 1997; Ulrich et al., 1993) and on the business results, such as innovativeness and greater productivity (Leonard-Barton, 1992). Mintzberg (1990) says the company performance is an important piece of feedback information on effectiveness and efficiency of the learning process. The study of Perez et al. (2004) has shown organisational learning has a significant impact on the company performance. On this basis, the following hypotheses can be put forward:

H₄: Organisational learning leads to improved financial results.
H₅: Organisational learning leads to improved non-financial results.

CONCEPTUALISATION OF MEASUREMENT SUB-MODEL

Having understood the hypothesized correlations between the latent variables, the following question is logically raised: 'How should these four constructs be operationalised and measured?' There are certainly various approaches available, since the number and the type of indicators to be used for the assessment of a certain construct, the number and the type of items to be included under an indicator and the methods for their integration are decided on the basis of validity and variability of specific measuring instruments. Table 1 presents constructs, indicators used for construct assessment, number of items summed up to give the value of an indicator and the theory or empirical research on the basis of which the measurement items were developed.

In short, the hypothesized model shall be composed of four constructs and 13 indicators, and will be of recursive nature, meaning that there shall be no cases of two variables appearing simultaneously, i.e. as a cause and a consequence to one another.

Development of Research Instrument

The questionnaire used has been under constant development and validation for more than 10 years. Dimovski (1994) used it on a sample of Ohio credit unions in order to measure the organizational learning process as a source of competitive advantage. Škerlavaj (2003) upgraded it to include the measures of non-financial performance, while he replaced the industry-specific measures of financial performance with two

Table 1. Specification of constructs

Latent Variables	Indicators and Number of Items from Questionnaire
Technology-Enhanced Learning	Information and communication infrastructure (ICI) – 9 items Education technology (ET) – 10 items Learning contents (LC) – 3 items
Organisational Learning	Knowledge acquisition (KAc) – 9 items Knowledge transmission (KTt) – 10 items Use of knowledge (UoK) – 10 items
Financial Performance	Return on assets (FP1) – 1 item Return on capital (FP2) – 1 item Value added per employee (FP3) – 1 item
Non-Financial Performance	Employee fluctuation (NFP1) – 1 item Share of loyal customers (NFP2) – 1 item Number of customer complaints (NFP3) – 1 item Supplier relations (NFP4) – 1 item

measures valid for all companies. For this study the operationalisation of all four constructs involved was improved and applied on a sample of Slovenian companies with more than 50 employees in 2007. The reason to include smaller companies is to improve the generalizability of the research findings. The measurement instrument used in this study has 22 items for the technology-enhanced learning construct, 29 items for the organizational learning construct, 3 items for the financial and 4 items for the non-financial performance. The pre-testing procedures were conducted in the form of interviews and studies with managers and focus groups of research and academic colleagues.

RESEARCH HYPOTHESES AND MODEL

Once the theoretical frame of the model is devised, illustration of conceptualisation by the means of a flow chart is to be tackled (Arh, Dimovski & Jerman-Blažič, 2008). Flow chart is a graphical representation of interrelations between various elements of a model. Measurement variables belonging to exogenous latent variables are marked with an x, while their measurement deviations are marked with a δ. Endogenous latent variable indicators are marked with a y, and measurement deviations with an ε. Structural equation deviations are ζ, exogenous latent variables are ξ, endogenous constructs are η, and one-way influence of exogenous latent variables on exogenous are γ. To describe relations between latent variables and their indicators (measurement variables) we use λ. The Figure 1 below is showing a conceptualised research model, presenting all basic constructs and hypothesized correlations between them. We aim at proving: (1) that the latent variable of technology-enhanced learning (TEL) has positive impact on organisational learning (OL), (2) financial (FP) and (3) non-financial performance (NFP); (4) that the latent variable of organisational learning (OL) as a process of knowledge creation leads to improved financial results (FP), as well as to (5) improved non-financial results (NFP); (6) that it is impossible to expect significant statistical correlations between financial performance (FP) and non-financial (NFP) performance.

RESEARCH PROCEDURE

The methodology applied to test our research model was structural equation modelling (SEM). This involves a combination of confirmatory factor analysis (CFA) and econometric modelling, which aims to analyse hypothesised relationships among the latent constructs, measured with observed indicators (measurement variables). Table 2 provides the procedure for data analysis.

Figure 1. Conceptualised research model

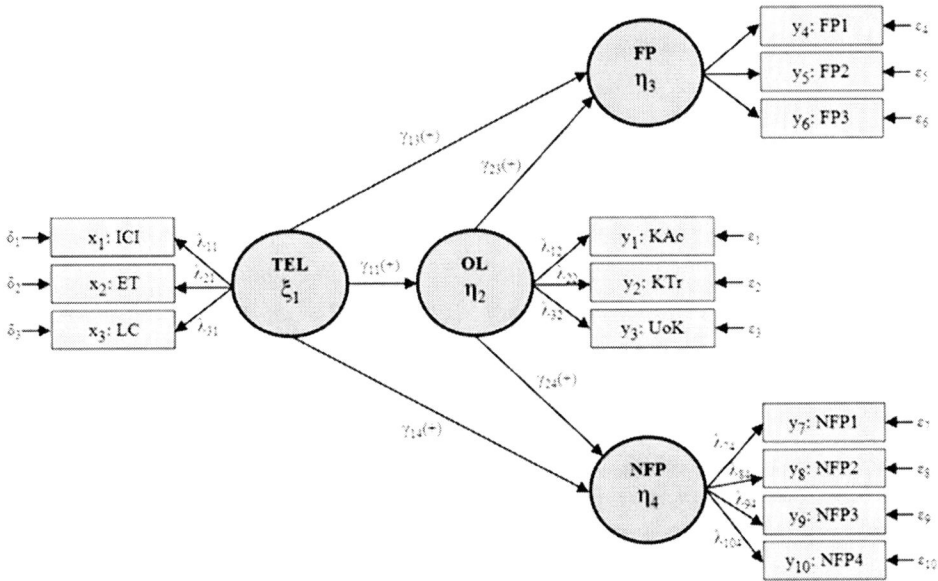

Table 2. Research pocedure

Stage	Analysis	Purpose
1.	Item Analysis	Investigation of sample characteristics Investigation of item means Investigation of item-to-total correlations
2.	Exploratory Factor Analysis	Exploration of loadings; removal of items with low loadings and high cross-loadings; Assessment of number of latent factors Assessment of reliability (Cronbach's alpha)
3.	Confirmatory Factor Analysis	Assessment of convergent validity Assessment of discriminant validity Assessment of construct reliability Assessment of correlations and multicollinearity
4.	Testing Hypothesis	Assessment of structural relationship (H1-H5) Parameter Estimates for Overall Measurement Model Convergent and Discriminant Validity
5.	Presentation of Results	Discussion of findings

First, the item analysis was performed to describe the sample characteristics, to investigate the item means, and to assess item-to-total correlations. Second, exploratory factor analysis was performed to explore whether the items load highly on their intended latent construct, and have low cross-loadings. After the exploratory factor analysis, reliability of the underlying factors was discussed in terms of Cronbach's alphas. Third, confirmatory analysis (CFA) was performed to ensure that the constructs are valid and reliable; this refers to the measurement part of the model. Consequently, CFAs (without any structural relationships) were performed with LISREL 8.80 to check whether the items meet the criteria for convergent and discriminant validity, as well as construct reliability. Properties of the four research constructs in the proposed model (Figure 1) and the five hypotheses were tested using LISREL 8.80 and PRELIS 2.30 packages for structural equation analysis and procedures. As estimation method for model evaluation and procedures, the maximum likelihood (ML) method was utilized. Structural equation modelling (SEM) is designed to evaluate how well a proposed conceptual model that contains observed indicators and hypothetical constructs explains or fits the collected data. It also provides the ability to measure or specify the structural relationships among the sets of unobserved (latent) variables, while describing the amount of unexplained variance. Clearly, the hypothetical model in this study was designed to measure structural relationships among the unobserved constructs that are set up on the basis of relevant theories, and prior empirical research and results. Therefore, the SEM procedure is an appropriate solution for testing the proposed structural model and hypotheses for this study.

Data Gathering and Sample

Based on the model's conceptualisation, a measurement instrument (questionnaire) was developed and sent in June 2007 to the CEOs or board members of all Slovenian companies with more than 50 employees, which accounted for 1215 companies. In the first three weeks 356 completed questionnaires were returned, five out of which were excluded from further analysis due to missing values. The response rate was 29.7%, which can be considered successful in the Slovenian context (using our primary data collection technique and no call backs). It is an indication that, beside academia, managers are also interested to know whether and in which circumstances investments in ICT and technology-enhanced learning pay off. We aimed at an audience of top and middle managers bearing in mind the idea of a strategic and to some degree even an interdisciplinary perspective of the companies in question, although there is some discrepancy between the desired and the actual structure of respondents. Based on the criterion of the average number of employees, in 2006 73.88% of the selected companies had between 50 and 249 employees, followed by 14.61% with 250 to 499 employees, while 11.51% of the companies had 500 to 999 employees. According to the company revenues in 2006, 33.15% of the Slovenian companies had the annual revenue of 2 to 7.3 million EUR. A somewhat smaller proportion (32.87%) of companies had the net income of 7.3 to 29.2 million EUR in this same period, 19.94% had the annual turnover of more than 29.2 million

Table 3. Structure of respondents (by industry)

Industry (EU NACE Rev.1)	Frequency	Percent (%)
A Agriculture, hunting and forestry	7	2
B Fishing	0	0
C Mining and quarrying	7	2
D Manufacturing	158	44.4
E Electricity, gas and water supply	15	4.2
F Construction	49	13.8
G Wholesale & retail, repair of motor vehicles, personal & household goods	41	11.5
H Hotels and restaurants	12	3.4
I Transport, storage and communication	14	3.9
J Financial intermediation	7	2
K Real estate, renting and business activities	16	4.5
M Education	2	0.6
N Health and social work	1	0.3
O Other community, social and personal services	27	7.6

euro, and only 14.04% have not reached the annual revenue threshold of 2 million euro. The questionnaire was mostly completed by middle management respondents (directors of functional departments). The top and middle management were almost equally represented within the sample.

Table 3 demonstrates the industry structure of the companies in question. Our respondents reported in almost half of all cases that their main industry was manufacturing, followed by 13.8% of companies in the construction business and 11.5% in the wholesale & retail, repair of motor vehicles, personal & household goods. One out of fifteen industries have only one company representative, there was no company from the fishery sector and only two companies working the field of education. This is logical since we excluded the non-profit and small businesses from our analysis.

Parameter Value Estimates

The results of structural equation analysis by LISREL were utilized to test the hypotheses proposed in this study. As discussed in the previous section, the relationships between the constructs were examined based on t-values associated with path coefficients between the constructs. If an estimated t-value was greater than a certain critical value ($p < .05$, t-value = 1.96) (Mueller, 1996), the null hypothesis that the associated estimated parameter is equal to 0 was rejected. Subsequently, the hypothesized relationship was supported.

The maximum likelihood (ML) method was used to estimate the parameter values. In this phase, the hypotheses posed in the conceptualisation phase are tested. Even though several methods can be used for this purpose, ML is the one most often used and has the advantage of being statistically efficient and at the same time specification-error sensitive because it demands only complete data and does not allow for missing values. All methods will, however, lead to similar parameter estimates on the condition that the sample is large enough and that the model is correct (Jöreskog & Sörbrom, 1993). Figure 2 shows a path diagram of our model (with completely standardised parameter estimates).

The Tpu construct demonstrated a statistically significant, positive and strong impact on the Ou. Namely, the value of the completely standardised parameter almost equals the margin of 0.70. However, Tpu did not exhibit any statistically significant impact on the Fp, meaning that the hypothesis 2 must be rejected. The Ol construct demonstrated a statistically significant positive and strong impact on the Fp and an even stronger one on the Nfp. This means that the hypotheses 4 and 5 can be considered empirically supported by the data at hand.

*Figure 2. Research model (completely standardised parameter values, *significant at p > 0.05)*

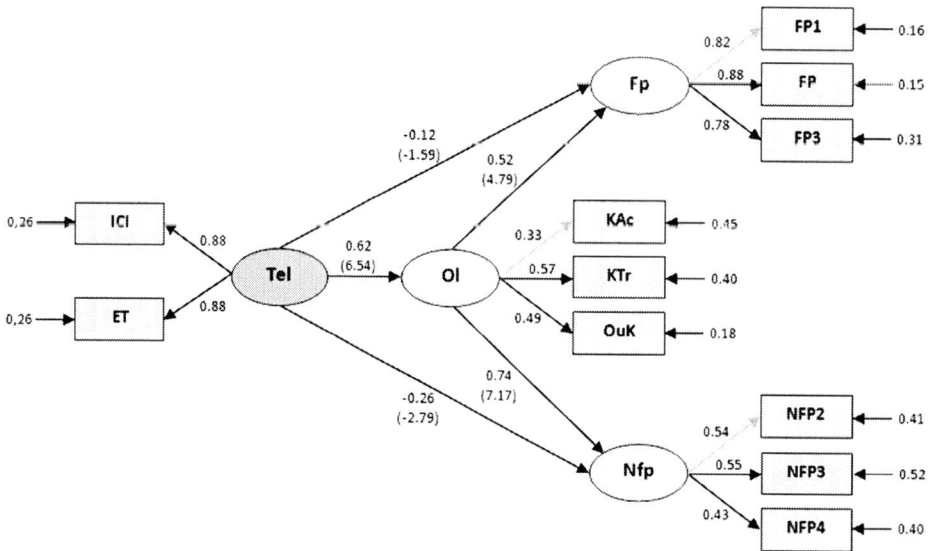

Global Fit Assessment

Bollen (1989) explained that the model fit relates to the degree to which a hypothesised model is consistent with the available data – the degree to which the implicit matrix of covariances (based on the hypothesised model) and the sample covariance matrix (based on the data) fit. The aim of the global fit assessment is to determine to what degree is the model as a whole consistent with the data gathered. Over the years numerous global fit indices have been developed. To every researcher's regret, none of them is superior to the others. Different authors favour different measures. Diamantopoulos and Siguaw (2000) recommend using several measures and at the same time provide reference values for every one of them (Table 4).

The most traditional value is χ^2 statistics. Using this fit indicator we test the hypothesis that the implicit covariance matrix equals the sample covariance matrix. Our goal was not to reject this hypothesis, however, in our case this hypothesis must be rejected (at a 5% level of significance). Nonetheless, quantifying the degree of misfit is often more useful than testing the hypothesis of exact fit, which χ^2 statistics are designed for. All other indices lead to the conclusion that the model is an appropriate representation of reality. The root means square error of approximation (RMSEA) is the most widespread measure of the global fit and in our case points

Table 4. Fit indices

Fit Indices	Reference Value	Model Value	Global Fit
Chi-square ($\chi 2$) of estimate model	($\chi^2/df < 2$)	89.29 (df = 38) = 2.34	No
Goodness-of-fit index (GFI)	$\geq .90$	.96	Yes
Root mean square residual (RMR)	$< .05$	.023	Yes
Root mean square error of approximation (RMSEA)	$\leq .05$	.062	Yes
CAIC	CAIC saturated model CAIC independent model	281.79	Yes
Adjusted goodness-of-fit index (AGFI)	$\geq .90$	.92	Yes
Non-normed fit index (NNFI)	$\geq .95$	.97	Yes
Normed fit index (NFI)	$\geq .90$	.96	Yes
Parsimony goodness-of-fit index(PGFI)	$\geq .50$	.55	Yes
Comparative fit index (CFI)	$\geq .90$	.98	Yes
Critical (CN)	N = 248.77	356	Yes

to the acceptable fitness of the model. The consistent Akaike information criteria (CAIC) of the model needs to be compared against the CAIC of the saturated and independent model, where smaller values represent a better fit. Standardised root mean square residual (standardised RMR) is a fit index calculated on the basis of standardised residuals (differences between elements of the sample and implicit covariance matrixes). The goodness-of-fit (GFI) index and the adjusted goodness-of-fit (AGFI) index are absolute fit indices which directly assess how well the co-variances based on the parameter estimates reproduce the sample covariances (Gebring &Anderson, 1993). All of the indices described above lead to the conclusion that the model can be regarded as an appropriate approximation of reality (at a global level).

SOLUTIONS AND RECOMMENDATIONS

The aim of this paper was to present the conceptualisation of a model for the assessment of the impact of technology-enhanced learning, and the respective information and communication technology on the business performance of Slovene companies with more than 50 employees. The theoretical and empirical grounds were studied in order to demonstrate the correlations between the aforementioned constructs with the basic aim to present a hypothesized research model as a concrete result.

The study focuses on the findings achieved through the estimation of the relations between information and communication technology and technology-enhanced learning, organizational learning and business performance, and their operation-alisation. In accordance with stakeholder theory and balanced scorecard, both the financial and non-financial aspects of business performance are considered. Within this approach, a structural equation model was conceptualised based on the prior theoretical and empirical foundations.

In the study, five hypothesis were tested: (1) technology-enhanced learning has a positive impact on organizational learning, (2) technology-enhanced learning has a positive impact on the financial business results, (3) technology-enhanced learning has a positive impact on the non-financial business results, (4) organizational learning as a process of knowledge creation has a positive impact on the financial performance, and (5) organizational learning has a positive effect on the non-financial performance. A sample of data collected was used through the survey questionnaire, which was circulated among the CEOs and presidents of the management boards of Slovenian companies with more than 50 employees in June 2007. Out of a total of 1215 questionnaires sent, 356 correctly completed questionnaires were returned, which means that the response rate was 29.7%. The questionnaire was structured in four parts. The first construct (technology-enhanced learning) was based on

22 measurement variables, the second construct (organizational learning) on 29 measurement variables related to the acquisition of knowledge, knowledge transfer and the use of knowledge. The third and the fourth constructs were designed with the intention of measuring the financial and non-financial company results (three measurement variables for the financial and four measurement variables for the non-financial results). Equation modelling methodology was used for the analysis in the empirical part of the study. The methodology of structural equation modelling enabled us to concretely determine whether the hypothetical links between the constructs or latent variables are valid or not.

The results of the survey prove a statistically significant, strong and positive impact of ICT and technology-enhanced learning on organizational learning, and a decisive influence of organizational learning on the financial and non-financial business results. The companies which systematically incorporated various advanced educational tools and systems into their daily work, and ensured high quality information and communication technology equipment recognized the importance of organizational learning as the most effective process for the production, dissemination and application of knowledge. Furthermore, the positive effects of organizational learning on the financial and non-financial business results confirm that this concept really guarantees the achievement of higher performance both in financial and non-financial terms. Knowledge is definitely one of the most important criteria of the competitive advantage, which is confirmed by the results of the study.

The study contributes to the technology-enhanced learning and organizational learning base of knowledge in the following three dimensions: (1) theoretical, (2) methodological, and (3) practical. Technology-enhanced learning contributes to sustainable competitive advantage through its interaction with other resources. Recent literature suggests that organizational learning is a process that plays an important role in enhancing company's competitive advantage (Lei, Slocum & Pitts, 1999), which may benefit from the judicious application of technology-enhanced learning. It has also been argued that a prerequisite for the firms to be successful is the completion of Tel with Ol. Within the broader conceptual framework, this study focuses on the relationship between technology-enhanced learning, organizational learning and business performance. As such, the conceptual model offers several research opportunities and provides a solid base for further empirical testing of hypotheses related to technology-enhanced learning and organizational learning.

REFERENCES

Argyris, C., & Schön, D. A. (1978). *Organizational Learning: A Theory of Action Perspective*. Reading, MA: Addison-Wesley.

Argyris, C., & Schön, D. A. (1996). *Organizational Learning II: Theory, Method and Practice*. Reading, MA: Addison-Wesley.

Arh, T., Dimovski, V., & Jerman-Blažič, B. (2008). *Model of impact of technology-enhanced organizational learning on business performance. V P. Cunningham, M. Cunningham (ur.), Collaboration and the knowledge economy: issues, applications, case studies, (str. 1521–1528)*. Netherlands: IOS Press.

Arh, T., Pipan, M., Jerman-Blažič, B. (2006). Virtual learning environment for the support of life-long learning initiative. *WSEAS transactions on advances in engineering education*, 4(4), str. 737–743.

Bollen, K. A. (1989). *Structural equations with latent variables*. New York: Wiley.

Carr, N. G. (2003). IT doesn't matter. *Harvard Business Review, 81*(5), 41.

Collins, C. J., & Smith, K. G. (2006). Knowledge exchange and combination: the role of human resource practices in the performance of high-technology firms. *Academy of Management Journal, 49*(3), 544–560.

Crossan, M., Lane, H. W., & White, R. E. (1999). An organizational learning framework: from intuition to institution. *Academy of Management Review, 24*(3), 522–537. doi:10.2307/259140

Davenport, T. H., De Long, D. W., & Beers, M. C. (1998). Successful knowledge management projects. *Sloan Management Review, 39*(2), 43–57.

Dewan, S., & Kraemer, K. L. (1998). International dimensions of the productivity paradox. *Communications of the ACM, 41*(8), 56–62. doi:10.1145/280324.280333

Diamantopoulos, A., & Siguaw, J. A. (2000). *Introducing LISREL*. London: SAGE Publications.

DiBella, J. A., & Nevis, E. C. (1998). *How Organizations Learn – An Integrated Strategy for Building Learning Capability*. San Francisco, CA: Jossey-Bass.

Dimovski, V. (1994). *Organisational learning and competitive advantage*. Unpublished doctoral dissertation, Cleveland State University.

Dimovski, V., & Colnar, T. (1999). Organizacijsko učenje. *Teorija in Praksa, 5*(36), 701–722.

Dinevski, D., & Plenković, M. (2002). Modern University and e-learning. *Media, culture and public relations, 2*, 137–146.

Dodgson, M. (1993). Organizational learning: a review of some literatures. *Organization Studies, 14*(3), 375–394. doi:10.1177/017084069301400303

Figueiredo, P. N. (2003). Learning processes features: How do they influence inter-firm differences in technological capability - Accumulation paths and operational performance improvement? *International Journal of Technology Management, 26*(7), 655–689. doi:10.1504/IJTM.2003.003451

Fiol, C. M., & Lyles, M. A. (1985). Organizational learning. *Academy of Management Review, 10*(4), 803–813. doi:10.2307/258048

Freeman, E. R. (1984). *Strategic Management – A Stakeholder Approach*. London: Pitman.

Freeman, E. R. (1994). Politics of Stakeholder Theory: Some Future Directions . *Business Ethics Quarterly, 4*, 409–422. doi:10.2307/3857340

Gerbing, D. W., & Anderson, J. C. (1988). An updated paradigm for scale development incorporating unidimensionality and measurement error. *JMR, Journal of Marketing Research, 25*, 186–192. doi:10.2307/3172650

Goh, S., & Richards, G. (1997). Benchmarking the learning capability of organizations. *European Management Journal, 15*(5), 575–583. doi:10.1016/S0263-2373(97)00036-4

Henry, P (2001). E-learning technology, content and services. *Education + Training, 43*(4), 251–259.

Huber, G. P. (1991). Organizational Learning: The Contributing Processes and the Literatures. *Organization Science, 2*(1), 88–115. doi:10.1287/orsc.2.1.88

Inkpen, A., & Crossan, M. M. (1995). Believing is seeing: Organizational learning in joint ventures. *Journal of Management Studies, 32*(5), 595–618. doi:10.1111/j.1467-6486.1995.tb00790.x

Jones, G. R. (2000). *Organizational Theory* (3rd ed.). New York: Prentice Hall.

Jöreskog, K. G., & Sörbrom, D. (1993). *LISREL 8: Structural Equation Modelling with the SIMPLIS Command Language*. London: Lawrence Erlbaum Associates Publishers.

Kaplan, R. S., & Norton, D. P. (1992). Balanced Scorecard – Measures That Drive Performance. *Harvard Business Review, 1–2*, 71–79.

Kirchner, P. A., & Pass, F. (2001). Web enhanced higher education: a Tower of Babel. *Computers in Human Behavior, 17*(4), 347–353. doi:10.1016/S0747-5632(01)00009-7

Lam, S. S. K. (1998). Organizational performance and learning styles in Hong Kong. *The Journal of Social Psychology, 138*(3), 401–403. doi:10.1080/00224549809600392

Lei, D., Hitt, M. A., & Bettis, R. (1996). Dynamic core competencies through meta-learning and strategic context. *Journal of Management, 22*(4), 549–569. doi:10.1177/014920639602200402

Lei, D., Slocum, J. W., & Pitts, R. A. (1999). Designing organizations for competitive advantage: The power of unlearning and learning. *Organizational Dynamics, 27*(3), 24–38. doi:10.1016/S0090-2616(99)90019-0

Leonard-Barton, D. (1992). The factory as a learning laboratory. *Sloan Management Review, 34*(1), 23–38.

Levitt, B., & March, J. G. (1998). Organizational learning. *Annual Review of Sociology, 14*, 319–340. doi:10.1146/annurev.so.14.080188.001535

MacManus, R., & Porter, J. (2005): *Web 2.0 for design: bootstrapping the social web.* Retrieved April 15th 2008, from: http://www.digital-web.com/articles/web_2_for_designers

Miner, A. S., & Mezias, S. J. (1996). Ugly duckling no more: pasts and futures of organizational learning research. *Organization Science, 7*(1), 88–99. doi:10.1287/orsc.7.1.88

Mintzberg, H. (1990). Strategy formation: Schools of thought . In Frederickson, J. W. (Ed.), *Perspectives of strategic management* (pp. 105–235). New York: Harper Business.

Mueller, R. O. (1996). *Basic Principles of Structural Equation Modelling: An Introduction to Lisrel and EQS.* New York: Springer.

Navarette, C. J., & Pick, J. B. (2002). Information technology expenditure and industry performance: The case of the Mexican banking industry. *Journal of Global Information Technology Management, 5*(2), 7–28.

Nonaka, I. (1994). A dynamic theory of organizational knowledge creation. *Organization Science, 5*(1), 14–37. doi:10.1287/orsc.5.1.14

Nonaka, I., & Takeuchi, H. (1996). A Theory of Organizational Knowledge Creation . *International Journal of Technology Management, 11*(7/8), 833–846.

O'Reilly, T. (2005). *What Is Web 2.0. Design Patterns and Business Models for the Next Generation of Software*. Retrieved November 10, 2009, from http://oreilly. com/web2 /archive/what-is-web-20.html

Péréz López, S., Montes Peón, J. M., & Vázquez Ordás, C.Managing knowledge: The link between culture and organizational learning. *Journal of Knowledge Management*, *8*(6), 93–104. doi:10.1108/13673270410567657

Raelin, J. A. (1997). A model of work-based learning. *Organization Science*, *8*(6), 563–578. doi:10.1287/orsc.8.6.563

Reychav, I., & Weisberg, J. (2009). Good for workers, good for companies: How knowledge sharing benefits individual employees. *Knowledge and Process Management*, *16*(4), 186–197. doi:10.1002/kpm.335

Roach, S. (1987). *America's technology dilemma: A profile of the information economy. Economics Newsletter Series*. New York: Morgan Stanley.

Robey, D., Boudreau, M., & Rose, G. M. (2000). Information Technology and Organizational Learning: a Review and Assessment of Research. *Accounting . Management and Information Technologies*, *10*, 125–155. doi:10.1016/S0959-8022(99)00017-X

Rosenberg, M. (2001). *E-Learning, Strategies for Developing Knowledge in the Digital Age. NewYork*. McGraw-Hill.

Senge, P. M. (1990). *The fifth discipline: art and practice of the learning organization*. New York: Doubleday.

Sevilla, C., & Wells, T. D. (1988). Contracting to ensure training transfer. *Training & Development*, *6*(1), 10–11.

Shrivastava, P. A. (1983). Typology of Organizational Learning Systems. *Journal of Management Studies*, *20*, 1–28. doi:10.1111/j.1467-6486.1983.tb00195.x

Simonin, B. L. (1997). The importance of collaborative know-how: An empirical test of the learning organization. *Academy of Management Journal*, *40*(5), 1150–1173. doi:10.2307/256930

Škerlavaj, M. (2003). *Vpliv informacijsko-komunikacijskih tehnologij in organizacijskega učenja na uspešnost poslovanja: teoretična in empirična analiza*. Unpublished Master's theses. Ljubljana: Ekonomska fakulteta.

Škerlavaj, M., & Dimovski, V. (2006). Study of the Mutual Connections among Information-communication Technologies, Organisational Learning and Business Performance. *Journal for East European Management Studies*, *11*(1), 9–29.

Slater, S. F., & Narver, J. C. (1995). Market orientation and the learning organization. *Journal of Marketing, 59*(3), 63–74. doi:10.2307/1252120

Sloan, T. R., Hyland, P. W. B., & Beckett, R. C. (2002). Learning as a competitive advantage: Innovative training in the Australian aerospace industry. *International Journal of Technology Management, 23*(4), 341–352. doi:10.1504/IJTM.2002.003014

Smith, R. (2008). Aligning Competencies, Capabilities and Resources. *Research Technology Management: The Journal of the Industrial Research Institute*, September-October.

Tippins, M. J., & Sohi, R. S. (2003). IT competency and firm performance: Is organizational learning a missing link? *Strategic Management Journal, 24*(8), 745–761. doi:10.1002/smj.337

Ulrich, D., Jick, T., & von Glinow, M. A. (1993). High-impact learning: Building and diffusing learning capability. *Organizational Dynamics, 22*(2), 52–66. doi:10.1016/0090-2616(93)90053-4

Varney, S. (2008). Leadership learning: key to organizational transformation. *Strategic HR Review, 7*(1), 5–10. doi:10.1108/14754390810880471

Wall, B. (1998). Measuring the Right Stuff: Identifying and Applying the Right Knowledge. *Knowledge Management Review, 1*(4), 20–24.

Zhang, D. *Media structuration – Towards an integrated approach to interactive multimedia-based E-Learning*. (Ph.D. dissertation, The University of Arizona, 2002. Zhang, D., & Nunamaker, J. F. (2003). Powering e-learning in the new millennium: an overview of e-learning and enabling technology. *Information Systems Frontiers, 5*(2), 207–218.

KEY TERMS AND DEFINITIONS

Balanced Scorecard (BSC): The balanced scorecard (BSC) is a strategic performance management tool – a semi-standard structured report supported by proven design methods and automation tools that can be used by managers to keep track of the execution of activities of staff within their control, and monitor the consequences arising from these actions. It is perhaps the best known of several such frameworks, and was widely adopted in the English speaking western countries and Scandinavia in the early 1990s. The BCS based on the use of three non-financial topic areas as prompts to aid the identification of the non-financial measures in addition to the one looking at the financial measures. The four perspectives are: financial, customer, internal business, and innovation and learning.

Confirmatory Factor Analysis: Confirmatory factor analysis (CFA) is a powerful statistical technique. CFA allows researchers to test the hypothesis of the existence of a relationship between the observed variables and their underlying latent construct(s). Researchers apply their theoretical knowledge, empirical research, or both, postulate the relationship pattern a priori and then tests the hypothesis statistically.

LISREL: LISREL is the pioneering software for structural equation modelling which includes statistical methods for complex data survey. LISREL was developed in 1970s by Karl Jöreskog and Dag Sörbom, both professors at the Uppsala University, Sweden.

Organizational Learning: Organizational learning is an area of knowledge within the organizational theory that studies models and theories about the ways an organization learns and adapts. Argyris and Schön (1978) were the first to propose models that facilitate organizational learning; others have followed in the tradition of their work. They distinguished between the single- and double-loop learning. In the single-loop learning, individuals, groups, or organizations modify their actions according to the difference between the expected and obtained outcomes. In the double-loop learning, entities (individuals, groups or organizations) question the values, assumptions and policies that led to the actions in the first place; if they are able to view and modify those, then the second-order or the double-loop learning has taken place. The double-loop learning is the process of learning about the single-loop learning.

Structural Equation Modelling: Structural equation modelling, or in short SEM, is a statistical technique for testing and estimating causal relationships using a combination of statistical data and qualitative causal assumptions. SEM allows both confirmatory and exploratory modelling, meaning it suits both theory testing and theory development. Factor analysis, path analysis and regression all represent special cases of SEM.

Technology Enhanced Learning: Technology-enhanced learning (TEL) refers to any learning activity supported by technology. TEL is often used as a synonym for e-learning, however, there are significant differences between the two; namely, TEL focuses on the technological support of any pedagogical approach that utilizes technology. However, it rarely includes the print technology or developments related to libraries, books and journals occurring in the centuries before computers.

Web 2.0: Web 2.0 is a category of new Internet tools and technologies created around the idea that those who consume the media, access the Internet, and use the web should not just passively absorb what is available; they should be rather active contributors, helping customize the media and technology for their own purposes, as well as those of their communities. Web 2.0 marks the beginning of a new era in technology – one that promises to help the nonprofits operate more efficiently, generate more funding, and affect more lives. These new tools include blogs, social networking applications, RSS, social networking tools, and wikis.

Chapter 13

Methodology and Software Components for E-Business Development and Implementation:
Case of Introducing E-Invoice in Public Sector and SMEs

Neven Vrček
University of Zagreb, Croatia

Ivan Magdalenić
University of Zagreb, Croatia

EXECUTIVE SUMMARY

Many benefits from implementation of e-business solutions are related to network effects which means that there are many interconnected parties utilizing the same or compatible technologies. The large-scale adoption of e-business practices in public sectors and in small and medium enterprises (SMEs)-prevailing economic environments will be successful if appropriate support in the form of education, adequate legislative, directions, and open source applications is provided. This case study describes the adoption of e-business in public sectors and SMEs by using an integrated open source approach called e-modules. E-module is a model which has process properties, data properties, and requirements on technology.

DOI: 10.4018/978-1-4666-2618-8.ch013

Therefore e-module presents a holistic framework for deployment of e-business solutions and such e-module structure mandates an approach which requires reengineering of business processes and adoption of strong standardization that solves interoperability issues. E-module is based on principles of service-oriented architectures with guidelines for introduction into business processes and integration with ERP systems. Such an open source approach enables the spreading of compatible software solutions across any given country, thus, increasing e-business adoption. This paper presents a methodology for defining and building e-modules.

ORGANISATIONAL BACKGROUND

Large-scale adoption of e-business practices is a complex task from many aspects and one of extremely important is the fact that all approaches, standards, guidelines or solutions should be widely accepted by collaborating organizations or at least interoperable. In that respect public sector can play important role because its e-government and e-business oriented momentum can trigger rest of the society to come into play especially SMEs which do not have resources and knowledge of multinational corporations. The interrelation of business and public sector is subtle but it is noticeable and quite important. On one hand free market should develop with as little government influence as possible (Smith, 1976) according to the *laissez-fair* principle and on the other, certain extent of government involvement is desirable in achieving broader public interest goals. According to Max Weber's theory of bureaucracy, main axis of public sector value chain (Porter, 1996; Heintzman, 2005) consists of providing public services and developing legislative. More recent approaches which deal with e-government broaden the perspective of public sector and it is defined as a mean to "achieve better government" (OECD, 2005), assist society with effectiveness and efficiency (Hachigian, 2002), acquire transparency, increase revenue growth, reduce costs of public administration, transform relationships with citizens, businesses, and government (Gartner Group, 2000; World Bank, 2009). Such approach fosters transformation in delivery of public services, increases effectiveness of public administration, and leads to stable and viable development of economy. Therefore it is important to notice that supportive business processes from public sector value chain could significantly influence economy and the most direct example of such approach is public procurement. The importance of public procurement has been recognized across EU and that is why European Commission included public procurement in its large scale pilot projects. Pan European Public Procurement Online (PEPPOL, 2008) is a pilot project with aim to develop good practices and implement standardization in this supportive family of business processes of public sector value chain but of great significance to the economy. By such approach public sector can influence Adam Smith's "invisible hand" and direct it towards adoption of e-business thus increasing competiveness of economy. This and other large scale pilots launched by European Commission such as Secure idenTity acrOss boRders linKed – STORK (STORK, 2009), Simple Procedures Online for Cross-border Services – SPOCS, SPOCS (2009) together with other EU directives and recommendations develop important e-business and e-government guidelines for member states but it must be noticed that there is still significant freedom left in implementation approaches which is solved within national borders of every member state. In many countries government sector is the largest single buyer and by such position it can impose standards and good practices which can have wide positive impact way beyond simple procurement logic. This is particularly important when small and medium-sized enterprises (SMEs) are majority of business sector and are expected to play a substantial role in the development and restructuring of economies. Some SMEs will certainly be able to cope with technological and business issues related to e-business implementation and practices, but the vast majority will be excluded from this process. If nothing is done, these companies will be left aside which will have tremendous impact on overall development of society. The reason for such situation lies in the fact that every development and implementation of information system is complex from technological point of view and requires deep insight into business processes in order to find out their operational and strategic significance which leads to decision how they should be supported by information and communication technologies (ICT). This gives companies competitive edge and increases overall competitiveness of economy. Such comprehensive analysis requires deep and at the same time heterogeneous knowledge, consumes organizational resources for significant time and entails strict methodology which, to the certain extent, reduces the risks of implementation. There are many published examples of this complexity and barriers which should be overcame to implement complex software solutions. One illustrative case is presented in study of adoption and implementation of IT in two public sector organizations where is shown how various factors, such as management, organization and capabilities of IT professionals, can affect final outcome of projects (Tarafdar, 2005). All mentioned critical success factors are scarce even in large companies and SMEs most often cannot bridge the gap which leads to e-business or information society. Unlike information system for single organization, e-business solutions are related with one additional obstacle – heavy and complex standardization which must be adopted by all networked enterprises in order to achieve interoperability and actually benefit from implemented technology. SMEs have little chances to jump in this global trend and therefore it is normal that there are certain initiatives which promote their inclusion into broader e-business community. In such circumstances public sector can play important role as trendsetter and early adopter. It also has direct mechanism to influence business sector through public procurement process. It must be noted that networked solutions have impact only if there is large scale of interoperable business partners which makes quite logical that public sector involves its suppliers in joint network which will penetrate e-business momentum and standards across given state. One approach is certainly development and promotion of open source solutions which do not require significant initial investments while providing access to modern technology to wide audience of public sector organizations and SMEs. However, it is evident that availability of software modules is not enough for their adoption by business community especially if their technological absorption capacity is low as in the case of SMEs. SMEs should be given entire methodological framework which will guide them through adoption and implementation of open source solutions. The idea of the work described by this article is to develop entire methodology followed by open source components which would enable various organizations (public sector and SMEs) to implement them into their business and integrate with already existing information systems. That would enable them to create network of electronically interconnected business partners so they could achieve certain level of interoperability. Development of this methodological framework is aligned with our previous scientific work in which we developed methodology for Strategic Planning of Information Systems (SPIS) which was published in several scientific articles and also used in numerous applied projects (Brumec, 1998, 2001, 2002; Vrček, 2007). However for open source purposes SPIS methodology had to be modified and extended. These modifications were related to development of generic business models of targeted organizations which were developed with idea to present wide range of possible business models. Second intervention in methodology was extension of SPIS in direction of development of open source service oriented architecture (SOA) capable of integration with various information systems in wide range of targeted organizations (public sector and SMEs). By such approach SPIS methodology was modified for development of e-modules where e-module is complex term which comprises various process, semantic, and software properties necessary for complex e-business interactions. In development of e-modules certain SPIS steps were fully implemented (e.g., business process modelling and related techniques e.g., BPR), some were added or modified, while other were described as guidelines to be applied on the course of implementation of e-modules.

Therefore this paper presents methodology for modelling and building e-modules based on previously developed and proven SPIS methodology. The presented variant of SPIS methodology was applied in an extensive case study demonstrating practical applicability of e-modules which enabled authors to justify and verify design choices.

The results described in this paper are derived from significant previous work. The most important is SPIS methodology which was developed in order to reduce risk of large scale IS projects. This was achieved by combining various methods into coherent framework. Methodology was theoretically elaborated and verified on real organizations in numerous large scale projects. Since elaboration of methodology goes beyond this paper, short overview of original SPIS methodology is presented in Table 1. However, original SPIS initially was not meant to be used for development of open source service oriented software modules and therefore in this work it has been adapted appropriately to make it aligned with such intention and wide targeted audience i.e., public sector organizations and SMEs.

Table 1. SPIS Methodology (adapted from Brumec, 1998)

Problem/step in IS design	Methods and techniques § -strategic, # -structured, ¤ -object oriented	Inputs and deliverables Inputs / Outputs	Usability Very powerful Powerful, Useful
1. Description of Business System (BS)	Interviewing	*Missions and goals of current BS* / Business strategy; Business processes (BP)	
2. Evaluation of the Impact of New IT on Business System	§ Balanced Scorecard § BCG-matrix § 5F-model § Value-chain model	*BP* / Performances of existing BS *Business strategy* / IS development priorities *Business strategy* / Information for top management *BP* / Basic (primary and support) business processes (BBP)	V P U V
3. Redefinition of Business Processes	# BSP-decomposition # Life cycle analysis for the resources	*BBP* / New organizational units (OU) *Basic system resources* / Business processes portfolio	P P
4. Business System Reengineering	§ BPR § SWOT	*Business Processes Portfolio* / New business processes (NBP) *Business Processes Portfolio* / SWOT analysis for NBP	P V
5. Estimation of Critical Information	§ CFS analysis (Rockart) # EndsMeans Analysis	*NBP* / Critical information for NBP NBP / Information for efficiency and effectivity improvement	P U
6. Optimization of New IS Architecture	# Matrix processes entities # Affinity analysis, Genetic algorithms	NBP / Business process relationships *Business processes relationships* / Clusters; Subsystems of IS	V P
7. Modeling of New Business Technology (BT)	# Work flow diagram (WFD) #Organizational flow diagram (OFD) # Activity flow diagram (AFD)	*NBP* / Responsibility for NBP *New OU* / Flows between new OU *NBP* / Activities for NBP	V P U

continued on following page

Table 1. Continued

Problem/step in IS design	Methods and techniques § -strategic, # -structured, ¤ -object oriented	Inputs and deliverables Inputs / Outputs	Usability Very powerful Powerful, Useful
8. Modeling of New Business Processes, Supported by IT	# Data flow diagram (DFD) # Action diagram (AD)	*NBP* / NBP supported by IT (IS processes); Data flows; Business Data *IS processes* / Internal logic of IS processes	V P
9. Evaluation of New IS Effects	# Simulation modelling	*IS processes* / Guidelines for BP improvements	U
10. Business Data Modelling	# ERA-model ¤ Object-model	*Business data* / ERA model *Business data* / Objects model	V P
11. Software Design	# HYPO diagram ¤ Transition diagram	*IS processes* / Logical design of program procedures (SW) *Data flows* / Events and transactions	V P
12. Detail Design of Programs and Procedures	# Action diagram ¤ Object scenario	*Logical design of program procedures (SW)* / Model of program logic *Object model; Events and transactions* / Object behaviour	P P
13. Data Model Development	# Relational model; Normalization	*ERA model* / Relational model	V
14. Software Development	# CASE tools and 4GL ¤ OO-CASE tools	*Model of program logic; Relational model* / Programs and procedures *Object Behaviour* / OO models and scenarios	P P
15. Implementation of New IS	Case study; Business games	*Programs and procedures* / Performances of new IS	P
16. Evaluation of New BS Performances	# Balanced scorecard	*Performances of existing BS; Performances of new IS* / Measure of success	V

Because of such complex and elaborated methodological framework this paper presents structured approach to development and implementation of e-business open source components. The intention is not just to describe and to build open source software, but also to clear provide business perspective for potential users. Similar approach is described in Mos (2008) where standards such as Business Process Modeling Notation (BPMN) (OMG, 2006), Business Process Execution Language (BPEL) (Jordan, 2007), and other SOA-related standards were also used but in simpler methodological framework. However utilizing SOA and e-business related standards in development methodology is important because they are presently most advanced and direct way from business processes to software functionality. The BPMN is gaining adoption as a standard notation for capturing business processes (Recker, 2005). The BPEL is emerging as a de facto standard for implementing business processes on the top of Web service technology (Ouyang, 2009).

Also, an integrated set of techniques which translate models captured using BPMN into BPEL is presented by Ouyang et al. (2009). As presented in Table 1, our methodology involves similar, but significantly extended approach. It is important to notice that SPIS methodology provides guidelines for business process reengineering and by this it goes beyond pure software development. This is important because it can help organizations which do not have appropriate resources to implement complex software solutions in their business processes by guiding them through adequate methodology emphasizing the need for rethinking the ways of doing business. In this sense this equally applies to profit and public sector keeping in mind that reached conclusions and methods of implementation will be different (e.g., to achieve certain change in public sector it is usually necessary to change relevant legal regulation).

Using SOA for solving interoperability inside organization and between organizations is important stream in scientific and professional community and several researchers describe such approach (Zimmermann, 2005; Specht, 2005). However, the emphasis in these and many other published research results is put on solving interoperability on technical and occasionally on process layer. Besides these two layers, our work is strongly focused on semantic layer of interoperability where meaning of data play important role because this aspect really should be coordinated, aligned with extremely complex standardization and widely accepted in order to involve larger number of heterogeneous organizations (public sector, SMEs, cross border transactions, etc.). We recommend acceptance of one international standard and its adjustment for given case study followed by incorporation in developed software modules. Embedding standardization in software components reliefs organizations that implement developed open source modules of acquiring complex standardization knowledge. It also helps in propagation of chosen standards across society which is necessary for its acceptance. International standards which provide information model of business documents are: Universal Business Language version 2.0 (UBL) (Bosak, 1999), GS1 XML (GS1, 2009), UN/EDIFACT standards (UN/CEFACT, 2008), OAGIS (OAGi, 1999), and CEN CWA documents (CEN, 2009). Our work is primarily based on UBL because of its acceptance in North European countries (NES, 2009) and we are continuously monitoring status and acceptance rate of other international standards.

This work is part of efforts of Croatia's government to introduce electronic business in the Republic of Croatia (MELE, 2007)[1], and is aligned with similar efforts across EU.

SETTING THE STAGE: E-INVOICE

This section briefly discusses why e-invoice has been chosen as an example in elaborated case study. E-invoice aspires to become the most common electronic document in the world. Also, it is a document that appears equally in business processes in public and business sector which makes possible wide standardization of business processes, semantics, regulation etc. As such invoice is equally interesting in public and private sector which makes it perfect case study for breakthrough towards broader e-business concepts. Yet, there are many obstacles and interoperability issues in the acceptance and implementation of e-invoice. That is why we still do not have global standardization related to e-invoice and its penetration rate varies among countries and business sectors with one common characteristic that SMEs are lagging behind. Public sector penetration rate is related to legal regulation in any given state which fluctuates significantly but in recent years there is strong trend showing that many states are trying to increase level of ICT use by putting it in official documents and legal acts (basically equalizing paper and electronic transactions). Beside direct impact of various modernization efforts on public services and governmental organizations (which mainly falls within framework of e-government) e-invoicing adoption trends in public sector must embrace business sector in one coherent network and this happens within framework of public procurement.

Important aspect is legal regulation of e-invoice. Since it serves as the basis for the value added tax, the government is passing laws and regulations that apply to it. In the European Union (EU) the cover document that regulates e-invoice is EU Directive 2006/112/EC of 28 November 2006 on the common system of value added tax (EU, 2006). This document serves as a guideline in implementation to the member states legislative and every state in EU applies this directive with its particularities. This causes problems at legal level of interoperability between states in EU which reflects on other interoperability levels (mainly semantic). If the e-invoice goes outside EU the situation becomes more complicated. The most common problems at legal level of interoperability are mandatory fields and request for electronic signature in e-invoice.

The basic request at the process level of interoperability is the alignment of business processes. Corresponding business messages that are exchanged among processes must convey the necessary and mutually understandable information. This is especially important in electronic communication where the best results are obtained when the business processes are fully automated. To avoid a partial semantic and business process alignment, the best solution is to accept the current international standards (i.e., these which are most widely accepted). However there are many acceptable standards and most important for e-invoice are listed. This myriad of standards which partially overlap and are not mutually exclusive is serious obstacle in their adoption because decision making is influenced by many factors.

The correct interpretation of fields in the electronic document is a challenge at semantic level of interoperability. For example, sometimes it is not clear what information is stored in a particular field and what is the domain of the data. In one standard the same information may be located in multiple fields, while in the other standard in just one field. Code lists that are used are not commonly accepted among states. Different standards use different documents for storing the same data, etc. There are many standards that are used for describing electronic documents. Figure 1 gives a non-exhaustive overview of the most important standard definitions, together with a timescale reflecting their appearance.

The used standardization should be unique at least at the state level but in globalized world it is normal that such efforts should overcome state borders and this trend is gaining momentum through various coordination committees and large scale pilot projects (e.g., PEPPOL). In that respect same principles apply to public and private sector and good solutions should be open for messages developed according to other standards which increases interoperability level.

There are even more standards that should be chosen from perspective of technical interoperability. For example, standards for applying requested level of security, standards for reliable messaging, standards for electronic signature and public key infrastructure, archiving, naming conventions, recommendations and guidelines etc. List of standards that can apply at this level of interoperability goes up to several dozen.

Figure 1. Overview of different business standards (Liegl, 2009)

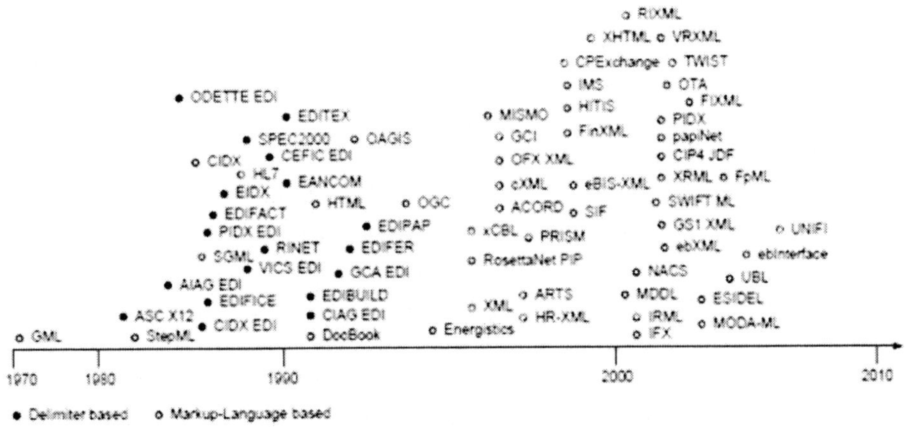

It is obvious that adoption of e-invoicing in public sector which would guide rest of organizations from other sectors and even entire society requires knowledge in different areas and, once implemented, this knowledge can be propagated to entire ecosystem which participates in public procurement.

E-module, as defined, presents implementation of chosen standards and serves as knowledge base for development of solutions for interchange of electronic documents. By such approach, on one place is gathered required knowledge needed for implementation of certain electronic interchange procedure and corresponding electronic documents. This knowledge is composed of several components: legislative, business processes, semantics of documents, technical details of communication, and requests for software. Many electronic documents in various sectors could be described through the same pattern of description which can significantly improve reusability of developed solutions.

CASE DESCRIPTION: E-MODULE DEFINITION

Development of e-modules was extension of SPIS to make it applicable on generic basis (i.e., without focus on concrete organization) and also that final product i.e., open source components are accompanied by entire methodological framework which will guide users through implementation process. Important aspect of the extension was consideration of strong standardization influence on e-business solutions (e.g., XML, UBL, SOAP, digital signature, CEN documents etc.) which is necessary for cross border transactions. Also methodology had to be adapted in respect to SOA paradigm developed in recent years (with new momentum related to cloud computing) on which entire e-module development was based. These components contributed to e-module development which is complex entity capable for supporting business processes that are on the boundary of the organization and that connect organization with its business environment.

E-module is a model that presents part of business process that can be performed electronically and contains process properties, data properties and requirements on technology. The structure of e-module allows that it can be put in various contexts and it is not tightly bound to one business process. Also implementation of e-modules does not require immediate changes in business processes and they allow gradual transition. This idea is presented by Figure 2 which presents parallel path allowing usage of e-module together with classical approach. Connection points shown in Figure 2 represent points in business process where business can be done either in traditional manner or electronically by using e-module. In the first phase of implementation, e-module is alternative way of doing business. It is expected that in mature phase, usage of e-module becomes preferable way of doing business.

Figure 2. Parallel path of using e-module

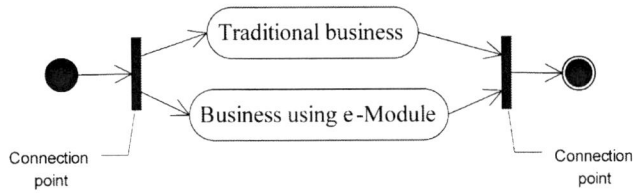

A description of e-module contains functional and technical requirements that can be solved by different technologies. This allows that created specifications exist longer and are independent of implementation technology.

E-Module is defined by the set of elements presented in Figure 3. Each e-module element is actually methodological step related to adapted SPIS methodology and various SPIS techniques are interrelated in development of e-module. Therefore e-module components directly reflect built in development methodology and that is why e-module is much more than just a software component. Understanding this fact is extremely important because many organizations do not have adequate absorption capacity (in all respects – knowledge, human resources, technology...)

Figure 3. E-module building elements

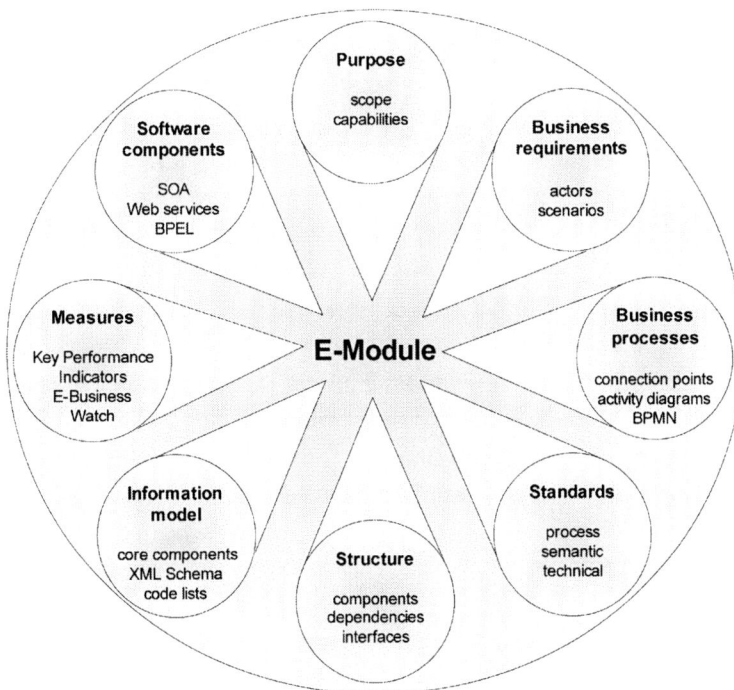

to adopt technology without entire framework which will guide them through the entire process. Such approach to open source development is new and it results from the fact that development of business solutions significantly differs from development and implementation of system software (e.g., LINUX). That is why e-module concept developed in this research comprises various building elements which make it applicable not only just into certain software environment (which is usually case with system software) but also integrates it into business processes that are going to be supported by e-module.

Each element from Figure 3 is defined and described in detail in following subsections. Appropriate example is provided for each element for the e-module e-invoice. Definition of real e-invoice module has been developed as a case study; it has more than two hundred pages accompanied by open source software components and is available freely online (full project results are available under Creative Commons License at web site http://www.edocument.foi.hr). This article describes only most significant parts which were extracted from entire documentation to demonstrate principles of building and using of e-modules.

Purpose of E-Module

Purpose gives general information about types of business processes where e-module can be used and what is its scope. It presents list of most important features and capabilities of e-module and gives answer on a question: "Why to use this module?".

Relation to SPIS Methodology

This is starting e-module building element and it is partly related to Step 1 and Step 2 of SPIS methodology i.e., *Description of Business System* and *Evaluation of the Impact of New IT on Business System*. However, it must be kept in mind that unlike SPIS e-module covers only certain business processes and not entire organization and that is why level of granularity is changed from coarse grained in SPIS to fine grained in e-module definition. In that respect mission and goals of e-module have to be clearly described with respect to the process level of particular business processes that are going to be supported by e-module. Therefore it can be concluded that purpose of e-module integrates first two steps of SPIS methodology downgraded from enterprise wide to process level of the generic enterprise.

E-Invoice Example

Purpose of e-invoice is to create, send, receive and verify electronic invoice. Exchange of electronic invoices should be done using different transport protocols based on

Figure 4. E-modules in procurement business process

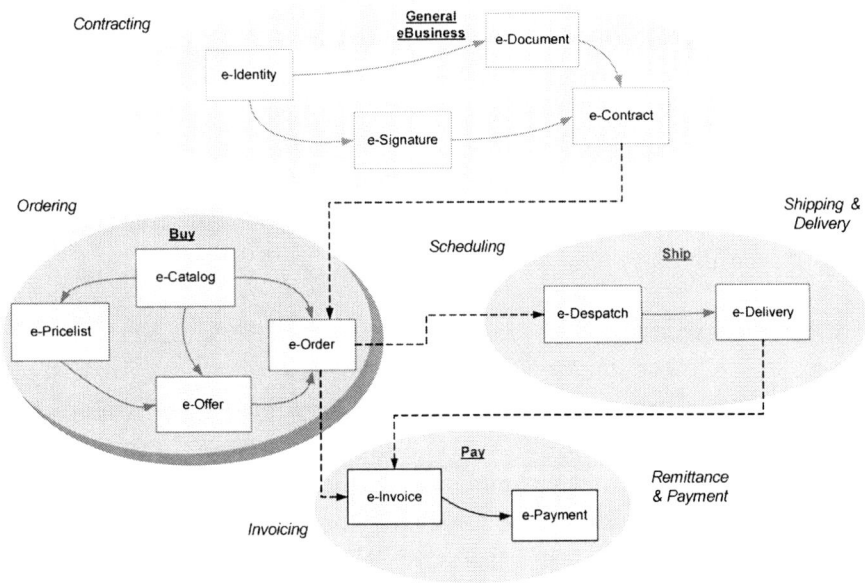

SOA principles. General role of e-invoice in the process of e-procurement is shown in Figure 4. Figure 4 shows e-modules which are identified as participants in procurement process. It is important to say that e-identity, e-signature and e-document are basis for all other e-modules and their functionality is contained in all modules.

Business Requirements

This component of e-module specifies business requirements which can be improved or solved by implementation of e-module. Business requirements are presented in the form of UML use case diagrams and in form of business scenarios.

Relation to SPIS Methodology

Business requirements element of e-module is derived from step 3 of SPIS methodology i.e., *Redefinition of Business Processes*. However, methods which are used are not identical as in SPIS. From original SPIS only resource life cycle analysis is used while BSP decomposition is omitted since it is applicable only at the organizational wide level. However certain UML diagrams are introduced in this part of e-module development cycle. They are used to present high level business interaction scenarios in which e-module participates.

E-Invoice Example

Business requirements for e-invoice are described by UML diagrams, actors, short description, pre-conditions, post-conditions, scenarios and remarks. The same form is used in CEN CWA 15668:2007 Business requirements specification - Cross industry invoicing. Acceptance of business requirements from EU reference documents strongly contributes to interoperability at the business level. Some of these requirements require reengineering of business processes and it is important that they influence architecture of e-modules

Business Processes

This component of e-module defines in detail business processes to which e-module applies. Business processes are defined in two ways: As-Is and To-Be business process models based on BPMN. As-Is model is detailed elaboration of selected generic business processes targeted by e-module as they are performed without usage of ICT. The purpose of this description is that potential users can identify area of application of certain e-module and to envisage the required level of change in business processes. Detailed As-Is model is important as reference point for comparison of organisational efficiency improvement which might be expected after the implementation of e-module. To-Be model is elaboration of changed business processes in order to optimize usage of ICT and to achieve maximum performance. As addition to this, all e-modules are developed according to principle that transition to new state does not have to be instantaneous. Therefore all solutions are developed in the manner that parallel existence of traditional and new business processes is possible as presented at the Figure 2. Through one path business is done electronically and the second path leads to traditional business processes. Relationship between As-Is and To-Be models is basis for cost benefit analysis which should justify gradual transition to electronic business based on implementation of e-modules.

Relation to SPIS Methodology

Business processes component of e-module comprises several steps from original SPIS methodology ranging from 4 to 9. Beside standard methods used in these steps in original SPIS one additional technique is part of e-module specification. This is Business Process Modelling Notation (BPMN) as widely adopted standard for business processes modelling. This notation also provides direct link to business process execution language (WS-BPEL) necessary for development of service oriented architectures (SOA). Since e-modules are developed according to SOA paradigm use of BPMN is very important. Beside that modern BPMN tools provide mechanisms for simulation modelling and for comparison among various business scenarios which is extensively used in e-modules to justify their implementation and presentation of cost benefit analysis.

E-Invoice Example

E-invoice describes two business processes: the process of publishing output invoice and the process of receiving incoming invoice. Both processes are described using BPMN and elaborated at several levels of detail. Because business processes differ within different industries invoicing is clear example where presentation can be made on generic level while leaving enough place for industry specific customization. Each vertical industry has some specificity and further plan of this research is to describe targeted business process in all major industries using BPMN.

Standards

There are three groups of standards which affect e-modules: process, semantic and technical standards. At each group there are number of standards that often overlap. Different countries, user groups or industry segments have various requirements or peculiarities and choice or recommendation of only one standard is not always the best choice. Therefore, this chapter brings a list of relevant standards in each area. Other chapters present which concrete standards from this extensive list were used for a particular purpose. Therefore e-module converges broad standardization area into specific set of standards suitable for concrete application. However, one of the important contributions of e-module description and elaboration is an overview of the standardization made by the experts which can serve as knowledgebase for implementation in different areas.

List of process standards includes national and international standards which describe business requirements and business processes where e-module can be applied. The examples of such standards are CEN CWA Business Requirements Specification (CEN, 2009) and UN/CEFACT-a Business Requirements Specifications (CEN, 2007). Process standards are also affected by national legislative especially in the domain of government. Other standards which also influenced e-module are process descriptions from Universal Business Language (UBL) (Bosak, 1999).

List of semantic standards includes national and international standards which describe content of documents and messages that are exchanged electronically. Examples of such standards are: UBL (Bosak, 1999), GS1 XML (GS1, 2009), OAGIS (OAGi 1999), CEN CWA (CEN, 2009).

List of technical standards includes standards that concrete implementations have to apply at the technical level. Examples of such standards which are sometimes combined with legislative are electronic signature, privacy and archiving standards. Some architectures, such as service oriented architecture which is basis for realization of e-modules, have additional demands on implementations (e.g., WS-Security, WS-Reliable Messaging etc.).

In development of e-modules relevant standards were systemized with clear description of their application and ways of deployment in actual software modules.

Relation to SPIS Methodology

SPIS does not have special step dedicated to standards. However interoperability is important aspect of e-business solutions and in that respect they heavily depend on standardization. Therefore this aspect of e-modules is different from original SPIS and methodology had to be extended with special step dedicated to standardization issues.

E-Invoice Example

Process standards: E-invoice process is described in CEN CWA 15668: Business requirements specification - Cross industry invoicing process (CEN, 2007), UN/CEFACT-a Business Requirements Specifications (BRS) Cross Industry Invoicing Process (UN/CEFACT, 2008), UBL version 2.0 (Bosak, 1999), UBL/NES Profile 4 - Basic Invoice Only, UBL/NES Profile 5 - Basic Billing, and UBL/NES Profile 8 - Basic Billing with Dispute Response (NES, 2009).

Semantic standards: Mandatory semantic elements are defined in EU directive 2006/112/EC (EU, 2006) and national legislative. Basic principle of building business documents from reusable semantic components is defined in Core Components Technical Specification version 2.01 (UN/CEFACT, 2003). An information model of e-invoice is defined in CEN CWA 15668. Business requirements specification - Cross industry invoicing process (CEN, 2007). Standards such as UBL 2.0, GS1 XML, and OAGIS also provide information models. Naming conventions for element names are defined in UBL Naming and Design Rules 2.0 (Cournane, 2006).

Technical standards: National legislative gives requirements concerning e-Identity, e-Signature, e-Documents, e-Commerce and Service Providers. Reliable exchange of business documents and messages is done using Web Services Reliable Messaging (Fremantle, 2009), and Business Process Execution Language (BPEL) (Jordan, 2007).

Figure 5. E-module architecture

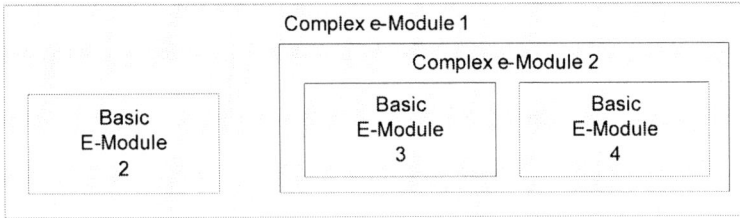

Structure

This component of e-module defines architecture of e-module and usage guidelines. E-module can be standalone or can be comprised from other e-modules. Figure 5 shows example of complex e-module 1 which uses functionality from Basic e-module 2 and complex e-module 2. Furthermore, e-module can interact with other e-modules by exchanging data or messages (implying that e-modules can work in tightly and loosely coupled architectures).

Another important aspect of e-modules is their interfaces. E-module communicates with environment and other e-modules through well defined interfaces. Authors identified four types of interfaces as shown in Figure 6.

Figure 6. E-module interfaces

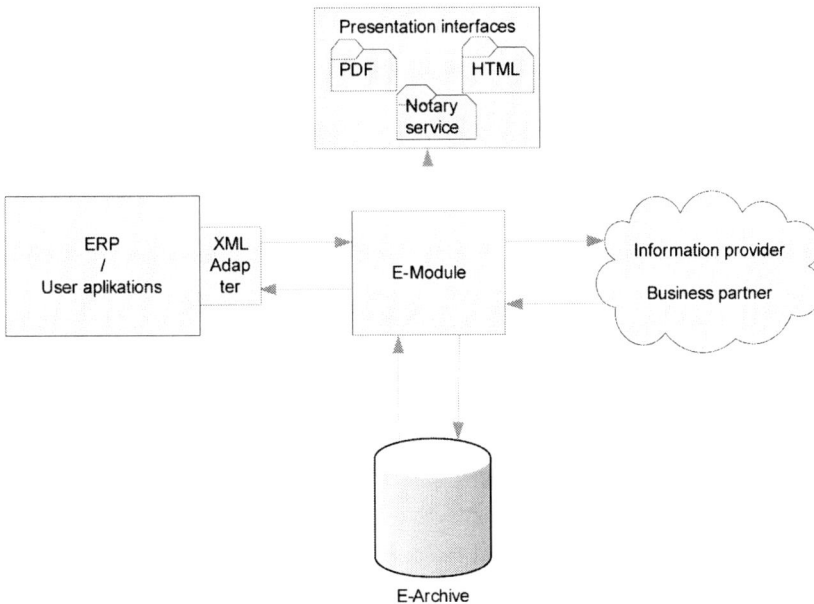

First interface is related to integration with the IS of the company. That is why e-module has interfaces for communication with user applications or ERP systems. E-module is based on XML in order to provide interoperability on technical and semantic level with various systems. This requires that all user applications have their own interface which is called XML Adapter. The purpose of XML Adapter is to convert data from legacy format to XML format and vice versa. Second interface is related to archiving. E-module has to communicate with e-Archive in order to fulfill possible legislative requirements for e-Documents (e.g., MOREQ 2, Accounting law, etc.). Third are presentation interfaces and they are used to present data from e-module in format more acceptable to human. Finally, e-module has to send and receive electronic messages among business partners or information providers which is realized through SOAP and other SOA related principles. This last interface takes care for reliable and secure transportation of electronic documents. In that respect it heavily relies on many SOA standards such as: WS-Reliable Messaging (Freemantle, 2009), WS-Security (OASIS, 2006), Web Services Description Language (W3C, 2007), WS-BPEL (Jordan, 2007), etc. By utilizing SOA and related standards e-module is more than just an ERP connector. It connects to ERP but also utilizes fully fledged transportation structure based on SOA mechanisms and enables full interconnection among business partners, information providers, banks, taxation authorities and any other interested parties.

Relation to SPIS Methodology

This component of e-module is developed according to step 14 (*Software Development*) from SPIS. However stronger emphasis is put on interface definition and that is why original SPIS set of techniques was extended with WSDL, BPEL, and WS-* family of standards and definitions.

E-Invoice Example

E-invoice is specialization of e-document and inherits properties and functionalities of e-module e-document. E-document uses e-signature and e-signature uses e-identity. E-invoice can receive data from e-modules: e-contract, e-order, e-despatch and e-delivery and send data to e-module e-payment. Structure of e-invoice is presented in Figure 7.

Figure 8 presents UML component diagram which denotes the most important interfaces of e-invoice and interfaces that e-invoice uses from other e-modules.

Figure 8 shows that usage of e-modules allows great reusability and that most interfaces of e-invoice are inherited from e-documents, e-signature and e-identity.

Figure 7. Structure of e-invoice

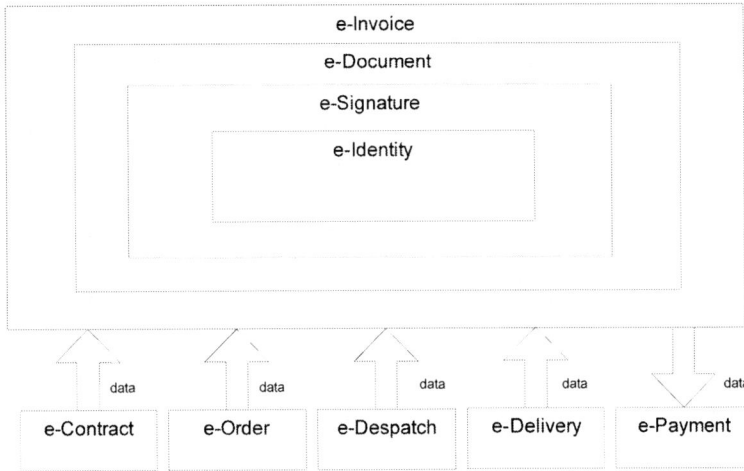

Figure 8. E-invoice component diagram

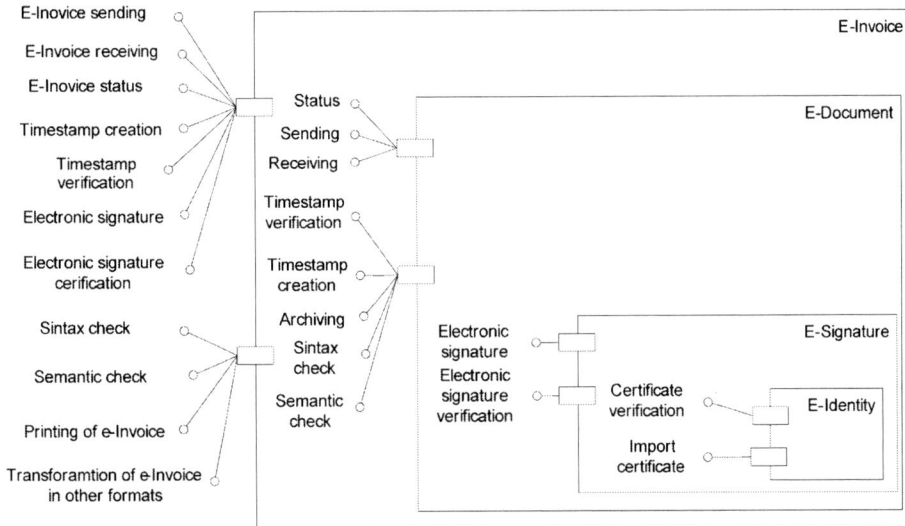

Structure of XML Adapter is shown in Figure 9. XML Adapter contains several layers. The base is XML Schema developed based on principles of Core Components (UN/CEFACT, 2003). Simple and Complex types from XML Schemas are implemented as object classes in concrete programming language (in this case Java). Object classes are grouped by creating functions and procedures for doing specific tasks. These functions and procedures are published as APIs with argument's definitions on business layer. Finally, APIs are used in user's applications or ERPs.

Figure 9. E-invoice XML Adapter structure

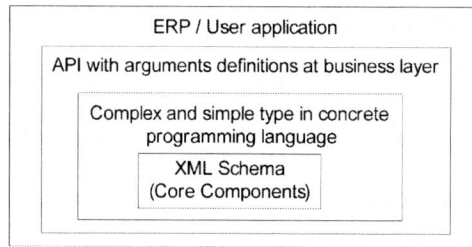

Information Model

Information model component of e-module defines format and semantics of data, and also documents and messages which are used in business processes covered by e-module. It is based on XML as today's first, and for all practical purposes the only solution for sharing structured data across different IT systems. The choice regarding semantics is harder and depends on particular appliance. It is important that data are semantically described which allows that the same data are interpreted in the same way at the source and at the end of communication. One way to accomplish this is to use internationally accepted classifications and taxonomies such as UNSPSC (2009) or NAICS (2009). This, however, solves only part of the problem. More general solution is offered by standard Core Components Technical Specification (CCTS) (UN/CEFACT, 2003). CCTS is accepted as ISO 15000-5 standard. CCTS describes methodology for building common set of semantic building blocks which represents general types of business data. CCTS defines a new paradigm in designing and implementation of reusable, syntax neutral information building blocks. CCTS serves as foundation for other standards such as Universal Business Language (Bosak, 1999), GS1 XML (GS1, 2009), UN/EDIFACT standards such as Cross Industry Invoice (UN/CEFACT, 2008) and CEN CWA documents (CEN, 2009). XML is accompanied by XML Schema which is used for defining documents and messages.

Besides definition of data, documents and messages, information model has to define code lists which can be used as restriction to some elements.

Therefore complete information model describes structure of the messages and for each message element defines its semantic meaning. From interoperability perspective, it is recommended that the creation of an information model is done by adapting existing standards to specific needs. To create an information model in this concrete case, we adapted standard UBL2.0 and it's built in mechanisms for adaptation. The main difference between here presented approach and other approaches is that we first built an information model of messages and then elaborated mapping of elements from information model to elements of UBL 2.0 messages. The advantage of this approach is easier conversion of messages into other formats. Validation of documents and messages is be done by using XML Schema for structure and data types. Advanced validation is done using XSLT Transformation (Clark, 1999) and Schematron (International Organization for Standardization, 2006).

Relation to SPIS Methodology

Information model of e-module is developed by using SPIS step 13 with strong extension related to XML standardization. Therefore this step extends relational modelling into XML domain and therefore it significantly improves original SPIS in that respect.

E-Invoice Example

Mandatory elements of invoice are defined by national legislative, EU directive 2006/112/EC (EU, 2006), EU DIRECTIVE 2010/45/EU and VAT elements in EU invoice as per CEN CWA 15575. It is recommended that invoice contain all elements which define payment instructions. Basic structure of invoice elements is presented in Figure 10. Header elements can appear only once in invoice. Elements that can appear more than once are part of invoice body. Both header and body can be extended by elements specific for vertical industries or by elements defined by bilateral agreements. The building of e-invoice information model is not just in taking over one of international standards, but adjustment of one or more standards for domicile purpose. Our information model is based on UBL 2.0 and is extended with some elements which are required by country and EU legislative. Therefore, approach in building of information model has to be based on certain international standard as a starting point and its adjustment according to given country and

Figure 10. Basic structure of invoice elements

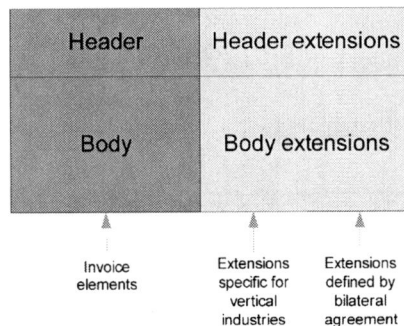

expected cross-border context. Such approach has already been adopted in some countries and projects, e.g., PEPPOL, UBL NES and Denmark.

Described approach can be systemized in following steps:

- Research and consideration of national and European legislation;
- Research and consideration of the specifics of business processes of payments, such as compliance with IBAN and SWIFT;
- Research and taking into account the business needs made by experts from public administration and business domains;
- Building of information model of invoice;
- Mapping of elements from information model to elements in UBL 2.0 standard;
- Creation of XML schemas by adopting existing UBL 2.0 XML schemas;
- Research of available code lists and their acceptance. Creation of own code lists according to specific country needs;
- Writing the implementation guidelines;
- Providing examples of usage.

Information model of electronic invoice has several hundreds of pages. Without software implementation of e-module it would take significant time, resources and knowledge to analyze this specification and launch development cycle in order to derive compatible software solution. Therefore e-module bridges the gap from complex specifications and their software implementation. That is why easily accessible open source approach is appropriate for increasing electronic invoice penetration rate.

Measures

This constitutive element of e-module defines measures and Key Performance Indicators (KPIs) which are used for tracking of usage of an e-module. Obtained statistic presents impact of an e-module on business processes and can be used by management in decision-making process. The same statistics can be aggregated by various criteria and enter composite indicators like Balanced Scorecard indicators or more aggregated like those in E-business Watch.

Relation to SPIS Methodology

One of the strong components of SPIS is strict adherence to business performance measurement. This means that organization's performance is monitored and all changes related to implementation of ICT solution are systematically recorded. That is why the idea of increasing organizational efficiency is built in the methodology from its very beginning. Therefore it is quite normal that e-modules must have performance measurement domain and this is entirely related to step 16 of SPIS.

E-modules collect and store all relevant data originated from activities in which modules participate. Also certain performance measurement indicators are derived from simulation modelling of As-Is and To-Be business processes. Simulation results are verified by concrete numbers obtained from operation of e-modules once they are actually implemented into concrete business process.

E-Invoice Example

Basic elements for measuring successfulness of e-Invoice are: ratio of electronic invoices in relation to total number of invoices, ratio of electronic invoices which contains identifiers of goods and services from e-order, ratio of data from e-contract incorporated in electronic invoice, ratio of electronic invoices which are result from data from e-Despatch or e-Delivery, ratio of e-Payment which resulted from data from electronic invoices.

Additional elements for measuring successfulness of e-invoice are: creation time of one electronic invoice compared to traditional process, ratio of business process speed-up compared with previous state, increase in transparency of costs, optimization of B2B processes, and minimization of storage and archival costs (Tanner, 2006).

Software Components

This constitutive element of e-module brings list of software components used for e-module. E-module can be implemented by various software components built by different authors and in different technologies as long as interfaces are kept consistent.

Relation to SPIS Methodology

This e-module element is related to step 15 of SPIS. However it is extended in direction of open source software development which means more detailed documentation adapted for wide audience to enable them to apply and further develop e-modules.

E-Invoice Example

Since entire framework is service oriented it is logical that developed software components for e-invoice are based on web services and service oriented architecture concepts, since in this way we can achieve high level of re-usability and independence of the technologies used for the concrete implementation of certain software modules. On the course of this case study following e-invoice constitutive software components were implemented:

- XML adapter - Java library for creating electronic invoices and conversion to XML format and vice versa that serves as the interface to ERP or other user programs.
- Web Service "Send electronic document" - Web service that takes invoice in XML format and electronically signs it, provides timestamp by relaying the call to time stamping service and sends it to the destination.
- Web service "Electronic signature" – for electronically signing documents and for verification of electronic signature for incoming invoices.
- Web Service "Electronic timestamp creation and verification".
- Web service "Log" - monitors and records all the important activity of software components
- Web Service "Receive electronic document" – receives an electronic document and saves a copy in the local database.
- Web service "Retrieve received electronic documents" – retrieves received electronic documents from the local database.

All developed services are orchestrated by using WS-BPEL.

Summarized Relationship of E-Module and SPIS

Discussion in previous chapter presents that e-modules were developed according to strict methodology. Figure 11 shows relationship of e-module elements and elements of SPIS methodology. All e-module elements, except two - Structure and Standards are mapped to elements of SPIS and some of them include more SPIS steps. E-module element Structure is not mapped because its purpose is to define internal structure of e-module and relationships between e-modules. E-module element Standards is also not mapped directly because it covers standardization of e-business oriented software components and messages, which has some specific rules. However it is important to note that e-module elements represent clear methodological framework and is actually a new methodology which solves specific problems of development of open source software for e-business and e-government.

Figure 11. Relationship between e-module and SPIS

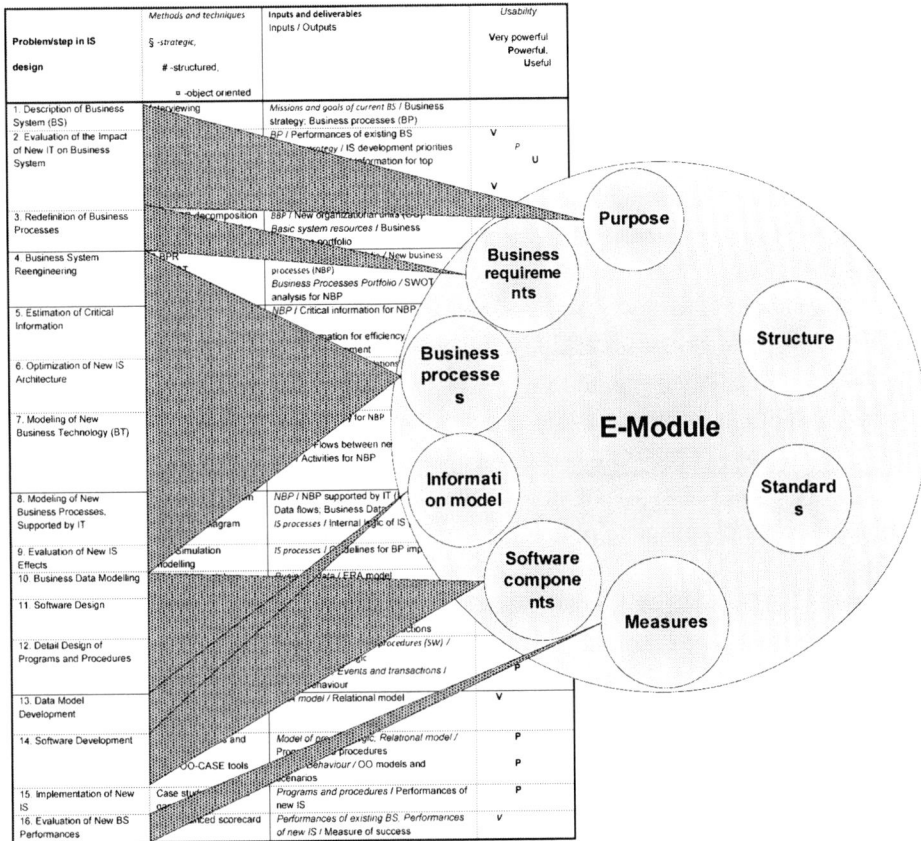

CURRENT CHALLENGES/PROBLEMS FACING THE ORGANISATION

This paper presents a detailed methodology for building and implementing open source software components called e-modules, with purpose to enable organizations to adopt e-business solutions and practices. This methodology is extension of already published methodology for building information systems called SPIS. Mature era of e-business which we are facing today requires extension of SPIS because the focus is not only on single organization and its information system but the framework was extended and enriched by standardization requirements to achieve adequate level of interoperability and enable cross border transactions. That is why open source e-modules and methodological framework which is embedded in them are important building blocks in progress of e-business across economic environment because large scale corporate solutions are expensive and cannot significantly increase e-business

293

penetration rate. E-modules enable creation of software components based on principles of service-oriented architecture and give entire methodology with precise guidelines for their introduction into business processes. Additionally e-modules have built in entire standardization requirements which enable dissemination of uniform standardization across country or any given area of their implementation. This gives strong momentum to adoption of e-business practices because e-modules disseminate same standardization and are mutually interoperable. By such approach wide area of users are directly influenced and involved in common standardization circle which leads to wide interoperability. This approach equally applies to public sector organizations because it reduces vendor dependencies and small and medium sized enterprises that cannot bridge the gap which leads to e-business or information society. Developed methodology was verified by its application in building concrete e-modules as presented in this article on example of e-module e-invoice.

The limitations of presented research and its results are in the fact that any open source development has to be sustainable through the community which would continuously contribute with new improvements. However it is hard to gather and maintain community around business oriented open source components due to very large and heterogeneous knowledge base on which e-modules are based. There is no guarantee that such community will sustain. Our future work is concentrated on promoting e-modules and their development for e-government and public services.

REFERENCES

W3C. (2007). *Web services description language (WSDL) version 2.0 part 1: Core language.* Retrieved from http://www.w3.org/TR/wsdl20/

Bosak, J., & McGrath, T. (1999). *Universal business language v2.0.* Retrieved from http://docs.oasis-open.org/ubl/cs-UBL-2.0/UBL-2.0.html

Brumec, J. (1998). Strategic planning of information systems. *Journal of Information and Organizational Sciences, 23*, 11–26.

Brumec, J., Dušak, V., & Vrček, N. (2001). The strategic approach to ERP system design and implementation. *Journal of Information and Organizational Sciences, 24*.

Brumec, J., & Vrček, N. (2002). Genetic taxonomy: The theoretical source for IS modelling methods. In *Proceeding of the ISRM Conference*, Las Vegas, NV (pp. 245-252).

Brumec, J., Vrček, N., & Dušak, V. (2001). Framework for strategic planning of information systems. In *Proceedings of the 7th Americas Conference on Information Systems*, Boston, MA (pp. 123-130).

CEN. (2007). *CEN CWA 15668: Business requirements specification - Cross industry invoicing process.* Retrieved from ftp://ftp.cenorm.be/PUBLIC/EBES/CWAs/CWA%2015668.pdf

CEN. (2009). *List of published ICT CEN workshop agreements.* Retrieved from http://www.cen.eu/cenorm/sectors/sectors/isss/cen+workshop+agreements/cwa_listing.asp

Clark, J. (1999). *W3C: XSL transformations (NAICS) (XSLT).* Retrieved from http://www.w3.org/TR/xslt

Cournane, M., & Grimley, M. (2006). *Universal business language (UBL) naming and design rules.* Retrieved from http://www.oasis-open.org/committees/download.php/20093/cd-UBL-NDR-2.0.pdf

EU. (2006). Council directive 2006/112/EC of 28 November 2006 on the common system of value added tax. *Official Journal of the European Union. L&C, L347*(1).

EU. (2010). Council directive 2010/45/EU of 13 July 2010 amending directive 2006/112/EC on the common system of value added tax as regards the rules on invoicing. *Official Journal of the European Union. L&C, L189*(1).

Fremantle, P., & Patil, S. (2009). *Web services reliable messaging.* Retrieved from http://www.oasis-open.org/committees/download.php/272/ebMS_v2_0.pdf

GS1. (2009). *Key features of GS1 XML.* Retrieved from http://www.gs1.org/ecom/xml/overview

Gartner Group. (2000). *Key issues in e-government strategy and management.* Stamford, CT: Gartner Group.

Hachigian, N. (2002). Roadmap for e-government in the developing world: 10 questions e-government leaders should ask themselves. In RAND Corporation (Ed.), *Working group on eGovernment in the developing world* (pp. 1-24). Los Angeles, CA: Pacific Council on International Policy.

Heintzman, R., & Marson, B. (2005). People, service and trust: Is there a public sector service value chain? *International Review of Administrative Sciences, 71*(4), 549–575. doi:10.1177/0020852305059599

International Organization for Standardization. (2006). *ISO/IEC 19757-3:2006: Information technology -- Document schema definition language (DSDL) -- Part 3: Rule-based validation – Schematron.* Retrieved from http://www.iso.org/iso/iso_catalogue/catalogue_tc/catalogue_detail.htm?csnumber=40833

Jordan, D., & Evdemon, J. (2007). *Web services business process execution language version 2.0*. Retrieved from http://docs.oasis-open.org/wsbpel/2.0/OS/wsbpel-v2.0-OS.html

Liegl, P. (2009). *Business documents for inter-organizational business processes*. Unpublished doctoral dissertation, Vienna University of Technology, Vienna, Austria.

Ministry of the Economy. Labour and Entrepreneurship (MELE). (2007). *Strategy for the development of electronic business in the Republic of Croatia for the period 2007–2010*. Retrieved from http://www.mingorp.hr/defaulteng.aspx?ID=1089

Mos, A., Boulze, A., Quaireau, S., & Meynier, C. (2008). Multi-layer perspectives and spaces in SOA. In *Proceedings of the 2nd International Workshop on Systems Development in SOA Environments*, Leipzig, Germany.

Northern European Subset (NES). (2009). *NES profiles*. Retrieved from http://www.nesubl.eu/documents/nesprofiles.4.6f60681109102909b80002525.html

OAGi. (1999). *OAGIS*. Retrieved from http://www.oagi.org/dnn/oagi/Home/tabid/136/Default.aspx

OASIS. (2002). *Message service specification version 2.0*. Retrieved from http://www.oasis-open.org/committees/download.php/272/ebMS_v2_0.pdf

OASIS. (2006). *Web services security (WSS)*. Retrieved from http://www.oasis-open.org/committees/tc_home.php?wg_abbrev=wss

OECD. (2005). *E-Government for better government*. Retrieved from http://www.oecd.org/document/45/0,3343,en_2649_34129_35815981_1_1_1_1,00.html

OMG. (2006). *Business process modeling notation (BPMN) version 1.0: OMG final adopted specification*. Retrieved from http://www.bpmn.org/

Ouyang, C., Van der Aalst, W. M. P., Dumas, M., Ter Hofstede, A. H. M., & Mendling, J. (2009). From business process models to process-oriented software systems. *ACM Transactions on Software Engineering and Methodology, 19*(1). doi:10.1145/1555392.1555395

PEPPOL. (2008). *eProcurement without borders in Europe*. Retrieved from http://www.peppol.eu/

Porter, M. E. (1996). What is strategy? *Harvard Business Review*, 61–78.

Recker, J., Indulska, M., Rosemann, M., & Green, P. (2005). Do process modeling techniques get better? A comparative ontological analysis of BPMN. In *Proceedings of the 16th Australasian Conference on Information Systems*.

Smith, A. (1976). The wealth of nations . In Mossner, E. C., Ross, I. S., Campbell, R. H., Raphael, D. D., & Skinner, A. S. (Eds.), *The Glasgow edition of the works and correspondence of Adam Smith*. Oxford, UK: Oxford University Press.

Specht, T., Drawehn, J., Thranert, M., & Kuhne, S. (2005). Modeling cooperative business processes and transformation to a service oriented architecture. In *Proceedings of the Seventh IEEE International Conference on E-Commerce Technology*, Munich, Germany (pp. 249-256).

SPOCS. (2009). *About the project*. Retrieved from http://www.eu-spocs.eu/index.php

STORK. (2009). *Stork at a glance*. Retrieved from https://www.eid-stork.eu/

Tanner, C., Wölfle, R., & Quade, M. (2006). *The role of information technology in procurement in the top 200 companies in Switzerland*. Aarau, Switzerland: University of Applied Sciences Northwestern Switzerland.

Tarafdar, M., & Vaidya, S. D. (2005). Adoption & implementation of IT in developing nations: Experiences from two public sector enterprises in India. *Journal of Cases on Information Technology*, 7(1), 111–135. doi:10.4018/jcit.2005010107

U. S. Census Bureau. (2009). *North American industry classification system*. Retrieved from http://www.census.gov/eos/www/naics/

UN/CEFACT. (2003). *Core components technical specification – Part 8 of the ebXML framework*. Retrieved from http://www.unece.org/cefact/ebxml/CCTS_V2-01_Final.pdf

UN/CEFACT. (2008). *Business requirements specification (BRS) for the cross industry invoice V.2.0*. Retrieved from http://www.unece.org/cefact/brs/BRS_CrossIndustryInvoice_v2.0.pdf

UN/CEFACT. (2009). *Business requirement specifications*. Retrieved from http://www.unece.org/cefact/brs/brs_index.htm

United Nations Standard Products and Services Code (UNSPSC). (2009). *Welcome*. Retrieved from http://www.unspsc.org/

Vrček, N., Dobrović, Ž., & Kermek, D. (2007). Novel approach to BCG analysis in the context of ERP system implementation . In Župančič, J. (Ed.), *Advances in information systems development* (pp. 47–60). New York, NY: Springer. doi:10.1007/978-0-387-70761-7_5

World Bank. (2009). *e-Government - Definition of e-government.* Retrieved from http://web.worldbank.org/WBSITE/EXTERNAL/TOPICS/EXTINFORMATION-ANDCOMMUNICATIONANDTECHNOLOGIES/ EXTEGOVERNMENT/0,c ontentMDK:20507153~menuPK:702592~pagePK:148956~piPK:216618~theSite PK:702586,00.html

Zimmermann, O., Doubrovski, V., Grundler, J., & Hogg, K. (2005). Service-oriented architecture and business process choreography in an order management scenario: Rationale, concepts, lessons learned. *Companion to the 20th Annual ACM SIGPLAN Conference on Object-oriented Programming, Systems, Languages, and Applications*, San Diego, CA (pp. 301-312).

ENDNOTES

[1] Government of Croatia has adopted Strategy for the development of electronic business in the Republic of Croatia for the period 2007 – 2010 (Min, 2007). The Strategy brings guidelines for faster development of e-business in Croatia. The Strategy is also basis for launching national projects which should support business entities to stay concurrent at domestic and international level. Projects are related to e-invoice, open source applications and interoperability. The purpose of these projects is to recognize and to deal with obstacles in adoption of electronic business. Another important aspect of mentioned projects is bringing international perspective anticipating the fact that Croatia is in the process of convergence with European Union (EU). All project results have to be aligned with EU recommendations, guidelines and strategies. Intention is that outcomes of the projects easily integrate with pan-European and global e-business development trends. One aim of these efforts was to develop and make widely available certain e-business open source software modules. This project was awarded to Faculty of Organization and Informatics, University of Zagreb and small outline of its results are presented in this article.

This work was previously published in the Journal of Cases on Information Technology, Volume 13, Issue 3, edited by Mehdi Khosrow-Pour, pp. 39-61, copyright 2010 by IGI Publishing (an imprint of IGI Global).

Chapter 14

Premium International for Credit Services:
Application of Value-Based Management

Eskandar Tooma
American University in Cairo (AUC), Egypt

Aliaa Bassiouny
American University in Cairo (AUC), Egypt

Nourhan El Mogui
American University in Cairo (AUC), Egypt

EXECUTIVE SUMMARY

Despite its success in creating a strong market for its product and growing its customer base, PICS is going through a restructuring phase to overcome a variety of operational and financial challenges. This case study examines the concept of value-based management (VBM) and how applying it to the company's restructuring process would help PICS'S management track its performance and make sound strategic decisions for the company. The protagonist is PICS CEO Mr. Paul Antaki, who is being presented with a proposal from 'Val-U' consultants on how VBM would create value for all PICS stakeholders.

The case follows through the history of PICS, presenting the business model and the market for its products. It then moves on to outline the financial position of PICS over the period 2002-2005, which shows that, despite double-digit growth in revenue, the company has suffered from poor bottom lines that have put the company in severe financial distress.

DOI: 10.4018/978-1-4666-2618-8.ch014

ORGANIZATIONAL BACKGROUND: THE HISTORY BEHIND PICS

On an early Sunday morning in his elegant office in Dokki, Zafer Paul Antaki, CEO of Premium International for Credit Services (PICS), was sitting at his desk, looking through some of the company's latest financials. Taking a sip of his morning coffee, he began flipping through a report from 'Val-U' Consultation. The report included several corporate success stories on the application of value-based management (VBM) and a full-fledged proposal on how the application of VBM could help PICS create value for all its stakeholders.

The first spark for PICS came to Antaki back in 2000, when he was Managing Director of Consolidated Casuals Ltd, a market leader in the fashion retail business in Egypt and a licensee of well-known European brands, including Naf Naf, Mexx and Daniel Hechter. Antaki introduced a loyalty program using a card, called Premium Card, that provided a payment plan for purchases made through the company's different outlets. Within a year, the demand for the Premium Card by both clients and merchants increased significantly. The success of the program captured Antaki's attention. He began thinking of how the company could capitalize and expand on the program in an emerging and growing market of credit card users. The involvement of new retail stores would better serve current customers, as well as attract potential customers.

After three years of study, the company formed a consortium with new business partners to establish PICS in 1997, with a 61 percent ownership for the Antaki family. The vision of the new shareholding company, which was managed by Paul Antaki as CEO, was to be the world's leading interest-free credit card provider and the leading role model for banks, end-users and merchants within the consumer credit card industry throughout Egypt and internationally, starting with the MENA region.

To fulfill this ambitious vision, PICS management put together a mission statement to guide their decisions:

- To develop Premium International's logistics and infrastructure for international deployment
- To offer the Premium Card through all major banks
- To be the preferred credit card amongst consumers by offering them excellent services, a strong marketing and retailing environment such as department stores, and online and catalogue shopping
- To be recognized by a large merchant network as the highest generator of customer purchases with continuous growth

Figure 1. Board of Directors' profile and organizational structure

Board of Directors Profile

Board Members		
Dr. Ibrahim Kamel *Chairman*	Kato Investments Group S.A.E Giza for Seeds & Herbs Co.	10%
Zafer Paul Antaki *CEO*	Founder of Premium International Consolidated Casuals LTD	38%
Rami E. Antaki *Board Member*	Co-founder of Premium International Managest International	23%
Nasser Chourbagy *Board Member*	Consolidated Casuals Ltd	14%
Ahmed El Gibaly *Board Member*	Co-founder of Premium International On Line Media S.A.E Xclusive Card	10%
Ayman Hamed Hamdy *Board Member*	Kato Investments Group S.A.E	5%

Organizational Structure

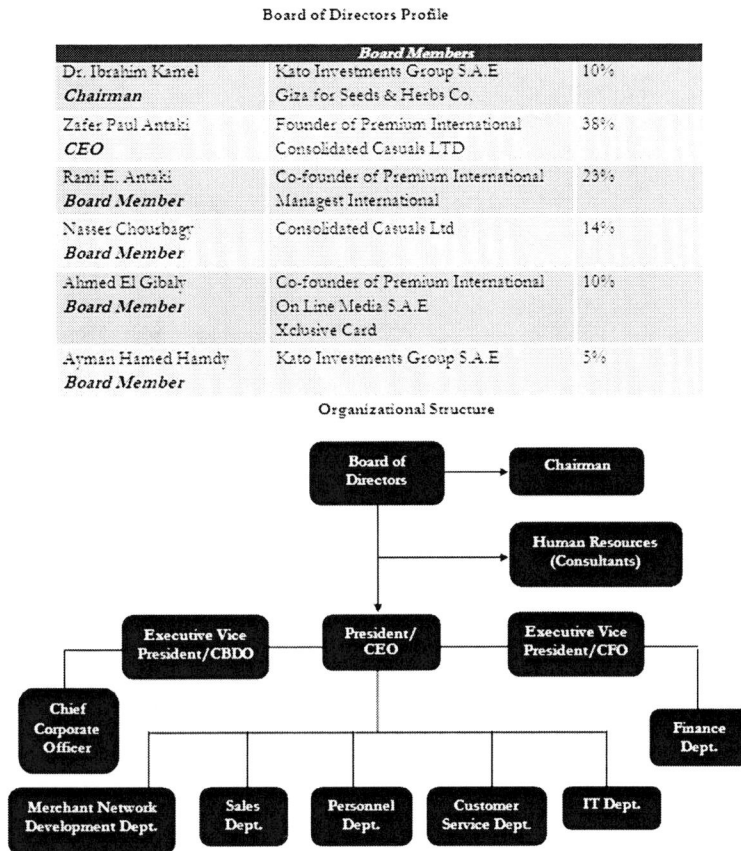

PICS™ became the first private sector credit card provider in the MENA region. The actual operation started in February 2002 after the official establishment of the first interest-free credit card, Premium Card, in Egypt. Through this step, PICS had validated a business model featuring an interest-free credit card designed to benefit consumers by improving their buying power rather than to maximize fees and interest charges.

PICS's uniqueness in the market of credit cards lies in being the only consumer credit card service provider offering 10 months interest-free payment plans for consumers. This feature distinguished its main product, Premium Card, from all other credit cards on the Egyptian market, giving PICS an edge and turning it into a market leader within a period of five years. The interest-free installment payment plans appealed to Egyptian society, especially the Muslim majority, since it did not entail any form of usury. Moreover, PICS'S extended network of merchant and bank

Figure 2. PICS progress

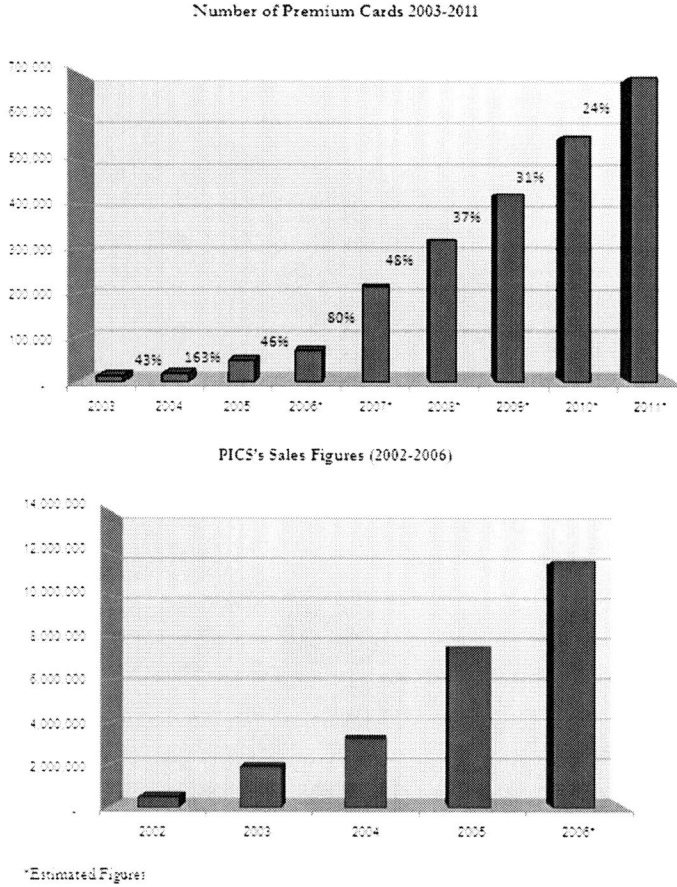

Number of Premium Cards 2003-2011

PICS's Sales Figures (2002-2006)

*Estimated Figures

alliances encouraged consumers to make use of the facilitated payment scheme. The number of subscribers had reached 70,000 customers by the end of 2006, despite the absence of above-the-line marketing activities.

The Local Market

Egypt is considered one of the most populous countries in the Middle East and the second most populous in the African continent. Egypt's population is approximately 80 million as of 2007, with 58 percent and 48 percent of the population living in rural and urban areas respectively, and a Muslim majority.

Egypt macroeconomic performance has improved since the 1990s. Through sound fiscal and monetary policies, the government of Egypt (GOE) has improved the inflation rate and budget deficits, and built up foreign reserves. Egypt has been moving towards a more market-oriented economy through government reform programs focusing on privatization and the enactment of new business legislation. Since the appointment of Prime Minister Ahmed Nazif's cabinet in 2004, Egypt has made substantial progress in developing its legal, tax and investment structure. More reforms are expected to follow.

Egypt is mainly a "cash-based" society, where only 30 percent of its money supply is in the form of bank deposits. The habit of holding cash is deeply rooted in the society. A study by the National Bank of Egypt conducted in March 2006 shows that the total number of credit cards issued in Egypt reached 2,738,555 in 2005. In contrast, in Saudi Arabia, more than 2 million cards are held by a population of nearly 24 million people, while in Kuwait, a population of just 2 million people holds more than 1 million cards. The low penetration of credit cards in Egypt can be seen as strong potential for the growth of this business. An analysis of the credit card market in Egypt by market structure and competition reveals the following:

- **Market Structure**

Credit card providers in Egypt are dominated by the public-sector bank, the National Bank of Egypt (NBE). It is worth mentioning that 36 percent of the total number of credit cards in Egypt are issued by NBE, with which Premium International has formed a strategic alliance.

Figure 3. Breakdown of credit card providers

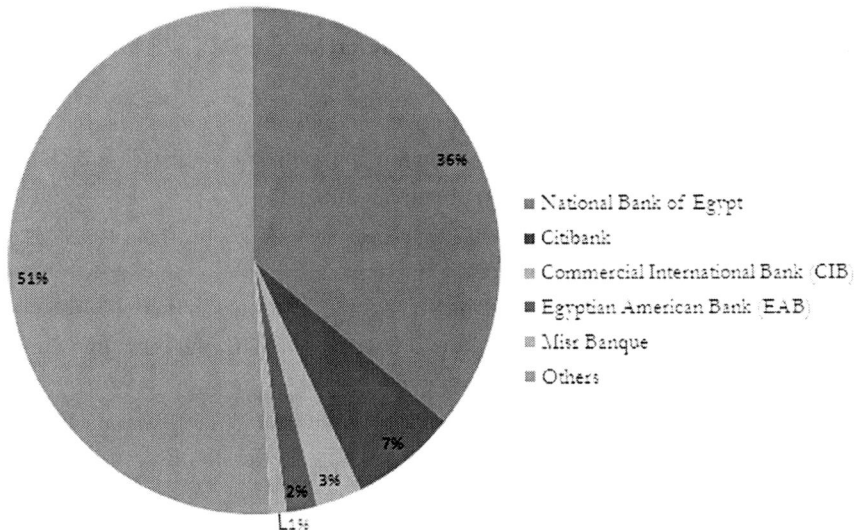

303

Figure 4. Comparison with competition

	Ahli Takseet	Tamima	Shams Ahli	Premium Card
Issuance Fees	100 (25 as an extra credit card)	Free	100	100
Renewal Fees	50 (25 as an extra credit card)	50	50	100
Max. Limit/card	150,000	50,000	50,000	50,000
Min. Limit/card	1000	1000	1000	1000
Min. Refund	10%	5%	5%	Equal Installments
Grace Period	25 days	25 days	25 days	25 days
APR	18%	18%	18%	18%
Advantages	Purchases from 65 outlets. Only 6 months interest free installments	Only 6 months interest free installments	Only 6 months interest free installments	450 different outlets. 10 equal free interest installments.

- **Competition**

Being a market-led company, Premium International focuses on delivering innovative products at exceptional service levels. Since the latest of its pioneer products, Premium Card, has become well recognized in the market, three main competitors have developed similar financial products. Tamima Company has developed "Tamima Viza MasterCard", Shams Company has produced "Shams Ahli Master Card", and National Bank of Egypt has introduced "Ahli Takseet Visa Card". Premium Card, however, has maintained its leadership position, being the only 10-month interest-free credit card.

SETTING THE STAGE: THE PICS BUSINESS MODEL

PICS takes pride in its innovative and unique product and its intact business model. Core to Premium Card's successful penetration is both the facilitation of payment and the card's usability in a wide range of retail outlets.

The business model is built on creating alliances with major banks and corporations to identify potential cardholders. PICS uses the banks' databases to identify, assess and select potential clients it wants to market the card to. PICS'S network of bank alliances helped the company attain a base of over 70,000 customers without incurring marketing expenditures.

Selecting potential customers, contacting them and successfully issuing a Premium Card is only one aspect of the process. Four parties are involved in the issuance of the card: *PICS, the partner-bank, the merchant and the customer.*

Figure 5. The PICS business model

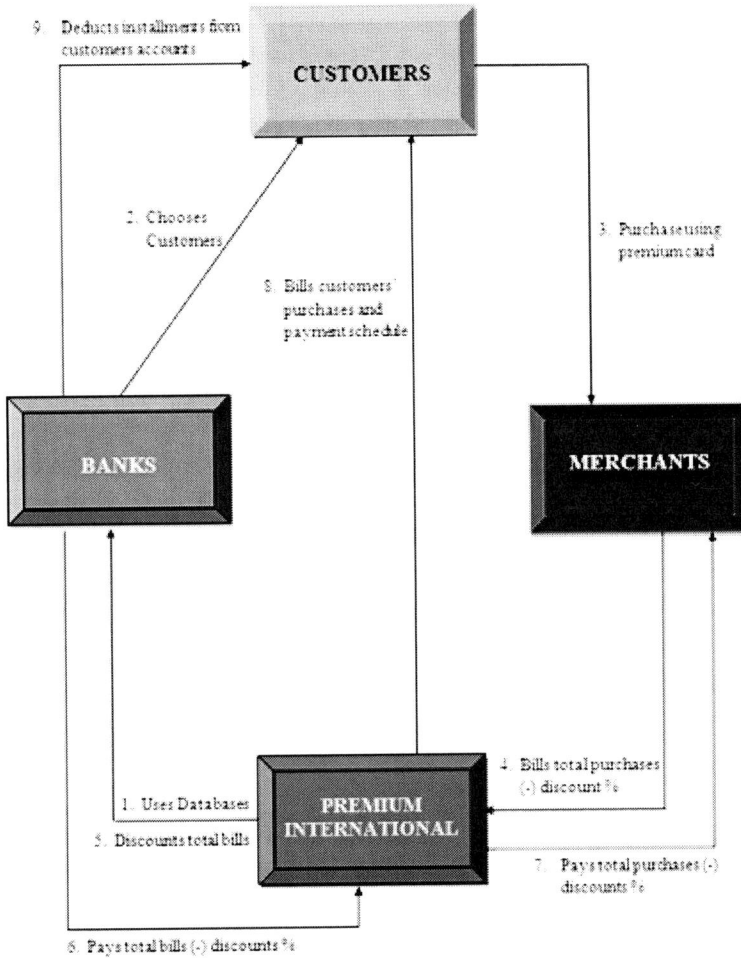

The money flow through this model is as follows:

- Monthly reports are sent to allied banks showing the value of issued cards, all purchase transactions during that month as well as installments due.
- The bank then pays Premium International the total amount after deducting the agreed-upon commission.
- The bank is responsible for collecting the installments from the clients' accounts.
- Premium International pays back the merchant after deducting the agreed-upon commission.
- Premium International also deducts the balance of customer installments in the system.

Key Players: The Customer

To illustrate how the model works, let us take the following example of Mrs. Bassiouny:

"Mrs. Bassiouny, who has just been issued a Premium Card with her bank, the National Bank of Egypt (NBE), and paid a fixed annual fee of LE 100, is shopping around at City Stars. She finds a LE 200 bag she likes in a shop that is a member of the PICS merchant network. Mrs. Bassiouny decides to use her Premium Card for the purchase. As soon as the purchase is made and her Premium Card is credited for the LE 200, PICS informs NBE of Bassiouny's purchase. Over the next 10 months, Bassiouny's account with NBE will be debited LE 20 a month."

The benefits of Premium Card are obvious to Mrs. Bassiouny. The card allows her to enjoy the privilege of buying on credit from 450 different renowned outlets in the domestic market and paying over a period of 10 months with no interest charge. For most customers like Bassiouny, the card has a minimum credit limit of LE 2,000, and is renewable annually for a fixed fee. The credit limit, which could be considered low, is actually quite adequate for most of Premium's target customers, who are mainly middle-class consumers.

To expand on this successful and innovative concept, PICS continuously develops new products and services for its clients. Some of the recent additions to PICS'S offerings include:

- **Premium Super Stores**

An established department store that combines several well-known brands under one roof. Premium Super Store is a sister company of PICS, founded to promote Premium Card. The first outlet was opened in City Stars Shopping Mall, among the largest malls in the Middle East, with expectations of more outlets in the future[1].

- **Individuals**

Instead of reaching customers through bank alliances, PICS has modified its business model to issue Premium Cards directly to individuals. This is usually done through corporate alliances. These types of alliances are formed through the development of direct relations with reputable organizations through which PICS targets employees as potential clients. The idea of targeting customers within certain organizations reduces the credit risk, since the credit value is guaranteed through the employee's salary.

Individual clients can also be reached through direct agreements with individuals who have bank accounts or credit cards with banks that Premium International does not have alliances with. In this case, the company guarantees its credit by requiring customers to sign a check for an amount representing 110 percent of the Premium Card credit limit, in the presence of sales or customer service staff, renewable upon the card's renewal.

- **VIP Cards**

PICS is studying the possibility of introducing a new set of cards, targeted at "A" class customers. These cards are proposed to have higher credit limits than the Classic Premium Card, and to be categorized by gender: "Silver and Gold Cards" for men who differentiate themselves by elegance, and "Ruby and Emerald Cards" for trendy, fashion-conscience women.

Key Players: The Banks

Most of PICS customers are acquired through banking alliances. Bank alliances are formed by either cross selling or bundling:

- **Cross Selling**

This involves an exchange of client databases between PICS and the bank. Through the bank's database, PICS is able to identify potential customers, get to know their credit history and contact them easily. PICS has formed such alliances with the National Bank of Egypt (NBE), Banque Misr and Housing and Development Bank. A large number of current Premium Card holders are originally NBE clients, mainly of the "B" and "C+" classes. The company is still studying the formation of new alliances, given that the average usage per card has not reached full potential. Allies under consideration include BNP-Paribas, Arab African International Bank (AAIB) and Citibank.

- **Bundling**

This involves the creation of joint packages between PICS and the bank for a new customer who is not an existing client of either party. It involves joining two related products and selling them as a single unit. PICS has successfully applied bundling with NBE by offering NBE Visa or Master Card with Premium Card.

Each card purchase entails a payment to PICS by the bank. However, in return for providing PICS with their databases and banking services, the bank will usually deduct a commission fee from the amount of each Premium Card purchase. The fee is negotiated between the two parties and varies from one bank to another. In the past, PICS used to pay an average commission fee of 7.5 percent to banks. This high fee was the main reason for PICS losses from 2002 until 2005.

To illustrate the dynamics of the relationship between banks and PICS, let us go back to our example. To get paid for Bassiouny's purchases, the bank will debit her monthly installments from her account and will pay PICS the total purchase amount less the commission fee. So, instead of paying LE 200 to PICS (which the bank takes through monthly installments), it will only pay PICS LE 200 - LE 15= LE 185.

Starting 2007, PICS has managed to extend its bank alliances. While most of its cards are issued by the National Bank of Egypt (El Ahly), PICS has also formed alliances with Bank Misr, Egyptian American Bank and Citibank.

Key Players: The Merchants

PICS's merchant network is central to the success of Premium Cards and the growth in the number of issuances. PICS currently has a network of 450 stores.

The expansion of the merchant network is very critical to PICS, since the greater the variety of merchants and retail outlets that give consumers the chance to use their Premium Cards, the greater the appeal and demand for the card. Because of the promotion of their outlets through PICS, the merchants give PICS a 10 percent discount on purchases made with the card. In the example of Mrs. Bassiouny, the loop is closed when PICS pays the merchant directly for Bassiouny's purchase. However, PICS will only pay the merchant LE 180, having deducted the 10% discount.

Key Players: The Company

PICS'S revenue stream in the above business model comes from two main sources, a fixed one and a variable one:

- **Fixed Revenue:** Card Issuances

Each time Premium issues a customer a Premium Card, they charge a fixed annual fee of LE 100 for bank customers and LE 200 for individual customers. For card issuances by banks, the bank usually takes a sales commission on every new card issued.

- **Variable Revenue**: Spread between Merchant Discount and Bank Commission.

Table 1. Key indicators

Average purchase amount/active card	LE 822/month
Average card limit	LE 2,500
Average used limit per active card	LE 710/month
% of cards with bad debts (PICS)	1.1%
% of cards with bad debts (Banks)	2.7%
Number of new cards acquired monthly	3400
Number of complaints	10/month
Attrition Rate	300 cards/month

*Figures are simple monthly averages over the past 6 months

In the previous example, PICS'S revenue from Bassiouny's purchase is LE 5, which is the difference between how much the bank paid PICS and how much PICS paid the merchant (LE185-LE180).

These two main sources of revenue are used by PICS to pay for all of its direct and indirect costs. The main costs to PICS are:

- Outgoing calls to potential customers to promote the Premium Card
- Incentives paid to sales personnel responsible for issuing new cards
- Direct costs of new card issuances (including customer application forms, card printing, envelopes, newsletters, merchant lists, mobile SMS, etc.)
- Direct costs of card renewals

PICS is continuously improving its service offerings, to ensure a continuous growth in their revenue stream. Some of their newly developed customer-oriented strategies include:

- **Information Technology (IT)**

Like all banking and credit service providers, IT is the backbone of the company. PICS is committed to surpassing other providers in its service level, and to consistently delivering quality services to both its clients and allies. Using its own in-house technologies, the company has designed and developed a fully operational card infrastructure, including merchant acquisition systems, card production, point of sales, a complete card-member reporting system and merchant system. Systems within the company are all coordinated using Premium's software, and are constantly being developed and upgraded to ensure high security levels and efficient flow of transactions.

- **Call Center**

A fully equipped call centre has been set up to respond to all consumer needs. PICS is driven by the belief that the most important thing for consumers is to use the service smoothly, get quick answers to their inquiries and be offered convenient solutions to any striking problem. The company strives to meet these needs by all possible means.

- **Customer Service**

PICS perceives customer satisfaction as one of its key success factors. Accordingly, the company ensures that customer-service employees are rigorously trained to work with customers, satisfying all their needs and providing all the assistance necessary. All complaints are carefully registered in the company's system and reports are distributed to various departments in order to identify and solve the problems customers face. PICS'S customer service department consists of more than 55 employees.

CASE DESCRIPTION: PICS'S FINANCIAL POSITION

Over the period 2002-2005, PICS was able to firmly establish a unique image, expand its client database, and achieve an increasing revenue growth rate. This success, however, was not reflected in the bottom line, as PICS suffered losses over the first four years of operation, amounting to a total of LE 5,356,488 in 2005. Although the company barely managed to break even in 2006, this was mainly due to large capital injections within this period that saved the company from bankruptcy and improved its ratio figures drastically.

PICS losses reflected ineffective operational management. PICS had suffered internally from the mismanagement of its commission system, paying bank commissions on purchases more than was discounted from merchants. Banks received not only a sales commission, but also an agreed-upon commission for every new issuance and card renewal. Indirect costs were also a major challenge, given the required quality standards for operations. As a result, costs exceeded revenues in two consecutive years: 2002 and 2003. In other words, despite the growing revenues and the success of the product, the rate of increase of costs was proportional to that of revenue, which made profits unlikely.

From an equity perspective, the ROE had improved from -3300% in 2002 to -39% towards the end of this time period. The main stimulus behind this, however, was the injection of capital that saved PICS from bankruptcy. A sum of LE1.95 million in 2004, followed by a further LE 4.95 million in 2005, helped the company acquire some financial stability before reaching breakeven in 2006.

PICS was committed to delivering outstanding service and innovative products. However, given the figures, expansion was impossible. A logical step was to hire a consultant to pump fresh ideas into the company and help implement an effective model that would increase profitability and control costs. VBM Models, such as those suggested by 'Val-U,' provide a holistic approach whereby the company can determine the key value drivers that contribute to its profits and returns and assess them against the various costs involved in the business. The outcome of this value-driven approach is a set of strategies that can help the company continue its revenue growth, and reflect this growth in the bottom line through various cost control strategies.

CURRENT CHALLENGE FACING THE ORGANIZATION

Discussions during several top management meetings have exposed the various pitfalls PICS has faced since its inception. The journey along the road ahead depends on how these challenges will be tackled. Despite the company's increasing

Figure 6. Historical financial statements for PICS

	2005	2004	2003	2002
Sales Revenue	7,561,716	3,266,616	1,923,190	487,940
COSS	(2,764,091)	(1,324,555)	(2,708,994)	(1,018,057)
Gross Profit	4,797,625	1,942,061	(785,804)	(530,117)
Less: Operating Expenses	(4,261,160)	(2,342,322)	-	(2,402,634)
Other Income	16,986	493	-	-
Operating Income/Loss	553,451	(399,768)	(785,804)	(2,932,751)
Less: Depreciation	(615,495)	(406,778)	(391,168)	(358,706)
EBIT	(62,044)	(806,546)	(1,176,972)	(3,291,457)
Interest Income			250	
Less: Interest Expense				56
Less: Taxes	-	-	-	-
Net P/L after tax	(62,044)	(806,546)	(1,176,722)	(3,291,401)
Unusual Items				
FX			1,417	9,419
Capital Loss				(30,610)
Net Profit/Loss	(62,044)	(806,546)	(1,175,305)	(3,312,592)

311

Figure 7. Historical financial statements for PICS

	2005	2004	2003	2002
Assets				
Current Assets				
Cash	4,257,888	445,777	496,366	153,570
Accounts Receivables	11,915,982	4,260,310	4,228,957	2,163,361
Receivables	5,932,989	3,064,912	3,117,882	1,975,341
Debtors	3,162,595	1,118,803	1,111,076	188,020
Receivables from affiliated companies	2,820,398	76,595		
Total Current Assets	16,173,870	4,706,087	4,725,323	2,316,931
Long term Assets				
Machinery			512,662	549,164
Equipment			73,914	63,051
Computers			88,408	44,693
Cars			88,888	102,923
Fixed Assets	1,131,978	765,153	763,873	759,831
Projects under implementation	421,796	562,395	834,999	1,107,603
Investment	220,000			
Total Long term Assets	1,773,774	1,327,548	1,598,872	1,867,434
Total Assets	17,947,644	6,033,635	6,324,195	4,184,365
Current Liabilities				
Short-term debt (merchants)	3,374,337	1,608,469	1,906,020	2,192,419
Account Payable	10,308,104	1,798,377	1,751,222	2,101,098
Creditors	2,621,692	5,871,235	7,054,853	3,103,442
Total Current Liabilities	16,304,133	9,278,081	10,712,095	7,396,959
Shareholders Equity				
Common Stocks (10 par, 1,000,000 shares authorized)	7,000,000	2,050,000	100,000	100,000
Accumulated Losses	(5,356,489)	(5,294,445)	(4,487,899)	(3,312,594)
Total Shareholders' Equity	1,643,511	(3,244,445)	(4,387,899)	(3,212,594)
Total Liab.& Shareholders' Eq.	17,947,644	6,033,636	6,324,196	4,184,365

revenues and reputable image, PICS incurred continuous losses in its first years, leading to financial problems. Shareholders managed to save the company through capital injections in 2004, 2005, and 2007 of LE 1,950,000, LE 4,950,000 and LE 5,000,000 consecutively. This gave rise to many questions, such as: Did the company over focus its efforts on obtaining alliances, while disregarding how to increase the current usage per present client? Why did the company have a negative factoring commission in 2002 / 2003? What would be the ideal value of bank commissions and merchant discounts? Other major questions revolved around the size of customers served, the targeted segments, and a more profitable approach to reach the end-user. A closer analysis of the aspect of 'who we serve and how' gave rise to questions like: Why did the company end up with a large database of clients, yet negative profits? What would be the appropriate mix of client categories – bank alliance / individuals - that would optimize profits? How would the increase in the

Figure 8. Historical financial statements for PICS

	2005	2004
Cash Flow from Operating Activities		
Net Loss	(62,044)	(806,546)
Loss in Sales Fixed assets	(1,563)	-
Depreciation	615,496	406,778
Change in Working Capital		
Increase in A P	7,026,052	47,155
Decrease in A P		(600,482)
Decrease in A R		47,578
Increase in A R	(7,655,672)	(959,619)
Cash Provided by Operating Activities	**(77,731)**	**(1,865,136)**
Cash Flow from Investment Activities		
Increase in long term Invest.	(220,000)	
Increase in Fixed Assets	(905,659)	
Decrease in Fixed Assets	65,500	
Cash Provided by Investment Activities	**(1,060,159)**	**(135,454)**
Cash Flow from Financing Activities		
Changes in Stockholders Equity	4,950,000	
Cash Provided by Financing Activities	**4,950,000**	**1,950,000**
Increase Cash	**3,812,110**	**(50,590)**
Beg. Cash	445,777	496,366
Net Increase in Cash	**4,257,887**	**445,776**

number of merchants PICS deals with, as well as bank alliances, benefit the business relative to other alternatives?

RECOMMENDED APPROACH: THE CONSULTANT

Antaki had invited 'VAL-U' to deliver a presentation on VBM during the next board meeting. He wanted the board and top management to become acquainted with the new idea, and gauge, through their discussions, to what extent the integration of VBM would become a success. Antaki also thought it would be a good idea to share some reports that introduced VBM before the meeting with 'VAL-U', to make sure the discussion would be fruitful. The following is a summary of the key points that appeared in the reports.

- **VBM Concept**

VBM is a management approach that unites company units towards a single goal, that of creating value. It suggests that all the different strategies, plans and performance targets within each function must be aligned with this ultimate goal. What creating value normally means is maximizing shareholder value. This consistent focus on value can be attained within a company through:

1. *Creating value (ways to increase or generate maximum future value = strategy),*
2. *Managing for value (governance, change management, organizational culture, communication, leadership) and,*
3. *Measuring value (valuation)* (Value-Based Management, n.d.)

There are two concepts that VBM stems from. The first is that a company's value is determined by its discounted future cash flows. Second, that value is created only when companies invest capital at returns that exceed the cost of that capital. VBM extends these concepts by focusing on how companies use them to make both major strategic and everyday operating decisions.

The proper execution of VBM entails an alignment of the company's overall objectives, analytical techniques and management processes. Accordingly, it centers the attention of management decision making on the key drivers of value. It is like restructuring towards certain focal points - key drivers of value - to achieve maximum value on a continuous basis. Its impact is often seen in improved economic performance.

Key Value Drivers

A company cannot directly affect value, but has to act on things it can influence, such as customer satisfaction, cost, capital expenditures, and so on. A key value driver is any variable that affects the company value. It is through these drivers of value that senior management learns to understand the rest of the organization and to create a dialogue about what it expects to be accomplished.

8:55am, Sunday, June 24th: The Meeting

'Val-U' executive team is setting up their presentation in one of PICS's meeting rooms. All of the top management team is present. Paul Antaki sits quietly at one end of the table, observing the attendees. The excitement of Val-U's team members is visible. "Can VBM be the miracle answer to getting PICS back on track and setting our strategies for the future?" he wonders thoughtfully. He looks forward to the presentation with interest.

REFERENCES

Management, V. B. (n.d.). *Business dictionary/management dictionary*. Retrieved from http://www.12manage.com/methods_value_based_management.html

ENDNOTE

[1]   There are currently three outlets open.

This work was previously published in Cases on Business and Management in the MENA Region: New Trends and Opportunities, edited by El-Khazindar Business Research and Case Center, pp. 76-88, copyright 2011 by Business Science Reference (an imprint of IGI Global).

Chapter 15

Use of the Concern–Task–Interaction–Outcome (CTIO) Cycle for Virtual Teamwork

Suryadeo Vinay Kissoon
RMIT University, Australia

EXECUTIVE SUMMARY

This chapter introduces the CTIO (Concern-Task-Interaction-Outcome) Cycle as a means of studying team member interaction using face-to-face and virtual interaction media in retail banking. The type of interaction is discussed in terms of different conceptual cycles having a linkage in the framing of the CTIO Cycle. In the past, routine teamwork using face-to-face communication was important. Today, with emerging technologies for retail banking organizations, teamwork through virtual communication has been gaining importance for increased productivity. This chapter addresses different problem-solving cycles, each of which relates to the mode of interaction medium (whether face-to-face or virtual) used by team members, facilitators, or managers to resolve problems in the workplace. The chapter focuses on understanding the relationship between face-to-face and virtual interaction variables. This is important to researchers in identifying retail banking trends using hybrid teams and virtual group networks with routine teamwork. Using virtual over face-to-face interactions in the different data life cycles linkages are gaining importance from the perspectives of data and information quality. This can be attributed to the increased use of technologies and virtual network features. Current trends are leading to the triangulation of continuous improvement, routine teamwork, and virtual teamwork in support of retail banking organizations achieving productive performance.

DOI: 10.4018/978-1-4666-2618-8.ch015

BACKGROUND

This chapter provides a background on an evolving approach to teamwork in the retail banking sector. The case refers to a new teamwork approach where routine teamwork is integrated with virtual teamwork using a continuous improvement initiative. The Concern-Task-Interaction-Outcome (CTIO) Cycle (Kissoon, 2007) is the continuous improvement initiative mapped from other conceptual problem-solving data life cycles.

The CTIO Cycle refers to the new evolving consultative, participative, virtual and interactive virtuous teamworking approach. It reflects the effect of employee interaction using both face-to-face and virtual interaction media in achieving productive performance for the organization (Kissoon, 2008a).

Routine teamwork is used in reference to face-to-face interaction, while virtual teamwork is used in reference to virtual interaction media. The CTIO Cycle was researched in a major Australian financial organization, which employs about 30,000 employees and 1,700 retail branches in all states of Australia.

The technology utilization of the financial organization relates to conferencing, teleconferencing, videoconferencing, voice mail, internet/intranet and many other networks features, as shown in Appendix 1. The players involved are the branch managers, team leaders, financial planners, home loan managers, personal bankers, customer service officers and tellers in retail banking branches.

CONTINUOUS IMPROVEMENT TEAMWORK (CIT) MODEL

The Continuous Improvement Teamwork (CIT) Model, demonstrated by stages in the CTIO cycle (shown in Figure 1), is a virtual teamwork approach. The circle in Figure 1 represents the continuous working towards resolution of a concern through face-to-face interaction or virtual interaction by team members. This approach is aligned with common organizational objectives of effective communication using emerging technologies (Kissoon, 2008a). The CIT Model is illustrative of an evolving participative, virtual approach to teamwork currently used by a major Australian banking organization with about 30,000 employees including its international branches. The company's objective for using the CIT Model is to achieve quality performance for its products and services.

The CIT Model is comprised of the following phases:

- **Concern (Issue):** A team member, or team members, identifies an issue related to organizational performance.

Figure 1. The CIT model realized through the CTIO cycle (Kissoon, 2007)

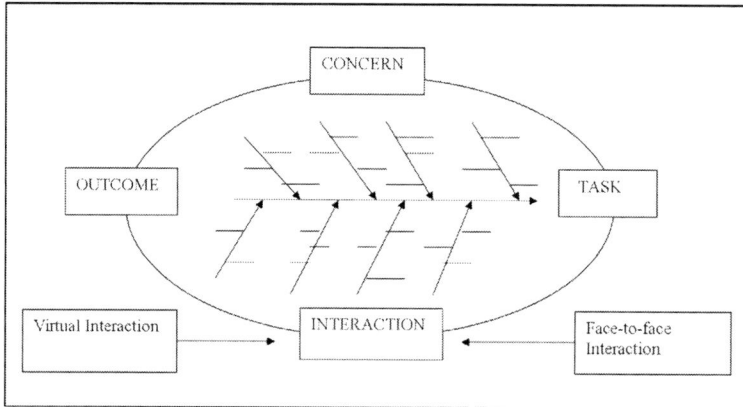

- **Task (Action):** The issue identified needs to be addressed as soon as possible through tasks by team members, facilitators, or managers working for the respective organization or as an external consultant.
- **Interaction (Involvement and Connection):** The various tasks are done through face-to-face interactions and/or virtual interactions through communication media between team members.
- **Outcome (Result):** The CIT is a continuous process in achieving successfully and productive outcomes for the benefit of the firm, team and stakeholders.

The CIT Model is part of the CTIO Cycle. The CIT Model is a classificatory framework (Kissoon, 2008a), comprised of the mapping of three knowledge domains: continuous improvement, teamwork, and e teamwork leading to the emergence of the Continuous Improvement Teamworking (CTIO) model. The CTIO Cycle is framed from other conceptual data life cycles (such as PDCA (Plan-Do-Check-Act) Cycle, DMAIC (Define, Measure, Analyze, Improve, Control) Cycle, Data Evolution Life Cycle, NEAT Methodology Data Life Cycle, and Information System Life Cycle). These process improvement approaches will be later explained.

This case illustrates the use of the CIT Model within the context of the CTIO Cycle. The CIT Model, evidenced through the CTIO Cycle (Kissoon, 2008a), was researched for about three years in a major leading Australian's service sector organization using both a deductive and inductive reasoning approach. The results from this participant observation study showed that synchronous conferencing, Internet online functional services, continuous improvement, and team meetings form the essential four core elements of the CIT Model/ CTIO Cycle. The study showed that the adoption of the CIT Model assists in improving retail banking operational activities and in achieving better performance (Kissoon, 2008b).

The CIT Model/CTIO Cycle is presented in this case based on observations made in the Australian retail banking sector. The use of the CIT Model/CTIO Cycle is appropriate for the banking sector, as interactions among team members is critical to operational effectiveness related to banking services.

Kissoon (2007) identified competition as a primary reason for the emergence of the CTIO Cycle and the adoption of the CIT Model. Without deregulation, which started in 1980`s, banking organizations would not have been so competitive. International banking organizations with expertise in retail banking were compelled to enter the domestic, Australian market due to competitive advantage. With the introduction of the Financial Services Reforms Act (FSRA) of 1988 by the Australian government, following the stock market crash in 1987, competition was encouraged (Hutley & Russel, 2005).

Increased competition means that efficiencies in operations and customer service are key to profitability. The CIT Model promotes effective communication internally among employees and externally with customers. With the increasing use of Internet and Web technologies, the CIT concept is integral to promoting both face-to-face and electronic teamwork (e-teamwork) in the efficient resolution of issues as well as meeting the needs of customers. The CIT Model is a continuous loop focused on problem-resolution. As part of the CTIO Cycle, it offers an organization the opportunity for effective communication within a process improvement loop.

Researchers and practitioners have identified the concepts of teamwork, e-teamwork, virtual communication, and continuous improvement as crucial parameters in the service sector. Each of these plays an important role in addressing customer concerns effectively. They are also part of the Total Quality Management (TQM). TQM is comprised of management practices that are applicable throughout the organization. TQM promotes organizational consistency such that customer needs are met (or exceeded). TQM also promotes process metrics and control mechanisms in order for an organization to continuously improve.

TQM continues to grow in popularity in organizational areas of service quality, data quality, information quality, and performance management. Each of these areas of TQM is supported by effective communication within and external to the organization. E-teamwork and virtual communication, in particular, allow for customer interaction transcending time and location boundaries.

A participant study was conducted by Kissoon (2008a) over a nine month time period. The results of the study showed that the CIT approach addresses organizational issues associated with the smooth, operational activities of a bank through the use of face-to-face interaction; as well as, through virtual interaction media used to communicate with internal and external customers.

The CTIO Cycle is different than other performance cycles; such as, the PDCA Cycle, NEAT Methodology data life cycle, Benchmarking Cycle, Kolb`s Cycle, and

RADAR Life Cycle, among others, as it involves the triangulation of traditional teamworking, virtual teamwork and Continuous Improvement (CI). Continuous Improvement is part of the management of all systems and processes (Evans & Dean, 2003). Interaction mode of team members in a Continuous Improvement approach is important when service quality is initiated in an organization. Continuous Improvement, from a virtual teamwork perspective, means that team members in performance cycles uses both routine teamworking integrated with CI and virtual teamworking integrated with CI. The knowledge contribution is the integration of traditional teamworking and virtual teamworking with CI in the performance and problem-solving cycles to achieve productive performance.

The concept of virtual teams was added to the concepts of TQM and teamwork in developing the existing CIT Model. This integration of concepts is referred to as the Continuous Improvement Teamwork (CIT) approach whereby the concepts of teamwork, virtual teamwork, and continuous improvement are amalgamated to foster better productive performance and improve customer service (Kissoon, 2008a). The key measures, for both face-to-face interaction and virtual interaction, are presented in Appendix 1.

Many other concepts and performance cycles also have a linkage to the CIT Model/ CTIO Cycle, as briefly illustrated in this chapter. These performance cycles are mainly focused in the service sector. Deming Planning, Doing, Checking and Acting (PDCA) Cycle; Six-Sigma Defining, Measuring, Analyzing and Improving (DMAIC) Cycle; Root Cause Hypothesis Analysis Cycle; Data Evolution Life Cycle; NEAT Methodology Data Life Cycle; Information System Life Cycle; Resulting, Approaching, Deploying, Assessing and Reviewing (RADAR) Cycle; Acceleration of Innovation ideas to Market (AIM) innovation Life Cycle, Ethnographic Research Cycle, Action Research Cycle, among others, have a linkage with the CIT Model which is realised through the CTIO Cycle.

CTIO CYCLE LINKAGES TO OTHER CONCEPTUAL CYCLES

Deming PDCA or Deming PDSA Cycle

The variant PDSA Cycle of the traditional Deming-Shewhart PDCA Cycle is a simple methodology for continuous improvement. The PDCA cycle helps team members solve problems. It provides the structure for work improvements so that a team can: (1) use process tools logically, (2) identify and analyse problems, (3) develop workable solutions, and (4) solve problems and ensure that they will not happen again (STA, 1996). This learning loop of planning, doing, checking, and acting is shown in Figure 2.

Figure 2. The PDCA cycle problem solving approach (Quality System, 1996)

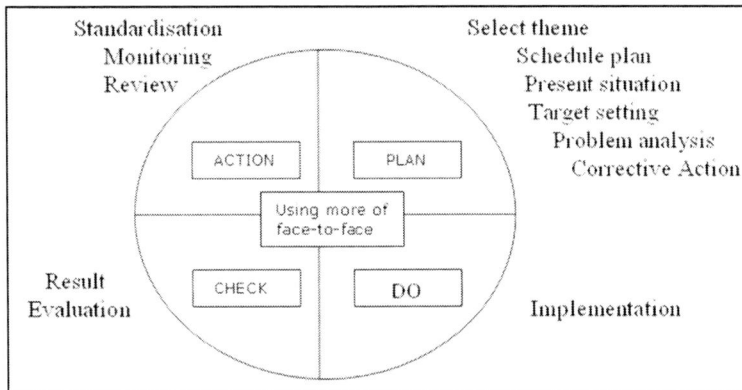

The CIT approach adopts the philosophy of the PDCA Cycle with its systematic problem-solving method. The CIT approach integrates teamwork into the process improvement cycle inclusive of traditional (routine) teamwork and virtual teamwork.

With globalisation, technological advances, virtual organizations, deregulation, and organizational competitiveness, the amalgamation of teamwork with virtual teamwork, as a hybrid team, is being envisaged. The use of hybrid teams has only recently emerged given technological and societal advances. However it is important to note that the original quality circles, which in the 1980's used the PDCA problem-solving approach, placed increasing emphasis on teamwork in organizational importance.

The Six-Sigma Methodology (DMAIC Cycle)

DMAIC Cycle, shown in Figure 3, is a problem-solving cycle related to improvement and achieving better customer service in the service sector. It is used by organizations to continuously monitor customer requirements and assess process performance. Six Sigma is a derivative of TQM (Total Quality Management) emerging in the late 1980's as a way for an organization to solve quality problems and maintain improvement. These process improvement techniques were first adopted by Motorola.

The successful completion of a Six Sigma team project is achieved through the effective use of teams. Team members, both virtuously and virtually, work together as a team to achieve organizational outcomes (e.g., process efficiencies, quality customer service). The benefit of combining the CIT Model with Six Sigma formal processes includes team efficiencies in job performance, effective use of virtual interaction media, convergence of team members into high performance,

Figure 3. The Kaizen DMAIC six-sigma cycle

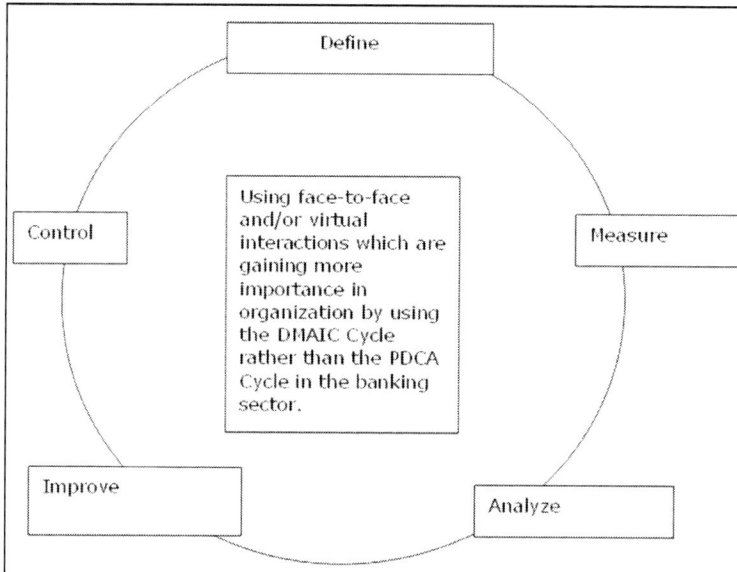

business-to-enterprise (B2E) teams, information quality, virtual working arrangements (e.g., telecommuting), e-training (electronic training), e-learning (electronic learning), and effective use of collaborative tools and other computer mediated communication. This breadth of benefits is typically not achievable by face-to-face interaction of team members working on process improvement associated with a project. The CIT approach illustrates the interaction of team members face-to-face and virtually with managers and other team members to work better as a dynamic team on any available project.

DMAIC Cycle Application in the Financial Services

The results of research with senior representatives from eleven financial services organizations showed that these financial institutions are leading exponents of lean, Six-Sigma and business Process Management Methods within the financial industry (Hayler & Nichols, 2007). These financial institutions are American Express, Bank of America, Credit Suisse, Dresdner Kleinwort Wasserstein, First Data Resources, JP Morgan Chase, Lloyds TSB, MBNA Consumer Finance, Merrill Lynch, Overseas Chinese Banking Corporation and UBS. Pande, Newman and Cavanagh (2000) identified Six Sigma as the organizational quality management system helping leading international organizations in saving millions of dollars by producing more satisfied customers. All four major Australian banking organizations are using Continuous Improvement and Six-Sigma problem-solving methodology (Figure 3) for achieving high performance of their organizations.

The Root Cause Hypothesis Analysis Cycle

The Root Cause Hypothesis Analysis Cycle (Hayler & Nichols, 2007) is illustrated in Figure 4 where the "Analyze" stage from any problem-solving cycle can be applied in process improvement as a cycle using both face-to-face interaction and virtual interaction of team members working on the project. The cycle is driven by generating and evaluating "hypotheses" (or "educated guesses") as to the cause of the problem. The causes are evaluated by using available data obtained from processes. Each of the hypotheses are refined or rejected according to the severity of the causes. The vital causes leading to the root causes are selected and confirmed for affecting the process in the process improvement cycle, which can be found by team members using both face-to-face and virtual interactions. Hence, root cause analysis is used to analyze the source of quality problems associated with quality improvement.

Similarly, in the "Task" stage of the CTIO Cycle, the Root Cause Hypothesis Analysis Cycle can be applied to detect the vital root causes affecting teamwork and virtual teamwork interactions showing a linkage of the conceptual cycles.

Figure 4. The root cause hypothesis analysis cycle (Hayler & Nichols, 2007)

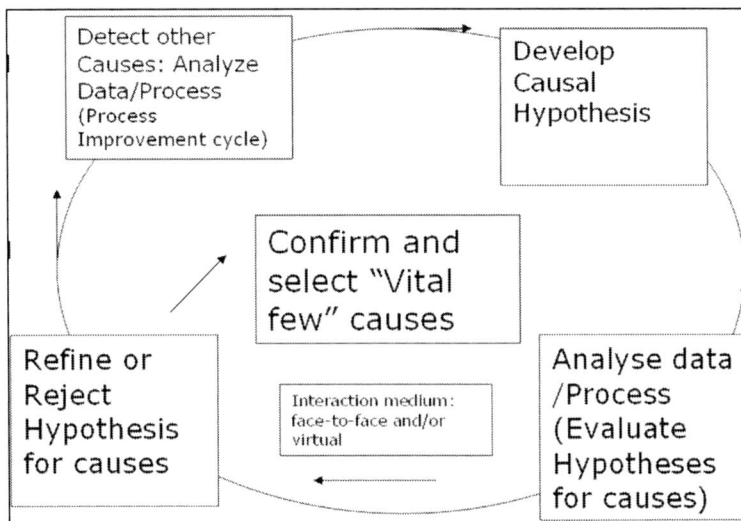

The Data Evolution Life Cycle

As described by Maier, Muegeli and Krejza (2007), a standard for information quality does not exist. The intuitive approach derives attributes for information quality based on personal experience (Wang, Reddy, & Kon, 1995; Miller, 1996; Redman, 1996; English, 1999), the empirical approach quantitatively illustrates the data consumer's point of view in the service sector about quality dimensions important to their tasks (Wang & Strong, 1996; Helfert, Zellner, & Sousa, 2002); and, the theoretical approach proposing quality dimensions that build upon established theory (Ballou & Pazer, 1985; Te`eni, 1993; Wand & Wang, 1996; Liu & Chi, 2002; as cited by Maier, Muegeli, & Krejza, 2007).

The data evolution lifecycle, shown in Figure 5, is normally used as a theoretical basis characterising the typical sequence of data evolution stages to derive four data quality stages. These consist of: (1) data collection, (2) organization, (3) presentation; and, (4) application (Liu & Chi, 2002; as cited by Maier, Muegeli, & Krejza, 2007). Each of these stages is derived through a task and an interaction medium, which can be either face-to-face and/or virtual. The objective is to effectively use collected information to focus on data quality. At each stage in the data evolution lifecycle, typical root causes of poor data quality as well as specific measurement attributes and models are derived through face-to-face and/or virtual interactions of team members.

Figure 5. The data evolution life cycle (Maier, Muegeli, & Krejza, 2007)

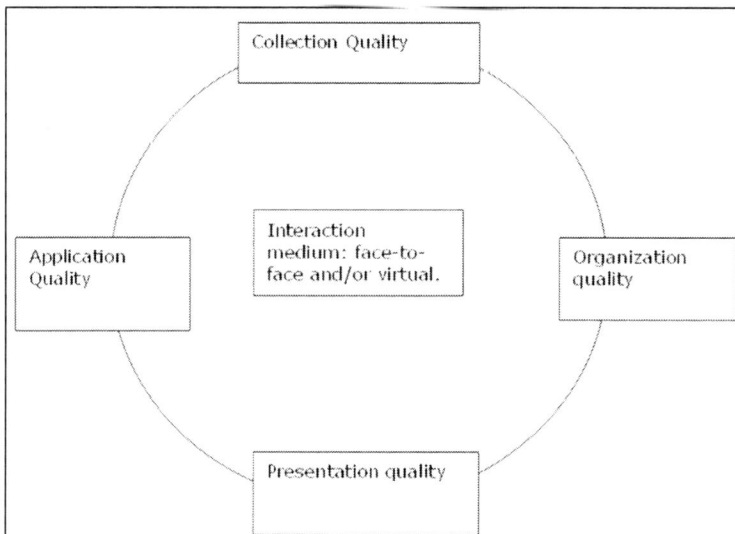

At Credit Suisse, this conceptual model is used for illustrating information quality issues with improvements in the customer investigational process (Maier, Muegeli, & Krejza, 2007). The process consists of two connected data evolution lifecycles. The first evolution lifecycle is the customer inquiry process. It is specified by team member interactions. The second data evolution lifecycle is initiated by the application of the customer inquiry data triggers. An illustration of this is: (1) An inquiry phase results in a new customer inquiry; and, (2) the reply phase produces a response to the customer inquiry.

The CTIO Model implements a similar cycle in addressing customer issues and other concerns. The overall objective is the reliance on hybrid teams for resolution outcome. The data-oriented view of the customer investigation process relates mostly to data quality. There is nothing mentioned about team interaction in the data evolutionary life cycle. As such, it is unknown as to how a team utilizes the data generated by the use of the model in arriving at a valid outcome. The CTIO Model illustrates the interaction type being used in a CIT approach to effectively use quality data. The research conducted on CIT is important, as it has shown that using various medium of communication, either or both face-to-face and/or virtually, is important for the effective operations of the organization.

The Customer Investigation Process (CIP) is illustrated, as described by Maier, Muegeli and Krejza (2007) and carried out through banking staff interaction at Credit Suisse. The Credit Suisse internal investigation process initiates the inquiry asked by the inquirer, which may be external such as government or internal, to identify the appropriate receivers or consignees associated with the specific inquiry. These receivers will then start to identify the departments and people that might have relevant information as owners of information archives. The receiver will consolidate all the information obtained from respective departments. When there are no accurate results, the same investigation process will be done with other departments and the request will be repeated until sufficient information collected. The final information dossier with a summary is normally sent to the inquirer. This work is quite complex and time consuming for Credit Suisse.

Though there are many people from various departments, nothing is mentioned on how the team members from Credit Suisse interact as a team using the CIT approach in addressing the concern raise by the inquirer. The CTIO model does illustrate how team members interact routinely and interactively in addressing customer concerns to come to the right solutions.

The NEAT Methodology Data Life Cycle

Many problems have emerged due to poor quality data collected through team member interaction, to which many software engineers can attest. To address these problems, the NEAT Methodology provides a systematic way in determining data quality for developing an improvement plan (Bobrowski, Marre & Yankelevich, 2002). The improvement plan constitutes both corrective and preventive actions in order to maintain the quality standards eventually met. The

The NEAT Methodology is typically based on the Goal Question Metric (GQM) framework. The NEAT Methodology identifies the need for making a diagnosis to assess based on its output and provides the convenience of implementing a corrective improvement action on the data while maintaining focus improvement expectations. The interaction media used is also important, as the NEAT Methodology facilitates organizations for evaluating the investment for improving its data. The NEAT Methodology (shown in Figure 6) is typically presented as a theoretical model of the data life cycle; and also, as a practical approach to performing evaluations in controlled environments (Bobrowski, Marre & Yankelevich, 2002).

The NEAT Methodology guides data quality evaluation by the implementation of six stages: elicitation; planning; measurement; diagnosis; treatment; and maintenance. Each stage is composed of several tasks (Bobrowski, Marre & Yankelevich, 2002). Each task is carried out by team member interaction.

The first stage in the NEAT Methodology is elicitation, which is the acquisition of information on the organizational data life cycle. This includes the evaluation of the state of the data. The stage involves a precise description of the actual state (a snapshot) over different subsets of data with two levels of quality: the target (optimum) level and the minimum level required. The second stage, planning, is the development of a plan for assessing quality. It includes the use of an evaluation

Figure 6. The NEAT methodology data life cycle (Bobrowski, Marre & Yankelevich, 2002)

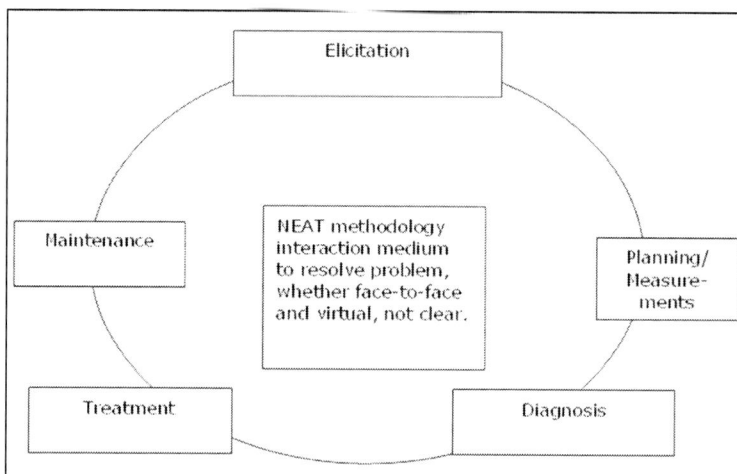

plan along with an explanation of how the evaluation plan is executed. The plan is updated with each task. The third stage, measurement, relates to the measurement of certain attributes using tools and techniques such as GQM tables, templates, and data analysis tools according to the measurement plan. The fourth stage is the diagnosis of data quality involving the interpretation of the measures and reporting of findings. Its main goal is to trigger actions that will change the status of data. The fifth stage, treatment, refers to treatment (corrective/preventive) and involves two main strategies. One strategy is to improve existing data accomplished through a corrective strategy, changing or deleting wrong data, and including the data needed by the organization. A second strategy is to improve the processes associated with data (data creation, consumption, updates, and so on). How these data are manipulated is of importance in terms of team members using the NEAT problem-solving methodology through face-to-face and virtual interaction. The latter, virtual interaction of team member, hinders incorporation of poor data into the system. The sixth stage, maintenance, provides a mechanism in maintaining quality once goals are met. This is strongly related to the treatment stage where data quality is monitored through time-based, systematic and periodic measurements, which in some cases are automated.

The NEAT Methodology is aligned with the CIT approach in terms of acquisition of information in the concern stage of the CTIO Cycle. The methodology performs certain phases that are part of the CTIO Model including planning, measurement and diagnosis. The interaction phase of the CTIO Cycle involves aspects of the NEAT Methodology treatment and maintenance phases where team interaction media offers critical support. The only difference found between the NEAT Methodology and the CTIO Cycle is the team interaction aspect. The CTIO Cycle uses both face-to-face and virtual teamworking. It is unclear which type of interaction media the NEAT Methodology uses as part of any of the six stages.

The Ethnographic Research Cycle

The cycle for collecting, recoding and analysing ethnographic data is illustrated in Figure 7 using the Ethnographic Research Cycle. This method has been implemented in most major Australian banking organizations. It was applied by Kissoon (2008a) in a participant observation study on the use of the CTIO Cycle. The process of showing the linkage and interaction media is illustrated in Figure 7.

The mode of ethnographic inquiry was used on a topic-oriented ethnography, which narrowed the focus to one or more aspects of CIT. The objective was to focus on the selective observation process regarding the adoption of virtual teamwork in the retail banking sector (Spradley, 1980). The process of narrowing participant observation was done by asking ethnographic questions related to the core elements

Figure 7. The Ethnographic Research Cycle, as Described by Spradley (1980) Used for The Observational Study. (The 5W-1H questioning skills technique has been introduced by the researcher to better focus on the selective observational aspects using both face-to-face and virtual interactions (Kissoon, 2008a)).

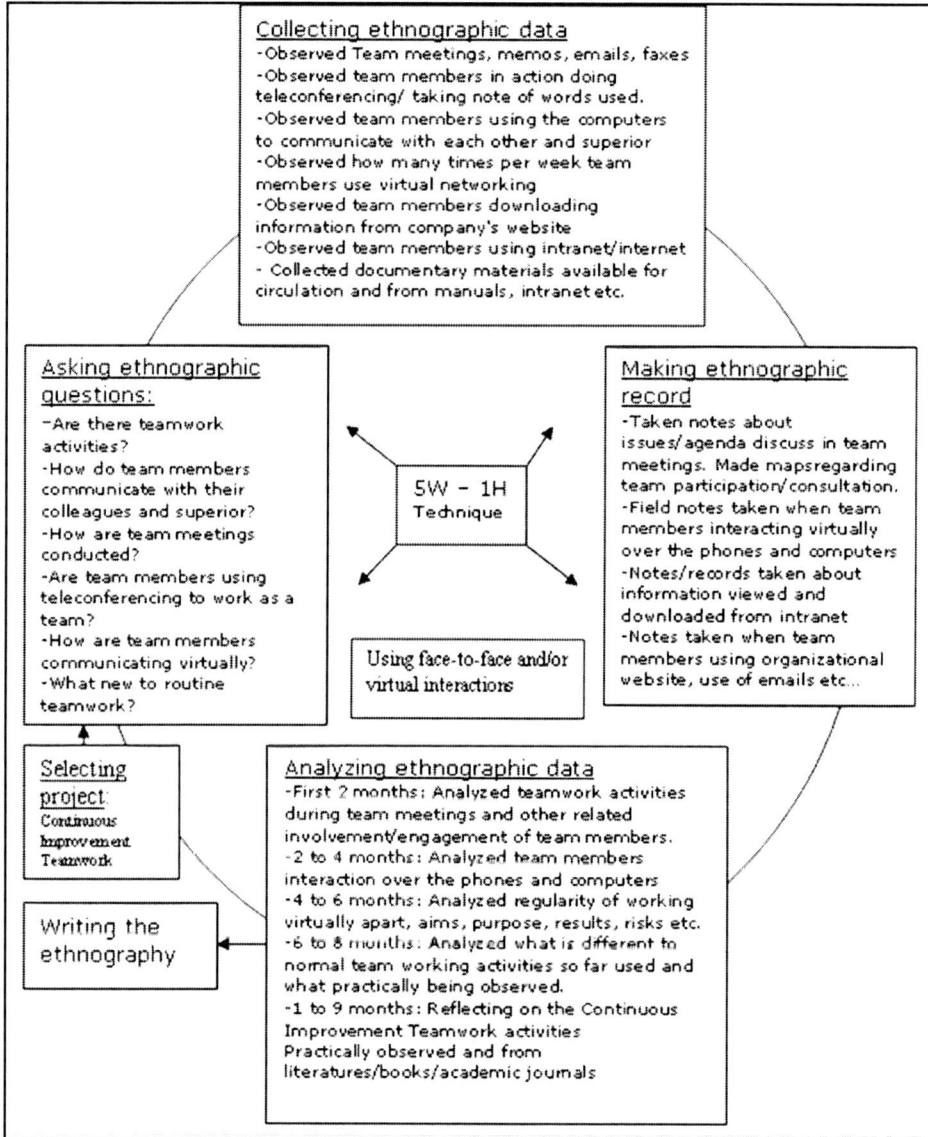

of the CIT Model/CTIO Cycle. Throughout the observational process of nine months, several questions were asked (refer to Figure 7). The researcher analysed the responses to reach a reliable and valid conclusion about the effectiveness of the CIT approach. The Ethnographic Research Cycle may be considered linked to the CTIO Cycle, as there is a continual search through the participant observation study to diagnose and realize the CIT approach inclusive of face-to-face and virtual interactions. Both the Ethnographic Research Cycle and the CTIO Cycle have common, problem-solving characteristics, which have been used in the service sector.

Other Conceptual Cycle Linkages Using Face-to-Face and Virtual Interactions

The Continuous Improvement Teamwork, realised through the CTIO Cycle using both face-to-face and virtual team interaction, is linked to other conceptual models such as: the Benchmarking Cycle; the Kolb`s Cycle; the Reverse Logistics and Supply Chain Continual Cycle; the Action Research Cycle (commonalities as a problem-solving approach); the Approach-Deployment-Results-Improvement(ADRI) Cycle of the Australian Business Excellence Framework. Table 1 presents a short description of each of these cycles.

The Information System Life Cycle, for example, consists of activities spanning the period between inspection and retirement of a system (Duggan & Reichgelt, 2006). The Information System Life Cycle searches for feasible influences in the planning of information during conceptualization, creation, consummation and consolidation. In the Information System Life Cycle, virtual teamwork may have a greater influence on project outcomes when compared to face-to-face, routine teamwork.

Table 1. Description of other performance cycles

Problem-solving cycle	Brief description of cycle	Interaction medium
Benchmarking Cycle	Measuring performance against that of best-in-class for development and realization of improvement goals.	More face-to-face
Kolb`s Cycle	Experiential cycle.	More face-to-face
Reverse Logistics and Supply Chain Continual Cycle	Used for goods being return into the processes for re-manufacturing.	Face-to-face and/or virtual
Action Research Cycle	Approach based on the assumption that the social world is changing, and the researcher and the research are part of this change.	Face-to-face
Approach-Deployment-Results-Improvement(ADRI) Cycle	Of the Australian Business Excellence Framework representing international best practices evident throughout the company.	Face-to-face and /or virtual

In the RADAR Cycle, as mentioned by Al-Zamany, Hoddell and Savage (2002), only the phases of assess, review and results have similarities to the CTIO Cycle. In these phases, both types of teamwork are deployed.

CURRENT CHALLENGES

The Panorama Of Information Systems Quality

The Information System (IS) community has embraced the underlying approach of continuous process improvement programs where process quality largely determines product quality (Deming, 1986; as cited by Duggan & Reichgelt, 2006). This was more evident in IS research in the field of 'quality management' (Harter *et al.*, 1998; Khalifa & Verner, 2000; Ravichandra & Rai, 2000; as cited by Duggan & Reichgelt, 2006). The key issues, including dimensions and implications of virtual teamwork in the panorama of IS quality, are reviewed and discussed in relation to the CIT Model/ CTIO Cycle.

Virtual Teamwork for Data and Information Dimension

According to Al-Hakim (2007), there is a distinction between data and information. Data are items, activities, events, things, figures, numbers, and transactions that are classified and stored but not organised to express specific meaning. Information, on the other hand, is data that have been organized in a way that gives them meaning for the recipient. It is commonly known that high data quality will result in high information quality; while poor data quality will result in poor information quality. As such, data quality impacts virtual teamworking when such information is used.

The Barings Bank, for example, had provided incorrect financial statements based on poor data quality resulting in economic scandals (Maier, Muegeli & Krejza, 2007). The use of a continuous improvement initiative supported by effective routine and virtual teamwork approaches in data collection activities will enhance information quality. Juran and Godfrey (1999), as cited by Al-Hakim (2007), define data quality as "fitness for intended use".

The emergence of the CIT approach, as seen in the financial institution by the researcher, illustrates the consideration by employees involved in retail operations, decision-making and planning and service quality to effectively use data and information through normal face-to-face interaction and virtual teamworking with the intention of meeting and exceeding customer expectations.

Al-Hakim (2007) mentioned that information quality is multi-dimensional meaning that organisations must use multiple measures to evaluate the quality of data and information. Wand and Wang (1996), as cited by Al-Hakim (2007), identified two subcategories of information quality dimensions namely data-related and system-related. The CIT approach through the CTIO Cycle relates to these two subcategories in essential measures and dimensions. For example, the face-to-face teamwork may be data-related and virtual teamwork may be system-related, which will continue to change as new technologies emerge.

Virtual Teamwork for Information Quality (IQ)

As mentioned by Koronios (2006), cited by AL-Hakim (2007), issues of information quality (IQ) in team member interaction is becoming very important in the modern organization in making decisions very quickly and in order to gain information superiority and competitive advantage. The concept of Information Quality has been brought to management's attention because of the widespread, successive waves of technology-driven innovations in information and communication technologies (ICT). Enabling technologies bring widespread connectivity, real-time access and large volumes of data and information for banking staff to use in daily interaction domains.

It is also becoming a customer requirement that organizations provide quality information (English and Perez, 2003; as cited by Al-Hakim, 2007). As a result, Australian financial institutions do not want to run the risk of legislation that requires quality information be provided by employees to internal and external customers. Furthermore, many financial institutions have found that the right approach is resolving information quality problems using a continuous, interaction process, instead of a single-phase interaction process, is the right approach. It may be that one solution may lead to new problems and employees at all levels have to work together in solving the information quality problems. This is where the CIT approach comes into play, as it is a continuous process of handling information quality through team interaction in resolving problems relevant to the organization. In the CIT approach, team members use both face-to-face and virtual interactions to handle information quality to alleviate potential problems and for increased performance.

Al-Hakim (2007) provides an example. On December 9, 2005, brokers at the Mizuho Securities tried to sell 610,000 shares at 1 yen (0.8 US cents) each. A "typing error", which is an information quality problem, introduced chaos into the Japan trading market. As a result of such chaos, Mizuho Securities incurred a loss of 27 billion yen or US $21 billion. The example illustrates that human interaction through virtual means, must provide for data input that is free-of-error (degree to which information is correct). It must also promote interpretability and objectivity of the information quality dimension. In the CIT approach, both face-to-face and virtual team interactions promote information quality thus limiting simple errors (e g., typing mistakes). The more interaction employees have in an organization, such as collaborative error checking and problem solving, the better chance for improved efficiencies and higher levels of performance.

Continuous Improvement for Information Quality Process Control

For customer satisfaction to be realised, organizations should consider continuous process improvement as a key management practice (Evans & Lindsay, 2005; as cited by Al-Hakim 2007). Effective team interaction, face-to-face or virtual, promotes the implementation of process improvements through collaborative problem-solving and information sharing. As mentioned by Al-Hakim (2007), process and people are no longer enough for achieving the required output without continuously improving upon procedures, policies and regulations. This is aligned with the concept of Continuous Improvement as a derivative of TQM that controls the conversion process. Information quality dimensions need to be based on the same principles of Total Quality for Service, which as listed by Evans and Lindsay (2005, p.18), are as follows: (1) Focus on customers and stakeholders; (2) consider participation and teamwork by everyone in the organization; and, (3) have a process focus with continuous improvement and learning.

The CIT illustrates a more focused and in-depth approach that is in alignment with Total Quality for Service. Both address key issues directly related to interaction and participation through face-to-face and virtual teamwork and through the use of the Continuous Improvement principles. Virtual teamwork, for achieving effective and efficient quality information, needs to be further researched. Much of the current research has focused on face-to-face teamwork and Continuous Improvement. The knowledge gap in Quality Information is the notion of integrating both face-to-face and virtual teamwork along with Continuous Improvement for effectively achieving results and improving performance.

The Continuous Improvement in an environment of Information Quality System, and as described by Al-Hakim (2007), illustrates the mechanism of the Information Quality System Process. Emphasis is placed on the importance of leveraging process and people using information quality (IQ) dimensions and information orientation. AS mentioned by Al-Hakim (2007), the term people refer to staff and users and the process means the operational activities being done effectively through interactions to achieve better outcome in service organizations. The process alone will not result in well achieved performance intended from the process without the involvement of the employees (Al-Hakim, 2007). The system and communication means for the employees to interact together are also important. The Information Quality dimensions and the Information Orientation form the control dimension of the IT system process. To have an Information Quality System, both the IQ dimensions and Information Orientation are important. The Information Dimensions relate to issues that are important to customers while the Information Orientation refers to an organization`s capability to effectively manage and use information.

The Information Dimensions and Information Orientation, in relation to the CTIO Cycle, focuses on virtual and routine interactions among employees in the banking sector such that they can work effectively as a team. As part of the Information Quality System, the Information Dimensions and Information Orientation are crucial for team members to interact virtually wit the objective of achieving quality customer service. Thus, the interaction evidenced by the CIT Model/CTIO Cycle shows the hybrid approach of using both face-to-face teamwork and e-teamwork in a continuous improvement environment as a viable means of achieving high performance. In the banking sector, the interaction of team members in meeting the customer's needs is very important in terms of using, maintaining, and promoting quality information. This is important in the banking sector given high information quality offers a competitive advantage. Customers are becoming very demanding seeking for efficient service and information quality through the process of Continuous Improvement.

Information is defined as data having been organised in a manner that gives meaning for the recipient (Turban *et al.*, 2005; as cited by Al-Hakim, 2007). For customers in the banking sector, "meaning to the recipient" can be interpreted as accurate, error-free, reliable, effective and efficient information in processing transactions and addressing concerns. To provide such information quality, people working in the banking sector need to work together using both face-to-face and virtual interaction media in a team environment. This requires the proper use of interactive systems and emerging technologies. It also requires adopting the concepts of TQM through the Continuous Improvement approach emphasizing quality customer service.

Information Quality Using Virtual Networks in Service Sector

As mentioned by Melkas (2007), networking and virtualization networks are calling for new ways of information quality utilizing well-being technology, which team members use to interaction using problem-solving approaches. There has been a growing use of virtual communication in many organizations. The real goal of information quality is to enhance customer satisfaction (English, 1999; Huang, Lee, & Wang, 1999; as cited by Melkas, 2007). Networking and virtualization is not the only concern for companies, but also for public organizations, cooperatives and non-governmental organizations, which are forming networks (Melkas, 2007).

A study done by Melkas (2007) has identified both weaknesses and strengths in network collaboration affecting management of information quality. There has been a rapid increase in networking and virtualization within many organizations. Many researchers in recent years have also studied virtual organizations, virtual enterprises and virtual teams (Duarte & Tennant, 2001; Handy, 1995; Holton, 2001; van Hout & Bekkers, 2000; Kotorov, 2001; Lipnack & Stamps, 1997; Miles & Snow, 1992; Putnam, 2001; Rouse, 1999; van der Smagt, 2000; Voss, 1996; as described by Melkas, 2007). Nevertheless, very little research has been devoted to organizational requirements placed of the effective utilization of hybrid team with CI. Both face-to-face and virtual teamwork would be used for improved operationalization of the retail banking service sector taking into account an increase in information technology. The quality of service provided to customers can be improved by the use of hybrid teams with CI.

As mentioned by Melkas (2007), the way the employee interprets the customer's message and transfers the information forward to the collaboration network may have a major impact on service quality. Thus, the interaction of the staff with other team members in the banking sector using information technology may have an impact on the quality of information and service provided to the customer. This is what led the researcher to investigate the CIT approach to study teamwork in the retail banking sector of a major Australian banking organization.

The research done by Melkas (2007) demonstrated that information quality planning by organization or network has been possible. This research had been a first attempt to study quality in the branch of safety telephone services in Finland and that the results of the information quality analysis can also be utilized in individual organization's quality management systems. An information quality analysis could form one element of a general quality assessment at the networked collaboration level. The valuable interview data have contributed to the basis for action and scientific recommendations. The results of this investigation were incorporated into the general quality recommendations that were recently formulated for the whole branch safety telephone services in Finland. This research has opened up two new insights into the directions of analysis and management of information quality and service networks based on virtualization.

CONCLUSION

With deregulation, reforms, competition, globalisation, enabling technologies, virtualisation and network technology, virtual communications is becoming as important as face-to-face communication. The mode of interaction of team members in a continuous improvement approach is important when quality is initiated in an organization. Similarly the major Australian bank which had undergone the study for justification of the CIT approach had embarked on a quality program in 2004.

The present research has investigated the key components and measures as illustrated in Appendix 1 that are enhancing the interaction in the CIT approach. Using the CTIO Model within the existing technological infrastructure, results in small improvements in response time from team members interacting in a virtual environment. The end result is significant benefits to customers in the banking sector. The various other linkages to process improvement and data quality approaches, as presented in this chapter may offer additional benefits in the implementation of the CIT approach and achieving continual improvement in response time. Thus, the CTIO Cycle framed from the other conceptual cycles and validated in the participant observation study (Kissoon, 2008a; Kissoon, 2008b) demonstrated the important of using a hybrid team for real-time interaction thus achieving performance efficiencies.

This chapter has shown a practical and theoretical linkage of the CTIO Model with other conceptual cycles using face-to-face and/or virtual interaction media. Face-to-face interactions related to routine teamwork and virtual interactions related to virtual teamwork are being integrated with Continuous Improvement initiatives for the banking sector to perform better. Without teamwork and virtual teamwork, all the practical project work would not have obtained productive performance in the same period of time. Data quality and information quality are key issues for the success of achieving productivity gain and performance in team member daily interaction medium.

REFERENCES

Al-Hakim, L. (2007). Information quality function deployment . In Al-Hakim, L. (Ed.), *Challenges of Managing Information Quality in Service Organizations* (pp. 26–50). Hershey, PA: IGI Global.

Al-Zamany, Y. Hoddell. S. E. J., & Savage, B. M. (2002). Self assessment and obstacles to their implementation in Yemen, TQM and change management. In S.K.M. Ho & J. Dalrymple (Ed.), *Proceedings of the 7ᵗʰ International Conference on ISO 9000 and TQM*. RMIT University, Melbourne, Australia.

Arvan, A. (1988). Those fabulous Japanese banks. *Bankers Monthly*, *105*(1), 29–35.

Ballou, D. P., & Pazer, H. L. (1995). Modelling data and process quality in multi-input, multi-output information systems. *Management Science*, *31*(2), 150–162. doi:10.1287/mnsc.31.2.150

Bobrowski, M., Marre, M., & Yankelevich, D. (2002). A Neat Approach for Data Quality Assessment. In Piattini, Calero & Genero (Ed.), Information and Database Quality (pp. 135-162), Hershey,PA: IGI Global.

Duarte, D. L., & Tennant Snyder, N. (2001). *Mastering virtual teams: Strategies, tools, and techniques that succeed.* San Francisco, CA: Jossey-Bass.

Duggan, E. W., & Reichgelt, H. (2006). *Measuring information systems delivery quality.* Hershey, PA: IGI Global.

English, L. P. (1999). *Improving data warehouse and business information quality: Methods for reducing costs and increasing profits.* New York: Wiley.

Evans, J. R., & Lindsay, W. M. (2005). *The management and control of quality* (6th ed.). Ohio: Thomson/South-Western.

Evans., J. & Dean, J. (2003). *Total quality management, Organization and strategy.* Ohio: Thomson/South-Western.

Handy, C. (1995, May-June). Trust and the virtual organization. *Harvard Business Review, 73*(3), 40–50.

Hayler, R., & Nichols, D. M. (2007). *Six Sigma for financial services, how leading companies are driving results with Lean, Six Sigma, and process improvement, profiles from global leaders including AMERICAN EXPRESS, BANK OF AMERICA, WACHOVIA, and LLOYDS TSB.* New York: McGraw-Hill.

Helfert, M., Zellner, G., & Sousa, C. (2002). Data quality problems and proactive data quality management in data-warehouse-systems. In *Proceedings of BIT-World 2002*, Guyaquil, Ecuador.

Holton, J. A. (2001). Building trust and collaboration in a virtual team. *Team Performance Management, 7*(3/4), 36–47. doi:10.1108/13527590110395621

Huang, K.-T., Lee, Y. W., & Wang, R. Y. (1999). *Quality information and knowledge.* Upper Saddle River, NJ: Prentice Hall PTR.

Hutley, P. S. B., & Russell, P. A. (3rd ed.). (2005). *An introduction to the Financial Services Reform Act, 2001.* Australia: LexisNexis Butterworths.

Kissoon, S. V. (2008a). Toward the conceptual model of Continuous Improvement Teamwork: A participant observation study. In F. Zhao (Ed.), *Information Technology Entrepreneurship and Innovation* (250-276). Hershey, PA: IGI Global.

Kissoon, S. V. (2007). Continuous improvement teamwork in the Australian banking sector. In *Proceedings of the 5th ANZAM and 1st Asian Pacific Operations Management Symposium 2007*. RMIT University, Melbourne, Australia.

Kissoon, S. V. (2008b). Ethnographic research cycle to evidence the Continuous Improvement Teamwork model. *Qualitative Research Journal, 8*(2), 134–136. doi:10.3316/QRJ0802134

Kotorov, R. (2001). Virtual organization: Conceptual analysis of the limits of its decentralization. *Knowledge and Process Management, 8*(1), 55–62. doi:10.1002/kpm.93

Lipnack, J., & Stamps, J. (1997). *Virtual teams: Reaching across space, time and organizations with technology*. New York: John Wiley & Sons.

Liu, L., & Chi, L. N. (2002). Evolutional data quality: A theory-specific view. In *Proceedings of 7th International Conference on Information Quality (ICIQ 2002)*, Cambridge, MA.

Maier, D., Muegeli, T., & Krejza, A. (2007). Customer investigation process at Credit Suisse: Meeting the rising demands of regulators. In Al-Hakim (Ed.), *Challenges of managing Information Quality in service Organizations* (pp. 52-76). Hershey, PA: IGI Global.

Melkas, H. (2007). Analyzing information quality in virtual networks of the services sector with qualitative interview data . In Al-Hakim, L. (Ed.), *Challenges of managing Information Quality in service Organizations* (pp. 187–212). Hershey, PA: IGI Global.

Miles, R. E., & Snow, C. C. (1992). Causes of failure in network organizations. *California Management Review, 34*(4), 53–72.

Miller, H. (1996). The multiple dimensions of information quality. *Information Systems Management, 13*(2), 79–82. doi:10.1080/10580539608906992

Pande, P. S., Newman, R. B., & Cavanagh, R. R. (2000). *The Six Sigma way, how GE, Motorola, and other top companies are honing the performance*. New York: McGraw-Hill.

Putnam, L. (2001). March/April). Distance teamwork: The realities of collaborating with virtual colleagues. *Online, 25*(2), 54–57.

Rouse, W. B. (1999). Connectivity, creativity, and chaos: Challenges of loosely-structured organizations. *Information & Knowledge Systems Management, 1*, 117–131.

Spradley, J. P. (1980). *Participant observation*. USA: Thomson Learning Academic Resource Centre. Te`eni, D. (1993). Behavioural aspects of data production and their impact on data quality. *Journal of Database Management, 4*(2), 30–38.

STA-Singapore Technologies Automobile. (1996). *Business improvement Hhandbook* (5th ed.). Singapore: Singapore Technologies.

van der Smagt, T. (2000). Enhancing virtual teams: Social relations and communication technology. *Industrial Management + Data Systems, 100*(4), 148-156.

Van Hout, E. J. Th., & Bekkers, V. J. J. M. (2000). Patterns of virtual organization: The case of the National Clearinghouse for Geographic Information. *Information Infrastructure and Policy, 6*, 197–207.

Voss, H. (1996, July/August). Virtual organizations: The future is now. *Strategy and Leadership*, 12–16. doi:10.1108/eb054559

Wand, Y., & Wang, R. Y. (1996). Anchoring data quality dimensions in ontological foundations. *Communications of the ACM, 39*(11), 86–95. doi:10.1145/240455.240479

Wang, R. Y., Reddy, M. P., & Kon, H. B. (1995). Toward quality data: An attribute-based approach. *Decision Support Systems, 13*(3-4), 349–372. doi:10.1016/0167-9236(93)E0050-N

Wang, R. Y., & Strong, D. M. (1996). Beyond accuracy: What data quality means to data consumers. *Journal of Management Information Systems, 12*(4), 5–33.

ADDITIONAL READING

Avkiran, N. (1997). Models of retail performance for bank branches: predicting the level of key business drivers . *International Journal of Bank Marketing, 15*(6). doi:10.1108/02652329710184451

Gujarati, D. N. (1998). *Basic econometrics*. New York: McGraw-Hill Higher Education.

Kissoon, S. (2008). Ethnographic research cycle to evidence the Continuous Improvement Teamwork model. *Qualitative Research Journal*, *8*(2), 134–136. doi:10.3316/QRJ0802134

Kock, N. (2005). *Business process improvement through e-collaboration: Knowledge sharing through the use of virtual groups*. Hershey, PA: IGI Global.

Maier, D., Muegeli, T., & Krejza, A. (2007). Customer investigation process at Credit Suisse: Meeting the rising demands of regulators. In Al-Hakim (Ed.), *Challenges of Managing Information Quality in Service Organizations* (52-76). Hershey, PA: Idea group Publishing.

Tagliaferri, L. E. (1982). As quality circles fade, a bank tries top-down teamwork. *American Bankers Association . ABA Banking Journal*, *74*(7), 98.

APPENDIX A

Variable	Results only for coding done on both variables
Face-to-face Interaction (FF)-Dependent variable (Y)	Continuous reinforcement (CR) = 19 change management (CM) = 22 six-sigma (SS) = 21, audio/video/T.V sets (AV) = 25 visual communication (VC) = 27 voice mail (VM) = 24 brainstorming (BR) = 22 computer assisted work (CA) = 2 training (TR) = 28 coaching/mentoring (CT) =16 continuous support (CS) =21 team convergence (TC) = 19
Virtual Interaction (VI)-Independent Variable (X)	Synchronous conferencing (SC) = 16 asynchronous conferencing (AC) = 14 audio conferencing (AU) = 19 computer conferencing (CC) = 24 e-learning (EL) = 25 electronic meeting (EM) = 15 search engine (SE) = 20 virtual group networking (VG) = 19 computer-mediated communication (CO) = 24 interactive multimedia communication (IM) = 15 WWW communication (WW) = 19 virtual working environment (VW) = 11

Results for the paired units obtained for both FF and VI variables following face-to-face interviews with 29 retail banking managers.

After obtaining these quantitative data, the bivariate analysis can be conducted to measure the relationship between face-to-face and virtual interactions variables. For example CR = 19 paired with SC= 21, CM = 22 paired with AC= 14 and follows the same order of paired-matching patterns up to TC= 19 paired with VW=11.

The contents of Appendix A show two types of data for face-to-face communication and virtual communication of team members working as problem-solving teams. The data represents the measures for the face-to-face interaction and virtual interaction variables paired together from the participant observation, as illustrated in Figure 7. For instance, computer assisted work was paired with virtual group networking in the participant observation study. Computer assisted work can be considered as peer-to-peer network, which is much like a company run by a decentralised management philosophy in which computers on the network used by team members on their desks communicate with each other as equals. Virtual group networking is similar to a company run by centralised management using a server computer where decisions are made centrally, which is more reliable and facilitates backup.

This work was previously published in Cases on Technology Innovation: Entrepreneurial Successes and Pitfalls, edited by S. Ann Becker & Robert E. Niebuhr, pp. 173-192, copyright 2010 by Business Science Reference (an imprint of IGI Global).

Chapter 16
Sharing Work Practice in the Distributed Organization

Inge Hermanrud
Hedmark University College, Norway

EXECUTIVE SUMMARY

Organizations today are looking for new ways to support knowledge-sharing and learning activities among their employees by the use of IT. The case describes how inspectors share their work experiences, reflect upon them, and learn from each other at a distance by using stories, pictures, and documents, which is made possible by the GoToMeeting tool™. In this case the GoToMeeting™ tool supports learning activities across geographical and organizational boundaries and contributes to efficient conditions for sharing inspection practices. The issues covered are learning activities facilitated by IT as well as the limitations of the tool in use.

ORGANIZATIONAL BACKGROUND

The inspection authority (herein referred to as the authority) discussed is a large distributed health and safety inspection authority in a Nordic country. The main task of the authority is to ensure that the work environment in the country is in accordance with the statutory requirements. The employees are based at several locations and they are given a high degree of individual autonomy. The employees

DOI: 10.4018/978-1-4666-2618-8.ch016

in this organization often work alone at small district offices or home offices. Over the years the inspectors have developed individual inspection practices, making it difficult to promote sharing and learning in the organization. Different districts involve different industries, which have also influenced inspection practices and created variations in competences among the distributed inspectors.

The authority is challenged by rapid changes within the domain for which it is responsible, such as changes regarding how clients behave and new insights from research – all of which might change the use of the legislation it oversees and with which its clients have to comply. The region 1 unit, 1 of 7 in the authority, has around 50 employees and of these around 40 are inspectors. The budget is approximately 40 million kroner (equal to US$6.6 million). The networks' mission is to ensure organizational learning in the authority on the topic area for which they are set up. The organizational culture among the inspectors can be described as a very independent work culture, in which the inspectors are used to working alone or in pairs and making their own decisions; they often work with their clients more than with their colleagues. Even though they often work alone and have few colleagues at the office, a sense of identity with a group and identity with the organization has been developed by telephone calls to colleagues conducting similar tasks or experts at the core of the organization (the directorate, see the organizational chart in Figure 1).

The inspectors conduct inspections of the use and storing of chemicals, installed ventilation facilities, and measures taken to prevent accidents at work. Usually they are at their office or home office when communicating with each other in the competence network meetings. This case focuses on the ability of GoToMeeting to

Figure 1. The organizational chart of the inspection authority

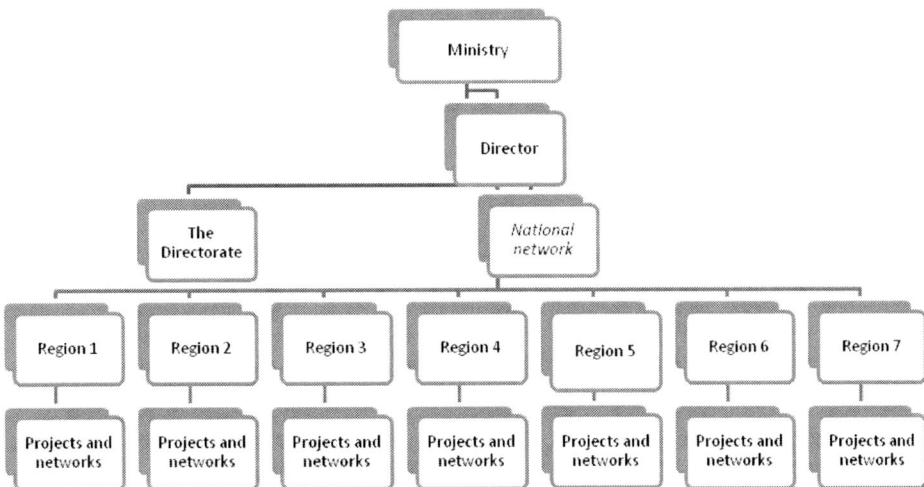

343

promote knowledge sharing by the representation of inspection practice online. In this context knowledge about chemistry or engineering, experiences, and the legislation has to be integrated. The IT infrastructure consists of many applications and newer and very old software. Sometimes the same information has to be reported in several systems.

Organizational Structure and Management Responsibilities

The organization has a long history that extends back more than a hundred years. The authority's mission is to encourage its clients to work systematically towards compliance with the laws and regulations. The organization has undergone substantial changes in the last seven years. The core of the organization, the directorate, has had its number of employees reduced, and responsibilities have been handed over to the seven regions in the authority. An organizational chart is presented in Figure 1.

The conducting of inspections by this authority is meant to take place in projects and organizational learning in the networks. The purpose of the national networks is to ensure knowledge sharing and learning across the regions. These networks are set up with coordinators from the regional networks. In Mintzberg's (1983) terminology the organization has reduced its techno-structure and moved towards more flexible forms of organizing using more project work and networking, much in line with the current trend in organizational design. The organization-specific argument for this design is that the inspectors are individually very knowledgeable, but very independent; they need to collaborate more in projects and networks to meet the challenges of the organization. The networks have so far meant a more or less permanent assignment to a specific competence network for the individual. Projects, on the other hand, run from one to three years.

The mode of learning that has dominated the organization until now comprises an apprentice conducting inspections with a senior inspector: in other words, face-to-face learning, in which the apprentice observes the senior inspector conducting inspections. While this organization used to have experts at its core, the expert knowledge now has to be developed in the regions – among dispersed inspectors in the intra-organizational networks set up by the management. They are now supposed to become experts collectively. This is to be achieved by setting up competence networks of inspectors. The inspectors within each region are assigned to one of four different networks, more or less based on their professional orientation or interest.

Inspectors work from regional headquarters, from one of the different local offices, or from home offices distributed all over their region. The distance between the different members in this region can be as much as 1,300 km, and owing to the limited budget they may only see each other face to face twice a year for 2 days. In addition, the inspectors are often on the move as they perform their tasks. The members of the network have different professional backgrounds, ranging from engineering and social science to law, some with lengthier professional education, like lawyers, to others with work experience from relevant industries. The organization employs a total of 500 inspectors, of whom approximately 40 work in region 1. The 40 inspectors in this region are assigned to 1 of 4 different competence networks. Each network is set up with a coordinator, but this assigned person has no formal authority or formal sanctions towards the network members. Each coordinator for each region is represented in national networks. The management responsibility in this context is to support the networks so that they develop the necessary knowledge and expertise to be able to conduct their tasks.

SETTING THE STAGE

External consultants suggested that the authority should set up competence networks in which the inspectors could develop their individual and collective competencies by reflecting upon their experiences and practices, and give input to the organization. The authority implemented competence network structures in 2005. The experiences in this case were collected in 2009 and 2010 through interviews and observations of actual meetings. GoToMeeting™ has been the selected collaborative IT for the teams since 2006, as well as for the competence networks in the organization. At the time the alternative tools for synchronic communication were:

a. Ordinary phone conferences (without screen sharing)
b. Videoconferencing (studio)
c. GoToMeeting™ (teleconferencing, screen sharing, and chat).

The competence networks have used the GoToMeeting™ tool. Since there were no videoconferencing studio facilities available at every district office and since many of the inspectors work from home offices, videoconferencing has rarely been used. Many of the participants would have to travel anyway. The selected tool, GoToMeeting™, we can argue, also had an advantage since the participants in the competence networks did not need to learn an extra tool: it was already in use.

Using Collaborative Tools to Nurture Communities of Practice

Research on the social aspects of learning has found that communities of practice enable learning in organizations (Wenger, 1998). A community of practice is an emergent social collective that self-organizes in order for the participants to help each other and share perspectives about work, enabling learning within the community

(Brown & Duguid, 1991; Lave & Wenger, 1991; Wenger, 1998, 2003). CoPs were previously conceptualized as a phenomenon emerging spontaneously in organizations; now it is believed that organizations may play a critical role in nurturing these communities (Newell, Robertson, Scarborough, & Swan, 2009). Communities of practice are viewed in the field of knowledge management as a means to deal with tacit knowledge, or the know-how that is not so easily articulated and transferable (Orlikowski, 2002; Galliers & Newell, 2003; Tsoukas, 2003). The role of collaborative IT in nurturing CoPs is to promote more interaction, sharing of artifacts, social networking, and collaboration among the organizational members.

In this view, knowledge is localized in social situations and the practices that people actually perform (Newell et al., 2009). Learning in communities occurs by carrying out tasks together, observing what others do, or sharing stories and practice reflection. Collaborative tools can in theory support all of these activities. The major tasks in knowledge management are to nurture or build communities of practice – sometimes across organizational or geographical boundaries – in which practitioners can learn from each other. The outcome of such knowledge-sharing processes could be the representation of individual practices and a collective diffusion of innovative work practices across space and time. CoPs are often seen as informal, organic, self-organized units of activity: "produced by its members through their mutual engagement ... that tend to escape formal descriptions and control" (Wenger, 1998, p. 118) and "who share a concern, a set of problems, or a passion about a topic, and who deepen their knowledge and expertise in this area by interacting on an ongoing basis" (Wenger, McDermott, & Snyder, 2002, p. 4). The elaboration of CoPs seems to assume that the members regularly work together, or as described by Orr (1996), regularly meet during lunchtimes and at meetings in which they share their work experiences. Some, however, do not have the opportunity to work together directly or meet regularly (daily, weekly) in other ways, since they are spread around large geographical areas. One alternative then can be to increase the interactions through the use of other media than face-to-face meetings, such as phone, email, videoconferences, and interactive ICT, as well as to try to create a community in which such a common focus and experiences can be shared. In a CoP members need to share information about:

1. Work activities so that they recognize that they are engaged in the same practice;
2. The artifacts, defined as objects or actions, to which the participants attach meaning;
3. Themselves and who knows what: who is the expert within an area or the members of specialized sub-groups of the community (Wenger, 1998).

Collaborative IT tools like GoToMeeting™ are particularly interesting because they combine access to whatever is stored in systems and each participant's PC and facilitate conversations about it. The tool might support the construction of collective meaning, an important feature of a CoP.

Varieties of Groups, Networks, Communities, and IT

Communities of practice have existed since individual craftsmen gathered to share issues, ideas, and solutions. Today technology acts as an enabler, linking dispersed individuals in terms of time and place and facilitating their interaction. Brown and Duguid (2000, p. 143) describe a continuum of networks from communities of practice defined as: "relatively tight-knit groups of people who know each other and work together directly ... typically face to face communities that continually negotiate with, communicate with, and coordinate with each other directly in the course of their work" to electronic networks of practice consisting of weak ties in which individuals may never get to know each other or meet face to face. A relatively new aspect of this phenomenon is the managerial ambition to integrate geographically spread units into one integrated unit using ICT and networks aiming to develop communication, collaboration, and learning horizontally in the organization (Newell et al., 2009), of which this case is an example (Table 1).

Table 1. Varieties of groups and networks from Wasko and Teigland (2006, p. 139), except the last column on the right, which describes the key features of the competence networks in this case

Macrostructural property	Work groups	Virtual team	Communities of practice	Electronic networks of practice	Competence networks
Control	Formal control, not voluntary	Formal control, not voluntary	No formal control, voluntary	No formal control, voluntary	Some formal control, e.g., managerial participation, evaluations, but not possible to force anyone to contribute
Communication channel	Face to face	Text-based computer-mediated (e-mail, intranet, can benefit from interactions face to face or on video)	Face to face	Text-based computer-mediated (like blogs, bulletin boards, and e-mail lists)	Screen sharing and telephone conferencing, e.g., text-, picture-, and voice-based, computer-mediated, and occasionally face to face

The competence networks in this case are somewhat controlled by the management since one manager (sometimes) participates in the meetings and the networks are evaluated by the organization. On the other hand, the assigned coordinator of each network cannot force anyone to contribute. While the participants in the competence networks perceive face-to-face interaction as the best setting for sharing practices, sharing via technology is seen as a good alternative due to long travel distances. The tool GoToMeeting is a highly rated (Lipschutz, 2007) web-based tool that allows everyone in a group meeting to share whatever is on each participant's computer. The tool contains features such as screen sharing, sharing of keyboard and mouse controls, web chat, and phone conferencing, and the tool is also integrated with e-mail and calendar (Outlook™) book meetings efficiently (http://www.gotomeeting.com). While it is possible to share everything you have on your computer and have a telephone meeting, the contenders do not see each other. When the networks are given tasks by the organization, such as answering hearings, these activities resemble a virtual team (Table 1), and the strength of GoToMeeting™ perceived in these activities is the ability to talk, read, and write together simultaneously.

The network size (Table 2) of the competence networks is small, since they are staffed with eight to fourteen members, but as they are linked to other networks in other regions by the national network, experiences could potentially be shared among hundreds of people (Figure 1). The members of each network are assigned by management, but the individual can suggest were to be assigned. Participation in

Table 2. Varieties of groups and networks from Wasko and Teigland (2006, p. 139) continues, except the last column on the right, which describes the key features of the competence networks in this case

Macrostructural property	Work groups	Virtual team	Communities of practice	Electronic networks of practice	Competence networks
Network size	Small	Small	Small	Large	Small, potentially large
Access	Restricted, assigned by formal control	Restricted, assigned by formal control	Restricted, locally bounded, limited to co-location	Open	Restricted, assigned by formal control, distributed participants
Participation	Jointly determined, specific task outcomes	Jointly determined, specific task outcomes	Jointly determined	Individually determined	Jointly and individually determined, a few times with some specific task outcomes

communities of practice is regarded as jointly determined, since individuals generally approach specific others for help. In electronic networks of practice, participation is individually determined; knowledge seekers have no control over who responds to their questions or the quality of the responses. In turn, knowledge contributors have no guarantee that the seekers will understand the answer provided or be willing to reciprocate the favor. The competence networks can, since they are not fully developed communities, therefore be described as a mixed participation context – both jointly and individually determined – and also sometimes with specific task outcomes (like answering a hearing). Access and participation are restricted and structured by the management, since the inspectors are assigned to a specific competence network, but ultimately the participation is dependent on mutual engagement. All in all the competence networks offer a mixed context.

Evolution of Communities and ICT Needs

An ICT perspective on communities of practice relates to how people use ICT to organize the social world to be able to learn. It is about how ICT enables the establishment and maintenance of ongoing relationships between people who have the potential to help each other. A tool is not a community of practice in itself, but it might enable people to share their experience and learn from others. Organizations use ICT to accommodate knowledge work and learning. However, the impact of ICT on sharing and learning is influenced by human agency, the physical properties of a particular ICT, and the context in which it is used (Newell et al., 2009). To develop communities of practice, according to Wenger et al. (2002), there is a need in the early stages to share information about individual competencies – sharing experiences to develop a sense of shared meaning, identity, and knowledge. In later stages the ICT can facilitate ongoing collaboration and the storing of experiences relevant to the community. A more detailed description of the needs in different stages is presented in Table 3.

The role of management in this approach, according to Wenger (2004, 2005) is to coach managers, fund activities, and supply the network with technology, facilitating arenas in which people can talk about their work and their practices. On the other hand, heavy reliance on ICT may be a burden on the community members, especially when they are not used to interacting with technology. A lack of competence, lack of self-confidence, and/or resistance to technology may reduce members' participation in the community (Dubé, Bourhis, & Jacob, 2006).

Mature communities of practice are often regarded as skilful in putting all kinds of tools to good use, regardless of their designer's intention (Wenger, White, & Smith, 2009). Wenger et al. (2009) describe several strategies for communities in their effort to build a community ICT structure. Strategies range from setting

Table 3. Wenger's communities evolution model (adapted from Dotiska, 2006, p. 259)

Stages	Main functions	IT enabling technologies
1	Connect, plan, commit	E-mail, e-conferencing (see, hear, text chat, present, and share information in a collaborative manner), listservers, online forums, Internet, corporate intranets
2	Form framework, create context	As above, plus remote login facilities, file transfer, information repositories
3	Operate, collaborate, grow, improve, mature	As above, plus online directories, analytical and decision-making tools, intelligent agents, e-surveying, and feedback facilities as well as portals
4	Sustain, renew, maintain, wind down	
5	Shut down	Knowledge repositories may remain for use by future communities

up a unique platform for the community to using existing internal and/or external tools. This case describes groups that build on and use what the organization offers. The ICT in use in the competence networks comprises e-mail, intranet, and the GoToMeeting™ tool. Web 2.0 applications in terms of wikis, blogs, and other social networking features are not part of any of the official applications in use so far, and freeware is forbidden due to virus problems and the potential leaking of sensitive information.

CASE DESCRIPTION

The main objective of this case is to explore the experience in a distributed organization, a public inspectorate, of using the GoToMeeting™ tool to facilitate knowledge-sharing activities. In this organization, which is often the case with older organizations, old and newer ICT tools and systems co-exist, but not all of them are used daily or by everybody. I can list as examples intranet, Internet, e-mail, and GoToMeeting™, as well as old and newer systems related to task handling, registration, and time management. The GoToMeeting™ tool was introduced into the organization at the same time as the competence networks were established; it has become an important tool in the inspectors' daily tasks in project work and is the main channel for the networks, which meet once a month online but only once or twice a year face to face. Five to ten participants attend the GoToMeeting™ meetings and the duration of the meeting is from one to two hours. GoToMeeting™ can be labelled as an audio-conferencing tool with web-based conference services, in which active and reflexive listening (like rephrasing participants' statements) is needed for smooth and effective communication (Munkvold & Akselsen, 2003).

Screen sharing and the use of text, illustrations, or pictures have further positive effects in this respect. The activities in an average meeting in the competence networks are described in Tables 4 and 5.

Table 4. Examples of activities taking place in the an average meeting in the competence networks

Activity	ICT in use
Logon sequence The individual logs onto the Web and teleconferencing (phone). All the necessary information regarding how and when to log on is provided by Outlook™.	Outlook e-mail and calendar, Web, and teleconferencing (phone)
Initial small talk ... ... about the weather or similar and sometimes rumours about what is going on in the organization are shared (3–4 minutes) among those who are online.	Phone
Who is here? The coordinator asks who is present, such as "Are you there Hans?", "I can see you are logged onto Elin!", and "Svein is sick". All of the participants say something in turn, like "yes, I am here". "Here, but I have to leave this meeting early, due to ...".	Phone/Web
Coordinator introduces the agenda for the meeting Word document presented (also sent by e-mail before the meeting)	Screen sharing
Change of screen control Coordinator lets the presenter (network participant or external expert) of the day control the screen	Screen sharing

Table 5. Examples of activities taking place further in the an average meeting in the competence networks

Activity	ICT in use
SHARING PART 1 **Experiences shared** PowerPoint presentations take place. Conversations are triggered by the help of stories, documents, and pictures.	Screen sharing: documents and pictures from PC and/or ePhorte or Vyr
SHARING PART 2 **Discussion, questions raised and answered** Sharing of experience, opinions, and ideas. Construction of meaning. What does the new information mean?	Teleconferencing. Sometimes participants during the meeting search the World Wide Web or intranet for answers to questions
Evaluation of the meeting Everyone is "forced" to say something. Comments are very short like: "it was okay", "I have nothing to say", "interesting topic", "well-organized meeting", "two hours without a break is too long", "remember to turn off the microphone when you are not talking – your noises disturb the others", "it is so sad that only a few took part in the discussion".	Phone

ePhorte™: A task-handling system, which includes a powerful search engine that makes it possible for the inspectors to search by case number and in free text.

Vyr™: The authority records the reported damage to a business and occupational injuries in a register called Vyr™. The authority and the competence networks use Vyr™ to analyse the registered data to monitor the situation within different branches. Figure 2 gives examples of what GoToMeeting™ looks like on screen.

The two snapshots are examples of text in an e-mail (snapshot 1) and a word document (snapshot 2) shared on GoToMeeting™. The participants just open their personal e-mail and share the content. On snapshot 2, on the right-hand side, note that the participants can also see who is logged on. The picture on the text page (Figure 3) is an example or what is shared and discussed in GoToMeeting™.

In the conversation and storytelling regarding this picture, the participants focus on the work processes related to this job, the problem of dust in work processes, and experiences regarding risk prevention efforts. These are then reflected on and made sense of. The picture illustrates how polluted air is taken out of the production hall through a point extraction, put onto the machine that produces the dust. The picture illustrates a solution to a more general problem situation for the inspectors. They often struggle to find effective solutions to fulfill the requirements of the legislation in a cost-efficient way for the inspected workplace, i.e., finding solutions that can work for both parties. When talking about these pictures, the presenter addresses attention to certain areas of the picture to illustrate how the problem can be solved or to show the problem to help in solving the problem.

So, what occurs at the face-to-face meetings that take place once or twice a year? The participants often visit a business as a group and later on discuss what they experienced there, or they invite an external expert lecturer or practitioner, or both, to talk about a topic.

GOTOMEETING FACILITATING LEARNING ACTIVITIES ACROSS BOUNDARIES

An ICT perspective on communities or networks of practice implies that we describe them by their ICT use. In the following I describe and discuss the competence networks through three different narratives. The experience is related by three inspectors: two senior members of staff, Tor and Stein, and one newcomer, Nils.

Figure 2. Snapshots 1 and 2

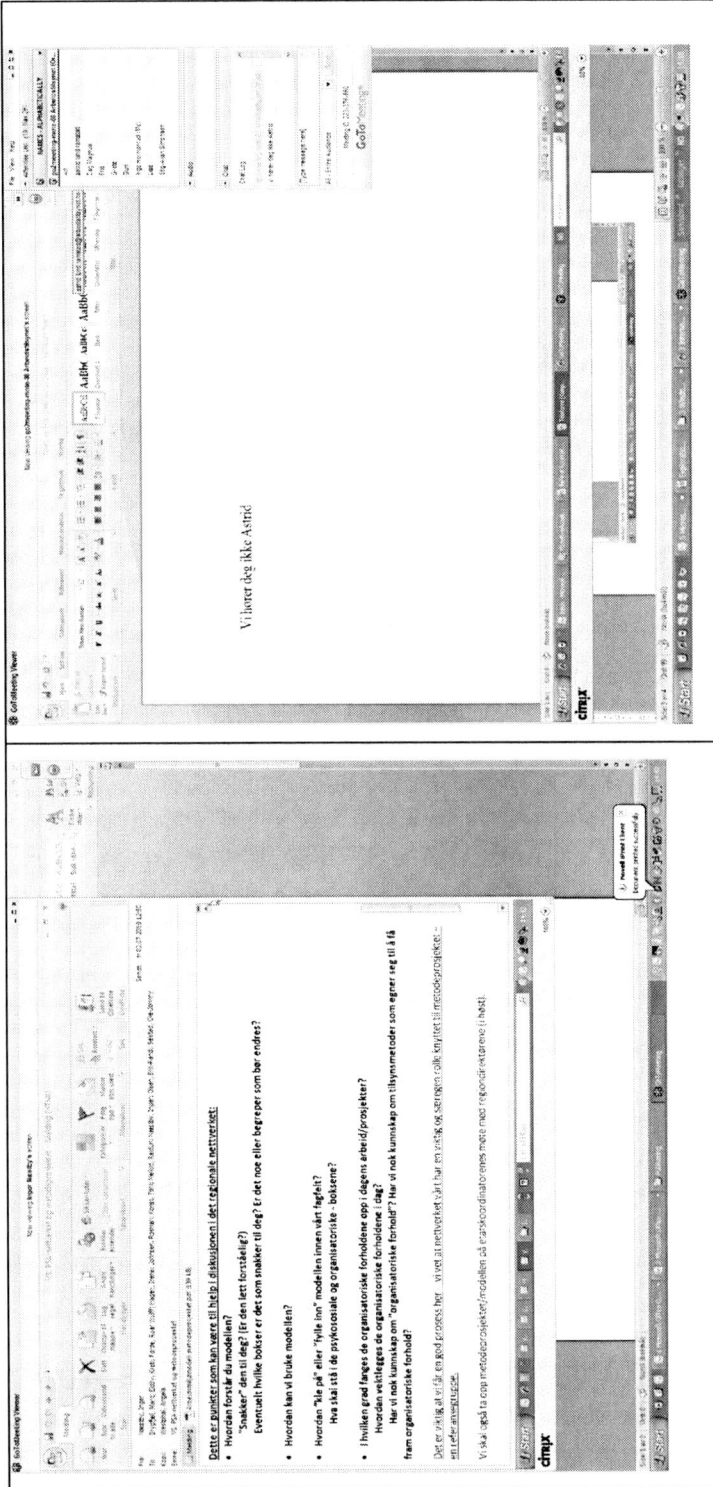

Figure 3. Example of what is shared and discussed in GoToMeeting™

GoToMeeting Facilitates the Sharing of Tor's "Workbench"

Tor has worked in the authority for 20 years, within different issues but mainly within engineering. He has also worked part-time as a lecturer at a university. He regards himself as very open-minded towards ICT. From the early days he has worked from his home office, where his boss has allowed him to try out the new technology. Tor is an early adopter of ICT. Today he has a fully equipped office at home, the same technology as at the office. He sees many opportunities for ICT-based sharing of knowledge related to his work, and he has used it on several projects. Additionally, he has been an assigned mentor and a union man online. He is assigned to a competence network for technical expertise.

Tor likes to use PowerPoint presentations when using the GoToMeeting™ tool, and he also likes to pick up files from his PC or intranet and present them as the discussion moves on. His intentions are threefold:

1. To enrich the discussion with cases presented orally, accompanied by the use of pictures and documents.
2. To help others to view and exploit the possibilities that the GoToMeeting™ tool offers.
3. To help others to look up and put together relevant information from the different systems that they have: intranet, Vyr™, and ePhorte™.

When using the GoToMeeting™ tool Tor can access rich illustrations regarding content and processes on inspected enterprises while he is elaborating on a given topic. To illustrate his work he uses his own "workbench" – his computer with access to everything he needs stored on it or available online. He shares the legislation he uses, how he interprets it, how he writes letters to inspected businesses, and their answers. He does this by presenting documents from the task-handling register, cases with which he has previously worked. He picks out an accident – a file describing what happened at the site, pictures of it, and the letters he wrote and how the business responded to them. He moves around between different applications to underline and illustrate his key points, as well as showing the others how to use the GoToMeeting™ tool. He stresses the importance of taking and attaching pictures to the case before putting it into the archive, which will be useful for task handling and for later sharing online on GoToMeeting™ in the competence network setting. This informs us that work activities and learning activities are dependent on each other. Taking pictures in the work context provides the means for later online knowledge sharing and learning. Several times Tor has run through accidents, sometimes the whole process, and at other times only what happened. Tor regards the tool as very efficient:

If the legislation is changing, pictures on screen can easily create a mutual understanding of the new legislation. Like when I present machines and equipment that are in line with the new rules. (Tor, senior member of staff)

In his view they are not ready for video-conferencing, but they may be in the future if the organization becomes more specialized and the need for communication and interaction internally within the organization increases.

Insight

GoToMeeting™ enables Tor to share his work practices as well as his ICT skills. Efficient online learning activities are dependent on resources created in work activities (like pictures).

Tor's story tells us that GoToMeeting™ can be a very useful tool for enhancing conversation sharing. It has the ability to gather people and their artifacts (documents and pictures) and the participants have conversations about the artifacts. For this purpose GoToMeeting™ is more efficient than face-to-face meetings, since the participants in GoToMeeting™ meetings, compared with those in face-to-face meetings, have easier access to documents. The results of the activity are justification, mutual understanding of the practice of others, and more collective practice. In other words, the processes and outcome promote a community. However, the sharing of documents and their conversations depends upon how open the participants are, and that differs. Some are more reluctant to disclose too much about what they actually do, as they are afraid of losing some of their flexibility when "in action", since new routines to increase the standardization can then be forced upon them.

Tor addresses a problem when using the GoToMeeting™ tool. The problem is the emergent "multitasking" during the GoToMeeting™ meetings in the competence network. The engagement in the discussions varies from participant to participant. Not everybody is interested in every issue all the time. They do not work with the issue discussed, or they have other opinions. Since nobody sees the individual, some are tempted to do other things while being logged on to the conference. This might not be true all the time, but the impression of a "lack of engagement" among some can turn into a vicious circle of "reduced engagement" in the network, hindering the participants from creating a community. To reduce this problem the coordinator is asked to involve everybody at the meetings, by addressing each and every participant directly.

GoToMeeting™ Enables Stein to Share His Practices, Which are Traceable in Documents

Stein is an experienced member of staff with more than 10 years' experience working with the authority. Previously, he worked for more than 10 years as a teacher. He is assigned to a competence network for technical expertise. He works from a regional office and has taken a university course about ICT use in the distributed environment, which addressed how to work together while not being together physically. On the course he learnt the importance of ensuring that everybody is heard and addressed during a GoToMeeting™ meeting. He speaks very highly of the GoToMeeting™ tool for sharing experiences. He puts it this way:

We are discussing something. I say, yes, but I have something on my PC, just give me the screen and I'll look up, and so I find it, and I find statements, pictures, or any other orders given before. So screen sharing is very useful. It is flexible (Stein, senior member of staff).

Stein regards it as too cumbersome to meet face to face often. Instead, he points out that by using the GoToMeeting™ tool the participants can share the documents needed if he runs into a similar case. He puts his point in this way:

We can't share by referring to what we remember, we need to find the case; our sharing must be traceable (Stein, senior member of staff).

In bureaucracies, such as this authority, action is taken on the basis of and recorded in written rules (Weber, 1971). This is also true regarding sharing and learning, as pointed out by Stein. Sharing and learning start with the recorded cases and the written rules in use. This implies that the sharing of documents is necessary to inform people about the legislation they use and how they use it when sharing their experience and knowledge.

Insight

Learning in bureaucracies occurs on the basis of and recorded in written rules.

The use of documents is a necessary resource for learning activities in a bureaucratically organizational context. In addition, to achieve "equal handling", documents are needed to understand the practice of others, and work as the window into it and contribute to the shared meaning and community.

GoToMeeting™ Enables Nils to Discuss and Learn from Practice Across the Organizational Boundary

Nils has worked for three years in the authority, from a regional office and mainly with industries. This is his first job after finishing college. Around half of his tasks are related to chemistry – the area for which the competence network to which he is assigned is set up. He thinks the meetings in his competence network have improved lately, since they are now are increasingly discussing professional issues – recent developments in research and the experiences of colleagues and other practitioners. For Nils, GoToMeeting™ is the best they have so far:

GoToMeeting™ is the best we have; you can invite external experts and practitioners – to develop a dialog between our authority, researchers, and our businesses (Nils, newcomer).

This use of GoToMeeting™ reveals networking outside and across the boundaries of the organization. Bringing different people together using GoToMeeting™ is possible. Everyone has access to a phone and to the World Wide Web, and that is all that is needed. When people with different backgrounds who are engaged in similar work start to have discussions, there is an extra "spin-off" effect, according to Nils. Practitioners and researchers start to share and discover solutions together. This is best achieved face to face, but is also possible using GoToMeeting™. Like Tor, Nils stresses the role of pictures and documents in sharing and learning using GoToMeeting™. Shared pictures can be of well-placed ventilation facilities in a welding shop to show why they are well placed. Sharing documents can be very useful because they give many ideas about what to look for when conducting inspections, according to Nils. Nils also argues for storing PowerPoint presentations presented at the network meetings on the intranet for later use. As he puts it:

When you need ideas and names of people to contact about a special issue, then the PowerPoint presentations can be very useful (Nils, newcomer).

Nils reveals an insight to us here. Useful informal contacts across the organizational boundaries are not only made up of people you know, but also names stored on your computer or intranet, accessible when needed in your work. These names and contact information contribute to access to a larger network of practice for the individual.

Insight

PowerPoint presentations contain names, which are useful for newcomers.

Even though GoToMeeting™ has several strengths, there are also limitations according to Nils. One dilemma exists between time and cost-efficient knowledge sharing and relation building. Nils states:

Face-to-face meetings are important, when you are using the phone, not seeing each other, then you don't get to know each other (Nils, newcomer).

Not getting to know each other means that the social network and the ties might not develop as strongly as they could. GoToMeeting™ seems not to be a sufficient tool to develop the stronger ties and the mutual recognition that define a fully developed community of practice. Since face-to-face meetings take time and travel costs are high over long distances, the participants need to find other ways to develop their relations, and, in particular, to develop the "know-who" – the experts among them within particular areas. One way is to select a richer media when sharing (like videoconferencing or more face-to-face interactions) or engage others (in particular people you do not know) in your project.

CURRENT CHALLENGES/PROBLEMS FACING THE ORGANIZATION

In this case GoToMeeting enables the sharing of work practices across distances through its ability to gather the inspectors, their documents, and their pictures – the objects and artefacts to which they attach meaning in their practice. By presenting accounts, documents, and pictures the inspectors are able to represent and reflect upon their work practices. GoToMeeting is regarded by Tor, Nils, and Stein (three engaged and dedicated network members) as a very useful tool for sharing and learning. GoToMeeting™ enables efficient sharing and learning activities across distances. Tor's sharing of ICT skills also seems to be a good practice, which the organization could look into for developing the use of GoToMeeting™ for further sharing and learning. The narratives highlight that collaborative IT can enhance "sharing conversations" when collaborating and when representing work practices.

On the other hand, pictures and documents that are useful when sharing knowledge are more or less stored "by chance" by the individual on a PC or the intranet, and are not very accessible for everyone. For some, often the case for experienced veteran employees, who are not so skilled in IT use, it is too difficult to import documents from the systems and into PowerPoint presentations for sharing on GoToMeeting™. Another serious problem is that it is hard to become acquainted with each other on GoToMeeting™. Participants who are not that interested or outspoken and who do not engage themselves in discussions are not well known among the rest of the network participants, making it difficult for the individual to work out who is the expert within an area, an important aspect of a community for advice seeking and learning. GoToMeeting™ facilitates the sharing of documents, but does not sufficiently support the development of social relations. Tools like Skype have video as well as screen sharing and could be a substitute for GoToMeeting™.

There is also a lack of sharing and learning across the seven regions in the authority. While experiences and practices are shared and reflected upon among a few people, the members of a regional competence network, experiences and practices are almost never shared across the different regions. The network members of a chemistry network in one region do not know what the chemistry network in another region has experienced, discussed, or learned. The situation is the same for other competence areas as well. To move forward, management and researchers should consider how to develop sharing and learning across networks and regions, supported by IT, to develop larger networks of practice for the individuals and for the competence networks.

Videoconferencing is suggested by the organization's IT department to replace GoToMeeting in the coming years. This is mainly due to the fact more daily interaction is needed since the planning and conducting of inspections is increasingly supposed to take place in projects and in collaboration with other authorities. This suggested IT change, if implemented, might have consequences for the competence networks, consequences that should also be considered by the management.

REFERENCES

Brown, J. S., & Duguid, P. (1991). Organizational learning and communities of practice: Toward a unified view of working, learning and innovation. *Organization Science, 2*, 40–57. doi:10.1287/orsc.2.1.40

Brown, J. S., & Duguid, P. (2000). *The social life of information*. Boston, MA: Harvard Business School Press.

Dotsika, F. (2006). An IT perspective on supporting communities of practice . In Coakes, E., & Clarke, S. (Eds.), *Encyclopedia of communities of practice in information and knowledge management* (pp. 257–263). Hershey, PA: Idea Group. doi:10.4018/978-1-59140-556-6.ch045

Dubé, L., Bourhis, A., & Jacob, R. (2006). Towards a typology of virtual communities of practice. *Interdisciplinary Journal of Information, Knowledge, and Management, 1*, 69–93.

Galliers, R., & Newell, S. (2003). Back to the future: From knowledge management to data management. *Information Systems and E-Business Management, 23*(3), 209–235.

Lave, J., & Wenger, E. (1991). *Situated learning: Legitimate peripheral participation*. Cambridge, UK: Cambridge University Press.

Lipschutz, R. P. (2007). *GoToMeeting 3.0 Review*. Retrieved September 13, 2010, from http://www.pcmag.com/article2/0,2817,2154128,00.asp

Mintzberg, H. (1983). *Structure in fives: Designing effective organizations*. Upper Saddle River, NJ: Prentice Hall.

Munkvold, B. E., & Akselsen, S. E. (2003). *Implementing collaboration technologies in industry: Case examples and lessons learned*. London, UK: Springer.

Newell, S., Robertson, M., Scarborough, H., & Swan, J. (2009). *Managing knowledge work and innovation*. Basingstoke, UK: Palgrave Macmillan.

Orlikowski, W. J. (2002). Knowing in practice: Enacting a collective capability in distributed organizing. *Organization Science, 13*(3), 249–273. doi:10.1287/orsc.13.3.249.2776

Orr, J. (1996). *Talking about machines: An ethnography of a modern job*. Ithaca, NY: Cornell University Press.

Tsoukas, H. (2003). Do we really understand tacit knowledge? In Easterby-Smith, M., & Lyles, M. A. (Eds.), *Handbook of organizational learning and knowledge* (pp. 410–427). Malden, MA: Blackwell.

Wasko, M. M., & Teigland, R. (2006). Distinguishing work groups, virtual teams, and electronic networks of practice . In Coakes, E., & Clarke, S. (Eds.), *Encyclopedia of communities of practice in information and knowledge management* (pp. 138–140). Hershey, PA: Idea Group. doi:10.4018/978-1-59140-556-6.ch027

Weber, M. (1971). *Makt og byråkrati: essays om politikk og klasse, samfunn.* Oslo, Norway: Gyldendal.

Wenger, E. (1998). *Communities of practice. Learning, meaning and identity.* Cambridge, UK: Cambridge University Press.

Wenger, E. (2003). Communities of practice and social learning systems . In Nicolini, D., Gherardi, S., & Yanow, D. (Eds.), *Knowing in organizations. A practice-based approach* (pp. 76–99). New York, NY: M. E. Sharpe. doi:10.1177/135050840072002

Wenger, E. (2004). Knowledge management as a doughnut: Shaping your knowledge strategy through communities of practice. *Ivey Business Journal, 1,* 1–8.

Wenger, E. (2005). *Technology for communities.* Retrieved September 19, 2010, from http://technologyforcommunities.com/CEFRIO_Book_Chapter_v_5.2.pdf

Wenger, E., McDermott, R., & Snyder, W. M. (2002). *Cultivating communities of practice.* Cambridge, MA: Harvard Business School Press.

Wenger, E., White, N., & Smith, J. D. (2009). *Digital habitats: Stewarding technology for communities.* Portland, OR: CPsquare.

This work was previously published in the Journal of Cases on Information Technology, Volume 14, Issue 1, edited by Mehdi Khosrow-Pour, pp. 46-60, copyright 2010 by IGI Publishing (an imprint of IGI Global).

Chapter 17

Investigating the Online Interactions of a Team of Test Developers Working in a Wiki Environment

Anna Filipi
Australian Council for Educational Research, Australia

Sophie Lissonnet
Australian Council for Educational Research, Australia

ABSTRACT

This chapter reports an investigation of online interactions occurring in the context of the development of a suite of foreign language tests known as the Assessment of Language Competence (ALC) (http://www.ucer.edu.au/alc/). The interactions took place in a wiki environment from 2007 to 2009. The aim of the investigation was twofold. The first was to identify the features of the organization of online postings in an asynchronous online environment and to compare them with the organization of face-to-face interaction. The second was to examine how expertise is invoked in interactions centered on the vetting of test items. The chapter uses selected findings from Conversation Analysis and applies them to the postings on the wiki. Findings from the analysis include the rarity of self-repair, similarities in the organization of sequence structure and the same orientations to affiliative behavior found in conversation.

DOI: 10.4018/978-1-4666-2618-8.ch017

INTRODUCTION

Previous research on the features of Computer-Mediated Communication, the bulk of which comes from educational settings, has focused in a very general sense on the differences between written and spoken interaction. Because it is communication in a written mode, but interactive in its delivery even if this does not occur in real time, traditional ways and forms of communication are being challenged. Indeed Smith (2003), while noting how Computer-Mediated Communication shares similarities with both written and spoken texts, pointed out that it also has characteristics which are unique to it. For example, there is an absence or reduction of paralinguistic and nonverbal features and a greater reliance on the bald written word which can lead to communication breakdown and challenges for the participants as they work to understand each other (Smith, 2003). Magnan Sieloff (2008) made reference to its uniqueness when speaking of technology as reconstructing how people go about communicating with each other. Not only is there an exchange in information, but this is co-constructed so that it becomes possible to "create new meaning collaboratively in new ways and at new rhythms" (p.1).

It is this co-construction of meaning which is precisely what is at the heart of spoken interaction from the perspective of Conversation Analysis. As a field of research in its own right, Conversation Analysis has provided both a set of findings and a set of tools for investigating naturally occurring real time interactions as they unfold moment by moment. The focus is on how people take turns and how turns are organized in sequences of talk (see Drew & Heritage, 2006; ten Have, 1999). According to Mazur (2004), online interactions provide conversation analysts with a potentially rich source of naturally occurring data to investigate various forms of communication including in work and instructional contexts. While it has for decades used transcriptions of audio or video recordings as primary sources of data, nowadays, Computer-Mediated Communication logs can be used to shortcut the transcription process, so that online turn-taking and sequence organization can be studied. Though they still need minor formatting to lend themselves to Conversation Analysis, "the text logs themselves contain "naturally occurring" conversant-generated indications of some of the sociolinguistic dimensions evinced in recordings of speech. The use of emoticons … are an example of this phenomenon quite prevalent in text-based on-line conversations" (p. 1083).

It is evident that Conversation Analysis lends itself very well to the study of online interaction, both to contexts that are informal and to contexts such as the one in the current study which are institutional in character deriving as they do from the world of work.

FINDINGS FROM CONVERSATION ANALYSIS

The findings from Conversation Analysis that are of relevance to the current analysis are assessments, repair, pursuit of a response, and aspects of sequence organization.

Assessments

In conversation, it has been found that speakers display a bias towards affiliative, and therefore closely connected and supportive actions over their opposite, disaffiliative and unsupportive ones (Clayman & Heritage, 2002; Heritage, 1984; Pomerantz, 1984a). Such a bias is made manifest through structural features in conversation associated with preferred and dispreferred 'turn shapes'. Commonly referred to as preference organization, an example of a preferred turn is a positive response to an invitation, while a dispreferred turn is a rejection, which will be marked in some way by pauses and dysfluency (see Schegloff, 2007).

Preference organization has been studied in specific sequential contexts. One such context that is relevant to the current study is the assessment. This has been found to be pervasively present in face-to-face interaction (Pomerantz, 1984a) although it is reported as being rare in asynchronous Computer-Mediated Communication (Tanskanen, 2007). Assessments involve speakers evaluating an activity or event as they converse with one another. Structurally, in conversational terms, on the production of a first assessment, a second assessment becomes a sequentially relevant next action. Pomerantz (1984a) has argued that a preference organization for agreement over disagreement holds for assessment environments. Speakers work to achieve agreement and strive to minimize the occurrence of disagreement. However, it is not possible to always avoid disagreement (Pomerantz, 1984a).

In the current data, the core of the work that occurs involves making assessments of the test materials. This is precisely what constitutes the role of the vetter. A key analytic interest is to examine how assessments are oriented to and what happens when there is a disagreement between a writer and a vetter. In other words, how does the normal display of affiliation play out in this environment?

Repair and Pursuit of a Response

Repair is a unique conversational phenomenon, which provides an organized system for dealing with breakdown in talk. Schegloff, Jefferson and Sacks (1977) and Schegloff (1987; 1992b; 1997; 2000a) have researched the ways in which hearers and speakers adjust their talk when breakdown occurs as a result of inadequate hearing or interpretation. An important point that emerges from this research is that sources of trouble do not induce repair. Rather it is as a result of repair initiation that something in the prior talk is found to be a source of trouble in need of remedy. The initiation will lead to some kind of outcome. Either there will be a solution or abandonment. Repair sequences can be initiated by the same speaker (referred to as self-initiated) or by the next speaker (referred to as other-initiated). Corrections can also be made by the same speaker (self-repaired) or by the next speaker (other-repaired). However, there is an overwhelming preference for self-initiated self-repair in conversation (Schegloff et al., 1977). This preference has also been reported to hold true for email interaction by Tanskanen and Karhukorpi (2008) in a study of concessive repair, a particular type of repair that entails retracting overstatements or potentially challenging statements that could provoke disagreement. Tanskanen and Karhukorpi (2008) found that in email interaction concessive repair occurs in the same turn and not in the next turn as is the case in face-to-face interaction. Tanksanen and Karhukorpi maintain that this provides evidence that in Computer-Mediated Communication, participants work to achieve affiliation by taking the perspective of the other participant. In other words, they work collaboratively to minimize conflict.

One resource that speakers can deploy as part of a broader repair strategy to facilitate communication is to pursue a response. Although not originally characterized in this way by Pomerantz (1984b), more recently in studies of very young children's talk both, Filipi (in press) and Forrester (2008) have shown that it is used as a "sequence implicated repair" phenomenon because it draws attention to the absence of an expected response.

The relevance of repair and pursuit of a response to the analysis of online interaction is obvious as they are implicated in meaning making. As noted, repair or communication breakdown has received attention particularly in studies of online interactions involving students learning a second language (Smith, 2003). Other aspects of communication such as (im)politeness and the mitigation of conflict (Graham, 2007; Harrison, 2000), concessive repair (Tanskanen & Karhukorpi, 2008) and the use of meta-pragmatic devices that focus on the communication act itself (*are you following me?*) rather than the content of the posting (Tanskanen, 2007), reveal the work that participants do to minimize actual and the potential for communication breakdown. They have all provided an increasingly rich picture of how participants co-construct meaning in online environments A focus on more general repair practices, particularly in a wiki environment, and the pursuit of a response, the focus of the current investigation, will contribute to this growing body of knowledge.

Sequence Organization

Sequence organization describes how turns at talk fit together structurally as relevant next actions to what has gone before. There are various types of sequences at the heart of this organization. One that is massively present in talk-in-interaction is the adjacency pair. This is a paired utterance composed of two turns (a first and second pair part) that "fit" together such as the question and answer pair.

While the adjacency pair can be considered a base sequence, sequences composed of a single utterance or clusters of sequences can be inserted between the first pair part and the second pair part (in which case they are not heard as an absence), or they can temporarily suspend the base sequence, as in side-sequences or asides (Jefferson, 1972). These are sequences that have nothing to do with the main business of the conversation.

All of the features just described emerge in the wiki interactions and as such provide a useful means of making comparisons between what happens in real time, face-to-face contexts and in asynchronous, online contexts.

Wikis at Work

Wiki technology is the brainchild of Ward Cunningham who wanted to create the simplest possible online database that could work. Wikis are commonly described as a collection of Web pages that anyone can edit.

According to Wood, Thoeny and Cunningham (2007), "When wikis succeed, they do so to a large degree because they meet the needs of so many different kinds of people" (p. 287). Wiki technology was chosen by the ALC team precisely because of its simplicity and ease of deployment. The team's rationale at the time of switching technology was that the team of 19 writers dispersed in a variety of locations and time zones could become operational in this environment with minimum training and technical support.

Wikis are by definition tools that support democratic participation and shared authorship. In such an environment the notion of authority and expertise is less relevant. People assume a number of roles when contributing to a wiki. They include: reader-researcher, contributor, editor, quality expert and administrator (Wood et al., 2007). In the case of the ALC, these personas are readily adopted by the writers, vetters and the project administrators, but they are dynamic and shifting, as determined by the local environment. Such shifts have been noted by Jaques and Salmon (2006) in their research of the exchanges operating in learning groups in both face-to-face and online environments. They described several critical factors, including the physical environment and people's relative positioning, which affect group dynamics and the free flow of communication. According to Jaques and Salmon (2006), the most salient change in group dynamics occurring in online interaction (in a school or university context) was the shift of authority from student to teacher.

An interesting question for the current study is to analyze how these roles emerge, shift and are co-constructed in the interactions as writers, vetters and the project manager work together to develop the tests, and whether any group defers to the other as the authority who has the ultimate say in what passes as a final test item.

Co-Constructing Expertise

Finding new ways of working in a computer-mediated environment can be somewhat unsettling to writers and vetters. As observed during the initial training session, writers and vetters appear to operate on subtly hierarchical arrangements in face-to-face situations. Writers may create their own internal hierarchy within a language group based on personal affinities and contact, they may even agree to defer to one another, but in their interactions with vetters and the project manager they expect their status as recruited language, (inter)cultural and pedagogical experts to be deferred to, and that their knowledge and experience be consulted.

As noted, many of the studies on online interaction have occurred in educational settings and have focused on the changes in teacher-student interaction in an online environment. The ALC wiki is an example of interactions that occur in the world of work. Writers, vetters and the project manager are recruited to undertake specific tasks. Unlike online educational settings, the risk of non-participation or disengagement is minimal. The most demanding adjustment for writers is to see their own sense of expertise being invoked as they accept or reject the vetters' assessments of their writing.

Research on workplace interaction has shown how the concurrent use of tools, instruments or graphic material, gesture and discourse form a coherent "grammar" of collaborative action (Goodwin, 1996). After observing the physical positioning and work interaction of two scientists sharing the use of a single device for two separate scientific research purposes aboard an oceanic research vessel, Goodwin (1995) concluded that human cognition is best approached as a corpus of "historically constituted and socially distributed processes including tools as well as multiple human beings situated in structurally different positions" (p. 46). A number of very basic comparisons can be drawn between Goodwin's vessel and the ALC wiki. Because of the online nature of the tools of working in a wiki environment, physical positioning matters less than status and identity positioning. Just like Goodwin's oceanic vessel, the wiki is a closed environment that forces experts from diverse disciplines to share a limited space, mitigate a range of personal and professional agendas and acknowledge each other's expertise. All these complex processes take place, often in full view of others in a rather un-buffered manner. Comments posted by vetters are sometimes received as "raw" and on occasion have been considered to be somewhat offensive. Once written, they sit in the allocated space for the duration of the writing cycle for all the team to see.

This is in sharp contrast with the more muted paneling process used for vetting items in a face-to-face environment, where speakers (usually two vetters and a writer) can interrupt each other, ask for and provide instant clarification, repair understanding immediately and use intonation and gesture as essential resources to create and display meaning.

One final issue that is pertinent to the current study of interactions in a work setting is the notion of how expertise emerges. Hall and Danby (2003) have paid particular attention to the co-construction of the expert category in professional meetings conducted in a professional educational setting. They analyzed interactions during a gathering of school and university staff intent on forming a partnership. In addition to Conversation Analysis, they also used membership category analysis (Hester & Eglin, 1997) in order to describe both people and activities as they interacted during formal meetings. Their analysis showed how participants "accomplish what might be seen as the attributes of a person belonging to the category of 'experts'" (Hall & Danby, 2004, p.4). By comparing the number of turns during the meeting, they noticed that the talk was dominated by a small number of participants, most notably the school principal and the dean of the faculty and two academic staff. The analysis showed how participants enact their everyday business through the partnership meetings and how they used words and turns to assert themselves as experts in the social worlds of education. A relevant question for the current investigation is how and when the expertise of vetters and writers is invoked through the online interactions, and like Hall and Danby's (2003) study, how roles are oriented to and shift as vetters and writers "do" the work of test development.

SETTING THE STAGE

The ALC certificate program of the Australian Council for Educational Research (ACER) (http://www.acer.edu.au/) is an annual multiple choice testing program in listening and reading comprehension for students from upper primary to senior secondary years of schooling. The tests are developed at three levels in Chinese, French, German, Indonesian, Italian and Japanese in a wiki environment. Test questions are written by a team of up to 19 writers from across Australia, all of whom are practising teachers or curriculum writers. The writing team is supported in its work by the test development staff at ACER. The ACER based ALC team trains the writers, vets the tests and provides advice and guidance on formatting as well as on the appropriateness and range of items for the level of learning. A team of language specialists is also contracted to provide advice on the language of each test once the vetting has been completed. When a final draft is completed, the tests are trialed with a small group of schools before going to the final production stage.

Maintaining version control of the tests in a collaborative writing arrangement and providing a possibility for the team of writers (not all of whom were living in geographical proximity to each other or to the test administrators and managers), provoked the major impetus for changing processes and adopting an online collaborative workspace.

In terms of organization, the wiki is designed around spaces, each containing pages. Each language is assigned two spaces, one each for the reading and listening units which comprise a stimulus and its accompanying test questions. In order to streamline both the discussions and the vetting, each unit is developed in a separate page of the wiki duly identified by a unique unit number. Comments relevant to the development and vetting of each unit are posted at the bottom of each wiki page.

Writers can elect to receive email alerts (or subscribe to an RSS feed) to stay informed of new postings added in their language space. The test development team, including the wiki administrator, can subscribe to a "daily digest" summarizing the postings to each page made in the last 24 hours. This feature of the wiki facilitates the ALC team's effort to minimize the response time to queries and comments posted by the writers. One of the immediate consequences is that items are monitored and vetted "as we go" instead of being batched and paneled at the end of the writing cycle. (For further details of the project, see Filipi and Lissonnet (2008)).

The interactions chosen for analysis were derived from over 2,000 postings taken from the 2008 and the 2009 test development. (Separate postings included single offerings such as "thanks".) In order to protect the identity of each member of the team, pseudonyms have been used. Other features that might reveal the identity of the team members in the transcripts have been replaced with "Target Language" as in Target Language background or Target Language country. These appear in brackets in the transcript. The transcripts themselves are formatted in italics while comments in the transcripts appear in single brackets in normal format. The postings were not edited, so some typographical errors may appear.

A Model for Online Moderation (and Student Teacher Interaction)

Working through a wiki was a new development for the test development team. In addition to the established expertise needed for the test development, it required additional skills to be developed, including a new shared set of competencies with no member of the actual writing team being more expert than the other. For this reason, Salmon's (2000) model of teaching and learning online through Computer-Mediated Communication was relevant as a way of briefly describing the key phases of interaction in the ALC wiki. Salmon's model developed from the analysis of 3000 messages posted to an online conferencing system by teachers and students enrolled in an Open University business course. It was largely devised to better understand the role teachers would have to play in their new capacity as e-moderators.

Salmon (2000) describes how the level of interactivity between participants in the Computer-Mediated Communication environment changes as the learners master specific technical skills. For each step Salmon also describes the type of e-moderating action that is required. The table below shows each phase of the test development and the kinds of technological skills acquired by the participants. (Note: Phase 3 and 4 are described by Salmon as the phases when the level and intensity of interaction between moderator and participant peak).

The main data selected for the following analysis was generated from the Knowledge Construction phase.

CASE DESCRIPTION

General Communication on the Wiki

While the majority of the interactions and postings in the wiki were focused on the development of the tests items, there was also a small set that were germane to general administration, formal evaluations of the experience of working through a wiki and, very rarely, "socializing." Analysis begins by examining this set of interactions with the aim of drawing out the organizational features that compare with face-to-face interaction. In order to uncover these similarities and differences, a useful approach is to consider the stance or voice (White, 2003) of the creator of the postings first.

Postings as Written Texts

What seems to have emerged in the analysis of the postings is that some writers have taken on a more distal "writing" stance to the postings while others have adopted a more proximal, "interactionist" approach. Evidence for making this claim is the presence or absence of a response to the postings from another member of the test development team, and whether the absence is noticed and oriented to as such by, for example, pursuing a response.

As noted above, pursuit of a response is part of a speaker's conversational "tool box." It is used as an option when a speaker is faced with a response that is hearably absent (Pomerantz, 1984b). While the action of not responding offers a possible display of recipient stance, it also offers a window on speaker stance. The following posting occurred during the evaluation phase of the test development (see Development phase in the table above).

Table 1. Salmon's model of online interaction and its relationship to wiki interaction as observed during test development

Description (Salmon)	Description (ALC)	Notes
Access and Motivation (Phase 1)	Set up phase and accessing the new system.	Participants check they can access the wiki from home and office. They test their password. They attend a briefing and training session. Some opposition to (or at least some reluctance to engage with) the new system is usually voiced at this point.
Online socialisation (Phase 2)	This is the phase during which participants establish online identities. They start to find others with whom to interact and play with the system).	In the case of the ALC, some of this happened during the training session and also through personal contact since some writers knew each other. This is also the phase where people get used to working differently. According to Salmon, induction is crucial and may determine future participation.
Information Exchange (Phase 3)	Participants share information about the course. They are both enthusiastic with the new system and the immediate, free-flowing information. They can also be overwhelmed by the volume of information available. Because they are still learning how to work the system, the moderator's role is to provide guidance and encouragement.	The ALC team gave rapid feedback to all requests and operated in Helpdesk mode throughout the writing phase. The team assisted writers who had trouble with accessing or navigating the system, or formatting test items.
Knowledge Construction (Phase 4)	Participants begin to interact with each other in more exposed and participative ways. During this phase they learn from others while at the same time asserting their beliefs.	Not all writers engaged in this knowledge construction with other members of the writing team preferring instead to confine this activity to engagement with the vetter only. Others were happy to engage with both vetters and other writers of the same language.
Development (Phase 5)	Participants look for more benefits from the system.	In the final phase of the ALC writing phase, writers were surveyed for feedback about working in the wiki. Some of them made comments regarding other features they would like to see implemented in the next year. This included the creation of a shared community space where writers could exchange links, tips, clipart or best practices.

Writer: There were no "hissy fits" or strident emails. It was clear that the people at ALC appreciated the fact that many of the writers also lead busy professional lives and thus the tone and pitch of the emails and messages reminding us to move on, get things done, etc were always reasonable and polite.

Because these specific comments were elicited in a formal evaluation process, there was no reply to this posting. Writers made reference to each other's comments, but did not engage with each other. They treated them as written postings not designed to receive a response.

Posts on the wiki

Participant stance to postings

←writing---interaction→

If all the postings were to be viewed as being on a continuum from written texts at one end to interaction at the other, then this posting would be at the writing end.

The majority of the postings, however, were more interactional. It is this set that will constitute the locus for the analysis, because one of the study's aims is to investigate how interaction is achieved in an asynchronous environment.

"Helpdesk" Postings

Postings about wiki features or how to get things done were most frequently produced in the form of the Question and Answer adjacency pair. These postings were much more conversational as a result. The example below typifies the kind of interaction in the talk about working on the wiki as opposed to talk about the items (the focus in the next sections).

Writer: I am finding it confusing to move from parent to children page. I think I am not doing it!! When I type TR I mean to be on the parent page. When I omit it I mean to be on the children page but how can I navigate between the two smoothly please??

Admin: You need to create a parent page (the translation of the text + question/s) and one child page (the text in the target language) for each text. To create the parent page, you need to be in the (Target Language) home space. Check by looking at the boxes that appear at the top of the new page. They should indicate the space (Target Language) and the home page (Target Language Home). Let me know how you go.

In the absence of para- and non-linguistic features, which is a key characteristic of Computer-Mediated Communication (Smith, 2003), there is a repeat of both the exclamation and question marks that mark the writer's attitude as one of frustration. The administrator seems to be orienting to this frustration as she not only answers the question, but she also opens up the possibility for further dialogue with an instruction to get back to her. This is not taken up because the problem gets resolved.

As well as the Question and Answer format, postings were also made in the form of unsolicited comments (such as an informing about moving an item to a different page or an enthusiastic embrace of the technology which did not invite a response), general problem comments such as having posted things in the wrong place (*Sorry! I accidentally attached my grid to a wrong space and I don't know how to remove it*), which were responded to through action, and in same pair types such as thanks and return thanks as in the following example.

Writer: With my school IT staff's assistance, I was able to work on the editing bar and get all the bolding job done. Thanks for your patience, Lynn.

Vetter: And thanks for your persistence.

This example comes at the end of a long process of trying to use the wiki function to bold relevant sections as required for formatting of the items. Unlike unsolicited comments, the vetter responds verbally. Like the Question and Answer, which routinely carries structural implications for the ensuing talk, in that a question makes an answer a relevant next action (Schegloff, 2007), there appears to be a similar constraint operating in this exchange. Indeed, in conversation a normal response to a thank-you is some kind of acknowledging turn such as "you're welcome". So the question becomes to what extent is this true for the interactions in the wiki which do not occur in real time? Are the participants held accountable? And is there a pursuit of a response?

Pursuing a Response

In the postings about the test items, some writers engage in an interaction while others simply accept the assessments without comment, and sometimes the vetter is compelled to pursue an action, for example when the changes requested do not appear. This could also then be linked to the notion of expertise or roles and stance towards them which are examined in the next main section.

One important difference between face-to-face interactions and the interactions on the wiki is that the latter do not occur in real time, therefore there can be quite a time delay between the posting of a question and a response to it. There is also the potential for questions not to be answered at all because they become irrelevant or are forgotten. This is evident in the example below. However, the vetter actually pursues the suggested edits, and in doing so, makes it clear that they must be acted on.

Vetter: Where would this announcement be heard? On a community radio station? In that case wouldn't the announcer be making the announcement on the family's behalf? I don't think an address would be given would it? Replace "If you find our dog, please ring 07113579 and we will come and collect him" with "if found ...", and delete "our children are crying". (Posted December 3, 2008.)

Vetter: Have changes been made? (Posted December 8, 2008.)

Writer: Julie, you are quite right. I have now changed it to be appropriate for a community radio station. (Posted December 12, 2008)

Vetter: Much more appropriate now. Thanks Melanie.

Here a series of questions are posted by the vetter which call into question the authentic like quality of the item. She then proceeds with providing a set of explicit edits she would like made. The posting lies dormant for five days at which point the vetter posts a follow-up question in the face of the absence of uptake. Noteworthy, is that the question, and therefore the pursuit, is not about whether the writer agrees or not with the suggested edits but rather whether the changes have been made. After a further time delay, the writer replies with a statement that makes evident that the vetter's pursued actions have been met. In other words, she has made the changes suggested. A final acknowledging posting by the vetter concludes the interaction and marks this as a successful completion of the pursuit. To sum up, the pursuit in this example is not of a feature of conversation such as an answer to a question, but rather of the action of editing.

Repair

Because the wiki provides an asynchronous environment, there are opportunities for participants to self-correct and to polish their postings before they are made public or to self-edit once they are posted, unlike synchronous environments and face-to-face interactions as noted by Tanskanen (2007). The self-repair is thus not made visible to the project team. Self-initiated self-repair is thus rare. Below is one of only two examples found in the corpus.

Writer: Should we mark the correct and bold the codes? (Posted at 12:01)

Sorry, I mean mark the correct answers. (Posted at 12.01)

Here the correction is made to the language form and not to the content, unlike the only other example of self-repair in the corpus. This is very rare because such slip-ups (such as omission of words or spelling errors) do occur quite often in the postings but they are not attended to because they are not essential to the meaning or can easily be retrieved from the posting as a whole.

Unlike conversation, it is therefore other-initiated self-repair or other-initiated other-repair that is more likely to occur than self-initiated self-repair in this environment, even though as noted above, they too are quite rare.

The next fragment provides an example of an other-initiated other-repair. Here the writer initiates repair on *3.10* (the test question number) which the vetter incorrectly referred to as *3.09* in the preceding posting.

Vetter: Or possibly the key for 309 is actually something like 'the pollution'

Writer: I assume you mean 3.10. I have changed the distracters and the key (made them longer). What do you think?

Vetter: Err, sorry, yes, I meant 310. The key is much more accurate, I think. Maybe another option as distractor could be

In face-to-face conversation, this kind of repair occurs in what is referred to as an insert sequence (Schegloff, 2007). As noted above, the insert is inserted into a base or main sequence of talk, and momentarily interrupts the "business" or topic of discussion. The repair similarly interrupts the discussion about the test item. However, it is dealt within the same posting. In other words, the repair is carried out directly without any confirmation check which would hand the space or floor back to the vetter to respond to. Indeed in the reply, the vetter delays answering the writer's question by building her response with an apology and a confirmation which also temporarily interrupt the discussions. Interestingly, she marks the beginning of her turn with "err" which gives it a very strong conversational flavor. Because the source of the error can easily be retrieved in the postings by the participants, there is no need to seek confirmation therefore it is possible that this kind of repair would be less common in online interaction than in face-to-face interaction. However, the other-initiated self-repair examples in the corpus are invariably about understanding the vetter's suggestions for edits to the test items. It is important to clarify the intended meaning in these postings. The following provides an example.

Writer: Not sure what you mean here ... Is that what you want me to put?

Vetter: Yes Peter, that's what I meant. 'Club members' might eliminate any clumbsiness (sp).

Here the writer asks for confirmation that he has understood the vetter's suggestions which she confirms in the next posting. This provides closure to the sequence so that the discussion moves onto the next item after acceptance of the suggestion by the writer.

Socialising

Finally, there are also occasions but very rare ones, when the participants post simple messages of a social nature. Below is one example. Here the writer welcomes a new vetter on board.

Vetter: This could be presented as a pie chart–to introduce a new text type?

Writer: Hi Joanne,

Welcome on board!

Why not? Lay-out/design is really in your hands.

Daniel.

Structurally it is treated as a side-sequence (Jefferson, 1972), because the response to the question is delayed. Like the insert sequence, it suspends the base sequence where the main activity–that of a suggestion about how to present the test item–is taking place. Similarly, the main business resumes on termination of the side-sequence. The other interesting features about this posting are the conventions of the written form–the address terms and greeting–and the infrequently occurring signing-off, even though it is evident who has made this posting. The writer is treating this interaction as a kind of formal introduction.

To sum up, there are features of these postings that share structural features of face-to face-interactions, namely, basic sequence structure including paired postings such as in Question and Answer, and base, insert and side-sequences. Because of communication and its possibility to breakdown, repair is also an important and fundamental feature. However, it is not very frequent. Self-initiated self-repair in particular is rare because the postings occur in a written mode where there is an opportunity to edit before posting or to return to and retrieve relevant information which is publicly available in order to more clearly understand the meaning if required. Finally there is also evidence that participants pursue a response as is the case in face-to-face interaction, however, much more likely in the current context, is the pursuit of an action such as editing. In the next section attention turns to assessments and the discussions around the test items.

Interactions Centred on Reaction to Feedback

The following set of examples form the nucleus of the ALC team's work. Analysis has revealed three patterns: Positively received feedback, negatively received feedback, and no response to feedback. The overriding focus will be to look at how the expertise of those involved emerges.

When Reaction to Feedback is Positively Received

The following example comes at the end of quite a protracted discussion between two vetters and one writer about a particular test item which was found to be in need of editing.

Vetter: I think the issue is that the distracters aren't all the same quality; there the answers to different questions—2 are for when can entry forms be submitted and two are for how. If we take out the option of being able to enter online that makes the following possible. I think the problem is that there is too much flexibility currently offered so it makes it hard to ask an item. (Altered test question follows.)

Writer: how about (Slightly amended test question follows.)

Vetter: Great minds think alike ... Yours is better though less reading and clearer. We could change by phone to by SMS then we'd have to go with on-line for B.

Writer: thank you.

Here the collaborative nature of the discussion as the writer and vetter work on improving the item to the satisfaction of both is evident. They have each contributed to this work, and they have done so in a supportive manner. In the first instance, the writer accepts the need to change the item as proffered in the vetter's assessment. Then they engage together in refining the question. This culminates in a positive assessment by the vetter directed at this collaborative effort (*great minds think alike*) and then more specifically to the writer, as is made evident in the shift to the second person singular *yours*. In response, the writer produces a "thank-you" which ends this sequence. Here "thank-you" works both as a response to the positive assessment and as a means of closing the discussion about this particular item. In other words all changes have now been made to improve this item so that the team can move onto the next one.

When Reaction to Feedback is Negatively Received

One way of responding to a less than positive assessment is to simply ask for a suggestion. Another is to simply disagree. Yet another is to ignore it. A fourth is to produce a justification or account for the choice. In the interests of space, only the latter can be analyzed. These are the more interesting responses because in building a justification or account for the design of the original test item, the writers invoke their own claim to some kind of expertise or knowledge. For example, they may invoke their native speaker competency: "*as a* (Target Language background) *person, born and bred in* (Target Language country), *I know that this is culturally appropriate*". They may also claim having greater access to native speakers: "*I worried about the preposition to use with "in the Antarctic" so consulted 2 native speaker pedagogues whose language expertise I value most highly*". Finally they may lay claim to a greater knowledge and familiarity with the country and its practices, as in this example: "*I thought it quite reasonable to assume that all of those things might be available for hire on a tropical Island. Ever been to* (name of island)*? You can hire all of those things there*".

In the example chosen for analysis below, there are two further illustrations of how the writers invoke expertise in the face of an assessment that suggests a problem with the item.

Vetter 1: I think this is OK, but I do feel we can manage without 'because' for the distractors. Removing it does not compromise the grammatical correctness. If someone asked me why I didn;t (sp) go to work yesterday I woudl (sp) say 'The office is too cold', definitely not 'Because the office is too cold.' Reducing the reading load is desirable.

Writer: Yes, I can drop the 'because' from the distractors, but have not done so yet. I will if you confirm your desire for it to be dropped, but I suggest you reconsider. Unlike you ... if someone asked me why I didn't go to work yesterday I would DEFI-NITELY say "Because the office is too cold". I ALWAYS answer 'why' questions with 'because'. I cannot imagine answering a 'why' question without 'because'. Indeed, I always taught my students to study the question word and choose the ap-

propriate response; i.e. to a 'who' question the answer is a name or a pronoun, to a 'where' question the answer is a place, to a 'why' question the answer is because.

This is a consequence of the instruction to, wherever possible, use complete questions rather than incomplete stems. Last year I would have framed this question as "Ina didn't go to school yesterday because ..." but with the new instruction to use complete questions the conjunction 'because' becomes part of the answer.

As I said, I will delete them if you confirm your instruction, but it is not the way that I would answer this question.

Vetter 2: I'm happy for you to retain 'because' Peter.

In this example the vetter's suggestion to remove "because" provokes the writer's disagreement. It is built with two invocations to expert knowledge. The first is about linguistic knowledge as displayed through the comment about the preservation of grammatical correctness if "because" is removed. The second invokes test development experience as displayed through the statement about relieving the cognitive load on the test taker as reader. In between, there is a statement about personal usage as well. This is marked by a shift in stance from the impersonal to a more personal one (marked linguistically by a shift in personal pronoun from "it" to "I" and from the passive to active construction, and then back again).

In his reply, the writer invokes his own expertise on two fronts. He lays claim to his competency as a user of the English language and recycles some of the vetter's words. Of particular note is how the vetter's "definitely", which already conveys a strong stance, is further upgraded by the writer through the use of capitalization and the accompanying "ALWAYS". He then invokes his pedagogical expertise as a teacher *(I always taught my students ... This is a consequence of the instruction to, wherever possible, use complete questions rather than incomplete stems).* This provides a mirror to the vetter's statement about strategy use (learner versus test-taker). Finally, he makes reference to the changed guidelines for writing test items which is a possible concession (though not one that emerges openly) that the repetition of "because" does jar *(Last year I would have framed this question as ....but with the new instruction to use complete questions the conjunction 'because' becomes part of the answer).* Structurally, this resembles the non-extreme concessive repair described by Tanskanen and Karhukorpi (2008) in email interactions.

Deferring to the Expertise of the Other

Clearly then there is some tension here caused by the differential experiences and knowledge bases that vetter and writer bring to the test development process. Yet, it is precisely these different kinds of expertise that are required to produce test items that will work and succeed in the test. How this is negotiated, worked on and resolved is an interesting question because it too reveals something about how the writers and vetters see their roles. In the above example, although the writer disagrees with the vetter's assessment, he opens with a statement that defers to the role of the vetter as having the last say on the item *(I can drop the 'because' from the distractors, but have not done so yet. I will if you confirm your desire for it to be dropped, but I suggest you reconsider).* This also emerges in his conclusion *(As I said, I will delete them if you confirm your instruction, but it is not the way that I would answer this question).* In opposition to this, the vetter does not directly insist on the change. It comes off more as a suggestion, albeit a fairly strong one. Interestingly, it is the second vetter who resolves the impasse–*I'm happy for you to retain 'because' Peter*–after which the discussion moves onto the next item.

The acceptance by the writers that the vetters have the final say also emerges in the absence of an agreement or disagreement, and there are copious examples in the corpus to show this. One such is where the writers make the change without providing any response or when they minimally acknowledge the vetter's suggestion *(done)*. Alternatively, they may respond with a request for feedback *(How is the change now?)*.

Likewise, a vetter may insist on a change. In the following example this is done by citing the set requirements *(we already have two double questions…we can't have anymore)*. This works to establish the final say on the matter and therefore invokes not so much the personal expertise of the vetter, but rather the role of vetter which confers upon it the right to reject.

Writer: This is the only double question in the set. I would like to keep q11 if I can. The students at this level have learned very limited topics.

Vetter: The question is too easy. All students need to do is match. Besides, we already have two double questions in B and we can't have anymore. We are four questions short. We can have an additional question in (Target Language).

Of course, as analyzed above, the writers can also claim a right to express a desire to retain the item as they originally wrote it. However, as well as providing a reason or account for its retention in a way that is less baldly expressed, the writer also qualifies it in some way. This is evident in the example where the writer challenges the vetter on linguistic and pedagogical grounds and again in the following posting by a writer–*I prefer to leave the street name as I feel that's what she would say as her comment is about living in the same street as well as the number-but if I'm over-ruled I won't have a breakdown over it.*

Finally, there are also examples where the vetters defer to the expertise of the writers (*I am not qualified to judge, but is ('I would like') ... a bit bald as a response?*), (*I can't comment on the suitability of the topic area, so please advise*), and may also explicitly acknowledge explanations proffered (*Thanks for the explanation*).

The notion of expertise is thus dynamic. It shifts as the writers and vetters defer to each other's knowledge bases as they discuss the test items one posting at a time. It is invoked when there is disagreement, when there is a need for an explanation or a decision to be made about the appropriateness of an item, and it emerges collaboratively.

SUMMARY AND CONCLUDING REMARKS

This study sought to investigate two questions. Firstly, how do the interactions in a work setting posted in an asynchronous wiki environment compare with face-to-face interactions? In terms of conversational structure, the following findings emerged.

- Self-initiated self-repair is rare because there are opportunities for the members of the wiki test development team to polish and edit their postings before they are made public. The team members also do not attend to minor spelling or other orthographic details as these do not interfere with meaning. Other-initiated self- or other-repair is also not very common but it certainly occurs more often than self-initiated self-repair. This finding is in contrast to Tanskanen and Karhukorpi's (2008) study for email exchanges and may have something to do with the setting and the explicit nature of the work being done, which is to clear up any misunderstandings which may otherwise result in a poorer test item. As in face-to-face interaction, the repair sequences momentarily interrupt the main business of the discussion until they are dealt with.

- The adjacency pair structure is also an important feature of these postings particularly the Question and Answer adjacency pair. As in conversation, the participants orient to the absence of a response, but they also pursue actions such as editing, made relevant by the work context. The presence of pursuit itself displays the orientation of the writer or vetter to the posting as interactional rather than as a more distal piece of written text.

- In terms of the organization of sequences, there are inserts and side-sequences in which the business other than the main one is dealt with before resumption of the main topic. There are also address terms to nominate recipient or addressee, as there are occasionally greetings—all features of face-to-face interaction but in contrast to face-to-face, there are also signings-off—a feature of writing.

- Finally, analysis has revealed that there is a bias towards affiliative and supportive actions as is the case in face-to-face conversation (Clayman & Heritage, 2002) despite the disagreements with assessments that sometimes arise. Participants orient to maximising successful exchanges, which is consonant with Tanskanen and Karhukorpi's (2008) findings on concessive repair in email exchanges.

The second question was centered on the notion of expertise and how it emerged. Analysis showed that the writers enacted their roles quite differently. While all writers deferred to the vetter as having a final say in what might pass as the final draft of an item, some accepted suggestions without comment, while others disagreed by invoking their own knowledge of the language (either English or the target language), pedagogy or the culture. This was less likely to occur when the vetters implicated less of themselves (for example "I use") and used more hedging ("I wonder if", "what about"). Expertise and the role of vetter or writer were fluid and dynamic and emerged locally as they worked on the test item evaluation. They were not fixed, a finding which echoes that of Hall and Danby's (2003) for teachers and academics working together.

Taken together these findings have several implications for training. Firstly, how feedback is given and received is an important consideration. The most positive interactions were those where vetter and writer collaborated and engaged in ways that brought their different but co-constructed knowledge perspectives into play. The way that negative feedback is given is also important. Although the purpose of the team is to evaluate the test items (and therefore the work of the writers), it is important to maintain a balance and pay attention to matters of face. In this regard, as part of wiki netiquette, one writer explicitly urged the need to "keep it nice" in her evaluation. In the words of another:

Writer: I think we ALL (writers and reviewers) need to be aware of just how easy it is to 'appear' abrupt and to be offensive when adding comments to work. I think the medium lends itself to quick comments which we tap out on the keyboard and which all of us would phrase more carefully in spoken word or in other forms of written communication. I know that I responded with very sharp tongue, a number of times, to what I perceived to be offensive comments; comments which I have no doubt were intended to be constructive criticism (which is welcome) but which, because of the nature of the communication, came across (to me) as something different. I am just as guilty because of my sharp responses. I apologize.

It is also important to explicitly state the roles of each member of the team and not take it as a given that each member knows what they might be. This is particularly so because of the writers' different cultural backgrounds (and therefore different perceptions and expectations) of their own roles and roles of others as well as their degree of familiarity with, and experience in, test writing.

Lastly, as the pursuit of a response or action indicated, there could be considerable delay between the posting of a comment and a response to it, such that the comment no longer became relevant or had been forgotten. Thus, although the interactions did not occur in real time, there was a "time relevancy" in operation and the members of the team oriented to this through the conversational resource of pursuit.

In conclusion, although different from face-to-face interactions, the online wiki interactions also share some important features. As is the case in comparisons between face-to-face conversation and institutionalized interaction, where conversation is held to have a "bedrock" status (Drew & Heritage, 1992) against which other types of talk are identified, there are differences between online interactions themselves as well as between face-to-face and online interaction. What those differences are in organizational and structural terms awaits further elucidation.

REFERENCES

Cavanagh, A. (1999). Behaviour in public? Ethics in online ethnography. *Cybersociology, 6*. Retrieved June 15, 2009, from http://www.cybersociology.com/files/6_2_ethicsinonlineethnog.html

Clayman, S., & Heritage, J. (2002). *The news interview: journalists and public figures on the air*. Cambridge: Cambridge University Press. doi:10.1017/CBO9780511613623

Drew, P., & Heritage, J. (1992). Analyzing talk at work: an introduction . In Drew, P., & Heritage, J. (Eds.), *Talk at work: interaction in institutional settings* (pp. 3–65). Cambridge: Cambridge University Press.

Drew, P., & Heritage, J. (Eds.). (2006). *Conversation analysis*. London: Sage.

Filipi, A. (2009). *Toddler and parent interaction: the organisation of gaze, pointing and vocalisation*. Amsterdam, Philadelphia: John Benjamins Publishing.

Filipi, A., & Lissonnet, S. (2008, September). Using wikis to create tests. *Teacher Magazine*, 20-22.

Forrester, M. A. (2008). The emergence of self-repair: a case study of one child during the early preschool years. *Research on Language and Social Interaction*, *41*(1), 99–128.

Goodwin, C. (1995). Seeing in depth. *Social Studies of Science, 25*, 237–274. doi:10.1177/030631295025002002

Goodwin, C. (1996). Transparent vision . In Ochs, E., Schegloff, E. A., & Thompson, S. A. (Eds.), *Interaction and grammar* (pp. 370–404). Cambridge: Cambridge University Press. doi:10.1017/CBO9780511620874.008

Graham, S. L. (2007). Disagreeing to agree: Conflict, (im)politeness and identity in a computer-mediated community. *Journal of Pragmatics, 3*, 742–759. doi:10.1016/j. pragma.2006.11.017

Hall, G., & Danby, S. (2003). Teachers and academics co-constructing the category of expert through meeting talk. *Proceedings of the Annual Conference of the Australian Association for Research in Education*. Retrieved June 15, 2009, from http://www.aare.edu.au/03pap/hal03027.pdf

Harrison, S. (2000). Maintaining the virtual community: use of politeness strategies in an email discussion group. In L. Pemberton & S. Shurville (Eds.), *Words on the web: computer mediated communication* (pp. 69-78). Exeter & Portland, OR: Intellect Books.

Heritage, J. (1984). *Garfinkel and ethnomethodology*. Cambridge: Polity Press.

Hester, S., & Eglin, P. (1997). Membership categorization analysis: an introduction . In Hester, S., & Eglin, P. (Eds.), *Culture in action: studies in membership categorization analysis* (pp. 1–23). Washington: International Institute for Ethnomethodology and University Press of America.

Jaques, D., & Salmon, G. (2006). *Learning in groups: a handbook for face-to-face and online environments*. Hoboken: Taylor & Francis.

Jefferson, G. (1972). Side sequences . In Sudnow, D. (Ed.), *Studies in social interaction* (pp. 294–338). New York: Free Press.

Magnan Sieloff, S. (Ed.). (2008). *Mediating discourse online: AILA Applied Linguistics (Series 3)*. Amsterdam, Philadelphia: John Benjamins Publishing.

Masur, J. (2004). Conversation analysis for educational technologists: theoretical and methodological issues for researching the structures, processes and meaning of on-line talk . In Jonassen, D. (Ed.), *Handbook of research for educational communications and technology* (pp. 1073–1098). New York: McMillan.

Pomerantz, A. (1984a). Agreeing and disagreeing with assessments: some features of preferred/dispreferred turn shapes . In Maxwell Atkinson, J., & Heritage, J. (Eds.), *Structures of social action: studies in conversation analysis* (pp. 57–101). Cambridge: Cambridge University Press.

Pomerantz, A. (1984b). Pursuing a response . In Maxwell Atkinson, J., & Heritage, J. (Eds.), *Structures of social action: studies in conversation analysis* (pp. 152–163). Cambridge: Cambridge University Press.

Salmon, G. (2000). *E-moderating: the key to teaching and learning online*. London, New York: Routledge.

Schegloff, E. A. (1992). Repair after next turn: the last structurally provided defense of intersubjectivity in conversation. *American Journal of Sociology, 97,* 1295–1345. doi:10.1086/229903

Schegloff, E. A. (1997). Third turn repair . In Guy, G. R., Feagin, C., Schiffrin, D., & Baugh, J. (Eds.), *Towards a social science of language: papers in honor of William Labov* (*Vol. 2*, pp. 31–40). Amsterdam, Philadelphia: John Benjamins.

Schegloff, E. A. (2000). When 'others' initiate repair. *Applied Linguistics, 21*(2), 205–243. doi:10.1093/applin/21.2.205

Schegloff, E. A. (2007). *Sequence organization in interaction: a primer in conversation analysis* (*Vol. 1*). Cambridge: Cambridge University Press.

Schegloff, E. A., Jefferson, G., & Sacks, H. (1977). The preference for self-correction in the organization of repair in conversation. *Language, 53,* 361–382. doi:10.2307/413107

Tanskanen, S.-K. (2007). Metapragmatic utterances in computer-mediated interaction . In Bublitz, W., & Hübler, A. (Eds.), *Metapragmatics in use* (pp. 87–106). Amsterdam, Philadelphia: John Benjamins.

Tanskanen, S.-K., & Karhukorpi, J. (2008). Concessive repair and negotiation of affiliation in e-mail discourse. *Journal of Pragmatics, 40,* 1587–1600. doi:10.1016/j.pragma.2008.04.018

ten Have, P. (1999). *Doing conversation analysis*. London: Sage.

White, P. (2003). Beyond modality and hedging: a dialogic view of the language of intersubjective stance. *Text*, *23*, 259–284. doi:10.1515/text.2003.011

Woods, D., Thoeny, P., & Cunningham, W. (2007). *Wikis for dummies*. Hoboken: John Wiley & Sons.

KEY TERMS AND DEFINITIONS

Affiliation: Participants work collaboratively to minimize conflict in their interactions both online and face-to-face.

Co-Constructed Expertise: Expertise is a dynamic process which emerges as participants work together. It shifts as the writers and vetters defer to each other's knowledge bases. It is invoked when there is disagreement or a decision to be made about the appropriateness of an item, and it emerges collaboratively.

Preference Organization: Refers to the bias for speakers to support each other's actions or assess each other's actions positively. An example of a preferred turn is a positive response to an invitation, while a dispreferred turn is a rejection of an invitation.

Pursuit of an Action: A resource that speakers can deploy as part of a broader repair strategy to facilitate communication. It draws attention to the absence of an expected response or action.

Repair: A unique conversational phenomenon; it refers to the ways in which hearers and speakers adjust their talk when breakdown occurs as a result of inadequate hearing or interpretation.

Sequence Organization: Describes how turns at talk fit together structurally as relevant next actions to what has gone before. One type of organization that is massively present in both face-to-face and online interaction is the paired utterance or adjacency pair. Examples include the question and answer, and a greeting and return greeting.

Stance: In the wiki postings, stance refers to how participants react to them. They may take on a distal "writing" stance to the postings or a more proximal, "interactionist" stance.

This work was previously published in Cases on Online Discussion and Interaction: Experiences and Outcomes, edited by Leonard Shedletsky & Joan E. Aitken, pp. 194-211, copyright 2010 by Information Science Reference (an imprint of IGI Global).

Chapter 18
A Use Case for Ontology Evolution and Interoperability:
The IEC Utility Standards Reference Framework 62357

Mathias Uslar
OFFIS – Institute for Information Technology, Germany

Fabian Grüning
OFFIS – Institute for Information Technology, Germany

Sebastian Rohjans
OFFIS – Institute for Information Technology, Germany

EXECUTIVE SUMMARY

Within this chapter, the authors provide two use cases on semantic interoperability in the electric utility industry based on the IEC TR 62357 seamless integration architecture. The first use case on semantic integration based on ontologies deals with the integration of the two heterogeneous standards families IEC 61970 and IEC 61850. Based on a quantitative analysis, we outline the need for integration and provide a solution based on our framework, COLIN. The second use cases points out the need to use better metadata semantics in the utility branch, also being solely based on the IEC 61970 standard. The authors provide a solution to use the CIM as a domain ontology and taxonomy for improving data quality. Finally, this chapter outlines open questions and argues that proper semantics and domain models based on international standards can improve the systems within a utility.

DOI: 10.4018/978-1-4666-2618-8.ch018

BACKGROUND

In the electric utility domain, several changes impose new requirements on the IT infrastructure of companies. In the past, the generating structure used to be very close aligned to the communication infrastructure. Electric energy was delivered top-down from the high voltage grid having large-scale generation attached to the lower voltage grid and the households. The corresponding communication infrastructure was arranged similar, as steering information be mainly passed down the vertical supply chain while data points from the field level were submitted to the SCADA (Supervisory Control and Data Acquisition System).

With the upcoming distributed power generation respectively the legal requirements imposed by federal regulation and the resulting unbundling, things have changed a lot. On the one hand, deploying new generation facilities like wind power plants or fuel cells, energy is fed into the grid at different voltage levels and by different producers – former customers having their own power generation can now both act as consumers and producers, which feed into the utilities' grid. Therefore, the communication infrastructure has to be changed. On the other hand, the legal unbundling leads to separation of systems, which have to be open to more market participants. Hence, this results in more systems that have to be integrated and more data formats for compliance with the market participants - the overall need for standards increases. This problem must be addressed by an adequate IT-infrastructure within the utility, supported by architectures like SOA (Service-oriented Architectures). Regarding this scope, the IEC (International Electrotechnical Commission) has developed data models, interfaces and architectures (Robinson, 2002) for both running the power-grid and automating the attached substations. Unfortunately, those standards have been developed by different working groups and therefore lack some harmonization although they have to be used in context (Uslar, 2006). Furthermore, the semantic techniques imposed by the CIM are not properly used. This contribution shows a possible solution for an integration based on semantic techniques for two use cases we would like to address, first general semantic ontology integration and second data quality management based on meta annotation.

The following contribution is as structured as follows. First, we give a brief introduction into the IEC TC 57 standards framework in Section 2 with a special focus on the two biggest domain ontologies available in the IEC TC 57 reference framework, the IEC 61970 family for IT integration with SCADA and the IEC 61850 family dealing with substation and distributed energy generation automation. We show the basic metrics for the two ontologies and excerpts on how they were developed and how their OWL serializations look like.

Afterwards, we summarize the current challenges imposed to the ontologies from practice. We argue that some of those challenges have already been addressed and outline the most striking problem when dealing with changing ontologies in the same domain, the need for constant integration and consistency.

Therefore, we introduce our domain specific alignment methodology, the COLIN framework and its results on the Common Information Model CIM and the IEC 61850 family in section 4.

Section 5 provides an example of using ontologies, especially, the CIM domain ontology to build an interoperable data quality management system called VDE and WDE comprising legacy systems using D2RQ.

Finally, the chapter concludes with a summary of the findings in this paper and an outlook of our future work. We emphasize on the actual benefits form using the ontologies as a technological basis and discuss both advantages and disadvantages.

SETTING THE STAGE

The IEC has the vision of enabling seamless integration of both data and functions for the electric utility domain using their standards reference framework. Within this standards framework, the so-called TC 57 seamless integration architecture, different working groups have developed several standards. Unfortunately, those groups have different ideas about what to standardize and the overall focus of the standardization efforts.

Two main standards families exist within the TC 57 framework, the so-called IEC 61970 family including the Common Information Model CIM and the IEC 61850 family for substation communication coping with the data exchanged between SCADA systems and the field devices. Those two families have been developed with a different technical background resulting in different serializations. The next section will give short introductions to those standards and provide a glimpse on the structure and sizes of the models to further understand the real world problem of integration of large structural heterogeneous ontologies.

The IEC 61970 Family: The Common Information Model CIM

The CIM (IEC, 2003) can be seen as the basic domain ontology for the electric utility domain at SCADA level. It is standardized in two different sub-families, namely the IEC 61970 family for the data model and OPC-based data models dealing directly with the day-to-day business of running the electric power grid.

Furthermore, the IEC 61968 family, which has to cover the needed objects to integrate the CIM into the overall utility having to exchange data with systems like

GIS (Geographical Information Systems), CSS (Customer Support System), or ERP (Enterprise-Resource Planning), is covered.

Overall, the CIM data model covers 53 UML packages covering roundabout 800 classes with more than 9200 attributes. A lot of effort and work has been put into the model to cover the most important objects for the electric utility domain. Furthermore, different serializations exist. First, XML and XML schema exist for building your own Enterprise Application Integration (EAI) messages (Uslar, Streekmann, Abels, 2007) based on the CIM and to use pre-defined messages built by the IEC.

Additionally, RDF serializations and RDF schemas used for modeling the graphs of power grids for electrical distribution exist, and, based on this work, an overall CIM OWL serialization for dealing with the concepts of the domain has been developed.

The following Figures and Tables 1, 2 and 3 show the extend and distribution of objects within the data model.

Table 1 provides an overview of the absolute allocation of the CIM model in revision 11_v01. Looking at the numbers, you see that there are two main packages, the IEC 61970 and IEC 61968 package, all others packages are smaller and not the very core of the CIM. The CIM is a fully object-oriented data model using

Figure 1. Top Level view on the CIM 11r_v00 packages

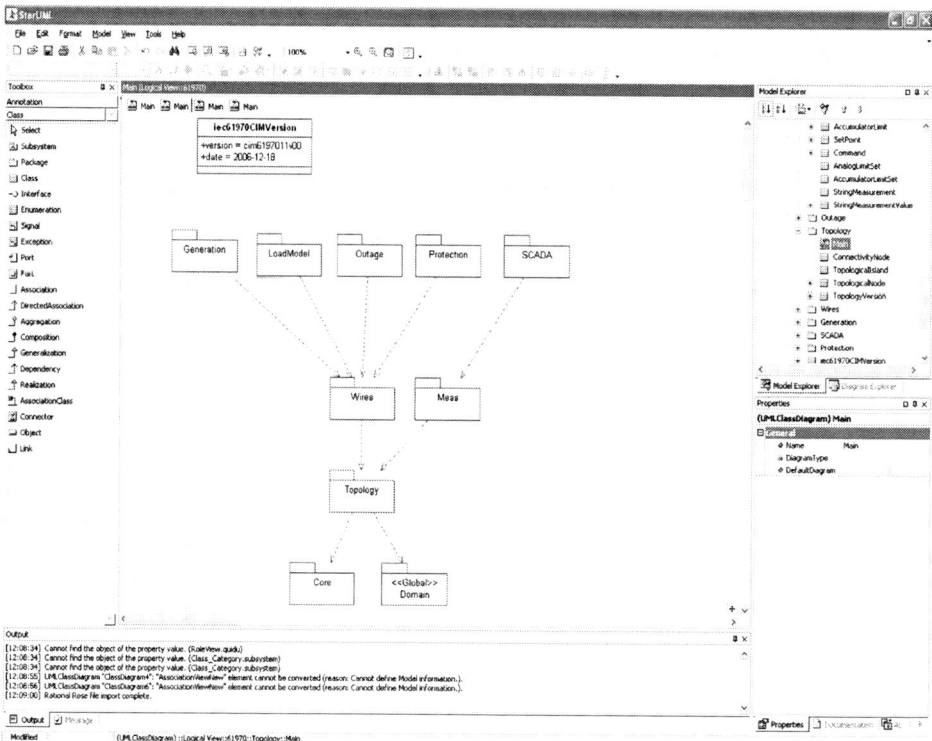

Table 1. Absolute allocation of the CIM11_v01-objects from the XMI-file

Package name	Number of sub packages	Number of classes	Number of native attributes	Number of inherited attributes	Number of total attributes	Number of associations
IEC 61970	12	293	780	1409	2189	126
IEC 61968	34	411	1021	4823	5844	502
Reservation	0	7	6	24	30	3
Market Operations	0	61	183	627	810	86
Financial	0	9	4	126	130	18
Energy Scheduling	0	19	25	198	223	35
IEC 61850	0	18	0	42	42	15
CIM11_v01	**53**	**819**	**2021**	**7249**	**9270**	**785**

Table 2. Absolute allocation of the CIM11_v01-objects from the XMI-file included in the IEC 61970 sub packages

Package name	Number of sub packages	Number of classes	Number of native attributes	Number of inherited attributes	Number of total attributes	Number of associations
Core	0	28	37	144	181	11
Domain	0	118	249	0	249	2
Load Model	0	13	12	149	161	10
Meas	0	27	40	152	192	22
Outage	0	4	13	21	34	4
Topology	0	4	9	18	27	4
Wires	0	39	165	301	466	24
Generation	2	48	225	562	787	41
SCADA	0	6	10	30	40	4
Protection	0	5	18	32	50	4
IEC 61970	**12**	**293**	**780**	**1409**	**2189**	**126**

all UML mechanisms like inheritance and packaging. Due to strong use of inheritance, the absolute numbers of attributes for the classes is rather high. The absolute number of associations between the classes is rather high compared the metrics for the classes, the CIM model is not tree-like organized with some classes on top, broadening going down the model layers but rather broad at all levels starting at subpackage layers and a fully meshed graph. Classes are strongly interwoven and changes cascade trough the model when they occur. Tables 2 and 3 show more detailed figures of the IEC 61970 and IEC 61968 packages.

Table 3. Absolute allocation of the CIM11_v01-objects from the XMI-file included in the IEC 61968 sub packages

Package name	Number of sub packages	Number of classes	Number of native attributes	Number of inherited attributes	Number of total attributes	Number of associations
Assets	6	169	470	2959	3429	185
Consumers	0	16	59	193	252	29
Core2	7	52	116	383	499	45
Documentation	6	30	86	249	335	48
ERP_Support	0	41	64	393	457	44
Work	8	54	135	445	580	103
GML_Support	0	48	89	201	290	48
IEC 61968	**34**	**411**	**1021**	**4823**	**5844**	**502**

Figure 2. Subview of the load model package: main view

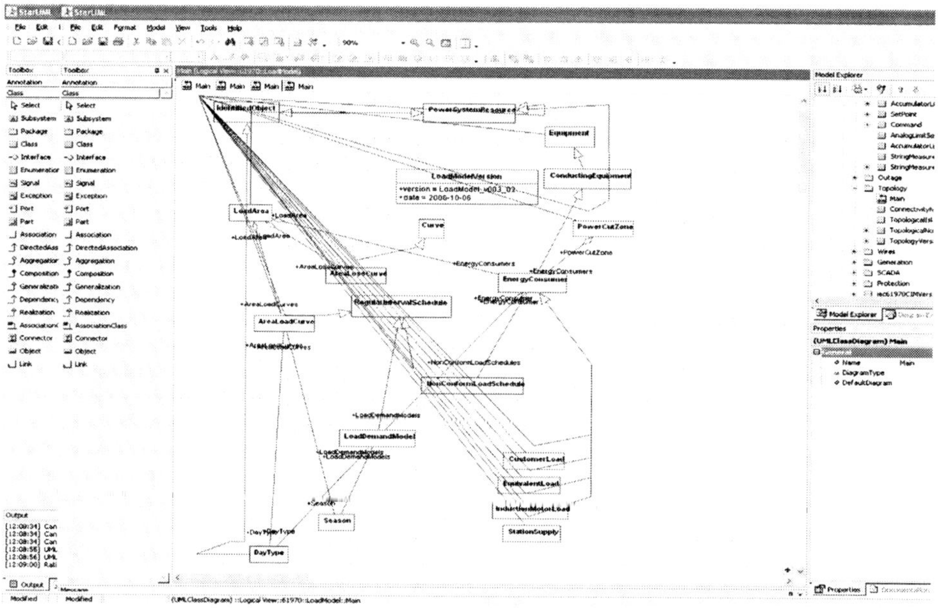

The idea of tracking those metrics was to find out the focus of the CIM. When IEC WG experts were asked, they could not name the largest or most detailed class. They could not name the largest packages or the most interwoven one. They did not know the distribution of viewpoints for the power-grid in their data models, which makes it very hard to find starting points for a good integration with other standards like the IEC 61850 one.

Therefore, we argue that that those figures and metrics are essential to the domain engineers and new users since they provide a good overview where the most detailed parts of the models lie and where the focus of the overall model is. Discussions with experts working with the CIM for years have shown that even they have not been aware where the most detailed parts were and that the IEC's focus has shifted since the first model due to new stakeholders bringing in their objects and relations.

From these figures, we can realize that different scopes exist and changes in those dense parts of the model have a stronger impact since inheritance is used more than in parts where only little objects actually exist. Figures 3 and 4 show the development of the CIM's data within the last 6 versions, i.e. 5 years. We see bumps in the model where large projects have created new objects needed not previously incorporated in the CIM. The biggest one was the integration of the IEC 61968 family that was introduced in the 10_v003 version. The CIM does not grow continually like big taxonomies known to integration experts; a lot of effort has to be spent on manually updating existing applications that is a difficult process.

Figure 5 shows excerpts from the model loaded into our mapping bench for both having an overview of the model and creating the metrics needed for our evaluation and mapping approaches for CIM and IEC 61850. It provides some insights on how each individual class is handled in terms of attributes and associations in the CIM model.

Figure 3. History of the number of packages, classes and associations included in the CIM

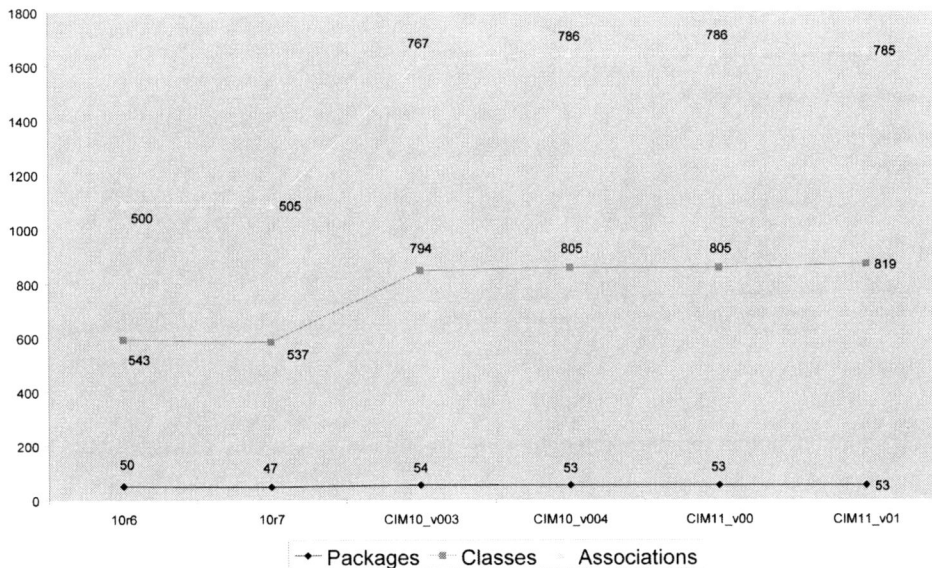

Figure 4. History of the number of native, inherited and total attributes included in the CIM

20000
18000
16000
14000
12000
10000
8000
6000
4000
2000
0
9270
8359
8545
8545
5117
5594
6376
6528
6528
7249
3691
4043
1426
1551
1983
2017
2017
2021
10r6
10r7
CIM10_v003
CIM10_v004
CIM11_v00
CIM11_v01
Native attributes
Inherited attributes
Total attributes

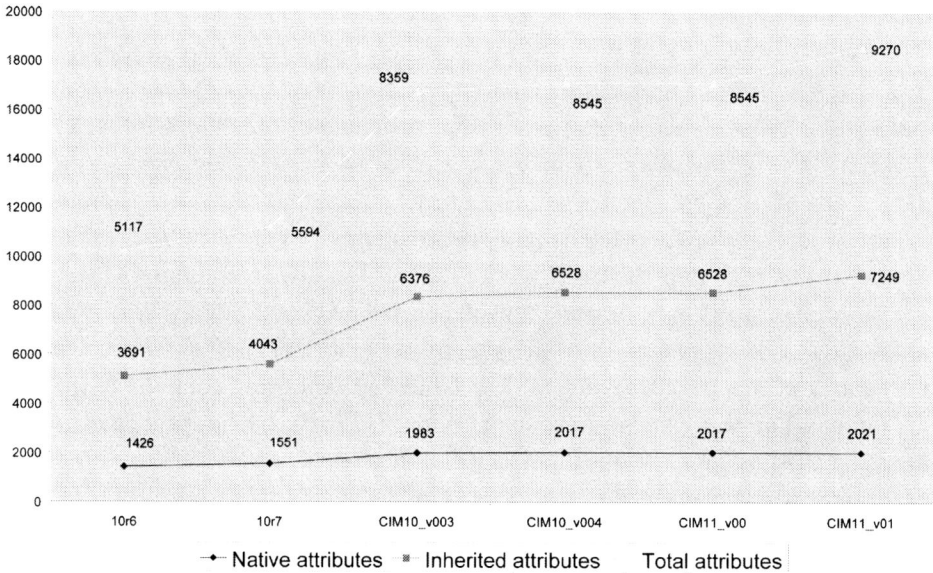

Figure 5. CIMBench showing the conductor class

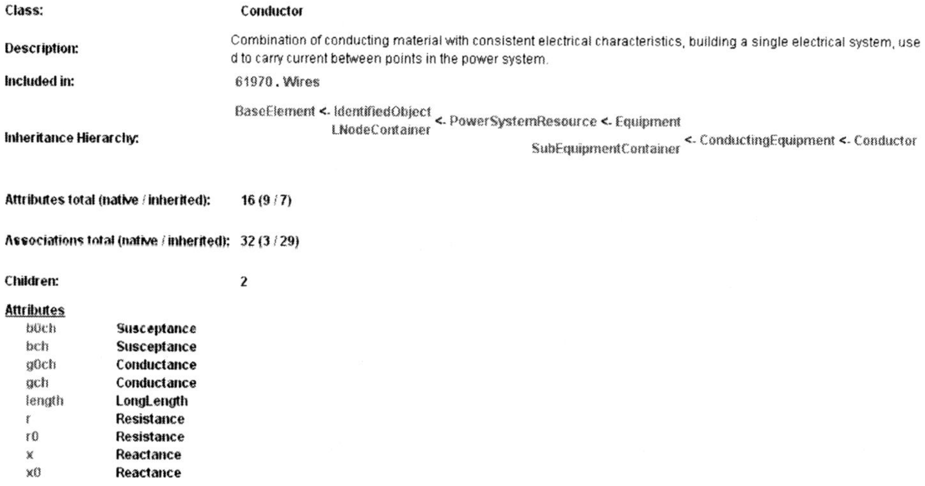

Class:
Conductor
Description:
Combination of conducting material with consistent electrical characteristics, building a single electrical system, use d to carry current between points in the power system.
Included in:
61970 . Wires
Inheritance Hierarchy:
BaseElement <- IdentifiedObject
LNodeContainer
<- PowerSystemResource <- Equipment
SubEquipmentContainer
<- ConductingEquipment <- Conductor
Attributes total (native / inherited):
16 (9 / 7)
Associations total (native / inherited):
32 (3 / 29)
Children:
2
Attributes
b0ch Susceptance
bch Susceptance
g0ch Conductance
gch Conductance
length LongLength
r Resistance
r0 Resistance
x Reactance
x0 Reactance

Figure 6. The OWL Serialization of the Conductor type and the resistance property r

```
<owl:Class rdf:about="http://iec.ch/TC57/2005/CIM-schema-cim10#Conductor">
<j.1:id rdf:datatype="http://www.w3.org/2001/XMLSchema#string"
>S.082.0657.26.278</j.1:id>
<rdfs:subClassOf>
<owl:Class rdf:about="http://iec.ch/TC57/2005/CIM-schema-cim10#ConductingEquipment"/>
</rdfs:subClassOf>
<rdfs:comment rdf:datatype="http://www.w3.org/2001/XMLSchema#string"
  >Combination of conducting material with consistent electrical characteristics, building a
  single electrical system, used to carry current between points in the power
  system.</rdfs:comment>
<rdfs:label xml:lang="en">Conductor</rdfs:label>
  <rdfs:isDefinedBy rdf:resource="http://iec.ch/TC57/2005/CIM-schema-
  cim10#Package_Wires"/>
</owl:Class>

<rdf:Property rdf:about="http://iec.ch/TC57/2005/CIM-schema-cim10#Conductor.r">
  <rdf:type rdf:resource="http://www.w3.org/2002/07/owl#FunctionalProperty"/>
<j.1:id rdf:datatype="http://www.w3.org/2001/XMLSchema#string"
S.082.0657.26.284</j.1:id>
  <rdfs:domain rdf:resource="http://iec.ch/TC57/2005/CIM-schema-cim10#Conductor"/>
  <j.1:hasStereotype rdf:resource="http://langdale.com.au/2005/UML#attribute"/>
  <rdf:type rdf:resource="http://www.w3.org/2002/07/owl#DatatypeProperty"/>
  <rdfs:isDefinedBy rdf:resource="http://iec.ch/TC57/2005/CIM-schema-
  cim10#Package_Wires"/>
<rdfs:label xml:lang="en">r</rdfs:label>
  <rdfs:comment rdf:datatype="http://www.w3.org/2001/XMLSchema#string">Positive
  sequence series resistance of the entire line section.</rdfs:comment>
  <rdfs:range rdf:resource="http://iec.ch/TC57/2005/CIM-schema-cim10#Resistance"/>
</rdf:Property>
```

For a better overview of how the CIM ontology is built, Figure 6 provides an example of how the ontology is actually built and serialized.

Section 2.2 of this contribution is going to show how we adopted the techniques used by the IEC and its working groups when dealing with the CIM to build a proper electronic model of the IEC 61850 family for substation communication. We will discuss why the overall data model is so different from the UML-model of the CIM and show the differences which make for difficult integration of both.

The IEC 61850 Family: Communication for Substations

The IEC TC 57 working group WG 10 has developed the IEC 61850 family dealing with substation automation systems and the corresponding communications. The standard itself is very large, comprising sub-standards of different kinds like communication protocols, data models, security standards etc.

The overall control system domain for IEC 61850 is system automation (Kostic et al, 2004). While the CIM focuses on energy management systems, the IT domains here are substation intra-application communication and, for the CIM, control-center intra-application communication. Both standards have a basic data model but the serializations differ completely. While only a small subset for engineering of substations needs a XML-serialization in IEC 61850, all CIM objects can be serialized using XML, RDF or OWL. In addition, the IEC 61850 family lacks a significant support of APIs – only an abstract communication interface is provided. Those differences lead to problems when coping in real-world projects with the IEC TC 57 reference framework.

The data model used within the context of IEC 61850 is based on a strictly hierarchical system having a tree-like taxonomy structure with three levels and composed data types – so called CDCs. Functions are integrated into the data model with a special focus on set points for control by the SCADA and data reports have to be implemented using queues and buffers. Those two features are not included in the CIM data model and therefore make harmonization a bit more difficult – we have to distinguish between different viewpoints for integration like engineering time, run-time and basic data model. So far, our approach works for basic data model and engineering time both has performance withdraws at run-time. The data model for

Figure 7. The logical node circuit breaker XCBR from [22]

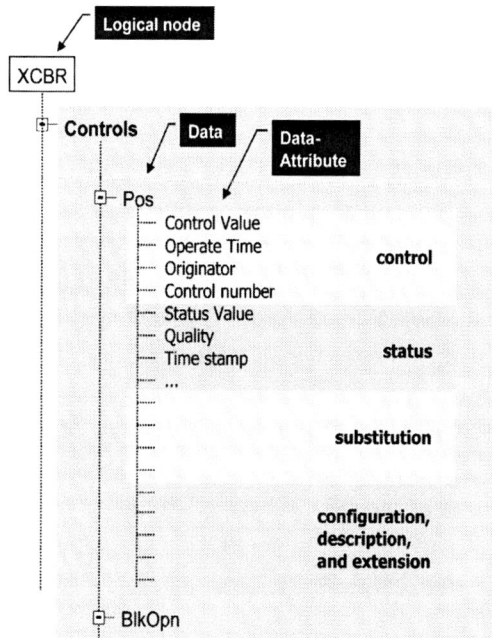

Table 4. Absolute allocation of the data objects according to the logical nodes information model concerning the sub standards IEC 61850-7-4, IEC 61850-7-410, IEC 61850-7-420 and IEC 61400-25-2

Package name	Number of native attributes	Number of inherited attributes	Number of total attributes	Number of native associations	Number of inherited associations	Number of total associations
IEC 61850-7-4	2	0	2	925	900	1825
IEC 61850-7-410	0	0	0	980	1000	1980
IEC 61850-7-420	44	0	44	630	500	1130
IEC 61400-25-2	40	0	40	189	170	359
IEC 61850	**86**	**0**	**86**	**2724**	**2570**	**5294**

IEC 61850 consists of just about 100 classes (so-called logical nodes LN) which have over 900 attributes (so-called data objects DOs) from the variety of around 50 base types (so-called common data classes CDCs) consisting of more or less simple types. These figures show that the standard is about as big as the CIM data model mentioned above. Figure 7 shows the tree-like structure of the individual logical nodes für the XCBR (circuit breaker) node.

Based on those facts, we have created both an electronic model and a serialization in OWL for the IEC 61850 family strictly adhering to the hierarchical model for a better acceptance with the IEC 61850 community, however risking the chance that the different modeling approach leads to a slightly more difficult mapping with the OO-based CIM model. The following table shows the overall figures for the whole standard data model dealing with IEC 61850-like data models for substation automation (61850-7-4), distributed energy producers (61850-7-420) and wind parks (61400-25-2) or hydro power plants (61850-7-410).

Individual systems are built from several logical nodes that may be combined to provide the data representation for a real world system as shown in Figure 8.

Next, we see a figure showing the tree-like hierarchy of our model of the standard in the CIMBench tool and a proper way to serialize the corresponding logical node (ZCAB) for a power cable. Please note already the difference between the modeling of a power line segment in the CIM where we have the syntax name "conductor" and the model for the IEC 61850 standard naming a line segment ZCAB.

In the later sections of this paper, we will see how we identified that both working groups of the IEC have built models which overlap and how to overcome this fallacy without having to change the whole standards.

Figure 8. Model and real-world system from [22]

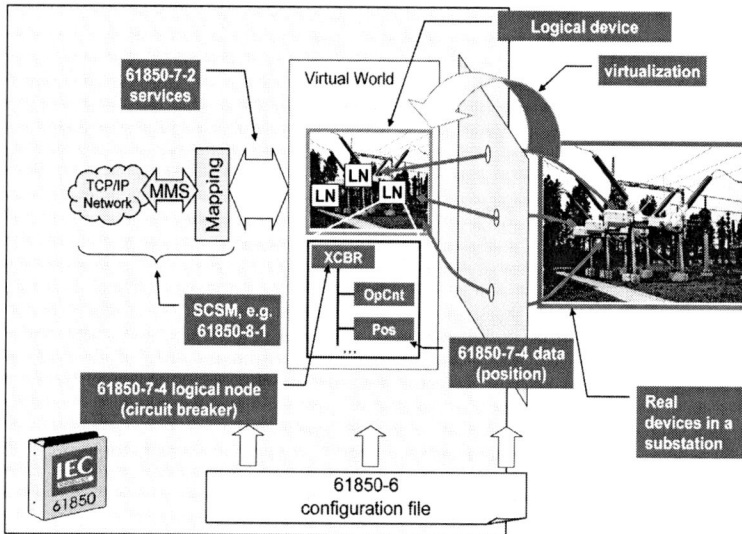

Figure 9. The CIMBench showing the power cable class

Class:	**ZCAB**
Description:	Power cable
Included in:	Logical Nodes
Inheritance Hierarchy:	CLN <- ZCAB
Attributes total (native / inherited):	0 (0 / 0)
Associations total (native / inherited):	13 (3 / 10)
Children:	0

Attributes

inherited from CLN

Associations

EEHealth	→ INS
EEName	→ DPL
OpTmh	→ INS

Figure 10. The OWL Serialization of the Cable logical node ZCAB and the operation time in hours property

```
<owl:Class rdf:ID="ZCAB">
        <rdfs:subClassOfrdf:resource="#Logical_Nodes"/>
        <rdfs:comment        rdf:datatype="http://www.w3.org/2001/XMLSchema#string"
        >Power cable</rdfs:comment>
</owl:Class>

<owl:ObjectProperty rdf:ID="_OpTmh_">
        <rdfs:comment rdf:datatype="http://www.w3.org/2001/XMLSchema#string"
        >Operation time
        </rdfs:comment>
        <rdfs:domain>
                <owl:Class>
                        <owl:unionOf rdf:parseType="Collection">
                                <owl:Class rdf:about="#ZCAB"/>
                        </owl:unionOf>
                </owl:Class>
        </rdfs:domain>
        <rdfs:range>
                <owl:Class>
                        <owl:unionOf rdf:parseType="Collection">
                                <owl:Class rdf:about="#INS"/>
                        </owl:unionOf>
                </owl:Class>
        </rdfs:range>
</owl:ObjectProperty>
```

In the next section, we will summarize our findings how the IEC and practioners deal and react to those two ontologies and identify challenges that are derived from the constant evolution of the domain ontologies. The most challenging problem will be the proper integration based on finding starting points form our metrics and integrating the semantics based on the labels and class names form the ontologies.

CURRENT CHALLENGES

As (Hepp, 2007) has already outlined, reality constrains the development of relevant ontologies even if proper semantics and serializations are available. However, the IEC still has taken the way to build their standards on rather large electronic models and taking modern techniques to facilitate the exchange of domain knowledge using OWL. Several problems have evolved which need to be resolved in order to further extend the use of such relevant early adopter projects for real-world OWL use. We have identified the following problems when dealing with our two large domain ontologies:

- Code-transformation techniques like MDSD (model-driven software development) have to be properly used to create both a holistic and, even more important, deterministic way to properly create the needed artifacts. Tooling is a key to deal with this problem.
- Visual editing is needed to help domain experts cope better with the formal semantics imposed by serializations like OWL – Protégé is not suitable for domain experts in the utility domain.
- A difference model to deal with new ontologies should be created to find out, what parts have changed in a new version of the ontology since it is far too large to find out manually.
- For finding out the impact of changes to individuals or interfaces, we have to deal with updates and additions to the model, deletions or changes in hierarchy and inheritance.
- A proper versioning of the ontologies (both schemes and instances) is needed.
- Checking instances for sub-profiles of the domain ontology should be done using standards reasoners like Pellet. The need for developing and updating custom reasoning and rule engines should not exist.
- The IEC has to create a maintenance process and a database format to deal with electronic models instead of using their processes originally developed for four-year maintenance cycles of paper standards.
- As more and more domain ontologies come up, more harmonization is needed since different groups see the world in a different manner. Since standards cannot easily be changed, federated and harmonized mapping ontologies should be created with least effort possible.

Challenges which are Nearly Solved

From the aforementioned problems and challenges, some have already been resolved by other projects. The model-driven development and transformation from the UML model to OWL and other serializations has been the focus of (Uslar, Streekmann, Abels, 2007). This lead to less efforts and a fast creation of needed serializations when changes to the model appeared.

A difference model to cope with changes to the CIM and finding out new parts for both instance data and schemes has been worked on in (Uslar, Dahlem, 2006). Currently, we built a checker for instance-based, mainly reasoning based CIM profile validation.

However, the most striking problem, which remains, is the fact, that the IEC versioning and standardization processes have not been adapted to the needs for electronic models. New versions of the standards are rolled out without having electronic models joining the bought paper documents and harmonization of the ontologies and models only gets little attention at all levels like engineering, basic data model and run-time. We argue that while the standards have overlapping semantics but different syntax and since products are already based on the standards, this fact leads to a resistance to fundamentally change the evolving standards while integration is necessary. Our solution is building mediation ontologies between the standards. The work conducted in this sector will be presented in section 4 of this contribution.

CASE DESCRIPTION 1: ONTOLOGY-BASED ALIGNMENT – THE COLIN FRAMEWORK

Of course, the data from both standards must be used in the same context, therefore, the SCADA and a mapping between structures from IEC 61850 must know a seamless integration of i.e. the functional description structure of a substation and IEC 61970. Furthermore, all data points and measurements from the field devices must be mapped from IEC 61850 semantics to IEC 61970 semantics. Without any doubt, those two scenarios are the most striking ones, but further scenarios exist.

Unfortunately, problems occur when trying to use the standards. The different working groups have used different naming schemes, object-oriented modeling vs. hierarchical modeling, different semantics, different tools and serializations and, the IEC 61850 model does not exist as an electronic model, just as tables within a proprietary text format (MS Word or PDF). Finally, all the standards have been made final international standards; therefore, they are being implemented by big vendors like ABB, Areva, or Siemens who rely on the stability of the standards and their products. The existing implementations cannot be harmonized at the meta-model level to a new, overall harmonized standard family comprising IEC 61850 and IEC 61970 without breaking several aspects. Hence, we have to deal with harmonization on a conceptual mediator layer.

To cope with all those problems and to facilitate integration, we have developed a methodology for integrating the standards that will be discussed in the next chapter. This method is based on ontology matching algorithms and will develop a bridge ontology for mediation between the two standard families.

Our "CIM Ontology aLigNment methodology" (abbrev.: COLIN) tries to overcome all the fallacies described in the previous sections by establishing a methodology for integrating utility standards taking the domain requirements and current research trends into account.

The approach taken to account as the scientific method was the design science approach by (Hevner et al, 2004). Our aim is to provide meaningful artifacts to evaluate the use of ontology-based integration and mediation in the context of the

IEC standards. The artifacts e.g. the created mediation ontologies are rigorously evaluated and put into different contexts. We have to distinguish between harmonization at schema level or at instance level, for example. The relevance of each artifact being developed must be clear. Furthermore, the transfer of the solution found into practice and showing the importance to both scientific audience and managerial audience is of high importance.

We will briefly introduce the results for the mapping of the IEC 61970 CIM family and the IEC 61850 family based on our ontologies in the next section. Using the design science approach described by Hevner, we have identified several use cases dealing with ontology-based integration. Firstly, we had to identify the standards that had to be integrated, we did an overview and developed ontology to express the concepts and relations the different standards had in general. Secondly, we had to identify at what point the integration should take place. We mainly used the quantitative analysis from section 2 of this chapter for this to find where certain aspects like generation, grid topology, and basic data types were located in the standards.

Here, it is necessary to distinguish between run-time and engineering time integration. Run-time integration deals with the integration of messages and signal instances and is much more complicated due to complexity and time criticality. The engineering integration that means integrations of schemata or, in our case, integration of ontologies has to deal with larger amounts of data but is not time critical to the same extent – it is more tedious but does not need to be performed every time you use the system due to its nature. The first use case we developed therefore was the integration of the data models of the IEC 61970 and IEC 61850 families described in section 2 of this contribution.

The CIM could already be used as an electronic OWL model since the IEC provides it this way. Therefore, we chose the CIM as our basic domain ontology for the electric energy domain and tried to model all the other standards as OWL ontologies, too. For the IEC 61850 family, the electronic model provided by the national German IEC mirror committee DKE was used and transferred from the proprietary format to the OWL ontology format as shown in section 2.2. Afterwards, we had our two very large domain ontologies reflecting the standards that can be obtained for evaluation from (OFFIS, 2008). The next step was choosing the (better say a) proper way to integrate the two ontologies.

As argued in the sections before, international standards cannot be easily changed – implementations exist and have to be taken into account when it comes to drastic changes in the overall models and standards. Therefore, we chose to integrate the standards with a minimum of changes to the original data models. One possible solution with the minimum impact on the standards is to align them using a mediator ontology (Euzenat, Shvaiko, 2007). From the beginning, we chose to use the INRIA alignment format (Shvaiko, 2006) to cope with the mappings between the standards we needed. This format is very easy to apply and well supported by nowa-days alignment tools like FALCON AO, HMatch or COMA ++ (Hong Hai, 2006).

One of our aims doing the integration was to find out whether the very large models could be integrated with minimum manual effort, e.g. mostly automatically. We tested the three aforementioned mapping tools with different configurations. In most cases, the results were not satisfying due to the different structures of the ontologies from the standards – the string matching approaches are very strong when strings are not abbreviated but as seen before, 61850: XCBR ist no good match for CIM:circuit breaker, we therefore had to rely on rdf:comments, labels and dictionaries using word stemming. Our idea was to keep the OWL ontologies as close as possible to the original standards, therefore reflecting their original hierarchies and depth structure. This has a strong impact on the overall mapping with automated matchers.

Based on the reference mediation ontology created by our domain experts, we got about 30 per cent of all the mappings correct in first place – therefore, we created a specialized mapping tool with a strong focus on the two standards, the so-called CIMBench. The main idea was to focus on string-based, lexical and diction-ary-based methods. We integrated all the descriptions form the standards into the data model elements of each individual class in the OWL files and supported them by a dictionary containing the proper descriptions for each term contained in the

Figure 11. The Mapping Bench Tool CIMBench

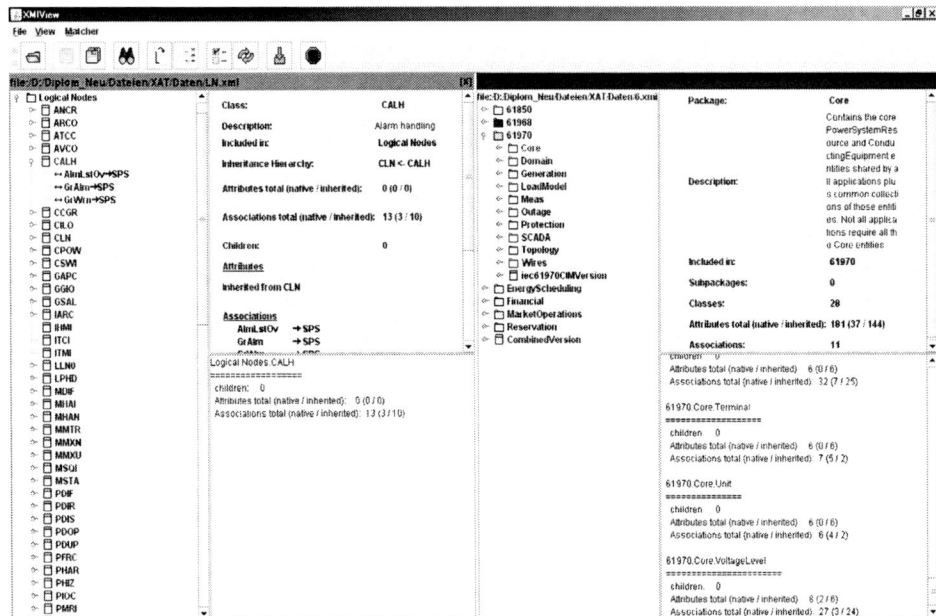

IEC 60050 Electropedia (IEC, 2008). The OWL ontology of the Electropedia was created by scraping the website using a custom Ruby script. The overall size of the resulting upper ontology for the electric energy sector is 15 megabytes, containing descriptions in English, French and German for each concept/class like breaker or cable.

Furthermore, the original ontologies were analyzed in a semantic way to find out different parts that could be mapped better due to their original purpose having the same focus. The CIM is divided into UML packages whereas the IEC 61850 model is divided into twelve groups of (logical) nodes having the same starting letter from A-Z, this means there are about 26 packages. An analysis performed on the intentions of each package lead to the following results for a partitioning shown in Figure 12.

The packages in the middle have been sliced from the large ontologies and have been mapped with the custom CIMBench mapper. This led to promising results as many false positives and basic mappings could be ruled out from the resulting alignments. The other packages and elements were mapped afterwards in order to find alignments that were not that obvious based on the basic semantics identified before. Still the packages, which were not covered by the intersection, contained very important alignments. As a final result, our custom made alignment algorithms based on string matching methods (for the rdf labels, comments and class names) like Levenshtein distance, Hamming distance and Jaro-Winkler distance combined and the input dictionaries like Electropedia combined with a word stemming for the IEC 61850 short names for classes provided promising results, we found about 180 proper alignments out of the 210 estimated by the experts. Unfortunately, due to the heterogeneous structure of the two ontologies, structure and hierarchy based matching provides less good results. The alignments can be downloaded at (OFFIS, 2008) or obtained from the authors. As future work, we want to specifically refine the packages and try to find better slicings for the pre-analysis of the standards. In

Figure 12. Intersection between the two standards

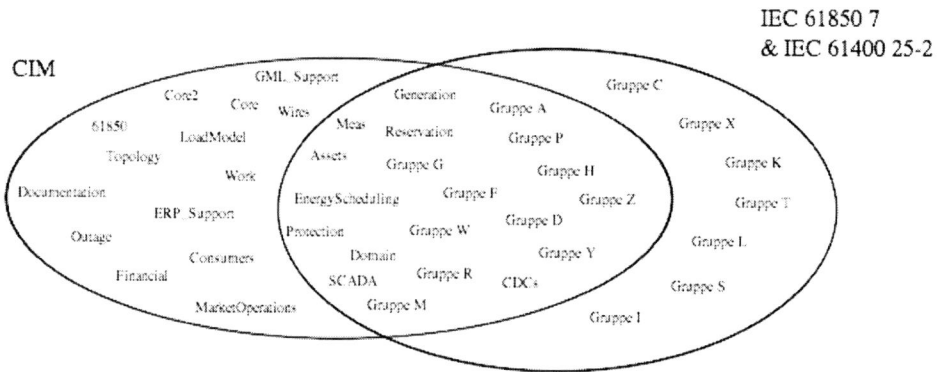

addition, integration for engineering time based on instances is a further aspect of the framework.

Using this harmonized IEC standards as a foundation, we argue that this leads to an integrated data and function model that can be used as one model for semantic annotation for Web services in the electric utility domain. Both standards already have Web services as interfaces defined like the interface reference model (IRM) in the IEC 61970 CIM family and the Web services interface for IEC 61850 models based on the wind power plant standards and distributed generation standards. Still, the strong semantic imposed by the data models for annotation is not properly used.

CASE DESCRIPTION 2: DOMAIN ONTOLOGIES AND DATA QUALITY ASPECTS

Domain ontologies like the CIM provide an excellent basis for data quality management approaches. In this section, we will discuss a methodology for data quality management for the utility domain that is focused on the use of the CIM as a domain ontology. Furthermore, a tool that automates most of its steps accompanies the methodology.

Motivation

Utility Domain's IT-Systems nowadays face different challenges: Liberalization of the energy domain lead to splitting of the former monopolists. The IT-Systems have to be adapted to be compliant with the new market rules, e.g. by providing information non-discriminating for all market participants (European Council and Parliament, 2003).

Another example is the integration of the new renewable energies. The increase of the number of power plants makes the automatic control for a lot more difficult so that automatic decision making becomes a necessity. As for the data, a completely new set of requirements emerges as traditionally data regarding technical equipment was used for informing technical staff and not for automatic decision-making. Therefore the demand regarding data quality rises, as humans are more fault-tolerant than algorithms for automatic control are.

Both the two discussed and further scenarios require a mechanism to provide information about the feasibility, i.e. whether or not the data quality is sufficient for such tasks. We will provide a process model that specifically for the databases of enterprises of the utility domain provides information about their data quality.

Methodologies for Data Quality Management

Several approaches for data quality management have been developed. To put our approach into relationship to those other methodologies, we will classify existing approaches first and give at least one example for every identified class. Afterwards, we will discuss the classification of our own approach in the context of data quality management in the utility domain with focus on data that is provided in the CIM format.

Universal Methodologies for Data Quality Management

Universal methodologies for data quality management structure the process of data quality management without any restrictions regarding their applicability. They can generally be divided into a two phases, where the first phase is used to identify the state of data quality of the databases to be analyzed and a second phase where actions are planned and executed to improve the situation where necessary.

One example of this class of methodologies is CDQM (Complete Data Quality Method) (Batini, Scannapieco, 2006)), which combines the advantages of two other methodologies, TDQM (Total Data Quality Method) and TQdM (Total Quality data Management), by providing both a technical and an economical view on the challenge of data quality management.

CDQM first analyses the interconnections between organizational units. The outcome is a matrix showing the inputs and outputs of data for every unit. Above that, the processes are modeled that are responsible for those data processings.

In the second step, the data quality among other performances of every organizational unit is measured to identify parts where bad data occurs.

Finally, the matrix is completed with costs to improve the data quality. With this information, it is possible to identify the most efficient way to improve the data quality for the whole organization.

Specialized Methodologies for Data Quality Management

As the universal methodologies provide a very general way for data quality management, they need a lot of fine-tuning when applying them to a certain domain. The idea behind specialized methodologies for data quality management is to reduce their applicability and therefore being able to be more precise about the steps to execute to gain a quality-managed database. We will introduce two methodologies in the following, afterwards pointing out their differences.

(Hinrichs, 2002) describes a methodology for data quality management that can be applied to data warehouses. By this specialization, it is possible to make statements about certain referential constraints, as data warehouses always have certain data structures that they are defined by.

(De Amicis, Batini, 2004) describe a methodology for data quality management for the data of the financial domain. By restricting its application to such a domain, it is possible to name certain authorities whose knowledge about the domain makes them experts for estimating certain data regarding their correctness.

Generally speaking, specialized methodologies for data quality management can either be specific for a certain kind of technology or domain. As certain domains tend to use similar technological solutions, this classification is not exclusive.

Putting our Methodology into Context

The methodology we are going to introduce here for data quality management for the utility domain clearly is a specialized methodology as discussed above. Furthermore, its specialization regards the domain, but as mentioned before, that also in some applications has technological implications. In our case, it can often be observed, that utilities prefer distributed information systems e.g. for customer relationship management and asset management. Our approach takes into consideration those implications as shown later on.

Domain Ontologies and their Advantages for Data Quality Management

We will provide several reasons why ontologies are an optimal basis for data quality management. Therefore, we will use the CIM as an example of a domain ontology for the utility domain. Especially when discussing metadata annotation in the second part of this subsection, we refer to the RDF-Serialization of the CIM as introduced before.

Avoiding the Object Identification-Problem

Data quality algorithms' tasks can be described as marking wrong data in a database. Wrong data can come in different appearances: Data can be missing, it can be inconsistent in relation to other data, and it can be wrong (e.g., a negative value for some measurement that can only be positive) or it can be outdated. The fifth possibility is that a real world entity is represented several times in a database. So-called duplicates are also errors.

To find such wrong data it is necessary to have a conceptualized view on the data, i.e. a complete description of the instances to cope with. In other words, it is only possible to apply an algorithm for e.g. duplicate detection in a meaningful way by comparing to instances of the same concept, e.g. transformers, with each other. It is not meaningful to compare two values without their relation to their correspondent instances as the same values appear often in databases without being wrong (e.g., many transformers will have the value "110" as a voltage level).

The task to assign data values to their correspondent instances so that such an instance becomes a meaningful representation of the real world entity is called object identification. In many databases, it is a difficult task to provide such an assignment as the databases' design often follows other design goals like reducing redundancy or being compatible with different software versions. In opposition to those systems, ontologies like the CIM provide a conceptualized view on the domain so that the data schema itself solves the object identification problem. Algorithms for detecting wrong data perform optimally on data that is described in such a way so that the CIM provides an excellent basis for data quality management.

It should be pointed out that while speaking of conceptualization we do not necessarily refer to an OWL ontology that uses all semantical constructs of e.g. OWL 2.0 to ensure its consistency and the consistency of the data of its instances. We rather use the term ontology in the data quality management context as the conceptualized view as discussed above, as the identification of incorrect, inconsistent, missing, outdated, and multiple representation of data is realized by numeric algorithms. The idea behind that is to construct a numeric metamodel for each ontology's concept that holds the information necessary to detect wrong data. Therefore, we avoid several problems that OWL and its open world assumption holds when it comes to the formulation of certain restriction like e.g. the need of existence of certain values.

Seamless Metadata Annotation

Data quality management makes intensive use of metadata annotation. We will give two examples of such tasks and conclude that the RDF-serialization of the CIM is very well suited for data quality management's metadata annotations.

The first example shows the necessity to annotate data at schema level. Beyond the already discussed need for a conceptualized view on data, data quality management also needs information about the data that a conceptualized view cannot deliver. An example are the scales of measurement of primitive data types as the way data is preprocessed for data quality management depends on that information. Therefore concepts are delivered by our own data quality management ontology that allow making statements like "The voltage level of transformers are interval scaled." which interact directly with the CIM's concepts. Ontologies are designed for such interactions contrary to e.g. relational database management systems so that they provide on optimal choice for data quality management.

The second example shows an annotation at instance level. Statements about data quality themselves are metadata as the state an estimation about wrong or correct data. Such a statement could be "The voltage level of the transformer with the name "Transformer X" seems to be wrong.". The developed data quality management ontology also provides concepts to make such statements about instances of CIM concepts. It shall be pointed out that RDF supports making statements about both concepts and instances optimally.

We have given two examples of different kinds of metadata annotations: One where statements were made on CIM's concepts and one where the annotations applied to instances of CIM's concepts. As the CIM is used in its RDF-serialization both use cases are supported optimally and suits the purpose as basis for data quality management's metadata annotation demands very well. The concepts to formulate those statements are defined in a data quality ontology provided by us.

Case Study: Data Quality Management for Utilities

The case study presented in this subsection shows a real world example where the methodology was applied to an enterprises database management system. We will explain the execution of the methodology's steps by examples and underline the support by the tool.

Introducing VDE and WDE

Our methodology for data quality management for the utility domain is called "VDE" ("Vorgehensmodell zum Datenqualitätsmanagement für Unternehmen der Energiewirtschaft" ~ "Methodology for data quality management for enterprises of the utility domain") and consists of five consecutive steps. Those steps are explained and accompanied by an example in the next subsection. It shall by pointed out that those steps are to be executed consecutively but whenever the outcome of one step is not sufficient for fulfilling the following steps backwards are allowed for improving the outcome similar as in the waterfall model for software development.

VDE is accompanied by WDE ("Werkzeug zur Unterstützung VDEs" ~ "Supporting tool for VDE"), a tool that provides either support for executing VDE's steps or fully automates them. In the following subsection, we will show how WDE fulfills its tasks.

Example Application of VDE and WDE

We will show an example application of how VDE with its supporting tool WDE is used to manage the data quality of a utility's data base management system. The provided use case is a real world example supported by the EWE AG (please visit http://www.ewe.de/). As we are not allowed to show details regarding the enterprise's data, their data schemas, or the outcome of the data quality evaluations, we will provide the description of the methodology's steps sufficiently anonymously.

1. Data selection: A domain expert has to make a selection of data that has to be integrated in the process of data quality management. This means to identify the specific databases of the distributed information system of a utility in question and its subsets that are to be analyzed. Of course, a first attempt could be to integrate all data into such a management, but as data quality management is costly it should be carefully evaluated which data needs data quality evaluation the most.

In our use case, we decided to integrate the data of the concepts "Substation", "Bay", "Switch", "ACLineSegment", and their "Location" and "Asset" information.

2. Mapping original database schemas on CIM concepts: As described above the conceptualized view and the data model provided by CIM respectively by RDF has many advantages for a data quality management approach. We therefore provide a possibility for mapping e.g. schemas of relational database management systems on the CIM. We use a technique named "D2RQ" which is both a mapping language and a tool that executes those mapping instructions. (Bizer & Seaborne, 2004) provide D2RQ.

Figure 13 shows a sample of such mapping instructions. The sample describes the mapping of the CIM concepts "Location" and "GmlPosition", where the further has a property to the latter and the latter has two literals, "GmlPosition.xPosition" and "GmlPosition.xPosition".

This step can be missed out if the data to be taken into account already exists in its CIM representation.

3. Providing necessary data annotations: As already discussed above, the conceptual view of the CIM is beneficial for data quality management, but further information about the data is needed for configuration of the data quality algorithms. Such information is the scales of measurements of the primitive data types.

Figure 14 shows such annotations, where both the properties "Asset.installationDate" and "Asset.statusDate" of the concept "EquipmentAsset" are marked as interval scaled.

Figure 13. Sample of mapping instructions for mapping a relational database management schema on the CIM

```
<?xml version="1.0" encoding="UTF-8"?>
<rdf:RDF
    xmlns:rdf="http://www.w3.org/1999/02/22-rdf-syntax-ns#"
    xmlns:rdfs="http://www.w3.org/2000/01/rdf-schema#"
    xmlns:cim="http://iec.ch/TC57/1999/rdf-schema-extensions-19990926#"
    xmlns:map="http://www.informatik.uni-oldenburg.de/dems/mapping#"
    xmlns:d2rq="http://www.wiwiss.fu-berlin.de/suhl/bizer/D2RQ/0.1#">

    <d2rq:ClassMap rdf:about="http://www.informatik.uni-oldenburg.de/dems/mapping#ClassMap_Location">
        <d2rq:uriPattern rdf:datatype="http://www.w3.org/2001/XMLSchema#string">http://iec.ch/TC57/1999/rdf-schema-extensions-19990926#Location_@@A.XKOORDINATE@@_@@A.YKOORDINATE@@</d2rq:uriPattern>
        <d2rq:class rdf:resource="http://iec.ch/TC57/1999/rdf-schema-extensions-19990926#Location"/>
    </d2rq:ClassMap>
    <d2rq:ClassMap rdf:about="http://www.informatik.uni-oldenburg.de/dems/mapping#ClassMap_GmlPosition">
        <d2rq:uriPattern rdf:datatype="http://www.w3.org/2001/XMLSchema#string">http://iec.ch/TC57/1999/rdf-schema-extensions-19990926#GmlPosition_@@A.XKOORDINATE@@_@@A.YKOORDINATE@@</d2rq:uriPattern>
        <d2rq:class rdf:resource="http://iec.ch/TC57/1999/rdf-schema-extensions-19990926#GmlPosition"/>
    </d2rq:ClassMap>

    <d2rq:PropertyBridge rdf:about="http://www.informatik.uni-oldenburg.de/dems/mapping#PropertyBridge_Location_Location_GmlPositions">
        <d2rq:belongsToClassMap rdf:resource="http://www.informatik.uni-oldenburg.de/dems/mapping#ClassMap_Location"/>
        <d2rq:property rdf:resource="http://iec.ch/TC57/1999/rdf-schema-extensions-19990926#Location.GmlPositions"/>
        <d2rq:refersToClassMap rdf:resource="http://www.informatik.uni-oldenburg.de/dems/mapping#ClassMap_GmlPosition"/>
    </d2rq:PropertyBridge>
    <d2rq:PropertyBridge rdf:about="http://www.informatik.uni-oldenburg.de/dems/mapping#PropertyBridge_GmlPosition_GmlPosition_xPosition">
        <d2rq:belongsToClassMap rdf:resource="http://www.informatik.uni-oldenburg.de/dems/mapping#ClassMap_GmlPosition"/>
        <d2rq:property rdf:resource="http://iec.ch/TC57/1999/rdf-schema-extensions-19990926#GmlPosition.xPosition"/>
        <d2rq:column rdf:datatype="http://www.w3.org/2001/XMLSchema#string">A.XKOORDINATE</d2rq:column>
    </d2rq:PropertyBridge>
    <d2rq:PropertyBridge rdf:about="http://www.informatik.uni-oldenburg.de/dems/mapping#PropertyBridge_GmlPosition_GmlPosition_yPosition">
        <d2rq:belongsToClassMap rdf:resource="http://www.informatik.uni-oldenburg.de/dems/mapping#ClassMap_GmlPosition"/>
        <d2rq:property rdf:resource="http://iec.ch/TC57/1999/rdf-schema-extensions-19990926#GmlPosition.yPosition"/>
        <d2rq:column rdf:datatype="http://www.w3.org/2001/XMLSchema#string">A.YKOORDINATE</d2rq:column>
    </d2rq:PropertyBridge>
</rdf:RDF>
```

4. Execution of data quality management and compilation of data quality reports: In addition to the annotations shown above there is also the necessity to label correct instances for every concept that was selected in the first step. The labeled data is used for training classifiers that are used to identify incorrect, inconsistent, and missing data as well as duplicates.

The forth step is executed automatically and the data quality reports contain data quality estimations on different aggregate levels: At the lowest level, the suspected

Figure 14. Sample of data annotations showing the annotations of scales of measurement

```
<?xml version="1.0" encoding="UTF-8"?>
<rdf:RDF
    xmlns:rdfs="http://www.w3.org/2000/01/rdf-schema#"
    xmlns:cim="http://iec.ch/TC57/1999/rdf-schema-extensions-19990926#"
    xmlns:rdf="http://www.w3.org/1999/02/22-rdf-syntax-ns#"
    xmlns:dqm="http://www.informatik.uni-oldenburg.de/dems/dataquality#">

    <rdfs:Class rdf:about="http://iec.ch/TC57/1999/rdf-schema-extensions-19990926#EquipmentAsset"/>

    <rdf:Property rdf:about="http://iec.ch/TC57/1999/rdf-schema-extensions-19990926#Asset.installationDate">
        <rdfs:domain rdf:resource="http://iec.ch/TC57/1999/rdf-schema-extensions-19990926#EquipmentAsset"/>
        <rdfs:range rdf:resource="http://www.w3.org/2000/01/rdf-schema#Literal"/>
    </rdf:Property>
    <dqm:PropertyAnnotation rdf:about="http://www.informatik.uni-oldenburg.de/dems/dataquality#PropertyAnnotation_Asset_installationDate">
        <dqm:hasProperty rdf:resource="http://iec.ch/TC57/1999/rdf-schema-extensions-19990926#Asset.installationDate"/>
        <dqm:isMeasurementTypeOf rdf:resource="http://www.informatik.uni-oldenburg.de/dems/dataquality#IntervalType"/>
        <dqm:belongsToClass rdf:resource="http://iec.ch/TC57/1999/rdf-schema-extensions-19990926#EquipmentAsset"/>
    </dqm:PropertyAnnotation>

    <rdf:Property rdf:about="http://iec.ch/TC57/1999/rdf-schema-extensions-19990926#Asset.statusDate">
        <rdfs:domain rdf:resource="http://iec.ch/TC57/1999/rdf-schema-extensions-19990926#EquipmentAsset"/>
        <rdfs:range rdf:resource="http://www.w3.org/2000/01/rdf-schema#Literal"/>
    </rdf:Property>
    <dqm:PropertyAnnotation rdf:about="http://www.informatik.uni-oldenburg.de/dems/dataquality#PropertyAnnotation_Asset_statusDate">
        <dqm:hasProperty rdf:resource="http://iec.ch/TC57/1999/rdf-schema-extensions-19990926#Asset.statusDate"/>
        <dqm:isMeasurementTypeOf rdf:resource="http://www.informatik.uni-oldenburg.de/dems/dataquality#IntervalType"/>
        <dqm:belongsToClass rdf:resource="http://iec.ch/TC57/1999/rdf-schema-extensions-19990926#EquipmentAsset"/>
    </dqm:PropertyAnnotation>
</rdf:RDF>
```

errors themselves are marked so that lists of errors can be compiled to be corrected by domain experts. At the next level, the ratio between correct and wrong instances is given per concepts. By these listings, ranges with increased data error rates can be identified. The final level is the data quality dimensions, namely correctness, completeness, consistency, and timeliness, where correctness contains the absence of duplicates. The data quality dimensions are defined by the data quality ontology by relating the outcome of the data quality algorithms to the data quality dimensions. Therefore it is possible to adapt the data quality reports by adjusting the ontology accordingly, e.g. making "absence of duplicates" a data quality dimension on its own if this characteristic is especially needful in the respective context.

5. Analysis of data quality reports: Those reports can be used to make decisions like deciding which of several databases should be the leading one or deciding whether money spent to increase the data quality of an enterprise's databases had its positive influence.

It should be pointed out that also the data quality management itself should be evaluated. As the outcome of the data quality management depends on e.g. the labeled data mentioned in step four, it is necessary to decide whether the data quality reports are correct. In case of bad performance the third step needs to be adjusted to improve the data quality management's performance as we already mentioned the steps backwards.

Evaluation and Recommendations for Data Quality Management for Utilities

The use case presented in the previous subsection allows us to draw conclusions regarding the quality of VDE with WDE's support. (Frank, 2006) defines criteria for evaluating methodologies that we will use in the following. Those criteria are divided into four perspectives, namely the economical perspective, the user perspective, the design perspective, and the epistemological perspective.

*   Economical perspective: VDE is designed to be applied in enterprises of the utility domain, as it uses the CIM as a domain ontology with its respective vocabulary and little configuration as shown in the steps one to three, so that the costs for applying the methodology are little. Therefore, the ratio between costs and benefit can be evaluated positively.
*   User perspective: On the one hand, both VDE and WDE are accompanied by a scientific work that explains motivation, design, and evaluation in detail. These aspects can be evaluated positively. On the other hand, VDE was only

applied on a copy of a live system, so that the acceptance by the users cannot be evaluated. It is not possible to except that users have difficulties with accepting the outcome of a data quality evaluation if its evidence them worse success than other users.

- Design perspective: The design decisions for VDE and WDE are discussed in detail in the accompanied work. Furthermore, the methodology is motivated by real world challenges and the vocabulary used for explanation fits the target audience. The design perspective can therefore be evaluated positively.
- Epistemological perspective: A methodology solves a class of problems and not only a specific one; it can be understood as a kind of scientific theory. Considering this, VDE has to be evaluated and critically questioned. As VDE and WDE are accompanied by a scientific work, the epistemological perspective is covered well.

Overall, VDE is a well fitting approach for the data quality needs for enterprises of the utility domain with its accompanied tool WDE that allows fast setup and quick generations of data quality reports. Especially the CIM proved to be an excellent basis for data quality management approaches.

REFERENCES

Batini, C., & Scannapieco, M. (2006). *Data quality*. Springer-Verlag.

Bizer, C., & Seaborne, A. (2004). *D2RQ -treating non-RDF databases as virtual RDF graphs*. Paper presented at the 3rd International Semantic Web Conference (ISWC2004), Hiroshima, Japan.

De Amicis, F., & Batini, C. (2004). A methodology for data quality assessment on financial data. In *Studies in communication sciences* (pp. 115-136).

Electropedia, I. E. C. (2008). Retrieved from http://www.electropedia.org.

European Parliament and the Council (2003). *Directive 2003/54/EU of the European Parliament and of the Council of 26 June 2003 concerning common rules for the internal market in electricity and repealing Directive 96/92/EC.*

Euzenat, S. (2007). *Ontology matching*. Heidelberg: Springer Verlag.

Frank, U. (2006). *Evaluation of reference models*. In P. Fettke, & P. Loos (Eds.), *Reference modeling for business systems analysis* (pp. 118-140). Idea Group.

Hepp, M. (2007). Possible ontologies: How reality constrains the development of relevant ontologies. *IEEE Internet Computing, 11*(1), 90–96. doi:10.1109/MIC.2007.20

Hepp; M. (2004). *OntoMeter: Metrics for ontologies.* 1st European Semantic Web Symposium (ESWS2004), Heraklion, Greece, May 10-12.

Hevner, A. R., March, S. T., Park, J., & Ram, S. (2004). Design science research in information systems. *Management Information Systems Quarterly, 28*(1), 75–105.

Hinrichs, H. (2002). *Datenqualitätsmanagement in data warehouse-systemen.* Phd thesis, University of Oldenburg, Germany.

Hong Hai, D. (2006). *Schema matching and mapping-based data integration: Architecture, approaches and evolution.* VDM Verlag Dr. Müller.

IEC - International Electrotechnical Commission. (2003). *IEC 61970-301: Energy management system application program interface (EMS-API) – Part 301: Common Information Model (CIM) Base.* International Electrotechnical Commission.

Kostic, T., Frei, C., Preiss, O., & Kezunovic, M. (2004). *Scenarios for data exchange using standards IEC 61970 and IEC 61850.* Cigre Paris 2004. IEEE Publishing.

OFFIS. (2008). *Ontologies for the utility domain.* Retrieved from http://www.offis.de/energie/ontologies

Robinson, G. (2002). Key standards for utility enterprise application integration (EAI). In *Proceedings of the DistribuTech 2002 Miami.* Pennwell.

Shvaiko (2006). *An API for ontology alignment* (Version 2.1).

Uslar, M. (2006). The common information model for utilities: An introduction and outlook on future applications. In R. Eckstein & R. Tolksdorf (Eds.), *Proceedings of the XML-Days 2006 in Berlin, XML-clearinghouse.de* (pp.135-148).

Uslar, M. (2008). Ontology-based Integration of IEC TC 57 Standards. In *Proceedings of the I-ESA 2008 Conference on Interoperability for Enterprise Systems and Applications, Fraunhofer IPK, Berlin.*

Uslar, M., et al. (2009). Untersuchung des Normungsumfeldes zum BMWi-Förderschwerpunkt. *e-Energy – IKT-basiertes Energiesystem der Zukunft.* Ministry of Economics, Germany.

Uslar, M., & Dahlem, N. (2006). Semantic Web technologies for power grid management. In R. Koschke, O. Herzog, K.-H. Rödiger & M. Ronthaler (Eds.), *Informatik 2007: Informatik trifft Logistik, Band 1, Beiträge der 37. Jahrestagung der Gesellschaft für Informatik e.V. (GI) 24.-27. September 2007.* In Bremen, 27(1), Gesellschaft für Informatik, Bonn, Köllen Verlag.

Uslar, Streekmann & Abels (2007). MDA-basierte Kopplung heterogener Informationssysteme im EVU-Sektor - ein Framework. In A. Oberweis, C. Weinhardt, H. Gimpel, A. Koschmider & V. Pankratius (Eds.), *eOrganisation: Service-, Prozess-, Market-Engineering*, 8. Internationale Tagung Wirtschaftsinformatik, 2, Universitätsverlag Karlsruhe.

Chapter 19
Streamlining Semantic Integration Systems

Yannis Kalfoglou
Ricoh Europe Plc, UK

Bo Hu
SAP Research CEC Belfast, UK

EXECUTIVE SUMMARY

Yannis Kalfoglou and Bo Hu argue for the use of a streamlined approach to integrate semantic integration systems. The authors elaborate on the abundance and diversity of semantic integration solutions and how this impairs strict engineering practice and ease of application. The versatile and dynamic nature of these solutions comes at a price: they are not working in sync with each other neither is it easy to align them. Rather, they work as standalone systems often leading to diverse and sometimes incompatible results. Hence the irony that we might need to address the interoperability issue of tools tackling information interoperability. Kalfoglou and Hu also report on an exemplar case from the field of ontology mapping where systems that used seemingly similar integration algorithms and data, yield different results which are arbitrary formatted and annotated making interpretation and reuse of the results difficult. This makes it difficult to apply semantic integration solutions in a principled manner. The authors argue for a holistic approach to streamline and glue together different integration systems and algorithms. This will bring uniformity of results and effective application of the semantic integration solutions.

DOI: 10.4018/978-1-4666-2618-8.ch019

If the proposed streamlining respects design principles of the underlying systems, then the engineers will have maximum configuration power and tune the streamlined systems in order to get uniform and well understood results. The authors propose a framework for building such streamlined system based on engineering principles and an exemplar, purpose built system, CROSI Mapping System (CMS), which targets the problem of ontology mapping.

THE NECESSITY FOR SEMANTIC INTEROPERABILITY

"We need interoperable systems."

Time has long gone when manufacturers designed and assembled artefacts as stand-alone objects, ready to be used for whatever purpose they had been originally conceived. The necessity for more and more complex devices and the industrialisation/standardisation of manufacturing processes have led to the engineering of very specialised components that can be reused for a variety of component-based systems, which neither have been designed nor assembled by a sole manufacturer and for a unique purpose.

Analogously, in our *information age*, a similar phenomenon has occurred to the ``manufacturing'' of information technology (IT) artefacts. Originally, software applications, databases, and expert systems were all designed and constructed by a dedicated group of software or knowledge engineers who had overall control of the entire lifecycle of IT artefacts. But this time has gone too, as software engineering praxis is shifting from the implementation of custom-made, stand-alone systems to component-based software engineering (COTS, ERP, etc.). Databases are gradually deployed in distributed architectures and subsequently federated, and knowledge-based systems are built by reusing more and more previously constructed knowledge bases and inference engines. A compelling example on this front is SAP Business One™, which contains 14 core modules specialised in the immediate and long-term needs (e.g. customer relationship management, finance, purchasing, etc.) of small or medium-sized enterprises (SMEs). Individual SMEs then decide which fields of business activity they want to support and align the relatively independent modules into an integral framework. While accessing a raft of functionalities through one seemingly unified interface, the users normally are not aware of the underlying integration effort that seamlessly juxtaposes heterogeneous data from different units of an organisation and different business policies.

Moreover, the World Wide Web, and its ambitious extension the Semantic Web, has brought us an unprecedented global distribution of information in the form of hypertext documents, online databases, open-source code, terminological repositories (like for example Wikitionary), web services, blogs, etc., all of which continually challenge the traditional role of IT in our society. As a result, the distributed nature of IT systems has experienced a dramatic explosion with major IT suppliers starting to provide on demand web-based services (empowered by Service Oriented Architectures) instead of all-in-one boxed products and localised solutions (fine-tuned against the legal system, currency, and accountancy policy in each country) instead of universal solutions.

But in contrast to traditional industrial manufacturing and composition of artefacts, the composition and interaction of IT components at the level of distribution on the Web is still at its infancy, and we are just grasping the scope of this endeavour: successful IT component interoperability beyond basic syntactic communication is very hard. Unlike with industrial manufacturing, our era's basic commodity around which all IT technology is evolving, namely *information*, is not yet well understood. While industrial and civil engineers know how to apply well-established mathematical models to derive an artefact's characteristics from the physical properties of its components, software engineers and knowledge workers lack the machinery that will enable them to do the same with information assets. The problem with understanding information is that we need ways with which we can reveal, expose and communicate the meaning (semantics) of information. But this has eluded any mechanistic approach to interoperability. Putting together different databases has proved to be successful only for closed environments and under very strong assumptions; the same holds for distributed artificial intelligence applications and interaction in multi-agent systems. While we were staying on entirely syntactic issues, it has been relatively easy to achieve component interoperability. For example, in the case of the Web, standardisation of hypertext representation using HTML, of hypertext location by means of URL/URIs, and of data transfer protocol via HTTP has boosted it to the great success it is today. But as soon as we try to deal with the meaning of information, looking for intelligent management of the information available on the (Semantic) Web, interoperability becomes a hard task.

The crux of the problem lies in the *heterogeneity* which is naturally inherited in independently constructed information systems. As most of the interoperability tasks faced today in distributed IT environments deal with integration of legacy and proprietary systems, the quest of engineers is to devise effective and practical solutions that leverage the existing assets. This is the state-of-the-practice as we are in financially challenging times and re-usability of existing assets, maximising their value and efficiency is a top priority from a cost-reduction perspective.

Solutions to the problem of heterogeneity are commonly dubbed, *integration* at a system level or *interoperability* at a task level. When the solution takes into account the "meaning" of information that needs to be integrated or used in support of interoperability, we often further refine the terminology as semantic integration or semantic interoperability. For example, a database schema matching algorithm that uses purely syntactic features of the schema (like table/column names) is not semantic whereas an ontology alignment algorithm that takes into account the codified meaning of ontology constructs that need to be aligned, it is. These comparisons are simplified views of what has become a versatile and dynamic mix of techniques and algorithms borrowed from a multitude of domains – like information retrieval, artificial intelligence, semantic web, database management – with a common goal: utilising as much semantic information as feasibly possible to enhance and improve the integration process of heterogeneous systems.

But, the versatile and dynamic nature of these solutions comes at a price: semantic integration solutions are available in abundance in both academic and commercial settings[1i]; however, these solutions are not working in sync with each other neither is it easy to align them. Rather, they work as standalone systems often leading to diverse and sometimes incompatible results leading to the irony that we might need to address the interoperability issue of tools tackling information interoperability. For example, in (Kalfoglou and Hu, 2006) the authors report an exemplar case from the field of ontology mapping where systems that used seemingly similar integration algorithms and data, yield different results which are arbitrary formatted and annotated making interpretation and reuse of the results difficult. This makes it difficult to apply semantic integration solutions in a principled manner.

One way to alleviate this problem is to apply a holistic approach and *streamline* by gluing together different integration systems and algorithms. This will bring uniformity of results and effective application of the semantic integration solutions. If the proposed streamlining respects design principles of the underlying systems, then the engineers will have maximum configuration power and tune the streamlined systems in order to get uniform and well understood results. This is the proposal we put forward in this work. Our working prototype is described in sections 3 and 4. Initially though, in the next section, we will provide a brief account on the historical context of semantic integration solutions with regards to their origins, state-of-practice and modern trends.

HISTORICAL CONTEXT AND TECHNOLOGY LANDSCAPE

Early work to tackle the semantic heterogeneity problem emerged in the eighties from the database community. In particular, the notion of federated databases where schemata are treated globally and exchanged between designers and among disparate systems, informed the requirements for techniques which assist database administrators to do schema matching.

Most of these techniques were based on syntactic features of the schemata used, and employed a variety of heuristics to kick off similarity measure algorithms, borrowed from the information retrieval community. A dominant technique has been the use of correspondence values, typically in the range 0..1, which supposedly captures the intended overlap of two mapped elements. These approaches had their deficiencies though, as it was often observed that schemata with virtually similar syntactic elements were describing different real world concepts. The crux of the problem was the lack of semantic information carried by the designated database schema elements. This information is important for the validity of the proposed mapping which made verification check of the proposed mappings by a human user, a necessity. This is one of the reasons why these approaches could not scale up.

In the mid to late nineties, more complex and richer knowledge representation models, namely ontologies, became popular and the advent of a global infrastructure for sharing semantics, the Semantic Web, necessitated the need to share ontologies. Sharing ontologies though presupposes some mapping between heterogeneous ontologies. Ontology mapping practice employs a variety of techniques: use of syntactic similarity, correspondence values (though sometimes more elaborated than a numerical range 0..1), and more advanced semantically rich techniques, mainly due to the knowledge representation origin of ontologies. For example, there are ontology mapping systems that exploit the hierarchical lattice found in ontology structures (partially ordered lattices), take advantage of ontology formalisms which allow certain semantic information to be attached to a particular element (from formal axioms to informal textual descriptions), and some use the underlying deductive mechanism to infer mappings (for example, use of Description Logics reasoning).

A popular technique has been the use of instance information. As both ontologies and database schemata are expected to be instantiated in the application domain (either directly with declared ontology instances or indirectly with an instantiated knowledge base that adheres to the ontology or a database that adheres to the schema).

Recently, the use of machine learning for computing correspondences has gain popularity. The underlying reason for that is that ontology or database schema mapping is, nowadays, an expensive endeavour. The proliferation of ontologies on the (Semantic) Web and the sheer number of database schemata call for automated support to compute correspondences in acceptable time. It appears that machine learning could be a solution to the problem of automating the matching task but there are some open issues, especially with regards to sourcing and training the background data used to feed the learning algorithms.

Finally, the use of heuristics was always an easily applicable and preferable choice for engineers. This is not a surprise to everyone who has attempted to do mapping: heuristics are cheap to develop, easy to deploy, and support automation. However, the main problem with heuristics is that they are easily defeasible. Even well-crafted heuristics that work for a particular case can fail in similar situations. Attempts to solve this problem go beyond the use of syntactic features, linguistic clues, and structural similarities and use as much semantic information as possible when building heuristics. They use the intended meaning of the concepts to be mapped. However, this is not always feasible as semantics are often not captured in the underlying formalism and a human expert is needed to provide their precise meaning.

To motivate the importance of semantic integration, we briefly present some key application areas where semantic heterogeneity occurs and there is a need for resolving it. This is not an exhaustive list but merely an indication of the diversity for the application domain of semantic integration[2].

Database Schema Integration: ``Given a set of independently developed schemas, construct a global view." (Rahm and Bernstein, 2001). The schemata often have different structure and the process of integration aims to unify matching elements. Matching is a whole field in its own right and is the core operation of schema integration.

Data warehouses: this a variation of the schema integration where the data sources are integrated into a data warehouse: "A data warehouse is a decision support database that is extracted from a set of data sources. The extraction process requires transforming data from the source format into the warehouse format." [Kalfoglou and Schorlemmer, 2003) These transformations could be assisted by database schema matching operations.

E-Commerce: Trading partners frequently exchange messages that describe business transactions. As each trading partner uses its own message format, this creates the problem of heterogeneity. That is, message formats may differ in their syntax (EDI structured, XML formatted, etc.) or use different message schemata. To enable systems to exchange messages, application developers need to convert messages between the formats required by different trading partners.

Semantic Query Processing: ``A user specifies the output of a query (e.g., the SELECT clause in SQL), and the system figures out how to produce that output (e.g., by determining the FROM and WHERE clause on SQL)' (Kalfoglou and Schorlemmer, 2003). The heterogeneity arises when the user specifies the query output in terms which are different from those used in the schema.

Ontology Integration (or Merging): Given two distinct, and independently developed ontologies, produce a fragment which captures the intersection of the original ontologies. This area is similar to that of schema integration but more difficult in nature due to the rich and complex knowledge representation structures found in ontologies.

Ontology Mapping: This is a subset of the previous area, mapping ontologies is a step towards integration and it is often the case that mapping ontologies is adequate for most interoperability scenarios on the Semantic Web.

Semantic Web Agents' Interoperability: A pre-requisite for Semantic Web agents to collaborate is their ability to understand and communicate their mental models. These are often model in the form of ontology and it is very likely to be distinct albeit modelling the same universe of discourse. Mapping their ontologies is a major area of interest where automated and scalable solutions are also sought due to the sheer size of agents involved in these scenarios.

In the next section we present the underlying principles for a unifying integration framework that aims to streamline and leverage on different integration systems.

SEMANTIC INTENSITY SPECTRUM

We observe a common trend for semantic integration practitioners to progress from semantically-poor to semantically-rich solutions. We therefore, use the metaphor of *semantic richness* to classify integration techniques along a *semantic intensity spectrum*. We mark several interim points to address string similarity, structure, context, extension, and intension awareness as different layers of semantic intensity (see Figure 1)

Figure 1.

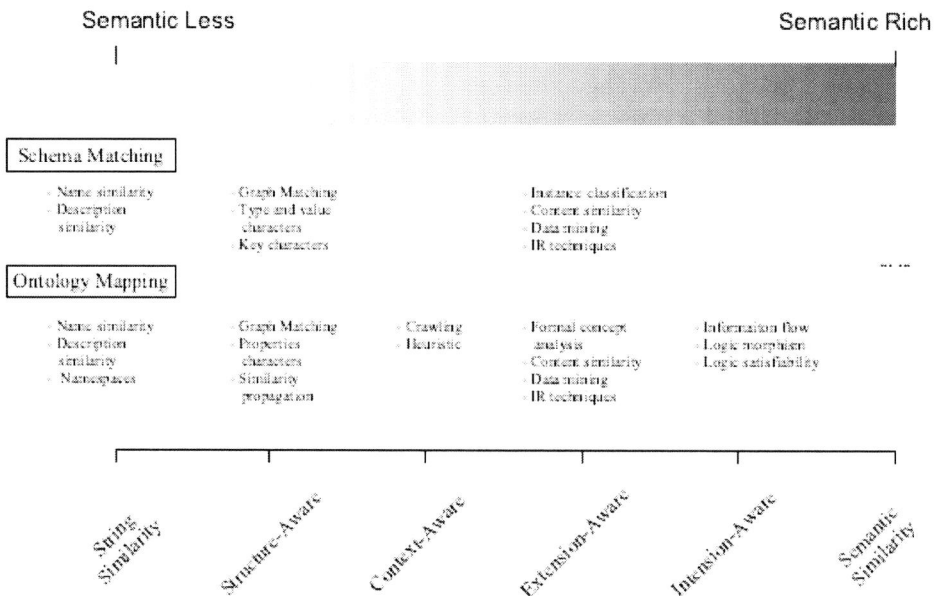

String Similarity: occupying the semantically-poor end of the spectrum, compares names of elements from different semantic models. A refinement of such techniques enhances the result by taking into account the textual descriptions (a.k.a., comments) associated with concepts and properties. These techniques are based on the assumption that concepts and properties names representing semantic similarity will have similar syntactic features. A string matcher usually first normalises the input string of names and/or descriptions via stemming and tokenisation. In the simplest form, the equality of tokens will be obtained and combined to give a score of the equality for the whole string. In a slightly more complicated form, similarity of two strings is computed by evaluating their substrings, edit distance, etc. Nowadays, pure string similarity measures are seldom used in practice, but rather in combination with external resources, like user-defined lexica and/or dictionaries.

Linguistic Similarity: at a position very close to the semantically-poor end, is an example of string similarity measures blended with some sense of semantics. For instance, pronunciation and soundex are taken into account to enhance the similarity when based purely on strings. Also, synonyms and hypernyms will be considered based on generic and/or domain-specific thesauri, e.g. WordNet, Dublin Core[3]. In many cases, user-defined name matches are often treated as useful resources. For lengthy descriptions, information retrieval techniques can be applied to compare and score similarities. As a basic group of matching techniques, linguistics usually are the initial step to suggest a set of raw mappings that other matchers can work with.

Structure-aware: refers to approaches that take into account the structural layout of ontologies and schemata. Going beyond matching names (strings), structural similarity considers the entire underlying structure. That is, when comparing ontologies there is a hierarchical, partially ordered lattice where ontology classes are laid out. Similarly, database schemata also use a lattice of connections between tables and classes, but not necessarily in a hierarchical fashion. Structure-aware techniques are seldom used solely in real-life mapping and matching applications. For instance, *PromptDiff* (Noy and Musen, 2002) leverages a series of heuristics to identify differences between two versions of ontology. Amongst the heuristics used are those based on structure information, e.g. the ``single unmatched sibling'' heuristic rule states that if two nodes, N1 and N2 are matching and each of them has exactly one unmatched child, N(C1) and N(C2), respectively, then N(C1) and N(C2) match.

In pure structural matching techniques, ontologies and schemata are transformed into trees with labelled nodes, thus matching is equivalent to matching vertices of the source graph with those of the targeted one. Similarity between two such graphs, G1 and G2 is computed by finding a subgraph of G2 that is *isomorphic* to G1 or vice versa. Although nodes of such graphs are labelled, their linguistic features rarely play a significant role in computing the similarity. Furthermore, labels of

Figure 2.

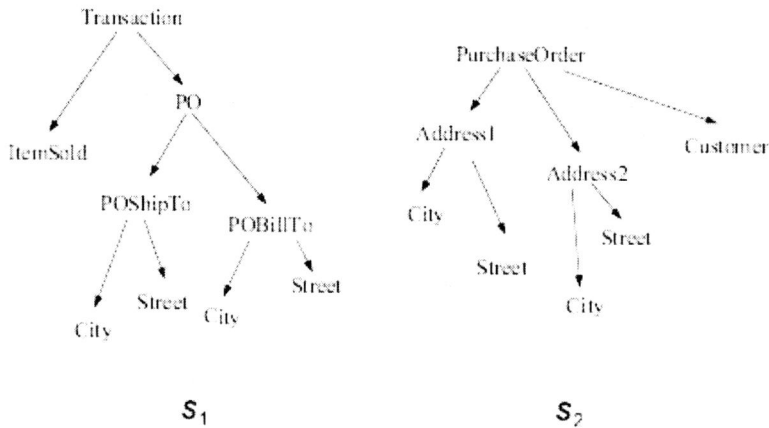

edges are normally ignored with the assumption that only one type of relation holds between connected nodes. For instance, suppose we have two fragments of e-Commerce schemata, one describing an arbitrary Transaction and the other one a PurchaseOrder (see Figure 2). Graph's isomorphism then gives us, among other possible mappings: PO ↔ PurchaseOrder, POShipTo ↔ Address1, and POBillTo ↔ Address2.

Analogous to pure *string similarity* methods, structure matching approaches, such as the one presented in (Wang et. al., 1994) are not common in practice, but they are usually enhanced with other matching techniques. We deliberately use the notion of *structure similarity* in a broad sense in order to accommodate many relevant methods that relate to each other, and which could, and sometimes are used in such a combined fashion.

Typically, algorithms that do structure to structure comparison use the properties found in these structures (transitivity, cardinality, symmetry, etc) as well as their tree form similarity (for example, similar branches). Other algorithms use information at the nodes other than label, for example, attributes such as datatype, property range and property domain, etc, (Milo and Zohar, 1998). These are used as if they were labels (strings) with the range of methods discussed above available for comparing them.

Context-aware: in many cases there are a variety of relations among concepts or schema elements which makes it necessary to differentiate distinct types of connections among nodes. This gives rise to a family of matching techniques which are more semantically rich than *structure similarity* ones.

Both database schema and ontology can be transferred into a labelled directed graph of which nodes could be elements and concepts, and edges, could be attributes and properties, respectively, with the names of attributes and properties as labels. A *context* defined in graph jargon, is an arbitrary node together with nodes that are connected to it via particular types of edges which at the same time satisfy certain criteria, e.g., a threshold of the length of paths.

Sometimes, *context-aware* approaches group and weigh the edges from and to a node to impose a view of the domain of discourse from the end user perspective. Depending on whether importing external resources is allowed, there are two types of context-awareness.

In the simplest form, algorithms that compare nodes from two schemata also traverse downwards several layers along the direction of edges from the node under consideration, or upwards against the direction of edges to the node under consideration. All the visited nodes, together with the information about edges connecting them (taxonomic relationships like part-of, subclass-of, etc) are evaluated as a whole to infer further mappings between nodes in the context. For instance, in Figure 3, the issue of whether "Norway" in S1 corresponds to "Norway" in S2 is evaluated together with the information provided by their ancestors along the part-of relationship path. It is evident that these two nodes do not match, as ``Norway" in S1 refers to a map of this country while ``Norway" in S2 refers to the country itself.

Anchor-Prompt (Noy et. al., 2001) is an example of exploiting context information in detecting and refining mappings between ontologies. If one sees ontologies as labelled graphs with nodes as concepts and edges as hierarchical relationships (superclass/subclass) and properties that have concepts as their domains and ranges, Anchor-Prompt can be understood as follows: it takes as input a set of mapping nodes, referred to as ``anchors", and traverses the paths of the same sorts (with the same labels) between the anchors.

Similar Concepts are Identified by Comparing the Nodes Along these Paths

Similarity flooding (Melnik, 2002) is an example of a *context-aware* approach. An arbitrary schema S_n is first transformed into a directed labelled graph. The initial mappings between two schemata, S_1 and S_2, are obtained using certain mapping techniques, e.g., a simple string matcher comparing common prefixes and suffixes of literals, and captured to a Pairwise Connectivity Graph (PCG). Nodes of a PCG are elements from $S_1 x S_1$, denoted as $N_{S1 x S2}$. An edge labelled $a : (m \times k) \rightarrow (n \times l)$ where $(m, n \in S_1$ and $k, l \in S_2)$ of a PCG means that an a edge is present in the original schemata between m and n as well as k and l, i.e. $a : m \subset n; a : k \subset l$.

Figure 3.

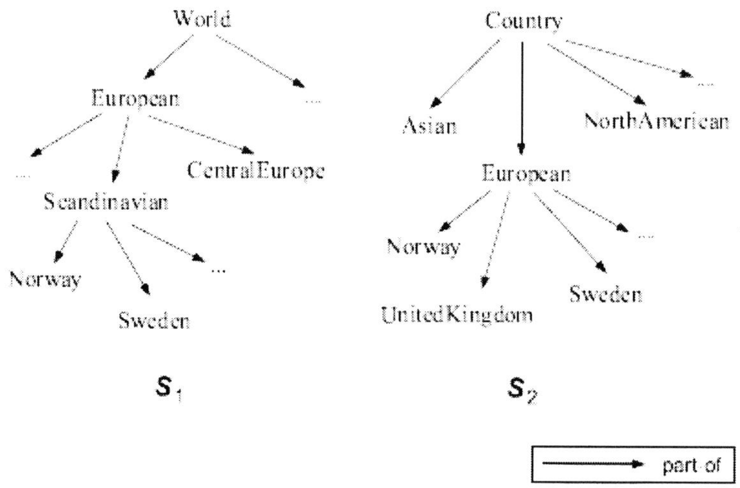

(a) "Norway" in different contexts

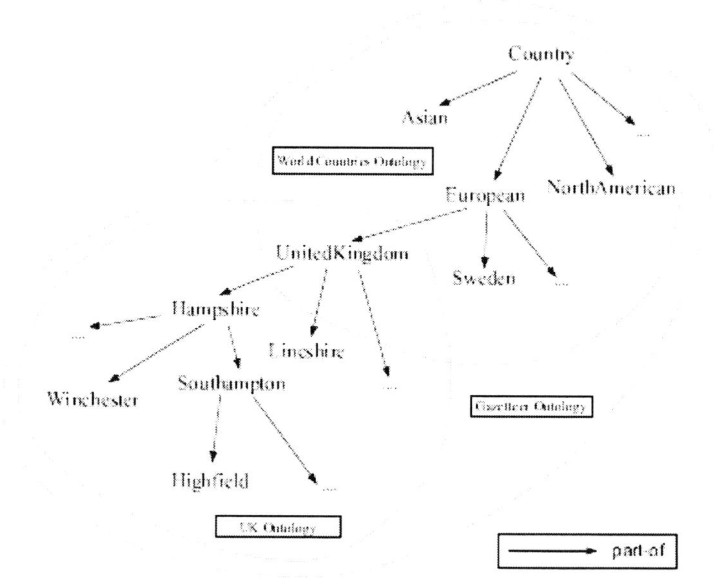

From a PCG, a similarity propagation graph is induced which assigns to each edge in the PCG a propagation coefficient to indicate the influence between nodes of the PCG. In other words, the weighted edges indicate how well the similarity of a given PCG node propagates to its neighbour. The accumulation of similarity is performed until a pre-set threshold is reached or terminated by the user after some maximal number of iterations. A series of filter methods are then adopted to reduce the size of the resultant mapping candidates and select the most plausible ones.

Following the same philosophy---similarity propagation, (Palopoli et. al., 2003) integrated multiple entity relationship (ER) schemata by using the following principle: similarity of schema elements depends on the similarity of elements in their vicinity (nearby elements influence match more than those farther away). ER schemata are first transformed into graphs with entities, relationships, and attributes as nodes. The similarity coefficient is initialised by standard thesauruses and re-evaluated based on the similarity of nodes in their corresponding vicinities.

With the use of *namespaces*, along comes another type of *context awareness*. As illustrated in Figure 3, "United Kingdom" belongs to both "World Countries Ontology" and "UK Ontology". Articulating these two ontologies summons the resolution of different namespaces that might involve string matchers in certain forms. An example of dealing with co-reference resolution of such namespaces is given in (Alani and Brewster, 2005).

Extension-aware: when a relatively complete set of instances can be obtained, semantics of a schema or ontology can be reflected through the way that instances are classified. A major assumption made by techniques belonging to this family is that instances with similar semantics might share features (Madhavan, 2003), therefore, an understanding of such common features can contribute to an approximate understanding of the semantics.

Formal Concept Analysis (FCA (Ganter and Wille, 1999)) is a representative of instance-aware approaches. FCA is a field of mathematics emerged in the nineties that builds upon lattice theory and the work of Ganter and Wille on the mathematisation of concept in the eighties. It is mostly suited for analysing instances and properties of entities (concepts) in a domain of interest. FCA consists of formal contexts and concept lattices. A formal context is a triple $K = \langle O, P, S \rangle$, where O is a set of objects, P is a set of attributes (or properties), and $S \subseteq O \times P$ is a relation that connects each object o with the attributes satisfied by o.

The intent (set of attributes belonging to an object) and the extent (set of objects having these attributes) are given formal definitions in (Ganter and Wille, 1999). A formal concept is a pair $\langle A, B \rangle$ consisting of an extent $A \subseteq B$ and an intent $B \subseteq P$, and these concepts are hierarchically ordered by inclusion of their extents. This partial order induces a complete lattice, the concept lattice of the context. FCA can be applied to semi-structured domains to assist in modelling with instances and properties in hierarchical, partially ordered lattices. This is the main structure most the mapping systems work with. Thus, FCA albeit not directly related to mapping, it is a versatile technology which could be used at the early stages of mapping for structuring a loosely defined domain. Data mining and information retrieval techniques are frequently exploited to winnowing away apparent discrepancy as well as discover the hidden correlations among instances. Some recent efforts along this line of research are presented in (Doan et. al., 2002) and (He and Chang, 2003).

Intension-aware: refers to the family of techniques that establish correlations between relations among extent and intent. Such approaches are particularly useful when it is impossible or impractical to obtain a complete set of instances to reflect the semantics.

Barwise and Seligman propose a mathematical theory, *Information Flow*, that aims at establishing the laws that govern the flow of information (Barwise and Seligman, 1997). It is a general theory that attempts to describe information flow in any kind of a distributed system. It is based on the understanding that information flow results from regularities in a distributed system, and that it is by virtue of regularities among the connections that information of some components of a system carries information of other components. As a notion of a component carrying information about another component, Barwise and Seligman followed the analogy of types and tokens where tokens and its connections carry information. These are classified against types and the theory of information flow aims to capture this aspect of information flow which involves both types and tokens.

When integration is our major concern, the same pattern arises: two communities with different ontologies (or schemata) will be able to share information when they are capable of establishing connections among their tokens in order to infer the relationship among their types. Kalfoglou and Schorlemmer argued for the relation of information flow to a distributed system like the (Semantic) Web, where the regularities of information flowing between its parts can be captured and used to do mapping (Kalfoglou and Schorlemmer, 2003). The mathematical background of information flow theory ensures that the corresponding types (concepts) respect token (instance) membership to each of the mapped types. Their approach is community-oriented, in the sense that communities on the (Semantic) Web own and control their data (instances) and they use them (i.e., classify them) against ontologies for the purpose of knowledge sharing and reuse. It is precisely this information of classifying your own instances against ontologies that is used as evidence for computing the mapping relation between communities' heterogeneous ontologies. It is evident that *information flow* goes beyond *extension-awareness* towards the tick marked by *intension-aware*.

Semantic Similarity, very close to the semantically-rich end lays the family of *logic satisfiability* approaches which focus on the logic correspondences. Logic constructors play a significant role in expressive formalisms, such as DLs, implying that the discovery of similarity is more like finding logic consequence. There has been a long debate regarding "semantics" (Ogde and Rich, 1923), (Smith, 2004) and (Uschold, 2003). Although none of the approaches has been unanimously agreed upon, in ontology engineering, capturing semantics with logic based (mainly DL-based) modelling languages and interpreting the formulae with model theories seem promising (c.f. the de facto standards, OWL/OWL1.1). The rationale behind such a phenomenon is that by formalising the definitions using constructs with clear interpretation, preferably machine-understandable, we prescribe the way how others, being human users or intelligent software agents, approach the semantics encoded in the definitions. There is a major assumption that enables such a vision: the intended semantics can be formalised by DLs or other logic languages and the formalisation can be uniformly interpreted. This gives rise to techniques reducing the matching/mapping problem to one that can be solved by resorting to logic satisfiability techniques. Concepts in a hierarchical structure are transformed into well-formed logic formulae (*wffs*). To compute the relationships between two set of *wffs* amounts to examine whether $(\phi, wffs_1, wffs_2)$ is satisfiable. ϕ is the set of relationships normally containing not only equivalence but also "more general than", "less general than", "disjoint with", etc.

The major difference among these approaches is on how the *wffs* are computed with respect to each concept (and/or label of concept). Bouquet, et. al. (2003) introduced an algorithm with the notions of *label interpretation* and *contextualization*, called CtxMatch. Each concept in a concept hierarchy is associated with a formula based on the WordNet senses of each word in the label of the concept. The senses associated with each label are refined according to the information provided by its ancestors and direct descendants. Matching of two concepts, C_1 and C_2, is then transformed into checking the satisfiability of a formula composed by contextualised senses associated with their labels and the known WordNet relations among senses expressed in logic formulae, e.g. $art\#1 \subseteq_{WordNet} humanities\#1$ denotes that, according to WordNet, the first sense of the word "art" is less general than the first sense of the word "humanities" where "art" and "humanities" are words from the labels of C_1 and C_2 respectively.

(Guinchiglia et. al. 2004) went one step further by distinguishing two different notions of concept, namely the *concept of label* and the *concept of node*. *Concept of a label* is context insensitive concerning only the WordNet senses of the labels of a concept. On the other hand, *concept of a node* is context-sensitive, its logic formula is computed as the "intersection of the concepts at labels of all the nodes from the root to the node itself." (Guinchiglia et. al., 2004). The concept of label matrix is constructed containing the relations exist between any two concepts of labels in the two hierarchies of which the matching is to be obtained. Based on such a matrix the concept of node matrix is calculated.

A significant caveat to this approach is that in real-life settings, humans tend to view the same things from different perspectives and thus formalise their knowledge in, possibly, fundamentally different ways. Therefore, logic-based approaches, though very close to the semantic rich end, still have a long way to go to faithfully capture the meaning of information. Technologies go beyond logic-based ones in SIS are yet to reach their maturity and will be discussed in Section 5. But first, we present a flexible modular architecture that enables a seamless integration of multiple ontology mapping strategies and combines arbitrary numeric similarities in a systematic manner.

A MULTI-STRATEGY APPROACH TO ONTOLOGY MAPPING

It is evident that current approaches demonstrate a wide diversity in terms of mapping capabilities and mapping results that cover all layers in the SIS mentioned in the previous section. Hence, we need to combine different technologies in order to achieve effective and efficient mapping. One way of doing this, is by using an architecture which is capable of accommodating diverse systems without sacrificing their functionality. We therefore proposed such an architecture that is characterized as a multi-stage and multi-strategy system comprising of four modules: *Signature Generation*, *Signature Selection* and *Processing*, *Aggregation* and *Evaluation*. We formalised that architecture in the CROSI system (Section 4.3) in which, different signatures of the input data (be it ontologies or other knowledge models) are generated. A subset of these signatures are selected to trigger different sorts of matchers. The resultant similarity values are compiled by multiple similarity aggregators running in parallel or consecutive order. The overall similarity is then evaluated to initiate iterations that backtrack to different stages. At multiple stages feedback loops enable fine-tuning of the system. A schematic depiction of the system is illustrated in Figure 4.

Unifying the Efforts

If sim() is defined to compute similarity between two ontology signatures, the multi-strategy approach that we envisioned can be formalised as follows:

$$sim(O,O') = aggregator\left(sim_i\left(sig_j(O), sig_j(O')\right)\right)$$

where $sig_j(O)$ extracts a particular signature *j* from ontology O.

Similarity functions $sim_i(O,O')$ instantiate one of the similarity measures discussed in Section 3. To show a full coverage of mapping capabilities, for individual similarity measures that are not ready at the moment, we implement a local copy

Figure 4.

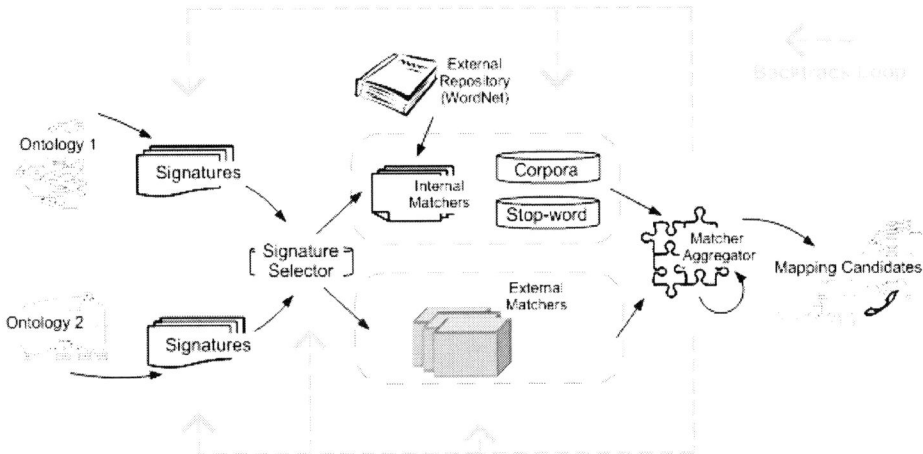

as the "internal matchers"; while for those that are provided by existing systems, we integrated them as "external matchers".

A multi-stage and multi-strategy approach is demonstrated by many systems, e.g. COMA (Do and Rahm, 2002), GLUE (Doan et. al., 2002), and QoM (Ehrig and Staab, 2004). Our approach, as illustrated in Figure 4, is different in that it allows: 1) multiple matchers: several heterogeneous matchers run independently producing intrinsic, yet different but complementary results; 2) use of existing systems which are treated as standard building blocks each of which is a plug and play component of the overall hybrid mapping system; 3) multiple loops: the overall similarity is evaluated by users or supervised learners to initiate iterations that backtrack to different stages of the process.

There are a number of challenges which we need to consider when building such a system: in ideal situations, each independent matcher considers an identical set of characteristics of the input ontologies and produces homogeneous output for further processes. However, this is seldom true in practice. There is currently no standard or common agreement on how an ontology mapping system should behave, i.e. no formal specification on what should be the input and how the system should output. If we consider some recent OWL based ontology alignment systems, we see intrinsic diversities: some take as input only names (URIs) of classes while others take the whole taxonomy; some generate as output abstract relationships (e.g. *more general than*, *more specific than*, etc) while others produce pairwise correspondences with or without confidence values; and some are stand-alone systems when others operate as Web services. Thus, the first and most imminent task for us was to derive a set of common ontology *signatures* that would cover all candidate ontology matching systems included in the CROSI framework and conceive a mechanism to unify heterogeneous outputs. For matchers that utilize specific aspects of ontologies, we fed them with ontology signatures that fully characterize the input ontologies no matter which representation language is used. In cases that matchers are treated as black-boxes --signature selection is not visible -- the entire ontologies are used. We parsed and lifted up all output using an extended SKOS representation (enriching SKOS with extra constructs for numeric similarities).

Making Combined Sense

Equally difficult to build are methods which process and aggregate results from different mapping systems (also refer to as *external matchers*). An unbiased measure is to run in parallel componental matchers each of which produces its own results. The output is then normalized and unified to facilitate accumulation and aggregation with numeric and non-numeric methods. A rift of aggregation methods were implemented and evaluated.

Weighted Average

When accumulating results, weighted average algorithms assumes the returns from different algorithms are in compatible formats and assign each algorithm a numeric weight that is decided manually based on the characteristics and the user's confidence in the algorithm.

$$sim_{overall}(\varepsilon, \varepsilon') = \frac{\sum_i w_i \bullet sim_i(\varepsilon, \varepsilon')}{\sum_i w_i}$$

where w_i is the weight of the ith similarity algorithm/tool and $sim_i()$ gives the mapping candidates of the ith algorithm.

Sigmoid Function

Instead of using predefined and static values, one can also adjust weights using Sigmoid function [12]. The rational behind such approach is that candidate alignments with higher similarity value should be emphasized and thus their contribution to the final result is amplified while the effects of least similar candidates should be largely diminished. Given function $sig(x) = 1/(1 + e{-}x)$, one can define the sigmoid function based similarity aggregation method as

the problem of aligning ontologies (Kalfoglou and Hu, 2005) in the context of the 2005 Ontology Alignment Evaluation Initiative (OAEI) contest[5]. Our experience with devising a purpose-build modular architecture and instantiating it with an ontology mapping system, CMS, helped us to understand better ways in which ontology mapping practice can be improve. First, results from multi-matchers are aggregated using multiple aggregators. Thus far, the selection of aggregation methods is left to the experience and domain knowledge of end users who would have to derive such knowledge from vast test data and the context of individual applications. Although labour-intensive, we see this as a sensitive approach as different matchers might focus on different aspects of ontologies and emphasise different outputs. A knowledgeable user of CMS would have to evaluate and justify such idiosyncrasies to make informed decisions. So far, this process is difficult to automate. Our experience indicates that in many cases the simple weighted average aggregator works, if not better than, as well as other approaches, especially when matcher weights are learnt from past performance based on user feedback. Alternatively, users can be assisted with sophisticated machine learning techniques to work out the most appropriate aggregator with respect to recurrent and largely similar tasks and data.

Second, the heterogeneous nature of different matchers – some external matchers produce pairwise equivalence with numeric values stating the similarity score while others output high level relationships, e.g. *same entity as*, *more specific than*, *more general than* and *disjoint with* expressed in high level languages such as OWL and RDF, and utilised in specialised vocabularies such as SKOS[6]. This suggests that output from different matchers has to be lifted to the same syntactical and semantic level. A unified representation formalism equipped with both numeric and abstract expressivity can facilitate the aggregation of heterogeneous matchers. In CMS, we extended SKOS with numeric similarities. A dedicated converter/parser acts as the interface of individual matchers (signature-specific ones and those adopted in a black-box fashion).

Third, multiple matchers give CMS a board coverage of many ontology signatures ranging from simple name/URL to the exact position of concepts in the concept hierarchy. Users are given the freedom to make adjustments according to their preferences and the task at hand by switching on and off certain signature processors and by including or excluding certain external matchers based on their past performance. Matchers designed for handling heavy-weight ontologies are obviously an over-kill for simple taxonomies and flat vocabularies. CMS provides an "omni-directional" framework to satisfy different requirements.

CONCLUDING REMARKS AND FUTURE DIRECTIONS

It is evident from the increasing number of participants in recent OAEI contests[7], there is a lot of interest and demand for semantically enriched ontology matching or semantic similarity tools due to: (i) the Semantic Web has grown out of its infancy with a large amount of data and services being annotated with one RDF model or another resulting in an imminent quest for aided data manipulation and service composition; (ii) techniques such as those reviewed in the previous sections have fallen into the incompatibility dilemma of "semantics or syntax" with the former as the ultimate goal to pursue and the latter as a compromise; and (iii) "semantics" has been ushered into a new territory with the Web 2.0 philosophy leading to a suite of new matching methodologies to be conceived and developed. Top-down semantics capture approaches start to give way to versatile grass-root initiatives allowing semantics to become explicit in collaborative activities. Instead of being imposed with a pre-defined unsolicited conceptual model, a community is given the freedom to negotiate and gradually build its consensus. Real world examples of this trend is the "schema last" metaphor used in building one of the largest sharable knowledge bases today in a true bottom up fashion[8]. Although arguably, we contend that such a "negotiating-reseeding-and-expanding" approach is an analogue of human learning and thus provide a high fidelity replica of human assigned meanings of information. A common term used to label these approaches as "emergent semantics".

Emergent Semantics

The promise of emergent semantics is that, as communities of users are getting more involved in the setting up of collaborative networks with the help of social software, then that very software, social software, should help us to capture the semantics used by communities as these emerge from social interactions. This promise has been put to work, to a certain extent and in certain scenarios. For example, (Zdhanova, 2005) proposed the involvement of user communities in ontology engineering, in particular, to validate ontology alignments. Furthermore, we saw that a dedicated event recently, (Dzbor et.al., 2005), focussed on the user aspects of the Semantic Web with emphasis on how users can be involved in certain engineering tasks. It is also an appealing prospect from the systems' maintenance point of view, as users, the ultimate target of information systems when they deployed, could be involved in their maintenance thus making sure that the system stays current and up to date. Sparse examples of this can be found in the software engineering literature with the engineering of experiences gathered throughout the life cycle of a project (see, for example, the work of (Basili et. al., 1999) on Experience Factory and Experience Bases). Similarly, organisational memories practitioners have experimented with user participation in their engineering tasks with some degree of success. For example, in the KnowMore system of (Abecker et.al., 2000) and the OntoProPer system of (Sure et al., 2000).

However, there are a number of issues which could potentially render the emergent semantics promise useless.

First, it relies on a relatively smooth and uniform representation of a community's interests. But, real world practice tells us that communities rarely employ uniform and common representations. In fact, they use a variety of norms and manifestations (Wenger, 1998). If we, the engineers, are to take advantage of the emergent semantics, then these manifestations should be analysed (ideally automatically), and represented in commonly agreed formats (like, for example, in an ontology) so that they can be shared in a distributed environment like the World Wide Web, and its extension the Semantic Web.

Second, little work has been done in resolving possible conflicts of representation. It is not uncommon for similar communities to use seemingly similar representations of the same domain concepts. Even if the sheer number of members that belong to these communities is a good enough indicator that these concepts are prevailing and should be part of a prospective ontology for the emerging domain, the fact that there are slight variations in representing or using the concept, calls for ontology mapping technology to resolve it.

Third, emergent semantics rely heavily on the use of machine learning technology and other statistical techniques, like OLAP. We do not despise the use of these technologies, but we are sceptical about the practicalities of deploying machine learning to capture and extract prevailing semantics from a community's log of information exchanges. As we know from machine learning theory, supervised learning methods are probably the most reliable ones (Wilks et al., 2005). But, they also require a lot of engineering in order to make sure that the right learning data set is fetched into the system, proper and timely updates to the learning strategy are made, timely maintenance of the learning rules is executed, etc. All these tasks are time consuming and require specialised knowledge of not only machine learning, but also of the domain in question. We do not see how this could scale up when we deal with subtle concept definitions where only a human expert in the domain is most likely to be capable to decode the information and associate the correct meaning to concepts.

This leaves us with other methods of machine learning which scale up dramatically well, but they also have serious flaws: unsupervised learning has seen some remarkable performance highs in recent years but the domains that it has been applied are well understood and devising the initial set of learning rules is not difficult, even with little knowledge of the domain in question. But in domains where a wide variety of concepts should be extracted and learned it is difficult to see how this approach could be applied with success.

One of the promising efforts in the context of emergent semantics is the use of collaboratively contributed web encyclopaedias, in particular Wikipedia. There has been an increasing research interest in deriving (formal or informal) semantics from Wikipedia (Weber and Buitelaar, 2006) (Wu and Weld, 2008). Equally, there is a growing but less mainstream approach that tries to maintain the formality of ontologies while, at the same time, exploit the flexibility, visibility and low overhead of mass contributions. Along this line of research, we discuss the approach deriving common background knowledge from Wikipedia.

Wikipedia as Background Knowledge

"How can we find out the semantics of a concept?" has been a question that plagues researchers of the conventional knowledge representation/engineering as well as the rapidly growing Semantics Web community. The diversity of human cognition has long been widely accepted. Even though we restrict the envisaged application to software agents, human factors cannot be ignored due to the fact that ontology creation and resource annotation tasks are still human labour intensive. For example, human reasoning is needed when the intended meanings of primary concepts and properties are less evident and difficult to be formally derived -- all the concerned parties must agree upon a list of words as the most basic building blocks to be the semantics carriers and the meanings of these words must "pick out the same individuals in the same context" (Steels and Kaplan, 1999). In other words, we should not hope that with a common language, formal or otherwise, the semantics and the way we understand them just become evident thereafter.

Discovering semantics requires understanding of idiosyncrasies and particulars in using the concept constructs so as to reproduce as faithfully as possible the context wherein ontological entities are created. Hence, in establishing a common understanding of ontologies, human factors have to be explored and somehow captured. In other words, when trying to grasp the semantics that the original modelers deliver, one needs to project his/her domain knowledge upon to those possessed by other modelers. In doing so, we accept a certain degree of imperfectness and replace the rigid model theory based semantics with one emerging from large scale collaborative contributions, such as Wikipedia[9]. The assumption is that tolerating approximation is more close to how humans observe and understand our surroundings. The merit of Wikipedia is evident from its scale, the versatile background of its contributors, and the structure of both its categories and the contents. Wikipedia is probably the biggest and most appealing collaboratively created source of encyclopaedic knowledge. It is a freely accessible, peer-reviewed Web encyclopaedic repository. Up to

November 2008, it collects more than 7 million articles in more than 250 different languages (among them are about 2,700,000 English ones). It contains both conventional encyclopaedias and articles about current affairs. The latter is constantly updated on a daily basis and usually by several contributors with different writing skills, story-telling techniques, and perspectives. This great diversity of the background of wikipedians (connotation for people who contribute to Wikipedia, among them about 10,000 are very active contributors) naturally reflects the variations of human cognition. Meanwhile, as an open access repository, Wikipedia articles are frequently reviewed and revised to ensure that the content is generally better and more comprehensive than other non-peer-reviewed web sources (Giles, 2005). In order to take advantage of such resource, we developed the following algorithm:

- Project a concept together with its conceptual context upon to Wikipedia as a well selected document repository which we treat as the background knowledge where the concept is defined;
- Identify the association between the Wikipedia articles and a concept's defining context (its conceptual neighbours) using conventional information retrieval methodologies;
- Distill a signature vector for each concept as the topics/titles of such articles whose weights may subject to a further refinement with the help of Singular Value Decomposition (SVD) to reveal hidden associations (Deerwester et al., 1990).

The resultant vector provides a simple and scalable method for measuring the semantic similarity between concepts from different ontologies. It might be of particular interest in ontology mapping aiming to facilitate knowledge sharing in distributed and peer-to-peer environments. In this scenario, dynamic and on-the-fly methods for establishing on demand consensus become more desirable and exact equivalences have given way to less perfect ones. Assuming each party has generated semantics-capturing vectors using Wikipedia, by passing such vectors, we can approximate ontology mapping with cosine distance between semantics-capturing vectors.

Towards Certified Ontologies

Despite the advantages and disadvantages of using emergent semantics and some encouraging results we mentioned above, we are cautiously optimistic about them. We believe that emergent semantics will continue to grow as more and more people will be drawn into these online communities using social software. We would like, therefore, to make the most out of their interactions and information exchanges on the Web and Semantic Web by capturing the semantics underlying their actions with respect to the pertaining problem of evaluation.

Communities alone though, will not be able to provide us with practical input with respect to evaluation unless we have ways of regulating and vetting their input. One way that this could be mechanised is with the use of certification. In the knowledge engineering domain, the issue of certification has been debated in the past (Shadbolt, 1999) in the context of certified knowledge bases. Recently, the issue of using ontologies as a commodity, and the commercial interest it has attracted has also been debated (O'Hara, 2001). We have also witnessed efforts that aim to certify and validate domain specific ontologies, like the work of (Eysenbach, 2001) with medical ontologies.

All these representative pieces of work emerge from different contexts and application domains but point to a workable approach: evaluation could be done by professionals and adhere to standards and practices approved by recognized bodies of prominence. We should also point to efforts that already exist in the commercial world, especially those that apply to the Web. For example, the commercial importance of the Web and the volume of trading online brought us technologies like SSL certificates for encrypting financially sensitive information and certification mechanisms like VeriSign's "verified by" trademarked certificates.

Similarly, at the syntactical level, some of the W3C family of languages, and other products related with the consortium's efforts, have clearly identifiable stickers on compatible web pages ("XHTML checkers", etc.) pointing to syntax validators and checkers or simply stating conformance to a standard.

Despite these activities though, the certification of ontologies, especially with respect to evaluation remains an issue largely unresolved and ignored by big standardisation bodies. We might have witnessed high profile efforts in ontology development, like the commercialisation of CyC (Lenat, 1995) or the IEEE sponsored work on SUO[10] but this does not mean that we have evaluation bodies that provide certificates of ontology quality assurance.

The problem with issuing certificates of ontology quality is two fold: on the technological level, we do not have a clear idea of what quality criteria and tests ontologies should satisfy in order to be accredited. On the political level, there is an issue of authority. Who will certify ontologies and how? How trustworthy will that organisation be and what, if any, will be the cost of certification. Will there be licensing issues and restrictions of use with respect to the ontology? How likely it is to reach at a standardisation level when talking about ontology evaluation?

Experience and industry reports on standardisation tells us that standards are hard to debate, difficult to enforce in an open-ended environment, hard to reconcile conflicting commercial interests, and take years to materialize. But, for ontology evaluation efforts to have more credible profile some sort of standardisation would be needed. One way of combining the strengths of emergent semantics we reviewed before and ideas from commercial efforts on certification and standards could be to use simple cataloguing technologies, like ranking.

Classification and Ranking

In (Alani et al., 2005), the authors reported on early efforts to come up with ranking mechanisms that allow us to classify ontologies according to their usage. Their domain of application is on searching for appropriate ontologies but the ranking mechanism is simple and could be adopted to support evaluation. Assuming that a community is willing to participate in a common effort to rank ontologies, such an approach could provide us with a majority's view on what is best and what to avoid. This is the premise of the ranking approach.

We do however, have certain issues to resolve before making it practical for evaluating ontologies: (a) how to monitor and regulate rankings in an open-ended environment? Reports that examined well crafted commercial efforts on using communal ranking (like for example the eBay feedback mechanism) has shown that it is easy to deceive authoritative systems in order to achieve personal gains (Resnick and Zeckhauser, 2002) (in the case of eBay feedback, a positive one could mean better deals for auctioneers). (b) What sort of features in an ontology users will be called upon to evaluate? That issue is related to the certification content discussed above and we see efforts such as in (Uschold, 1999) as an early step towards a consensual set of features that evaluated ontologies should demonstrate. Furthermore, in (Lozano-Tello, 2004) a more detailed and extensive list of characteristics for ontology classification has been proposed. (c) Will all participating users have equal opinion weighs? For example, in the case of the FMA ontology, should an anatomist's opinion have greater importance than an ontology engineer's? Common sense might dictate that he should, but there might be subtle knowledge representation related issues that only the ontology engineer will be qualified to resolve.

Evaluation of ontologies themselves is a difficult issue. It cannot be seen as orthogonal to other ontology development and use issues, especially not in an environment like the Web and the Semantic Web. The promise of accessing, retrieving, and re-using a variety of ontologies in these environment necessitates an evaluation strategy that is (a) open to users, transparent in nature and with references to the standards it adheres to or certificates it holds, (b) amendable, easy to change and adopt to different use cases, (c) domain specific, and reflect opinions of various stakeholders, not only of ontology engineers.

But, these are hard to achieve goals. In the short to medium term we should look for mid term solutions that we can build and experiment with, before engaging to long term evaluation research. In the last part of the paper, we elaborate on a rough roadmap of the short to medium future. Standards and certification is an area that needs more work. In fact, when it comes to ontology evaluation, it is in its infancy. However, we want to avoid the painfully slow process of standardisation. There are lessons learnt and experiences we can build upon. For example, in the context of the IEEE SUO effort, there have been debates on using ISO standards to evaluate the content and appropriateness of ontologies[11]. Despite the fact that views and opinions expressed there are subjective, it is a good start.

We also see an increasing interest in using emergent semantics and engaging user communities. That could prove to be a useful and practical input to the evaluation problem. The commercial interest in ontologies nowadays also brings us closer to certification and standards. As academic and neutral interest stakeholders we should inform possible attempts for certification as to what the quality features that ontologies need to exhibit should be and leave the prolong arguments on how to enforce them to the politicians. Licensing is also an issue that should be considered closely with evaluation. Appropriate licensing should provide certain assurances on evaluation.

The practical research questions on what sort of evaluation technology we need should be part of the ontology development and language communities. The Semantic Web community at the moment focuses on applications and infrastructure issues. Having closed a successful circle on developing languages to materialise the Semantic Web, researchers and practitioners are focussing on attracting commercial and public interest by demonstrating Semantic Web technology and its advances. But, evaluation of ontologies, a cornerstone for achieving the full potential of the Semantic Web, is not complete yet.

Last, but not least, in an era where user communities matters the most, we need to raise the awareness of this issue and demonstrate its importance. As researchers, we need to share experiences, good and bad, on related efforts and learn from each others mistakes. Open source and publicly available tools should be on the agenda so that we can reach to a consensus quicker. We should not be afraid to constructively critique and despise ill-defined ontologies as this will raise the quality standards. Most importantly, we should work with examples, tools, and use cases that are easy to replicate in neutral settings. One of the fruitful directions is that of using Wikipedia as background knowledge.

ACKNOWLEDGMENT

The work described in this manuscript is a result of many years of research and development by the authors under the auspices of a multitude of programmes and projects: CROSI, a Hewlett Packard Laboratories sponsored project (2004-2005); Advanced Knowledge Technologies (AKT) Interdisciplinary Research Collaboration

(IRC) programme (2000-2007) sponsored by the UK EPSRC under Grant number GR/N15764/01; OpenKnowledge, a European Commission funded Specific Targeted Research Project (STREP) under contract number FP6-027253. The views and conclusions contained herein are those of the authors and should not be interpreted as necessarily representing official policies or endorsements, either expressed or implied, of the HP CROSI, UK EPSRC AKT IRC, EC OpenKnowledge, RICOH Europe Plc or SAP institutions.

REFERENCES

Abecker, A., Bernardi, A., Hinkelmann, K., Kuhn, O., & Sintek, M. (2000). Context-aware, proactive delivery of task-specific knowledge: The KnowMore project. [ISF]. *International Journal on Information Systems Frontiers, 2*(3/4), 139–162.

Alani, H., & Brewster, C. (2005). Ontology ranking based on analysis of concept structures. In *Proceedings of the 3rd International Conference on Knowledge Capture (K-Cap'05),* Banff, Canada (pp. 51-58).

Alani, H., Dasmahapatra, S., Gibbins, N., Glasser, H., Harris, S., Kalfoglou, Y., et al. (2002). Managing reference: Ensuring referential integrity of ontologies for the Semantic Web. In *Proceedings of the 13th International Conference on Knowledge Engineering and Knowledge Management (EKAW'02),* Siguenza, Spain (pp. 317-334).

Barwise, J., & Seligman, J. (1997). Information flow: The logic of distributed systems (Cambridge Tracts in Theoretical Computer Science 44). Cambridge, UK: Cambridge University Press.

Basili, R. V., Shull, F., & Lanubile, F. (1999). Building knowledge through families of experiments. *IEEE Transactions on Software Engineering, 25*(4), 456–473. doi:10.1109/32.799939

Bouquet, P., Magnini, B., Scrafini, L., & Zanobini, S. (2003). A SAT-based algorithm for context matching. In *Proceedings of the 4th International and Interdisciplinary Conference on Modeling and Using Context (Context03).*

Deerwester, S., Dumais, S., Landauer, T., Furnas, G., & Harshman, R. (1990). Indexing by Latent Semantic Analysis. *Journal of the American Society for Information Science American Society for Information Science, 41*(6), 391–407. doi:10.1002/(SICI)1097-4571(199009)41:6<391::AID-ASI1>3.0.CO;2-9

Do, H.-H., & Rahm, E. (2002). COMA: A system for flexible combination of schema matching approaches. In *Proceedings of the 28th International Conference on Very Large Databases (VLDB'02),* Hong Kong, China.

Doan, A., Madhavan, J., Domingos, P., & Halevy, A. (2002). Learning to map between ontologies on the Semantic Web. In *Proceedings of the 11th International World Wide Web Conference (WWW 2002)*, Hawaii, USA.

Dwork, C., Kumar, S., Naor, M., & Sivakumar, D. (2001). Rank aggregation methods for the Web. In *Proceedings of the 10th International Conference on World Wide Web* (pp. 613-622).

Dzbor, M., Takeda, H., & Vargas-Vera, M. (Eds.). (2005). *Proceedings of the User-SWeb: Workshop on End User Aspects of the Semantic Web (UserSWEB'05), CEUR (137)WS.* Retrieved from http://sunsite.informatik.rwth-aachen.de/Publications/CEUR-WS//Vol-137

Ehrig, M., & Staab, S. (2004). QOM - quick ontology mapping. In *Proceedings of the 3rd International Semantic Web Confernece (ISWC'04)*, Hiroshima, Japan (LNCS 3298, pp. 683-697).

Euzenat, J. (2004). An API for ontology alignment. In *Proceedings of the 3rd International Semantic Web Confernece (ISWC'04),* Hiroshima, Japan (LNCS 3298, pp. 698-712).

Eysenbach, G. (2001). An ontology of quality initiatives and a model for decentralized, collaborative quality management on the (semantic) World Wide Web. *Journal of Medical Internet Research, 3*(4), e34. doi:10.2196/jmir.3.4.e34

Fagin, R., Kumar, R., & Sivakumar, D. (2003). Efficient similarity search and classification via rank aggregation. In *Proceedings of the ACM SIGMOD International Conference on Management of Data.*

Ganter, B., & Wille, R. (1999). *Formal concept analysis: Mathematical foundations.* Berlin, Germany: Springer.

Giles, J. (2005). Internet encyclopaedias go head to head. *Nature, 438*(7070), 900–901. doi:10.1038/438900a

Guinchiglia, F., Shvaiko, P., & Yatskevich, M. (2004). S-Match: An algorithm and an implementation of semantic matching. In *Proceedings of 1st European Semantic Web Symposium (ESWS'04),* Crete, Greece, (pp. 61-75).

He, B., & Chang, K. C. (2003). Statistical schema matching across Web query interfaces. In *Proceedings of SIGMOD Conference* (pp. 217-228).

Kalfoglou, Y., & Hu, B. (2005). CMS: CROSI mapping system - results of the 2005 ontology alignment contests. In *Proceedings of the K-Cap'05 Integrating Ontologies workshop,* Alberta, Canada.

Kalfoglou, Y., & Hu, B. (2006). Issues with evaluating and using publicly available ontologies. In *Proceedings of the 4th International EON workshop,* Edinburgh, UK.

Kalfoglou, Y., Hu, B., Reynolds, D., & Shadbolt, N. (2005). *CROSI project: Final report* (CROSI project deliverable). University of Southampton and HP Labs Bristol.

Kalfoglou, Y., & Schorlemmer, M. (2003). Ontology mapping: the state of the art. *The Knowledge Engineering Review, 18*(1), 1–31. doi:10.1017/S0269888903000651

Kalfoglou, Y., & Schorlemmer, M. (2003b). IF-Map: An ontology mapping method based on information flow theory. *Journal on Data Semantics, 1,* 98–127.

Lenat, D. (1995). Cyc: A large scale investment in knowledge infrastructure. *Communications of the ACM, 38,* 11.

Lozano-Tello, A., & Gomez-Perez, A. (2004). ONTOMETRIC: A method to choose the appropriate ontology. *Journal of Database Management, 15*(2), 1–18.

Madhavan, J., Bernstein, P. A., Kuang, C., Halevy, A., & Shenoy, P. (2003). Corpus-based schema matching. In *Proceedings of the IJCAI'03 Workshop on Information Integration on the Web (IIWeb-03),* Acapulco, Mexico.

Melnik, S., Garcia-Molina, H., & Rahm, E. (2002). Similarity flooding: A versatile graph matching algorithm and its application to schema matching. In *Proceedings of the 18th International Conference on Data Engineering (ICDE)* (pp. 117-128).

Miller, G. A. (1990). WORDNET: An online lexical database. *International Journal of Lexicography, 3*(4), 235–312. doi:10.1093/ijl/3.4.235

Milo, T., & Zohar, S. (1998). Using schema matching to simplify heterogeneous data translation. In *Proceedings of the 24rd International Conference on Very Large Data Bases (VLDB'98),* New York, NY, USA (pp. 122-133).

Noy, F. N., & Musen, M. (2002). PROMPTDIFF: A fixed-point algorithm for comparing ontology versions. In *Proceedings of the 18th National Conference on Artificial Intelligence, (AAAI'02),* Edmonton, Alberta, Canada (pp. 744-751).

Noy, N., & Musen, M. (2003). The PROMPT suite: Interactive tools for ontology merging and mapping. *International Journal of Human-Computer Studies, 59*(6), 983–1024. doi:10.1016/j.ijhcs.2003.08.002

Noy, N., Sintek, M., Decker, S., Crubezy, M., Fergeson, W., & Musen, M. (2001). Creating Semantic Web contents with Protege-2000. *IEEE Intelligent Systems, 16*(2), 60–71. doi:10.1109/5254.920601

O'Hara, K., & Shadbolt, N. (2001). Issues for an ontology for knowledge valuation. In *Proceedings of the IJCAI'01 workshop on E-Business and the Intelligent Web,* Seattle, WA, USA.

Ogden, C., & Richards, I. (1923). *The meaning of meaning: A study of the influence of language upon thought and of the science of symbolism.* San Diego, CA: Harcourt Brace Jovanovich.

Palopoli, L., Terracina, G., & Ursino, D. (2003). DIKE: A system supporting the semi-automatic construction of cooperative information systems from heterogeneous databases. *Software. Practice, 33*(9), 847–884.

Rahm, A., & Bernstein, A. (2001). A survey of approaches to automatic schema matching. *The Very Large Databases Journal, 10*(4), 334–350. doi:10.1007/s007780100057

Resnick, P., & Zeckhauser, R. (2002). Trust among strangers in Internet transactions: Empirical analysis of eBay's reputation system. *Advances in Applied Mircroelectronics, 11.*

Shadbolt, N., O'Hara, K., & Crow, L. (1999). The experimental evaluation of knowledge acquisition techniques and methods: History, problems, and new directions. *International Journal of Human-Computer Studies, 51,* 729–755. doi:10.1006/ijhc.1999.0327

Smith, B. (2004). Beyond concepts: Ontology as reality representation. In *Proceedings of the International Conference on Formal Ontology and Information Systems (FOIS 2004),* Turin.

Steels, L., & Kaplan, F. (1999). Bootstrapping grounded word semantics. In T. Briscoe (Ed.), *Linguistic evolution through language acquisition: Formal and computational models.* Cambridge, UK: Cambridge University Press.

Sure, Y., Maedche, A., & Staab, S. (2000). Leveraging corporate skill knowledge - from ProPer to OntoProPer. In *Proceedings of the 3rd International Conference on Practical Aspects of Knowledge Management (PAKM2000),* Basel, Switzerland.

Uschold, M. (2003). Where are the semantics in the Semantic Web? *AI Magazine, 24*(3), 25–36.

Uschold, M., & Jasper, R. (1999). A framework for understanding and classifying ontology applications. In *Proceedings of the IJCAI-99 Workshop on Ontologies and Problem-Solving Methods (KRR5),* Stockholm, Sweden.

Wang, J. T.-L., Zhang, K., Jeong, K., & Shasha, D. (1994). A system for approximate tree matching. *IEEE Transactions on Knowledge and Data Engineering, 6*(4), 559–571. doi:10.1109/69.298173

Weber, N., & Buitelaar, P. (2006). Web-based otnology learning with ISOLDE. In *Proceedings of the Workshop on Web Content mining with Human Language, International Semantic Web Conference (ISWC'06),* Athens, USA.

Wenger, E. (1998). *Communities of practice: The key to knowledge strategy.* Cambridge, UK: Cambridge University Press.

Wilks, Y., Webb, N., Setzer, A., Hepple, M., & Capitzone, R. (2005). Machine learning approaches to human dialogue modelling. In *Advances in natural multimodal dialogue systems.* Amsterdam: Kluwer Academic Publishers.

Wu, F., & Weld, D. (2008). Automatically refining the Wikipedia infobox ontology. In *Proceedings of the 17th International Conference on World Wide Web* (pp. 635-644).

Zdhanova, A., & Shvaiko, P. (2006). Community-driven ontology matching. In *Proceedings of the 3rd European Semantic Web Conference (ESWC'06),* Budva, Montenegro.

ENDNOTES

[1]   See, for example the list in http://www.ontologymatching.org/
[2]   A more elaborate list appears in the CROSI project report accessible from: http://www.aktors.org/crosi/deliverables/
[3]   http://dublincore.org/
[4]   The project's software is available as open source and accessible from: http://sourceforge.net/projects/ontologymapping/
[5]   Source data and reference alignments are available from: http://oaei.inrialpes.fr/2005/
[6]   http://www.w3.org/TR/skos-reference/
[7]   http://oaei.ontologymatching.org/

[8]   The Freebase knowledge base from Metaweb technologies - http://www.
       metaweb.com/8
[9]   http://en.wikipedia.org/.
[10]   http://suo.ieee.org/
[11]   http://suo.ieee.org/email/msg12376.html

Chapter 20

The Interplay between Practitioners and Technological Experts in the Design Process of an Archaeology Information System

Tommaso Federici
Università degli Studi della Tuscia, Italy

Alessio Maria Braccini
Università LUISS Guido Carli, Italy

EXECUTIVE SUMMARY

This case describes the design and development process of a computer-based information system for the management of archaeological finds and related documents. Adaptive Structuration Theory is used as the conceptual framework to analyse the role and actions of different people involved in the design and development process, during the different stages of the case. The case addresses key issues, such as an initiative taking place in an organizational context where users show different needs, profiles and levels of information technology literacy. It focuses primarily on the interactions between practitioners and technological experts during the design and development process. Another matter of interest comes from the fact that, in this sector, no other information system for finds management was already available. Moreover, this case targets the domain of archaeology that has not received so much attention by Information Systems literature to date.

DOI: 10.4018/978-1-4666-2618-8.ch020

ORGANIZATIONAL BACKGROUND

The case presented here concerns a project to design and develop an Information System (IS) to support all the management activities of archaeological finds and their related documents. This is a domain where technology has rarely been employed for such usage (Braccini & Federici, 2010, p. 139) and where several different professionals usually work separately. In order to achieve the best possible results, the promoters planned the project to take into account the novelty of the projects aims, as well as the preliminary need to share knowledge and exigencies among all the involved professionals.

The project was then based on two fundamental choices: the participation of most of the final users, first in the requirements definition, and later in the design discussion; and the adoption of an iterative process along which the many different cultures (of archaeologists, restorers, storekeepers and technological experts) may eventually converge on a solution able to answer to everybody's requirements.

The designed IS has a wide scope and adopts advanced technologies and solutions that will be described in the paper. Nevertheless, the main theme of this case is the presence of many different actors and the interplay among them during the long process of designing and developing the system. To investigate this phenomenon, we applied Adaptive Structuration Theory (AST) which is devoted specifically to describing the social aspects of human interactions in a technological context.

Even though this case deals with the field of finds and document-management systems in archaeology, arguably a neglected topic in IS studies, some considerations regarding the system and its development process also hold true for other domains. In particular, some specific problems addressed by the system described in this paper are linked directly to the nature of the objects (finds and related documents) and are close to those experienced in other domains that manage perishable and valuable assets, such as ancient books, paintings or artworks in museums. Moreover, the issues faced in the development process, regarding the roles and actions of final users and technology experts, are in our opinion also applicable to generic development processes that try to design an operational IS to support managerial operations, particularly when the multi-disciplinarity of the users and novelty of the solution come into play.

General Problems Regarding Finds Management

The management of archaeological finds is a process that encompasses all the activities performed on a find, including excavation, restoration, study, conservation and exhibition (Braccini & Federici, 2010). To perform all these activities, information is crucial but it is often not managed properly.

Each object that comes out of the soil during an excavation is not only a discovery of the past but also a potential valuable source of information. Just for the fact of being discovered in a certain place, at a certain depth, close to certain other objects, each find is a testimony of the presence and activities of mankind in that location. However, not every find is an object worth displaying in an exhibition. The largest part of finds is formed merely by small fragments that can only in a few cases be used to rebuild (virtually or physically) a partial or complete object. Their contribution to the unveiling of cultural heritage is still crucial since they bring with them valuable informative potential. For example, in 1900, the discovery of a part of a gear-wheel-based mechanism in the shipwreck of *Antikythera,* built approximately between 80 and 50 B.C., significantly contributed after decades of study to shift the date of the workmanship of complex mechanical machines from the first century B.C. to the fourteenth century A.D. This discovery that deeply altered our knowledge about the technological level of the ancient Greeks was achieved even though the mechanism discovered was only partial, and its original form, function, and shape could not be rebuilt with the parts discovered from the shipwreck. They were derived thanks to the contribution and information exchange of many scholars (de Solla Price, 1975; Edmunds & Morgan, 2000).

Each archaeological find, starts a new life cycle through which it will cross several stages (among them storage, cleaning, restoration, study, exhibition, grouping or consolidation), sometimes repeatedly (Braccini & Federici, 2010). During this life cycle, many different players (such as archaeologists, restorers, storekeepers, archivists, photographers and others) may perform different activities on the find. Each of these activities produces new information and can change the nature of the find, for example, the combination in a single object of fragments found in different moments. At the same time, every action can alter the stock of information embedded in the find, such as the aforementioned example of *Antikythera* where a raw metal mass covered by corrals only revealed a wheel-geared calculation machine after an X-Ray inspection (Freeth *et al.,* 2006).

Organizational Setting in Finds Management

Archaeologists, restorers, storekeepers, archivists, photographers and others often perform their activities on the finds in different places, in different organizational units and usually at different points of time. They frequently work following individual methodologies and context pressure, as in the case of urgent excavations during the construction of crucial infrastructures, such as highways or railways. For example, during the construction of the high-speed railway from Rome to Naples (204.6 km long) there were 130 interventions on archaeological finds discovered during the excavations. Of the sites discovered, 20 were defined as being of high scientific relevance (http://www.fsitaliane.it/). For each intervention, cooperation between the building side and the archaeology side is required to devise actions that can simultaneously safeguard the cultural heritage and the successful completion of the building project. Timely decisions are crucial to respect schedule and costs of the construction project. Whenever possible, finds are quickly removed from the site. In this case, the activities that might normally performed be on site are postponed to a later moment.

Figure 1 shows the typical organizational structure of a European archaeological department. The chart shows that professionals with the same profile may work in different divisions, usually without direct connections. Moreover, each archaeological department has an exclusive (commonly regional) territorial competence, and even though it is subject to national laws about finds conservation and cataloguing, it is partially autonomous in its way of acting. At the same time, as some activities are highly specialized, each professional (namely archaeologists, restorers and archivists) may develop individual practices. For all these reasons, many different procedures are carried on in Europe and to a certain extent, within the same department.

In the finds management sector, both organizational and technological structures are unfit to support an effective and worthwhile management cycle. On one hand, organizational structures such as procedures, workflows and hierarchies are neither strict nor incontrovertible. They may differ on the basis of each organizational practice, each professional way of working, and also as a result of external pressures (as in the aforementioned case of urgent excavations during a construction project). On the other hand, the technological structures do not substantially exist. This does not mean that no technology at all is used in archaeology. Several technologies and

Figure 1. Typical organizational structure of an Archaeological Department

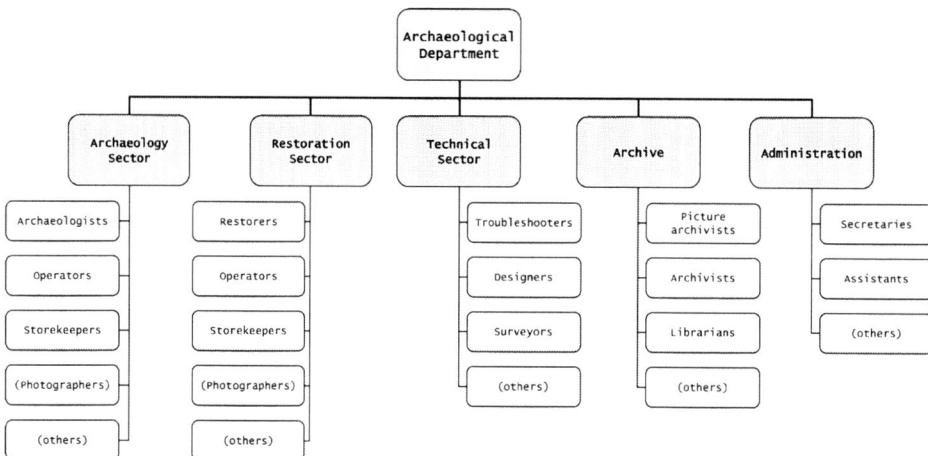

electronic tools have been designed and adapted for the needs of archaeology (Voorrips, 1998). These are mainly extensions of Geographic Information Systems (GIS) that help archaeologists to track sites or finds geographically (Cosmas *et al.*, 2001; Fronza *et al.*, 2002; Tokmakidis *et al.*, 2004; Wüst *et al.*, 2004; Braccini & Federici, 2010). Such tools are then targeted at only one kind of professional out of the many that work on finds, and only target one piece of information, the geographic location, related to a find.

The Need of an IS for Finds Management

The sharing and management of all the information on a find is vital to fully exploiting its informative potential, and giving value to its discovery and its expensive conservation. Despite the importance of the possible information brought by each find, finds management practices do not follow routines and procedures that are capable of fully exploiting the potential richness of information. Information regarding a find is usually not specifically managed with proper IS (Kintigh, 2006; Karmacharya *et al.,* 2008), almost always not filed in digital archives, and rarely transferred to people not involved in the single events (Watrall & Siarto, 2007). Data is usually recorded without any sort of formalized protocol, using paper and pencil in personal notes, and on the sides of the wooden or plastic boxes where finds are kept and stored. Rarely is data keyed into computers, in this case into private files with different formats and content, because the different players usually have different information requirements. This makes the data more difficult to be transferred and interoperated (Lauzikas, 2005). Sometimes information merely remains in the mind of a single individual. Moreover, many of the people working in this field show low levels of IT literacy. All these elements hinder information sharing among those involved in archaeology.

The absence of proper management procedures for information related to finds can produce many problems. For example, when the finds do not have an aesthetic value and are thus not suitable to be shown in exhibitions, in the absence of information (date, state, location, and depth of discovery) they turn into scientifically dumb objects with expensive conservation costs. Also, when the information regarding the storage depot is also not properly managed, finds stored there can be forgotten and, with the absence of information about their location or their need for conservation interventions, they can be damaged by the action of time and atmospheric agents. For instance, during a large urban renovation project in the centre of Rome in 1939, many finds discovered and catalogued in the same site were stored in 500 boxes in anticipation of the decision on their final destination. Owing to the events of the Second World War, these boxes were forgotten. They were only recently rediscovered (September 2010) in the basement of a building in Rome (Fulloni,

2010). These boxes were found to contain finds with a high, sometimes priceless, scientific and aesthetic value. It has been estimated that it will take approximately two years to properly study, catalogue, photograph and restore (if needed) all the contents of these boxes.

Another significant issue comes from keeping finds and documents separately, often in different buildings and with different storing organizations. This reason, together with diverse cataloguing practices, makes matching a find and its related documentation, such as photos, drawings and reports, very difficult, and sometimes nearly impossible.

Given the context described in the previous sections, the creation of a brand new computer-based Information System (IS) to track events and manage information on finds is a big challenge. On the one hand, such a system has to be designed in detail to achieve its aims, and on the other hand, organizational structures are neither fit (diverse, unstandardized procedures), nor ready (novelty of IT use in operations) to adopt it profitably.

The Preliminary Context of the Examined Archaeological Departments

The case presented here involves seven European Archaeological Departments, from Italy, France, Spain and Portugal, all partners of the *Recouvrement du Potentiel Informatif des Sites Archéologiques Démontés* project called hereafter giSAD. The seven departments were (and still are) very different in terms of laws, practices, territorial extension, number and type of finds managed (Table 1).

The seven departments also varied according to their previous technological experiences and equipment (Table 2).

However, before the start of the giSAD project (2003), all of them operated in a condition similar to that described in the organizational background section, and experienced the same problems with finds' conservation, safety and exploitation.

Owing to the lack of correct, updated and shared information, activities on finds could not be planned and sometimes (for example, when the person who had worked on a find was not on hand for the necessary clarifications) it happened that an object could not be identified, or it was even impossible to know where it was stored. Such issues were increasingly relevant considering the amount of archaeological discoveries each year that are often kept in inappropriate places, such as cellars, passages, or even grottos at the same archaeological sites. The figures in Table 3 can be of help to better appreciate the relevance of such issues.

The Monuments Department of the Italian Region VdA has been trying to address such concerns since 1992. The solution then identified was that of designing a software devoted to gathering information about managed finds. This experimen-

Table 1. Description of the seven Archaeological Departments partner in the giSAD project

Department	Country	Territory	Official Competences	Supervised Structures
Direzione Beni Archeologici e Paesaggistici della Regione VdA	Italy	Region	Maintenance and safeguarding of archaeological sites and finds	1 Museum 4 Archaeological areas 2 Depots
Soprintendenza per i Beni Archeologici di E	Italy	Region	Maintenance and safeguarding of archaeological sites and finds	4 National Museums 3 Archaeological areas ±50 depots
Soprintendenza Archeologica di R	Italy	Town	Maintenance and safeguarding of archaeological sites and finds	2 National Museums ±80 Archaeological areas >20 Depots
Soprintendenza Archeologica di CO	Italy	Two Provinces	Maintenance and safeguarding of archaeological sites and finds	2 Museums >30 Archaeological areas ±40 Depots
Atelier du Patrimoine de la Ville de M	France	Town	Support and supervision of the projects regarding archaeological sites	5 Depots
Direccion General de Cultura de la Comunidad Autonoma de la Region de M	Spain	Region	Supervision of the historical and archaeological heritage	5 Museums
Division Culturelle de la Câmara Municipal de RM	Portugal	Municipality	Supervision of the historical, cultural and archaeological heritage	2 Museums (+2 in preparation at that time) 1 Depot

tal software, named Arkeokeeper, was developed by external developers in collaboration with an internal professional who worked as a restorer. The high level of newness for a software in this field, together with the presence of a sole professional, and therefore of a unique point of view, were probably the cause of relevant limitations of Arkeokeeper. First, this system had a narrow scope as regards finds management as it was especially conceived to meet restorers' needs (Pedelì & Pesciarelli, 1997). Second, it presented several rigidities with regard to work routines and did not cover all relevant information.

As a result, it was used mainly in the Restoration sector of the Department. In fact, even though other users recognized the need of software for their work and tried to adopt Arkeokeeper, they ended up abandoning it because of its limitations and constraints. Nevertheless, the experimentation with Arkeokeeper had the ben-

Table 2. Technological experiences and equipment of the seven departments at the beginning of the giSAD project

Monument Departments	Previous Technological Experience	Equipment
Direzione Beni Archeologici e Paesaggistici della Regione VdA	Development of an IS to manage finds restoration Cataloguing software GIS	Intranet with 28 PCs connected
Soprintendenza per i Beni Archeologici di ER	Cataloguing software GIS to manage risks map	Local network in each building: direction, museum, depot (35, 8, and 9 PCs)
Soprintendenza Archeologica di R	Cataloguing software GIS	Intranet with >300 PCs connected
Soprintendenza Archeologica per CO	Individual spreadsheets	Some PCs
Atelier du Patrimoine de la Ville de M	Individual database	1 Apple notebook connected to an Intranet
Direccion General de Cultura de la Comunidad Autonoma de la Region de M	GIS to manage risks map	Local network in each office
Division Culturelle de la Câmara Municipal de RM	Individual spreadsheets	Local network in each building

Table 3. Figures on archaeological finds management: minimum and maximum values (approximate) among the partners

Voice	Min	Max
Number of managed archaeological sites	300	1,000
Number of excavation campaigns performed	500	3,000
Number of boxes stored in depots	10,000	100,000
Number of discovered finds	100,000	1,000,000
Cubic meters (m3) of finds stored in the depots	30,000	100,000
Square meters (m2) occupied by finds in the depots	1,000	10,000

efit of making most of the professionals in the Monument Department of the VdA Region aware of the possibility of facing their daily issues with a customized IS. This awareness provided the impulse to the start the giSAD project some years later.

SETTING THE STAGE

Theory and Methodology

The primary aspect that this case describes concerns the interaction among practitioners and technological experts during the development process of an IS for finds and document management in archaeology. When an IS is introduced to manage the activities of groups of actors in contexts similar to those described above, unexpected outcomes can be produced because of the interplay among social structures, structural features and human agency. Users might distort and misinterpret the intended way of using the technology. The actual appropriation of the technology could then be different from the intended one (Schultze & Orlikowski, 2004).

An influential theory tackling the social dynamics between human actors and information and communication technology in the landscape of IS studies is Giddens' Structuration Theory (ST) (DeSanctis & Poole, 1994; Pozzenbon & Pinsonneault, 2005; Jones & Karsten, 2008). ST is a general theory of the social organization centred on the concept of the relationships between individuals and society. According to Giddens, phenomena are determined by both social structures (i.e., properties of the society) and human actions (Jones & Karsten, 2008). Every human action is performed in a context of pre-existing social structures governed by specific, but variable in time, sets of norms and laws. Every action is therefore partially predetermined by the contextual rules under which it occurs.

ST views groups and organizations as systems. These systems are produced by human agency (human actions) that creates structures. Systems and structures can reproduce themselves through a structuration process that can be stable or evolve over time. This theory has been applied extensively to explain the organizational adoption of computing and other technologies (DeSanctis & Poole, 1994) but in spite of this attention, ST completely neglects the Information and Communication Technology (ICT) artefact (Jones & Karsten, 2008). To overcome this limitation, scholarship has attempted to extend and adapt Giddens' ST to include the technology variable more explicitly (Pozzenbon & Pinsonneault, 2005). Among these works, DeSanctis and Poole (1994) proposed the Adaptive Structuration Theory (AST).

The AST still points at human agency but also addresses the ICT artefact directly, recognizing its role in shaping human action. The ICT artefact is described in AST by further concepts that have been added to Giddens' theory. Those concepts are: *structural features, spirit* and *appropriation*. These concepts have found a broad acceptance for the study of ICT in organizations (Markus & Silver, 2008).

The *structural features* are rules, resources, or capabilities offered by the system that govern how information is gathered, manipulated and managed by the users

(DeSanctis & Poole, 1994). The *structural features* can restrain or empower final users when performing their activities using the technology.

The *spirit* is the general intent related to the values and the goals underlying a given set of *structural features*. The *spirit* is the official line with which the technology is presented to the people. In the absence of procedures and norms that clarify how a certain technology has to be used, the *spirit* helps users in interpreting the features and understanding how to use them (DeSanctis & Poole, 1994).

Given the structuration process through which systems and structures are reproduced when a technology is implemented, a complex pattern of users' interaction and actors' interplay leads to *appropriation*. *Appropriation* can then be examined to tell how a specific rule or resource of the technology is brought into action (DeSanctis & Poole, 1994). *Appropriation* can be of different kinds. First, users might appropriate the whole system or just a portion. *Appropriation* can then be faithful (consistent with spirit and structural features) or unfaithful (in the opposite case). Finally, when appropriating technology, final users usually show an attitude that can be of comfort (when they are confident and relaxed with the technology), respect (when they perceive that the technology can be useful for their needs), or challenge (when they commit themselves to work hard using the technology) (De Sanctis & Poole, 1994).

The AST is used in this case since it tackles the interactions among users groups and the technology, which is close to the focus of our paper. In this case, we have decided to apply the AST to investigate a development process rather than a post-implementation process, also because this case involved a pilot experimentation by users in real activities during the design phase. Since the canonical method of AST is very complex, to ease readability of the paper we have decided to structure the case description following the elements proposed by Boudreau and Robey (2005) in terms of sequence of events (*inertia*, *reinvention* and *improvised learning*), and groups of actors (*promoters and leaders*, *technology experts* and *final users*).

Data for the case was collected from project reports, minutes of meetings and direct observation. One of the authors of this paper participated directly in all the activities described below. The other had access to relevant project documentation and interview transcriptions.

Promotion and Design of the giSAD Project

In the situation described in the 'Preliminary context of the examined Archaeological Departments' section of this paper, having experimented the potentiality of using software to improve the finds management, in 2001 the Italian Region VdA, by means of its Co-financed Projects and Research Direction under the Monuments Department, promoted a project named giSAD, co-financed by the European

Union. A partnership was established with other six regional Monuments Departments, three from Italy and one each from France, Portugal and Spain (Table 1). The Monuments Department of the Region VdA, in its role as first promoter, was the main partner of the project.

As stated above, even though each partner's context was slightly different, they operated in the field of archaeological heritage management in a scenario similar to the one described at the beginning of this paper. The involvement of several partners in similar conditions, although with possible different practices, was a deliberate choice, with the aim of extending the experiences and the needs to be analysed and addressed by the project.

The project intended to design and develop an operational IS (Pedelì, 2008), addressing multiple objectives common to all the partners: the exploitation of the huge amount of finds not studied; the availability of much more information based on more trustworthy data; the improvement in resources usage; the achievement of a higher finds' protection; and the reduction of management costs. In the background, the initiative promoters had also more general intents (the *spirit*), which can be classified in three dimensions (Table 4).

In order to point out the human agency in the emergence of structures, the people intervening in the project can be classified into three groups: project promoters and leaders (PL); technology experts (TE); and final users (FU). These groups, their roles and the output expected to be provided by each of them, are described in Table 5.

In the archaeological context, the role of each individual appears hugely relevant, because of the multiplicity of involved disciplines and the high level of everyone's specialization. At the same time, it must be noticed that the final users group was composed of people who, while sharing similar competences and roles, came from different departments and so possibly adopted diverse practices.

Taking into account the innovation brought by the project to the environment, giSAD was planned involving several phases and stages to iteratively present and discuss the outputs produced so far with the users (Table 6), in order to provoke

Table 4. Dimensions of the intents characterizing the 'spirit' of the initiative

Dimension	Description
Integration	Promoting continuous cooperation among the diverse professionals, through the use of the same platform
Knowledge management	Fostering the creation of knowledge through the availability and sharing of much more information
Ease of adoption	Minimizing the initial impact on users' daily practices and the changes in organizational structures (roles, rules …)

Table 5. Groups involved in the giSAD project

Group	Description	Role	Output
PL	Most interested persons in innovation in each Department External IS Project Management expert	Local Project leaders of the seven departments Global project leaders	Project plan Sessions reports Project plan adaptation Project reports
TE	External established experts without any specific knowledge of archaeological procedures at the beginning of the project	Designers of technical aspects of the system Developers of the system	Initial technical design Final technical design Developed system
FU	Different professionals from the seven departments: archaeologists, restorers, storekeepers, archivists, photographers, archivists and others	Setters of requirements (information and way of use) Verifiers of the compliance Users of the final system	Requirements document Multilingual system thesaurus

Table 6. Phases of the project with outputs and people involved (summarized)

Phases	Outputs	Main Actors
1. Analysis of practices and needs	Set of information needed (on the characteristics of finds, depots, archives, events …); thesaurus for each piece of information; map of the events to be managed	PL, FU
2. Preliminary design of the system (performed only on the basis of documents)	Documents including technical solutions (database model, structure of the software, hardware …) and new workflow model	TE
3. Trial of pilot software (pre-existing)	Acceptance and hints by the users about the software Arkeokeeper (limited to some functions in respect of the target one)	FU
4. Discussion on the preliminary design and trial results	List of comments, suggestions and criticism by the users, both on pilot experience and new software design	PL, TE, FU
5. Revised software design	Detailed project to proceed at the system development	TE, FU
6. Development	Final software to be implemented	PL, TE

new suggestions and reframe individuals' old ideas. At the same time, another two crucial decisions made during the project setting were:

- The involvement of all the roles engaged in different moments of finds management (archaeologists, restorers, archivists, storekeepers, photographers) which usually work separately;
- The schedule of plenary sessions, including every professionalism in the analysis phase and, later, for the IS project discussion.

Such decisions pursued the aim of accumulating and sharing as much knowledge as possible, in order to overcome the limited sharing and narrowness in scope formerly experienced by the Monument Department of the Region VdA with its pilot software Arkeokeeper. Just having in mind similar objectives, it was considered the future diffusion of the new IS to as many as possible other cultural heritage departments, in order to create a larger community of practices behind the system (Federici, 2010).

CASE DESCRIPTION

This case describes the history of the giSAD project whose aim was the design and the development of an IS to manage the entire life cycle of archaeological finds. The IS was later named ArcheoTRAC (Information Systems for the Tracking, Recovery, Assessment and Conservation of the Archaeological and Documental Heritage).

The case history is structured as a sequence of three different stages with the following contents:

- Stage 1: *initial inertia*.
    - This stage encompasses the first and the second phases of the giSAD project (cf. Table 6).
    - It describes the interest shown by the final users in the initial phases, and the way the technical experts were involved in the activities.
- Stage 2: *improvised learning*.
    - This stage encompasses the third and the fourth phases of the giSAD project (cf. Table 6).
    - It describes the reactions and the comments of the final users on the preliminary study elaborated by the technical experts. This stage also describes the results and experience of the final users during the trials of Arkeokeeper;
- Stage 3: *reinvention*.
    - This stage encompasses the last two phases of the giSAD project (cf. Table 6).
    - It concerns the reactions of technological experts to the problems and the difficulties highlighted by final users in the previous stages. It also deals with the deriving structure and features of the ArcheoTRAC information system eventually developed.

Stage 1: Initial Inertia

When the project started, almost all the users from the various departments were very curious. They were particularly interested in discovering possible ways of innovating their work ('*it's time to have more modern and efficient tools to improve our work*'). At least at the beginning, their attitude towards the technology was one of respect. At the same time, their experience with managerial software was very low. They were not used to keying data into a piece of software, and using it later to retrieve the information. They feared being restricted or bound by the system in their daily work. Moreover, they were also not used to cooperating with other professionals (working in the same or in different fields) in their tasks. The final users approached the start of the project showing great interest and some difficulties, as with any similar innovation.

For their part, the technical experts (consultants with no previous experience in the archaeological domain) were introduced to the project only at the end of the analysis phase (phase 1 in Table 6). They did not have any previous contact with the final users. The technical experts made sense of the needs and the exigencies of the users on the basis of available documents. When elaborating the first version of the software design, owing to the lack of interaction with final users and their cultural bias, they placed too much emphasis on the security and efficiency objectives with the intent of achieving a total process certainty, data completeness and trustworthiness in the software use. The technical experts also paid much attention to the issue of distributing the same piece of software to several partners operating in partially different situations. For this reason, whilst also considering the will of diffusing the IS widely, they chose to use open source environments, in order to lower the adoption barriers, and designed a system with fully scalable solutions (i.e., from a sole personal computer up to a large client server network, using only bar codes or even smart-tags, and so on), to ease its adaptation to the different economic and technical contexts of the partners.

The first design of the system by technical experts then followed a purely rational approach, with excessive focus on aspects such as the data model, the workflow model, the architecture of the system, the number of mandatory data and similar. By doing so, the technical experts produced a system design in which the structural features were too bounded for final users. Such a design implied indeed a correspondent organizational structuration (in terms of procedures, flow of events, task content, and so on) that could not always find a correspondence in the real world. For example in the aforementioned case of an excavation of finds discovered in a construction site, the urgency is on taking the decision regarding how to proceed the construction without damaging the finds and delaying the construction project. The decision can vary from taking the finds away, to burying them once more, or also leaving them where they are, modifying the construction plan. The alternative to take, and the subsequent actions, cannot be known in advance (i.e., when the construction project begins) because it strictly depends on what will actually be found under the ground.

Stage 2: Improvised Learning

Following this preliminary design of the system, the central phase of the project focused on its presentation and discussion with the final users. An important step in this phase was the examination of the reactions of the same users after the trial of Arkeokeeper. The spirit with which such a pilot was introduced was that of showing to the users the consequences of a complete automation and rationalization of all the daily activities of the professionals. All these discussions took the form of informal brainstorming sessions. In each session a diverse set of professionals (the intended final users of the software to be developed), with their individual skills, faced a group of technological experts. These sessions were facilitated with the support and mediation of the project leaders.

The general sentiment of the final users on the preliminary design of the system elaborated by the technical experts was that it posed too many constraints and prescriptions on many aspects of their work. The reactions clearly showed the differences in the work practices of each user.

An aspect that was criticized was the restrictive data model ('*I could guess that an internal automatic code can help* you *to univocally identify a find, but* I *need a mnemonic code created by* myself'). Moreover, following the rational design approach, the designed system used standardized forms, none of which appeared to be particularly targeted at the needs of a specific kind of user ('*you put that data in this form, I don't know who's meant to use it, but I don't need it, and it confuses me*'). The data that was needed to complete the forms appeared to compel final users' work too much ('*we cannot key in that data all the time at this stage of the process, even if it would be both correct and useful*'). Finally, overall, the final users found the underpinning workflow of the pilot software to be too rigid and restrictive ('*yes, we agree, yours would be an ideal flow, but we can hardly follow it. Let's think of an open excavation: we must bring away all the finds in a certain time, no matter the complete registration of their data*'). All these elements are evident signs of the initial fears of final users who actually found their activities hampered or constrained by the software that was originally intended to support them. At the same time, they are also evident signs of the cultural bias of the technical experts, which makes them distant from users' position. The structural features of the initial design were then not in line with users' needs to start any kind of appropriation. As a result, final users rejected the initial design.

In contrast, the choices made by the technical experts with regard to using open source as the environment and the scalability of the system (which obviously were not discussed in detail in technical terms), was really appreciated by the final users as they promised an easier adaptation to their different contexts and the possibility of sharing the system with a larger community of users in the future. While rejecting the designed software, the final users were simultaneously still finding these latter features useful for their needs, showing again a respectful attitude towards (at least part of) the technology.

Critical comments were also registered during and after the evaluation of the planned trial of Arkeokeeper. As already mentioned, the software used in the trial had only been developed with the profile of the restorer in mind and had features targeted to support their (and only their) activities. For all the other professionals, the software presented constraints such as the rigid workflow and the usage of the 'finds parcel' concept that was unusual for most users. All these elements led to some misinterpretation of the features and functionalities of the software by the final users during the pilot trial.

As a result, many users abandoned the trial in advance even before the term fixed by the project. Even though it was shorter, their experience with the software still produced some results, in the sense expected by the project promoters. The final users, having experienced the usefulness of a computerized system in their work to record and manage data, tried to replicate the experience and achieve some benefits by starting their own individual *shadow systems* (McAfee *et al.,* 2004). Many users tried to use simple systems based on spreadsheets or databases running on their own PCs. Obviously every system was different in terms of the data collected, the structure, the codification and the completeness.

Stage 3: Reinvention

The experience of the second stage of the project was very helpful for technical experts who learnt many lessons during the meeting with the final users. The peculiar aspects of the field of application, the archaeological sector, then emerged quite clearly in terms of the differences among the organizations, and the variety of cultures during the discussions. All the issues identified by the final users in the design and the pilot software were still relevant enough to convince project partners to modify the original spirit of the initiatives. Among the objectives of the project, technical experts, promoters and leaders decided to emphasize more the 'ease of adoption' dimension, even in favour of reducing the weight of other objectives. This also resulted in a shift in the spirit of the technology; this was rethought with the objective of providing a support to the final users' activities, reducing to a minimum, and if possible avoiding, possible limitations.

The original design of the system was then reconsidered. The new concept was designed interactively with the final users. The new concept involved many changes in the technical structures and led to a less prescriptive and limited system.

With regard to the architecture of the system, to enable it to be suitable to the different needs of different kinds of users, the main aspects that needed to be modified were:

- The data model;
- The set of mandatory data;
- The views and the navigation tools used by users to browse the different functionalities of the system;
- The workflow model.

Concerning the data model, the new concept included an extensible 'core' model with information common to all the partners and professionals. With the new concept any user now has the chance to obtain, in certain cases, new fields as extensions to such a core model (i.e., for other individual codes of the finds). These fields will automatically appear in the specified form.

Whenever possible, the set of mandatory data has been reduced to a minimum in each usage scenario: for example, with the new concept, a find can be registered initially without the specification of its material or discovery location. These details can be added at a second point in time.

To reconcile the need for each user to have a comfortable view, tailored to their specific needs while safeguarding the heterogeneity of the needs of the different groups of final users of ArcheoTRAC, the forms and navigation tools were altered for each professional profile. The option to add data or change the position of these elements in the software is available to each user at any time.

Finally, to reduce the degree of constraint during activities on the finds, the workflow model initially designed by the technical experts rationalizing an ideal process for managing finds (Figure 2), was deconstructed in a collection of events, which can be called up by users in many different compositions, without any sort of constraint (Figure 3). Each user can insert data on a new find, starting from the event considered more appropriate for that circumstance, and then proceed with any other event (or stop there), without the need to follow a chronological sequence.

To ensure traceability of events, which is a crucial feature for the work of all professionals, the system can rebuild the history of each find ex-post by aggregating all the atomic events that relate to a specific find. With this feature the system produces a timeline of treatments, movements and all other activities the find has received, starting from the collection of sparse events related to that specific find.

Figure 2. Initial strict workflow (simplified) designed by TE

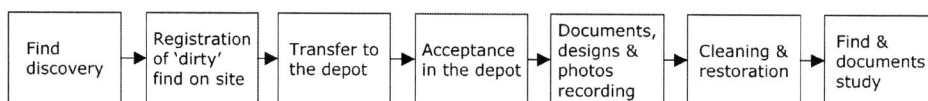

Figure 3. Final design based on a collection of events (reduced), with some example of real use

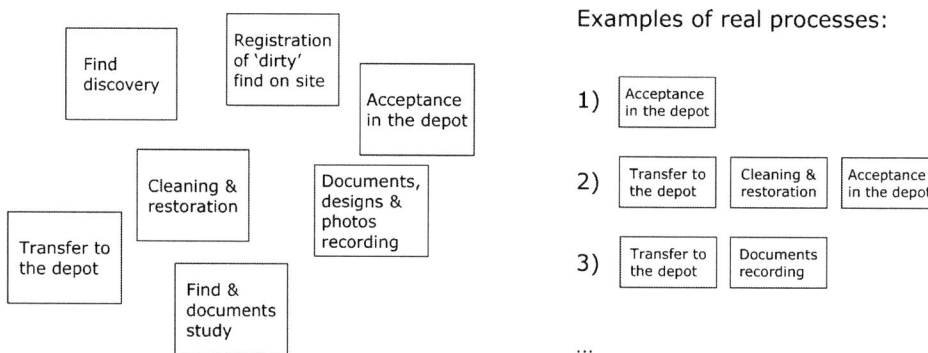

Again for the need for traceability of finds, another feature was added to the new concept of the system to automatically build a network of relationships among different finds. This feature can be used to identify finds that are closely related to another one. The connections among the finds can derive either from a scientific activity, or by a restoration action.

Most of the choices about technological design of the system were made to cope primarily with the different technological levels of the partner and, subsequently, with those of other organizations wishing to implement it (Federici, 2010). The final system was been developed using open source software technologies, both as development and operational environments (Table 7).

ArcheoTRAC is a web-based (Figure 4), natively multi-lingual, IS system that can be used either in-house or via the application service provision (ASP) mechanism. On its client side, ArcheoTRAC requires the final user to have only a web browser to use the system. The server side can run either on Unix or Windows architectures. Users' authentication and authorization, using badges, has been implemented to ensure security and confidentiality.

The system is designed to be used throughout the network (Figure 5), either using workstations and notebooks over wireless or cable LANs (Local Area Networks), or using reinforced notebooks over UMTS/HSDPA networks to work directly on the site of discovery or excavation. A scalable design has been chosen for

Table 7. Software chosen to develop and to operate ArcheoTRAC

Environment	Software	Use	Licence
Development	Abator	Code generator for iBatis	Apache License 2.0
	Tibco General Interface	AJAX framework and IDE	BSD License
	Eclipse	IDE for development	GNU General Public License version 2
Operation	Apache Tomcat	Application Server#J2EE-compliant	Apache License 2.0
	Spring Framework	Framework MVC J2EE-based	Apache License 2.0
	iBatis Java	Object Relation#Mapping Framework	Apache License 2.0
	ACEGI	Framework for authentication	Apache License 2.0
	MySQL	Database Management System	GNU General Public License version 2
	Metro	Web services framework	Apache License 2.0

Figure 4. Screen view of a form of the depot management module

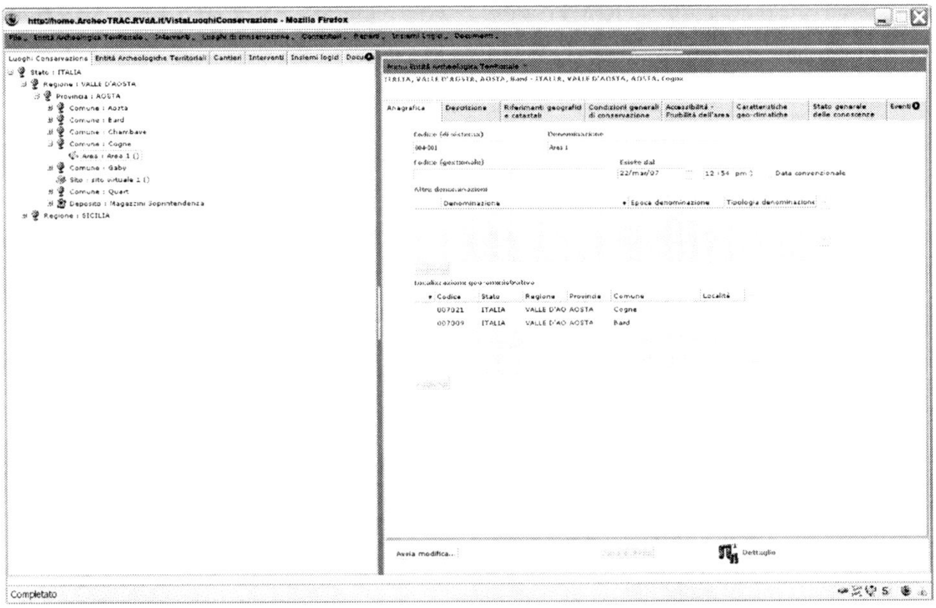

Figure 5. Different conditions of ArcheoTRAC use

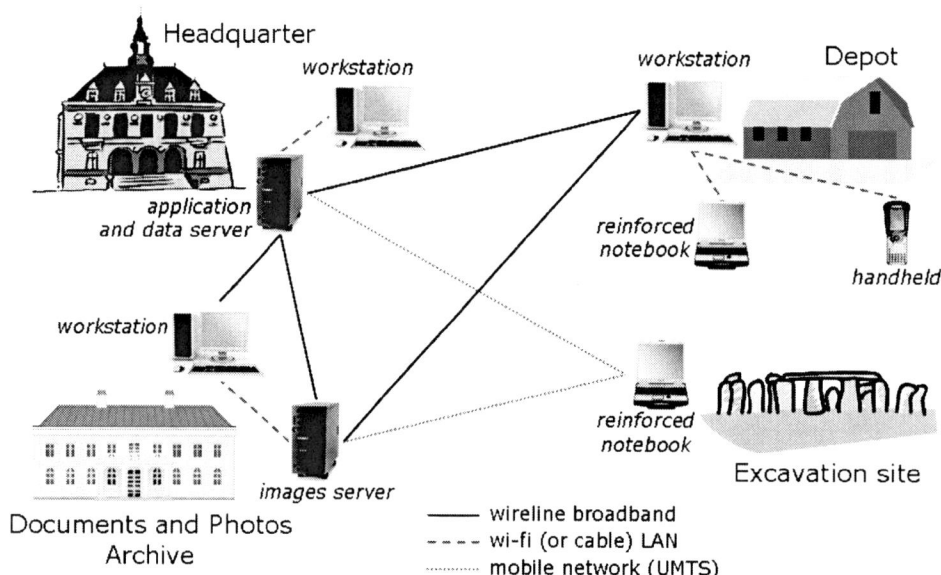

the main features of the system. ArcheoTRAC can, therefore, either use Radio Frequency Identification (RFID) tags or bar codes to catalogue boxes or finds (Federici, 2010). Handheld devices with a bar code or RFID reader can be used to speed up operations.

ArcheoTRAC was developed by adopting an incremental approach: the six modules (Figure 6) were completed separately and tested one by one, starting from the "Finds management" module (the core one) and then proceeding with "Archaeological Sites management", "Excavations management", and so on. This choice was taken both because of the huge complexity of the entire system, and owing to the opportunity to reduce the number of final users involved each time.

Figure 6. Modules of the ArcheoTRAC system in its first version

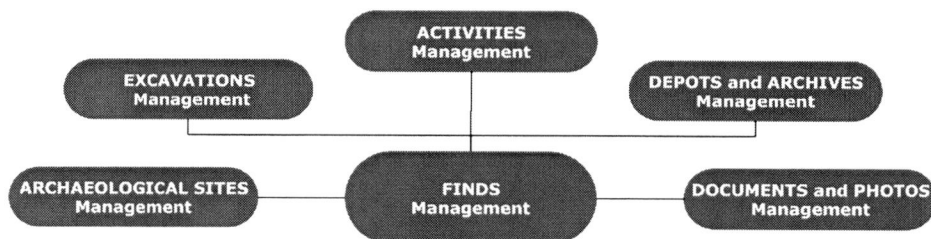

By the end of 2007, the development of the ArcheoTRAC system was finally complete. The design and development process took a very long time (about four years) as a result of the lengthening produced by the necessity to blend many different points of view. First, all the final users from different departments had to share their knowledge and needs, in order to create a wish list of system features and a common thesaurus to be used for labels, texts and voices in the dropdown menus. Later, technical experts with no skill in archaeology had to present and discuss their proposal of solutions for the system with the final users (experienced practitioners with low or no IT literacy). The increase in time should, however, be considered as a source of improvement, because the resulting system was then based on the best possible combination of knowledge and experience, and the designed solutions were shared consciously by all the players. A different way of proceeding might have been shorter but it would probably have resulted in the rejection of the system by most of the users excluded from the definition of needs, or from the stages of discussion with the technical experts.

The implementation plan was designed to minimize the impact on the adopting structures, in terms of investments in technological equipment, overheads on the ordinary activities to be carried on, and effort for people to be trained. For this reason, a programme was planned to implement one or more modules of the IS in a single area at a time (i.e., firstly a depot, then an excavation site). Moreover, the introduction started with a simpler technology set (i.e., a PC or a LAN with some printers), to move step by step towards a more advanced one (i.e., bar code use with printers and readers, or RFID tags with printers and handhelds), once the former was sufficiently known and adopted by users.

At the beginning of 2008, an experimental programme was started to validate the system against the requirements. This pilot was performed with selected users of the main partner (the VdA Region), already involved in the design activity. During the evaluation, the users asked for minor changes to further customize the views in the system. However, as a first result, it could be observed that the first users started to use ArcheoTRAC in a short time and expressed quite positive judgements regarding their experience, since they noticed some speeding up in their work and an increased opportunity to keep and organize information previously dispersed across various locations. It can be said that the final users are moving from a respectful to a comfortable or even challenging attitude in the appropriation of the system.

CURRENT CHALLENGES/PROBLEMS
FACING THE ORGANIZATION

Archaeology runs at a very slow speed. This limitation is aggravated by the public nature of the monuments departments. Owing to the lack of human and economic resources, the full implementation of the system experienced a delay. A year later, another important Italian partner started a larger pilot, but it was halted after few months (only end user training and system set-up were completed by that time), because of a change in the leading management. For this reason, no further conclusion can be drawn from such experimentation.

The realization of a large, flexible and technologically up-to-date IS in the virgin context of archaeology has to be considered as a positive result by itself. The success is even greater because such a result has been reached involving all the professionals, and through a constructive and improving interaction between practitioners and technological experts, which often leads to a dead-end. Nevertheless, the partner organizations have still to face some challenges in order to consider the initiative as fully successful.

First of all, they want to make sure of the full achievement of the expected improvements in the finds management activities, in terms of:

- The exploitation of the huge amount of finds not studied, through the recovery and sharing of their information potential;
- A better use of resources, by estimating intervention costs, and planning them on the basis of their possible information contribution;
- Higher finds protection;
- A greater collaboration and involvement of all professionals.

To evaluate the reaching of this objective, the changes in the users' behaviours should be observed once ArcheoTRAC is fully deployed in all sectors of the departments.

Moreover, the project promoters want to evaluate to what extent the structure and features of ArcheoTRAC really meet the needs and attitudes of a larger number of users. The software, as already stated, was finally designed avoiding most of the possible constraints. However, the individual practice of some users, or a specific urgency, may ask for much greater freedom. At the same time, new, still unthought-of, ways of using the software may appear as either faithful or unfaithful appropriation. The promoters are interested in these emergences of appropriation: on the one hand, to judge the quality of the designed solutions; on the other hand, to single out new improvements and add-ons for the software.

Finally, the giSAD project was conceived as a sort of community of various experts, in order to share their knowledge and practices. A further challenge for the promoters is now that of diffusing the software and it's embedded new management approach, to other monuments departments in Europe. Their adoption of Archeo-TRAC could extend the knowledge exchanged and increase the critical mass beyond the software even more. With such an aim, a specific set of rules and steps to enter the community of ArcheoTRAC adopters has been designed.

REFERENCES

Boudreau, M., & Robey, D. (2005). Enacting integrated information technology: A human agency perspective. *Organization Science, 16*(1), 3–18. doi:10.1287/orsc.1040.0103

Braccini, A. M., & Federici, T. (2010). An IS for archaeological finds management as a platform for knowledge management: The ArcheoTRAC Case. *VINE: The Journal of Information and Knowledge Management Systems, 40*(2), 136–152.

Cosmas, J., Itagaki, T., Green, D., Grabczewski, E., Weimer, F., Van Gool, L., et al. (2001). 3D MURALE: a multimedia system for archaeology. In *Proceedings of the Conference on Virtual Reality, Archaeology, and Cultural Heritage* (pp. 297-306). New York, NY: ACM.

De Solla Price, D. (1975). *Gears from the Greeks: the Antikythera Mechanism: A Calendar Computer from ca. 80* BC. New York, NY: Science History.

DeSanctis, G., & Poole, M. (1994). Capturing the complexity in advanced technology use: Adaptive Structuration Theory. *Organization Science, 5*(2), 121–147. doi:10.1287/orsc.5.2.121

Edmunds, M. G., & Morgan, P. (2000). The *Antikythera* mechanism: Still a mystery of Greek astronomy? *Astronomy & Geophysics, 41*(6), 6.10-6.17.

Federici, T. (2010). OS e Tecnologie Avanzate per la Valorizzazione della Conoscenza nel Settore Archeologico. *Archeologia e Calcolatori, 2*, 259–263.

Freeth, T., Bitsakis, Y., Moussas, X., Seiradakis, J. H., Tselikas, A., & Mankou, E. (2006). Decoding the ancient Greek astronomical calculator known as the Antikythera mechanism. *Nature, 444*(30), 587–591. doi:10.1038/nature05357

Fronza, V., Nardini, A., & Valenti, M. (2002). An integrated information system for archaeology data management: latest developments. In *Proceedings of CAA2002: Conference on the Digital Heritage of Archaeology* (pp. 147-153). Retrieved from http://archeologiamedievale.unisi.it/NewPages/Testi/fronza02.pdf

Fulloni, A. (2010). *Fori Imperiali, il mistero delle 500 casse: Bronzi, mosaici, affreschi e persino una tela di lino: riemergono i reperti catalogati nel '39. Ora in caveau.* Retrieved from http://roma.corriere.it/roma/notizie/cronaca/10_settembre_12/fori-impieariali-mistero-500-casse-1703745805200.shtml

Jones, M., & Karsten, H. (2008). Gidden's Structuration Theory and information systems research. *Management Information Systems Quarterly, 32*(1), 127–157.

Karmacharya, A., Cruz, C., Boochs, F., & Marzani, F. (2008). Managing knowledge for spatial data: A case study with industrial archaeological findings. In *Proceedings of the International Conference on Digital Heritage in the New Knowledge Environment: Share Spaces & Open Paths to Cultural Context,* Athens, Greece.

Kintigh, K. (2006). The promise and challenge of archaeological data integration. *American Antiquity, 71*(3), 567–578. doi:10.2307/40035365

Lauzikas, R. (2005). Digitization of cultural heritage: model of an integral, three-dimensional spatio-temporal thesaurus. *Archeologia e Calcolatori, 16,* 93–112.

Markus, L., & Silver, M. (2008). A foundation for the study of IT effects: A new look at DeSanctis and Poole's concepts of structural features and spirit. *Journal of the Association for Information Systems, 9*(10-11), 609–632.

McAfee, A., McFarland, F., & Wagonfeld, A. (2004). Enterprise IT at Cisco. *Harvard Business Review*.

Niederman, F., Birggs, R., de Vreede, G., & Kolfschoten, G. (2008). Extending the contextual and organizational elements of Adaptive Structuration Theory in GSS research. *Journal of the Association for Information Systems, 9*(10-11), 633–652.

Pedelì, C. (2008, December 8-14). *An information system for the ordinary management of the archaeological and documental patrimony: overview of the conceptual model.* Paper presented at the 6th International Conference on Science and Technology in Archaeology and Conservation, Rome, Italy.

Pedelì, C., & Pesciarelli, R. (1997). ArkeoKeeper: A computer recorder and controller of conservation and restoration work on the archaeological mobile finds. In *Proceedings of the 8th Journée d'études de la SFIIC,* Chalon-sur-Saône, France.

Poole, M. S., & DeSanctis, G. (1990). Understanding the use of group decision support systems: the theory of adaptive structuration . In Fulk, J., & Steinfield, C. (Eds.), *Organizations and communication technology* (pp. 173–193). Newbury Park, CA: Sage.

Pozzenbon, M., & Pinsonneault, A. (2005). Challenges in conducting empirical work using structuration theory: Learning from IT research. *Organization Studies*, *26*(9), 1353–1376. doi:10.1177/0170840605054621

Schultze, U., & Orlikowski, W. (2004). A practice perspective on technology-mediated network relations: The use of Internet-based self-serve technologies. *Information Systems Research*, *15*(1), 87–106. doi:10.1287/isre.1030.0016

Tokmakidis, K., Kalyvioti, M. E., & Nankou, P. (2004). *Geographic information system applied in archaeological site.* Paper presented at the Archeological Surveys Workshop on Spatial Information System for Archaeology (WAS3), Athens, Greece.

Voorrips, A. (1998). Electronic information systems in archaeology: Some notes and comments. *Archeologia e Calcolatori*, *9*, 251–267.

Watrall, E., & Siarto, J. (2007). IAKS: A proposal for a Web 2.0 archaeological knowledge management system. In *Proceedings of the International Cultural Heritage Informatics Meeting* Toronto, ON, Canada.

Wüst, T., Neibiker, S., & Landolt, R. (2004). Applying the 3D GIS Dilas to archaeology and cultural heritage projects – requirements and first results. *International Archives of Photogrammetry Remote Sensing and Spatial Information Sciences*, *35*(5), 407–412.

This work was previously published in the Journal of Cases on Information Technology, Volume 14, Issue 1, edited by Mehdi Khosrow-Pour, pp. 26-45, copyright 2010 by IGI Publishing (an imprint of IGI Global).

474

Compilation of References

Abecker, A., Bernardi, A., Hinkelmann, K., Kuhn, O., & Sintek, M. (2000). Context-aware, proactive delivery of task-specific knowledge: The KnowMore project. *International Journal on Information Systems Frontiers, 2*(3/4), 139–162.

Ajzen, I. (1991). The theory of planned behavior. *Organizational Behavior and Human Decision Processes, 50*, 179–211. doi:10.1016/0749-5978(91)90020-T

Alani, H., & Brewster, C. (2005). Ontology ranking based on analysis of concept structures. In *Proceedings of the 3rd International Conference on Knowledge Capture (K-Cap '05),* Banff, Canada (pp. 51-58).

Alani, H., Dasmahapatra, S., Gibbins, N., Glasser, H., Harris, S., Kalfoglou, Y., et al. (2002). Managing reference: Ensuring referential integrity of ontologies for the Semantic Web. In *Proceedings of the 13th International Conference on Knowledge Engineering and Knowledge Management (EKAW '02),* Siguenza, Spain (pp. 317-334).

Alavi, M., & Leidner, D. (1997). Knowledge management systems: Emerging views and practices from the field. *Proceedings of the 32nd IEEE Hawaii International Conference on System Sciences.*

Al-Hakim, L. (2007). Information quality function deployment. In Al-Hakim, L. (Ed.), *Challenges of Managing Information Quality in Service Organizations* (pp. 26–50). Hershey, PA: IGI Global.

Alkin, K., & Okay, E. (2008). *The process of alignment with Basel II by SMEs in Turkey and recommendations* (pp.68, 74). (Istanbul Chamber of Trade, Publication No: 2008-4).

Allen, D. (2007). Cost/Benefit analysis for implementing ECM, BPM systems. *The Information Management Journal, 41*(3), 34.

Alter, S. (1980). *Decision support systems: Current practice and continuing challenge.* Reading: MA Addison Wiley.

Al-Zamany, Y. Hoddell. S. E. J., & Savage, B. M. (2002). Self assessment and obstacles to their implementation in Yemen, TQM and change management. In S.K.M. Ho & J. Dalrymple (Ed.), *Proceedings of the 7ᵗʰ International Conference on ISO 9000 and TQM.* RMIT University, Melbourne, Australia.

AMR Research (currently part of Gartner inc.). (2005). *Market Analytix Report: ERP 2004-2009.*

Compilation of References

Antonacopoulou, E. P., & FitzGerald, L. (1996). Reframing competency in management development. *Human Resource Management Journal*, *6*, 27–46. doi:10.1111/j.1748-8583.1996.tb00395.x

Antonides, G. (1998). *An attempt at integration of economic and psychological theories of consumption. European Perspectives on Consumer Behavior*. Prentice Hall, Europe.

Anwar, N., Kanok-Nukulchai, W., & Batanov, D. (2005). Component based, information oriented structural engineering applications. *Journal of Computing in Civil Engineering*, *19*(1), 45–57. doi:10.1061/(ASCE)0887-3801(2005)19:1(45)

Ardagna, C. A., Damiani, E., Frati, F., & Reale, S. (2007). Secure Authentication Process for High Sensitive Data E-Services: A Roadmap. *Journal of Cases on Information Technology*, *9*(1), 20–35. doi:10.4018/jcit.2007010102

Argyris, C., & Schön, D. A. (1978). *Organizational Learning: A Theory of Action Perspective*. Reading, MA: Addison-Wesley.

Argyris, C., & Schön, D. A. (1996). *Organizational Learning II: Theory, Method and Practice*. Reading, MA: Addison-Wesley.

Arh, T., Pipan, M., Jerman-Blažič, B. (2006). Virtual learning environment for the support of life-long learning initiative. *WSEAS transactions on advances in engineering education*, *4*(4), str. 737–743.

Arh, T., Dimovski, V., & Jerman-Blažič, B. (2008). *Model of impact of technology-enhanced organizational learning on business performance. V P. Cunningham, M. Cunningham (ur.), Collaboration and the knowledge economy: issues, applications, case studies, (str. 1521–1528)*. Netherlands: IOS Press.

Arvan, A. (1988). Those fabulous Japanese banks. *Bankers Monthly*, *105*(1), 29–35.

Augier, M., & Knudsen, T. (2004). The architecture and design of the knowledge organization. *Journal of Knowledge Management*, *8*(4), 6–20. doi:10.1108/13673270410548450

Autry, C. W., Griffis, S. E., & Goldsby, T. J. (2005). Warehouse management systems: Resource commitment, capabilities, and organizational performance. *Journal of Business Logistics*, *26*(2), 165–182. doi:10.1002/j.2158-1592.2005.tb00210.x

Awad, E., & Ghaziri, H. (2004). *Knowledge management*. Upper Saddle River, NJ: Prentice Hall.

Ballou, D. P., & Pazer, H. L. (1995). Modelling data and process quality in multi-input, multi-output information systems. *Management Science*, *31*(2), 150–162. doi:10.1287/mnsc.31.2.150

Bancroft, N. (1996). *Implementing SAP R/3*. Greenwich, CT: Manning Publication Co.

Bandura, A. (2001). Social cognitive theory: An agentic perspective. *Annual Review of Psychology*, *52*, 1–26. doi:10.1146/annurev.psych.52.1.1

Barwise, J., & Seligman, J. (1997). Information flow: The logic of distributed systems (Cambridge Tracts in Theoretical Computer Science 44). Cambridge, UK: Cambridge University Press.

Basili, R. V., Shull, F., & Lanubile, F. (1999). Building knowledge through families of experiments. *IEEE Transactions on Software Engineering*, *25*(4), 456–473. doi:10.1109/32.799939

Batini, C., & Scannapieco, M. (2006). *Data quality*. Springer-Verlag.

Beck, U., Giddens, A., & Lash, S. (1994). *Reflexive modernization. Politics, tradition and aesthetics in the modern social order.* Cambridge: Polity Press.

Berglund, M., Laarhoven, G., & Wandel, S. (1999). Third-party logistics: Is there a future? *International Journal of Logistics Management, 10*(1), 59–71. doi:10.1108/09574099910805932

Bingham, D. (1999). *Food and beverage companies need to integrate information enterprise-wide.* Beverage Online.

Bizer, C., & Seaborne, A. (2004). *D2RQ -treating non-RDF databases as virtual RDF graphs.* Paper presented at the 3rd International Semantic Web Conference (ISWC2004), Hiroshima, Japan.

Bjorklund, D. F. (1995). *Information processing approaches: An introduction to cognitive development.* Washington, D.C.: Brooks-Cole.

Bobrowski, M., Marre, M., & Yankelevich, D. (2002). A Neat Approach for Data Quality Assessment. In Piattini, Calero & Genero (Ed.), Information and Database Quality (pp. 135-162), Hershey, PA: IGI Global.

Bollen, K. A. (1989). *Structural equations with latent variables.* New York: Wiley.

Bosak, J., & McGrath, T. (1999). *Universal business language v2.0.* Retrieved from http://docs.oasis-open.org/ubl/cs-UBL-2.0/UBL-2.0.html

Bose, R. (2004). Knowledge management metrics. *Industrial Management & Data Systems, 104*(6), 457–468. doi:10.1108/02635570410543771

Boudreau, M., & Robey, D. (2005). Enacting integrated information technology: A human agency perspective. *Organization Science, 16*(1), 3–18. doi:10.1287/orsc.1040.0103

Bouquet, P., Magnini, B., Scrafini, L., & Zanobini, S. (2003). A SAT-based algorithm for context matching. In *Proceedings of the 4th International and Interdisciplinary Conference on Modeling and Using Context (Context03).*

Boxall, P. (1996). The strategic HRM debate and the resource-based view of the firm. *Human Resource Management Journal, 6,* 59–70. doi:10.1111/j.1748-8583.1996.tb00412.x

Braccini, A. M., & Federici, T. (2010). An IS for archaeological finds management as a platform for knowledge management: The ArcheoTRAC Case. *VINE: The Journal of Information and Knowledge Management Systems, 40*(2), 136–152.

Brazel, J. F., & Dang, L. (2008). The effect of ERP system implementations on the management of earnings and earnings release dates. *Journal of Information Systems, 22*(2), 1–21. doi:10.2308/jis.2008.22.2.1

Brown, J. S., & Duguid, P. (1991). Organizational learning and communities of practice: Toward a unified view of working, learning and innovation. *Organization Science, 2,* 40–57. doi:10.1287/orsc.2.1.40

Brown, J. S., & Duguid, P. (2000). *The social life of information.* Boston, MA: Harvard Business School Press.

Brumec, J., & Vrček, N. (2002). Genetic taxonomy: The theoretical source for IS modelling methods. In *Proceeding of the ISRM Conference,* Las Vegas, NV (pp. 245-252).

Compilation of References

Brumec, J., Dušak, V., & Vrček, N. (2001). The strategic approach to ERP system design and implementation. *Journal of Information and Organizational Sciences, 24*.

Brumec, J., Vrček, N., & Dušak, V. (2001). Framework for strategic planning of information systems. In *Proceedings of the 7th Americas Conference on Information Systems*, Boston, MA (pp. 123-130).

Brumec, J. (1998). Strategic planning of information systems. *Journal of Information and Organizational Sciences, 23*, 11–26.

Bukowitz, W., & Williams, R. (2000). *The knowledge management fieldbook*. London: Prentice Hall.

Burns, T., & Stalker, G. M. (1961). *The management of innovation*. London: Tavistock.

Business Maps of India. (2010). Pharmaceutical companies in India. Retrieved November 11, 2011, from http://business.mapsofindia.com/india-company/pharmaceutical.html

Carr, N. G. (2003). IT doesn't matter. *Harvard Business Review, 81*(5), 41.

Cavanagh, A. (1999). Behaviour in public? Ethics in online ethnography. *Cybersociology, 6*. Retrieved June 15, 2009, from http://www.cybersociology.com/files/6_2_ethicsinonlineethnog.html

CEN. (2007). *CEN CWA 15668: Business requirements specification - Cross industry invoicing process*. Retrieved from ftp://ftp.cenorm.be/PUBLIC/EBES/CWAs/CWA%2015668.pdf

CEN. (2009). *List of published ICT CEN workshop agreements*. Retrieved from http://www.cen.eu/cenorm/sectors/sectors/isss/cen+workshop+agreements/cwa_listing.asp

Centre for Retail Research. (2009). *The global retail theft barometer 2009*. Nottingham, UK: Author. Retrieved November 10, 2009, from http://www.globalretailtheftbarometer.com/pdf/GRTB_2009_ENGLISH.pdf

Chakravarthy, B. (1997). A new strategy framework for coping with turbulence. *Sloan Management Review*, (Winter): 69–82.

Chatterjee, D., Grewal, R., & Sambamurthy, V. (2002). Shaping up for e-commerce: Institution enablers of the organizational assimilation of Web technologies. *Management Information Systems Quarterly, 26*(2), 65. doi:10.2307/4132321

Chomsky, N. (1996). *Language and problems of knowledge*. Mendocino, CA: MIT Press.

Chou, D., Tripuramully, H., & Chou, A. (2005). BI and ERP integration. *Information Management & Computer Security, 13*(5), 340–349. doi:10.1108/09685220510627241

Clark, J. (1999). *W3C: XSL transformations (NAICS) (XSLT)*. Retrieved from http://www.w3.org/TR/xslt

Clayman, S., & Heritage, J. (2002). *The news interview: journalists and public figures on the air*. Cambridge: Cambridge University Press. doi:10.1017/CBO9780511613623

Collins, C. J., & Smith, K. G. (2006). Knowledge exchange and combination: the role of human resource practices in the performance of high-technology firms. *Academy of Management Journal, 49*(3), 544–560.

Compeau, D. R., & Higgins, C. A. (1995). Computer self-efficacy: Development of a measure and initial test. *Management Information Systems Quarterly, 19*, 189–211. doi:10.2307/249688

Cosmas, J., Itagaki, T., Green, D., Grabc-zewski, E., Weimer, F., Van Gool, L., et al. (2001). 3D MURALE: a multimedia system for archaeology. In *Proceedings of the Conference on Virtual Reality, Archaeology, and Cultural Heritage* (pp. 297-306). New York, NY: ACM.

Council of Supply Chain Management Professionals. (2008). *CSCMP*. Retrieved from http://www.cscmp.org

Cournane, M., & Grimley, M. (2006). *Universal business language (UBL) naming and design rules.* Retrieved from http://www.oasis-open.org/committees/download.php/20093/cd-UBL-NDR-2.0.pdf

Coyle, J. J., Bardi, E. J., & Langley, C. J. Jr. (2003). *The Management of Business Logistics: A Supply Chain Perspective*. Cincinnati, OH: South-Western.

CRM2day. (2004). *Business intelligence.* Retrieved from www.crm2day.com/bi

Crossan, M., Lane, H. W., & White, R. E. (1999). An organizational learning framework: from intuition to institution. *Academy of Management Review*, *24*(3), 522–537. doi:10.2307/259140

Daft, R. (2007). *Understanding the theory and design of organizations*. Thomson South-Western.

Daft, R. L., & Lengel, R. H. (1986). Organizational information requirements, media richness and structural design. *Management Science*, *32*, 554–571. doi:10.1287/mnsc.32.5.554

Dalkir, K. (2005). *Knowledge management in theory and practice*. Amsterdam: Elsevier.

Data monitor. (2001). *Business intelligence from data to profit.* Retrieved from www.researchandmarkets.com

Davenport, T., & Hansen, M. (1998). *Knowledge management at Andersen consulting.* Case 9-499-032, Harvard Business School Press, Boston.

Davenport, T. (1998). Putting the enterprise into the enterprise system. *Harvard Business Review*, *76*(4), 121–131.

Davenport, T. H., De Long, D. W., & Beers, M. C. (1998). Successful knowledge management projects. *Sloan Management Review*, *39*(2), 43–57.

Davis, F. D. (1989). Perceived usefulness, perceived ease of use, and user acceptance of information technology. *Management Information Systems Quarterly*, (September): 319–338. doi:10.2307/249008

De Amicis, F., & Batini, C. (2004). A methodology for data quality assessment on financial data. In *Studies in communication sciences* (pp. 115-136).

De Mooij, M. (2003). Convergence and divergence in consumer behavior: Implications for global advertising. *International Journal of Advertising*, *22*(2), 183–202.

De Sanctis, G., & Poole, M. S. (1994). Capturing the complexity in advanced technology use: Adaptive structuration theory. *Organization Science*, *5*, 121–147. doi:10.1287/orsc.5.2.121

De Solla Price, D. (1975). *Gears from the Greeks: the Antikythera Mechanism: A Calendar Computer from ca. 80 BC*. New York, NY: Science History.

Deerwester, S., Dumais, S., Landauer, T., Furnas, G., & Harshman, R. (1990). Indexing by Latent Semantic Analysis. *Journal of the American Society for Information Science American Society for Information Science, 41*(6), 391–407. doi:10.1002/(SICI)1097-4571(199009)41:6<391::AID-ASI1>3.0.CO;2-9

DeLone, W., & McLean, E. (1992). Information systems success: The quest for the dependable variable. *Information Systems Research, 3*(1), 60–95. doi:10.1287/isre.3.1.60

DeLone, W., & McLean, E. (2003). The DeLone and McLean Model of Information Systems success: A ten-year update. *Journal of Management Information Systems, 19*(4), 9–30.

Denton, D. K., & Wisdom, B. L. (1992). Shared vision. In Thompson, A. A. Jr, Fulmer, W. E., & Strickland, A. J. III, (Eds.), *Readings in strategic management* (pp. 52–56). Boston: Irwin.

DeSanctis, G., & Poole, M. (1994). Capturing the complexity in advanced technology use: Adaptive Structuration Theory. *Organization Science, 5*(2), 121–147. doi:10.1287/orsc.5.2.121

Dewan, S., & Kraemer, K. L. (1998). International dimensions of the productivity paradox. *Communications of the ACM, 41*(8), 56–62. doi:10.1145/280324.280333

Diamantopoulos, A., & Siguaw, J. A. (2000). *Introducing LISREL*. London: SAGE Publications.

DiBella, J. A., & Nevis, E. C. (1998). *How Organizations Learn – An Integrated Strategy for Building Learning Capability*. San Francisco, CA: Jossey-Bass.

Dimovski, V. (1994). *Organisational learning and competitive advantage*. Unpublished doctoral dissertation, Cleveland State University.

Dimovski, V., & Colnar, T. (1999). Organizacijsko učenje. *Teorija in Praksa, 5*(36), 701–722.

Dinevski, D., & Plenković, M. (2002). Modern University and e-learning. *Media, culture and public relations, 2*, 137–146.

Ding, D., & Chen, J. (2007). Supply chain coordination with contracts game between complementary suppliers. *International Journal of Information Technology & Decision Making, 6*(1), 163–175. doi:10.1142/S0219622007002332

Do, H.-H., & Rahm, E. (2002). COMA: A system for flexible combination of schema matching approaches. In *Proceedings of the 28th International Conference on Very Large Databases (VLDB '02)*, Hong Kong, China.

Doan, A., Madhavan, J., Domingos, P., & Halevy, A. (2002). Learning to map between ontologies on the Semantic Web. In *Proceedings of the 11th International World Wide Web Conference (WWW 2002)*, Hawaii, USA.

Dodgson, M. (1993). Organizational learning: a review of some literatures. *Organization Studies, 14*(3), 375–394. doi:10.1177/017084069301400303

Donnelly, J. H. (1970). Marketing notes and communications: Attitudes toward culture and approach to international advertising. *Journal of Marketing*, 60–63.

Dotsika, F. (2006). An IT perspective on supporting communities of practice. In Coakes, E., & Clarke, S. (Eds.), *Encyclopedia of communities of practice in information and knowledge management* (pp. 257–263). Hershey, PA: Idea Group. doi:10.4018/978-1-59140-556-6.ch045

Drew, P., & Heritage, J. (1992). Analyzing talk at work: an introduction. In Drew, P., & Heritage, J. (Eds.), *Talk at work: interaction in institutional settings* (pp. 3–65). Cambridge: Cambridge University Press.

Drew, P., & Heritage, J. (Eds.). (2006). *Conversation analysis*. London: Sage.

Drickhamer, D. (2005, September). Labor management software: The final profit frontier. *Material Handling Management*. Retrieved January 28, 2009, from http://mhmonline.com

Drucker, P. (1998). The next information revolution. *Forbes*. Retrieved from www.forbes.com

Drucker, P. (2006). *Classic Drucker*. Harvard Business School Publishing Corporation.

Duarte, D. L., & Tennant Snyder, N. (2001). *Mastering virtual teams: Strategies, tools, and techniques that succeed*. San Francisco, CA: Jossey-Bass.

Dubé, L., Bourhis, A., & Jacob, R. (2006). Towards a typology of virtual communities of practice. *Interdisciplinary Journal of Information, Knowledge, and Management*, *1*, 69–93.

Duggan, E. W., & Reichgelt, H. (2006). *Measuring information systems delivery quality*. Hershey, PA: IGI Global.

Dwork, C., Kumar, S., Naor, M., & Sivakumar, D. (2001). Rank aggregation methods for the Web. In *Proceedings of the 10th International Conference on World Wide Web* (pp. 613-622).

Dzbor, M., Takeda, H., & Vargas-Vera, M. (Eds.). (2005). *Proceedings of the User-SWeb: Workshop on End User Aspects of the Semantic Web (UserSWEB'05), CEUR (137) WS*. Retrieved from http://sunsite.informatik.rwth-aachen.de/Publications/CEUR-WS//Vol-137

Earl, M. J. (1996). Information Systems Strategy…Why Planning Techniques are not the Answer. *Business Strategy Review*, *7*(1), 54–58. doi:10.1111/j.1467-8616.1996.tb00115.x

Edenius, M., & Borgerson, J. (2003). To manage knowledge by intranet. *Knowledge Management*, *7*(5), 124–136. doi:10.1108/13673270310505430

Edmunds, M. G., & Morgan, P. (2000). The *Antikythera* mechanism: Still a mystery of Greek astronomy? *Astronomy & Geophysics*, *41*(6), 6.10-6.17.

Edwards, J. S., Handzic, M., Carlsson, S., & Nissen, M. (2003). Knowledge management research and practice: Visions and directions. *Knowledge Management Research & Practice*, *1*(1), 49–60. doi:10.1057/palgrave.kmrp.8500005

Ehrig, M., & Staab, S. (2004). QOM - quick ontology mapping. In *Proceedings of the 3rd International Semantic Web Confernece (ISWC'04)*, Hiroshima, Japan (LNCS 3298, pp. 683-697).

Electropedia, I. E. C. (2008). Retrieved from http://www.electropedia.org.

Compilation of References

English, L. P. (1999). *Improving data warehouse and business information quality: Methods for reducing costs and increasing profits*. New York: Wiley.

EU. (2006). Council directive 2006/112/EC of 28 November 2006 on the common system of value added tax. *Official Journal of the European Union. L&C, L347*(1).

EU. (2010). Council directive 2010/45/EU of 13 July 2010 amending directive 2006/112/EC on the common system of value added tax as regards the rules on invoicing. *Official Journal of the European Union. L&C, L189*(1).

Euromonitor International. (2009). *Convenience Stores - India*. London, UK: Author.

European Parliament and the Council (2003). *Directive 2003/54/EU of the European Parliament and of the Council of 26 June 2003 concerning common rules for the internal market in electricity and repealing Directive 96/92/EC.*

Euzenat, J. (2004). An API for ontology alignment. In *Proceedings of the 3rd International Semantic Web Confernece (ISWC'04)*, Hiroshima, Japan (LNCS 3298, pp. 698-712).

Euzenat, S. (2007). *Ontology matching*. Heidelberg: Springer Verlag.

Evans., J. & Dean, J. (2003). *Total quality management, Organization and strategy*. Ohio: Thomson/South-Western.

Evans, D., & Yen, D. C. (2005). E-government: An analysis for implementation: Framework for understanding cultural and social impact. *Government Information Quarterly, 22*(3), 354–373. doi:10.1016/j.giq.2005.05.007

Evans, J. R., & Lindsay, W. M. (2005). *The management and control of quality* (6th ed.). Ohio: Thomson/South-Western.

Eysenbach, G. (2001). An ontology of quality initiatives and a model for decentralized, collaborative quality management on the (semantic) World Wide Web. *Journal of Medical Internet Research, 3*(4), e34. doi:10.2196/jmir.3.4.e34

Fagin, R., Kumar, R., & Sivakumar, D. (2003). Efficient similarity search and classification via rank aggregation. In *Proceedings of the ACM SIGMOD International Conference on Management of Data.*

Fan, M., Stallaert, J., & Whinston, A. (2000). The adoption and design methodologies of component-based enterprise systems. *European Journal of Information Systems, 9*, 25–35. doi:10.1057/palgrave.ejis.3000343

Federici, T. (2010). OS e Tecnologie Avanzate per la Valorizzazione della Conoscenza nel Settore Archeologico. *Archeologia e Calcolatori, 2*, 259–263.

Figueiredo, P. N. (2003). Learning processes features: How do they influence inter-firm differences in technological capability - Accumulation paths and operational performance improvement? *International Journal of Technology Management, 26*(7), 655–689. doi:10.1504/IJTM.2003.003451

Filipi, A., & Lissonnet, S. (2008, September). Using wikis to create tests. *Teacher Magazine*, 20-22.

Filipi, A. (2009). *Toddler and parent interaction: the organisation of gaze, pointing and vocalisation*. Amsterdam, Philadelphia: John Benjamins Publishing.

Fiol, C. M., & Lyles, M. A. (1985). Organizational learning. *Academy of Management Review, 10*(4), 803–813. doi:10.2307/258048

Fordham University. (n.d.). *Royal licenses to export and import, 1205-1206*. Retrieved from http://www.fordham.edu/halsall/source/carol-devillis.html

Forrester, M. A. (2008). The emergence of self-repair: a case study of one child during the early preschool years. *Research on Language and Social Interaction, 41*(1), 99–128.

Fox, W. M. (1995). Sociotechnical system principles and guidelines: past and present. *The Journal of Applied Behavioral Science, 31*, 91–105. doi:10.1177/0021886395311009

Francalanci, C. (2001). Predicting the implementation effort of ERP projects: Empirical evidences on SAP R/3. *Journal of Information Technology, 16*(1), 33–48. doi:10.1080/02683960010035943

Frank, U. (2006). *Evaluation of reference models*. In P. Fettke, & P. Loos (Eds.), *Reference modeling for business systems analysis* (pp. 118-140). Idea Group.

Freeman, E. R. (1984). *Strategic Management – A Stakeholder Approach*. London: Pitman.

Freeman, E. R. (1994). Politics of Stakeholder Theory: Some Future Directions. *Business Ethics Quarterly, 4*, 409–422. doi:10.2307/3857340

Freeth, T., Bitsakis, Y., Moussas, X., Seiradakis, J. H., Tselikas, A., & Mankou, E. (2006). Decoding the ancient Greek astronomical calculator known as the Antikythera mechanism. *Nature, 444*(30), 587–591. doi:10.1038/nature05357

Fremantle, P., & Patil, S. (2009). *Web services reliable messaging*. Retrieved from http://www.oasis-open.org/committees/download.php/272/ebMS_v2_0.pdf

Fronza, V., Nardini, A., & Valenti, M. (2002). An integrated information system for archaeology data management: latest developments. In *Proceedings of CAA2002: Conference on the Digital Heritage of Archaeology* (pp. 147-153). Retrieved from http://archeologiamedievale.unisi.it/NewPages/Testi/fronza02.pdf

Fryling, M. (2005). ERP implementation dynamics. *Information Science and Policy*. University at Albany. State University of New York, Oct. 2005.

Fulloni, A. (2010). *Fori Imperiali, il mistero delle 500 casse: Bronzi, mosaici, affreschi e persino una tela di lino: riemergono i reperti catalogati nel '39. Ora in caveau*. Retrieved from http://roma.corriere.it/roma/notizie/cronaca/10_settembre_12/fori-impieariali-mistero-500-casse-1703745805200.shtml

Fussell, S. R., & Benimoff, I. (1995). Social and cognitive processes in interpersonal communication: Implications for advanced telecommunications technologies. *Human Factors, 37*, 228–250. doi:10.1518/001872095779064546

Gable, G., Sedera, D., & Chan, T. (2003). Enterprise systems success: A measurement model. *Proceedings of the 24th ICIS,* (pp. 576-591). Seattle, Washington.

Gable, G., van Den Heever, R., Erlank, S., & Scott, J. (2001). Large packaged application software maintenance: A research framework. *Journal of Software Maintenance and Evolution: Research and Practice, 13*(6), 351–371. doi:10.1002/smr.237

Compilation of References

Galliers, B. (1999). Towards the integration of e-business, knowledge management and policy considerations within an information systems strategy framework. *The Journal of Strategic Information Systems, 8*(3), 229–234. doi:10.1016/S0963-8687(00)00023-8

Galliers, R. D., Swatman, P. M. C., & Swatman, P. A. (1995). Strategic Information-Systems Planning - Deriving Comparative Advantage from Edi. *Journal of Information Technology, 10*(3), 149–157. doi:10.1057/jit.1995.19

Galliers, R., & Newell, S. (2003). Back to the future: From knowledge management to data management. *Information Systems and E-Business Management, 23*(3), 209–235.

Galloway, L. (2006). E-Learning Winter Showcase and Learning Symposium Highlights Best Practices and Innovative Approaches. *T+D, 60*(2), 14.

Ganter, B., & Wille, R. (1999). *Formal concept analysis: Mathematical foundations.* Berlin, Germany: Springer.

Gartner Group. (2000). *Key issues in e-government strategy and management.* Stamford, CT: Gartner Group.

General Accounting Office. (2007). *Internal Control Weaknesses Governmentwide Led to Improper and Abusive Use of Premium Class Travel.* Washington, DC: Author.

General Accounting Office. (n.d.). *Federal Travel Regulations.* Washington, DC: U.S. Government Printing Office. Retrieved June 25, 2008, from http://www.gpoaccess.gov/cfr/

Gephart, R. P., Boje, D. M., & Thatchenkery, T. J. (1996). Postmodern management and the coming crises of organizational analysis. In Gephart, R. P. (Eds.), *Postmodern Management and Organization Theory* (pp. 1–20). Thousand Oaks, CA: Sage.

Gerbing, D. W., & Anderson, J. C. (1988). An updated paradigm for scale development incorporating unidimensionality and measurement error. *JMR, Journal of Marketing Research, 25*, 186–192. doi:10.2307/3172650

Giddens, A. (1984). *The constitution of society: Outline of the theory of structuration.* Cambridge, UK: Polity Press.

Giddens, A. (1991). *Modernity and self-identity. Self and society in the late modern age.* Stanford, CA: Stanford University Press.

Giles, J. (2005). Internet encyclopaedias go head to head. *Nature, 438*(7070), 900–901. doi:10.1038/438900a

Goh, S., & Richards, G. (1997). Benchmarking the learning capability of organizations. *European Management Journal, 15*(5), 575–583. doi:10.1016/S0263-2373(97)00036-4

Gonsalves, A. (2004, March 5). *Albertsons Launches RFID Initiative.* Retrieved January 29, 2009, from http://www.networkcomputing.com

Goodhue, D. L., & Thompson, R. L. (1995). Task-technology fit and individual performance. *Management Information Systems Quarterly,* (June): 213–232. doi:10.2307/249689

Goodwin, C. (1995). Seeing in depth. *Social Studies of Science, 25*, 237–274. doi:10.1177/030631295025002002

Goodwin, C. (1996). Transparent vision. In Ochs, E., Schegloff, E. A., & Thompson, S. A. (Eds.), *Interaction and grammar* (pp. 370–404). Cambridge: Cambridge University Press. doi:10.1017/CBO9780511620874.008

Gottschalk, P. (1999). Strategic information systems planning: the IT strategy implementation matrix. *European Journal of Information Systems*, *8*(2), 107–118. doi:10.1057/palgrave.ejis.3000324

GovTrip. (2007). *The Department of the Interior Selects Northrop Grumman's Gov-Trip!* Retrieved June 25, 2008, from http://www.govtrip.com/govtrip/site/document.jsp?docID=807

GovTrip. (n.d.). *Implementation*. Retrieved June 25, 2008, from http://www.govtrip.com/govtrip/site/section_more.jsp?sid=4

Graham, S. L. (2007). Disagreeing to agree: Conflict, (im)politeness and identity in a computer-mediated community. *Journal of Pragmatics*, *3*, 742–759. doi:10.1016/j.pragma.2006.11.017

Greer, C. R. (1995). *Strategy and human resources. A general managerial perspective*. Englewood Cliffs, NJ: Prentice-Hall.

Gregor, S., & Benbasat, I. (1999). Explanations from intelligent systems: Theoretical foundations and implications for practice. *Management Information Systems Quarterly*, *23*, 497–527. doi:10.2307/249487

GS1. (2009). *Key features of GS1 XML*. Retrieved from http://www.gs1.org/ecom/xml/overview

Guinchiglia, F., Shvaiko, P., & Yatskevich, M. (2004). S-Match: An algorithm and an implementation of semantic matching. In *Proceedings of 1st European Semantic Web Symposium (ESWS'04)*, Crete, Greece, (pp. 61-75).

Gustafson, L. T., & Reger, R. K. (1995). Using organizational identity to achieve stability and change in high velocity environments. *Academy of Management Journal, Best Papers Proceedings*, 464-468.

Gustin, C., Daugherty, P., & Ellinger, A. (1997). Supplier selection decisions in system/software purchases. *International Journal of Purchasing and Materials Management*, *33*(4), 41–47.

Hachigian, N. (2002). Roadmap for e-government in the developing world: 10 questions e-government leaders should ask themselves. In RAND Corporation (Ed.), *Working group on eGovernment in the developing world* (pp. 1-24). Los Angeles, CA: Pacific Council on International Policy.

Hall, G., & Danby, S. (2003). Teachers and academics co-constructing the category of expert through meeting talk. *Proceedings of the Annual Conference of the Australian Association for Research in Education*. Retrieved June 15, 2009, from http://www.aare.edu.au/03pap/hal03027.pdf

Hall, E. T. (1977). *Beyond Culture*. Garden City, NY: Anchor Press/Doubleday.

Hall, E. T. (1983). *The Dance of Life*. Garden City, NY: Anchor Press/Doubleday.

Hamel, G., & Prahalad. (1993). Strategy as stretch and leverage. *Harvard Business Review*, (March-April): 75–85.

Compilation of References

Hammer, M., & Champy, J. (1993). *Reengineering the corporation: A manifesto for the business revolution.* New York, NY: Harper Business.

Handy, C. (1995, May-June). Trust and the virtual organization. *Harvard Business Review, 73*(3), 40–50.

Harrington, H. J. (1991). *Business process improvement.* US: McGraw-Hill.

Harrison, S. (2000). Maintaining the virtual community: use of politeness strategies in an email discussion group. In L. Pemberton & S. Shurville (Eds.), *Words on the web: computer mediated communication* (pp. 69-78). Exeter & Portland, OR: Intellect Books.

Hayler, R., & Nichols, D. M. (2007). *Six Sigma for financial services, how leading companies are driving results with Lean, Six Sigma, and process improvement, profiles from global leaders including AMERICAN EXPRESS, BANK OF AMERICA, WACHOVIA, and LLOYDS TSB.* New York: McGraw-Hill.

He, B., & Chang, K. C. (2003). Statistical schema matching across Web query interfaces. In *Proceedings of SIGMOD Conference* (pp. 217-228).

Heintzman, R., & Marson, B. (2005). People, service and trust: Is there a public sector service value chain? *International Review of Administrative Sciences, 71*(4), 549–575. doi:10.1177/0020852305059599

Helfert, M., Zellner, G., & Sousa, C. (2002). Data quality problems and proactive data quality management in data-warehouse-systems. In *Proceedings of BIT-World 2002,* Guyaquil, Ecuador.

Henry, P. (2001). E-learning technology, content and services. *Education + Training, 43*(4), 251–259.

Hepp; M. (2004). *OntoMeter: Metrics for ontologies.* 1st European Semantic Web Symposium (ESWS2004), Heraklion, Greece, May 10-12.

Hepp, M. (2007). Possible ontologies: How reality constrains the development of relevant ontologies. *IEEE Internet Computing, 11*(1), 90–96. doi:10.1109/MIC.2007.20

Heritage, J. (1984). *Garfinkel and ethnomethodology.* Cambridge: Polity Press.

Hester, S., & Eglin, P. (1997). Membership categorization analysis: an introduction. In Hester, S., & Eglin, P. (Eds.), *Culture in action: studies in membership categorization analysis* (pp. 1–23). Washington: International Institute for Ethnomethodology and University Press of America.

Hevner, A. R., March, S. T., Park, J., & Ram, S. (2004). Design science research in information systems. *Management Information Systems Quarterly, 28*(1), 75–105.

Hinrichs, H. (2002). *Datenqualitätsmanagement in data warehouse-systemen.* Phd thesis, University of Oldenburg, Germany.

Hoeing, C. (2001). Beyond e-government: building the next generation of public services. *Government Executive, 33*(14), 49–60.

Hofstede, G. (1980). *Culture's Consequences: International Differences in Work-Related Values.* London: Sage Publications.

Hofstede, G. (1991). *Cultures and Organizations: Software of the Mind.* New York: McGraw-Hill.

Holsapple, C., & Whinston, A. B. (1996). *Decision support systems: A knowledge based approach.* Minneapolis, MN: West Publishing.

Holton, J. A. (2001). Building trust and collaboration in a virtual team. *Team Performance Management*, *7*(3/4), 36–47. doi:10.1108/13527590110395621

Hong Hai, D. (2006). *Schema matching and mapping-based data integration: Architecture, approaches and evolution.* VDM Verlag Dr. Müller.

How Products are Made. (2011). *The manufacturing process of soap.* Retrieved October 13, 2011, from http://www.madehow.com/Volume-2/Soap.html#ixzz3qH1Q5YLh

Huang, K.-T., Lee, Y. W., & Wang, R. Y. (1999). *Quality information and knowledge.* Upper Saddle River, NJ: Prentice Hall PTR.

Huber, G. P. (1991). Organizational Learning: The Contributing Processes and the Literatures. *Organization Science*, *2*(1), 88–115. doi:10.1287/orsc.2.1.88

Hutley, P. S. B., & Russell, P. A. (3rd ed.). (2005). *An introduction to the Financial Services Reform Act, 2001.* Australia: LexisNexis Butterworths.

IEC - International Electrotechnical Commission. (2003). *IEC 61970-301: Energy management system application program interface (EMS-API) – Part 301: Common Information Model (CIM) Base.* International Electrotechnical Commission.

Ifinedo, P. (2006a). Extending the Gable et al. enterprise systems success measurement model: A preliminary study. *Journal of Information Technology Management, 17*(1), 14-33.

Ifinedo, P., & Nahar, N. (2007). ERP system success: An empirical analysis of how two organizational stakeholder groups prioritize and evaluate relevant measures. *Enterprise Information Systems*, *1*, 25–48. doi:10.1080/17517570601088539

Inkpen, A., & Crossan, M. M. (1995). Believing is seeing: Organizational learning in joint ventures. *Journal of Management Studies*, *32*(5), 595–618. doi:10.1111/j.1467-6486.1995.tb00790.x

International Organization for Standardization. (2006). *ISO/IEC 19757-3:2006: Information technology -- Document schema definition language (DSDL) -- Part 3: Rule-based validation – Schematron.* Retrieved from http://www.iso.org/iso/iso_catalogue/catalogue_tc/catalogue_detail.htm?csnumber=40833

Jaques, D., & Salmon, G. (2006). *Learning in groups: a handbook for face-to-face and online environments.* Hoboken: Taylor & Francis.

Jarzabkowski, P. (2008). Shaping strategy as a structuration process. *Academy of Management Journal*, *51*, 621–650.

Jefferson, G. (1972). Side sequences. In Sudnow, D. (Ed.), *Studies in social interaction* (pp. 294–338). New York: Free Press.

Jessup, L., & Valacich, J. (2006). *Information Systems Today: Why IS Matters* (2nd ed.). Old Tappan, NJ: Prentice Hall.

Jones, G. R. (2000). *Organizational Theory* (3rd ed.). New York: Prentice Hall.

Jones, M., & Karsten, H. (2008). Gidden's Structuration Theory and information systems research. *Management Information Systems Quarterly*, *32*(1), 127–157.

Jones, P., Clarke-Hill, C., Shears, P., Comfort, D., & Hillier, D. (2004). Radio frequency identification in the UK: Opportunities and challenges. *International Journal of Retail & Distribution Management*, *32*(3), 164–171. doi:10.1108/09590550410524957

Jordan, D., & Evdemon, J. (2007). *Web services business process execution language version 2.0.* Retrieved from http://docs.oasis-open.org/wsbpel/2.0/OS/wsbpel-v2.0-OS.html

Jöreskog, K. G., & Sörbrom, D. (1993). *LISREL 8: Structural Equation Modelling with the SIMPLIS Command Language*. London: Lawrence Erlbaum Associates Publishers.

Kahai, S. S., Sosik, J. J., & Avolio, B. J. (1997). Effects of leadership style and problem structure on work group process and outcomes in an electronic meeting system environment. *Personnel Psychology*, *50*, 121–146. doi:10.1111/j.1744-6570.1997.tb00903.x

Kahl, S. (1999). What's the 'value' of supply chain software? *Supply Chain Management Review*, *4*(4), 59–67.

Kalfoglou, Y., & Hu, B. (2005). CMS: CROSI mapping system - results of the 2005 ontology alignment contests. In *Proceedings of the K-Cap'05 Integrating Ontologies workshop*, Alberta, Canada.

Kalfoglou, Y., & Hu, B. (2006). Issues with evaluating and using publicly available ontologies. In *Proceedings of the 4th International EON workshop*, Edinburgh, UK.

Kalfoglou, Y., Hu, B., Reynolds, D., & Shadbolt, N. (2005). *CROSI project: Final report* (CROSI project deliverable). University of Southampton and HP Labs Bristol.

Kalfoglou, Y., & Schorlemmer, M. (2003). Ontology mapping: the state of the art. *The Knowledge Engineering Review*, *18*(1), 1–31. doi:10.1017/S0269888903000651

Kalfoglou, Y., & Schorlemmer, M. (2003b). IF-Map: An ontology mapping method based on information flow theory. *Journal on Data Semantics*, *1*, 98–127.

Kallinikos, J. (2004). Deconstructing information packages: Organizational and behavioral implications of ERP systems. *Information Technology & People*, *17*, 8–30. doi:10.1108/09593840410522152

Kamaladevi, B. (2010). Customer experience management in retailing. *Business Intelligence Journal*, *3*(1), 37–54.

Kaplan, R. S., & Norton, D. P. (1992). Balanced Scorecard – Measures That Drive Performance. *Harvard Business Review*, *1–2*, 71–79.

Karmacharya, A., Cruz, C., Boochs, F., & Marzani, F. (2008). Managing knowledge for spatial data: A case study with industrial archaeological findings. In *Proceedings of the International Conference on Digital Heritage in the New Knowledge Environment: Share Spaces & Open Paths to Cultural Context*, Athens, Greece.

Keskin, E. (2008). *Access to financing for SME's in the EU and Turkey*. REX/264 EU-Turkey Joint Consultative Committee, 25th meeting of the EU-Turkey Joint Consultative Committee Paris, France, 18-19 November, 2008.

Khaled, M. (2006). *Toward building a knowledge management system in a design firm: The case of Khatib and Alami structural department*. Master's thesis, American University of Beirut, Lebanon.

Kintigh, K. (2006). The promise and challenge of archaeological data integration. *American Antiquity*, *71*(3), 567–578. doi:10.2307/40035365

Kirchner, P. A., & Pass, F. (2001). Web enhanced higher education: a Tower of Babel. *Computers in Human Behavior*, *17*(4), 347–353. doi:10.1016/S0747-5632(01)00009-7

Kissoon, S. V. (2007). Continuous improvement teamwork in the Australian banking sector. In *Proceedings of the 5th ANZAM and 1st Asian Pacific Operations Management Symposium 2007*. RMIT University, Melbourne, Australia.

Kissoon, S. V. (2008a). Toward the conceptual model of Continuous Improvement Teamwork: A participant observation study. In F. Zhao (Ed.), *Information Technology Entrepreneurship and Innovation* (250-276). Hershey, PA: IGI Global.

Kissoon, S. V. (2008b). Ethnographic research cycle to evidence the Continuous Improvement Teamwork model. *Qualitative Research Journal*, *8*(2), 134–136. doi:10.3316/QRJ0802134

Knowledge @ Wharton. (n.d.). *Home page*. Retrieved November 12, 2011, from http://knowledge.wharton.upenn.edu

Kolsaker, A., & Lee-Kelley, L. (2007). G2C e-Government: Modernisation or transformation? *Electronic Government*, *4*(1), 68–75. doi:10.1504/EG.2007.012180

Kostic, T., Frei, C., Preiss, O., & Kezunovic, M. (2004). *Scenarios for data exchange using standards IEC 61970 and IEC 61850*. Cigre Paris 2004. IEEE Publishing.

Kotorov, R. (2001). Virtual organization: Conceptual analysis of the limits of its decentralization. *Knowledge and Process Management*, *8*(1), 55–62. doi:10.1002/kpm.93

Kraut, R. E., Rice, R. E., Cool, C., & Fish, R. S. (1998). Varieties of social influence: The role of utility and norms in the success of a new communication medium. *Organization Science*, *9*, 437–453. doi:10.1287/orsc.9.4.437

Krumbholz, M. (2000). Implementing enterprise resource planning packages in different corporate and national cultures. *Journal of Information Technology*, *15*(4), 267–280. doi:10.1080/02683960010008962

Kuhn, T. S. (1996). *The structure of scientific revolutions*. Chicago: University of Chicago Press.

Kumar, K., & Van Hillegersberg, J. (2000). ERP: Experience and evolution. *Communications of the ACM*, *43*, 23–26.

Kumar, V., Maheshwari, B., & Kumar, U. (2001). An investigation of critical management issues in ERP implementation: Empirical evidences from Canadian organizations. *Technovation*, *23*(10).

Lake, M. (2009). The art of creation in science: A consonant paradox. *Market Times*, *19*, 278–197.

Lam, S. S. K. (1998). Organizational performance and learning styles in Hong Kong. *The Journal of Social Psychology*, *138*(3), 401–403. doi:10.1080/00224549809600392

Lauriola, M., Levin, I. P., & Hart, S. S. (2007). Common and distinct factors in decision making under ambiguity and risk: A psychometric study of individual differences. *Organizational Behavior and Human Decision Processes*, *104*, 130–149. doi:10.1016/j.obhdp.2007.04.001

Compilation of References

Lauzikas, R. (2005). Digitization of cultural heritage: model of an integral, three-dimensional spatio-temporal thesaurus. *Archeologia e Calcolatori*, *16*, 93–112.

Lave, J., & Wenger, E. (1991). *Situated learning: Legitimate peripheral participation*. Cambridge, UK: Cambridge University Press.

Layne, K., & Lee, J. (2001). Developing fully functional e-Government: A four stage model. *Government Information Quarterly*, *18*(2), 122–136. doi:10.1016/S0740-624X(01)00066-1

Lee, P. M., & O'Neill, H. M. (2003). Ownership structures and R&D investments of US and Japanese firms: Agency and stewardship perspectives. *Academy of Management Journal*, *46*, 195–211.

Lei, D., Hitt, M. A., & Bettis, R. (1996). Dynamic core competencies through meta-learning and strategic context. *Journal of Management*, *22*(4), 549–569. doi:10.1177/014920639602200402

Lei, D., Slocum, J. W., & Pitts, R. A. (1999). Designing organizations for competitive advantage: The power of unlearning and learning. *Organizational Dynamics*, *27*(3), 24–38. doi:10.1016/S0090-2616(99)90019-0

Lenat, D. (1995). Cyc: A large scale investment in knowledge infrastructure. *Communications of the ACM*, *38*, 11.

Leonard-Barton, D. (1992). The factory as a learning laboratory. *Sloan Management Review*, *34*(1), 23–38.

Levitt, B., & March, J. G. (1998). Organizational learning. *Annual Review of Sociology*, *14*, 319–340. doi:10.1146/annurev.so.14.080188.001535

Levitt, T. (1983). The globalization of markets. *Harvard Business Review*, 92–102.

Liegl, P. (2009). *Business documents for inter-organizational business processes*. Unpublished doctoral dissertation, Vienna University of Technology, Vienna, Austria.

Light, B. (2001). The maintenance implications of the customization of ERP software. *Journal of Software Maintenance and Evolution: Research and Practice*, *13*(6), 415–429. doi:10.1002/smr.240

Lipnack, J., & Stamps, J. (1997). *Virtual teams: Reaching across space, time and organizations with technology*. New York: John Wiley & Sons.

Lipschutz, R. P. (2007). *GoToMeeting 3.0 Review*. Retrieved September 13, 2010, from http://www.pcmag.com/article2/0,2817,2154128,00.asp

Liu, L., & Chi, L. N. (2002). Evolutional data quality: A theory-specific view. In *Proceedings of 7th International Conference on Information Quality (ICIQ 2002),* Cambridge, MA.

Lozano-Tello, A., & Gomez-Perez, A. (2004). ONTOMETRIC: A method to choose the appropriate ontology. *Journal of Database Management*, *15*(2), 1–18.

Luthans, F., & Doh, J. P. (2009). *International management, culture, strategy, and behavior*. McGraw Hill.

MacManus, R., & Porter, J. (2005): *Web 2.0 for design: bootstrapping the social web*. Retrieved April 15th 2008, from: http://www.digital-web.com/articles/web_2_for_designers

Madapusi, A., & Kuo, C. (2007). Assessing data and information quality in ERP systems. *Proceedings of the Decision Sciences Institute Annual Meeting*, Arizona.

Madapusi, A., Kuo, C., & White, R. (2007). A critical factors approach to ERP information quality and decision quality. *Proceedings of the Decision Sciences Institute Annual Meeting*, Arizona.

Madhavan, J., Bernstein, P. A., Kuang, C., Halevy, A., & Shenoy, P. (2003). Corpus-based schema matching. In *Proceedings of the IJCAI'03 Workshop on Information Integration on the Web (IIWeb-03)*, Acapulco, Mexico.

Magnan Sieloff, S. (Ed.). (2008). *Mediating discourse online: AILA Applied Linguistics (Series 3)*. Amsterdam, Philadelphia: John Benjamins Publishing.

Maier, D., Muegeli, T., & Krejza, A. (2007). Customer investigation process at Credit Suisse: Meeting the rising demands of regulators. In Al-Hakim (Ed.), *Challenges of managing Information Quality in service Organizations* (pp. 52-76). Hershey, PA: IGI Global.

Management, V. B. (n.d.). *Business dictionary/management dictionary*. Retrieved from http://www.12manage.com/methods_value_based_management.html

Manz, C. C., & Stewart, G. L. (1997). Attaining flexible stability by integrating total quality management and socio-technical systems theory. *Organization Science*, *8*, 59–70. doi:10.1287/orsc.8.1.59

March, J. G. (2006). Rationality, foolishness, and adaptive intelligence. *Strategic Management Journal*, *27*(3), 201–214. doi:10.1002/smj.515

Markus, L., & Silver, M. (2008). A foundation for the study of IT effects: A new look at DeSanctis and Poole's concepts of structural features and spirit. *Journal of the Association for Information Systems*, *9*(10-11), 609–632.

Markus, M., & Robey, D. (1988). Information Technology and organizational change: Causal structure in theory and research. *Management Science*, *34*, 583–598. doi:10.1287/mnsc.34.5.583

Masur, J. (2004). Conversation analysis for educational technologists: theoretical and methodological issues for researching the structures, processes and meaning of online talk. In Jonassen, D. (Ed.), *Handbook of research for educational communications and technology* (pp. 1073–1098). New York: McMillan.

Maznevski, M. L., & Chudoba, K. M. (2000). Bridging Space Over Time: Global Virtual Team Dynamics and Effectiveness. *Organization Science*, *11*, 473–492. doi:10.1287/orsc.11.5.473.15200

McAfee, A., McFarland, F., & Wagonfeld, A. (2004). Enterprise IT at Cisco. *Harvard Business Review*.

McAfee, R., Glassman, M., & Honeycutt, E. (2002). The effects of culture and human resource management policies on supply chain management strategy. *Journal of Business Logistics*, *23*(1), 1–18. doi:10.1002/j.2158-1592.2002.tb00013.x

McCracken, G. (1989). Culture and consumer behavior: An anthropological perspective. *Journal of the Market Research Society. Market Research Society*, *32*(1), 56–73.

McDonald, k., et al. (2002). *Mastering SAP business information warehouse*. Canada: Wiley Publishing.

Compilation of References

McElroy, M. (2003). *The new knowledge management: Complexity, learning and sustainable innovation.* Boston: Butterworth-Heinemann.

Melkas, H. (2007). Analyzing information quality in virtual networks of the services sector with qualitative interview data. In Al-Hakim, L. (Ed.), *Challenges of managing Information Quality in service Organizations* (pp. 187–212). Hershey, PA: IGI Global.

Melnik, S., Garcia-Molina, H., & Rahm, E. (2002). Similarity flooding: A versatile graph matching algorithm and its application to schema matching. In *Proceedings of the 18th International Conference on Data Engineering (ICDE)* (pp. 117-128).

Mensching, J., & Corbitt, G. (2004). EPR data archiving- a critical analysis. *Journal of Enterprise Information Management, 17*(2), 131–141. doi:10.1108/17410390410518772

Meyer, M., & Zack, M. (1996). The design and implementation of information products. *Sloan Management Review, 37*(3), 43–59.

Mezher, T., Abdul-Malak, M. A., Ghosn, I., & Ajam, M. (2005). Knowledge management in mechanical and industrial engineering consulting: A case study. *Journal of Management Engineering, 21*(3), 138–147. doi:10.1061/(ASCE)0742-597X(2005)21:3(138)

Michael, S. (2004). GSA E-Travel mandatory. *Federal Computer Week, 18*(1), 14.

Miles, R. E., & Snow, C. C. (1992). Causes of failure in network organizations. *California Management Review, 34*(4), 53–72.

Miller, G. A. (1990). WORDNET: An online lexical database. *International Journal of Lexicography, 3*(4), 235–312. doi:10.1093/ijl/3.4.235

Miller, H. (1996). The multiple dimensions of information quality. *Information Systems Management, 13*(2), 79–82. doi:10.1080/10580539608906992

Milo, T., & Zohar, S. (1998). Using schema matching to simplify heterogeneous data translation. In *Proceedings of the 24rd International Conference on Very Large Data Bases (VLDB '98),* New York, NY, USA (pp. 122-133).

Miner, A. S., & Mezias, S. J. (1996). Ugly duckling no more: pasts and futures of organizational learning research. *Organization Science, 7*(1), 88–99. doi:10.1287/orsc.7.1.88

Min, H. (2006). The applications of warehouse management systems: An exploratory study. *International Journal of Logistics: Research and Applications, 9*(2), 111–126.

Ministry of the Economy. Labour and Entrepreneurship (MELE). (2007). *Strategy for the development of electronic business in the Republic of Croatia for the period 2007–2010.* Retrieved from http://www.mingorp.hr/defaulteng.aspx?ID=1089

Mintzberg, H. (1983). *Structure in fives: Designing effective organizations.* Upper Saddle River, NJ: Prentice Hall.

Mintzberg, H. (1987). Crafting Strategy. *Harvard Business Review*, 66–75.

Mintzberg, H. (1990). Strategy formation: Schools of thought. In Frederickson, J. W. (Ed.), *Perspectives of strategic management* (pp. 105–235). New York: Harper Business.

Mintzberg, H. (1994). The fall and rise of strategic planning. *Harvard Business Review,* (January-February): 107–114.

Mintzberg, H. (1996). Learning 1, planning 0. *California Management Review*, *38*(4), 92–93.

Mintzberg, H., & Ghoshal, S. (2003). *The Strategy Process: Concepts, Contexts, Cases*. Upper Saddle River, NJ: Pearson Education.

Morris, M. G., & Venkatesh, V. (2000). Age differences in technology adoption decisions: Implications for a changing work force. *Personnel Psychology*, *53*, 365–401. doi:10.1111/j.1744-6570.2000.tb00206.x

Mos, A., Boulze, A., Quaireau, S., & Meynier, C. (2008). Multi-layer perspectives and spaces in SOA. In *Proceedings of the 2nd International Workshop on Systems Development in SOA Environments*, Leipzig, Germany.

Mueller, R. O. (1996). *Basic Principles of Structural Equation Modelling: An Introduction to Lisrel and EQS*. New York: Springer.

Mueller, R. O. (1996). *Basic Principles of Structural Equation Modelling: An Introduction to Lisrel and EQS*. New York: Springer.

Mukherjee, A., & Patel, N. (2005). *FDI in retail sector*. New Delhi, India: Academic Foundation.

Munkvold, B. E., & Akselsen, S. E. (2003). *Implementing collaboration technologies in industry: Case examples and lessons learned*. London, UK: Springer.

Murphy, P. R., & Poist, R. E. (1993). In search of warehousing excellence: A multivariate analysis of HRM practices. *Journal of Business Logistics*, *14*(2), 145–164.

Murray, A. (2007). Overcoming Resistance to Change. *KM World*, *16*(9), 24.

Murray, P., & Donegan, K. (2003). Empirical linkages between firm competencies and organisational learning. *The Learning Organization*, *10*(1), 51. doi:10.1108/09696470310457496

Nah, F. H., Faja, S., & Cata, T. (2001). Characteristics of ERP software maintenance: A multi-cause study. *Journal of Software Maintenance and Evolution: Research and Practice*, *13*(6), 339–414. doi:10.1002/smr.239

Navarette, C. J., & Pick, J. B. (2002). Information technology expenditure and industry performance: The case of the Mexican banking industry. *Journal of Global Information Technology Management*, *5*(2), 7–28.

Newell, S., Robertson, M., Scarborough, H., & Swan, J. (2009). *Managing knowledge work and innovation*. Basingstoke, UK: Palgrave Macmillan.

Ngwenyama, O. K., & Lee, A. S. (1997). Communication richness in electronic mail: Critical social theory and the contextuality of meaning. *Management Information Systems Quarterly*, (June): 145–166. doi:10.2307/249417

Nicolaou, A. (2004). *ERP system implementation drivers of post-implementation success*. Decision Support in an Uncertain and Complex World: The IFIP TC8/WG8.3 International Conference, 2004, (pp. 589-597).

Nicolaou, A., & Bhattacharya, S. (2007). Organizational performance effects of ERP systems usage: The impact of post-implementation changes. *International Journal of Accounting Information Systems*, *7*(1), 18–35. doi:10.1016/j.accinf.2005.12.002

Niederman, F., Birggs, R., de Vreede, G., & Kolfschoten, G. (2008). Extending the contextual and organizational elements of Adaptive Structuration Theory in GSS research. *Journal of the Association for Information Systems*, *9*(10-11), 633–652.

Niederman, F., Mathieu, R., Morley, R., & Kwon, I. (2007). Examining RFID applications in supply chain management. *Communications of the ACM, 50*(7), 93–101. doi:10.1145/1272516.1272520

Nonaka, I. (1994). A dynamic theory of organizational knowledge creation. *Organization Science*, *5*(1), 14–37. doi:10.1287/orsc.5.1.14

Nonaka, I., & Takeuchi, H. (1996). A Theory of Organizational Knowledge Creation. *International Journal of Technology Management*, *11*(7/8), 833–846.

Northern European Subset (NES). (2009). *NES profiles.* Retrieved from http://www.nesubl.eu/documents/nesprofiles.4.6f60681109102909b80002525.html

Northrop Grumman Systems. (2007). *Online Booking Engine Sign In.* Retrieved November 5, 2007, from http://www.govtrip.com

Northrop Grumman. (2007). *Complete Document Processing Manual.* Retrieved November 5, 2007, from http://www.govtrip.com/govtrip/site/redir.jsp?docID=717

Northrop Grumman. (n.d.). *Federal Civilian Agencies.* Retrieved June 25, 2008, from http://www.it.northropgrumman.com/serve/agencies.html

Noy, F. N., & Musen, M. (2002). PROMPT-DIFF: A fixed-point algorithm for comparing ontology versions. In *Proceedings of the 18th National Conference on Artificial Intelligence, (AAAI'02)*, Edmonton, Alberta, Canada (pp. 744-751).

Noy, N., & Musen, M. (2003). The PROMPT suite: Interactive tools for ontology merging and mapping. *International Journal of Human-Computer Studies*, *59*(6), 983–1024. doi:10.1016/j.ijhcs.2003.08.002

Noy, N., Sintek, M., Decker, S., Crubezy, M., Fergeson, W., & Musen, M. (2001). Creating Semantic Web contents with Protege-2000. *IEEE Intelligent Systems*, *16*(2), 60–71. doi:10.1109/5254.920601

O'Brien, J., & Marakas, G. (2005). *Introduction to Information Systems* (13th ed.). New York: McGraw-Hill.

O'Leary, D. (2002). *Enterprise resource planning systems: System lifecycle, electronic commerce, and risk.* Cambridge, UK: Cambridge University Press.

O'Reilly, J. (2007). Market insight survey: 3PL perspectives. *Inbound Logistics, July*, 107.

O'Reilly, T. (2005). *What Is Web 2.0. Design Patterns and Business Models for the Next Generation of Software.* Retrieved November 10, 2009, from http://oreilly.com/web2/archive/what-is-web-20.html

OAGi. (1999). *OAGIS.* Retrieved from http://www.oagi.org/dnn/oagi/Home/tabid/136/Default.aspx

OASIS. (2002). *Message service specification version 2.0.* Retrieved from http://www.oasis-open.org/committees/download.php/272/ebMS_v2_0.pdf

OASIS. (2006). *Web services security (WSS).* Retrieved from http://www.oasis-open.org/committees/tc_home.php?wg_abbrev=wss

OECD. (2005). *E-Government for better government.* Retrieved from http://www.oecd.org/document/45/0,3343, en_2649_34129_35815981_1_1_1_1,00.html

OFFIS. (2008). *Ontologies for the utility domain.* Retrieved from http://www.offis.de/energie/ontologies

Ogden, C., & Richards, I. (1923). *The meaning of meaning: A study of the influence of language upon thought and of the science of symbolism.* San Diego, CA: Harcourt Brace Jovanovich.

O'Hara, K., & Shadbolt, N. (2001). Issues for an ontology for knowledge valuation. In *Proceedings of the IJCAI'01 workshop on E-Business and the Intelligent Web,* Seattle, WA, USA.

Olszak, C., & Ziemba, E., (2006). Business intelligence systems in the holistic infrastructure development - supporting decision-making in organizations. *Interdisciplinary Journal of Information, Knowledge, and Management, 1.*

Olszak, C., & Ziemba, E. (2007). Approach to building and implementing business intelligence system. *Interdisciplinary Journal of Information, Knowledge, and Management, 2,* 135–148.

OMG. (2006). *Business process modeling notation (BPMN) version 1.0: OMG final adopted specification.* Retrieved from http://www.bpmn.org/

Orlikowski, W. J. (1996). Improvising organizational transformation over time: A situated change perspective. *Information Systems Research, 7,* 63–92. doi:10.1287/isre.7.1.63

Orlikowski, W. J. (2002). Knowing in practice: Enacting a collective capability in distributed organizing. *Organization Science, 13*(3), 249–273. doi:10.1287/orsc.13.3.249.2776

Orr, J. (1996). *Talking about machines: An ethnography of a modern job.* Ithaca, NY: Cornell University Press.

Ouyang, C., Van der Aalst, W. M. P., Dumas, M., Ter Hofstede, A. H. M., & Mendling, J. (2009). From business process models to process-oriented software systems. *ACM Transactions on Software Engineering and Methodology, 19*(1). doi:10.1145/1555392.1555395

Palopoli, L., Terracina, G., & Ursino, D. (2003). DIKE: A system supporting the semi-automatic construction of cooperative information systems from heterogeneous databases. *Software. Practice, 33*(9), 847–884.

Pande, P. S., Newman, R. B., & Cavanagh, R. R. (2000). *The Six Sigma way, how GE, Motorola, and other top companies are honing the performance.* New York: McGraw-Hill.

Parr, A., & Schanks, G. (2000). A model of ERP project implementation. *Journal of Information Technology, 15*(4), 289–304. doi:10.1080/02683960010009051

Pasternack, B., & Viscio, A. (1998). *The center less corporation: A new model for transforming your organization for growth and prosperity.* New York.

Pava, C. (1986). Redesigning socio-technical systems design: Concepts and methods for the 1990s. *The Journal of Applied Behavioral Science, 22,* 201–221. doi:10.1177/002188638602200303

Pedelì, C. (2008, December 8-14). *An information system for the ordinary management of the archaeological and documental patrimony: overview of the conceptual model.* Paper presented at the 6th International Conference on Science and Technology in Archaeology and Conservation, Rome, Italy.

Pedelì, C., & Pesciarelli, R. (1997). Arkeo-Keeper: A computer recorder and controller of conservation and restoration work on the archaeological mobile finds. In *Proceedings of the 8th Journée d'études de la SFIIC,* Chalon-sur-Saône, France.

PEPPOL. (2008). *eProcurement without borders in Europe.* Retrieved from http://www.peppol.eu/

Péréz López, S., Montes Peón, J. M., & Vázquez Ordás, C. Managing knowledge: The link between culture and organizational learning. *Journal of Knowledge Management, 8*(6), 93–104. doi:10.1108/13673270410567657

Péréz López, S., Montes Peón, J. M., & Vázquez Ordás, C. Managing knowledge: The link between culture and organizational learning. *Journal of Knowledge Management, 8*(6), 93–104. doi:10.1108/13673270410567657

Pfeffer, J., & Salancik, G. R. (1978). *The external control of organizations: A resource dependence perspective.* New York: Harper & Row.

Plumlee, M. A. (2003). The effect of information complexity on analysts' use of that information. *Accounting Review, 78,* 275–296. doi:10.2308/accr.2003.78.1.275

Pomerantz, A. (1984a). Agreeing and disagreeing with assessments: some features of preferred/dispreferred turn shapes. In Maxwell Atkinson, J., & Heritage, J. (Eds.), *Structures of social action: studies in conversation analysis* (pp. 57–101). Cambridge: Cambridge University Press.

Pomerantz, A. (1984b). Pursuing a response. In Maxwell Atkinson, J., & Heritage, J. (Eds.), *Structures of social action: studies in conversation analysis* (pp. 152–163). Cambridge: Cambridge University Press.

Poole, M. S., & DeSanctis, G. (1990). Understanding the use of group decision support systems: the theory of adaptive structuration. In Fulk, J., & Steinfield, C. (Eds.), *Organizations and communication technology* (pp. 173–193). Newbury Park, CA: Sage.

Porter, M. E. (1979). *How competitive forces shape strategy.* New York: Free Press.

Porter, M. E. (1996). What is strategy? *Harvard Business Review,* (November-December): 61–78.

Powanga, M., & Powanga, L. (2008). Deploying RFID in logistics: Criteria and best practices and issues. *Business Review (Federal Reserve Bank of Philadelphia), 9*(2), 1–10.

Pozzenbon, M., & Pinsonneault, A. (2005). Challenges in conducting empirical work using structuration theory: Learning from IT research. *Organization Studies, 26*(9), 1353–1376. doi:10.1177/0170840605054621

Prahalad, C. (2004). Why selling to the poor makes for good business. *Fortune, 150*(10), 70–72.

Ptak, C., & Schragenheim, E. (2000). *ERP: Tools, techniques and applications for integrating the supply chain.* London, UK: Series on Resources Management, St Lucie Press/APICS.

Putnam, L. (2001). March/April). Distance teamwork: The realities of collaborating with virtual colleagues. *Online, 25*(2), 54–57.

Quinn, J. B. (1992). Managing strategic change. In A. A. Thompson, Jr., W. E. Fulmer & A. J. Strickland III (Eds.), *Readings in Strategic Management* (4th ed., pp. 19-42). Boston: Irwin. (Reprinted from *Sloan Management Review, 21,* 3-20).

Raelin, J. A. (1997). A model of work-based learning. *Organization Science, 8*(6), 563–578. doi:10.1287/orsc.8.6.563

Rahm, A., & Bernstein, A. (2001). A survey of approaches to automatic schema matching. *The Very Large Databases Journal, 10*(4), 334–350. doi:10.1007/s007780100057

Raisch, S., & Birkinshaw, J. (2008). Organizational ambidexterity: Antecedents, outcomes, and moderators. *Journal of Management, 34,* 375–409. doi:10.1177/0149206308316058

Raman, A., DeHoratius, N., & Ton, Z. (2001). Execution: The missing link in retail operations. *California Management Review, 43*(3), 136–152.

Rasmussen, N., Goldy, P., & Solli, P. (2002). *Financial business intelligence: Trends, technology, software selection and implementation.* New York, NY: Wiley.

Raub, S., & Von Wittich, D. (2004). Implementing knowledge management: Three strategies for effective CKOs. *European Management Journal, 22*(6), 714–724. doi:10.1016/j.emj.2004.09.024

Razzaque, M., & Sheng, C. (1998). Outsourcing of logistics functions: A literature survey. *International Journal of Physical Distribution & Logistics Management, 28*(2), 89–107. doi:10.1108/09600039810221667

Recker, J., Indulska, M., Rosemann, M., & Green, P. (2005). Do process modeling techniques get better? A comparative ontological analysis of BPMN. In *Proceedings of the 16th Australasian Conference on Information Systems.*

Resnick, P., & Zeckhauser, R. (2002). Trust among strangers in Internet transactions: Empirical analysis of eBay's reputation system. *Advances in Applied Mircroelectronics, 11.*

Reychav, I., & Weisberg, J. (2009). Good for workers, good for companies: How knowledge sharing benefits individual employees. *Knowledge and Process Management, 16*(4), 186–197. doi:10.1002/kpm.335

Reychav, I., & Weisberg, J. (2009). Good for workers, good for companies: How knowledge sharing benefits individual employees. *Knowledge and Process Management, 16*(4), 186–197. doi:10.1002/kpm.335

Ritzer, G. (2005). Structuration theory. *Contemporary Sociology: A Journal of Reviews, 36,* 84-85.

Roach, S. (1987). *America's technology dilemma: A profile of the information economy. Economics Newsletter Series.* New York: Morgan Stanley.

Robey, D., & Boudreau, M. (1999). Accounting for the contradictory organizational consequences of information technology. *Information Systems Research, 10,* 167–185. doi:10.1287/isre.10.2.167

Compilation of References

Robey, D., Boudreau, M., & Rose, G. M. (2000). Information Technology and Organizational Learning: a Review and Assessment of Research. *Accounting. Management and Information Technologies*, *10*, 125–155. doi:10.1016/S0959-8022(99)00017-X

Robinson, G. (2002). Key standards for utility enterprise application integration (EAI). In *Proceedings of the DistribuTech 2002 Miami*. Pennwell.

Robinson, J. H. (1904). *Readings in European history* (*Vol. I*). Ginn and Co.

Rogers, E. M. (1983). *Diffusion of innovations*. New York: Free Press.

Rogers, E. M., & Kincaid, D. L. (1981). *Communication networks: Toward a new paradigm for research*. New York: Free Press.

Rogin, J. (2006). GAO: DOD overstated travel system savings. *Federal Computer Week*, *20*(34), 12.

Rosenberg, M. (2001). *E-Learning, Strategies for Developing Knowledge in the Digital Age. New York*. McGraw-Hill.

Rouse, W. B. (1999). Connectivity, creativity, and chaos: Challenges of loosely-structured organizations. *Information & Knowledge Systems Management*, *1*, 117–131.

Russell, S. H. (2000). Growing world of logistics. *Air Force Journal of Logistics*, *24*(4), 15.

Rutner, C., & Langley, J. Jr. (2000). Logistics value: Definition, process and measurement. *International Journal of Logistics Management*, *11*(2), 73–83.

Salmon, G. (2000). *E-moderating: the key to teaching and learning online*. London, New York: Routledge.

Sauvage, T. (2003). The relationship between technology and logistics third-party providers. *International Journal of Physical Distribution & Logistics Management*, *33*(3), 236–253. doi:10.1108/09600030310471989

Scarff, A. (2006). Advancing knowledge sharing with Intranet 2.0. *Knowledge Management Review*, *9*(4), 24–27.

Schallert, M. (2003). Business process redesign in travel management in an SAP R/3 upgrade project--a case study. *Annals of Cases on Information Technology*, *5*, 319–327. doi:10.4018/978-1-59140-061-5.ch021

Schegloff, E. A. (1992). Repair after next turn: the last structurally provided defense of intersubjectivity in conversation. *American Journal of Sociology*, *97*, 1295–1345. doi:10.1086/229903

Schegloff, E. A. (1997). Third turn repair. In Guy, G. R., Feagin, C., Schiffrin, D., & Baugh, J. (Eds.), *Towards a social science of language: papers in honor of William Labov* (*Vol. 2*, pp. 31–40). Amsterdam, Philadelphia: John Benjamins.

Schegloff, E. A. (2000). When 'others' initiate repair. *Applied Linguistics*, *21*(2), 205–243. doi:10.1093/applin/21.2.205

Schegloff, E. A. (2007). *Sequence organization in interaction: a primer in conversation analysis* (*Vol. 1*). Cambridge: Cambridge University Press.

Schegloff, E. A., Jefferson, G., & Sacks, H. (1977). The preference for self-correction in the organization of repair in conversation. *Language*, *53*, 361–382. doi:10.2307/413107

Schein, E. (1992). *Organizational Culture and Leadership*. San Francisco: Jossey-Bass.

Schein, E. H. (1985). *Organizational Culture and Leadership*. San Francisco: Jossey Bass.

Schultze, U., & Orlikowski, W. (2004). A practice perspective on technology-mediated network relations: The use of Internet-based self-serve technologies. *Information Systems Research, 15*(1), 87–106. doi:10.1287/isre.1030.0016

Seddon, P. B. (1997). A re-specification and extension of the DeLone and McLean model of IS success. *Information Systems Research, 18*(3), 240–253. doi:10.1287/isre.8.3.240

Sedera, D., Gable, G., & Chan, T. (2004). Measuring enterprise systems success: The importance of a multiple stakeholder perspective. *Proceedings of the 12th European Conference on Information Systems*, (pp. 1-13). Turku, Finland.

Semler, S. W. (1997). Systematic agreement: a theory of organizational alignment. *Human Resource Development Quarterly, 8*, 23–40. doi:10.1002/hrdq.3920080105

Senge, P. M. (1990). *The fifth discipline: art and practice of the learning organization*. New York: Doubleday.

Senge, P. M. (1990). *The fifth discipline: art and practice of the learning organization*. New York: Doubleday.

Sevilla, C., & Wells, T. D. (1988). Contracting to ensure training transfer. *Training & Development, 6*(1), 10–11.

Shadbolt, N., O'Hara, K., & Crow, L. (1999). The experimental evaluation of knowledge acquisition techniques and methods: History, problems, and new directions. *International Journal of Human-Computer Studies, 51*, 729–755. doi:10.1006/ijhc.1999.0327

Sheppard, B. H., Harwick, J., & Warshaw, P. R. (1988). The theory or reasoned action: A meta-analysis of past research with recommendations for modifications and future research. *The Journal of Consumer Research, 15*, 325–343. doi:10.1086/209170

Shrivastava, P. A. (1983). Typology of Organizational Learning Systems. *Journal of Management Studies, 20*, 1–28. doi:10.1111/j.1467-6486.1983.tb00195.x

Shvaiko (2006). *An API for ontology alignment* (Version 2.1).

Siau, K., & Long, Y. (2006). Using Social Development Lenses to Understand E-Government Development. *Journal of Global Information Management, 14*(1), 47–62. doi:10.4018/jgim.2006010103

Simonin, B. L. (1997). The importance of collaborative know-how: An empirical test of the learning organization. *Academy of Management Journal, 40*(5), 1150–1173. doi:10.2307/256930

Simon, M., & Houghton, S. M. (2003). The relationship between overconfidence and the introduction of risky products: Evidence from a field study. *Academy of Management Journal, 46*, 139–149.

Sine, W. D., Mitsuhashi, H., & Kirsch, D. A. (2006). Revisiting Burns and Stalker: Formal structure and new venture performance in emerging economic sectors. *Academy of Management Journal, 49*, 121–132.

Škerlavaj, M. (2003). *Vpliv informacijsko-komunikacijskih tehnologij in organizacijskega učenja na uspešnost poslovanja: teoretična in empirična analiza*. Unpublished Master's theses. Ljubljana: Ekonomska fakulteta.

Compilation of References

Škerlavaj, M., & Dimovski, V. (2006). Study of the Mutual Connections among Information-communication Technologies, Organisational Learning and Business Performance. *Journal for East European Management Studies*, *11*(1), 9–29.

Slater, S. F., & Narver, J. C. (1995). Market orientation and the learning organization. *Journal of Marketing*, *59*(3), 63–74. doi:10.2307/1252120

Sloan, T. R., Hyland, P. W. B., & Beckett, R. C. (2002). Learning as a competitive advantage: Innovative training in the Australian aerospace industry. *International Journal of Technology Management*, *23*(4), 341–352. doi:10.1504/IJTM.2002.003014

Smith, B. (2004). Beyond concepts: Ontology as reality representation. In *Proceedings of the International Conference on Formal Ontology and Information Systems (FOIS 2004)*, Turin.

Smith, R. (2008). Aligning Competencies, Capabilities and Resources. *Research Technology Management: The Journal of the Industrial Research Institute*, September-October.

Smith, A. (1976). The wealth of nations. In Mossner, E. C., Ross, I. S., Campbell, R. H., Raphael, D. D., & Skinner, A. S. (Eds.), *The Glasgow edition of the works and correspondence of Adam Smith*. Oxford, UK: Oxford University Press.

Soh, C., & Tay-Yap, J. (2000). Cultural fits and misfits: Is ERP a universal solution? *Communications of the ACM*, *43*(4), 47–51. doi:10.1145/332051.332070

Specht, T., Drawehn, J., Thranert, M., & Kuhne, S. (2005). Modeling cooperative business processes and transformation to a service oriented architecture. In *Proceedings of the Seventh IEEE International Conference on E-Commerce Technology*, Munich, Germany (pp. 249-256).

SPOCS. (2009). *About the project.* Retrieved from http://www.eu-spocs.eu/index.php

Spott, D. (2000). Componentizing the enterprise applications packages. *Communications of the ACM*, *43*(4), 63–90. doi:10.1145/332051.332074

Spradley, J. P. (1980). *Participant observation*. USA: Thomson Learning Academic Resource Centre. Te`eni, D. (1993). Behavioural aspects of data production and their impact on data quality. *Journal of Database Management*, *4*(2), 30–38.

Srivastava, S. C., & Teo, T. S. H. (2007). E-Government Payoffs: Evidence from Cross-Country Data. *Journal of Global Information Management*, *15*(4), 20–40. doi:10.4018/jgim.2007100102

Stacey, R. D. (2005). Values, spirituality and organizations: a complex responsive processes perspective. In D. Griffin & R. Stacey, D. (Eds.), *Complexity and the Experience of Leading Organizations* (pp. 93-123). London: Routledge.

Stacey, R. D. (2007). *Strategic Management and Organisational Dynamics: The Challenge of Complexity* (5 ed.). Upper Saddle River, NJ: Prentice Hall.

Stacey, R. D. (2001). *Complex Responsive Processes in Organizations: Learning and Knowledge Creation (Complexity & Emergence in Organizations)*. London: Routledge.

Stacy, R. D. (1992). *Managing the unknowable. Strategic boundaries between order and chaos in organizations.* San Francisco: Jossey-Bass.

STA-Singapore Technologies Automobile. (1996). *Business improvement Hhandbook* (5th ed.). Singapore: Singapore Technologies.

Stedman, C. (1999, November 1). Failed ERP gamble haunts Hershey. *Computerworld.* Retrieved April 16, 2006, from www.computerworld.com

Stedman, C. (2002). Maximizing the ERP investment. *Competitive Financial Operations: The CFO Project, 1*, 1–6.

Steels, L., & Kaplan, F. (1999). Bootstrapping grounded word semantics. In T. Briscoe (Ed.), *Linguistic evolution through language acquisition: Formal and computational models.* Cambridge, UK: Cambridge University Press.

Stones, R. (2005). *Structuration theory.* New York: Palgrave-Macmillan.

STORK. (2009). *Stork at a glance.* Retrieved from https://www.eid-stork.eu/

Suerdem, A. (1993). Social de(re)construction of mass culture: Making (non) sense of consumer behavior. *International Journal of Research in Marketing, 11*, 423–443.

Sure, Y., Maedche, A., & Staab, S. (2000). Leveraging corporate skill knowledge - from ProPer to OntoProPer. In *Proceedings of the 3rd International Conference on Practical Aspects of Knowledge Management (PAKM2000),* Basel, Switzerland.

Synnott, W. R. (1987). *The information weapon: Winning customers and markets with technology.* New York: John Wiley & Sons.

Tallon, P. P., Kraemer, K. L., & Gurbaxani, V. (2000). Executives' perceptions of the business value of information technology - A process-oriented approach. *Journal of Management Information Systems, 16*(4), 145–173.

Tan, F. B., & Hunter, M. G. (2002). The repertory grid technique: A method for the study of cognition in information systems. *Management Information Systems Quarterly, 26*, 39–57. doi:10.2307/4132340

Tanner, C., Wölfle, R., & Quade, M. (2006). *The role of information technology in procurement in the top 200 companies in Switzerland.* Aarau, Switzerland: University of Applied Sciences Northwestern Switzerland.

Tanskanen, S.-K. (2007). Metapragmatic utterances in computer-mediated interaction. In Bublitz, W., & Hübler, A. (Eds.), *Metapragmatics in use* (pp. 87–106). Amsterdam, Philadelphia: John Benjamins.

Tanskanen, S.-K., & Karhukorpi, J. (2008). Concessive repair and negotiation of affiliation in e-mail discourse. *Journal of Pragmatics, 40*, 1587–1600. doi:10.1016/j.pragma.2008.04.018

Tarafdar, M., & Vaidya, S. D. (2005). Adoption & implementation of IT in developing nations: Experiences from two public sector enterprises in India. *Journal of Cases on Information Technology, 7*(1), 111–135. doi:10.4018/jcit.2005010107

Taylor, H., & Karlin, S. (1993). *Introduction to stochastic modeling.* London: Academic Press.

Taylor, S., & Todd, P. A. (1995). Understanding information technology usage: A test of competing models. *Information Systems Research, 6*, 144–176. doi:10.1287/isre.6.2.144

ten Have, P. (1999). *Doing conversation analysis*. London: Sage.

Terry, D. J., Hogg, M. A., & White, K. M. (1999). The theory of planned behavior: Self-identity, social identity and group norms. *British Journal of Psychological Society, 38*, 225–244. doi:10.1348/014466699164149

Teubner, A. (2007). Strategic information systems planning: A case study from the financial services industry. *The Journal of Strategic Information Systems, 16*(1), 105–125. doi:10.1016/j.jsis.2007.01.002

Tihanyi, L., Johnson, R. A., Hoskisson, R. E., & Hitt, M. A. (2003). Institutional ownership differences and international diversification: The effects of boards of directors and technological opportunity. *Academy of Management Journal, 46*, 195–211.

Tippins, M. J., & Sohi, R. S. (2003). IT competency and firm performance: Is organizational learning a missing link? *Strategic Management Journal, 24*(8), 745–761. doi:10.1002/smj.337

Titah, R., & Barki, H. (2005). E-Government Adoption and Acceptance: A Literature Review. *International Journal of Electronic Government Research, 2*(3), 23–57. doi:10.4018/jegr.2006070102

Tokmakidis, K., Kalyvioti, M. E., & Nankou, P. (2004). *Geographic information system applied in archaeological site*. Paper presented at the Archeological Surveys Workshop on Spatial Information System for Archaeology (WAS3), Athens, Greece.

Torres, L., Pina, V., & Acerete, B. (2005). E-government developments on delivering public services among EU cities. *Government Information Quarterly, 22*(2), 217–238. doi:10.1016/j.giq.2005.02.004

Treasury Board of Canada Secretariat. (n.d.). *Proactive Disclosure*. Retrieved December 30, 2008, from http://www.tbs-sct.gc.ca/pd-dp/index-eng.asp

Triggs, D. (1993). Justifying investment in technology. *Logistics Information Management, 6*(5), 20–27. doi:10.1108/09576059310045934

Trist, E. (1971). New directions of hope. *Regional Studies, 13*, 439–451. doi:10.1080/09595237900185381

Tsoukas, H. (2003). Do we really understand tacit knowledge? In Easterby-Smith, M., & Lyles, M. A. (Eds.), *Handbook of organizational learning and knowledge* (pp. 410–427). Malden, MA: Blackwell.

TUIK- Turkish Statistical Institute. (2003). *General census of industry and establishments*. Retrieved from https://www.tuik.gov.tr

Turban, E., Aronson, J. E., Liang, T. P., & Sharda, R. (2007). *Decision support and business intelligence systems*. New York: Prentice Hall.

Tversky, A., & Kahneman, D. (1983). Extensional versus intuitive reasoning: The conjunction fallacy in probability judgment. *Psychological Review, 90*, 293–315. doi:10.1037/0033-295X.90.4.293

U. S. Census Bureau. (2009). *North American industry classification system*. Retrieved from http://www.census.gov/eos/www/naics/

U.S. General Services Administration. (2003, August 15). Bush Administration's E-Travel Initiative Under Way: GSA Awards E- Travel Contract Expected to Save Millions. *PR Newswire, 1*. Retrieved December 4, 2008, from http://www.gsa.gov/Portal/gsa/ep/contentView.do?contentType=GSA_BASIC&contentId=12920&noc=T

U.S. Government. (2002). *E-government strategy: Implementing the President's* management *agenda for e-Government: Simplified delivery of services to citizens.* Retrieved September 30, 2008, from http://www.whitehouse.gov/omb/inforeg/egov-strategy.pdf

U.S. Government. (n.d.). *About E-Gov.* Retrieved November 12, 2007, from http://www.whitehouse.gov/omb/egov/g-1-background.html

Ulrich, D., Jick, T., & von Glinow, M. A. (1993). High-impact learning: Building and diffusing learning capability. *Organizational Dynamics, 22*(2), 52–66. doi:10.1016/0090-2616(93)90053-4

UN. (2008). *United Nations e-Government Survey 2008.* Retrieved December 30, 2008, from http://unpan1.un.org/intradoc/groups/public/documents/un/unpan028607.pdf

UN/CEFACT. (2003). *Core components technical specification – Part 8 of the ebXML framework.* Retrieved from http://www.unece.org/cefact/ebxml/CCTS_V2-01_Final.pdf

UN/CEFACT. (2008). *Business requirements specification (BRS) for the cross industry invoice V.2.0.* Retrieved from http://www.unece.org/cefact/brs/BRS_CrossIndustryInvoice_v2.0.pdf

UN/CEFACT. (2009). *Business requirement specifications.* Retrieved from http://www.unece.org/cefact/brs/brs_index.htm

United Nations Standard Products and Services Code (UNSPSC). (2009). *Welcome.* Retrieved from http://www.unspsc.org/

Uschold, M., & Jasper, R. (1999). A framework for understanding and classifying ontology applications. In *Proceedings of the IJCAI-99 Workshop on Ontologies and Problem-Solving Methods (KRR5),* Stockholm, Sweden.

Uschold, M. (2003). Where are the semantics in the Semantic Web? *AI Magazine, 24*(3), 25–36.

Uslar, M. (2006). The common information model for utilities: An introduction and outlook on future applications. In R. Eckstein & R. Tolksdorf (Eds.), *Proceedings of the XML-Days 2006 in Berlin, XML-clearinghouse.de* (pp.135-148).

Uslar, M. (2008). Ontology-based Integration of IEC TC 57 Standards. In *Proceedings of the I-ESA 2008 Conference on Interoperability for Enterprise Systems and Applications, Fraunhofer IPK, Berlin.*

Uslar, M., & Dahlem, N. (2006). Semantic Web technologies for power grid management. In R. Koschke, O. Herzog, K.-H. Rödiger & M. Ronthaler (Eds.), *Informatik 2007: Informatik trifft Logistik, Band 1, Beiträge der 37. Jahrestagung der Gesellschaft für Informatik e.V. (GI) 24.-27. September 2007.* In Bremen, 27(1), Gesellschaft für Informatik, Bonn, Köllen Verlag.

Uslar, M., et al. (2009). Untersuchung des Normungsumfeldes zum BMWi-Förderschwerpunkt. *e-Energy – IKT-basiertes Energiesystem der Zukunft.* Ministry of Economics, Germany.

Uslar, Streekmann & Abels (2007). MDA-basierte Kopplung heterogener Informationssysteme im EVU-Sektor - ein Framework. In A. Oberweis, C. Weinhardt, H. Gimpel, A. Koschmider & V. Pankratius (Eds.), *eOrganisation: Service-, Prozess-, Market-Engineering*, 8. Internationale Tagung Wirtschaftsinformatik, 2, Universitätsverlag Karlsruhe.

Vaidyanathan, G. (2005). A framework for evaluating third-party logistics. *Communications of the ACM*, *48*(1), 89–94. doi:10.1145/1039539.1039544

van der Smagt, T. (2000). Enhancing virtual teams: Social relations and communication technology. *Industrial Management + Data Systems, 100*(4), 148-156.

Van Hout, E. J. Th., & Bekkers, V. J. J. M. (2000). Patterns of virtual organization: The case of the National Clearinghouse for Geographic Information. *Information Infrastructure and Policy*, *6*, 197–207.

Van Wert, J. M. (2002), E-government and performance: a citizen-centered imperative. *The Public Manager,* 16-20.

Varney, S. (2008). Leadership learning: key to organizational transformation. *Strategic HR Review*, *7*(1), 5–10. doi:10.1108/14754390810880471

Verspoor, M., & Lowie, W. (2003). Making sense of polysemous words. *Journal of Language Learning*, *53*, 547–586. doi:10.1111/1467-9922.00234

Vijayaraman, B., & Osyk, B. (2006). An empirical study of RFID implementation in the warehousing industry. *International Journal of Logistics Management*, *17*(1), 6–15. doi:10.1108/09574090610663400

Voices of Words. (2010). Blog. Retrieved November 15, 2011, from http://ahssan.wordpress.com

Voorrips, A. (1998). Electronic information systems in archaeology: Some notes and comments. *Archeologia e Calcolatori, 9,* 251–267.

Voss, H. (1996, July/August). Virtual organizations: The future is now. *Strategy and Leadership*, 12–16. doi:10.1108/eb054559

Vrček, N., Dobrović, Ž., & Kermek, D. (2007). Novel approach to BCG analysis in the context of ERP system implementation. In Župančič, J. (Ed.), *Advances in information systems development* (pp. 47–60). New York, NY: Springer. doi:10.1007/978-0-387-70761-7_5

W3C. (2007). *Web services description language (WSDL) version 2.0 part 1: Core language.* Retrieved from http://www.w3.org/TR/wsdl20/

Wall, B. (1998). Measuring the Right Stuff: Identifying and Applying the Right Knowledge. *Knowledge Management Review*, *1*(4), 20–24.

Wand, Y., & Wang, R. Y. (1996). Anchoring data quality dimensions in ontological foundations. *Communications of the ACM*, *39*(11), 86–95. doi:10.1145/240455.240479

Wang, L., Bretschneider, S., & Gant, J. (2005) Evaluating Web-Based E-Government Services with a Citizen-Centric Approach. In *Proceedings of the 38th Annual Hawaii International Conference on Systems Sciences,* Big Island, Hawaii.

Wang, J. T.-L., Zhang, K., Jeong, K., & Shasha, D. (1994). A system for approximate tree matching. *IEEE Transactions on Knowledge and Data Engineering*, *6*(4), 559–571. doi:10.1109/69.298173

Wang, R. Y., Reddy, M. P., & Kon, H. B. (1995). Toward quality data: An attribute-based approach. *Decision Support Systems, 13*(3-4), 349–372. doi:10.1016/0167-9236(93)E0050-N

Wang, R. Y., & Strong, D. M. (1996). Beyond accuracy: What data quality means to data consumers. *Journal of Management Information Systems, 12*(4), 5–33.

Wasko, M. M., & Teigland, R. (2006). Distinguishing work groups, virtual teams, and electronic networks of practice. In Coakes, E., & Clarke, S. (Eds.), *Encyclopedia of communities of practice in information and knowledge management* (pp. 138–140). Hershey, PA: Idea Group. doi:10.4018/978-1-59140-556-6.ch027

Watrall, E., & Siarto, J. (2007). IAKS: A proposal for a Web 2.0 archaeological knowledge management system. In *Proceedings of the International Cultural Heritage Informatics Meeting* Toronto, ON, Canada.

Weber, N., & Buitelaar, P. (2006). Web-based otnology learning with ISOLDE. In *Proceedings of the Workshop on Web Content mining with Human Language, International Semantic Web Conference (ISWC '06),* Athens, USA.

Weber, M. (1971). *Makt og byråkrati: essays om politikk og klasse, samfunn.* Oslo, Norway: Gyldendal.

Webster's Dictionary. (1978). *Webster's new 20th century dictionary.* New York: Harper-Collins.

Webster, J. (1998). Desktop video teleconferencing: Experiences of complete users, wary users, and nonusers. *Management Information Systems Quarterly,* (September): 257–286. doi:10.2307/249666

Weiss, L. (1999). *Collection and connection: The anatomy of knowledge sharing in professional service firms.* Chicago.

Wenger, E. (1998). *Communities of practice: The key to knowledge strategy.* Cambridge, UK: Cambridge University Press.

Wenger, E. (2005). *Technology for communities.* Retrieved September 19, 2010, from http://technologyforcommunities.com/CEFRIO_Book_Chapter_v_5.2.pdf

Wenger, E., White, N., & Smith, J. D. (2009). *Digital habitats: Stewarding technology for communities.* Portland, OR: CPsquare.

Wenger, E. (1998). *Communities of practice. Learning, meaning and identity.* Cambridge, UK: Cambridge University Press.

Wenger, E. (1998). *Learning, meaning, and identity.* Cambridge, UK: Cambridge University Press.

Wenger, E. (2003). Communities of practice and social learning systems. In Nicolini, D., Gherardi, S., & Yanow, D. (Eds.), *Knowing in organizations. A practice-based approach* (pp. 76–99). New York, NY: M. E. Sharpe. doi:10.1177/135050840072002

Wenger, E. (2004). Knowledge management as a doughnut: Shaping your knowledge strategy through communities of practice. *Ivey Business Journal, 1,* 1–8.

Wenger, E., McDermott, R., & Snyder, W. M. (2002). *Cultivating communities of practice.* Cambridge, MA: Harvard Business School Press.

Compilation of References

West, D. M. (2008). *Improving Technology Utilization in Electronic Government around the World, 2008.* Retrieved December 29, 2008, from http://www.brookings.edu/~/media/Files/rc/reports/2008/0817_egovernment_west/0817_egovernment_west.pdf

White, P. (2003). Beyond modality and hedging: a dialogic view of the language of intersubjective stance. *Text, 23,* 259–284. doi:10.1515/text.2003.011

Wiig, K. (1993). *Knowledge management foundations.* Arlington, TX: Schema Press.

Wikipedia. (n.d.). *Soap.* Retrieved November 12, 2010, from http://en.wikipedia.org/wiki/Soap

Wilde, G. J. S. (2001). *Target risk.* Toronto: PDE Publications.

Wilks, Y., Webb, N., Setzer, A., Hepple, M., & Capitzone, R. (2005). Machine learning approaches to human dialogue modelling. In *Advances in natural multimodal dialogue systems.* Amsterdam: Kluwer Academic Publishers.

Williamson, E. (2006, September 27). Report Criticizes Pentagon's New Travel Booking System. *The Washington Post,* A.25.

Wolfe, R. A. (1994). Organizational innovation: Review, critique and suggested research directions. *Journal of Management Studies, 31,* 405–427. doi:10.1111/j.1467-6486.1994.tb00624.x

Woods, D., Thoeny, P., & Cunningham, W. (2007). *Wikis for dummies.* Hoboken: John Wiley & Sons.

Workman, M. (2005). Expert decision support system use, disuse, and misuse: A study using the theory of planned behavior. *Journal of Computers in Human Behavior, 21,* 211–231. doi:10.1016/j.chb.2004.03.011

Workman, M. (2007). Advancements in technology: New opportunities to investigate factors contributing to differential technology and information use. *Journal of Management and Decision Making, 8,* 221–240.

Workman, M., & Bommer, W. (2004). Redesigning computer call center work: A longitudinal field experiment. *Journal of Organizational Behavior, 25,* 317–337. doi:10.1002/job.247

World Bank. (2009). *e-Government - Definition of e-government.* Retrieved from http://web.worldbank.org/WBSITE/EXTERNAL/TOPICS/EXTINFORMATIONANDCOMMUNICATIONANDTECHNOLOGIES/EXTEGOVERNMENT/0,contentMDK:20507153~menuPK:702592~pagePK:148956~piPK:216618~theSitePK:702586,00.html

Wu, F., & Weld, D. (2008). Automatically refining the Wikipedia infobox ontology. In *Proceedings of the 17th International Conference on World Wide Web* (pp. 635-644).

Wunnenberg, C. A. Jr. (1977). Productivity in the warehouse: Who needs to automate? *Management Review,* (October): 55–59.

Wüst, T., Neibiker, S., & Landolt, R. (2004). Applying the 3D GIS Dilas to archaeology and cultural heritage projects – requirements and first results. *International Archives of Photogrammetry Remote Sensing and Spatial Information Sciences, 35*(5), 407–412.

Xu, H., Nord, J., Brown, N., & Nord, D. (2002). Data quality issues in implementing an ERP. *Industrial Management & Data Systems, 102*(1), 47–58. doi:10.1108/02635570210414668

Yen, D. C., Chou, D. C., & Chang, J. (2002). A synergic analysis for Web-based enterprise resource planning system. *Computer Standards & Interfaces, 24*(4), 337–346. doi:10.1016/S0920-5489(01)00105-2

Zdhanova, A., & Shvaiko, P. (2006). Community-driven ontology matching. In *Proceedings of the 3rd European Semantic Web Conference (ESWC '06)*, Budva, Montenegro.

Zhang, D. *Media structuration – Towards an integrated approach to interactive multimedia-based E-Learning.* (Ph.D. dissertation, The University of Arizona, 2002. Zhang, D., & Nunamaker, J. F. (2003). Powering e-learning in the new millennium: an overview of e-learning and enabling technology. *Information Systems Frontiers, 5*(2), 207–218.

Zimmermann, O., Doubrovski, V., Grundler, J., & Hogg, K. (2005). Service-oriented architecture and business process choreography in an order management scenario: Rationale, concepts, lessons learned. *Companion to the 20th Annual ACM SIGPLAN Conference on Object-oriented Programming, Systems, Languages, and Applications*, San Diego, CA (pp. 301-312).

About the Contributors

Mehdi Khosrow-Pour (DBA) received his Doctorate in Business Administration from the Nova Southeastern University (FL, USA). Dr. Khosrow-Pour taught undergraduate and graduate information system courses at the Pennsylvania State University – Harrisburg for 20 years where he was the chair of the Information Systems Department for 14 years. He is currently president and publisher of IGI Global, an international academic publishing house with headquarters in Hershey, PA (www.igi-global.com). He also serves as executive director of the Information Resources Management Association (IRMA) (www.irma-international.org) and executive director of the World Forgotten Children's Foundation (www.world-forgotten-children.org). He is the author/editor of over twenty books in information technology management. He is also the editor-in-chief of the *Information Resources Management Journal*, the *Journal of Cases on Information Technology*, the *Journal of Electronic Commerce in Organizations* and the *Journal of Information Technology Research* and has authored more than 50 articles published in various conference proceedings and journals.

* * *

Asem Abdul-Malak is a Professor of Engineering Management at the American University of Beirut. He earned a BS in Civil Engineering from Beirut Arab University, and Master and PhD in Construction Management from University of Texas at Austin in 1986 and 1990 respectively. His research interests include Construction management, decision support tools for project and construction management, construction planning and scheduling, cost estimating and bidding for construction, administration and resolution of construction claims and disputes, materials management for large construction projects, and work process design for engineering and construction enterprises.

Amit Agrahari is an Assistant Professor of Information Systems at the Indian Institute of Management, Lucknow. Before joining IIM Lucknow, he worked with

Infosys Technologies Ltd for over two years as a member of its research lab and worked on Business Process Management. He is a Fellow of XLRI Jamshedpur, India. He has published in *Journal of e-Commerce in Organization, Journal of Internet Commerce* and has co-edited a book titled *"e-Procurement in Emerging Economies: Theory and Cases"* published by Idea Group Publishing, USA.

Tushar Agrawal is a management graduate from Shri Shankaracharya Group of Institutions, India.

Sami Akabawi is a professor of Information Systems in the Management Department, School of Business at the American University in Cairo, Egypt, since 1983. Akabawi has been active participant in the local and regional business community in the capacity of ICT consultant and advisor to many institutions. During his career, he has provided extensive professional consultancy services to many Egyptian and regional industrial and trading organizations for the development, use, and adoption of ICT and information systems within their management and operational business processes. Akabawi's current research interests cover the architecting, design, development, and implementation of ICT infrastructures; adoption and institutionalization of enterprise systems; impacts of the use of ICT artifacts on the human agency's behavior particularly in developing countries environment. He holds a Ph.D. in Computer Science from the City University, London (1977), a Master of Science in Computer Science from London University (1973), and a Bachelor of Science in Industrial Engineering from Cairo University (1967).

Ramazan Aktas is Professor and Chair of Business Administration Department at TOBB University of Economics and Technology. He has over 25 years' experience teaching graduate and undergraduate business courses including financial management, financial analysis, entrepreneurship, and introduction to business. He has taught many seminars to businesspeople on subjects like financial statement analysis, financial mathematics, risk management, SMEs, entrepreneurship, et cetera. He is also the director of the Continuing Education Center of TOBB University of Economics and Technology. His interest areas are corporate finance, financial markets and institutions, investment and portfolio analysis, and SMEs analysis. Prof. Aktas holds a B.S. in Business Administration from Military Academy, Ankara-Turkey, a Master's degree in Middle East Technical University, Ankara-Turkey, and a Ph.D. in Business Administration from Ankara University, Political Science Faculty. He has written 7 books and many articles in business publications.

Mustafa Al Shawi is a Professor of IT in Construction at the University of Salford. He holds many international advisory posts in various countries and a consultant to the World Bank. He is also the Editor in Chief of the international journal *Construction Innovation: Information, Process, Management* and the author of more than hundred publications in fields such as integrated computer environments, databases, object oriented databases, IT strategies, CAD, planning automation, and IS success factors. Professor Alshawi is the founder of five innovative postgraduate courses ranging from PG Diploma, MSc, Master of Research, and PhD (without residence). His leading work in management of information in collaborative environments, integrated databases in construction and computer integration are internationally known. His computer environments, such as SPACE and WISPER, have set up a vision for future work practices, which enable different professionals to share and exchange project information.

Tanja Arh graduated of Computer Science at the Faculty of Organizational Sciences, University of Maribor. She obtained her Master's degree at the Faculty of Organizational Sciences, University of Maribor. She is a PhD candidate at Faculty of Economics, University of Ljubljana. She works in Laboratory for Open Systems and Networks at Jožef Stefan Institute as a researcher in the field of e-learning and organizational learning. Her current research is performed mostly for European-wide research programmes (GLOBAL, iCoper, e4VET, etc.) with focus on e-learning, applications of ICT in education, education and transfer of knowledge, human resource development and organizational learning. Tanja Arh is member of Executive Board of Slovenian Project Management Association. She is Technical editor of Slovenian scientific journal Project Management Review.

Aliaa Bassiouny holds a BBA as well as an MBA, both with a specialization in finance from the American University in Cairo. She is currently a PhD candidate at ESADE Business School. Ms. Bassiouny has played a variety of roles at AUC. She has delivered several training modules in executive financial training programs as well as teaches undergraduate finance courses. Ms. Bassiouny is also involved with a variety of financial research and has worked as research associate in the finance unit on research papers as well as case studies.

Borka Jerman Blažič is working as a head of the Laboratory for Open Systems and Networks at Jožef Stefan Institute, Slovenia and as a full professor at the University of Ljubljana, Faculty of Economics in Slovenia. The main field of applications and research are computer communications, internet technologies, security in networking, privacy and internationalisation of Internet services, etc. She is a member of many professional associations and is appointed expert to UNECE UN (Economic Commission for Europe), appointed member of UNECE/CEFAT Team of specialist on Internet enterprise development, appointed member of eTEN management committee of EU, member of FP7 PC on security, chair of the Execom of the Internet Society of Europe (www.isoc-ecc.org), member of New York Academy of science 1999, IEEE, ACM, distinguished member of Slovene Society for Informatics, member of IEEE on Computers, ACM. She is also chair of Slovenian Standardisation Committee on ICT as well as chair of the Slovenian chapter of Internet Society and a member of the European ICT Standardisation Board. She is holding Plaque of appreciation of Thai branch of IFIP and ACM for her services in Internet development. She has published more than 80 papers in refereed journals, 154 communications scientific meetings, 15 chapters in scientific books, 6 books and other 142 non-classified contributions.

Linda L. Brennan is a professor of management at Mercer University in Macon. She conducts research and consults in the areas of technology impact assessment, process and project management, and instructional effectiveness. Her most recent book, *Computer-Mediated Relationships and Trust: Organizational and Managerial Implications*, was published by IGI Global in 2008. Dr. Brennan's prior work experience includes management positions at The Quaker Oats Company and marketing and systems engineering experience with the IBM Corporation. A licensed professional engineer, she received her Ph.D. from Northwestern University, her MBA from the University of Chicago, and her B.I.E. from the Georgia Institute of Technology.

Alessio Maria Braccini (1977, Italy) is a PhD Research Fellow at the CeRSI research center of the LUISS Guido Carli University in Rome, and he teaches Information Systems Management at the Faculty of Economics of the same University. In the past years he has been actively involved in research activities managed by the CeRSI research center. As author or co-author, he has published research papers, books, and book chapters (the full list is available at http://www.cersi.it/abraccini). His research appeared on the Communications of AIS, VINE – The Journal of Knowledge Management Systems, and the International Journal of Electronic Commerce Studies. His current research interest, besides information systems for archaeology, concerns the assessment of IT business value, and the impact that ICT might have on organizational behaviour of digital natives.

Vlado Dimovski is a full professor of management and organizational theory at the University of Ljubljana, Faculty of Economics in Slovenia. He holds B.A. degrees in Economics and Philosophy, M.A. in Economics, and Ph.D. in Management and Finance. As an academician Dimovski has taught and researched at various universities and institutions, and has published numerous articles in recognized journals. His academic research interests cover learning organization, competitiveness, corporate strategy, developing knowledge-based organizations, and labor markets. Besides his university position, professor Dimovski was the State Secretary for Industry (1995–97), the president of the Center for International Competitiveness (1997–2005), and Minister for Labor, Family and Social Affairs (2000–2004).

Ibrahim El-Khatib is the head of the Structural Engineering Department at XYZ and has a PhD in Structural Engineering.

Nourhan El-Mougi works in the Marketing Research field, passionate of analyzing figures to identify innovative market opportunities. She holds great enthusiasm in helping others learn and grow. She started her career as a Teaching Assistant in Statistics, Calculus and other related topics while working on her MBA degree. She joined TNS Global, Marketing Research Agency, in 2008 for 2 years. In that time, attained TNS Special Award for excellent performance, and was nominated for TNS Research Knowledge Box (TKB) among a group of TNS worldwide nominees. Recently, she joined Vodafone as a Consumer Insight Senior Specialist focusing on the understanding, analysis and opportunity identification of the Consumer segment. Nourhan holds a Bachelor degree in Statistics from Cairo University with grade of Very Good with honors, and an MBA from AUC with GPA 3.52. She is passionate of horse-riding, traveling and embracing new experiences.

Anna Filipi at the time of writing, was a Senior Research Fellow at the Australian Council for Educational Research and Project Director for the Assessment of Language Competence certificates. Her research interests include the application of the findings and methods of Conversation Analysis to the study of language acquisition (both First and Second) and spatial language as well as her more recent interest in online interactions in a work setting. She is also interested in bilingualism and teacher education. She is currently living in Switzerland where she continues to work as a Consultant for ACER.

Tommaso Federici (1960, Italy) is adjunct professor of Information Systems Management and Organization Theory at the University of Tuscia, in Viterbo, Italy. He has also taught at other universities (University "La Sapienza" and LU-ISS G.Carli University, in Rome, Italy) and Schools of management. As author or co-author, he published papers, articles and books (a list of them is available at: www.tommasofederici.it). He is fascinated by the innovation process, particularly when a new IT artifact is introduced for the first time into a class of organizations. This is a frontier territory to be understood according to multiple perspectives and by following a multi-disciplinary approach. Beside the innovation in the archaeological sector, other recent research domains are: e-procurement and FLOSS, both regarded as boosters to foster organizational change in the public sector, and the ERP introduction in the SMEs segment.

Harald Fardal is an Assistant Professor Vestfold University College. His research focuses on the processes involved in IT/IS strategy development and in IT/IS projects, and especially on how the competence of end users can strengthen these processes. Fardal teaches courses in IS-management and methodology.

Ahu Genis-Gruber is Assistant Professor in Business Administration Department at TOBB University of Economics and Technology where she teaches organizational theory, organizational behavior, management theories, cross cultural management, and human resource management. Her interest areas are international management, cross cultural management, merger and acquisitions, and e-commerce. Dr. Genis-Gruber holds a B.S. in Labor Economics and Industrial Relations from Ankara University, Political Science Faculty, a Master's degree (Mag.rer.soc.oec.) in Social and Economic Sciences from Johannes Kepler University, Linz-Austria and a Ph.D. (Dr.rer.soc.oec.) in Social and Economic Sciences from Johannes Kepler University, Linz-Austria.

Fabian Gruning Fabian Grüning studied computer science at the University of Oldenburg, Germany. From 2005 on he started to work as a research assistent at the OFFIS - Institute for Information Systems both in third party founded projects as well as teaching. He currently finishes his PhD-Thesis "Data Quality Management for the Utility Domain" which contains a process model for data quality management that is adjusted to meet the requirements companies of the utility domain have for efficient application of a data quality management in the specific domain. It is accompanied by a supporting tool that automizes the steps of the process model.

Sumeet Gupta is heading the Department of Business Administration at Shri Shankaracharya Institute of Technology and Management, India. He received PhD (Information Systems) as well as MBA from National University of Singapore. He also worked as a research fellow with The Logistics Institute – Asia Pacific, Singapore, where he worked on consultancy projects with SAP A.G., DFS Gallerias, ASEAN secretariat, and EDB Singapore. He has published several papers in top tier international journals (*Decision Support Systems, International Journal of e-Commerce, European Journal of Operations Research, Information Resources Management Journal, Information and Management, Psychology and Marketing, Electronic Markets*, and *Omega-An International Journal of Management Science, International Journal of Electronic Business*) and Conferences (International Conference of Information Systems, AMCIS, ECIS, AOM and POMS. He has received Accredited Management Teacher Certification from All India Management Association, India. His research interests are in supply chain management, virtual community, Internet security and privacy, as well as technology adoption.

Bogdan Hoanca is Associate Professor of Management Information Systems at the University of Alaska Anchorage (UAA). Before that, he co-founded, started up and sold a company that builds components for fiber optic communications. He also helped start and consulted with a number of other startup companies in optical fiber communications. Bogdan received a Ph.D. in Electrical Engineering from the University of Southern California in 1999. Prof. Hoanca authored and co-authored two case studies, two patents, ten journal papers, eight book chapters and more than thirty conference papers. His current research interests include information security, e-learning and societal implications of technology.

Inge Hermanrud holds an Associate Professor position at Hedmark University College, Norway where he teaches courses in Strategy, IT, Communication and Innovation. His research focuses on ICT use in knowledge sharing and organizational learning.

Heba Hodeeb was born in November 1st, 1983. She graduated with highest honors from the American University in Cairo with major in Business Administration, concentrating in Marketing and a minor in Economics. During her undergraduate studies, she participated as a delegate in the International Student Leadership Conference. After her graduation, she started her career in a multinational beverage company located in Cairo and worked as a Sales Analyst and Project Coordinator for three years. She was then chosen to be an elected pioneer of Mohammed Bin Rashid Al Maktoum scholarship in order to pursue her MBA studies at the American University in Cairo. She is currently married and has children.

Bo Hu is a researcher in SAP Research (CEC Belfast). He received his PhD in Computer Science from the Robert Gordon University, Aberdeen in 2004. Between 2002 and 2008, He worked as a Research Fellow in the Intelligence, Agent, Multimedia Group (IAM), School of Electronics and Computer Science, University of Southampton. His main research interest is in knowledge management, Semantic Web, context modelling and context awareness, and the application in e-learning and e-healthcare.

Dolly Jaisinghani is a management graduate from Shri Shankaracharya Group of Institutions, India.

Saket Jhunjhunwala is a management consultant working with Accenture, Mumbai in their retail vertical. Before joining Accenture, he worked with Reliance Retail Limited (RRL), one of the leading and biggest retailers in India. In RRL he was responsible for creation of standard operation procedures for store operations used across the formats of Reliance Retail India. He has more than six years of experience, overall eight years, on Business Process Management and Process Reengineering and has worked with Ernst & Young India Limited and Infosys Technologies Limited among others. He holds a masters degree in management and a bachelors in science.

Yannis Kalfoglou is a Technology Innovation Consultant with RICOH Europe Plc, and a Visiting Senior Research Fellow with the University of Southampton. He has published extensively in the field of semantic interoperability and integration and he is a pioneer in ontology mapping technology. He holds a PhD in Artificial Intelligence from the University of Edinburgh and several years post doctoral experience in the field of Artificial Intelligence, Knowledge Engineering and Management and the Semantic Web. He participated in national and international funding programmes on the use of AI technologies on the Web. He led industrially funded projects on the provision of services in the field of semantic interoperability. He participates in several programme committees for national and international research consortia and he has consulted venture capitalist funds on the use of semantic technologies.

Aundrea Kell attended the University of Alaska Fairbanks, earning a BA in sociology. She will graduate with an MBA from the University of Alaska Anchorage in 2009. Ms. Kell is an MIS business systems analyst with one of the largest federal credit unions in the country. Her previous professional experience has been in the airline and utility industries. She is active in Toastmasters International and the Alaska Chapter of the Project Management Institute.

Mohamad Khaled: BS in Civil Engineering from Beirut Arab University in 2001 and Master of Engineering Management from the American University of Beirut in 2006. Working for XYZ firm as a Structure Engineer since 2001. Currently, I am a project engineer working on many projects including high rise buildings in Dubai.

Suryadeo Vinay Kissoon has about 15 years practical work experience in general management. Corporate member and chartered quality professional with Chartered Quality Institute (U.K). Accredited trainer for training in field of quality management and finance in industry and tertiary education. Previously worked as operations manager in a major manufacturing company for about 12 years administering about 150 employees. He has been working in some major Australian organizations in

514

fields of banking and finance, customer service and railway industries. Five nomi-
nations and quality awards nationally and internationally as operations manager.
One nomination in quality award and one employee excellence award in Australia.
Best paper award by a Ph.d candidate in 2007 in the international Association of
Qualitative Research conference. Author has been involved as part-time consultancy
and lecturer for nearly ten years in fields of HRM, quality management, service
quality, financial management, strategic management, marketing management,
supply chain management, logistic system analysis and production management.
Author has been working extensively with quality circles (PDCA), kaizen teams
(application of Six Sigma DMAIC methodology), workplace improvement teams,
process improvement team and virtual teams. Author has also been working on
TQM, Continuous Improvement, ISO 9000, EMS, HACCP, Information Quality
Systems and some other quality management principles and methodologies. He has
also been involved in research project works and written about 20 papers in various
fields of management.

Sophie Lissonnet has a Masters in Information Management and a Masters in
Indigenous Studies. She works as an indexer and digital repository officer at the
Cunningham Library (Australian Council for Educational Research) in Melbourne.
In 2008, she was invited by the ALC team to set up and support the ALC wiki for
the purpose of test development.

Ivan Magdalenić is assistant at the University of Zagreb, Faculty of Organization and Informatics in Varaždin, Croatia. He received his B.S. and M.S. degrees in
Electrical Engineering with a major in Telecommunications and Information Science
from the University of Zagreb, in 2000 and 2003, respectively. The research topic
of his Master thesis was "Business Documents Interchange". He has been working as a research assistant at the Faculty of Electrical Engineering and Computing,
University of Zagreb from 2000 to 2003. He received his Ph.D. degree in Computer
science 2009. The thesis title was "Dynamic generation of ontology supported Web
services for data retrieval". His research interests are in e-Business, Web technology,
Semantic Web technology and generative programming. He is leader of technical
committee in project of Introduction of e-Invoice in Croatia and he is a member of
National council for electronic business. He is author and coauthor of many scientific
and technical studies and research papers.

Toufic Mezher is a Professor of Engineering Management at the American University of Beirut. He earned a BS in Civil Engineering from University of Florida,
and a Master and ScD in Engineering Management from George Washington University in 1988 and 1992 respectively. His research interests include Sustainable

Development, Renewable Energy Management and Policy, Building Knowledge-Based Economies and Innovation Systems, etc.

Shari Pierre is an MBA student at the University of Alaska Anchorage. Her undergraduate degrees are in Marketing and Management, and she currently works at Fed-AK. At Fed-AK, she is a Budget Analyst, and is responsible for the management of millions of dollars annually. When not working, Ms. Pierre volunteers in her church and local community. She is a member of the Phi Kappa Phi Honor Society, Golden Key Honour Society, and Alpha Kappa Alpha Sorority, Inc. Ms. Pierre is scheduled to graduate from the MBA program in Spring 2009.

Ritika Rathi is a management graduate from Shri Shankaracharya Group of Institutions, India.

Sebastian Rohjans Sebastian Rohjans has joined the OFFIS - Institute for Information Systems in late 2008. He holds a computer science degree from the University of Oldenburg with a minor in business and wrote his thesis about ontology-based integration. He is now working in industrial setting projects having the same scope. His research interests include semantic web services, the OPC unified architecture and ontology based mediation.

Hafez Salleh is a Deputy Dean(Undergraduate)/Senior Lecturer in the Faculty of Built Environment, University of Malaya, Malaysia. He obtained a BSc, MSc and PhD Degree from School of the Built Environment and top rated, 6* Research Institute for the Built and Human Environment, University of Salford, United Kingdom. He has 15 years experience in both academia and industry practice and has been an active researcher and research supervisor. He has supervised and supported a wide range of post graduate research students in various research themes. His main research interests are IT/IS performance evaluation and management, project management and sustainable design. His previous research was the development of IT/IS Readiness Model that focuses on evaluation of organizational readiness prior IT/IS investment. He is currently working on the theme of IT/IS evaluation in construction with a particular interest in the links between 'hard' and human issues. He is also the technical committee member of Malaysian Construction Industry Master Plan (CIMP) 2005-2015, Strategic Thrust 6: Leveraging Information Technology and Editorial Board Members, Journal of Surveying, Construction and Property.

Jan Oddvar Sørnes (PhD Norwegian University of Science and Technology, 2004) is an Associate Professor and Vice Dean of research at Bodø Graduate School of Business in Norway. His research focuses on organizational communication, cross-cultural communication, and on stakeholder dialogue in the energy industry. He teaches doctoral courses in qualitative methods and several undergraduate and graduate courses related to his research interest.

Cheryl A. Tibus is an assistant professor of management at Mercer University in Macon, Georgia. She conducts research and consults in the areas of leadership, strategy, and human resource management. Dr. Tibus spent over 25 years in corporations including roles of Vice President in both public and private organizations. Most recently she was the executive in charge of a key system implementation project and the senior human resources executive of a privately held firm. She received her doctorate at the George Washington University.

Eskandar Tooma is an associate professor of finance and holds the British Petroleum endowed chair with the Department of Management at The American University in Cairo. He is a member of the American Economic Association (AEA), the American Finance Association (AFA), and also is the Secretary General of the African Finance Association. Professor Tooma obtained his B.A. in Business from The American University in Cairo and Adelphi University. Dr. Tooma holds two M.S. degrees, the first in Finance and the second in International Economics from Adelphi and Brandeis Universities, respectively. Finally, he holds a Ph.D. in Finance from Brandeis University. Professor Tooma is a specialist in financial economics. His writings focus on volatility dynamics and forecasting in emerging stock markets as well as market microstructure. Subsequent research is in the areas of asset pricing, portfolio theory, and stock market regulations. Currently, he is focusing on research in the area of agent based modelling and stock market simulations as well as writing finance case studies that are used worldwide as teaching aids in both graduate and undergraduate courses. Professor Tooma combines academic experience with practical exposure through assuming a variety of public and private professional posts. He was senior advisor to the Capital Market Authority for 2.5 years, as well as a member of a variety of committees including the EGX30 Index Committee, Market Advancement Committee at the Egyptian Stock Exchange, an advisor and member of the Derivatives and Commodities Exchange Committee with the Ministry of Investments, and an advisor to the Ministry of International Cooperation on Egypt's Debt Swap Experience. Privately, he has advised leading institutions including but not limited to: Citadel Capital, Beltone Financial, EFG-Hermes, AAIB, and Osoul Fund Management. Dr. Tooma is a co-owner and board member of Premium International for Credit Services as well as a board member of Orascom Housing Communities, Orascom Investment Fund, Egyptian Resorts Company, Roward Tourism, and Regina Food Industries, among others. Professor Tooma is currently advising leading real estate and development groups on financial and restructuring issues. He sits on the boards of one of the largest real estate funds in the region and is a financial advisor to Orascom for Hotels and Development (OHD).

Mathias Uslar Since 2004, after having finished his studies of informatics with a minor in legal informatics and business, Mathias Uslar joined the OFFIS –Institute in Oldenburg Germany where he is working in the Utility Informatics branch. His main interests are standardization and utility EAI. He also brings in his expertise to both national and international standardization boards. He is also the director of the Center for It Standards in the Energy Domain, abbreviated CISE (http://www. ccise.de).

Neven Vrček is full professor at the University of Zagreb, Faculty of Organization and Informatics, Varaždin, Croatia. His area of research and professional interest are Software Engineering and Electronic Business. He is member of various professional and scientific associations related to wide aspects of ICT use and organizational development. Occasionally he works as business and ICT consultant.

Michael Workman received his Ph.D. from Georgia State University, and has over 50 reviewed research publications. He came to academic life in 2001 with nearly thirty years of experience in the computer industry where he began as a software engineer, then moved into management. Reflecting on problems he faced, his research area investigates how to exploit technologies, tasks, and human factors to improve how well people work. Prior to coming to Florida Tech, Michael was an assistant and associate professor of information systems at the Florida State University.

Index

A

B

C